Foundations of Bilingual Education and Bilingualism

BILINGUAL EDUCATION AND BILINGUALISM
Series Editors: Professor Nancy H. Hornberger, *University of Pennsylvania, Philadelphia, USA*
and Professor Colin Baker, *University of Wales, Bangor, Wales, Great Britain*

Recent Books in the Series
Power, Prestige and Bilingualism: International Perspectives on Elite Bilingual Education
    Anne-Marie de Mejía
Identity and the English Language Learner
    Elaine Mellen Day
Language and Literacy Teaching for Indigenous Education: A Bilingual Approach
    Norbert Francis and Jon Reyhner
The Native Speaker: Myth and Reality
    Alan Davies
Language Socialization in Bilingual and Multilingual Societies
    Robert Bayley and Sandra R. Schecter (eds)
Language Rights and the Law in the United States: Finding our Voices
    Sandra Del Valle
Continua of Biliteracy: An Ecological Framework for Educational Policy, Research, and Practice
in Multilingual Settings
    Nancy H. Hornberger (ed.)
Languages in America: A Pluralist View (2nd Edition)
    Susan J. Dicker
Trilingualism in Family, School and Community
    Charlotte Hoffmann and Jehannes Ytsma (eds)
Multilingual Classroom Ecologies
    Angela Creese and Peter Martin (eds)
Negotiation of Identities in Multilingual Contexts
    Aneta Pavlenko and Adrian Blackledge (eds)
Beyond the Beginnings: Literacy Interventions for Upper Elementary English Language
Learners
    Angela Carrasquillo, Stephen B. Kucer and Ruth Abrams
Bilingualism and Language Pedagogy
    Janina Brutt-Griffler and Manka Varghese (eds)
Language Learning and Teacher Education: A Sociocultural Approach
    Margaret R. Hawkins (ed.)
The English Vernacular Divide: Postcolonial Language Politics and Practice
    Vaidehi Ramanathan
Bilingual Education in South America
    Anne-Marie de Mejía (ed.)
Teacher Collaboration and Talk in Multilingual Classrooms
    Angela Creese
Words and Worlds: World Languages Review
    Martí, P. Ortega, I. Idiazabal, A. Barreña, P. Juaristi, C. Junyent, B. Uranga and E. Amorrortu
Language and Aging in Multilingual Contexts
    Kees de Bot and Sinfree Makoni

For more details of these or any other of our publications, please contact:
Multilingual Matters, Frankfurt Lodge, Clevedon Hall,
Victoria Road, Clevedon, BS21 7HH, England
http://www.multilingual-matters.com

BILINGUAL EDUCATION AND BILINGUALISM 54
Series Editors: Nancy H. Hornberger and Colin Baker

Foundations of Bilingual Education and Bilingualism

Fourth Edition

Colin Baker

MULTILINGUAL MATTERS LTD
Clevedon • Buffalo • Toronto • Sydney

Library of Congress Cataloging in Publication Data
Baker, Colin
Foundations of Bilingual Education and Bilingualism/Colin Baker, 4th ed.
Bilingual Education and Bilingualism: 54
Includes bibliographical references and index.
1. Education, Bilingual. 2. Education, Bilingual–Great Britain. 3. Bilingualism.
4. Bilingualism–Great Britain. I. Title. II. Series.
LC3715.B35 2006
370.117–dc22   2005021289

British Library Cataloguing in Publication Data
A catalogue entry for this book is available from the British Library.

ISBN 1-85359-865-8/ EAN 978-1-85359-865-4 (hbk)
ISBN 1-85359-864-X/ EAN 978-1-85359-864-7 (pbk)

Multilingual Matters Ltd
UK: Frankfurt Lodge, Clevedon Hall, Victoria Road, Clevedon BS21 7HH.
USA: UTP, 2250 Military Road, Tonawanda, NY 14150, USA.
Canada: UTP, 5201 Dufferin Street, North York, Ontario M3H 5T8, Canada.

Typeset by Archetype-IT Ltd (http://www.archetype-it.com).
Printed and bound in the United States of America.

Contents

Introduction

The fourth edition of this book is intended as a comprehensive and modern introduction to bilingual education and bilingualism. Written from a cross-disciplinary perspective, the book covers a wide range of topics: individual and societal concepts in minority and majority languages; childhood developmental perspectives; general bilingual education issues, bilingual classrooms, and political and ideological perspectives. Bilingualism and multilingualism relates to, for example, use of two or more communication systems, identity and personality, thinking, education and culture. All of these are encapsulated in this book.

In compiling successive editions, increasingly tough decisions had to be made as to what to include and exclude, what to present in detail and what to summarize, what assumptions to explore and what to take 'as read'. I have often been asked: 'Why don't you put Chapter X earlier?' I agree, everything should be earlier. Other frequently asked questions are 'Why don't you expand on Y?'; 'Why don't you leave out Z because it is irrelevant to me?' and 'Why can't we have an edition just for our region?'. 'Why isn't a chapter in an earlier edition still included?' What follows are some explanations.

An attempt is made to balance the psychological and the sociological; macro and micro education issues; the linguistic and the sociopolitical with discussion at individual and societal levels; and to be inclusive of major international concerns in bilingualism, multilingualism and bilingual education. Faced with the social and political challenges that surround bilinguals, students will find in this book an attempt to analyze constructively those problems and recognize the positive values and virtues of a future multilingual world.

This book starts with definitional, sociological and psychological issues that are essential to understanding bilingual/multilingual children, and bilingual education. Later discussions of bilingual education and bilingual classrooms are built on that foundation. However, the book is more than a cross-disciplinary foundation with a series of education layers built on top. Within the boundaries of clarity in writing style and structuring, explicit inter-connections are made between chapters.

In writing the book, a constant challenge has been 'From whose perspective?' There are majority language mainstream viewpoints, relatively advantaged minority language viewpoints and various disadvantaged minority language viewpoints. There are left-wing and right-wing politics, activist and constructivist ideas. The book attempts to represent a variety of viewpoints and beliefs. Where possible, **multiple perspectives** are shared. Readers and reviewers have kindly pointed out some of the hidden and implicit assumptions made, and kindly provided alternative viewpoints that I have tried to represent faithfully in the text. Where there are conclusions and dominating perspectives, I alone stand responsible.

Another issue has concerned generalization and contextualization. The book was written for an international audience to reflect ideas that transcend national boundaries. The book attempts to locate issues of international generalizability. Unfortunately, space limits discussion of a variety of regional and national language situations. There are other writings that will provide necessary contextualization (e.g. the *Encyclopedia* by Baker & Jones, 1998). Where particular situations have been discussed (e.g. US debates), it is often because of the thoroughness of documentation and the depth of analysis in the surrounding literature.

In an attempt to make the contents of this book relevant to a variety of contexts and regions, various chapters focus on **integrating theories**. From one individual research study, it is usually impossible to generalize. A study from Europe may say little about North America. Results on six-year-olds may say nothing about sixteen- or sixty-year-olds. Research on middle-class children speaking French and English in a dual language school may say little or nothing about children from a lower social class in a bilingual environment where the second language is likely to replace the first language. From a gray mass of research and sometimes from a paucity of research, a theoretical framework will attempt to outline the crucial parameters and processes. Thus a theoretical framework on a particular area of bilingualism may attempt to do one or more of the following: attempt to explain phenomena; integrate a diversity of (apparently contradictory) findings; locate the key parameters and interactions operating; be able to predict outcomes and patterns of bilingual behavior; be capable of testing for falsification or refinement; express the various conditions that will allow the theory to be appropriate in a variety of contexts.

However, in providing a relatively comprehensive synthesis of bilingualism, multilingualism and bilingual education, the danger lies in suggesting that there is a systematic coherence to the subject. While some teachers and many students want 'recipes' and clear assertions, the current state of our knowledge and understanding rarely provides that clarity. The book therefore attempts to represent contested positions, varied viewpoints and the limitations of research and theory.

Instructors, in particular, will wish to know what are the specific changes in the fourth edition. First, there are many minor changes. For example, references have been updated (there are 454 new references), research findings added and corrections made. Second, and importantly, there are new or more thoroughly covered topics: the politics of testing bilinguals, the use of censuses to survey bilinguals, endangered languages, language planning, language revitalization and resurrection, language and nationalism, the spread of English as a global language, the advantages and disadvantages of English as a second or third language, the early development of bilinguals, trilingualism and trilingual education, identity and multiple identities, recent changes in bilingual education in the United States (e.g. No Child Left Behind), the achievement gap in bilinguals, the educational mainstreaming of bilingual children, Dual Language schools, heritage language education, content and language integrated learning (CLIL), the recent politics of bilingual education, the economic advantages of bilingual education, effective practices in bilingual schools and classrooms, multilingual literacy and multiliteracies, biliteracy, dual language books, gifted bilingual children, gender, bilingualism in the economy, multilingualism and the Information Communications Technology revolution.

There is a **Reader** to accompany this book entitled *Bilingual Education: An Introductory Reader* (2006) published by Multilingual Matters Ltd. This Reader contains a selection of the most important and influential contributions on bilingualism and bilingual education and is edited by Ofelia García (Teachers College, New York) and myself. Each is a 'classic' or a pivotal paper.

ORGANIZATION OF THE BOOK

The starting point of the book is an introduction to the language used in discussing bilingual education and bilingualism. Not only are important terms introduced, but also key concepts, distinctions and debates which underpin later chapters are presented. There are important dualisms and paradoxes throughout the study of bilingualism and multilingualism: for example, the individual bilingual person as different from groups and societies where bilinguals live; the linguistic view compared with the sociocultural and sociopolitical view; language skills and language competences; subtractive and additive forms of bilingualism. The opening chapters (1 to 8) present foundational issues that precede and influence discussions about bilingual education. Before we can sensibly talk about bilingual education we need to tackle questions such as:

- Who are bilinguals and multilinguals?
- How does bilingual education fit into minority language maintenance, language decay and language revival?
- How does a child become bilingual or trilingual?
- What effect does the home and the neighborhood play in developing bilingualism and multilingualism?
- Does bilingualism have a positive or negative effect on thinking?

Chapters 9 to 16 focus on the many aspects of bilingual education. They commence with a broad discussion of different types of bilingual education, followed by an examination of the effectiveness of those types. After a focus on systems of bilingual education, the book proceeds to examine bilingual classrooms, multiliteracies and biliteracy and key bilingual education strategies. The underlying questions are:

- What forms of bilingual education are more successful?
- What are the aims and outcomes of different types of bilingual education?
- What are the essential features and approaches of a classroom fostering bilingualism?
- What are the key problems and issues of bilingual classrooms?

Chapters 17 and 18 are central to understanding bilingualism and bilingual education. They consider the political and cultural dimensions that surround bilingualism in society (and bilingual education in particular). Different views of the overall value and purpose of bilingualism join together many of the threads of the book. The finale of the book (chapter 19) takes a look at the present and future with themes of multilingualism and the Internet, employment, mass media, economy and tourism.

Thus the concluding issues of the book include:

- Why are there different viewpoints about language minorities and bilingual education?
- Why do some people prefer the assimilation of language minorities and others prefer linguistic diversity?
- Why are Deaf people an important group to study both as bilinguals and as recipients of bilingual education?

STUDY ACTIVITIES

Study activities are placed at the end of each chapter. These are designed for students wishing to extend their learning by engaging in various practical activities. Such activities are flexible and adaptable. Instructors and students will be able to vary them according to local circumstances. More study activities are found in the Reader that accompanies this text.

FINALE

To end the beginning. The motivating force behind this book is to introduce students to the modern and ever-increasing world of bilingualism, multilingualism and bilingual education. The book has been written for minority language students seeking to understand and preserve, and for majority language students seeking to become more sensitized. The book is an attempt to contribute to the preservation and celebration of a linguistically and culturally diverse world. Bilinguals and multilinguals help preserve the 'beauty of diversity' of the world.

Acknowledgements

The idea of this introductory text derived from a fellow Essex gentleman, Mike Grover. He wrote one simple sentence in the early 1990s that has affected my academic life ever since: 'Consider writing THE textbook on Bilingual Education'. My Essex *'fanks ma(t)e'* go to Mike of Multilingual Matters for not only trusting me with this responsibility, but also for his continual encouragement, risk taking and friendly, facilitative style. Ken Hall in Multilingual Matters has worked with me patiently, meticulously and expertly in the production of all the books. A tower of strength and always helpful, Ken has made successive projects smooth and successful. *Merci beaucoup, Ken.* And recently Tommi Grover and Anna Roderick showed how evolution works among publishers with a new generation constantly giving wise, astute, sensitive, tactful and efficient advice.

Multilingual Matters perceptively appointed Ofelia García as Academic Consultant when this project began. I received detailed, sensitive, wise and judicious advice from her. Much gratitude is owed to Ofelia who helped to shape the book. *Muchas gracias.*

In the previous three editions, I recorded my grateful thanks to those who helped in the construction of those editions. I wish to repeat my sincere gratitude to: Jasone Cenoz, Tony Cline, Jim Crawford, Jim Cummins, Nancy Dorian, Viv Edwards, Peter Garrett, Nancy Hornberger, Annick De Houwer, Sharon Lapkin, Hilaire Lemoine, Christer Laurén, Karita Mard, Stephen May, Bernard Spolsky, Merrill Swain, Terry Wiley and not least my previous Head of School, Iolo Wyn Williams, who gave me the freedom to write. My current Head, Dr Janet Pritchard, has kindly given me the opportunity and encouragement to continue my scholarly activity.

For the fourth edition, various scholars constructively gave expert advice on improvements and needed developments: Hugo Baetens Beardsmore, Claudine Brohy, Tony Cline, Margaret Deuchar, Viv Edwards, Tamar Gollan, Annick De Houwer, John Maher, Terry McCarty and Bernard Spolsky. The whole draft manuscript was thoroughly reviewed by Aneta Pavlenko who provided a wealth of new ideas from the combined perspectives of a teacher, multilingual, and highly expert scholar. Her depth of understanding across so many multidisciplinary areas, plus her insights into the sequence and structure, have been highly influential in this fourth edition. Sylvia Prys Jones wrote the *Encyclopedia of Bilingualism and Bilingual Education* (1998) with me, and during three years of cooperation, I learnt much from such a brilliant intellect. The chapter on 'Bilingualism in the Modern World', and the discussion on one-parent bilingual families owes much to Sylvia's superlative contribution to the *Encyclopedia*. Continuous dialogue with Cen Williams (a colleague at Bangor) and Meirion Prys Jones, Chief Executive of the Welsh Language Board, has been a constant source of encouragement and enlightenment. *Diolch i chi.*

Working on bilingualism has always been inspired by a bilingual family: my Welsh wife, Anwen, three bilingual offspring (Sara, Rhodri and Arwel) who still daily teach me the gifts of bilingualism that go beyond language, and a grandson (Ioan Tomos) who allows me to observe closely without the responsibility of parenthood. Their loving support is always appreciated. *Diolch yn fawr iawn am bopeth.*

The help and support given me by all those mentioned above has been extremely generous and far more than is deserved. However, the responsibility for all that is not perfect is totally mine.

Colin Baker

Note

Permissions: Every attempt has been made to contact copyright holders and gain permissions where needed. If there are any omissions, we will be pleased to correct them in a future edition.

CHAPTER 1

Bilingualism: Definitions and Distinctions

CHAPTER 1

Bilingualism: Definitions and Distinctions

INTRODUCTION

Since a bicycle has two wheels and binoculars are for two eyes, it would seem that bilingualism is simply about two languages. Multilingualism is then about three or more languages. The aim of this chapter is to show that the ownership of two or more languages is not so simple as having two wheels or two eyes. Is someone bilingual if they are fluent in one language but less than fluent in their other language? Is someone multilingual if they rarely or never use one of their languages? Such questions need addressing before other topics in this book can be discussed.

To understand the answers to these questions, it is valuable to make an **initial distinction between bilingualism and multilingualism as an individual characteristic, and bilingualism and multilingualism in a social group, community, region or country.** Bilingualism and multilingualism can be examined as the possession of the individual. Various themes in this book start with bilingualism as experienced by individual people. For example, a discussion of whether or not bilingualism affects thinking requires research on individual monolinguals, bilinguals and multilinguals. From sociology, sociolinguistics, politics, geography, education and social psychology comes a different perspective. Bilinguals and multilinguals are usually found in groups. Such groups may be located in a particular region (e.g. Basques in Spain), or may be scattered across communities (e.g. the Chinese in the US). Bilinguals may form a distinct language group as a majority or a minority. For example, linguists study how the vocabulary of bilingual groups change across time. Geographers plot the density of bilinguals in a country. Educationalists examine bilingual educational policy and provision for minority language groups.

The first distinction is therefore between bilingualism (and multilingualism) as an individual possession and as a group possession. This is usually termed **individual bilingualism and societal bilingualism**. Like most distinctions, there are important links between the two parts. For example, the attitudes of individuals towards a particular minority language may affect language maintenance, language restoration, language shift or language death in society. In order to understand the term 'bilingualism', some important further distinctions at the **individual** level are discussed in this chapter. [While bilingualism and multilingualism are different, where there is similarity, multilingualism is (for the sake of brevity) combined under bilingualism.] An introduction to bilingualism and multilingualism as a group possession (societal bilingualism) is provided in chapters 3 and 4.

If a person is asked whether he or she speaks two or more languages, the question is ambiguous. A person may be **able** to speak two languages, but tends to speak only one language in practice. Alternatively, the individual may regularly speak two languages, but competence in one language may be limited. Another person will use one language for conversation and another for writing and reading. An essential distinction is therefore between **language ability** and **language use**. This is sometimes referred to as the difference between degree and function.

TERMINOLOGY

Before discussing the nature of language use and abilities, a note about **terminology**. Entry into the many areas of bilingualism and bilingual education is helped by understanding often-used terms and distinctions. There exists a range of terms in this area, for example language ability, language achievement, language competence, language performance, language proficiency and language skills. Do they all refer to the same entity, or are there subtle distinctions between the terms? To add to the problem, different authors and researchers sometimes tend to adopt their own specific meanings and distinctions.

Some Dimensions of Bilingualism

Bilinguals and multilinguals can be analyzed along the following over-lapping and interacting dimensions:

(1) **Ability**: some bilinguals actively speak and write in both languages (**productive** competence), others are more passive bilinguals and may have **receptive** ability (understanding or reading). For some, their ability in two or more languages is well developed. Others may be moving through the early stages of acquiring a second language. Ability is thus on a dimension or continuum (Valdés *et al.*, 2003) with dominance and development varied across people.

(2) **Use**: the **domains** where each language is acquired and used are varied (e.g. home, school, street, phone, TV). An individual's different languages are often used for different purposes.

(3) **Balance of two languages**: rarely are bilinguals and multilinguals equal in

their ability or use of their two languages. Often one language is **dominant**.

(4) **Age**: when children learn two languages from birth, this is often called **simultaneous** or infant bilingualism. If a child learns a second language after about three years of age, it is termed **consecutive** or **sequential** bilingualism. Chapters five and six consider age issues in detail.

(5) **Development: Incipient** bilinguals have one well developed language, and the other is in the early stages of development. When a second language is developing, this is **ascendant** bilingualism, compared with **recessive** bilingualism when one language is decreasing, resulting in temporary or permanent **language attrition.**

(6) **Culture**: Bilinguals become more or less **bicultural** or **multicultural**. It is almost possible for someone (e.g. a foreign language graduate) to have high proficiency in two languages but be relatively **monocultural**. In comparison, some monolinguals move towards biculturalism. A process of **acculturation** accompanies language learning when immigrants, for example, learn the majority language of the host country. **Bicultural competence** tends to relate to: knowledge of language cultures, feelings and attitudes towards those two cultures, behaving in culturally appropriate ways, awareness and empathy, and having the confidence to express biculturalism.

(7) **Contexts**: Some bilinguals live in bilingual and multilingual **endogenous communities** that use more than one language on an everyday basis. Other bilinguals live in more monolingual and monocultural regions and **network** with other bilinguals by vacations, phone and email, for example. Where there is an absence of a second language community, the context is **exogenous** (e.g. Russian bilinguals in the US). Some contexts may be **subtractive**, where the politics of a country favors the replacement of the home language by the majority language (e.g. Spanish being replaced by English in the US). This particularly occurs among **immigrant** bilinguals (e.g. in the US and UK). Other contexts are **additive** such that a person learns a second language at no cost to their first language as occurs in **elite** or prestigious bilinguals.

(8) **Elective bilingualism** is a characteristic of individuals who choose to learn a language, for example in the classroom (Valdés & Figueroa, 1994; Valdés, 2003). Elective bilinguals typically come from majority language groups (e.g. English-speaking Americans who learn French or Arabic). They add a second-language without losing their first language. **Circumstantial bilinguals** learn another language to function effectively because of their circumstances (e.g. as immigrants). Their first language is insufficient to meet the educational, political and employment demands, and the communicative needs of the society in which they are placed. Circumstantial bilinguals are groups of individuals who must become bilingual to operate in the majority language society that surrounds them. Consequently, their first language is in danger of being replaced by the second language, – a **subtractive** context. The

difference between elective and circumstantial bilingualism is thus valuable because it immediately raises differences of prestige and status, politics and power among bilinguals.

AN INDIVIDUAL'S USE OF BILINGUALISM

Language cannot be divorced from the **context** in which it is used. Language is not produced in a vacuum; it is enacted in changing dramas. As props and scenery, audience, co-actors and actresses, the play and the role change, so does language. A pure linguistic approach to two language competences is not sufficient. Communication includes not only the structure of language (e.g. grammar, vocabulary) but also who is saying what, to whom, in which circumstances. One person may have limited linguistic skills but, in certain situations, be successful in communication. Another person may have relative linguistic mastery, but through undeveloped social interaction skills or in a strange circumstance, be relatively unsuccessful in communication. The social environment where the two languages function is crucial to understanding bilingual usage. Therefore, this section considers the **use** and **function** of an individual's two languages.

An individual's **use** of their bilingual ability (**functional bilingualism**) moves away from the complex arguments about language proficiency that tend to be based around school success and academic performance. Functional bilingualism moves into language production across an encyclopedia of everyday contexts and events. Functional bilingualism concerns when, where, and with whom people use their two languages (Fishman, 1965). The table below provides examples of the different targets (people) and contexts (often called **domains**) where functional bilingualism is enacted in different role relationships.

Examples of Language Targets	Examples of Language Contexts (Domains)
1. Nuclear Family	1. Shopping
2. Extended Family	2. Visual and Auditory Media (e.g. TV, Radio, CD, DVD)
3. Work Colleagues	3. Printed Media (e.g. Newspapers, Books)
4. Friends	4. Cinema/Discos/Theater/Concerts
5. Neighbors	5. Work
6. Religious Leaders	6. Correspondence/Telephone/Official Communication
7. Teachers	7. Clubs, Societies, Organizations, Sporting Activities
8. Presidents, Principals, Other Leaders	8. Leisure & Hobbies
9. Bureaucrats	9. Religious Meetings
10. Local Community	10. Information and Communications Technology (e.g. computers, phones)

Language Choice

Not all bilinguals have the opportunity to use both their languages on a regular basis. Where a bilingual lives in a largely monolingual community there may be little choice about language use from day-to-day. However, in communities where two or more languages are widely spoken, bilinguals may use both their languages on a daily or frequent basis. When bilinguals use both their languages, **language choice** is not haphazard or arbitrary. If the other person is already known to the bilingual, as a family member, friend or colleague, a relationship has usually been established through one language. If both are bilingual they have the option of changing to the other language (e.g. to include others in the conversation), although old habits die hard.

If the other person is not known, a bilingual may quickly pick up clues as to which language to use. **Clues** such as dress, appearance, age, accent and command of a language may suggest to the bilingual which language it would be appropriate to use. In bilingual areas of Canada and the United States for example, employees dealing with the general public may glance at a person's name on their records to help them decide which language to use. A person called Pierre Rouleau or Maria García might be addressed first in French or Spanish, rather than English.

An individual's own attitudes and preferences will influence their choice of language. In a minority/majority language situation, older people may prefer to speak the minority language. Younger folk (e.g. second-generation immigrants) may reject the minority language in favor of the majority language because of its higher status and more fashionable image. Heller (1982, p. 108) shows how in a conversation, perceptions about language and **identity** affect language choice, as in the following example from Quebec:

> I stopped in a garage . . . and struggled to explain . . . that my windshield wipers were congelé and I wanted to make them fonctionner. He listened in mild amusement and then said: 'You don't have to speak French to me, madame. I am not a separatist'.

In situations where the native language is perceived to be under threat, some bilinguals may avoid speaking the majority or dominant language to assert and reinforce the status of the other language. French-Canadians in Quebec sometimes refuse to speak English in shops and offices to emphasize the status of French.

Li Wei *et al.* (1992), in a study of a Chinese community in northern England, indicate that the degree of contact with the majority language community is a factor in language choice. Their research shows that Chinese speakers who were employed outside the Chinese community were more likely to choose to speak English with other Chinese speakers. In contrast, those Chinese immigrants who worked in family businesses, mainly catering, and had less daily contact with English speakers, were more likely to use Chinese with other Chinese–English bilinguals.

Some minority languages are mostly confined to a **private** and domestic role. This happens when a minority language has historically been disparaged and

deprived of status. In Western Brittany in France, for example, many Breton speakers only use their Breton in the family and with close friends. They can be offended if addressed by a stranger in Breton, believing that such a stranger is implying they are uneducated and cannot speak French (C. Baker & S.P. Jones, 1998).

An individual may also **switch** languages, either deliberately or subconsciously, to accommodate the perceived preference of the other participant in the conversation. The perception of which language is regarded as more prestigious or as more accommodating may depend on the nature of the listener. To gain acceptance or status, a person may deliberately and consciously use the majority language. Alternatively, a person may use a minority language as a form of affiliation or belonging to a group. (Codeswitching is discussed in chapter 5.)

BILINGUAL AND MULTILINGUAL ABILITY

The Four Language Abilities

If we confine the question 'Are you bilingual?' to ability in two (or more) languages, the issue becomes 'what ability'? There are four basic language abilities: **listening, speaking, reading and writing**. These four abilities fit into two dimensions: receptive and productive skills; oracy and literacy. The following table illustrates:

	Oracy	Literacy
Receptive skills	Listening	Reading
Productive skills	Speaking	Writing

The table suggests avoiding a simple classification of who is, or is not, bilingual. Some speak a language, but do not read or write in a language. Some listen with understanding and read a language (passive bilingualism) but do not speak or write that language. Some understand a spoken language but do not themselves speak that language. To classify people as either bilinguals or monolinguals is thus too simplistic. Or, to return to the opening analogy, the two wheels of bilingualism exist in different sizes and styles.

The four basic language abilities do not exist in black and white terms. Between black and white are not only many shades of gray; there also exist a wide variety of colors. The multi-colored landscape of bilingual abilities suggests that each language ability can be more or less developed. Reading ability can range from simple and basic to fluent and accomplished. Someone may listen with understanding in one context (e.g. shops) but not in another context (e.g. an academic lecture). These examples show that the four basic abilities can be further refined into sub-scales and dimensions. There are **skills within skills**, traditionally listed as: pronunciation, extent of vocabulary, correctness of grammar, the ability to convey exact meanings in different situations and variations in style. However, these skills tend to be viewed from an academic or classroom perspective. Using a language on the street and in a shop require a greater accent on social competence with language (e.g. the idioms and 'lingo' of the street).

The range and type of sub-skills that can be measured is large and debated. Language abilities such as speaking or reading can be divided into increasingly microscopic parts. What in practice is tested and measured to portray an individual's bilingual performance is considered later in the book. What has emerged so far is that a person's ability in two languages are multidimensional and will tend to evade simple categorization.

Minimal and Maximal Bilingualism

So far, it has been suggested that deciding who is or is not bilingual or multilingual is difficult. Simple categorization is arbitrary and requires a value judgment about the minimal competence needed to achieve a label of 'bilingual'. Therefore, a classic definition of bilingualism such as 'the native-like control of two or more languages' (Bloomfield, 1933) appears too extreme and maximalist ('native like'). The definition is also ambiguous (what is meant by 'control' and who forms the 'native' reference group?). At the other end is a minimalist definition, as in Diebold's (1964) concept of **incipient bilingualism**. The term *incipient bilingualism* allows people with minimal competence in a second language to squeeze into the bilingual category. Tourists with a few phrases and business people with a few greetings in a second language could be incipient bilinguals. Almost every adult in the world knows a few words in another language. The danger of being too exclusive is not overcome by being too inclusive. Trawling with too wide a fishing net will catch too much variety and therefore make discussion about bilinguals ambiguous and imprecise. Trawling with narrow criteria may be too insensitive and restrictive.

Valdés (2003) pictures bilinguals is existing on a **continuum**, where A and B are the two languages. The first letter is the dominant language, and font sizes and case suggest different proficiencies:

   A   Ab Ab Ab Ab Ab AB AB aB aB Ba Ba Ba Ba Ba   B
Monolingual   Monolingual

Who is or is not categorized as a bilingual will depend on the purpose of the categorization. At different times, governments, for example, may wish to include or exclude language minorities. Where a single indigenous language exists (e.g. Irish in Ireland), a government may wish to maximize its count of bilinguals. A high count may indicate government success in language planning. In comparison, in a suppressive, assimilationist approach, immigrant minority languages and bilinguals may be minimized (e.g. Asian languages in the UK in the Census – see chapter 2).

Is there a middle ground in-between maximal and minimal definitions? The danger is in making arbitrary cut-off points about who is bilingual or not along the competence dimensions. Differences in classification will continue to exist. One alternative is to move away from the multi-colored canvas of proficiency levels to a portrait of the everyday use of the two languages by individuals (see earlier).

Balanced Bilinguals

The literature on bilingualism frequently spotlights one particular group of bilinguals whose competences in both languages are well developed. Someone who is approximately equally fluent in two languages across various contexts may be termed an equilingual or ambilingual or, more commonly, **a balanced bilingual**. As will be considered in chapter 7, balanced bilinguals are important when discussing the possible thinking advantages of bilingualism.

Balanced bilingualism is sometimes used as an idealized concept. Fishman (1971) argued that rarely will anyone be equally competent across all situations. Most bilinguals will use their two languages for different purposes and with different people. For example, a person may use one language at work; the other language at home and in the local community.

Balanced bilingualism is also a problematic concept for other reasons. The balance may exist at a low level of competence in the two languages. Someone may have two relatively undeveloped languages that are nevertheless approximately equal in proficiency. While this is within the literal interpretation of 'balanced' bilingual, it is not the sense employed by many researchers on bilingualism. The implicit idea of balanced bilingualism has often been of 'appropriate' competence in both languages. A child who can understand the delivery of the curriculum in school in either language, and operate in classroom activity in either language would be an example of a balanced bilingual.

Is 'balanced bilingualism' of use as a term? While it has limitations of definition and measurement, it has proved to be of value in research and theory (see chapter 7). However, categorizing individuals into such groups raises the issue of comparisons. Who is judged normal, proficient, skilled, fluent or competent? Who judges? The danger is in using monolinguals as the point of reference, as will now be considered.

An argument advanced by Cook (1992, 2002a) and Grosjean (1985, 1994, 2001) is that there are two contrasting views of individual bilinguals. First, there is a monolingual or **fractional** view of bilinguals, which evaluates the bilingual as 'two monolinguals in one person'. There is a second, **holistic** view which argues that the bilingual is not the sum of two complete or incomplete monolinguals, but that he or she has a unique linguistic profile. The monolingual view is that normal or 'pure' to have own language, and therefore bilinguals are studied from that perspective. The multi-competence view is that bilingualism and multilingualism are normal with different consequences for how language is studied (e.g. acquisition, use, storage, thinking, integration / interconnection / separation, (Cook, 2002a)).

THE MONOLINGUAL VIEW OF BILINGUALISM

Many teachers, administrators, politicians and researchers look at the bilingual as **two monolinguals in one person**. For example, if English is a bilingual's second language, scores on an English reading or English attainment test will often be compared against monolingual scores and averages. A bilingual's English language competence is often measured against that of a native monolingual English speaker (e.g. in the US and the UK). This is unfair because it derives from a monolingual view of people. It is also unfair because bilinguals will typically use their two languages in different situations and with different people. Thus bilinguals may be stronger in each language in different domains.

One expectation from this fractional viewpoint will be for bilinguals to show a proficiency comparable to that of a monolingual in both their two languages. If that proficiency does not exist in both languages, especially in the majority language, then bilinguals may be denigrated and classified as inferior. In the United States, for example, children of immigrant families, or of other language minority families, are often officially federally categorized as LEP (Limited English Proficient). In northern Europe, bilinguals who appear to exhibit a lack of proficiency in both languages may be described as 'semilingual'.

While areas such as Africa, India, Scandinavia and parts of Asia often see bilingualism as the norm, in countries such as the United States and England, the dominant view of the world is monolingual (Brutt-Griffler & Varghese, 2004). Although between a half and two-thirds of the world's population is bilingual to some degree, the monolingual is often seen as normal in these two countries, and the bilingual as an oddity or as inferior. This 'inferior' viewpoint, for example that bilinguals have two half developed languages, is encapsulated in the debate about 'semilingualism'.

'Semilingualism'/'Double Semilingualism'

Bilinguals tend to be dominant in one of their languages in all or some of their language abilities. This may vary with context and may change over time with geographical or social mobility. For others, the dominance may be relatively stable across time and place. The topic of dominance will be considered in chapter 2 when tests are discussed. For the present, a group has been proposed, one that is distinct from balanced and dominant bilinguals. Sometimes termed pejoratively as **semilinguals** or double semilinguals, the group is regarded as not having 'sufficient' competence in either language. This section will suggest that such a label is more politically motivated than accurate or commonplace.

Hansegård (1975; see Skutnabb-Kangas, 2000) described **semilingualism** in terms of deficiencies in bilinguals when compared with monolinguals on the following: display a small vocabulary and incorrect grammar, consciously think about language production, stilted and uncreative with each language, and finds it difficult to think and express emotions in either language.

The notion of semilingualism, or **double semilingualism**, has received much criticism (e.g. Skutnabb-Kangas, 2000; Wiley, 1996a, 2005c; MacSwan, 2000). There are major **problems** with the term. **First**, the term took on disparaging and belittling overtones, particularly in Scandinavia and with **immigrant** groups in the US. Semilingualism may be used as a negative label that invokes expectations of underachievement and a self-fulfilling prophecy. It is most frequently applied to immigrant groups and 'blames the victim'.

Second, if languages are relatively undeveloped, the origins may not be in bilingualism *per se*, but in the economic, political and social conditions that evoke under-development. This is a theme considered in detail in later chapters. The danger of the term semilingualism is that it locates the origins of under-development in the internal, individual possession of bilingualism, rather than in external, societal factors that co-exist with bilingualism. Thus the term may be used as a political rather than a linguistic concept.

Third, most bilinguals use their two languages for different purposes and events. Language may be specific to a context. A person may be competent in some contexts but not in others. Some children are competent in the school context, but are less competent in the vernacular of the street. Some are competent in a language for religious purposes, but less so in the home.

Fourth, the educational tests that are most often used to measure language proficiencies and differentiate between people may be insensitive to the qualitative aspects of languages and to the great range of language competences. Language tests may measure a small, unrepresentative sample of a person's daily language behavior (see chapter 2). Thus 'deficiencies' are often an artifact of narrow academic tests. Standardized tests of language proficiency fail to measure the discourse patterns that children from different cultures use with considerable competence.

> Test scores [are] based on specific language and literacy tests of the school. These tests, in turn, reflect particular literacy practices and social expectations favoring groups that control institutions. Also, because school tests are based on 'standard' academic language, there is an implicit bias against language variation within L1 (i.e., there is a bias against speakers of non-standard and creolized varieties of L1. In interpreting results based on standardized tests, practitioners sometimes claim that students have 'no language', meaning that they have no standard academic language. (Wiley, 1996a, pp. 167–168)

Fifth, the comparison with monolinguals may not be fair. It is important to distinguish whether bilinguals are 'naturally' qualitatively and quantitatively different from monolinguals in their use of their two languages (as a function of being bilingual). An apparent deficiency may be due to unfair comparisons with monolinguals.

The criticisms raise serious doubts about the value of the term 'semilingualism'. However, this does not detract from the fact that there are language abilities on which people do differ, with some people being at the earlier stages of development, others where there is rapid language loss (Davies, 2003). Being at an early stage or undergoing language loss may not be the result of being bilingual. Economic and social factors or educational provision may, for example, be the cause.

Rather than highlight the apparent 'deficit' in language development, the more equitable and positive approach is to emphasize that, when suitable **conditions** are provided, competence in language is capable of development to high levels. When a 'language deficit' is perceived, a more proper approach is to locate the causes in, for example, the type of tests used, material deprivation, in the quality of treatment in schooling and not in language itself (see chapters 9, 15 and 17).

THE HOLISTIC VIEW OF BILINGUALISM

Cook (1992, 2002a, 2002b) and Grosjean (1985, 1994, 2001) present a more positive alternative view of bilinguals, as those with **multi-competences**. Grosjean uses an analogy from the world of athletics, and asks whether we can fairly judge a sprinter or a high jumper against a hurdler. The sprinter and high jumper concentrate on one event and may excel in it. The hurdler concentrates on two different skills, trying to combine a high standard in both. With only a few exceptions, the hurdler will be unable to sprint as fast as the sprinter or jump as high as the high jumper. This is not to say that the hurdler is a worse athlete than the other two. Any comparison of who is the best athlete makes little sense. This analogy suggests that comparing the language proficiency of a monolingual with a bilingual's dual language or multilingual proficiency is similarly unjust.

However, this raises the question, should bilinguals only be measured and compared by **reference to other bilinguals**? When for example, someone learns English as a second language, should that competency in English only be measured against other bilinguals? In countries like Wales for instance, where first-language Welsh-speaking children compete in a largely English-language job market against monolingual English speakers, the dominant view is that they should be given the same English assessments at school.

Any **assessment** of a bilingual's language proficiency should ideally move away from the traditional language tests (with their emphasis on form and correctness), to an evaluation of the bilingual's general communicative competence. This appraisal would be based on a totality of the bilingual's language usage in all domains, whether this involves the choice of one language in a particular domain, or a mixing of the two languages.

There is sometimes a political reality that deters the blossoming of a holistic view of the bilingual. In Australia, much of Canada, the United States and the United Kingdom, the dominant English-speaking monolingual politicians and administrators will not accept a different approach or standard of assessment (one for monolinguals, another for bilinguals).

Yet the bilingual is a complete linguistic entity, an integrated whole. Bilinguals use their two languages with different people, in different contexts and for different purposes. Levels of proficiency in a language may depend on which contexts (e.g. street and home) and how often that language is used. Communicative competence in one of a bilingual's two languages may be stronger in some domains than in others. This is natural and to be expected. Any assessment of a bilingual's competence in two languages needs to be sensitive to such differences of when, where and with whom bilinguals use either of their languages. Such an assessment should reveal the multi-competences of bilinguals (Cook, 1992, 2002a).

CONVERSATIONAL FLUENCY AND ACADEMIC LANGUAGE COMPETENCE

So far, the chapter has centered on the variety of language abilities and the danger of categorization using a small or biased selection of language sub-skills. One issue has been whether the variety of sub-skills can be reduced to a small number of important dimensions. Hernández-Chávez *et al.* (1978), for example, suggested there are 64 separate components to language proficiency. In comparison, many reading tests tacitly assume that reading can be reduced to one dimension. Oller's (1982) claimed that there was one overall, global language dimension. An overlap between different academic language tests was sufficient for Oller and Perkins (1980) to suggest that there exists a single factor of **global language proficiency**.

The idea of a single language factor is contentious as the evidence indicates that there are both global and specific aspects of language proficiencies. Oller's (1982) idea of a global language factor is based on quantitative testing. As will be considered later in the book, such tests leave qualitative differences between people unexplored. There is also an emphasis on language in an academic context. This leaves the out-of-school communicative profile of people relatively ignored.

Oller's (1982) much disputed claim for one global language factor provides a starting point for a distinction between two different language abilities. Oller's (1982) language proficiency factor has been allied to the language abilities needed to cope in the classroom. Most (but not all) language tests are closely linked to the cognitive, academic language skills of the classroom. Reading and writing tests are obvious examples. The notion of a curriculum based language competence led various authors to make an important distinction. Apart from **academically related language competence**, it has been proposed that there is a conceptually distinct category of **conversational competence** (Cummins, 2000b). Skutnabb-Kangas and Toukomaa (1976) proposed a difference between **surface fluency** and **academically related aspects of language competence**. Surface fluency would include the ability to hold a simple conversation in the shop or street and may be acquired fairly quickly (e.g. in two or three years) by second language learning. To cope in the curriculum, conversational language competence may not be enough. Academically related language competence in a second language may take from five to eight years or longer to acquire. This theme is considered in detail later in the book when a contentious distinction is made between basic interpersonal communicative skills and cognitive/academic language proficiency (BICS and CALP – see chapter 8). Such a distinction between two levels of language competence is important as it involves disputing Oller's (1982) 'single factor' language skill.

> If language abilities are multicolored, and if bilinguals have a range of colors in both languages, then positive terms are needed to portray the variety. Calling bilinguals LEP (**Limited English Proficiency**) students in the US seems negative and pejorative. For example, in the US, Title III of the Elementary and Secondary Education Act of 1965, as reauthorized by the 'No Child Left Behind Act' of 2001 is entitled 'Language Instruction of Limited English Proficient and Immigrant Students'. Such a label can accentuate children's perceived deficiency rather than their proficiencies, children's perceived 'deprivation' rather than their accomplishments, their lower, marginalized, minority status through majority eyes rather than their bilingual potentiality. Such a label highlights past and present performance rather than potentialities and the possibility of functioning well in two or more languages.

The chapter now continues by considering various language structure theories. Theories about the structure of language competence provide an integrating consideration of the themes of the definition of bilingualism.

THE STRUCTURE OF LANGUAGE COMPETENCE

The language theories of the 1960s (e.g. Lado, 1961; Carroll, 1968) tended to center on language skills and components. The skills comprise listening, speaking, reading and writing and the components of knowledge comprise grammar, vocabulary, phonology and graphology. These earlier models did not indicate how skills and knowledge were integrated. For example, how does listening differ from speaking? How does reading differ from writing? Earlier models fail to probe the competence of 'other' people in a conversation. In a conversation, there is negotiation of meaning between two or more people. Real communication involves anticipating a listener's response, understandings and misunderstandings, sometimes clarifying one's own language to ensure joint understanding and relationships of similar and different status and power.

It has also been suggested that such skill and knowledge models tend to ignore the sociocultural and sociolinguistic context of language. Earlier models tended to be linguistic and ignore the settings and social contexts where language is used. A more sociolinguistic approach will examine actual content and context of communication called 'speech acts' or the 'ethnography of communication'. This approach includes looking at the rules of dual language usage among bilinguals, their shared knowledge in conversation, and the culturally, socially and politically determined language norms and values of bilingual speech events.

Various holistic models of language competence have been developed. One example will be briefly outlined.

Bachman's Model of Language Competence

A major model of language competence was proposed by Bachman (1990), refined by Bachman and Palmer (1996) and with a critique by McNamara (2003). Bachman's model is valuable in that it considers both **language competence and language performance**. The model includes not only grammatical knowledge but also knowledge of how to use language in a particular communicative context. To fully define, refine and enable the testing of communicative competence, Bachman (1990) proposed a model that is summarized in the following table.

Language Competence
1. Organizational Competence
    (i)   Grammatical (e.g. Syntax, Vocabulary)
    (ii) Textual (e.g. Written and oral cohesion)
2. Pragmatic Competence
    (i)   Illocutionary Competence (e.g. speech strategies, language functions)
    (ii) Sociolinguistic Competence (e.g. sensitivity to register, dialect, cultural figures of speech)

To explain the table: for Bachman (1990), communicative competence is composed of two major components: organizational competence and pragmatic competence. **Organizational competence** is broken down into two parts, grammatical competence and textual competence. Grammatical competence comprises knowledge of vocabulary, syntax, morphology and phonology/graphology. For example, a person needs to arrange words in a correct order in a sentence with appropriate endings (e.g. high, high**er**, high**est**). Textual competence involves 'the knowledge of the conventions for joining utterances together to form a text, which is essentially a unit of language – *spoken or written* – consisting of two or more utterances or sentences' (Bachman, 1990, p. 88).

Pragmatic competence is composed of two sub-parts: illocutionary competence and sociolinguistic competence. Following Halliday (1973), Bachman (1990) lists four language functions as part of **illocutionary competence**: ideational (the way we convey meanings and experiences), manipulative (using language in an instrumental way to achieve ends), heuristic (the use of language to discover new things about our world and solving problems), and the imaginative function (using language beyond the 'here and now' (e.g. for humor or fantasy).

The second part of pragmatic competence is **sociolinguistic competence**. Sociolinguistic competence is sensitivity to the context where language is used, ensuring that language is appropriate to the person or the situation. This may entail sensitivity to differences in local geographical dialect, sensitivity to differences in register (e.g. the register of boardroom, baseball, bar and bedroom). Sociolinguistic competence also refers to sensitivity to speaking in a native-like or natural way. This will include cultural variations in grammar and vocabulary (e.g. Black English). Another part of sociolinguistic competence is the ability to interpret cultural references and figures of speech. Sometimes, to understand a particular conversation, one needs inner cultural understanding of a specific language. A Welsh figure of speech such as 'to go round the Orme' (meaning 'to be long-winded') is only fully understandable within local northern Welsh cultural idioms.

In order to represent language as a dynamic process, the listed components given in the table must be regarded as interactive with each other. Therefore the notion of **strategic competence** is important, where individuals constantly plan, execute and assess their communication strategies and delivery. Bachman and Palmer (1996) see such strategic competence as cognitive executive processes that govern language behavior. In a revision of the model, Bachman and Palmer (1996) added the personal characteristics of the individual language user to the model (topical knowledge and affective schema). Critiques of this model are provided by McNamara (1996) and Skehan (1998).

Since competence in a language is viewed as an integral part of language performance and not abstracted from it, measuring language competence cannot just use pencil and paper tests, but also need to investigate the language of genuine communication. Instead of tests that are artificial and stilted (e.g. language dictation tests), **communicative performance testing** involves creative, unpredictable, contextualized conversation. However, predicting 'real world' performance from such tests, and the 'one sidedness' that ignores the reality that conversations are jointly constructed and negotiated, remain problematic. This suggests that it will be difficult to measure communicative proficiency in an unbiased, comprehensive, valid and reliable way. Simple classroom tests are likely to be but a partial measure of the bilingual's everyday performance.

Discussions of language competence often move to questions about measurement (e.g. of students). To what extent can we measure someone's performance in their two languages? How can we portray when, where and with whom people use their two languages? What are the problems and dangers in measuring bilinguals? These questions provide the themes for the next chapter.

CONCLUSION

Defining exactly who is or is not bilingual is essentially elusive and ultimately impossible. Some categorization, however, is often necessary and helpful to make sense of the world. Therefore categorizations and approximations may be required. Definitions in a phrase (e.g. Bloomfield's (1933) 'native-like control of two languages') offer little help. Intrinsically arbitrary and ambiguous in nature, they can be easily criticized and are difficult to defend.

A more helpful approach may be to locate important distinctions and dimensions surrounding the term 'bilingualism' that refine thinking about bilingualism (Baetens Beardsmore, 1986). The fundamental distinction is between bilingual ability and bilingual usage. Some bilinguals may be fluent in two languages but rarely use both. Others may be much less fluent but use their two languages regularly in different contexts. Many other patterns are possible.

A person's use of their two languages asks questions about when, where and with whom? This highlights the importance of considering domain or context. As a bilingual moves from one situation to another, so may the language being used in terms of type (e.g. Spanish or English), content (e.g. vocabulary) and style. Over time and place, an individual's two languages are never static but ever changing and evolving.

In terms of ability in two languages, the four basic dimensions are listening, speaking, reading and writing. With each of these proficiency dimensions, it is possible to fragment into more and more microscopic and detailed dimensions (e.g. pronunciation, vocabulary, grammar, meaning and style). Those sub-dimensions can subsequently be further dissected and divided.

Creating a multidimensional, elaborate structure of bilingual proficiency may make for sensitivity and precision. However, ease of conceptualization and parsimony require simplicity rather than complexity. Therefore simple categorization is the paradoxical partner of complex amplification. This chapter has focused on the categories of balanced bilingualism, semilingualism, and one-factor ideas of language ability. These categories have received some depth of discussion and critical response in the research literature. As will be revealed in later chapters, these categories also relate to central research on bilingualism and bilingual education.

The chapter considered theories of the structure of language competence. In particular, the focus has been on linking a linguistic view of language competence with a communicative view. Language can be decomposed into its linguistic constituents (e.g. grammar, vocabulary). It is also important to consider language as a means of making relationships and communicating information. This important dualism will follow us through the book: ability and use; the linguistic and the social; competence and communication.

KEY POINTS IN THIS CHAPTER

- There is a difference between bilingualism as an individual possession and two or more languages operating within a group, community, region or country.
- At an individual level, there is a distinction between a person's ability in two languages and their use of those languages.
- Bilinguals typically use their two languages with different people, in different contexts and for different purposes.
- Language abilities are listening, speaking, reading and writing. Thinking in a language is sometimes seen as a fifth language ability.
- Balanced bilinguals with equal and strong competence in their two languages are rare.
- There is a difference between a monolingual or fractional view of bilinguals

and a holistic view. The fractional view sees bilinguals as two monolinguals inside one person. The holistic view sees bilinguals as a complete linguistic entity, an integrated whole.

- The term 'semilingual' or 'double semilingualism' has been used to describe those whose languages are both under-developed. However, the label has tended to take on negative, political and personally pejorative connotations.
- A distinction is made between the kind of language required for conversational fluency and the type of language required for academic, classroom operations.
- Language competence includes not only linguistic competence (e.g. vocabulary, grammar) but also competence in different social and cultural situations with different people.

SUGGESTED FURTHER READING

BAKER, C. & JONES, S.P., 1998, *Encyclopedia of Bilingualism and Bilingual Education*. Clevedon: Multilingual Matters.

BHATIA, T.K. & RITCHIE, W.C. (eds), 2004, *The Handbook of Bilingualism*. Malden, MA: Blackwell.

EDWARDS, V., 2004, *Multilingualism in the English-speaking World*. Oxford: Blackwell.

GROSJEAN, F., 2001, Bilingualism, individual. In R. MESTHRIE (ed.), *Concise Encyclopedia of Sociolinguistics*. Oxford: Elsevier Science.

SKUTNABB-KANGAS, T., 2000, *Linguistic Genocide in Education – Or Worldwide Diversity and Human Rights?* Mahwah, NJ: Erlbaum.

See also the Special Issue of the *International Journal of Bilingual Education and Bilingualism*, 2004, volume 7, 2&3, for a recent conceptualization of bilinguals and bilingualism.

A valuable WWW site for general searching on bilingualism is maintained by the School of Education at the University of Birmingham (UK): **http://www.edu.bham.ac.uk/bilingualism/database/biweb.htm**

STUDY ACTIVITIES

(1)   Do you consider yourself and/or people known to you as bilingual or multilingual? Would you describe yourself, or someone known to you, as 'balanced' in ability and use of two or more languages? Which language or languages do you think in? Does this change in different contexts? In which language or languages do you dream, count numbers, pray and think aloud?

(2)   This activity can be based on self-reflection or you may wish to interview someone who is bilingual or multilingual. Make a table or diagram to illustrate how one person's dual or multilingual ability and language usage has changed and developed since birth. Write down how different contexts have affected that change and development. The diagram or table should illustrate the life history of someone's languages indicating changes over time and over different contexts.

(3)   In a school with which you are most familiar, find out how students are labeled and categorized in terms of their languages. Who applies what labels? Which students are seen positively and negatively? Are there consequences of labels?

Is there interest in the language competences and language use of multilingual students?

CHAPTER 2

The Measurement of Bilingualism

The Measurement of Bilingualism

INTRODUCTION

Having discussed definitions, dimensions and distinctions, the topic of measuring bilinguals and multilinguals both elaborates and illuminates that discussion. Problems of defining bilinguals are illustrated when there is measurement and categorization of such individuals and groups. This chapter, therefore, begins by clarifying the different reasons for measuring bilinguals and multilinguals. This occurs not only in education but also in society (e.g. censuses). Illustrations are then given of such measurement with ways of profiling the language ability and use of individuals and language groups. It is important to develop a critical awareness of language measurement, both in the internal limitations of measurement and the politics surrounding language testing.

It is customary to try to categorize the complexity of individual differences in bilingualism. We make sense of our world by continual classification. People are constantly compared and contrasted. Yet the simplification of categorization often hides the complexity of reality. Sorting often simplifies unsympathetically. Individual differences are reduced to similarities. Yet over-complexity can be unwelcome and confusing. Complications can confound those needing order and pattern. The measurement of bilinguals attempts to locate similarities, order and pattern.

THE PURPOSES OF THE MEASUREMENT OF BILINGUALS

Measurement of bilinguals can take place for a variety of purposes, and it is valuable to differentiate between some of these overlapping aims.

Distribution

An example of the measurement of bilinguals is **census questions** requesting information about ability or usage in two or more languages (e.g. in US, Canada,

Ireland). Such census data allow a researcher to estimate the size and distribution of bilinguals in a particular area. For example, a survey of 850,000 children in London schools revealed the presence of over 300 different languages (Baker & Eversley, 2000). Geographers map the proportion and location of regional and minority language groups (C.H. Williams, 2004). For an example, see the Ethnologue web site: **http://www.ethnologue.com/**

Selection

Bilinguals may be distinguished as a 'separate' group for selection purposes. For example, a school may wish to allocate children to classes, streams, groups or tracks based on their degree of bilingual proficiency or language background. Bilinguals may be assessed for **placement** in special education classes (see chapter 15). A different example is measuring bilinguals at the outset of research. An investigation may require the initial formation of two or more groups (e.g. 'balanced' bilinguals, 'partial' bilinguals and monolinguals).

Summative

Summative means 'totaling up' to indicate the destination a person has reached in their language learning journey. **Summing up** someone's language proficiency may occur, for example, at the end of a semester or a school year. When measuring the current performance level of a person, a wide variety of language proficiency and achievement tests are available (e.g. reading comprehension, reading vocabulary, spelling, grammar). Such tests may be used in schools to measure the four basic language abilities. In a minority language context, emphasis is often on measuring proficiency in both the minority language and the majority language.

   In the United States, emphasis on minority language groups becoming proficient in English has been a dominant issue in the testing of bilinguals (see chapter 9). Thus in most US schools, language testing is solely in English, with second language competence ignored (Carrisquillo & Rodríguez, 2002).

   With proficiency testing, the measurement of bilinguals becomes fused with second language testing and the general area of language testing. Apart from general language tests, there are measures of the relative dominance of a person's two languages and the mixing of a person's two languages (sometimes pejoratively termed 'interference' – see chapter 5). Such tests spotlight the particular characteristics of bilinguals as different from second language learners and first language development. Examples are provided later in this chapter.

Formative

Language proficiency tests are often used for summative judgments. In comparison, a test or assessment device that gives feedback during learning, and to aid further development is **formative assessment**. A student may be profiled on a precise breakdown of language skills to provide facilitative feedback to the teacher that directly leads to action. This is the notion of formative testing. If the test reveals areas where a child's language needs developing, there can be immediate intervention and remedial help. A diagnosis of a problem in language may lead to the formation of a plan to effect a remedy. The assessment of bilinguals is considered in chapter 15.

THE ASSESSMENT OF BILINGUALS IN SCHOOL

Criterion Referenced Language Tests: A Curriculum Approach to Language Testing

A recent shift in testing has been away from norm referenced tests to criterion referenced tests. This is partly due to the movement in language education towards communicative skills, curriculum objectives and mastery learning. What is the distinction between norm referenced and criterion referenced tests?

Language proficiency tests are usually classified into norm referenced and criterion referenced tests; the former usually being summative tests, the latter mostly being formative tests. Standardized **norm referenced tests** essentially compare one individual with others, as in an IQ test. A norm referenced test of reading ability, for example, may enable the teacher to compare one student with a national or regional average (norm). The student can then be exactly placed in an ordered list (e.g. in the top 16%).

A **criterion referenced test** moves away from comparing one person with another. Instead it profiles an individual child on a particular language skill. The profile will test what a child can and cannot do on a precise breakdown of language skills. The parallel is with a car driving test. There are a variety of components to driving (e.g. backing around a corner, three-point turn, starting on a steep hill). Proficiency in driving often requires being able to satisfy an examiner on these sub-skills. Comparisons with other drivers are unimportant. An individual's mastery of specific tasks is the criterion for passing or failing.

Specifying driving criteria is easier than identifying language criteria, hence the analogy is not exact. The sub-components of language proficiency will be contested, and may not be easily definable or measurable. Apart from language skills, there are the qualitative aspects of language that are not simply reducible for testing (e.g. the emotive, status and poetic functions of languages).

One advantage for bilinguals of criterion referenced testing over norm referenced testing is the point of comparison. Norm referenced testing may compare bilinguals with monolinguals. The norm becomes the native speaker (Davies, 2003). Various authors (e.g. Frederickson & Cline, 1996; Cook, 2002a; Grosjean, 1985, 1994) regard such comparison as unfair and invalid (see chapter 1).

In criterion referenced testing, the bilingual can be profiled on specific language skills. In theory, **unfair comparisons** between bilingual and monolingual may then be avoided. In practice, however, criterion referenced tests *can* be used to create comparisons between children (e.g. monolingual native speakers and bilinguals), between groups of children and between schools. Behind every criterion lurks a

---

Language Test Terminology

- **Language skills** tend to refer to highly specific, observable, measurable, clearly definable components such as handwriting.
- **Language competence** is a broad and general term, used particularly to describe an inner, mental representation of language, something latent rather than overt. Such competence refers usually to an underlying system inferred from language performance.
- **Language performance** hence becomes the outward evidence for language competence. By observing general language comprehension and production, language competence may be implied.
- **Language ability** and **language proficiency** tend to be used more as 'umbrella' terms and therefore used somewhat ambiguously. For some, language ability is a general, latent disposition, a determinant of eventual language success. For others, it tends to be used as an outcome, similar but less specific than language skills, providing an indication of current language level. Similarly, language proficiency is sometimes used synonymously with language competence; at other times as a specific, measurable outcome from language testing. However, both language proficiency and language ability are distinct from language achievement.
- **Language achievement** (attainment) is usually seen as the outcome of formal instruction. Language proficiency and language ability are, in contrast, viewed as the product of a variety of mechanisms: formal learning, informal non-contrived language acquisition (e.g. on the street) and of individual characteristics such as 'intelligence'.

---

norm. The norm is usually the point of departure for setting a criterion (Davies, 2003).

An advantage of criterion referenced language tests is that they may facilitate feedback to the teacher that directly leads to action. This is the notion of formative testing. If the test reveals areas where a child's language requires developing, further action can be taken. One illustration of testing language proficiency by criterion referenced tests is given by Harris (1984, see also Harris & Murtagh, 1999). Focussing on the attainment of Irish listening and speaking objectives, the table below specifies the test items. The number of items to measure each objective ranged from three (control of syntax of questions) to 25 items (general comprehension of speech). Fourth grade children were assessed for their mastery of 140 separate items.

Harris' (1984) language tests are based on phonology (pronunciation), morphology (knowledge of the functions of words), syntax (grammar structures) and lexicon (vocabulary). In contrast, the Council of Europe's Common European Framework of Reference for language assessment (Council of Europe, 2001) particularly concerns language communication and use. The Common

Listening Objectives	Speaking Objectives
1. Sound discrimination	1. Pronunciation
2. Listening vocabulary	2. Speaking vocabulary
3. General comprehension of speech	3. Fluency of Oral description
4. Understanding morphology of verbs	4. Control of morphology of verbs
5. Understanding morphology of prepositions	5. Control of morphology of prepositions
6. Understanding morphology of qualifiers	6. Control of morphology of qualifiers
7. Understanding morphology of nouns	7. Control of morphology of nouns
8. Understanding syntax of statements	8. Control of syntax of statements
9. Understanding syntax of questions	9. Control of syntax of questions

European Framework 'provides a common basis for the elaboration of language syllabuses, curriculum guidelines, examinations, textbooks, etc. across Europe' (Council of Europe, 2001, p. 1). The Framework defines levels of **proficiency** that allow assessment of learners' progress irrespective of age, language or region. To reach the first language proficiency level of the Framework (called the Breakthrough Level), a learner should be able to demonstrate a basic ability to communicate and exchange information in a simple manner. An assessment task to demonstrate this might be asking simple questions about a menu or passing on simple instructions.

Such assessment tasks are important because they tend to accent what a child can do, rather than typical classroom tests which focus on what cannot be done. Communicative skills, knowledge and understanding are profiled rather than marks, percentages or grades. **Competence** is highlighted rather than errors and deficiencies. Such tasks compare the learner with a scheme of language development, rather than comparing the child with other children. Such tests are formative, giving direct feedback and 'feedforward' to enable curriculum decisions about individual learners.

Criterion referenced language tests should provide direct feedback into the following areas (Baker, 1995):

- teaching decisions (e.g. diagnosis of curriculum areas not mastered by an individual student);
- reporting to, and discussing achievement with parents;
- locating children needing special support and the type of curriculum support they need;
- identifying children for accelerated learning;
- informing about standards in the class in terms of curriculum development through a subject.

In the US, single tests to measure bilinguals' proficiency are becoming less common than multiple criteria (Carrasquillo & Rodríguez, 2002). Structured approaches (e.g. published standardized tests, checklists) are often joined by inspection of portfolios of students' work (e.g. assignments, journals) and teachers' own insightful observations.

Self-rating on Proficiency

Students may be asked to assess their language strengths and weaknesses. An example to illustrate self-rating on language proficiency follows:

Can you understand:	English?	Spanish?	Can you speak:	English?	Spanish?
Yes – fluently	☐	☐	Yes – fluently	☐	☐
Yes – fairly well	☐	☐	Yes – fairly well	☐	☐
Yes – some	☐	☐	Yes – some	☐	☐
Yes – just a little	☐	☐	Yes – just a little	☐	☐
No – not now	☐	☐	No – not now	☐	☐

Can you read:	English?	Spanish?	Can you write:	English?	Spanish?
Yes – fluently	☐	☐	Yes – fluently	☐	☐
Yes – fairly well	☐	☐	Yes – fairly well	☐	☐
Yes – some	☐	☐	Yes – some	☐	☐
Yes – just a little	☐	☐	Yes – just a little	☐	☐
No – not now	☐	☐	No – not now	☐	☐

LIMITATIONS IN MEASUREMENT

Self-rating covers the basic four language abilities across two languages (e.g. Spanish and English). The answers are possibly too broad (e.g. there are many graduations possible in between each of the answers. Apart from this problem of scaling, there are other problems frequently encountered with measuring language competence. These may be listed as:

(1) **Ambiguity**. Words such as 'speak', 'understand', 'read' and 'write' include a wide variety of levels of proficiency. The range is from those with minimal proficiency to Bloomfield's (1933) maximum notion of 'native-like control of two languages'. Tests also often contain only a small and unrepresentative sample of the totality of language proficiencies.

(2) **Context**. A bilingual may be able to understand a language in one context (e.g. a shop) and not in another context (e.g. academic lecture). Another bilingual may be able to read newspapers but not textbooks. Proficiency and usage will vary with changing environments. A response summated across contexts is required. This may not be sensitive to different levels of proficiency across different contexts.

(3) **Social desirability/Subjectivity**. Respondents may consciously or unconsciously give a 'halo' version of themselves. Self-ratings are vulnerable to exaggeration or understatement. People may say they are fluent in a second language (when in reality they are not) for identity, self-esteem or status reasons. Others may indicate they do not speak a language when they can. This may occur, for example, in a low prestige, 'subtractive' (see chapter 4) minority language environment where the introduction of the second language may replace the first language. Questions about proficiency can be interpreted as political referendum or attitudinal questions.

(4) **Acquiescent response**. There is a slight tendency of respondents to answer 'yes' rather than 'no' in self rating questions. It appears preferable to be positive rather than negative. This also tends to hold with a preference for 'Agree' rather than 'Disagree' and 'Like Me' rather than 'Not Like Me'.

(5) **Self-awareness**. A self rating depends on accuracy of knowledge about oneself. For one person, the frame of reference may be other neighborhood children who are not so fluent. When compared to children in another community, apparent fluency may be less. What is competent in one environment may seem less competent in another. The age, nature and location of the reference group may cause self-assessment not to be strictly comparable across a representative sample of people. A child may also self-rate on surface fluency and not be aware of much less fluency in cognitively demanding language tasks (Skutnabb-Kangas, 2000).

(6) **Point of reference**. There is a danger of using monolingual proficiency and performance as the point of comparison (see chapter 1).

(7) **Test aura**. Another danger is of raising language measurement to the level of scientific measurement with an accompanying exaggerated mystique. More 'natural' forms of language sampling may be given lower status (e.g. recording natural conversation) as they rarely carry the mystique of educational and psychological (psychometric) measurement, but may provide more authentic samples of language.

(8) **Narrow sampling of dimensions of language**. Language measurement may unwittingly be perceived as something tangible and concrete (as when measuring height and weight). Rather, language tests mostly contain a specification of language skills that is debatable.

(9) **Insensitivity to change**. It is customary and seen as good practice to produce measurement which is reliable over time and across occasions (give consistent scores for the same individual over weeks or months). However, the paradox is that such measurement may be insensitive to change within individuals. Test scores need an expiry date (e.g. not valid after one year).

(10) **Labeling**. Test scores are apt to create labels for individuals (e.g. someone is seen as having low performance) which create expectations (e.g. of further underachievement) that may lead to a self-fulfilling prophecy.

COMMUNICATIVE LANGUAGE TESTING

In attempting to assess a bilingual's competence in two languages, there is a danger of using a simple paper and pencil test believing the test will provide a faithful estimation of everyday language life (McKinnie & Priestly, 2004). Multiple choice language tests, dictation, reading comprehension tests and spelling tests are much used paths in the testing of academic language skills (see Clapham & Corson, 1997). Reducing everyday language competence to tests of specific skills is like measuring Michelangelo's art solely by its range of colors.

The tape recording of interviews or storytelling to measure oral proficiency is frequently used (McKinnie & Priestly, 2004). A radical alternative is seeing how bilinguals perform in both languages in a range of **real communicative situations**. Observing a bilingual in a shop, at home, at work and during leisure activity might seem the ideal way of measuring bilingual competence. This idea is time-consuming and may be biased by the presence of the researcher. Being a 'research' situation, it is sometimes intrusive into individual privacy and may be unrepresentative across time and place.

However, the greater danger lies in only viewing languages inside an academic context. The classroom is one language domain where language minority students from different cultural contexts may not reveal their wealth of language talents. Such academic testing is often more suited to elective bilinguals (see chapter 1) whereas circumstantial bilinguals require their language abilities and uses to be portrayed across out-of-school domains to be realistic and representative.

In order to collect *realistic and representative* data, we need to know how situations (domains) relate to one another. We also need to know the sample of language performance that relates adequately to all round language competence (see chapter 1).

A particular emphasis in language testing is on **communicative competence**. While tests of spelling, grammar, written comprehension and reading abound, the importance of using languages in realistic, everyday settings is reflected in current testing movements. The ideal is expressed by Skehan (1988, p. 125):

> Genuine communication is interaction-based, with more than one participant; unpredictable and creative, i.e. genuine communication may take the participants in unforeseen directions; is situated in a context which is both linguistic/discoursal and also sociocultural; has a purpose, in that participants will be trying to achieve something by use of language, e.g. to persuade, to deceive, etc.; uses authentic stimulus materials, and avoids contrived, specially produced materials; is based on real psychological conditions, such as time pressure; and is outcome evaluated, in that successful performance is judged in terms of whether communicative purposes have been achieved.

A test of language proficiency which meets Skehan's (1988) criteria is probably impossible to achieve. A test that truly measures purposeful communication across sufficient contexts without tester effects is improbable. For some, the answer is simply not to test. For others, a best approximation is accepted. A test may therefore be used that measures the more limited notion of **performance** rather than the wider idea of competence.

A test that attempts to approximate the conditions outlined by Skehan (1988) is an **oral interview**, an example of which is given below.

International English Language Testing System (IELTS)

The IELTS tests the English language proficiency of non-native speakers of English (for example, those who intend to study in Universities through the medium of English). There are Listening, Speaking, Reading and Writing tests. IELTS is accepted by most Australian, British, Canadian, New Zealand and many American Universities for admission purposes. For example, the UK General Medical Council normally requires a minimum score of 7.0 in each individual section of the IELTS test before a non-native speaker of English is allowed to commence medical training in the UK.

As part of an IELTS interview that comprises the Speaking Test, a candidate answers basic questions for 11 to 14 minutes about topics such as: where you live, clothes, travel, family, free time and shopping. Questions on shopping might ask:

- Do you like shopping? Why or why not?
- What kind of things do you like to buy?
- When do people in your area usually do their shopping?
- What are some of the advantages and disadvantages of large shops?

Candidates receive scores on a scale from one to nine, with allocation based on a rigorous and detailed system of performance descriptors (fluency and coherence; lexical resource; grammatical range and accuracy; pronunciation). The nine bands and their descriptive statements are as follows:

Band 9 Expert User
Has fully operational command of the language: appropriate, accurate and fluent with complete understanding.

Band 8 Very Good User
Has fully operational command of the language with only occasional unsystematic inaccuracies and inappropriacies. Misunderstandings may occur in unfamiliar situations. Handles complex detailed argumentation well.

Band 7 Good User
Has operational command of the language, though with occasional inaccuracies, inappropriacies and misunderstandings in some situations. Generally handles

complex language well and understands detailed reasoning.

Band 6 Competent User
Has generally effective command of the language despite some inaccuracies, inappropriacies and misunderstandings. Can use and understand fairly complex language, particularly in familiar situations.

Band 5 Modest User
Has partial command of the language, coping with overall meaning in most situations, though is likely to make many mistakes. Should be able to handle basic communication in own field.

Band 4 Limited User
Basic competence is limited to familiar situations. Has frequent problems in understanding and expression. Is not able to use complex language.

Band 3 Extremely Limited User
Conveys and understands only general meaning in very familiar situations. Frequent breakdowns in communication occur.

Band 2 Intermittent User
No real communication is possible except for the most basic information using isolated words or short formulae in familiar situations and to meet immediate needs. Has great difficulty understanding spoken and written English.

Band 1 Non User
Essentially has no ability to use the language beyond possibly a few isolated words.

See: (http://www.ielts.org/)

Such interview procedures may not reflect reality. Does genuine communication take place between strangers, in a contrived, artificial context? Is the language repertoire of a person truly elicited? Is 'interview language' representative of a person's everyday language functioning? Can we generalize from oral communicative tests based on a single type of test, given on a single occasion, based on a test interview which is not a typical event in real life? To what extent are language abilities comprehensively sampled in an interview? There are doubts about whether such interview procedures can validly imitate and investigate real communicative competence. At the same time, they are a compromise between artificial pencil and paper tests and the impracticality of the detailed observation of individuals across many domains.

A POLITICAL VIEW OF LANGUAGE TESTING

Language testing is not a neutral activity. For example, language tests are sometimes introduced to achieve curriculum change. Indeed, there is almost no more
powerful route to educational policy control or curriculum change than tests that
almost force the teacher to 'teach for the test'. Centrally or locally imposed language
tests define what skills are to be accented (e.g. communicative competence or
literacy) and what languages are to be promoted (e.g. the majority language at the
expense of minority languages). Language tests can include or exclude, gate-keep
or motivate, stagnate or innovate. Behind language tests are often agendas,
motives, ideology and politics. A language testing policy is typically the language
policy operationalized (Shohamy, 2001).

Language testing relates to cultural, social, political, educational and ideological agendas that shape the lives of all students and teachers. Such language tests
are deeply embedded in cultural, educational and political debates where
different ideologies are in contest. Elana Shohamy (1997, 2001) therefore proposes
a perspective she terms '**critical language testing**' that views test-takers as **political subjects in a political context**. An example is high stakes assessment in the US
(see chapter 9).

Critical language testing asks questions about whose formal and hidden agendas
tests relate to, and what sort of political and educational policies are delivered
through tests. Critical language testing argues that language testers must ask them
selves what sort of vision of society language tests create, and for what vision of
society tests are used? For example, are language tests intended to fulfill pre-defined
curricular or proficiency objectives, or are there other hidden aims, maneuvers or
manipulations?

Critical language testing asks questions about **whose knowledge** the tests are
based on? What is the intended or assumed status of that knowledge (e.g. 'truth' or
something that can be negotiated and challenged)? What is the meaning of
language test scores, and to what degree are they prescriptive, final and absolute, or
to what extent are they open to discussion and interpretation?

Critical language testing thus widens the field of language testing by
relating it to political and social debates.

> Tests have become tools which, in the name of objectivity, have created and
> perpetuated new subjective powers, and defined and dictated society's knowl-
> edge by building on the fear and trust of the public who are affected by their
> results. Tests have become tools which are used to perpetuate power and
> control, to screen and keep out those who are not part of the mainstream
> knowledge. Thus tests, originally developed for democratizing purposes,
> have become authoritative and centralized tools which are being manipulated
> in the hands of 'a few'. This is perpetuated by the symbolic values of tests in
> most modern societies. Tests have become symbols of quality, standards,
> achievements and high level order. (Shohamy, 2001, p. 159)

EXAMPLES OF THE MEASUREMENT OF BILINGUALS IN RESEARCH

A full inventory of bilingual measurement devices would be immense and is not provided (see Hornberger & Corson (1997) and Clapham & Corson (1997) for comprehensive surveys of this area). The examples given below help to make some essential points and tend to represent the styles most often used in research on bilinguals.

Language Background Scales

Language background or functional bilingualism scales are self-rating scales. They endeavor to measure actual **use** of two languages as opposed to proficiency. An example for schoolchildren is now presented (adapted from Baker, 1992; see Extra & Yagmur, 2004 for a multilingual example):

Here are some questions about the *language* in which you talk to different people, and the *language* in which certain people speak to you. There are no right or wrong answers. Leave an empty space if a question is inappropriate.

In which language do YOU speak to the following people? Choose just one of these answers

	Almost always in Spanish	In Spanish more often than English	In Spanish and English about equally	In English more often than Spanish	Almost always in English
Father					
Mother					
Brothers/Sisters					
Friends in the Classroom					
Friends on the Playground					
Friends outside School					
Teachers					
Neighbors					
Grandparents					
Other relatives					

In which language do the following people speak TO YOU?

	Almost always in Spanish	In Spanish more often than English	In Spanish and English about equally	In English more often than Spanish	Almost always in English
Father					
Mother					
Brothers/Sisters					

	Almost always in Spanish	In Spanish more often than English	In Spanish and English about equally	In English more often than Sapnish	Almost always in English
Friends in the Classroom					
Friends on the Playground					
Friends outside School					
Teachers					
Neighbors					
Grandparents					
Other relatives					

Which language do YOU use with the following?

	Almost always in Spanish	In Spanish more often than English	In Spanish and English about equally	In English more often than Spanish	Almost always in English
Speaking on the Telephone					
Text Messaging					
Computer/Internet/WWW					
Watching TV/Videos/DVDs					
Listening to Radio					
Listening to Cassettes/CDs					
Newspapers/Comics					
Reading Books					
Shopping					
Playing Sport					
Clubs/Societies					
Earning Money					
Religion					
Other Leisure Activities					

This scale has limitations besides the problems of ambiguity and 'social desirability' considered later. It is not exhaustive of targets (people) or of domains (contexts). Language activity with uncles and aunts, discos, correspondence, organizations, hobbies and travel are not included, for example. The choice of items included in such a scale is somewhere between an all-inclusive scale and a more narrow sample of major domains. At first glance, it may appear that the more inclusive a scale is the better. There is a problem, illustrated by Baker and Hinde (1984: 46):

> A person who says she speaks Welsh to her father (mostly away at sea), her grandparents (seen once a year), her friends (but tends to be an isolate), reads Welsh books and newspapers (only occasionally), attends Welsh Chapel (marriages and funerals only) but spends most of her time with an English speaking mother and in an English speaking school might gain a fairly high 'Welsh' score.

This example suggests that the 'to whom' question is insufficient. Frequency of usage in such contexts and with certain targets needs adding. To accompany 'to whom and where', a 'how often' and 'why' question is necessary. Also, such scales do not indicate networking or status and power in relationships which are important in language shift and language attitudes. Further problems of language background and functional bilingualism scales are discussed by Baker and Hinde (1984) and Baker (1985).

Language Use Surveys

The language background of a **language group** needs to include many different contextual dimensions. Listed below are some of the contexts that need to be included in such a language use or language census survey (examples are from the European Commission, 1996):

- Geographical (areal) extent of the language; number and density of users.
- Legal status of language; use of the language in bureaucracy; effect of local and central government on the language.
- Recent and past immigration and emigration affecting the language.
- Use of the language by parents with their children and between siblings; use of the language in new and existing marriages.
- Use of language in Elementary and Secondary education, Vocational, Technical, Adult, Continuing and Higher Education; language learning classes.
- Literacy and biliteracy of the language group.
- Unemployment in the language group. Types of employment among language group (e.g. socioeconomic status).
- Amount of language activism among the language group, especially in younger age groups.
- Cultural vitality of the language group; institutions dedicated to supporting the language and culture.
- Attitudes of speakers and non speakers to the language. Optimism or pessimism surrounding the language.

Language Balance and Dominance Measures

Various tests have been devised to gauge the relative dominance or balance of a bilingual's two languages. While such measures have been used in research, they have also been important in US education. Because instruction for US language minority children was historically mandated to take place in the child's dominant language, some measure of language dominance was needed. This may be through, for example, English language and Spanish language proficiency tests.

Five examples of psychometric tests are given below:

- **Speed of reaction in a word association task.** This seeks to measure whether a bilingual can give an association to stimulus words more quickly in one language than the other. No particular difference would seem to indicate a balanced bilingual. For example, a word such as 'house' may be presented, then measuring the time taken to produce an association (e.g. window). When a person is consistently quicker in giving associations in one language than another, the likelihood is that one language is dominant. However, dominance is different from competence. A person may be competent in two or more languages while being dominant in one. Similarly, there could be equal dominance and a low level of competence in both languages. Also, some cultures do not value speed of reaction, preferring accuracy. Thus there may be a cultural bias in the use of such tests.
- **Quantity of reactions to a word association task.** Bilinguals are measured for the number of associations given within one minute when a stimulus word (e.g. 'color') is presented. An approximately equal number of responses in two languages might indicate a balance between those languages.
- **Detection of words using both languages.** Words in both languages are extracted from a nonsense word such as DANSONODEND. The letters in the nonsense words must be equally representative of both languages. This is not easily achievable, and depends on relatively similar alphabets and scripts.
- **Time taken to read** a set of words in the respondent's two languages.
- **Amount of mixing** the two languages, the quantity of borrowing and switching from one language to another.

A major **problem** with such balance and dominance tests lies in the representativeness of the measure of language proficiency and performance. In this respect, such tests would appear to tap only a small part of a much larger and more complex whole (language ability or language use). The tests cover a small sample of language sub-skills that might be tested. Dominance will vary by domain and across time, being a constantly changing personal characteristic. It is possible to be approximately equally proficient in two languages, yet one may be dominant. Speed of processing may provide evidence about balance but not about dominance in actual language use, in different sociocultural contexts and over time (Valdés & Figueroa, 1994).

LANGUAGE CENSUSES

The Belgian census of 1846 was one of the first national censuses to ask language questions. Other countries were soon to follow Belgium's lead: Switzerland in 1850, Ireland in 1851, Hungary in 1857, Italy in 1861, Canada in 1871, Austria and Finland in 1880, India and Scotland in 1881, the United States in 1890, Wales in 1891 and Russia in 1897 (Ó Gliasáin, 1996). Other countries such as Venezuela, Bolivia and

Australia have more recently asked language questions in a census. Such censuses are often perceived by governments as providing relatively accurate measures of the number of language speakers in local communities, regions and countries.

Languages in the United States' Census

The **United States census** was instituted at the beginning of the United States political system in Article 1 Section 2 which stated that political representation in the House of Representatives was to be based on a population census. The census has been taken every 10 years since 1790, when Secretary of State, Thomas Jefferson, supervised the first census. A question on race was included in that first 1790 census. The first time a question was asked about 'languages spoken at home' was in 1890 (with a question on Hispanic origin being introduced in 1970 and 'ancestry' in 1980, see Macías, 2000). Increasingly, census data helps states and localities 'benchmark' and measure progress in meeting their objectives and legislatively mandated targets. Thus a census does not just provide information. It also can assist or invoke political action (e.g. the 1910 US Census spurring the Americanization campaign).

Two examples are given below of census questions on language from two different US censuses, the first from 1910 and the second from 2000. These examples illustrate how **census questions** are constructed in a way that does not always give accurate and comprehensive information about use of languages, and also reveals implicit official attitudes towards the use and maintenance of minority languages.

The United States Census of 1910
In the 1910 United States census, advice was given to enumerators when asking respondents about the mother tongue of members of the household. The extracts given below illustrate notions from a bygone era.

Extracts from Advice to Enumerators in the United States 1910 Census

'127. The question of mother tongue should not be asked of any person born in the United States'

'133. Column 17. Whether able to speak English; or, if not, give language spoken. This question applies to all persons age 10 and over. If such a person is able to speak English, write English [on the form]. If he is not able to speak English – and in such cases only – write the language which he does speak, as French, German, Italian.'

Note that:
- The question of mother tongue excluded those born in the United States. This indicates an assumption that all those born in the United States would be able to speak English, and that the maintenance of minority languages or bilingualism in English and a minority language was not considered.
- A person's ability in languages other than English was ignored if they were able to speak English.

- Ability in a heritage language was counted only if a person was unable to speak English.
- The language of the under-10-year-olds was ignored.

The United States Census of 2000

In 2000, a Census of the population was taken throughout the United States. Starting in January 2000 with visits to very remote areas and in March 2000 with postal delivery, Census 2000 questionnaires were made available in six languages – English, Spanish, Chinese, Tagalog, Vietnamese, and Korean. Language Assistance Guides were produced in 49 languages apart from English. Two questionnaires were used. A short questionnaire was sent to every household in the US, requesting information on individuals (e.g. gender, race, Hispanic origin, home ownership and age). A longer questionnaire was sent to about one in six of all US households. The longer questionnaire asked about ancestry, residence five years ago (migration), income and education. It also included a question about home languages. Question 11 on the 2000 Census form was phrased as follows:

Question 11

(a) **Does this person speak a language other than English at home?**

  ❑ Yes
  ❑ No *Skip to 12*

(b) **What is this language?**
  (*For example: Korean, Italian, Spanish, Vietnamese*)

(c) **How well does this person speak English?**

  ❑ Very well
  ❑ Well
  ❑ Not well
  ❑ Not at all

This question is more comprehensive than the 1910 language question. It asks about the use of a minority language in the home irrespective of command of English. It also asks a more searching question about the level of ability in English, which is the dominant question.

The **US 2000 Census** showed an increase in the percentage of residents 5 years old and over speaking a language other than English at home.

Year	Numbers Speaking a Language Other than English	Percentage of US Population
1980	23.1 million	11.0%
1990	31.8 million	13.8%
2000	46.9 million	17.9%

Of US residents who reported speaking other languages at home in the 2000 Census, 59.9% speak Spanish, 21.3% speak another Indo-European language, 14.8% speak Asian and Pacific Island languages, and 4.0% speak other languages. In Arizona, California, Hawaii, New Mexico, New Jersey, New York, Texas over 25% of the population speak another language in the home. Three hundred and twenty-two home languages were reported in the 2000 Census. The 10 languages with the highest number of speakers are: English (215.4 million), Spanish (28.1 million), French (1.6 million), Cantonese (1.5 million), German (1.4 million), Tagalog (1.2 million), Vietnamese and Italian (both with 1.0 million), Korean (0.9 million) and Russian (0.7 million). Of indigenous languages, Navaho recorded 178,015 speakers, Pennsylvania Dutch with 83,720 speakers and Yupik with 16,910 speakers.

For more information:
http://www.census.gov/
http://www.usefoundation.org/foundation/research/lia/
For interactive US language maps: http://www.mla.org/census_main

LIMITATIONS OF LANGUAGE CENSUSES

Language census data contain a set of limitations, even when there is a long tradition of census compilation.

- Census questions about home language, mother tongue and first language are often **ambiguous**. In the 2001 Canadian Census, one of the three language questions was 'Can this person speak English or French well enough to conduct a conversation?' This reveals the ambiguity of census questions. The term 'speak well enough' may be interpreted in different ways by different people. What one person considers 'well enough' may be at a different level of fluency to another. A brief conversation in the shop can be at a different level from a conversation in the classroom or in a President's office. Sometimes the questions do not distinguish between language use and language ability (see chapter 1). Thus a question, 'Do you speak English?' does not specify whether the question is about everyday use of language, ability to speak the language irrespective of regular use, or both use and ability. Some can but don't. Others do but with difficulty.
- Questions on census forms do not usually include the **four language abilities**: understanding a language, speaking, reading and writing. Thus oracy may be evaluated and not literacy.
- Questions about contexts or **domains** of language use (e.g. home, school, religion, street, shopping) are rarely asked. Therefore, a response is very generalized across many domains and insensitive to where languages are used.
- Census data may rapidly become **out of date** when factors such as migration, social upheaval, war or a high birthrate mean that the language situation is rapidly changing.
- Language questions can be **politically inflammatory**. For example, in the

1846 Belgian census the language question was restricted to asking what language was usually spoken by respondents. Soon after, language censuses in Belgium began asking questions about knowledge of the official languages of Belgium. Since there was a mixture of official and unofficial (autochthonous) languages in use in Belgium, the restriction of such questions to official languages provoked argument and debate. In such Belgian language census questionnaires, all those over 14 years of age had to complete and sign the questionnaire. This also provoked contention and controversy. The outcome was that, in 1961, the majority of parliamentarians in Belgium decided to suspend the language censuses in Belgium to avoid further dispute.

- Not all censuses include questions on language. Some censuses ask about **ethnic groups**, which may not correspond to language groups. This occurred in the 2001 Census in England where there was no language census question but a question on ethnic origins (http://www.statistics.gov.uk/)
- Conversely, a language question in a census may be treated by respondents as referring to **identity**. For example, in Ireland, a non-Irish speaker may wish to be seen as Irish and therefore answer the Irish language question affirmatively. Thus a census language question may be interpreted as an attitude question. People from a particular ethnic group may feel they ought to say that they speak the indigenous or heritage language even if they do not. It may be regarded as socially desirable to say one speaks a language, and speaks it well. The opposite may also occur. If a minority language is disparaged and of low status, a speaker of that language may claim not to speak the language. Answers to questions about language on a census form may thus reflect 'a pose', a socially desirable answer and not everyday behavior.
- Censuses do not usually cover all of the **population** of a country despite considerable efforts to be inclusive. Some of the population may refuse to respond through the mail system, or to answer census personnel calling at their dwelling. Other people are out of reach or difficult to track down. Itinerants, illegal immigrants and the homeless, for example, may be missed by the census.

CONCLUSION

Just as dimensions and categorizations can never capture the full nature of bilingualism, so measurement usually fails to capture fully various conceptual dimensions and categorizations. Just as the statistics of a football or an ice hockey game do not convey the richness of the event, so language tests and measurements are unlikely to fully represent an idea or theoretical concept. Complex and rich descriptions are the indispensable partner of measurement and testing. The stark statistics of the football or ice hockey game and the colorful commentary are complementary, not incompatible.

Language background scales to measure language usage and a plethora of tests to measure language proficiency exist. The latter includes norm and criterion referenced language tests, self-rating scales and language dominance tests. Particular attention in this chapter has been given to criterion referenced tests measuring mastery of specific language objectives. Suitable for both first and second languages, sometimes based on theoretical principles, sometimes eclectic, such tests tend to relate directly to the process of teaching and learning.

KEY POINTS IN THE CHAPTER

- Bilinguals are measured both for their proficiency and use of their languages. Examples include census surveys of languages in a population, selection for different classes in school according to language ability, assessment of competency following second language learning.
- Language background scales measure a person's use of their languages in different domains and in different relationships.
- Language balance and dominance measures seek to gauge the relative strength of each language of a bilingual.
- Communicative language testing attempts to measure a person's use of language in authentic situations
- Criterion referenced language tests seek to provide a profile of language sub-skills whereas norm referenced tests compare a person with other people.
- 'Critical language testing' examines whose knowledge the tests are based on, and for what political purposes the tests will used. It regards test-takers as political subjects in a political context.
- Language censuses are used in many countries to measure the extent and density of speakers of different languages. There are problems with terms used, validity of the questions and reliability of the answers.

SUGGESTED FURTHER READING

CLAPHAM, C. and CORSON, D. (eds), 1997, *Language Testing and Assessment.* Volume 7 of the *Encyclopedia of Language and Education.* Dordrecht: Kluwer.
HORNBERGER, N. and CORSON, D. (eds), 1997, *Research Methods in Language and Education.* Volume 8 of the *Encyclopedia of Language and Education.* Dordrecht: Kluwer.
LYNCH, B., 2003, *Language Assessment and Programme Evaluation.* Edinburgh: Edinburgh University Press.
SHOHAMY, E., 2001, *The Power of Tests: A Critical Perspective on the Uses and Consequences of Language Tests.* London: Longman.
VALDÉS, G. and FIGUEROA, R.A., 1994, *Bilingualism and Testing: A Special Case of Bias.* Norwood, NJ: Ablex.

STUDY ACTIVITIES

(1) Using a local school(s), find out what tests are used to measure language achievement in the classroom. These may be listening, speaking, reading, writing or language development tests. Find out whether these are norm refer-

enced or criterion referenced tests. For what purposes are these tests being used? How fair are these to bilingual children?

(2) Use the Language Background Scale (modified to suit your context) on yourself or someone you know. This may also be used with a class of students. Examine the answers given and sum up in words or in numbers the balance and use of languages. If used with a group of students, are there groups or clusters of students? Are there those dominant in one language, those dominant in another language and those with an approximate balance between two languages? What is the profile of multilinguals?

(3) Using the library or the Internet, gather detailed information about one country's language census (e.g. US, Canada, East Africa, Wales, Ireland, Scotland (Gaelic), Australia, India, Bolivia, Venezuela, Caucasus Region). What were the major findings? What problems are there in the wording of the question(s)? What other limitations do you find in the survey?

(4) Using the WWW, a library or local schools, investigate one or more of the following tests, and assess their strengths and weakness when used with bilingual students in the classroom (e.g. selection, placement, formative and summative judgments): TOELF, Peabody Picture Vocabulary Test, WAIS vocabulary subtest, MacArthur Communication Development Inventories, Bilingual Syntax Measure, the SPEAK test.

CHAPTER 3

Endangered Languages: Planning and Revitalization

Introduction

Endangered Languages

Language Policies

Language Planning

A Theoretical Model of Language Revitalization
Status Factors
Demographic Factors
Institutional Support Factors

A Theory of Language Reversal
Steps in Reversing Language Shift
Limits and Critics

Conclusion

CHAPTER 3

Endangered Languages: Planning and Revitalization

INTRODUCTION

How would you feel if you were the **last speaker** of your language? Marie Smith, the last speaker of the Alaskan Eyak language, gave her answer (Nettle & Romaine, 2000, p. 14): 'I don't know why it's me, why I'm the one. I tell you, it hurts. It really hurts.' Richard Littlebear (1999), a Native American Cheyenne member, tells of his meeting with Marie Smith. 'I felt that I was sitting in the presence of a whole universe of knowledge that could be gone in one last breath. That's how fragile that linguistic universe seemed.'

To be told that a loved one is dying or dead is one of the most unpleasant experiences of life. To talk about a dead language or a dying language sounds academic and without much sentiment. Yet languages have no existence without people. A language dies with the last speaker of that language. For humanity, that is a great loss. It is like an Encyclopedia formed from that language and culture being buried. Three further examples will illustrate.

- In Cameroon in 1994/95, a researcher, Bruce Connell, visited the last speaker of a language called **Kasabe** (or Luo). In 1996, he returned to research that moribund language. He was too late. The last speaker of Kasabe had died on 5th November 1995 taking the language and culture with him. Connell reports that the last speaker was survived by a sister who could understand but not speak Kasabe, and whose children and grandchildren did not understand the language (Crystal, 2000). Simply stated, on 4th November 1995 Kasabe existed. On 5th November it was dead.

- On the 8th October 1992 a northwestern Caucasian language called **Ubykh** died. A linguist, Ole Andersen arrived in the Turkish village of Haci to interview the last speaker, Tefvik Esenc, only to learn that he had died just a couple of hours earlier (Crystal, 2000; Nettle & Romaine, 2000). His three sons were unable to talk to their father in Ubykh as they had become Turkish speakers. Tefvik Esenc had composed his own gravestone eight years earlier: 'This is the grave of Tefvik Esenc – the last person able to speak the language they called Ubykh.'

*   The last native speaker of **Cupeño** died in California in 1987, of **Catawba Sioux** in 1980, and of **Wappo** in 1990 (Nettle & Romaine, 2000).

ENDANGERED LANGUAGES

There is no exact agreement as to the **number of living languages** in the world. There is, however, growing agreement that many or most are dying languages (Nettle & Romaine, 2000). Grimes (2000) lists 6809 living languages in the world, while Mackey (1991) suggests 6170 living languages. Moseley and Asher's (1994) *Atlas of the World's Languages* specifies close to 5900 discrete languages, while Bright (1992) lists 6300 living languages. A UNESCO *Atlas of the World's Languages in Danger of Disappearing* (Wurm, 2001) estimates 5000 to 6000 languages in existence. The variation in estimate is due, for example, to the difficulty in defining a language (e.g. as different from a dialect), and problems of gathering reliable, valid and comprehensive information about languages in large expanses such as Africa, South America and parts of Asia (e.g. see Batibo (2005) on the 2000 languages of Africa).

There are thus **approximately 6000 languages** in the world today. An overview of Krauss (1992), Grimes (2000), Wurm (2001) and Martí *et al.* (2005) suggests the following approximate distribution of those languages:

The Distribution of Languages in the World	
	Approximate % of the world's languages
Europe	3%
Canada	2%
USA	2%
Central & South America	11%
Africa	32%
Asia	32%
Pacific countries	18%

Languages of the World: Estimated number of L1 & L2 speakers	
Chinese Mandarin	1200 million
English	750 million
Hindi	490 million
Spanish	310 million
Russian	230 million
Bengali	210 million
Arabic	200 million
Portuguese	190 million
German	128 million
Japanese	126 million

Will all those 6000 languages survive? According to Michael Krauss (1992, 1998) of the Alaska Native Research Center, between 20% to 50% of the world's existing languages are likely to die or become perilously close to death in the next 100 years. Wurm (2001) estimates that 50% of the world's languages are endangered. The US Summer Institute of Linguistics (see: http://www.ethnologue.com/) has calculated that, in the year 2000, 417 languages could be classified as nearly extinct, that is with only a few elderly speakers still living. The distribution of that 417 languages is: Africa (37), North and South America (161), Asia (55), Europe (7) and The Pacific (157).

In the long term: 'It is a very realistic possibility that 90% of mankind's languages will become extinct or doomed to extinction' (Krauss, 1995, p. 4). This estimated 90% death:10% safe ratio is based on the following argument:

- 50% of the world's languages are no longer being reproduced among children. Thus many of these 50% of languages could die in the next 100 years unless there are conservation measures.
- An additional 40% are threatened or endangered. Economic, social and political change is one such threat. For example, such a threat is found in countries where there are a large number of languages and where centralization, economic and social development for example, will take priority over language survival. Nine countries have more than 200 languages: Australia, Brazil, Cameroon, India, Indonesia, Mexico, Nigeria, Papua New Guinea and Zaire. These nine countries account for about 3300 of the world's 6000 languages. Another dozen countries have more than 100 languages each (e.g. Burma, Chad, Ethiopia). Many of these countries have relatively small numbers of speakers of the different languages. Assimilation, urbanization, centralization, uniformity and economic pressures will make future generations prefer majority languages.

As few as 600 languages (10%) may survive, although Krauss (1995, p. 4) believes this is too optimistic and suggests that 'it does not seem unrealistic to guess on these bases that 300 languages may be deemed safe'. The IUCN Red List of Threatened Species (http://www.redlist.org) lists 24% of mammals, 12% of birds and 3% of fish as 'critically endangered', 'endangered' or 'vulnerable'. There are consequently enthusiastic conservation measures. If 90% of the world's languages are vulnerable, **language planning** measures to maintain linguistic and cultural diversity are urgently required (Grenoble & Whaley, 1998) as is an ecology of languages (Mühlhäusler, 2002).

David Crystal (2000) suggests that there are five basic arguments why retaining **language diversity** is essential:

(1) It is widely agreed that ecological **diversity is essential**. The concept of an ecosystem is that all living organisms, plants, animals, bacteria and humans survive and prosper through a network of complex and delicate relationships (Skutnabb-Kangas, 2000). Damaging one of the elements in the ecosystem will result in unforeseen consequences for the whole of the system. Nettle and

Romaine (2000) argue that cultural diversity and biological diversity are insep-arable. For example, where forests are decimated, so are the homelands of people speaking a minority language. Where biodiversity and rich ecosystems exist, so do linguistic and cultural diversity (see Terralingua map: http://www.terralingua.org/). Evolution has been aided by genetic diversity, with species genetically adapting in order to survive in different environments. Diversity contains the potential for adaptation. Uniformity holds dangers for the long-term survival of the species. Uniformity can endanger a species by providing inflexibility and inadaptability. The range of cross fertilization becomes less as languages and cultures die and the testimony of human intel-lectual achievement is lessened. In the language of ecology, the strongest ecosystems are those that are the most diverse. That is, diversity is directly related to stability; variety is important for long-term survival. Our success on this planet has been due to an ability to adapt to different kinds of environment over thousands of years (atmospheric as well as cultural). Such an ability is born out of diversity (Skutnabb-Kangas, 2000).

(2) **Languages express identity**. Identity concerns the shared characteristics of members of a group, community or region. Identity helps provide the security and status of a shared existence. Sometimes identity is via dress, religious beliefs, rituals, but language is almost always present in identity formation and identity display. Language is an index, symbol and marker of identity (see chapter 18).

(3) **Languages are repositories of history**. Languages provide a link to a personal-ized past, a means to reach the archive of knowledge, ideas and beliefs from the past. 'Every language is a living museum, a monument to every culture it has been vehicle to' (Nettle & Romaine, 2000, p. 14). The range, richness and wealth of cultures, homelands and histories are lost. This limits the choice of pasts to preserve, and the value of life past and present. It is analogous to humanity losing one of its whole libraries built over years. The Sicilian poet, Ignazio Buttitta (1972), expressed it thus:

> Shackle a people, strip them bare, cover their mouths: they are still free.
> Deprive them of work, their passports, food and sleep: they are still rich.
> A people are poor and enslaved when they are robbed of the language inherited from their parents: it is lost forever.

Batibo (2005), in discussing the potential demise of many of Africa's 2000 languages, provides the example of medicine. If African languages die, so will centuries of knowledge of the powers of natural medicines: 'some of the traditional medicines used by some of these communities have proved to be effective in treating complex diseases such as cancer, asthma, leprosy and tuberculosis, as well as chronic cases of STD, bilharzias and anaemia' (p. 41).

However, the Latin language died, but some of its culture and the Roman influence continued although diminished (Edwards, 2002). The stored knowledge and understandings in oral languages (without literacies) may die with the death of that language. Yet written text may store accumulated meanings after language death, although translations will often lose a degree of stored insight and nuance.

(4) **Languages contribute to the sum of human knowledge**. Inside each language is a vision of the past, present and future so that when a language dies its vision of the world dies with it. If the world is a mosaic of visions, one part of that mosaic is lost. Language not only transmits visions of the past but also expressions of social relationships, individual friendships with local landscapes, a wealth of organizing experiences, rules about social relation-ships as well as ideas about art, craft, science, poetry, song, life, death and language itself. A language contains a way of thinking and being, acting and doing. Different languages contain different understandings of people as individuals and communities, different values and ways of expressing the purpose of life, different visions of past humanity, present priorities and our future existence.

Language lies at the heart of human education, culture and identity. When a language dies so does culture, identity and knowledge that has been passed down from generation to generation through and within that language. Knowledge about local land management, lake and sea technology, plant culti-vation and animal husbandry may die with a language. Each language contains a view of the universe, a particular understanding of the world. If there are 6000 living languages, then there are 6000 overlapping ways to describe the world. That variety provides a rich mosaic.

Crystal (2000) suggests that there are a number of solutions to avoid language death (see chapter 4). While the solutions will be different for languages at different stages of survival and revitalization, he suggests that an endangered language will progress if its speakers:

- increase their prestige within the dominant community;
- increase their wealth relative to the dominant community;
- have access to a stable economic base;
- increase their legitimate power in the eyes of the dominant community;
- increase the number of domains in which their language is used;
- have a critical mass in communities and regions;
- have a strong presence in the educational system;
- have a literacy in that language;
- make use of electronic technology;
- have a strong sense of ethnic identity;
- have internal and external recognition as a group with unique unity;
- resist the influence of the dominant culture or are protected and formally recognized by that dominant culture.

(5)   **Languages are interesting in themselves**. David Crystal (2000) argues that language itself is important, each language having different sounds, grammar and vocabulary that reveal something different about linguistic organization and structure. The more languages there are to study, the more our understanding about the beauty of language grows.

LANGUAGE POLICIES

The solution to avoiding language death involves **language policy-making**, with interventions to arrest the decline of a language. This is also termed minority language **revitalization** (see King (2001) for a discussion of terminology). Some majority languages, particularly English, have expanded considerably during the last century. Small minority languages are in danger of extinction and therefore need extra care and protection. A free language economy will mean the extinction of many languages. **Language planning** is essential to avoid such trends (Cooper, 1989).

In contrast, a language policy-maker who is concerned only for majority languages will regard protecting rare languages as expensive and unnecessary, and will wish to standardize the variety of language in the country. In the US, for example, many politicians prefer monolingualism to bilingualism. The preference is for the assimilation of minority language communities into a more standardized, monochrome language world.

It is important to note **variations in attitude** to the language environment. C.H. Williams (1991a) sums up differing 'environmental' attitudes to the survival and spread of minority languages. First, the **evolutionist** will follow Darwin's idea of the survival of the fittest. Those languages that are strong will survive. The weaker languages will either have to adapt themselves to their environment, or die. The biological evolutionary metaphor assumes that language loss is about survival of the fittest: if a language fails to adapt to the modern world, it deserves to die. Natural selection (Social Darwinism) suggests the inevitability of weaker forms dying. A different way of expressing this is in terms of a free, *laissez-faire* language economy. Languages must survive on their own merits without the support of language planning.

There are criticisms of this evolutionary viewpoint. (1) Survival of the fittest is too simplistic a view of evolution. It only accents the negative side of evolution: killing, exploitation and suppression. (2) There are human-made reasons why languages die due to political and economic policies. **Language shift** (in terms of numbers of speakers and uses) occurs through deliberate decisions that directly or indirectly affect languages and reflects economic, political, cultural, social and technological change. It is therefore possible to analyze and determine what causes language shift rather than simply believing language shift occurs by accident. Social and political factors, and not just 'evolution', are at work in language loss. Power, prejudice, discrimination, marginalization and subordination are some of the causes of language decline and death. The history of Native American languages in the United States is an example of language genocide and eradication rather than suicide or natural change (see chapters 9 and 11). Language loss is thus not 'evolutionary' but determined by politicians, policy-makers and peoples (May, 2001). (3) Evolutionists who argue for an economic, cost–benefit approach to languages, with the domination of a few majority languages for international communication, hold a narrow view of the function of languages. Languages are not purely for economic communication. They are also concerned with human culture, human heritage, the value of a garden full of different languages rather than the one variety. (4) Those who support an evolutionary perspective on languages will typically support the spread of majority languages and the replacement of minority languages. Those who advocate monolingualism often feel that their particular culture and perspectives are the only legitimate varieties – all others are inferior and less worth preserving. A more positive view of evolution is **interdependence** rather than constant competition. Cooperation for mutually beneficial outcomes can be just as possible as exploitation (C.H. Williams, 1991a, 1999).

The second approach to languages is that of **conservationists** (Williams, 1991a). Conservationists will argue for the maintenance (and increasingly the enrichment) of variety in the language garden. For conservationists, language planning must care for and cherish minority languages, revitalizing and invigorating. Just as certain animal species are now deliberately preserved within particular territorial areas, so conservationists will argue that threatened languages should receive special status in heartland regions (or on reservations). Native Indian languages in North America and the Celtic languages in Britain and France have invoked the conservationist argument. In Ireland, certain areas (Gaeltacht) are officially designated for Irish language conservation.

The third attitude to languages is that of **preservationists** (Williams, 1991a). Preservationists are different from conservationists by being more conservative and seeking to maintain the status quo rather than to develop the language. Preservationists are concerned that any change, not just language change, will damage the chances of their language surviving. Such a group is therefore traditionalist, anti-modern in outlook. Whereas conservationists may think globally and act locally, preservationists will tend to think locally and act locally.

One example of language preservation may be when language is closely tied in with religion. The historical survival of Pennsylvania German within the **Amish** community in the US has been a classic illustration of a preservationist approach to language. The Pennsylvania Germans, sometimes called the Pennsylvania Dutch, came to the US from Germany in the early 18th century. They originally settled in farming communities in southeastern and central Pennsylvania. The language is a German dialect related to that spoken in the German Palatinate along the Rhine river. Distinctive in dress, these Protestant Old Order Amish and Old Order Mennonite sectarians speak Pennsylvania German (a German dialect) at home and in the community. English is learnt at school since it is the language of instruction. English is also increasingly spoken with outsiders (Huffines, 1991). Archaic forms of German are used in Protestant religious worship. The language of the community has thus been preserved within the established boundaries of that community. However, particularly among the non-sectarian Pennsylvania Germans, the language is dying (Huffines, 1991). As English replaces the High German used in religious worship, the *raison d'être* for the use of Pennsylvania German in the home and community disappears. Religion has preserved the language. As religious practices change, preservation changes to transformation.

LANGUAGE PLANNING

If the world's languages are to be retained, then immediate policy interventions and impactive strategies are needed via language planning. **Language planning**, also called language engineering, refers to 'deliberate efforts to influence the behavior of others with respect to the acquisition, structure, or functional allocation of their language codes' (Cooper, 1989, p. 45). Traditionally, such language planning involves three integrated lines of attack (Hornberger, 1994; Wiley, 1996b; Kaplan & Baldauf, 1997; Dogancay-Aktuna, 1997): **status planning** (e.g. raising the status of a language within society across as many institutions as possible), **corpus planning** (e.g. modernizing terminology, standardization of grammar and spelling) and **acquisition planning** (creating language spread by increasing the number of speakers and uses by, for example, interventions with parents, language learning in school, adult language classes, literacy).

The bedrock of language planning is acquisition planning. The **inter-generational transmission** of a language (parents passing their language(s) onto their children) and language learning in bilingual education is an essential but insufficient foundation for language survival and maintenance (Baker, 2003a).

Status planning is found in a variety of policies: political movements seeking recognition or official status for a language (both minority languages like Māori and Welsh, and majority languages like English in the United States), as well as religious and nationalist movements seeking revitalization of a language such as Hebrew in Israel. Status planning is political by nature, attempting to gain more recognition, functions and capacity for a language. By maintaining use in, and sometimes spreading into new language domains, a language may hopefully be secured and revitalized (e.g. official use of that language in courts of law, local (regional) and central government, education, mass media and as many public, private and voluntary institutions as possible). Through laws, rights (see chapter 17) and constitutions, but also by persuasion and precedent, status planning attempts to conserve, revitalize or spread a language. Special attention is often given to modernization – to ensure that the language is used in modern, influential spheres (e.g. computers, Internet, television, radio, advertising, newspapers and magazines).

However, while individuals may be influenced by such changes in status of a language, such actions are not guaranteed to maintain a language. To influence language change, status planning has to affect everyday usage in the home and street, family and work relationships, and not just official usage (Welsh Language Board, 1999). Thus opportunity planning for daily use of the minority language is

Language planning has tended to proceed by trial and error and not by well-conceived prioritization. Richard Littlebear's (1996, p. 1) litany on failed language planning measures with Native American languages tells of that history:

'Probably because of [a] tradition of failure, we latch onto anything that looks as though it will preserve our languages. As a result, we now have a litany of what we have viewed as the one item that will save our languages. This one item is usually quickly replaced by another.

For instance, some of us said, 'Let's get our languages into written form' and we did and still our Native American languages kept on dying.

Then we said, 'Let's make dictionaries for our languages' and we did and still the languages kept on dying.

Then we said, 'Let's get linguists trained in our own languages' and we did, and still the languages kept on dying.

Then we said, 'Let's train our own people who speak our languages to become linguists' and we did and still our languages kept on dying.

Then we said, 'Let's apply for a federal bilingual education grant' and we did and got a grant and still our languages kept on dying.

Then we said, 'Let's let the schools teach the languages' and we did, and still the languages kept on dying.

Then we said, 'Let's develop culturally-relevant materials' and we did and still our languages kept on dying.

Then we said, 'Let's use language masters to teach our languages' and we did, and still our languages kept on dying.

Then we said, 'Let's tape-record the elders speaking our languages' and we did and still our languages kept on dying.

Then we said, 'Let's video-tape our elders speaking and doing cultural activities' and we did and still our languages kept on dying.

Then we said, 'Let's put our native language speakers on CD-ROM' and we did and still the languages kept on dying.

. . . In this litany, we have viewed each item as the one that will save our languages – and they haven't.'

essential. Also people's choices about language may be governed by their perceptions of the 'market', and be neither easily influenced nor rational (as is supposed by rational interventions in language planning).

Corpus planning is a typical part of language planning where languages are precarious and when they are resurgent. A common process for all languages, majority and minority, is to modernize vocabulary. Science and information communications technology (ICT) are just two examples where standardized terminology is created and spread. An alternative is the increasing use of 'loan words' (e.g. English words used in Spanish, possibly leading eventually to

'Spanglish' or preference for English). Schools, books and magazines, WWW, television and radio all help to standardize a language and hence new concepts need an agreed term. The Catalans, Basques, Welsh and Irish are examples of countries who formally engage in corpus planning through centrally funded and coordinated initiatives. Another example is France which, since the establishment of the Académie Française, has tried to maintain the purity of French and halt the influence of English (see Baker & Jones, 1998).

Being prescriptive about 'correctness' in a language and insisting on the purity of spoken or written language (e.g. US politicians insisting on standard English and not Ebonics or Black English in schools), relates to prestige speech styles. In the UK, speaking 'Queen's English' (Received Pronunciation) with a 'high class' accent connects with power and position, upward mobility and affluence. To speak non-standard or dialect English in the US and UK often relates to being seen as less intelligent, inferior, less educated and cultured, and less trustworthy. Teachers' judgments of students' intelligence and personality are affected by such students' languages and accents. Listening to the language variety of a person evokes social stereotypes and expectations, coloring the behavior of the listener toward the speaker. Thus when corpus planning is about purity and normalization, there is a danger that linguistic policy becomes political, with power and status going to those with the purity of language (Spolsky, 1998).

Acquisition planning is particularly concerned with language reproduction in the family and language production at school. In all minority languages, there are families who use the majority language with their children. In Wales, where both parents are Welsh speaking, 8% of parents speak English and not Welsh to their children. If this occurs across successive generations, the language will rapidly decline. All minority languages need a supply line, and if families fail to reproduce such languages in children, bilingual education has to attempt to make up the shortfall (Baker, 2005).

Parents may believe that there are economic, employment or educational advantages of speaking a majority language (e.g. English) to their children and not the minority language. Or that majority language has such high prestige in the neighborhood that parents feel the minority language has scars. Such attitudes can have an immediate effect on the fate of a language. A lack of **family language reproduction** is a principal and direct cause of language shift. In this scenario, a minority language can die within a two or three generations unless bilingual education can produce language speakers who then find everyday purposes (e.g. economic, social, religious) for that language.

Language acquisition planning is therefore partly about encouraging parents to raise their children bilingually. Edwards and Newcombe (2005) portrays a scheme whereby midwifes, nurses and health workers provide expectant mothers and new parents with information about the many benefits of bilingualism. This intervention attempts to lead new parents to make a deliberate and rational choice about the languages of the home, choice in pre-school education and later bilingual education.

Language Planning: The Approach in Wales

ACQUISITION
(1) Family Language Reproduction
(2) Bilingual Education – pre-school to University
(3) Adult Language Learning

STATUS – societal
(1) Institutionalization e.g. use in local and national government and organizations
(2) Modernity e.g. use on television, WWW

USAGE / OPPORTUNITY- individual
(1) Economic, workplace – instrumental
(2) Culture, leisure, sports, social, religious, social networks – integrative

CORPUS
(1) Linguistic Standardization (e.g. by dictionaries, school, TV)
(2) Public Vernacular (Clear or Plain Welsh)

Where there is a shortfall in language maintenance in families, **education** becomes the principal means of producing more language speakers (Baker, 2003a). Through bilingual education, language learning but also adult classes (e.g. Ulpan), the potential numbers of minority language speakers can be increased (e.g. French speakers in Canada, Quechua (Quichua) speakers in Peru).

It is possible to plan for the status, corpus and acquisition of a language and yet not affect the **daily language usage** of ordinary people. Language planning has to impact on individual language life. Languages decline when speakers drop in number and their daily usage diminishes. Therefore, language planning has to relate to everyday language life as enacted in homes, streets, schools, communities, workplaces and leisure activities. In Wales, such planning involves interventions in the economy so that minority language speakers can function in Welsh in employment (Welsh Language Board, 1999). 'No local economy, no community; no community, no language.' Such planning also involves targeting key local cultural, leisure, social and community institutions where minority languages speakers will use their language, form relationships and networks using that language. Planning also needs to empower local communities directly, enabling everyday language life to be enacted through a minority language. Opportunities for 'teenagers and twenties' to use their minority language is particularly crucial as they are the next generation of parents, and hence the fate of a minority language partly rests on these shoulders.

However, even the most advanced and dynamic **language planning** may not be enough to save a threatened minority language (Tollefson, 2002). Such languages will typically die unless there is language planning; they may also die despite robust language planning (J. Edwards, 2002). Languages may die unless there is intervention; they may die even if there is intervention. Such planning can attempt to persuade parents and speakers; it cannot control. It is nearly impossible to plan for a less dominant role for English or control its spread across domains and dominions. Language planning also has to be part of wider economic, social and political processes and policy-making, sensitive to regional and area differences and traditions.

Cooper (1989, p. 98) provides a classic scheme for understanding language planning by asking a series of key questions:

- **Which actors** (e.g. elites, influential people, counter-elites, non-elite policy implementers)
- **attempt to influence which behaviors** (e.g. the purposes or functions for which the language is to be used)
- **of which people** (e.g. of which individuals or organizations)
- **for what ends** (e.g. overt (language-related behaviors) or latent (non-language-related behaviors, the satisfaction of interests)
- **under what conditions** (e.g. political, economic, social, demographic, ecological, cultural)
- **by what means** (e.g. authority, force, promotion, persuasion)
- **through what decision-making processes and means**
- **with what effect or outcome?**

This relatively comprehensive set of questions makes some important points. First, language planning may be generated by different groups. For example, poets, linguists, lexicographers, missionaries, soldiers as well as administrators, legislators and politicians may become involved in language planning. Cooper (1989) argues, however, that language planning is more likely to succeed when it is embraced or promoted by elite groups or counter-elites. Such elites tend to work primarily from their own self-interests. Language planning is motivated by efforts to secure or reinforce the interests of particular people. However, language planning may positively affect the masses by adding to their self-identity, self-esteem, social connectedness and economic and employment opportunities.

A consideration of language planning runs the danger of over-emphasizing its importance in overall political planning. Language planning is rarely high priority for governments. **First**, there is often piecemeal political pragmatism rather than planning. The revival of Hebrew is often quoted as one triumphant and successful example of language planning, with now over five million speakers. Yet the rapid advance of Hebrew in Israel appears to have occurred by improvisation and diverse ventures rather than by carefully structured, systematic and sequenced language planning (Spolsky & Shohamy, 1999). **Second**, political and economic decisions usually govern language decisions. Language decisions are subsidiary and minor concerns of those in power, whose pervading interests are more frequently about power and purse. Language is usually an outcome from other decisions rather than a determinant of social, political or economic policies. Yet, as the European Commission has increasingly stressed, minority language issues and the need for bilingualism and multilingualism in a future Europe are relevant to European cultural and economic development, to peacefulness and equality in society. Bilingualism is one part of interconnected politics. Third, language planning depends on winning hearts and minds (e.g. of parents). Top-down government language planning cannot control, merely attempt to influence. Therefore, bottom-up language planning is also needed (Hornberger, 1997; Piller, 2001). Local decision-making, planning at a community level so that there is local ownership, empowerment and commitment is a crucial balance to top-down approaches.

Language status and corpus planning require full consideration of bilingualism and not just planning for the minority language. Where minority languages exist, there is usually the need to be bilingual if not multilingual. Minority language monolingualism is usually impracticable and unfavorable to individuals (e.g. for employment). A bunker 'monolingualism' approach to a minority language and culture may be tantamount to language death.

A THEORETICAL MODEL OF LANGUAGE REVITALIZATION

To revive a language, an *a priori* model is needed that gives broad ideas about a revival strategy and priorities regarding language planning. Such a model would attempt to 'predict whether a particular language will expand or contract' (King, 2001, p. 15).

In an attempt to create a model rather than a list of the many factors involved in **language vitality**, Giles *et al.* (1977) and Giles (2001) propose a three category model: status factors, demographic factors and institutional support factors, which combine to give more or less minority **language revitalization**.

Status Factors

A key issue in language status is whether the language minority is in the ascendancy (superordinate) or is subordinate. The **economic status** of a minority language is likely to be a key element in language vitality. Where, for example, a minority language community experiences considerable unemployment or widespread low income, the pressure may be to shift toward the majority language. Guest workers, immigrants and refugees looking for social and vocational mobility may place a high value on education in the majority language. The importance of an economic dimension to a minority language is explored in detail in chapter 19.

The **social status** of a language – its prestige value – will be closely related to the economic status of a language and will also be a powerful factor in language revitalization. When a majority language is seen as giving higher social status and more political power, a shift towards the majority language may occur. Where a minority language is seen to co-exist with unemployment, financial poverty, social deprivation and few amenities, the social status of the language may be negatively affected.

A language's **symbolic status** is also important in language vitality. A heritage language may be an important symbol of ethnic identity. Is there a paradox emerging in the relationship between majority and minority languages? Majority languages such as English have high status as languages of international communication. At the same time, globalism and internationalism (e.g. increasing Europeanization) appears to awaken a basic need for rootedness, for an anchor in a local language and a local cultural community. Becoming European can revive and reawaken the need to belong to one's local heritage and historical groups. In becoming part of a larger whole, a local identity may be essential and fundamental. The push to become a member of the global village seems to lead to a strong balancing pull towards primary roots.

Demographic Factors

The second of Giles *et al.*'s (1977, Giles, 2001) factors concerns the **geographical distribution** of a language minority group. One part of this is two or more languages having their own rights in different areas within a country (see chapter 17); or, in Ireland, there being designated heartland areas where some protection and maintenance of the Irish language is encouraged (Gaeltacht). A second part of this factor is the **number of speakers** of a certain language and their **saturation** within a particular area (Evas, 2000). The high numbers of Spanish speakers in Miami, for example, has been a component of Latino vitality, both economic and cultural, within that area.

However, within urban and rural areas, a low number or low density of minority language speakers may not stop language use. If those speakers interact in social networks on a regular basis (e.g. work, leisure, religion) then language vitality may still occur. Also important in the language maintenance equation is the demographics of biliteracy and multiliteracy (see chapter 14). Where bilingualism exists without biliteracy, there is an increased likelihood of language decay. When someone can speak a minority language but not read or write in that language, the range of functions and uses of that language is diminished. Bilingualism without biliteracy also means a decrease in the status of that language, and less chance of a linguistically stable language.

It seems possible for a small language minority to survive when surrounded by the majority language. Three examples will illustrate that small numbers of minority language speakers can still provide a lively minority language social network, even when surrounded by a majority language community. **First**, when some language groups have strong religious beliefs, they may prefer not to interact with majority language speakers. Such is the case of the Old Order Amish, Pennsylvania Germans. They continued to speak Pennsylvania German at home and in the community and created strong boundaries in their language usage. **Second**, when minority language speakers can travel easily between the homeland and their current area of residence, the minority language may be invigorated and strengthened (e.g. Puerto Ricans in New York; Mexicans in Texas and California; the Turkish minority in northern Greece). **Third**, in a large city or in border areas, a small number of minority language speakers may be socially and culturally active in their minority language. Such speakers may interact regularly and create a strong network.

The idea of demographic factors relates to mixed, **inter-language marriages**. In such marriages, the higher status language will usually have the better chance of survival as the home language. With inter-language marriages specifically, and with language minority communities in general, there is likely to be movement across generations. For example, immigrants may lose their heritage language by the second or third or fourth generation. This highlights the vital importance of languages in the home as a major direct cause in the decline, revival or maintenance of a minority language.

As a generalization with many exceptions, a minority language is more likely to be preserved in a rural than an urban area. Once the migration of rural people to urban areas occurs, there is an increased chance of the minority language losing its work function. In the office and in the factory, the dominant language is likely to be the majority language with a decrease in the minority language. In rural areas, the language of work and cultural activity is relatively more likely to be the historical language of that area (Robinson, 1996). There will be important exceptions (e.g. where an urban ethnic group generates its own industries, or is sited in a particular part of a city, or congregates regularly for religious purposes).

Institutional Support Factors

Language vitality is affected by the extent and nature of a minority language's use in a wide variety of institutions in a region. Such institutions will include national, regional and local government, religious and cultural organizations, mass media, commerce and industry, and not least education. The absence or presence of a minority language in the **mass media** (television, radio, newspapers, magazines, Internet and computer software) at the very least affects the prestige of a language (see chapter 19). Strong representation in the mass media also gives a minority language both status and a feeling of being modern.

Religion can be a strong and important vehicle for the maintenance of a majority and a minority language. The use of classical Arabic in Islam, Hebrew in Judaism, and German among the Protestant Old Order Amish in Pennsylvania all illustrate that religion can be a preserver of language. The revitalization of Hebrew among Jews both in Israel and elsewhere has strong connections with historic religious identity (Spolsky & Shohamy, 1999). Through its holy books, tracts and pamphlets, traveling missionaries and teachers, a relatively standard form of a language may evolve.

Providing **administrative services** in a minority language serves to give status to that language. It also increases the usefulness of that minority language for communication. The use of languages within educational institutions is probably an essential but not sufficient condition for language maintenance. Where **schooling** in a minority language does not exist, the chances of the long-term survival of that language in a modern society may be severely diminished. Where the minority language is learnt and used in the school situation, the chances of survival are greatly increased but not guaranteed. Education by itself cannot enable a minority language to become revitalized. Potential does not always translate into production, particularly as peer groups have their own values and preferences in language use. Also, Hornberger and King (2001) suggest that when a language minority have control of schools themselves, they may not want their heritage language to be used in the school curriculum, preferring the use of the majority language.

A distinction is made between objective and subjective representations of **ethnolinguistic vitality** (Giles, 2001). An objective measure of such vitality might compare TV programs, newspapers, and sales of music in the minority and majority language. However, what might be more important is perceived ethnolinguistic vitality by minority language speakers. It is their subjective view that more affects their language behavior. 'Indeed, high-perceived vitality is proposed to be necessary to preserve a whole range of language maintenance and survival strategies' (Giles, 2001, p. 473). For example, two Spanish speakers in San Francisco may experience similar language contexts. Yet one may perceive Spanish positively, the other negatively. As their social networks change (e.g. work, leisure) and as politics changes (e.g. legislation about English or Spanish), so may their perceptions. Vitality is not static but malleable.

Giles *et al.*'s (1977) theory of language vitality has been criticized by Husband and Khan (1982). **First**, they suggest that the dimensions and factors are not separate and independent of each other. In reality, these elements interact, inter-relate and are often mutually dependent on each other. **Second**, different language contexts have widely differing processes and recipes that affect language vitality. Success in some contexts is achieved by a process of democratic change and consensus, in other contexts by conflict, protest and opposition (see chapters 17 & 18). Indeed, low perceived ethnolinguistic vitality may on occasions stir-up language minority activists, rousing and mobilizing them into action. The historical, social, economic, cultural and political processes that operate in any language community vary considerably (e.g. compare US immigrant communities with Native Americans; or colonial India, francophone Quebec and the indigenous language minority of Ireland).

We also need a historical and sociological perspective, for example, to help explain patterns of interaction that relate to language revitalization. Thus C.H. Williams (2000) suggests there are often five historical stages in minority language revitalization: (1) **idealism** (e.g. to construct a vision of language revival); (2) **protest** (e.g. to mobilize people to change the use or status of a minority language); (3) **legitimacy** (e.g. to attain language rights for the minority language, in order to secure its survival and enhance its status); (4) **institutionalization** (e.g. to secure the presence of the language in key agencies of the state, such as public administration, law, education, employment and commercial activity); and (5) **parallelism** (e.g. to extend the minority language to as many social domains as possible, such as sport, media, entertainment, public services, private industry).

Hyltenstam and Stroud (1996) place factors that affect languages into three categories: societal, speech community, individual. At the **societal** level, important factors include: political-legal conditions, the ideologies of the majority language society and sociocultural norms, economic conditions (industrialization, urbanization, communications, labor market), and education.

At the **speech community** level, key variables include: demography (size, geographical distribution, immigration and migration, age and gender distribution, endogamy/exogamy), language characteristics (e.g. official status of the language, dialects, standardization and modernization, bilingualism, proficiency and use), opportunities for use across different domains, and institutional use (e.g. religion, education, culture), mass media). At the **individual** level, there is personal language behavior and choice, including: use, proficiency, confidence in use, and attitudes.

A THEORY OF LANGUAGE REVERSAL

A major contribution to the theory of attempting the reversal of language shift is by Joshua **Fishman** (1991, 1993, 2001b, 2001c). Fishman (1991) noted that the assumption has been that minority languages, like patients in a hospital or doctor's surgery, will ultimately die. Therefore all one can do is to understand the causes of death and illness, and attempt to overcome those causes for as long as possible. Instead, Fishman (1991) argued that language shift needs to take the jump of modern medicine by attempting 'not only to combat illness, but to cultivate "wellness"' (p. xii).

Fishman (1991, 2000) seeks to answer the question 'what are the priorities in planning language shift?' For example, what is the point of pouring money into minority language mass media and bilingual bureaucracy when home, family, neighborhood and face-to-face community use of the minority language is lacking? It is like blowing air into a punctured balloon. Blowing minority language air in through the mass media and legislation does not make a usable balloon, because of the unmended hole.

Fishman (1991) provides a list of **priorities** to halt language decline and attempt to reverse language shift. This plan attempts to achieve **social justice** and support **cultural pluralism and cultural self-determination**. The destruction of minority languages is the destruction of intimacy, family and community, often involving oppression of the weak by the strong, subjugating the unique and traditional by the uniform and central. Thus, Fishman argues for 'greater sociocultural self-sufficiency, self-help, self-regulation and initiative' (p. 4) among linguistic communities. However, Fishman warns of the danger of language as the sole focus for shift.

A different warning is given to those who believe that reversing language shift is purely about the accumulation of **power and money** by a minority language group (e.g. as has been said about the use of Hebrew and Welsh). Believing that language minorities who are attempting language reversal and resurrection are concerned with achieving power and increasing wealth is simplistic and misguided. Fishman (1991) argues that human values, feelings, loyalties and basic life-philosophies are present in the complex reasons for language change. Language activists often have ideals, commitments, even altruism that makes their motives more than just power and money. Minority languages and cultures, in their desire for a healthy existence, may be sometimes irrational or super-rational. This is similar to religion, love, art and music where there are personal elements that transcend conscious rationality, and go beyond self-interest in power and money.

Fifth, to help understand language revitalization, Fishman (1991) clarifies the relationship between language and culture in terms of three links:

(1)   **A language indexes its culture.** A language and its attendant culture will have grown up together over a long period of history, and be in harmony with each other. Thus the language that has grown up round a culture best expresses that culture. Its vocabulary, idioms, metaphors are the ones that best explain at a cognitive and emotive level that culture.

(2)   **A language symbolizes its culture.** To speak German in the USA, during World War I, and in France and Britain during World War II was not appropriate nor acceptable. Not that the allies were at war with the German language. Rather, the German language symbolized the enemy. Therefore, that language was inappropriate in allied countries. A language tends to symbolize the status of the culture with which it is associated. Speaking English often symbolizes money and modernity, affluence and achievement. English may also symbolize colonial subjugation. A language that is apparently dying may symbolize low status and low income.

(3)   **Culture is partly created from its language.** Much of a culture is enacted and transmitted verbally. The songs, hymns, prayers of a culture, its folk tales and shrewd sayings, its appropriate forms of greeting and leaving, its history, wisdom and ideals are all wrapped up in its language. The taste and flavor of a culture is given through its language; its memories and traditions are stored in its language. An example is a saying or a figure of speech in a minority language that requires a long explanation in another language. Even then that pithy saying may sacrifice some of its meaning and feeling in translation. At the same time, culture is derived from many more sources than language. For example, there are many different cultures which all use the Spanish language.

Steps in Reversing Language Shift

Fishman's (1990, 1991, 1993, 2001c) Graded Intergenerational Disruption Scale (GIDS) is an aid to understanding language planning and attempted **language reversal** from an international perspective. Just as the Richter scale measures inten-

Fishman's (1990, 1991) Graded Intergenerational Disruption Scale for Threatened Languages

Stage 8   Social isolation of the few remaining speakers of the minority language. Need to record the language for later possible reconstruction.

Stage 7   Minority language used by older and not younger generation. Need to multiply the language in the younger generation.

Stage 6   Minority language is passed on from generation to generation and used in the community. Need to support the family in intergenerational continuity (e.g. provision of minority language nursery schools).

Stage 5   Literacy in the minority language. Need to support literacy movements in the minority language, particularly when there is no government support.

Stage 4   Formal, compulsory education available in the minority language. May need to be financially supported by the minority language community.

Stage 3   Use of the minority language in less specialized work areas involving interaction with majority language speakers.

Stage 2   Lower government services and mass media available in the minority language.

Stage 1   Some use of minority language available in higher education, central government and national media.

sity of earthquakes, so Fishman's scale gives a guide to how far a minority language is threatened and disrupted in international terms. The higher the number on the scale, the more a language is threatened. The idea of stages is that it is little good attempting later stages if earlier stages are not at least partly achieved. Various foundations are needed before building the upper levels. The value of the scale is not just in its eight sequenced steps or stages. Rather it provides a sense of prioritization for reversing languages in decline. The eight stages are briefly summarized above.

Limits and Critics

While Fishman (1991) is careful to point out that one stage is not necessarily dependent on a previous stage, there are priorities. The more advanced stages cannot usually be secured unless the fundamental stages are either first built or repaired. The danger is in advancing on all fronts. Attempting to win individual battles without having a strategy for the whole war does not champion success. There is also a danger in working solely for tangible, newsworthy, easily recognized victories (Fishman, 1993). Changing the language of road signs, tax forms and gaining minority language presence on television are battles that have been fought and won in some minority language regions. It is more difficult, but more important, to support and encourage the minority language for communication in daily family and community life. For Fishman (1991, 1993), it is the informal and intimate spoken language **reproduced across generations** that is the ultimate pivot of language shift.

Fishman (1991) is particularly guarded about how much **bilingual education** can achieve in reversing language shift. There is sometimes the belief that, where families do not transmit the minority language, the school is there to do it instead. Where parents do not bring up their children in the minority language, the school is expected to be the substitute minority language parent. The school may initiate second language acquisition in the minority language. But few students rather than many may use the school-learnt language throughout life, particularly in parenting their children. Even when a child successfully learns minority language oracy and literacy skills in school, unless there is considerable support in the community and the economy outside school, that language may wither and die. A classroom-learnt second language may become a school-only language.

For that language to survive inside the individual, a person needs to become bonded in language minority **social networks** while at school, and particularly after leaving school. There needs to be pre-school, out-of-school and after-school support and reward systems for using the minority language. The minority language needs to be embedded in the family–neighborhood–community experience and in the economics of the family. Unless this happens, it is unlikely that bilingually educated children will pass on the minority language to the next generation. Thus, for Fishman (1991, 1993), each stage needs examining for how it can be used to feed into Stage 6 – the inter-generational transmission of the minority language.

Fishman's (1991) eight stages must be seen as overlapping and interacting. In language revival, it is not the case of going one step or stage at a time. The myriad of factors in language reversal link together in complex patterns (Spolsky, 2004). A language at Stage 2 may still be securing elements of previous stages. A language at Stage 6 may be engaged in long-term planning to secure higher stages. Hornberger and King (2001) indicate that 'reversing Quechua language shift in the Andes has not neatly climbed up the RLS stages of the framework' (p. 186).

Also, different communities and different geographical areas may be at different stages within the same nation (Bourhis, 2001a). The use of the minority language in business and the local economy may vary considerably from rural to urban areas, social class to social class, and according to closeness of access to airports, roads, railways and sea links.

Glyn Williams (1992), in a **critique** of Fishman, has argued that the presupposition is that change is gradual, mechanical, evolutionary and cumulative. He suggests that the viewpoint of Fishman tends to be of a consensus nature, concerned with integration, equilibrium, order and cohesion. Williams (1992) regards the work of Fishman as politically conservative with a consequent limited discussion of deviance, power, struggle and conflict. The preference is to play down the conflict while ignoring power relationships, thereby not expressing the anger, discrimination and frustration felt by language minority groups and their members. This theme is returned to when considering Paulston's (1980) equilibrium and conflict paradigms in chapter 18.

Spolsky (2004, p. 215) suggests that the danger of Fishman's scale is that it 'puts too much emphasis on language and language management, and so distracts attention from the social and economic factors which are likely to be the major sources of changes in . . . language shift'. Ó Riagáin (2000) and Hornberger and King (2001) also argue that Reversing Language Shift does not indicate the **economic processes and interventions** that are so important for language revival. For parents to raise their children in the minority language, for schools to have a strong reason for content teaching through the minority language, economic and employment incentives and rewards are crucial to language revival, but not sufficient in themselves (Fishman, 2001b). Economic prescriptions are needed to provide a strong rational for intergenerational transmission. Integrative motives and cultural sentiment may not be enough to persuade parents, educators and students to use the minority language. The economic base of the language community can be a vital safeguard to the maintenance of a threatened language. The state, and not just the local language community is thus important (e.g. in economic regeneration of a language minority area). Material dimensions of success (individual and societal) and economic advancement have grown in importance in a consumerist society. Because these areas are often controlled by majority language groups, a power struggle becomes vital. As Pierre Bourdieu (1991, p. 57) declared: 'those who seek to defend a threatened language, – are obliged to wage a total struggle. One cannot save the value of a competence unless one saves the market, in other words, the whole set of political and social conditions of production of the producers/consumers.'

CONCLUSION

This chapter commenced with the current concerns about the future of over 6000 languages, many of which are dying. Forecasts of wide-scale language decline and death are met with calls to retain language diversity. Such retention of the world's languages requires intervention: language planning. Such language planning requires a reproduction and production line among the young, via families and schools. For parents and schools to be motivated to pass on minority languages, there must be reasons: instrumental and integrative, economic, employment, social and cultural, sometimes religious. The fate of minority languages requires an understanding of how two languages interact in society.

Language planning is aided by conceptual frameworks regarding language vitality, revitalization and language reversal. Sometimes such language groups shift to insignificance even death. At other times they attempt to spread and not just survive. One argument for the survival of languages has been that as languages die, so does part of the totality of human history and culture. Theory of language revitalization is also about the realities of everyday futures for children.

KEY POINTS IN THIS CHAPTER

- The languages of the world are rapidly declining in number with predictions of 50–90% of the world's languages dying or near death in the next century. The world's language and cultural diversity is thus endangered.
- Language planning is needed for language maintenance, revitalization and reversing language shift. Language planning includes acquisition planning (home and education), status planning (e.g. in key institutions) and corpus planning (e.g. standardization and modernization).
- Language vitality concerns three factors: (1) economic, social and symbolic status; (2) geographical density and distribution of language minority speakers; (3) institutional support factors (e.g. religion, administration, mass media, education and community).
- Fishman's model of Reversing Language shift has eight stages that reflect different conditions in the health of a language and steps needed to revive a language.
- The transmission of a minority language in a family is an essential foundation for the re-building of that language.

SUGGESTED FURTHER READING

BATIBO, H.M., 2005, *Language Decline and Death in Africa: Causes, Consequences and Challenges.* Clevedon: Multilingual Matters.
CRYSTAL, D., 2000, *Language Death.* Cambridge: Cambridge University Press.
EDWARDS, V., 2004, *Multilingualism in the English-speaking World.* Oxford: Blackwell.
FISHMAN, J.A., 1991, *Reversing Language Shift.* Clevedon: Multilingual Matters.
FISHMAN, J.A. (ed.), 2000, *Can Threatened Languages be Saved?* Clevedon: Multilingual Matters.
GILES, H. and COUPLAND, N., 1991, *Language: Contexts and Consequences.* Milton Keynes: Open University Press.
MARTÍ, F et al. (eds), 2005, *Words and Worlds. World Languages Review.* Clevedon: Multilingual Matters.
NETTLE, D. and ROMAINE, S., 2000, *Vanishing Voices: The Extinction of the World's Languages.* Oxford: Oxford University Press.
SKUTNABB-KANGAS, T., 2000, *Linguistic Genocide in Education – Or Worldwide Diversity and Human Rights?* Mahwah, NJ: Erlbaum.

WEBSITES

Ethnologue, Languages of the World
http://www.ethnologue.com/

International Clearinghouse for Endangered Languages
http://www.tooyoo.l.u-tokyo.ac.jp/ichel/ichel.html

Linguasphere: Register of the World's Languages and Speech Communities
http://www.linguasphere.org/

Terralingua: Partnerships for Linguistic and Biological Diversity
http://www.terralingua.org/

UNESCO Redbook of Endangered Languages
http://www.tooyoo.l.u-tokyo.ac.jp/Redbook/index.html

Foundation for Endangered Languages
http://www.ogmios.org/home.htm

STUDY ACTIVITIES

(1) Find out how many different languages are spoken in your area (local or regional). List the names of these languages and in which regions they are spoken as an indigenous language. Through interviews with language minority members, or through a library search, provide a brief example of that language (on paper or on tape). Are the languages in your list 'native' or 'immigrant' languages in your area? Are they spoken by different generations or more by older generations? Is there preservation and maintenance of the language, or is the language declining?

(2) Using the Ethnologue WWW site (http://www.ethnologue.com/), map endangered languages within a particular region. Compare this with the Terralingua map: http://www.terralingua.org/) and write an information box on your map about diversity in that region.

(3) Grand Chief Mike Mitchell related the following words of his grandfather (Kirkness, 2002, p. 18): 'What would happen to the Creator's law if the robin couldn't sing its song anymore? We would feel very bad: We would understand that something snapped in nature's law. What would happen if you saw a robin and you heard a different song, if it was singing the song of a seagull? You would say, "Robin, that's not your language; that's not your song." To this Chief Mitchell added: 'It was not meant for us to lose our language; we broke the cycle, and today we have nothing to stand on if our language is going to die.' Using either a poem, picture or prose, express this sentiment in your own words.

(4) Use the 22 item Subjective Ethnolinguistic Vitality Questionnaire by Bourhis *et al.* (1981) or its adaptation by Harwood *et al.* (1994) to measure the ethnolinguistic vitality of a minority language as perceived by a small sample of speakers of that language. Compare their answers to a small sample of speakers of the majority language in that area. Try to explain the differences in answers.

(5) Search on the WWW for information on one revived language (e.g. Manx Gaelic in the Isle of Man, Hebrew, Basque, Catalan, Welsh). What is the recent history of the language in numbers and use across domains? What revival efforts have been made? What interventions have been particularly successful?

(6) Read Landry and Bourhis (1997) and any other articles on 'linguistic land-scapes'. Then take photographs of signs (e.g. street names, sings on shops, notices, adverts, graffiti) from one important street in a shopping area in your neighborhood. Analyze the pictures for the way two languages are represented (e.g. different size, lettering, colors). Who decided which languages to use? What does this say about language status and vitality in your neighborhood? How might different linguistic landscapes affect the choice of languages by people in your neighborhood?

CHAPTER 4
Languages in Society

Introduction

Diglossia

Additive and Subtractive Contexts

Language Shift and Language Maintenance

Language Decline and Death

Language Resurrection

Language Conflict

Language and Nationalism

English as a Global Language
The Spread of English
The Future of English

Conclusion

CHAPTER 4

Languages in Society

INTRODUCTION

Bilinguals are present in every country of the world, in every social class and in all age groups. Numerically, bilinguals and multilinguals are in the majority in the world: it is estimated that they constitute between **half and two thirds of the world's population**. The bilingual population of the world is growing as international travel, communications and mass media, emigration and a planetary economy create the global village.

Bilingual individuals do not exist as separated islands. Rather, people who speak two or more languages usually exist in **networks, communities and sometimes in regions**. People who speak a minority language within a majority language context may be said to form a speech community or language community.

Bilingualism at the individual level is half the story. The other essential half is to analyze how **groups** of language speakers behave and change. Such an examination particularly focuses on the movement and development in language use across decades. Such movement in a minority language is often downwards. A language minority is rarely stable in its size, strength or safety. Therefore, examining the politics and power situation in which minority languages are situated becomes important (see chapters 17 & 18).

This chapter focuses on the idea that there is no language without a language community. Since language communities do not usually exist in isolation from other communities, it becomes important to examine the **contact** between different language communities. The rapid growth of information (e.g. across the Internet) and inter-continental travel has meant that language communities are rarely if ever stable. Some languages become stronger (e.g. English); other languages tending to decline, even die. Some languages thought to be dead may occasionally be revived (e.g. Manx Gaelic in the Isle of Man). This chapter therefore seeks to examine **language communities, language contact, language change and language conflict**. This will reveal that decisions about bilingual education are part of a much wider whole. That is, bilingual education can only be properly understood by examining the circumstances of language communities in which such education is placed.

This chapter takes a **sociolinguistic perspective**. Sociolinguistics is the study of language in relation to social groups, social class, ethnicity and other interpersonal factors in communication. The chapter examines central sociolinguistic concepts such as diglossia, language shift, language maintenance, language death and language spread (including the rise of global English in bilingualism). There is also a linguistic view of these topics (e.g. change in syntax, semantics and lexicon) that is not covered in this or the preceeding chapter (see Romaine, 1995, 2000a; Dixon, 1997 for a linguistic discussion of these topics).

DIGLOSSIA

The term bilingualism is typically used to describe the two languages of an individual. When the focus changes to two languages in society, the term often used is **diglossia** (Ferguson, 1959; Fishman, 1972, 1980; A. Hudson, 2001; also triglossia – Batibo, 2005). While the term **diglossia** has become broadened and refined, it was originally derived from the Greek word for having two languages. In practice, a language community is unlikely to use both languages for exactly the same purpose; it is more likely to use one language in certain situations and for certain functions, the other language in different circumstances and for different functions. For example, a language community may use a minority language in the home, for religious purposes and in social activity, but use the majority language at work, in education and when experiencing the mass media.

Ferguson (1959) first described **diglossia** in terms of two varieties of the same language (dialects). Fishman (1972, 1980) extended the idea of diglossia to two languages existing side by side within a geographical area. Ferguson's (1959) original description distinguishes between a high language variety (called H) and a low variety (called L). This distinction can also be between a majority (H) and minority (L) language within a country, which is a rather non-neutral and discriminatory

Context		Majority Language (H)	Minority Language (L)
1.	The home and family		✔
2.	Schooling	✔	
3.	Mass Media and WWW	✔	
4.	Business and commerce	✔	
5.	Social and cultural activity in the community		✔
6.	Correspondence with relatives and friends		✔
7.	Correspondence with government departments	✔	
8.	Religious activity		✔

distinction. In both situations, different languages or varieties may be used for different purposes as the table above illustrates.

The example shows that languages may be used in different situations, with the low variety more likely to be used in informal, personal situations; the high or majority language being more used in formal, official communication contexts. It is typically embarrassing or belittling to use the low variety of language in a situation where the high variety is expected.

The distinction between high and low languages is possibly more about the status and power of languages than about the languages as language varieties. The table above suggests that different language situations usually make one language more **prestigious** than the other. The majority language will often be perceived as the more eminent, elegant and educative language. The high variety is usually seen as the door to both educational and economic success.

The concept of diglossia can be usefully examined alongside the concept of bilingualism. Fishman (1980) combines the terms **bilingualism** and **diglossia** to portray four language situations where bilingualism and diglossia may exist with or without each other. The following table, based on Fishman (1980; see G. Williams (1992) and A. Hudson (2002) for critiques) portrays this relationship.

		DIGLOSSIA	
		+	−
INDIVIDUAL BILINGUALISM	+	1. Diglossia and Bilingualism together	3. Bilingualism without Diglossia
	−	2. Diglossia without Bilingualism	4. Neither Bilingualism nor Diglossia

The first situation is a language community containing **both individual bilingualism and diglossia**. In such a community, almost everyone will be able to use both the high language (or variety) and the low language (or variety). The high language is used for one set of functions, the low language for a separate set of functions. For example, the high language is used for education and government while the low language is used in the family and local neighborhood.

The second situation outlined by Fishman (1972, 1980) is **diglossia without bilingualism**. In such a context there will be two languages within a particular geographical area. One group of inhabitants will speak one language, another group a different language. This tends to be a theoretical case, with few, if any, strong examples. Historically, in a colonial situation a ruling power group might speak the high language, with the larger less powerful group speaking only the low language. For example, English (e.g. in India) or French (e.g. in Haiti) were spoken by the ruling elite, with the indigenous language(s) spoken by the masses.

The third situation is **bilingualism without diglossia**. In this situation, most people will be bilingual and will not restrict one language to a specific set of purposes. Either language may be used for almost any function. Fishman (1972, 1980) regards such communities as unstable and in a state of change. Where bilingualism exists without diglossia, the prediction is that the majority language will become even more powerful and extend its use. The other language may decrease in its functions and decay in status and usage.

However, this is not the only outcome. In Wales, for example, an attempt is being made for the minority language (Welsh) to be increasingly available in hitherto English language domains (e.g. in education, television, pop music), thus giving bilinguals a choice of language. It is believed in Wales that allowing separate functions for Welsh will relegate the language to low status and subordinate uses only. Welsh would have sentimental and not instrumental (e.g. economic) value. Thus the Welsh view is that diglossia in Wales leads to language decline (except where the minority language has prestigious uses, such as for religious purposes). Similarly, Romaine (2002) in the context of Māori indicates that **functional separation** may 'seem an admission of defeat, tantamount to accepting that a minority language can survive only through separation from a modern world and by remaining undeveloped.' (p. 139). In addition, Sridhar (1996) suggests that rather than compartmentalization of languages in a diglossic situation, the reality is an overlapping and intermeshing use of languages.

Both Fishman (1972, 1980) and Hudson (2002) disagree, believing that keeping up with the prestige and power of a world-wide language such as English is impossible, impractical and unrealizable. If a minority language attempts to take over (or share) the functions of the majority language, it is doomed to fail as the majority language will be too powerful, too high status, and impossible to defeat. They argue that each language having its own separate set of functions and space, without threatening each other, is needed for minority language survival. Otherwise, minority language shift and demise may occur. Fishman in particular argues that trying to reclaim all functions for the minority language sets the wrong goal for that language. Instead, the minority language must be safeguarded in the home and community, with **intergenerational transmission** particularly accented.

However, family language reproduction does not exist in a vacuum. Parents and children are influenced by the status and prestige of language in society (e.g. its use in institutions and government). If status functions operate in the majority language, the message to parents and children is about the power of the majority rather than the minority language. Thus, increasing the functions for a minority language is also about sending the right signals to parents and teachers.

The fourth situation is where there is **neither bilingualism nor diglossia**. One example is where a linguistically diverse society has been forcibly changed to a relatively monolingual society. In Cuba and the Dominican Republic, the native languages have been exterminated. A different example would be a small speech community using its minority language for all functions and insisting on having no relationship with the neighboring majority language.

Boyd and Latomaa (1999) empirically tested this four-fold typology among nine language groups (e.g. Turkish, Vietnamese, Finnish and English speakers in the Nordic region in places such as Helsinki, Copenhagen, Göteborg and East Finnmark). By rating the parents' and children's degree of bilingualism and type of diglossia, they found the typology to have a limited predictive value. Part of the problem was that language groups could not be easily allocated to the four 'cells' as there are underlying continuous dimensions in both bilingualism and diglossia. Also, when elements such as language stability and maintenance were examined in each of the language groups, the typology did not always fit the data. For example, Boyd and Latomaa (1999, p. 320) found that 'For the Americans in Göteborg and Copenhagen, high levels of bilingualism and low levels of diglossia do not seem to have led to instability and language shift in the younger generation.'

Fishman (1980) argues that diglossia with and without bilingualism tends to provide a relatively stable, enduring language arrangement. Yet such stability may be increasingly rare. With the growing ease of travel and communication, increased social and vocational mobility, a more global economy and more urbanization, there tends to be more contact between language communities. As we shall see later in this chapter, language shift tends to be more typical than language stability. Changes in the fate and fortune of a minority language occur because the separate purposes of the two languages tend to change across generations. The **boundaries** that separate one language from another are never permanent. Neither a minority language community nor the uses that community makes of its low/minority language can be permanently compartmentalized. Even with the **territorial principle** (a language being given official status in a specific geographical area), the political and power base of the two languages changes over time. However, keeping boundaries between the languages and compartmentalizing their use in society is regarded as important for the weaker or lower variety to survive.

The **territorial principle** occurs when language rights or laws apply to a specific region. For example, in Belgium there are three designated regions where Flemish, French and German speakers have language rights inside their regions, but not outside those regions in the remainder of Belgium (Nelde *et al.*, 1992). Switzerland is another example. In contrast, the **personality principle** applies when status to the language is given to individuals or groups wherever they travel in a country (Paulston, 1997). For example, in Canada francophones have the theoretical right to use French wherever they travel across Canada (although most areas outside Quebec do not have French language service provision). The 'personality' refers to the linguistic status of the person.

An attempted merging of the territorial and personality principles when applied to language rights has been termed the **'asymmetrical principle'** or 'asymmetrical bilingualism' (Reid, 1993). As conceived by its Canadian advocates (e.g. in Quebec), the principle gives full rights to minority language speakers and fewer rights to the speakers of a majority language. This is a form of positive discrimination, seeking to discriminate in favor of those who are usually discriminated against. The argument is that the minority language can only survive if it is given protection and preferential treatment. Some of the functions of a minority language will be regulated, so as to preserve that language. This may result in enforcement and 'language policing' rather than (or as well as) winning hearts and minds by education and persuasion. We return to the underlying question of individual and minority group language rights in chapter 17.

An argument for the maintenance and spread of a language is often based on its historic existence within a **defined geographical boundary** (e.g. Welsh in Wales; Basque in the Basque Country). The 1999 Coolangatta Statement on Indigenous Rights in Education declared that 'Indigenous peoples have strong feelings and thoughts about landforms, the very basis of their cultural identity. Land gives life to language and culture' (Benally & Viri, 2005). As the indigenous language of the region, language rights may be enshrined in law. For example, Welsh speakers have certain language rights in Wales (e.g. 1993 Welsh Language Act allowing, among other things, the use of Welsh in courts of law) but not when they cross into England or mainland Europe. But what status do immigrant languages have when they cannot claim either territorial or personality rights?

Such a geographical argument for an indigenous language has unfortunate implications for **immigrant language minorities** (Stubbs, 1991). Do languages belong to regions and territories and not to the speakers of those languages, or to groups of speakers of those languages wherever they may be found? Do immigrant languages in the United States, Canada, United Kingdom and Germany not 'belong' as they are not indigenous languages? Do such immigrant languages only belong in the home country (e.g. Korean in Korea, Turkish in Turkey)? Should immigrant language minorities either speak the language of the territory or return to the home country? In Europe, there are many indigenous (or autochthonous) languages that are seeking preservation status in the European Community. Almost no status is accorded to the immigrant languages of Europe (e.g. the various Asian languages such as Panjabi, Urdu, Bengali, Vietnamese, Korean, Hindi and Gujerati).

An immigrant language retains distinctive attributes (e.g. as revealed in its uses and functions, customs and rituals, culture and shared meanings, communication styles and literature; see Allardt, 1979). One example is the **Pennsylvania Amish** who decided to ensure the continuity of their heritage language by reserving an exclusive place for that language at home, and reserving English for school and for contacts with the outside secular world. One language was reserved for particular societal functions, another language for distinctly separate functions. This compartmentalization ideally exists in a relatively stable arrangement.

In language communities, the functions and boundaries of the two languages will both affect and be reflected in **bilingual education** policy and practice. In a diglossic situation, is the high or low variety of language used in the different stages of schooling, from kindergarten to university? If the low variety is used in the school, in which curriculum areas does it function? Is the low variety just used for oral communication or is biliteracy a goal of the school's curriculum? Are science, technology and computing taught in the high or low variety? Is the low variety just allowed for a year or two in the elementary school with the higher variety taking over thereafter (e.g. transitional bilingual education in the US, see chapter 10)? Does the school deliberately exclude the low variety as a medium for classroom learning? The purposes and functions of each language in a diglossic situation are both symbolized and enacted in the school situation. This links with chapter 10 where different forms of bilingual education are examined.

ADDITIVE AND SUBTRACTIVE CONTEXTS

This highlights the potential importance of different functions for the minority and majority language. Where different languages have different functions, then an additive rather than a subtractive bilingual situation may exist. An **additive** bilingual situation is where the addition of a second language and culture is unlikely to replace or displace the first language and culture (Lambert, 1980). For example, English-speaking North Americans who learn a second language (e.g. French, Spanish) will not lose their English but gain another language and some of its attendant culture. The 'value added' benefits may not only be linguistic and cultural, but social and economic as well.

When the second language and culture are acquired (e.g. immigrants) with pressure to replace or demote the first language, a **subtractive** form of bilingualism may occur. This may relate to a less positive self-concept, loss of cultural or ethnic identity, with possible alienation or marginalization. For example, an immigrant may find pressure to use the dominant language and feel embarrassment in using the home language.

When the second language is prestigious and powerful, used in mainstream education and in the jobs market, and when the minority language is perceived as of low status and value, minority languages may be threatened. Instead of addition, there is subtraction; division instead of multiplication.

Lambert's (1974) distinction between additive and subtractive bilingualism has been used in two different ways. First, additive bilingualism is used to refer to positive cognitive outcomes from an **individual** being bilingual (see chapter 7). Subtractive bilingualism hence refers to the negative affective and cognitive effects of bilingualism (e.g. where both languages are 'under developed'). Landry *et al.* (1991) suggest this first use is too narrow, with a second use of additive and subtractive bilingualism being more appropriate. This wider use of additive and subtractive bilingualism relates to the enrichment or loss of minority language, culture and ethnolinguistic identity at a **societal** level. In additive bilingualism, language minority members are proficient (or becoming proficient) in both languages, and have positive attitudes to the first and second language (Landry *et al.*, 1991).

LANGUAGE SHIFT AND LANGUAGE MAINTENANCE

With changes of season and weather come growth and death, blossoming and weakening. Minority language communities are similarly in a constant state of change. Such language shift may be fast or slow, upwards or downwards, but never absent.

Generally, **language shift** is used in the language planning literature to refer to a downwards language movement (Hornberger, 2002). That is, there is a reduction in the number of speakers of a language, a decreasing saturation of language speakers in the population, a loss in language proficiency, or a decreasing use of that language in different domains. The last stages of language shift are called **language death**. **Language maintenance** usually refers to relative language stability in number and distribution of its speakers, its proficient usage by children and adults, and its retention in specific domains (e.g. home, school, religion). **Language spread** concerns an increase – numerically, geographically or functionally – in language users, networks and use (Cooper, 1989; Hornberger, 2002).

However, there is a **danger** in the ways these terms are used. First, the terms are ambiguous and may refer to the numerical size of the language minority, their saturation in a region, their proficiency in the language or the use of the language in different domains. Second, these are predominantly sociolinguistic concepts. Linguists have their own use of these terms (e.g. referring to changes in grammar and vocabulary over time – see Aitchison, 1991; McMahon, 1994; Romaine, 1995, 2000a; Dixon, 1997).

A variety of factors create **language shift**. For example, out-migration from a region may be vital to secure employment, a higher salary or promotion. In-migration can be forced (e.g. the capture of slaves) or voluntary (e.g. guest workers). Sometimes this movement of minority language groups occurs within a particular geographical area. Within a country, marriage may also cause a shift in bilingualism. For example, a bilingual person from a minority language community may marry a majority language monolingual. The result may be majority language monolingual children. Increasing industrialization and urbanization in the 20th century have led to increased movement of labor. With the growth of mass communications, information technology, tourism, road, sea and air links, minority languages seem more at risk. Bilingual education, or its absence, will also be a factor in the ebb and flow of minority and majority languages.

A relatively comprehensive list of factors that may create **language maintenance and shift** was given by Conklin and Lourie (1983) (see also Gaarder, 1977, pp. 141f). This list (tabulated on the following pages) essentially refers to immigrants rather than indigenous minorities, but many factors are common to both groups. What is missing from this list is the power dimension (such as being in subordinate status – e.g. many Puerto Ricans in New York City).

This concludes the initial consideration of important factors in language shift. It has been shown that such shifts are particularly related to economic and social change, to politics and power, to the availability of local social communication networks between minority language speakers and to the legislative and institutional support supplied for the conservation of a minority language. While such factors help clarify what affects language shift, the relative importance of these

FACTORS ENCOURAGING LANGUAGE MAINTENANCE	FACTORS ENCOURAGING LANGUAGE LOSS
A. Political, Social and Demographic Factors	
1. Large number of speakers living closely together.	Small number of speakers well dispersed.
2. Recent and/or continuing in-migration.	Long and stable residence.
3. Close proximity to the homeland and ease of travel to homeland.	Homeland remote or inaccessible.
4. Preference to return to homeland with many actually returning.	Low rate of return to homeland and/or little intention to return and/or impossible to return.
5. Homeland language community intact.	Homeland language community decaying in vitality.
6. Stability in occupation.	Occupational shift, especially from rural to urban areas.
7. Employment available where home language is spoken daily.	Employment requires use of the majority language.
8. Low social and economic mobility in main occupations.	High social and economic mobility in main occupations.
9. Low level of education to restrict social and economic mobility, but educated and articulate community leaders loyal to their language community.	High levels of education giving social and economic mobility. Potential community leaders are alienated from their language community by education.
10. Ethnic group identity rather than identity with majority language community via nativism, racism and ethnic discrimination.	Ethnic identity is denied to achieve social and vocational mobility; this is forced by nativism, racism and ethnic discrimination.
B. Cultural Factors	
1. Mother-tongue institutions (e.g. schools, community organizations, mass media, leisure activities).	Lack of mother-tongue institutions.
2. Cultural and religious ceremonies in the home language.	Cultural and religious activity in the majority language.
3. Ethnic identity strongly tied to home language.	Ethnic identity defined by factors other than language.
4. Nationalistic aspirations as a language group.	Few nationalistic aspirations.
5. Mother tongue the homeland national language.	Mother tongue not the only homeland national language, or mother tongue spans several nations

FACTORS ENCOURAGING LANGUAGE MAINTENANCE	FACTORS ENCOURAGING LANGUAGE LOSS
6. Emotional attachment to mother tongue giving self-identity and ethnicity.	Self-identity derived from factors other than shared home language.
7. Emphasis on family ties and community cohesion.	Low emphasis on family and community ties. High emphasis on individual achievement.
8. Emphasis on education in mother tongue schools to enhance ethnic awareness.	Emphasis on education in majority language.
9. Low emphasis on education if in majority language.	Acceptance of majority language education.
10. Culture unlike majority language culture.	Culture and religion similar to that of the majority language.

C. Linguistic Factors

1. Mother tongue is standardized and exists in a written form.	Mother tongue is non-standard and/or not in written form.
2. Use of an alphabet which makes printing and literacy relatively easy.	Use of writing system which is expensive to reproduce and relatively difficult to learn.
3. Home language has international status.	Home language of little or no international importance.
4. Home language literacy used in community and with homeland.	Illiteracy (or aliteracy) in the home language.
5. Flexibility in the development of the home language (e.g. limited use of new terms from the majority language).	No tolerance of new terms from majority language; or too much tolerance of loan words leading to mixing and eventual language loss.

(Adapted from Conklin & Lourie, 1983).

factors is debatable and unclear. There are various levels of establishing **causes** of language shift, levels such as the political, the economic, the psychological (e.g. at the individual or home level) and at the sociolinguistic level. A list of the relative importance of these factors is simplistic because the factors interact and intermingle in a complicated equation. Such a list does not distinguish the more important factors in language shift. Nor does it reveal the processes and mechanisms of language shift. It is thus difficult to predict which minority languages are more or less likely to decline, and which languages are more or less likely to be revived. A frequent, if generalized, **scenario for immigrants** is given by R. García and Diaz (1992, p. 14) and called three generation shift:

Most US immigrant groups have experienced a language shift to English as a consequence of assimilation into American life. The first generation immigrants sustain their native or first language while learning English. The second generation, intent upon assimilation into a largely English-speaking community, begin the shift towards English by using the native language with first generation speakers (parents, grandparents, others) and English in more formal settings. By slow degrees, English is used in contexts once reserved for the first language. Encroachment of English into the domain of the first language serves to destabilize the native language.

Eventually, third generation speakers discontinue the use of the native language entirely. The shift completes when most of the third generation are monolingual English speakers'.

However, a '**three generation shift**' is not the only possible pattern. Paulston (1994) cites the Greeks in Pittsburgh as experiencing a four generation shift. She attributes this slower shift to the use of a standardized, prestigious written language; access to an institution teaching Greek language and literacy (i.e. Greek churches in Pittsburgh); and arranged marriages with one partner being a monolingual Greek speaker from Greece. In contrast, the three generation shift among Italians in Pittsburgh is attributed to their speaking a non-standard, non-written dialect of Italian with little prestige; no religious institutional support as they shared English language Roman Catholic services with, for example, Irish priests, nuns and laity; and marriage to Roman Catholics with religious compatibility being more important than language compatibility. Also, the Pennsylvania Amish (see earlier in the chapter) historically avoided a three or four generation shift by retaining strong boundaries between them and the outside world.

A **five stage shift** from minority language monolingualism to majority language monolingualism is proposed by Batibo (2005) as fitting many African minority languages, and was found by Von Gleich and Wölck (1994) in Peru: (1) monolingualism in Quechua (Quichua), (2) bilingualism but Quechua stronger than Spanish, (3) bilingualism with Quechua and Spanish approximately balanced, (4) bilingualism but Spanish dominant over Quechua, (5) monolingualism in Spanish. However, the idea of 'stages' can be misleading as change is continuous across many language dimensions (see chapters 1 and 2).

Amongst Panjabi, Italian, Gaelic and Welsh communities in Britain, there are occasional **fourth generation** individuals who sometimes wish to revive the language of their ethnic origins. For some, assimilation into the majority language and culture does not give self-fulfillment. Rather, such revivalists seek a return to their roots by recovering the language and culture of their ethnic heritage. In Europe, with increasing pressure towards a European identity, language minority members seem increasingly aware of the benefits of a more distinctive and intimate local identity. The pressure to become part of a larger whole seems to result in a **counter-balancing** need to have secure roots within a smaller and more domestic community. A local language is valuable in this more particular identity. Bilingualism provides the means to be international and local.

LANGUAGE DECLINE AND DEATH

Another way of identifying the causes of language shift is to examine a dying language within a particular region (Dorian, 1989, 1998; Grenoble & Whaley, 1998). Susan Gal (1979) studied in detail the replacement of Hungarian by German in the town of Oberwart in eastern Austria. After 400 years of relatively stable Hungarian–German bilingualism, economic, social and family life became more German language based. For Gal (1979) the issue was not the correlates of language shift, but the process. For example (p. 3), while industrialization was related to language decline in Oberwart, the crucial question became: 'By what intervening processes does industrialization, or any other social change, effect changes in the uses to which speakers put their languages in everyday interactions?'

Gal (1979) showed how **social changes** (e.g. industrialization and urbanization) change social networks, relationships between people, and patterns in language use in communities. As new environments arise with new speakers, languages take on new forms, new meanings and create new patterns of social interaction. Indeed, Ó Riagáin (1997) suggests that Irish is better understood in terms of **social networks** of Irish speakers and not by communities. Where ability to speak Irish is insufficient, then the structure and operation of Irish language social networks becomes challenged. As levels of Irish language ability and confidence decrease, so does usage in social networks. This particularly occurs after fluent Irish speakers leave school and Irish language attrition occurs among 20 and 30 year olds, especially in the workplace. Consequently, their social networks increasingly use the English language.

Another celebrated study is by Nancy Dorian (1981). Dorian carried out a detailed case study of the decline of Gaelic in east Sutherland, a region in the north-east Highlands of Scotland. In the history of the region, English and Gaelic co-existed with English generally being perceived as the high status 'civilized' language and Gaelic the 'savage' language of lower prestige. In this region of east Sutherland, the last two groups to speak Gaelic were the 'crofters' (farmers of a small amount of land) and the fishing community. Surrounded by English speaking communities, these fisher-people originally spoke only Gaelic and later became bilingual in English and Gaelic. The fisher-folk thought of themselves, and were thought of by their neighbors, as of lower social status. They tended to marry within their own group. When the fishing industry began to decline, the Gaelic speaking fishing-folk began to find other jobs. The **boundaries** between the Gaelic speakers and the English speakers began to crumble. Inter-marriage replaced in-group marriage, and 'outside' people migrated to the east Sutherland area. Over time, the community gave up its fisher identity and the Gaelic language tended to decline with it.

In the 20th century, Gaelic in east Sutherland declined across the generations. Whereas grandparents spoke (and were spoken to) only in Gaelic, parents would speak Gaelic to other people but use English with their children and expect their children to speak English in reply. The children were able to understand Gaelic from hearing their parents speak it, but were not used to speaking it themselves:

> The home is the last bastion of a subordinate language in competition with a dominant official language of wider currency . . . speakers have failed to transmit the language to their children so that no replacement generation is available when the parent generation dies away. (Dorian, 1981, p. 105)

A different and controversial perspective is given by John Edwards (1985). When languages die, Edwards asks, are they murdered or do they commit suicide? In the histories of the native Indian languages of Canada and the US, and particularly in the histories of the African languages of those who became slaves, there is evidence of murder. In histories of the Irish, Gaelic and the Welsh language it is sometimes argued that the language has been murdered by English and England's dominant rule over the peripheries of Britain. However, it is debated whether the 'destruction' of Celtic languages has been deliberate and conscious, or through negligence and indifference.

When minority language speakers become bilingual and prefer the majority language, the outcome for the minority language may be decline, even death. Yet, where people are determined to keep a language alive, it may be impossible to destroy a language. **Language activists**, pressure groups, affirmative action and language conservationists may fight for the survival of the threatened language. In Puerto Rico, the government introduced English into schools to attempt bilingualization of the island. Over two-thirds of the population remain functionally monolingual in Spanish. M.C. Resnick (1993) has shown that nationalism, political uncertainty and the relationship between language and identity have made some groups of Puerto Ricans resistant to language change and the use of English.

For Edwards (1985, 1994a, 2002), **language shift** often reflects a pragmatic desire for social and vocational mobility, an improved standard of living, a personal cost–benefit analysis. This provides a different slant on the language garden analogy. One answer to the environmentalist who wishes to preserve a garden of great beauty is that, when the priority is food in the stomach and clothes upon the back, 'you can't eat the view'. Sometimes, there may be a gap between the rhetoric of language preservation and harsh reality. This is illustrated in a story from Bernard Spolsky (1989b, p. 451):

> A Navajo student of mine once put the problem quite starkly: if I have to choose, she said, between living in a hogan a mile from the nearest water where my son will grow up speaking Navajo or moving to a house in the city with indoor plumbing where he will speak English with the neighbors, I'll pick English and a bathroom!

However, where there are oppressed language minorities who are forced to live in segregated societies, there is often little choice of where to live and work. In the quote, the Navajo may have had the choice. In actuality, many language minorities have little or no real choice. Thus, electing for language suicide is misleading. Attribution of suicide is a way of 'blaming the victim' and diverting a focus on the determination of real causes of language shift. Freedom of choice is more apparent than real. There is often no viable choice among language minority speakers.

Language shift and the erosion of minority languages have been related to the growth of a few powerful majority languages such as English, Spanish, Arabic, Mandarin and Hindi/Urdu. For some, bilingualism is threatened by such growth. Such a threat is especially suggested where bilingualism is based on English and a minority language and this is considered later in the chapter.

However, the chapter continues by the more positive and optimistic possibilities of language resurrection with the example of Manx Gaelic. This particularly reveals the major part that education can play in the fast decline of a minority language and in slow resurrection.

LANGUAGE RESURRECTION

Manx Gaelic is a Celtic language, closely related to the Gaelic spoken in Scotland and Irish in Ireland. It is spoken on the Isle of Man, a small island set between Ireland and England (Gawne, 2003). In a survey of 1874, close to 50% of the island's population were found to speak Manx Gaelic, numbering around 12,350 speakers. However, the 1872 Education Act banned Manx Gaelic in schools. If Manx was spoken by a child in school, a whipping could result. While not the only cause of language decline, banishment from schools triggered a fast shift to English. A language expelled from education sends a message to parents, that the language is becoming obsolete, of no employment or economic value. The language transmission of Manx Gaelic in the home no longer prepared children for school, employment success or sociability.

By 1931, the Isle of Man Census showed only 531 speakers of Manx remaining. In 1974, Edward (Ted) Maddrell died. He was regarded as the last native speaker of Manx Gaelic. Thereafter, the word among international linguists was that Manx was dead (e.g. Grimes, 2000). In the 1981 decennial Census on the Isle of Man, a language question was symbolically eradicated.

However, there remained a few second language speakers of Manx. Even at the lowest point (the 1961 Census), there were 165 recorded (second language) speakers (0.3% of the population), thus making revival possible. By the 1991 Census, an increase to 643 speakers had occurred, and the 2001 Census counted 1689 speakers out of a population of 75,315 (2.2%). 47% of these were under 19 years of age (Gawne, 2003). Remarkably, a few of these speakers in 2001 were **new native speakers** having been spoken to in Manx Gaelic by their fluent second language parents from birth. Manx Gaelic is thus being resurrected.

The Manx Gaelic revival continues, inspired by the enthusiasm and dedication of a small number of 'heritage language' enthusiasts. This revival is particularly driven by the desire for an Isle of Man identity that is separate and different from only having a general British identity. A Manx language medium unit in a mainstream school is successfully operating (Gawne, 2003), plus there are second language Manx Gaelic classes in Elementary (for approximately 1,200 students) and High Schools (for approximately 350 students).

The main point of this illustration is that a language can be very rapidly massacred by its ban from all schools and its non-transmission in the home. The revival of a language via schooling is very slow. A language can be cut down within a few decades, but takes much time to grow from small seedlings and even longer to spread. The revival in education does not only start with young children; it needs *a priori* the training and availability of teachers who can operate in the revived language. Teachers thus join crusading parents, language activists and language planners as the human foundation of language salvage and salvation. As Hyltenstam & Stroud (1996) suggest, apart from the societal and speech community levels of analysis of language change, there is the individual person level in revival. Teachers and their students are important individuals in such revitalization efforts.

LANGUAGE CONFLICT

Contact between ethnic groups with differing languages does not always occur in a peaceful and harmonious fashion (Nelde, 1997). There are sometimes tensions, rivalries and disputes. Such disputes do not always lead to conflict, although, as in the case of Indonesia, Ethiopia, Rwanda, Bosnia, Serbia and the Middle East, ethnic conflicts do develop. As an extreme, there can be 'linguistic cleansing'. When there is extreme inter-ethnic conflict and civil war, an attempt to enforce the language of the ascendant group may be attempted.

Thus as one instrument of **social control**, languages can be a component in social conflict. For example, a monolingual and centralized bureaucracy may believe that multilingualism is like Babel: when there is linguistic diversity, there is a state of chaos, with resulting effects on law and order, economy and efficiency. Monolingualism is seen as a stable condition, multilingualism as linguistic imperfection leading to problems and conflicts. This theme is followed in chapter 17.

When languages (e.g. official, national, ethnic, indigenous, in-migrant languages) enter such conflicts between groups, language tends to become a marker or a **symbol** of the conflict, rather than the real source of the conflict, which is often racial, ethnic, religious, economic or cultural. When there are struggles for power and dominance between groups in society, language is often the surface feature or focal point of the deeper-seated conflicts underneath.

For example, in the **United States** there are conflicts about the place of English and in-migrant languages. Conflicts about the place accorded to in-migrant languages in bilingual education, for example, hide deeper concerns about political dominance, status, defense of economic and social position, as well as concerns about cultural integration, nationalism and an American identity. Thus language minorities may, on the surface, appear as a threat to national unity, with language acting as a symbol of the threat. Underneath, the conflict is more about economic and political advantage, political power and ethnic or national solidarity and identity.

The real source of the conflict is often rooted in political power struggles, economic tensions and issues about rights and privileges. Social and economic disadvantages often tend to underlie language conflicts. Language is a usually a secondary sign of primary or fundamental causes of conflict. Nevertheless, politicians and administrators often seize upon language as if it were the cause, and sometimes as if it were the needed remedy. Underlying causes are thus ignored or avoided. In essence, conflicts cannot occur between languages, they only occur between the speakers of those languages. Thus, the idea of language conflict can be a misnomer.

LANGUAGE AND NATIONALISM

Language has been an important symbol of national identity. Nationalism concerns a consciousness of belonging to an imagined separate people, located in a defined territory, bound by a belief in a common culture and history, with common institutions and desiring to achieve or maintain political autonomy. Language helps create that consciousness. **Nationalism** is often said to have emerged after the French Revolution and became a major determinant of political policy and change throughout much of the 19th and 20th century. The French Revolution marks one turning point in the emergence of democracy and the equal participation of all citizens in the process of government. Democracy evoked the need for national unity and the call for a **common national language** that would transcend regional or ethnic differences. In France, the necessity for a country '*une et indivisible*' led to the disparagement and attempted eradication of regional languages and cultures. Thus the French revolution marked the emergence of the modern nation, with its emphasis on assimilation and supra-ethnic unity for political reasons.

Yet, particularly in the latter half of the 20th century, **minority ethnic groups** became concerned about their particular identity. This led to a desire to maintain their languages and cultures and to achieve a measure of political self-determination. Minority languages represent important markers of ethnic identity, but the maintenance of regional ethnic identities has been seen as contrary to the unity of the nation. Thus, attempts have been made by governments to eradicate minority languages and establish the majority language in their place, by means of education and compulsory use of the majority language in public and official life.

In recent decades, a 'space for each race', a territory for each nationality that many nationalists prefer, has been challenged by a chain of cosmopolitan cities. The rise of multilingual cities with their linguistically, culturally, economically diverse populations is an example of the challenge to nationalism. Cities such as Brussels, London, New York and Montreal now contain multinational and transitional peoples, with a multitude of languages, identities and cultures.

The concept of a **supra-ethnic nation** state has been perceived as a necessity in many African and Asian countries in the post-colonial era. For countries such as

Kenya, Tanzania and Nigeria, for instance, which consist of many local ethnic groups, maintenance of supra-ethnic unity has been regarded as vital for economic and technological development. However, the imposition of a nation state structure on diverse ethnic groups is at the root of many internal conflicts within modern African nations. One practical outcome of this is the need for a majority language for international relations, official life and education, and local vernaculars being used in the home and neighborhood. This shows that the concept of a nation does not inevitably mean cultural assimilation and the eradication of local languages.

For many people, nationalism has **negative connotations** to it. It is associated with 20th century fascism in Germany, Italy and Spain. One danger of extreme nationalistic views is that they overlap with some form of racism and language imperialism. Far from an ideology that embraces the equality of nations and the right of all nations to flourish independently, racist nationalism maintains that some 'races' and languages are superior to others. Afrikaner nationalism in South Africa was traditionally based on the myth of the white man's superiority. The racist ideology of Nazis and neo-Nazis represents an extreme form of nationalism based on the myth of racial purity (e.g. the Third Reich in Germany and neo-Fascism). This is also evident in contemporary British (English) nationalism where, for example, extreme right wing groups express their nationalism with explicit racism and hatred of languages other than English.

The basis of **United States nationalism** also relates to recent support for the increased dominance of English over immigrant languages. Unlike the Irish, US nationalism cannot be based on historical territory given the massive immigration into the United States. Unlike the Arabs, there is no long shared history, and no overall religious dimension such as Islam that unites people into nationhood. While political feeling, for example against Communism and terrorism, has been used as a means of creating nationalist sentiment, US nationalism is instead based around dimensions such as political freedom, emancipation, social and economic mobility, individual freedoms and liberties, individual enterprise, economic advantage and military advantage, and the superiority of US military, political and economic power in the world. United States nationalism is thus based in modernity rather than history, on a shared economic and political aspiration rather than on long ownership of territory, and is based on self-determination and strong patriotism. Such a basis for US nationalism has implications for language policy in the US. Such policy favors the replacement of immigrant languages by English.

Language is often viewed as a badge of **loyalty**. For some, language is the pre-eminent badge that expresses a sense of belonging to a national group. Language becomes a symbol of independence of a separate nation and of a separate people. Language becomes important to gain and sustain language group cohesion. The Basques as a national group define their boundaries and separatism by who speaks, and who does not speak, the Basque language. Language comes to represent an attitude to independence and separation. Thus the Quebecois in Canada make French a symbol of their drive for more independence from Canada.

Nevertheless, language is not essential to either nationalism or ethnicity.

Concerns about loyalty, self-determination and political independence do not necessarily require a separate language. African nationalism is not based on language. Given the many different languages and dialects in Africa, language is clearly not a common denominator in African self-determination, membership and loyalty, nor in the desire for self-determination and political independence from Europe. In countries such as Pakistan, it is religion that tends to be the cement and symbol of loyalty rather than language. Thus language is a valuable but not an essential condition for nationalism to survive and thrive.

Bilingualism has been seen as an obstacle to nationalism (and not as an advantage) by both majority and minority language groups. This brings into play the distinction between majority language and minority language nationalism. For the Basques and Catalans to express a sense of separate nationhood, it has become important to emphasize the Basque and Catalan language and to protest about Spanish. Given that a minority language is always in danger of being swamped by a majority language, bilingualism can be seen as an unstable state, a halfway house for people who are moving from the minority language to the majority language. This is not the only possible view about the connection between bilingualism and nationalism. Bilingualism can be supported by nationalism, particularly in areas where there are a variety of ethnic groups, and where a group is in a numerical minority but uses a majority language as its mother tongue.

Political changes throughout the world are changing the concept of nationhood. In **China**, with 55 designated 'national minorities' and a recent growth in English, language policy 'is among the most critical and complex issues' (Blachford, 2004a, p. 154) with an intention to 'attain national unity by integrating the national minorities into the Han and Communist culture and at the same time maintain political stability by addressing the concerns of the minority population (Blachford, 2004b, p. 99).

In Europe, with the growth of the European Union and the drive towards Europeanization, a sense of more global identity rather than a purely national identity has begun. In the world of the Internet, the global economy and ease of transport between countries, the growth of economic and political interdependence in the world, new forms of loyalty and identity are beginning to occur. Thus **supra-nationalism** is beginning to have effects on language. The move towards supra-nationalism may have a positive effect on bilingualism. The drive to share a wider identity (e.g. to be European or part of the global village) may lead to a reaction among individuals. To belong to a supranational group may initially require local loyalty, a rootedness in local group cohesion, a sense of belonging to a community first of all before being able psychologically to identify with large supranational groups. Thus bilingualism in the majority and the minority language may become important in gaining a feeling of rootedness in the locality, as well as belonging to an increasingly larger identity.

The political dominance of English as a world language has meant more pressure towards being bilingual or multilingual in English and other languages. In countries such as Brunei and Malaysia, the value of English for access to information and the world-wide trade has led to the rise of English bilinguals in both countries.

ENGLISH AS A GLOBAL LANGUAGE

The situation of English and its relation to bilingualism is not uniform throughout the world but varies according to a multitude of factors, including the local political situation, other languages spoken in the country, inter-ethnic relations and cultural attitudes. The situation of English can be divided into three broad categories: countries where English is the first language of the majority of the population; countries where English is spoken widely as a second language and enjoys official status; countries where English has no official status but is used (e.g. in business, multinational communications). The world pre-eminence of English lies in that it is a first, second and foreign language and is found across the globe in all three categories (V. Edwards, 2004). These three categories will now be considered in turn.

(1) In many countries, **English is the first language** and often the only language of the majority of the population. In the United States, Australia, Canada, UK, Ireland and New Zealand, the majority of the population are monolingual English speakers. These are sometimes called the 'inner circle counties'. This has not always been the case. Historically, the spread of English in the wake of political and economic expansion has led to the decline and sometimes death of indigenous languages in all these countries. In Ireland, the English language gradually superseded Irish in the 19th century, and although the Irish language is still the official language of Ireland and has great symbolic significance for the majority of Irish, it is regularly spoken by a minority (e.g. 6%) of the population. In the US, the indigenous Native American languages and other ethnic languages spoken by in-migrants from Europe yielded to English, which became a symbol of national cohesion. This has led to conflict, and today, minority groups in many of these countries, (such as the Māori in New Zealand and Welsh speakers in Wales), are struggling to preserve their national languages in the face of English domination.

(2) In many countries of the world, **English co-exists with other language**s in a bilingual or multilingual situation. In former British colonies or 'outer circle countries', English has often remained the official language or one of the official languages (V. Edwards, 2004). It is still used widely in official contexts and education (e.g. South Africa, India). English is not spoken as a first or home language by the majority of the population. It may only be spoken by an exclusive social elite, only be used in certain contexts (e.g. official and formal contexts). English speakers may only be competent to use it in certain communicative situations (see Baker & Jones, 1998 for an extended discussion).

(3) In many 'expanding circle' countries of the world, **English has no official status**, and may not be spoken at all by the vast majority of the population. In these countries, however, English is acknowledged as an important and prestigious language, and people may be exposed to it in particular domains (e.g. Japan, China). For example in the former Soviet republics, bilinguals used to speak their local language plus Russian. Now it tends to be moving to the local language plus English. In other Eastern Europe countries (e.g. Slovenia), English has no official status but is increasingly spoken by younger people. There may be considerable

emphasis on the teaching of English as a foreign language in schools and also in business and industry. English language films may be shown with subtitles on television and in the cinema, and English pop songs may be heard on the radio. Many English words may have been borrowed into the indigenous language, and English may be used widely in advertising to suggest power, popularity and prestige.

The Spread of English

The spread of English, like that of other prestigious languages throughout time, has come about in a variety of ways, including political domination, the subordination of vernacular languages, trade, colonization, emigration, education, religion and the mass media. Through such channels, the English language has penetrated to the furthest reaches of the globe. However, the influence of each of these factors, and the level of intent in domination or market-led change, is much contested (e.g. Phillipson, 1992, 2003; Brutt-Griffler, 2002; Anderson, 2003; Ramanathan, 2005; whole issue of Journal of Language, Identity and Education (2005) 4(2)).

Approximately 375 million people in the world speak English as a first language (Graddol, 1997). With English based Creoles and Pidgins, this rises to over 400 million speakers (Crystal, 1997a). The number of English second language speakers is more contentious, with figures between 100 million and 400 million often quoted. Crystal's (1997a) overview suggests 350 million and Graddol (1997) 375 million. The variations are due to guesses or estimates being required in many countries, and to the criteria for inclusion as a second language speaker (see chapter 1) being variable – see Crystal (1995, 1997a). The numbers who have learnt English as a foreign language also varies very widely with estimates ranging from 100 million to 1000 million depending on how much 'learning' has occurred. In all, Crystal's (1997a) 'middle of the road' estimate is of a grand total of 1200 to 1500 million English speakers in the world.

Numbers of speakers is less important than the **prestigious domains and functions** into which English has spread and often dominates. The international **prestige of English** and English-speaking nations and the popularity of Anglo-American culture has given the English language associations of status, power and wealth. Access to English means access to valued forms of knowledge and access to affluent and prestigious social and vocational positions.

As a global language, English dominates many prestigious domains and functions: international communication, science, technology, medicine, computers, research, books, periodicals, transnational business, tourism, trade, shipping, aviation, advertising, diplomacy, international organizations, mass media, entertainment, news agencies, internet, politics, youth culture and sport.

Crystal (1997b) indicates that 80% of information on the WWW is stored in English and that English language radio programs are received by over 150 million people in 120 countries. He estimates that over 50 million children study English at the elementary school level and over 80 million study it at secondary level (these figures exclude rapidly growing numbers in China).

Such a widespread use of English ensures that Anglo culture, Anglo institutions, and Anglo ways of thinking and communicating are spreading. English then tends to displace some of the functions of other languages and even displace the languages themselves.

The Future of English

Estimates for the future of English are shown in the following graphs, with Spanish added as a point of comparison in the second graph (adapted from Crystal, 1997a; Graddol, 1997).

The **advantages and disadvantages** of English are much debated by scholars (e.g. Phillipson, 1992; Crystal, 1997a; Holborow, 1999; Hall & Eggington, 2000; Brutt-Griffler, 2002; Ramanathan, 2005; whole issue of Journal of Language, Identity and Education (2005) 4(2)). On one side there are those who regard English as, for example, valuable for international and intercultural communication, *de facto* the global language, a relatively neutral vehicle for communication (e.g. in areas of inter-ethnic tensions and battles for the predominance of one ethnic group over another), giving access to high quality higher education. A developing country that encourages the learning and use of English in trade and business may facilitate economic and employment opportunities. However, English is not alone in this scenario, with Spanish and Arabic, for example, also having prestigious economic and employment associations.

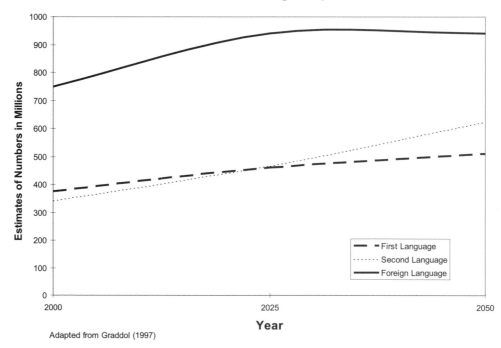

Estimates for Numbers of English Speakers in the World

Adapted from Graddol (1997)

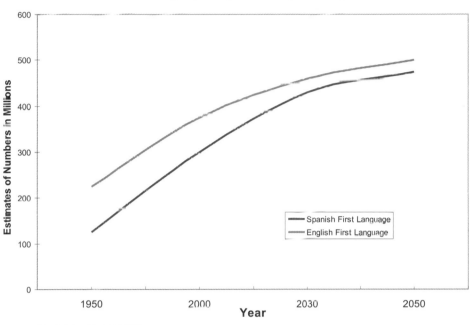

Estimates of First Language English and Spanish Speakers 1950-2050

Adapted from Graddol (1997)

Many people on all continents have been willing to learn and accept English as a **universal utilitarian language**. Such learners have been willing to embrace English, not for Anglo-American enculturation, but as an international language that facilitates trade and commerce, and international and multinational communication. Communication in English is regarded by such learners as a means of communication to an economic or political (rather than a cultural or social) end. In such situations, the stigma of a colonializing English is being replaced by a positive attitude about the multinational functionality of English. However, 'long shadows' of inequality and divisiveness, class divides and subordination remain. Such English may increasingly be a post-colonial hybrid language, appropriated and nativized 'to fit and reflect local ways of thinking, knowing, behaving, acting and reasoning' (Ramanathan, 2005, p. vii).

A growth of the English language in a region often provides a menu for different communicative and cultural behaviors. A switch from Japanese to English may encourage behaviors that are more Anglo-American than Japanese (e.g. in less signaling of status and power in relationships). 'McCommunication' suggests that when English is exported, so are its norms of behavior.

On the other side there is critical perspective that sees English as part of **linguistic imperialism**, dominance by the US and other English speaking countries, a means of reproducing structural, cultural, educational and economic inequalities, maintaining capitalist economic advantages and control, and oppressing weak minority languages and their peoples.

Thus Gandhi (1927) accused English of being an intoxicating language, denationalizing a country such as India, and encouraging mental slavery to Anglo forms of thinking and culture. He argued that English has been used in some multilingual societies to internally colonize, and to preserve the power of ruling elites. English has imposed linguistic uniformity that is culturally, intellectually, spiritually and emotional restricting. Other languages are then portrayed as confining, ethnocentric, divisive, alienating and anti-nationalistic. Asserting the dominance of English can become a means by which power elites justify exclusion and sustain inequality.

The relationship between **Islam and English** is a topic of current concern as a result of issues such as 9/11 (Karmani & Pennycook, 2005), the employment of Anglophone armies in Islamic lands (e.g. Iraq), the varied politics of the 'war against terrorism' and invasion, the legacy and resurgence of Christian missionary work especially of a fundamentalist nature (Pennycook & Makoni, 2005), and the connection of English with social elites and privilege in Islamic countries.

Rahman (2005) claims that there are three Islamic responses to English: acceptance of English and assimilation into Anglophone culture; rejection and resistance based of religion and preferred identity and values; and pragmatic utilization so as to share power and knowledge, raise wealth and social status, and 'learn the language of your enemy' (Karmani & Pennycook, 2005). While there may sometimes be a clash of cultural values and a polarizing conflict between Islam and western, Anglophone culture, this is not the necessary preferred position of Islam. Mohd-Asraf (2005) suggests that the Qur'an invokes proselytizing by the learning of other languages, and the gaining of wisdom from other cultures through their languages. So long as a child is socialized thoroughly into the Muslim way of life, then Mohd-Asraf (2005) argues that bilingualism and biculturalism have additive effects. This is because Islam is more than a world religion, being a whole way of life, a source of identity, a worldview, a political force, regionally allied to oil rich reserves, and not least concerned with Arabic as a holy and, for some, a daily language (Karmani, 2005). If a child is rooted strongly in such Islamic identity and culture, then Mohd-Asraf (2005) regards learning English as enabling rather than conflicting, so long as English and Anglophone culture does not come to dominate.

Yet it is not the language that is dominating but the people who use it. A language such as English is not intrinsically dominating. No language is more suited to oppression, domination, westernization, secularization or imperialism than another. It is the speakers of that language who are the oppressors and dominators. Whether English is empowering or divisive it is those who, for example, impose, teach, learn and use it that make it so. The danger is that language is made the symbolic scapegoat for political and economic domination, which are, in fact the consequences of people and politics.

Also, as Davies (1996) warns, guilt about **colonization** and a desire to retreat to linguistic 'nature and innocence' should not prevent us in acknowledging that English gives access to personal status, modernization (e.g. technology, science), a global economy and international communication (Graddol, 1997; Graddol & Meinhof, 1999). Often students are very motivated to learn English. For example, in the European Union, some 83% of pupils are reported to be learning English compared with 32% learning French and 16% learning German (Laitin, 1997).

However, the advantages for individuals in the globalization of English need to be understood against the **elitism** and hegemony that is often attached to English (Pennycook, 1994; Wiley & Lukes, 1996; Wiley, 2005b; Dicker, 2003; McGroarty, 1997). Tollefson (1986) found that English in the Philippines was used as a means of 'creating and maintaining social divisions that serve an economy dominated by a small Philippine elite, and foreign economic interests' (p. 186). Thus, while social psychology might view the role of English in the Philippines as 'instrumental motivation', at root there is a contest about political power and material wealth. There is nothing politically neutral about majority language speakers.

In the **United States**, some 98% of adults speak some level of English or varieties of English such as Ebonics (see Ramirez *et al.*, 2005). African American varieties of English in the US demonstrate that 'standard English' and Ebonics exist in a power hierarchy, with an attempted suppression of variation, and norms derived from written, school-based English and not from oral Englishes, 'which explains why children mist go to school to *learn* their "native" language . . . advantaging some students while disadvantaging others' (Wiley, 2005b, p.6).

For some, the spread of English has been connected to the decline and death of many indigenous languages (e.g. Phillipson, 1992). The dissemination of Anglo-American culture is claimed to have caused the weakening and eradication of local, indigenous cultures. Such a widespread use of English means that Anglo culture, Anglo institutions, and Anglo ways of thinking and communicating are spread. English then tends to displace the functions of other languages and even displace the languages themselves. For example, in technology, communications and entertainment, English has sometimes become the dominant language in a country. It can take over some of the internal functions of other languages in a country (e.g. in business, mass media) and become the means of the external link in, for example, politics, commerce, science, tourism and entertainment.

Where English has rapidly spread, the danger is that it does not encourage bilingualism but rather a shift towards English as the preferred language, especially in schools. English has sometimes become an official language or a national language (e.g. Singapore, India, Kenya) and a local vernaculars may be viewed as a substandard languages, languages of the socially or politically dominated, and languages with much lower status and prestige. Advanced schooling, for example in Kenya, has often required English to be the principal medium of language in the classroom. The use of vernaculars in the classroom will then be seen as of lower status, for the poor or less socially and economically mobile peoples. In India, English has often functioned as a *lingua franca*, particularly among highly educated elite groups (although Hindi has also become a common language of India).

There are exceptions to the growth of English in various countries of the world. Where a country has a 'great tradition', the place of English may be restricted to particular modern and separate functions. For example, in Arabic and Islamic countries, and in some oriental countries such as Malaysia, the strong promotion of religion or nationalism may help restrain English from infiltrating a variety of domains. Yet in other countries such as Singapore and India, English has been adopted as a unifier between different regions and as a common language. In India, there are 15 languages that have constitutionally guaranteed status, with English and Hindi being the main languages of intercommunication between different regions.

When there are reactions against English as a colonizing language, the arguments tend to take on different dimensions: that English creates anti-nationalism and is likely to destroy native cultures; that English will introduce materialism and values that may destroy the religion of the people (e.g. Islam, Hinduism, Buddhism); that a people learning English will be rootless, in a state of flux and transition; that decadent western values such as sexual permissiveness, drugs and lack of respect for elders will be transmitted by the language; that English will bring divisions both in the country, in the community and in families, separating those who speak the native languages and those who prefer to move towards English; that there will be alienation from traditional culture, heritage values and beliefs, plus a lack of individual and unique identity.

English language learning is changing as globalization increases (Block & Cameron, 2002). Globalization implies using English increasingly for economic purposes, and English as owning rich linguistic capital. Bilingualism also is becoming a commodity (see chapter 19). The communication skills required by new information technologies means that languages become a valuable commodity: 'individuals who command two languages are attractive to businesses competing in multiple, or multilingual markets (Block & Cameron, 2002, p. 7).

CONCLUSION

This chapter has focused on languages at the group, social and community level. Two languages within a region is termed diglossia. Majority and minority languages are frequently in contact, sometimes in conflict. The relationship between the two languages tends to shift constantly as a consequence of a variety of changeable cultural, economic, linguistic, social, demographic and political factors.

Indigenous languages are located in a defined territory and will claim the territorial principle for their preservation. Immigrant language minorities may lay claim to the personality principle: their language group having unifying ethnic characteristics and identity. But the future of languages goes wider and deeper. The history of nationalism and the modern role of global English suggests that languages are fated according to wider social, economic, political issues. The future of the world's languages, and the future of English as the international language, is not only about the behavior of individuals but also about economic, social and symbolic values attached to different languages, about institutional support, and not least about regional and global politics.

KEY POINTS IN THIS CHAPTER

- Diglossia is used to describe and analyze two languages existing together in a society in a relatively stable arrangement through different uses attached to each language.
- The territorial principle is a claim to the right to a language within a geographical area while the personality principle is a claim to the right to use a language based on an individual's ownership of a language that belongs to them wherever they travel within their country (e.g. Canada).
- Minority languages can decline by three generation shift, from grandparents being monolingual in the minority language, to their grandchildren being monolingual in the majority language. Bilingual parents in the second generation are a half-way house.
- Language resurrection is slow and starts with a few often enthusiasts.
- Language has been a key symbol of national identity and as a badge of loyalty.
- The English language is spreading rapidly, mostly as a second and foreign language. Its advantages and disadvantages as an international language are much contested, as are its effects on the future of minority languages. Bilingualism and multilingualism in English and another language or languages is globally increasing.

SUGGESTED FURTHER READING

BLOCK, D. & CAMERON, D. (eds), 2002, *Globalization and Language Teaching*. London: Routledge.
BRUTT-GRIFFLER, J., 2002, *World English: A Study of Its Development*. Clevedon: Multilingual Matters.
CRYSTAL, D., 1997, *English as a Global Language*. Cambridge: Cambridge University Press.
KAPLAN. R.B. (ed.), 2002, *The Oxford Handbook of Applied Linguistics*. Oxford: Oxford University Press.
MESTHRIE, R. (ed.), 2001, *Concise Encyclopedia of Sociolinguistics*. Oxford: Elsevier Science.
ROMAINE, S., 2000, *Language in Society: An Introduction to Sociolinguistics* (2nd edition). Oxford: Oxford University Press.
SPOLSKY, B., 1998, *Sociolinguistics*. Oxford: Oxford University Press.

STUDY ACTIVITIES

(1) As a group activity or with a partner, make an abbreviated list of the factors of language shift from Conklin and Lourie (1983). On a five-point scale (5 = very important, 4 = fairly important, 3 = neither important or unimportant, 2 = fairly unimportant, 1 = unimportant), rate your perception of the strength of these factors in language shift.

(2) What are the status, domain use and functions of English in your area? Have they changed in the last decade? Interview three of four local people who may have a well informed view of the future of English in your area. Do they expect English to grow in your area? If so, how and why?

(3) Locate several families of immigrants in your area. Is the 'three generation shift' pattern evident in some or most of those families? What have been the

changes in language use and status since immigration in those families? What reasons do the families give for language change? What factors seem to aid language preservation?

CHAPTER 5

The Early Development of Bilingualism

CHAPTER 5

The Early Development of Bilingualism

INTRODUCTION

This chapter looks at the various ways in which young children become bilingual. There are various routes to bilingualism, some from birth, others later (see chapter 6). Such **routes** include: acquiring two languages early on in the home; acquiring a second language in the street, in the wider community, in the nursery school, elementary or high school; and, after childhood, learning a second or foreign language by adult language classes and courses or by informal interaction with others. This chapter outlines different major routes to becoming bilingual early (e.g. before formal schooling) and examines some of the central issues involved in this private form of language planning (Piller, 2001).

As the previous chapters of this book have illustrated, a discussion of bilingualism has to include psychological, linguistic, social and educational factors. Later in the book, it will be shown that political factors are also crucial in understanding bilingualism and bilingual education. While psychologists and linguists have studied the development of children's two languages, it may be valuable to examine simultaneously the social **context** in which children acquire their languages. For example, being a member of an immigrant community, an elite group, a majority or minority language group are important societal or 'macro' influences in the acquisition of bilingualism (Bayley & Schecter, 2003). Valdés (2003) and Piller (2001) outline the different experiences of middle and upper class privileged bilinguals (e.g. children of diplomats, expatriates learning two prestigious languages), majority language children living in minority language communities, and minority language children living in majority language communities (e.g. immigrants, American Indians). In each of these groups, societal pressures and family language planning may be supportive or conflicting, affecting choices, access and language outcomes. There are also 'micro' environments such as the street, crèche, nursery, school, local community and the extended family that similarly foster bilingualism. Such contexts tend to make bilingual use in a child a constantly **shifting** rather than a stable phenomenon.

The variety of individual differences and social contexts makes simple generalizations about the development of bilingualism difficult and dangerous. The chapter therefore commences with a basic typology of the development of childhood bilingualism.

TYPES OF CHILDHOOD BILINGUALISM

It is possible that as many children worldwide grow up to become bilinguals as monolinguals, and possibly more become bilinguals than monolinguals (Tucker, 1998). Some children become bilinguals almost effortlessly from birth. Others learn a language in school or later as adults. An initial distinction is between **simultaneous and sequential childhood bilingualism**. Simultaneous childhood bilingualism refers to a child acquiring two languages at the same time from birth, sometimes called infant bilingualism, bilingual acquisition and bilingual first language acquisition. For example, where one parent speaks one language to the child, and the other parent speaks a different language, the child may learn both languages simultaneously (Barron-Hauwaert, 2004). An example of sequential childhood bilingualism is when a child learns one language in the home, then goes to a nursery or elementary school and learns a second language (Thompson, 2000). There are no exact boundaries between simultaneous and sequential bilingualism, although the age of acquisition is likely to be influential, as this chapter will show.

Nursery and kindergarten education can enable a child to acquire a second language without formal instruction in that language (Baker & Jones, 1998; Thompson, 2000). In the **pre-school** education context, language development may be supported through sessions that emphasize understanding and meaning rather than attention to language form. In such sessions, Winsler *et al.* (1999) found that Spanish-speaking Mexican-American children attending a bilingual (Spanish–English) pre-school gained linguistically compared to those who stayed at home. Such children developed in their Spanish language proficiency as much as home-based children, as well as developing greater English proficiency. Such early bilingual education did not lead to native language loss.

In contrast, second language classes for children and adults usually foster bilingualism through direct instruction (see chapter 6). This leads to a distinction between informal **language acquisition** and more formal **language learning** (Krashen, 1985). However, the boundary between acquisition and learning is not distinct (e.g. informal language acquisition can occur in a second language class). There is a movement towards making second language acquisition more naturalistic in an educational setting, developing communicative competence in a less formal way (see chapters 1 & 6). Thus, the distinction between naturally becoming bilingual and being taught to become bilingual has imprecise borders.

THE SIMULTANEOUS ACQUISITION OF BILINGUALISM AND MULTILINGUALISM

Parents, members of the public and politicians are sometimes prejudiced and believe that acquiring two languages from birth must be detrimental to a child's language growth. In past times, it has been wrongly claimed that simultaneous acquisition will muddle the mind or retard language development (see chapter 7). On the contrary, babies appear **biologically ready** to acquire, store and differentiate two or more languages from birth onwards (Meisel, 2004; Genesee, 2003). Infant bilingualism is normal and natural, with evidence that it is typically beneficial in many ways: cognitively (see chapter 7), culturally (see chapter 18), communicatively (see chapter 1), for higher curriculum achievement (see chapters 11 and 12), and to increase the chances of employment and promotion (see chapter 19).

To acquire successfully two languages from birth, babies need to be able to (a) differentiate between the two languages and (b) effectively store the two languages for both understanding (input) and production (output). Research suggests infants have these capacities and thus infant bilingualism is very viable (Deuchar & Quay, 2000; Genesee, 2001, 2003; Genesee *et al.*, 2004; Meisel, 2004).

Differentiation Between Two Languages in the Infant

Infants show language discrimination very early. Memory for language sounds even operates in the **fetal stage**, such that the processes of bilingual acquisition may have started before birth (Boysson-Bardies, 1999). Upon birth, newborns immediately prefer their mother's voice to any other mother, but not if the mother's recorded voice is played backwards. Also, newborns respond more to prose passages read to them regularly before birth than to new prose, even when not read by the mother. Thus an infant is not just recognizing the mother's voice. There is also immediate sound discrimination. There appears to be an immediate receptive language differentiation in the newborn particularly in intonation (Genesee, 2003). This can be extended from monolingualism to bilingualism as Mehler *et al.* (1988) found that newborns can distinguish their parents' native language sounds from unfamiliar foreign language sounds.

Maneva & Genesee (2002) found that in the **babbling stage**, a child (around 10 to 12 months of age) exposed to two languages from birth (a) has a tendency to babble in their stronger language, (b) demonstrates language-specific babbling features of each language, but (c) may not babble with context-specific accuracy. Language specific patterns and some speech differentiation may thus occur before the first birthday.

Recent research has found that bilingual children (two years old or earlier) know which language to speak 'to whom' and in 'what situation' (Quay, 1994; De Houwer, 1995; Lanza, 1997; Nicoladis & Genesee, 1997; Nicoladis, 1998; Deuchar & Quay, 2000; Meisel, 2004). Very young children easily switch languages and **differentiate** their two languages, but there is individual variation. For example, Deuchar and Quay (1999, 2000) found that a bilingual child as young as, and younger than, two years of age uses two languages in contextually sensitive ways. In the last five months of a child's second year (1:7 to 2:0), utterances were beginning to be matched to the context (e.g. which language to use with each parent). That is, an appropriate language was used in particular locations. 'Our results show that a child as young as 1;7 appears to be able to take account of a range of complex factors in language choice. These included not only the language of the interlocutor, but also the location of the interaction' (Deuchar & Quay, 2000, p. 111).

The ability to use the appropriate language with a particular person occurs very early. Nicoladis (1998) found that social awareness of the **one parent – one language** routine seemed to have encouraged an awareness of translation equivalents and two separate language systems. 'Children's understanding of the appropriate social use of their two languages may lead to an understanding that the translation equivalents in their vocabulary belong to two distinct input languages' (Nicoladis, 1998, p. 105).

Genesee *et al.* (1996) found that '**appropriate language matching**' is found in two year olds from bilingual homes when talking to strangers. Children rapidly and accurately accommodated the monolingualism or bilingualism of a stranger and talked in the appropriate language. A study of a Dutch and English bilingual aged three showed that the child would accurately choose the appropriate language when speaking with a monolingual person (De Houwer, 1990). Also, the child was much more ready to use both languages (i.e. codeswitching) in conversation with people she knew to be fluent bilinguals. The study suggests that bilingual children tend to mix languages less when addressing monolinguals, but move relatively more between two languages when addressing bilinguals. This sensitivity to interaction with others appears in older bilinguals, but Comeau *et al.* (2003) also found such sensitivity in two year old bilinguals (age between 2;0 and 2;7).

The **age** at which a child differentiates their two language systems and rarely code-mixes will differ considerably from child to child, with the interaction between adults and the child, the nature of the adult input, increasing self awareness in the child, adjusting to adult norms, varying context, and the child's relative proficiency in each language being influential (Deuchar & Muntz, 2003).

Deuchar & Quay (2000) found that mixed utterances in a young child could be accounted for by 'a gap in lexical resources: that is, the child uses a word from an inappropriate language because she does not have the word from the appropriate language in her vocabulary (p. 113). This suggests that codemixing is partly about **language proficiency** levels in the child, but that such mixing is temporary and decreases with dual language proficiency. Young children code mix, for example, to fill gaps in their language proficiency. Bilingual adults occasionally also do this when they cannot immediately remember a word or phrase in a language. For adults, this tends to be viewed as being pragmatic; for young children (in contradiction and incorrectly) as a problem. As children grow older, they acquire the language abilities found in their parents and community.

As Toribio (2004) suggests: 'intra-sentential codeswitching is not a random mixture of two flawed systems; rather, it is rule-governed and systematic, demonstrating the operation of underlying grammatical restrictions. Proficient bilinguals may be shown to exhibit a shared knowledge of what constitutes appropriate intra-sentential code-switching' (p. 137).

Codeswitching is affected by the language model provided by parents and significant others in the family and community. If parents code-switch regularly, then their children may imitate. If parents discourage codeswitching (e.g. by clear language separation), then less mixing may occur. What is culturally appropriate, the norm of the community, and what is valued by parents and others will have an important influence (Luykx, 2003), as may the extent of the child's repertoire in each language. Such codeswitching is not evidence of a lack of differentiation between languages in the child. If a child knows that the parent, for example, can understand both languages, then codeswitching may seem valuable in relaying a message.

Thus a variety of factors may affect a **child's language choice**: exposure to the two languages in different contexts, the attitudes of parents to the two languages and to mixing the languages, the language competences and metalinguistic abilities of the child, personality, peer interaction, exposure to different forms of language education, as well as sociolinguistic influences such as the norms, values and beliefs of the community (Nicoladis & Genesee, 1997).

In conclusion about differentiation, Genesee (2002) suggests that 'it is now generally accepted that bilingual children can use their developing languages differentially and appropriately from the one word stage onward, and certainly from the age when there is evidence of syntax in their spoken language' (p. 173).

Storing Two Languages

Until recently, many academics believed that a child exposed to two languages from birth initially operated like a monolingual with a single language system. Volterra and Taeschner (1978) suggested a three stage model with bilingual children moving from mixing languages to partial separation to fuller separation. The debate was about whether a young bilingual child develops two separate linguistic systems or just one overall integrated system (the unitary language hypothesis – see Nicoladis, 1998), or as Deuchar and Quay (2000) suggest, no initial system followed by language differentiation. Research does not support the old idea that children initially use their two languages as a single or 'unitary language system' (Genesee, 2001, 2002). Genesee's (2001) review of this research on the **storage** of a child's two languages finds that 'contrary to earlier conceptualizations, it is generally agreed now that the languages of the bilingual child are represented in underlying differentiated ways' (p. 158). However, he suggests that the two languages develop both autonomously and inter-dependently, and this is partly a function of transfer between types of language combination (e.g. French–English compared with Mandarin–English). This is further discussed in terms of bilingualism and the brain in chapter 7.

Language Choices of Parents

When parents can potentially use more than one language with their children, there is language choice in raising their children. Piller (2001) refers to this as private language planning. Where parents have the ability to speak both languages to their children, there may be a latent understanding or occasionally a conscious strategy about which language to use with the child from birth upwards. However, Piller (2002) found that many couples do not make a conscious decision about which language(s) to use in the home. Such language choice may derive from a habit formed from the first interaction between the couple, compensation (e.g. using one's native language in return for not living in the homeland) and identity (projecting a desired self-image). Tuominen (1999) found that parents' attitudes to languages, their preferred identity, and an overall cost-benefit analysis were influential in a choice. Other influences include the extended family and friends. **Children** themselves can be surprisingly in control and their own preferences can be highly influential (Tuominen, 1999). Other families may not have that luxury of various options (e.g. less educated or disadvantaged minority language parents in a majority language community). Multilingual extended families may have increased choices of language, particularly if coming from 'elite' circumstances.

Bilingual parents may choose to use just one of their languages with the child. For varied reasons, a mother, for example, may use just Spanish with the child. A different situation is when one parent speaks one language to the child and the other parent speaks a different language (Barron-Hauwaert, 2004). For example, the mother may speak Spanish to the child and the father may speak English. Few families obtain an equal balance between the two languages (e.g. as parents may speak to each other in one language). A third circumstance is when bilingual parents both speak the minority language to their children, leaving the child to learn the majority language outside the home.

Parents make **language choices** in terms of conscious, subconscious and spontaneous decisions that are overall (general) and local (specific) (Pavlenko, 2004). Piller (2002) found that parental choice of family languages relates to desired language, cultural and gender identity, for example. That is, societal contexts in which the family is placed affect language choices.

Such choices may be relatively stable across time, but there are also choices that reflect a local, particular **event** (e.g. when a stranger enters the house everyone changes to the majority language). Thus, strategies and choices are often pragmatically flexible in family language situations, as visitors and contexts change. For example, a visit of a monolingual friend may trigger the need for everyone to use a different language. Or the family attend a religious meeting where everyone uses a holy language.

Emotions affect language choice and strategies. Different languages may be used by parents to convey the emotions of praise and discipline, love and instructions, such that parents are often multilingual and not monolingual in language interactions with their children (Pavlenko, 2004). 'Many [parents] draw on multiple linguistic repertoires, uttering "I love you" in one language, endearments in another, and "Go clean your room!" in yet another' (Pavlenko, 2004, p. 200). Pavlenko (2004) portrays the example of codeswitching when the parent moves from, for example, English to Russian to signify 'I mean what I say!'

Bilingualism in childhood is also influenced by factors outside of parents and the home. With recent immigrants, the parents may speak the heritage language, but the children (especially teenagers) speak to each other in the language of the street, school and television. Playing with neighborhood children, making friends in and out of school with majority language speakers and use of the mass-media may help create bilingualism in the child. An alternative scenario is when the grandparents and other relations use a different language with the child than the home language. For example, Chinese children in the United States may speak English at home and at school, but acquire at least a passive understanding of Cantonese or Mandarin through regular visits to extended family members.

TYPES OF SIMULTANEOUS ACQUISITION

There are **broad categories** of early childhood bilingualism based on the language or languages spoken by the parents to the children and the language of the community (Harding-Esch & Riley, 2003; Romaine,1995; Piller, 2001). Not all children fit neatly into such categories. For example, De Houwer (2005) suggests that the most typical input pattern a bilingual child receives is a combination of hearing some people only speaking one language plus hearing other people speaking both languages on a regular basis. Some families also are exceptions (e.g. one of the parents always addresses the child in a language that is not his/her native language). There will also be an uneven distribution in the use of two or more languages, and that tends to change over time as family, social and educational circumstances, and language use opportunities vary. A bilingual child rarely or never has an equal balance in two-language experience. Hence, balanced bilingualism (see chapter 1) is more of a myth than a reality.

Categories of Early Childhood Bilingualism

One person – one language
The parents have different languages, one of which is often the dominant language of the community. The parents each speak their own language to the child from birth, but tend to speak one language to each other. (Example: mother speaks English; father speaks Dutch; the community language is Dutch.) This has often been suggested as a successful strategy. However, it tends to imply incorrectly that it is only the family that influences language acquisition. Community influences are also important (e.g. pre-school, extended family, mass media). A particular example is when children are raised in multilingual cities (e.g. Brussels, New York, Sydney), and the diverse language experience may add much variation to this strategy.

Home language is different from outside the home
There is much variation within this category (e.g. in terms of parental first language, neighborhood, language of schooling). What is central is that the child acquires one language in the home, and a different language outside the home. Both parents will use the same language in the home, and the child will acquire another language

formally or informally outside the home. One parent may be using their second language. (Example: father is a native English speaker but uses fluent Japanese with his child; mother speaks Japanese; the community language is English.) The parent's language may be the same as the local neighborhood, or it may be different. If it is different, then the child may, for example, acquire the second language at school.

One further variation can produce multilingualism. If each parent speaks a different language to the child from birth, the child may gain a third language outside the home. This often results in trilingualism. (Example: mother speaks German; father speaks Spanish; the community language is English.)

Mixed language

The parents speak both languages to the children, frequently using both languages with the child. Codeswitching and codemixing is acceptable in the home and the neighborhood. The child will typically codeswitch with other bilinguals but not with monolinguals. However, some domains (e.g. school) may expect separation of language code. The community may have a dominant language or not. (Example: mother and father speak Maltese and English; the community language is Maltese and English.)

Delayed introduction of the second language

Where the neighborhood, community and school language is a higher status and dominant language, parents may delay exposure to that dominant language. For example, parents may exclusively speak Navajo in the home until the child is two or three years of age, then add English. The tactic is to ensure a strong foundation in a heritage language before the dominant language outside the home becomes pervasive.

One main **limitation** of the Harding-Esch & Riley (2003) and Romaine (1995) category system is that most types are concerned with 'prestigious bilingualism', where there is a relatively stable additive bilingual environment and a family commitment to bilingualism. In communities where subtractive bilingualism operates, and assimilation (see chapter 18) is politically dominant, childhood bilingualism can be much less stable. Piller (2001) also suggests that, of the four types listed above, types one and two have come to be regarded as successful strategies, and that types three and four are more negatively evaluated. However, this masks a social class difference. Types one and two are associated particularly with 'elite' and middle class families. Types three and four are often found among relatively economically disadvantaged heritage language groups, immigrants and working class families.

Also, there are **agencies** other than the family that can play a major role in early childhood bilingualism. Before the age of three, the language experience with neighbors, networks of friends, crèche, mass media and the nursery school may be a particularly important part of becoming bilingual. The chapter continues by focusing on the better documented routes to childhood bilingualism.

CASE STUDIES OF EARLY BILINGUALISM

Some of the earliest research on bilingualism concerns detailed case studies of children becoming bilingual (see Deuchar & Quay (2000) and Yamamoto (2001) for a review). For example, Ronjat (1913) described a case of the mother speaking German and the father speaking French in a French community. Ronjat's (1913) case study introduced the concept of '**one parent - one language**'. That is, the case study announced the idea that a very effective method of raising children bilingually was for each parent to speak a separate language to the child.

While there have been a number of case studies of children growing up bilingually since Ronjat's first study, one of the most detailed of case studies is Leopold's (1939 to 1949). Leopold's classic study of his daughter Hildegard was based on the father speaking German in the home and the mother speaking English. **Leopold** was a phonetician by training and made a comprehensive record of the development of Hildegard's speech, which he published in four books.

One important aspect of Leopold's studies is the **shifting balance** of the two languages in childhood. When Hildegard went to Germany, her German became stronger. When back in the United States and attending school, Hildegard's English became the dominant language. Many bilingual situations are changeable, where, at an individual level (and not just at a societal level), the languages shift in dominance. Hildegard, for example was reluctant to speak German during her mid-teens, with German becoming the weaker language. Leopold's second daughter, Karla, understood German but spoke very little German to her father. In childhood, Karla was a passive bilingual. Yet at the age of 19, Karla visited Germany where she was able to change from receptive German to productive German, managing to converse relatively fluently in German.

Other examples of shifting bilingualism in childhood are given by Fantini (1985) who details a child's shift between English, Italian and Spanish, and Yukawa (1997) who examines three cases of first language Japanese loss and re-acquisition. Yamamoto (2002) found in Japan that 'Many parents testify, however, that in spite of their full-fledged care, their children have not developed active bilingual abilities' (p. 545). De Houwer (2003) found that among some 2500 bilingual families, 1 in 5 children reared bilingually do not later use one of those languages. But as Quay (2001) aptly concludes: 'passive competence is valuable as the potential exists for his two weaker languages to be activated and used more actively later on . . . The status of strong and weak languages can change over the course of the child's life' (p. 194). De Houwer (2005) suggests that **passive competence** can rapidly change to productive competence by a dramatic increase in input and a need to speak that language (e.g. visiting monolingual grandparents, a vacation).

Apart from the 'one parent - one language' method of raising children bilingually, there are other case studies showing **different approaches** (see Schinke-Llano, 1989; Romaine, 1995). Two of these approaches have already been mentioned: each parent speaking a different language to the child; and parents speaking a minority language to the child who acquires a second language in the community or extended family. A third approach occurs where both parents (and the community) are bilingual and use both their languages with the children. Romaine (1995) considers this 'a more common category than it might seem on the basis of its representation in the literature' (p. 186). For example, along the US–Mexico border there are many communities where English and Spanish is mixed. This is supported by Lyon (1996) who found that, in families in Wales, mixed language input with little apparent self-monitoring or awareness was quite typical. E. García (1983) showed that a parental mixing of languages can still lead to a child communicating effectively in two languages so long as the child learns that the two languages have relatively distinct forms and uses.

An example of parents using both languages with their first-born is by Deuchar & Quay (2000). A simplified profile of such dual language use with Deuchar's daughter (from 10 months to 2 years and 3 months) follows:

Mother: Born in UK, native speaker of English, learnt fluent Spanish in adulthood.

Father: Born in Cuba, later lived in Panama and then UK, native speaker of Spanish, began learning English at high school and became fluent in English.

Language spoken to daughter by mother: English up to age 1, then Spanish. Spanish used by the mother when talking to the father; English when in the company of English speakers (e.g. crèche) or in a specific context (e.g. University campus).

Language spoken to daughter by father: Spanish except when English speaker present, then he used English.

Language spoken to daughter by maternal grandmother / carers / crèche: English.

Community: English.

Trips abroad: Spanish.

What is significant in this case study is that the daughter experienced her parents speaking both languages, with the **context** providing the rule-bound behavior. Both parents were fluent and effective role-models in both languages, although each parent was a native speaker of one language and a learner of a second language. The switching between English to Spanish was not random but governed by the situation (e.g. presence of others, crèche). This illustrates a danger of the 'one language one parent' model in that it can restrict discussion to the home, as if the parents are almost the only language influence. In contrast, siblings, extended families, carers, crèche, pre-schooling, friends of the family and many varying contexts (e.g. religious, geographical mobility) often have an additional language effect (Yamamoto, 2001). Parents may be able to plan language use when together as a nuclear family (e.g. one parent-one language). However, once other people enter the house, and especially in the child's language experience outside the home, parental control is limited (Deuchar & Quay, 2000).

One-Parent Families and Bilingualism

Most case-studies of bilingual children have been based on two-parent families. Books dealing with raising children bilingually tend to assume the presence of two parents in the family home. By accident rather than design, this implies that a one-parent family has little or no chance of raising a child bilingually. This is not true. Two examples will illustrate this.

(1) A second language is often acquired outside the home. In parts of Africa, children acquire one language at home or in the neighborhood and another language (or even two or three) at school or in inter-ethnic communication in urban areas. Children of immigrant United States communities may acquire Spanish, for example, in the home and neighborhood, and learn English at school. A single parent who speaks French but resides in the US may decide to make French the family language so that the children may have the opportunity of bilingualism. In cases like these, the absence of a father or mother does not necessarily hinder a child's bilingual development.

(2) In some cases, the maintenance of a family's bilingualism may be challenged by the absence of a parent. In cases such as those in (1) above, where one parent speaks the dominant language of the community to the children, and the other parent uses a minority language with them, the death or departure of the second parent may mean that the family becomes monolingual. However, if the remaining parent is committed to the maintenance of the family's bilingualism, it can be accomplished in various ways (see Baker & Jones, 1998).

The disruption of a family by death or divorce is typically traumatic for both parents and children. At times of great mental and emotional stress, when many practical difficulties and changes have to be faced, bilingualism may seem low on the list of priorities. However, single-parent families are often adept at meeting challenges and may look for ways of maintaining a child's bilingualism without causing further disruption to the child's life. In addition, where a child has undergone such stress, it may be wise, if possible, to avoid the added trauma of losing a language, a culture and an intrinsic part of the child's identity.

TRILINGUALISM

Many people are multilingual and not just bilingual. For example, some Swedish people are fluent in Swedish, German and English. Many individuals in the African and Indian continents speak a local, regional and official or international language. In Zaire, children may learn a local vernacular at home, a regional language such as Lingala or Kikongo in the community or at school, and French as they proceed through schooling. Early trilingualism, when a child is exposed to three languages from birth, is more rare than trilingualism achieved through schooling (e.g. two languages learnt at school). Particular examples of trilingual schooling are found in the Basque Country (Basque, Spanish, English – see Lasagabaster, 2000, L. Etxeberría, 2004), Catalonia (Catalan, Spanish, English – see Muñoz, 2000), Finland (Finnish,

Swedish, English – see Björklund & Suni, 2000), Friesland (Frisian, Dutch, English – see Ytsma, 2000) and Romania (Romanian, Hungarian and English – see Iatcu, 2000).

One route to **trilingualism** is parents speaking two different languages to their children at home. The children then take their education through a third language. Alternatively, the children pick up a third language from the grandparents, carers, visitors, playmates or the mass media. The majority language of the community is likely to influence the relative strengths of the three languages. The relative proficiency in each of the three languages may also change over time. Stable trilingualism seems less likely than stable bilingualism.

There are few case studies of the development of **trilingual children** (see Quay (2001) and C. Hoffmann (2001) for reviews) and even less demographics (but see De Houwer, 2004 for a survey of trilingual families in Flanders). One case study (C. Hoffmann, 1985) concerns Spanish (acquired mostly from the father and *au pairs*), German (acquired mostly from the mother and visits), and English (acquired mostly among peers and in school). The one parent - one language 'rule' was followed. English came to be dominant as the school experience and peer relationships developed.

Quay (2001) researched a child raised in German (spoken by the father to the child and the language used between mother and father) and English (used by the mother when addressing the child). Both parents were fluent in Japanese which was the language of the local community (e.g. where their son attended daycare that operated in Japanese). There was a change in language exposure over the first two years, for example due to visits abroad and changes in the father's work schedule (see below, adapted from Quay, 2001). Such changes are quite common for early trilinguals and bilinguals.

Age of child	% English heard	% German heard	% Japanese heard
Birth to 11 months	70%	30%	0%
11 months to 1;0 year (attending daycare)	50%	20%	30%
1;0 to 1;5 months	43%	23%	34%
1;5 to 1;6	45%	10%	45%

The table shows that this child was less exposed to German than English. At 1;3 it was not apparent that the child understood much German. Yet after two weeks in Germany at 1;3 the mother reports that he 'shocked us with how much he understood in German when spoken to by the extended family' (Quay, 2001, p. 174). This is also a common experience for families: understanding (and speaking) a second or third language quickly grows once there is sufficient exposure and incentive. However, Quay (2001) also shows that the child was a developing trilingual rather than an active trilingual. This child preferred to speak Japanese to his parents as he had more lexical resources in Japanese, and his parents understood and accepted his Japanese utterances. He tended to be a **passive trilingual**, understanding English and German, but speaking Japanese.

A case study by DeWaele (2000) follows Livia, a girl raised in Dutch by her mother, French by her father, with English acquired in the London neighborhood. The mother and father use Dutch when speaking together, making Dutch the dominant language of the family. English quickly became her 'default language' when meeting new children in London. From five months to two and a half years, Livia learnt Urdu from a childminder, thus becoming quadralingual at an early age. By one year and two months she had a passive knowledge of some 150 French, Dutch, Urdu and English words. Multiword utterances in Dutch and French appeared at two years two months. Awareness of her languages (metalinguistic awareness – see chapter 7) came before her second birthday, for example, in suggesting that the mother duck in her bath was Dutch-speaking. The **value of multilingualism** was also understood at a very early age: 'If she doesn't get the cookie she ordered in one language, she code-switches to the other, just to make sure we understand her request' (DeWaele, 2000, p. 5). However, by five years of age, status and **acceptance** by peers had become important. Her father reports that she 'does not want me to speak French to her at school and addresses me . . . in English, or whispers French in my ear' (DeWaele, 2002, p. 547). She wanted to avoid standing out from her peers, even in multiethnic London.

In a review of **research on trilingualism**, Cenoz and Genesee (1998, p. 20) conclude that 'bilingualism does not hinder the acquisition of an additional language and, to the contrary, in most cases bilingualism favors the acquisition of a third language'. Cenoz (2003, p. 82) also suggests that 'Studies on the effect of bilingualism on third language acquisition tend to confirm the advantages of bilinguals over monolinguals in language learning.' The cognitive advantages of bilingualism such as a wider linguistic repertoire, enhanced learning strategies, cognitive flexibility and metalinguistic awareness (see chapter 7) and the development of enhanced linguistic processing strategies may help explain this positive effect of bilingualism on acquiring a third language (Cenoz, 2000, 2003). The linguistic interdependence hypothesis (see chapter 8) also suggests that positive influences may occur from bilingualism to trilingualism (Cenoz, 2003). Where advantages are not present, the context is typically subtractive. This is returned to briefly in chapter 12.

Clyne *et al.* (2004) found multiple positive social, cultural and cognitive **advantages for trilingualism**. Such trilinguals were found to be effective and persistent language learners, whose bilingualism is a language apprenticeship for further language learning. They conclude that 'acquiring a third language at school boosts students' confidence in their bilingualism and makes them appreciate their home language more, in some cases even leading to a desire to maintain their heritage language in the future and pass it on to the next generation' (p. 49). Clyne *et al.* (2004) also found that acquisition of a third language awakens and deepens interest in other languages, cultures and countries, creating more multicultural and global citizens.

Trilingualism has become a growth area in research that has sociolinguistic, psycholinguistic, social and cultural identity, political and educational dimensions (see Cenoz & Jessner, 2000; C. Hoffmann & Ytsma, 2004). Many recent studies of trilingualism analyze the current and future place of English as the most important language of wider communication, not only in science and commerce but also in travel and technology (e.g. the Internet) – see Cenoz & Hoffmann (2003).

CODESWITCHING AND CODEMIXING

One issue frequently raised by parents and teachers of children of differing ages is when one language is mixed with another. Terms such as Hinglish, Spanglish, Tex-Mex and Wenglish (respectively for Hindi-English, Spanish-English, Texan-Mexican and Welsh-English) are often used in a derogatory fashion to describe what may have become accepted language borrowing within a particular community. However, in some domains, a separation of languages may be the acceptable norm. For example, in formal classroom teaching and learning, codeswitching may be disfavored.

Codeswitching may also be less acceptable for political, social or cultural reasons. If a power conflict exists between different ethnic groups, then language may be perceived as a prime marker of a separate identity, and codeswitching may seem disloyal.

Monolinguals may have negative attitudes to codeswitching, believing that it shows a deficit, or a lack of mastery of both languages. However, it tends to be those who are more fluent in a language that code-switch (Meisel, 2004). Yet bilinguals themselves may be defensive or apologetic about their codeswitching and attribute it to laziness or sloppy language habits. However, codeswitching is a valuable linguistic tool. It does not typically happen at random. There is usually purpose and logic in changing languages. It is using the full language resources that are available to a bilingual, usually knowing that the listener fully understands the code-switches. One main language (called the matrix language) provides the grammatical frame or rules for grammar (Myers-Scotton, 2002). Codeswitching thus involves a **rule-bound** (e.g. word order, verb endings) use of the secondary language, as the second language insertions will fit those matrix language rules.

If codeswitching is very prevalent in a language group, it is sometimes regarded as a sign that the minority language is about to disappear. Bilingualism is then associated with a move from a heritage language to a majority language. Identifying the matrix (main, dominant) language that provides the rules from codeswitching becomes a key indicator of the health of a minority language. For example, if the matrix language is Navajo and there are English insertions, this indicator for the future of Navajo will be positive. However, if the **grammatical frame** is English, this indicator for Navajo may be negative.

Very few bilinguals keep their two languages completely separate, and the ways in which they mix them are complex and varied. Grosjean (1992) distinguishes between the 'monolingual mode' (when bilinguals use one of their languages with monolingual speakers of that language) and the 'bilingual mode' when bilinguals are in the company of other bilinguals and have the option of switching languages.

Even in the 'monolingual mode', bilinguals occasionally switch their languages inter-sententially.

Various terms have been used to describe switches between languages in conversation. The term '**codemixing**' has sometimes been used to describe changes at the word level (e.g. when one word or a few words in a sentence change). A mixed language sentence such as '*Leo un magazine*' (I read a magazine) might be called codemixing. In contrast, '*Come to the table. Bwyd yn barod*' (food is ready) might be called codeswitching. The first phrase is in English; the second in Welsh. Codeswitching has generally been used to describe any switch within the course of a single conversation, whether at word or sentence level or at the level of blocks of speech. However, Muysken (2000) prefers codemixing as the more general term, but distinguishes between insertions (e.g. immigrants who insert or borrow words while their languages are uneven), alternation (e.g. relatively stable bilinguals such as French/Dutch speakers in Brussels living in a context where languages are kept relatively separate), and congruent lexicalization (e.g. where there is a tradition of mixing grammatically similar languages such as Dutch and Frisian with vocabulary being used from both languages).

Language borrowing has been the term used to indicate foreign loan words or phrases that have become an integral and permanent part of the recipient language. Examples are '*le weekend*' from English into the French language and '*der Computer*' from English into the German language. All languages borrow words or phrases from other languages with which they come into contact. Codeswitching may often be the first step in this process. Myers-Scotton (1992) argues against trying to establish criteria to distinguish between code-switches and loans. Code-switches and loans are not two distinct and separate entities. Rather, they form a continuum. As Eastman (1992, p. 1) suggested: 'efforts to distinguish codeswitching, codemixing and borrowing are doomed.'

'**Language interference**' was a term that was once used to refer to when people acquiring two languages mixed their languages. Many bilinguals regard this as a negative and pejorative term, revealing a monolingual's perspective and suggesting that there is a problem when a bilingual speaks. For the child, switching between languages may be to convey thoughts and ideas in the most personally efficient manner. The child may also realize that the listener understands such switching. Given that such 'interference' is typically temporary in a child's bilingual development, the more neutral terms '**transfer**' and '**cross-linguistic influence**' (see Sharwood Smith, 1989) may be preferable.

The discussion of codeswitching will now be considered from a sociolinguistic perspective. Those interested in a linguistic perspective (e.g. 'where in a sentence can a speaker change languages?') may consult Myers-Scotton (1993, 1997), Muysken (2000), Poplack and Meechan (1998), Romaine (1995) and Toribio (2004).

Code-switches have a variety of purposes and aims. Codeswitching will vary according to who is in the conversation, what the topic is, and in what kind of context the conversation occurs. The languages used may be negotiated and may change with the topic of conversation. Also, social, economic, political and symbolic factors can influence codeswitching (Treffers-Daller, 1992, 1994; Stroud, 2004). For example, competition among language groups, the relationships between the language majority and language minority, the norms of the community and inter group relations in a community may have a major effect on the use of codeswitching. Twelve over-lapping **purposes of codeswitching** will now be considered.

(1)   Code-switches may be used to **emphasize** a particular point in a conversation. If one word needs stressing or is central in a sentence, a switch may be made (e.g. 'get out of the mud, *hogyn drwg* [bad boy]

(2)   If a person does not know a word or a phrase in a language, that person may **substitute** a word in another language. This often happens because bilinguals use different languages in different domains of their lives. A young person may, for instance, switch from the home language to the language used in school to talk about a subject such as mathematics or computers. Myers-Scotton (1972) describes how a Kikuyu university student in Nairobi, Kenya, switched constantly from Kikuyu to English to discuss geometry with his younger brother.'*Atiriri angle niati has ina degree eighty; nayo this one ina mirongo itatu.*' Similarly, an adult may code-switch when talking about work, because the technical terms associated with work are only known in that language. Man and Lu (2006) found that in Hong Kong schools both teachers' and students' major reason for codeswitching was that there was no direct translation of words between English and Cantonese.

(3)   Words or phrases in two languages may not correspond exactly and the bilingual may switch to one language to **express a concept that has no equivalent** in the culture of the other language. For example, a French–English bilingual living in Britain may use words like 'pub' or 'bingo hall' when speaking French, because there are no exact French equivalents for these words.

(4)   Codeswitching may be used to **reinforce** a request. For example, a teacher may repeat a command to accent and underline it (e.g. '*Tuisez-vous les enfants*! Be quiet, children!'). In a majority/minority language situation, the majority language may be used to underline authority. In a study conducted at a hospital in Mid-Wales (G. Roberts, 1994), it was found that nurses repeat or amplify commands to patients in English in order to emphasize their authority (e.g. '*Peidiwch a chanu'r gloch Mrs Jones* – don't ring the bell if you don't need anything!'). A Spanish-speaking mother in New York may use English with her children for short commands like 'Stop it! Don't do that!' and then switch back to Spanish.

(5)   Repetition of a phrase or passage in another language may also be used to **clarify** a point. Some teachers in classrooms explain a concept in one language, and then explain it again in another language, believing that repetition adds reinforcement and completeness of understanding.

(6)   Codeswitching may be used to express **identity**, communicate friendship or family bonding. For example, moving from the common majority language to

the home language or minority language which both the listener and speaker understand well may communicate friendship and common identity. Similarly, a person may deliberately use codeswitching to indicate the need to be accepted by a peer group. Someone with a rudimentary knowledge of a language may inject words of that new language into sentences to indicate a desire to identify and affiliate. The use of the listener's stronger language in part of the conversation may indicate deference, wanting to belong or to be accepted. Stroud's (2004) research shows that codeswitching between Portuguese and Ronga in Mozambique relates to social identities that are constructed in tensions between competing political, economic and cultural pressures.

(7) In **relating a conversation** held previously, the person may report the conversation in the language or languages used. For example, two people may be speaking Spanish together. When one reports a previous conversation with an English monolingual, that conversation is reported authentically – for example, in English – as it occurred.

(8) Codeswitching is sometimes used as a way of **interjecting** into a conversation. A person attempting to break into a conversation may introduce a different language. Interrupting a conversation may be signaled by changing language.

(9) Codeswitching may be used to **ease tension and inject humor** into a conversation. Man and Lu (2006) found that teachers in Hong Kong schools used codeswitching for such an effect. If discussions are becoming tense in a committee, the use of a second language may signal a change in the 'tune being played'. Just as in an orchestra, different instruments may be brought in during a composition to signal a change of mood and pace, so a switch in language may indicate a need to change mood within the conversation.

(10) Codeswitching often relates to a **change of attitude or relationship**. For example, when two people meet, they may use the common majority language (e.g. Swahili or English in Kenya). As the conversation proceeds and roles, status and ethnic identity are revealed, a change to a regional language may indicate that boundaries are being broken down. A code-switch signals there is less social distance, with expressions of solidarity and growing rapport indicated by the switch. A study of Italian immigrants into the United States at the turn of the 20th century (Di Pietro, 1977) showed that the immigrants would tell a joke in English and give the punch line in Italian, not only because it was better expressed in that language, but also to emphasize the shared values and experiences of the minority group.

Conversely, a **change** from a minority language or dialect to a majority language may indicate the speakers' wish to elevate their own status, create a distance between themselves and the listener, or establish a more formal, business relationship. Myers-Scotton and Ury (1977) describe a conversation between a Kenyan shop keeper and his sister, who had come in to buy some salt. After exchanging greetings in their own Luyia dialect, the brother switches to Swahili in front of the other customers and says: '*Dada, sasa leo unahitaji nini?*' (Sister, what do you need today?) For the rest of the conversation, the brother speaks in Swahili and the sister in the Luyia dialect. The brother's code-switch to Swahili, the business language of Kenya, indicates to his sister that, although they are closely related, he must maintain a business relationship with her. She should not expect any favors or to receive anything for free.

(11) Codeswitching can also be used to **exclude** people from a conversation. For example, when traveling on the metro (subway, underground), two people speaking English may switch to their minority language to talk about private matters, thus excluding others from the conversation. Bilingual parents may use one language together to exclude their monolingual children from a private discussion. A doctor at a hospital may make a brief aside to a colleague in a language not understood by the patient. However, monolinguals sometimes feel threatened and excluded by codeswitching, even when that is usually not the intention of the speakers.

(12) In some bilingual situations, codeswitching occurs regularly when certain topics are introduced (e.g. money). Spanish–English bilinguals in the South West United States often switch to English to discuss money. For example, a person may say 'La consulta era (the visit cost) twenty dollars'. This reflects that English is the language of commerce, and often the dominant language of the mathematics curriculum.

Familiarity, projected status, the ethos of the context and the perceived linguistic skills of the listeners affect the nature and process of codeswitching (Martin-Jones, 2000; Simon, 2001). This suggests that codeswitching is not just linguistic; it indicates important social and power relationships.

A variety of factors may affect the **extent** to which older children and adults switch between their languages (Romaine, 1995). The perceived status of the listeners, familiarity with those persons, atmosphere of the setting and perceived linguistic skills of the listeners are examples of variables that may foster or prevent codeswitching. Such factors operate as young as two years of age. Whereas a two-year-old's mixing of language has tended to be seen as 'interference' or a lack of differentiation between languages, research has shown that codeswitching by two-year-olds can be context-sensitive (e.g. according to who is being addressed), as discussed earlier in this chapter (Deuchar & Quay, 2000).

The chapter concludes by examining a topic related to codeswitching: children acting as interpreters for their parents and others (Kaur & Mills, 1993). Bilingual children (and adults) are frequently expected to act as go-betweens by interpreting from one language to another. Such an interpreter's role also illustrates how bilingual development impacts on other aspects of child development such as personality and family relationships.

CHILDREN AS LANGUAGE INTERPRETERS AND BROKERS

In language minority families, children sometimes act as **interpreters** or **language brokers** for their parents and others (Valdés, 2003). For example, in first and second generation immigrant families, parents may have little or no competency in the majority language. Therefore, their children act as interpreters in a variety of contexts (as do 'hearing' children with deaf parents). Rather than just transmit information, children act as information and communication brokers (Tse, 1995, 1996a, 1996b), often ensuring the messages are 'culturally translated' as in the following example:

> Father to daughter in Italian: '*Digli che è un imbecille!*' (Tell him he is an idiot!)
> Daughter to trader: 'My father won't accept your offer.'

Language minority students can be important language brokers between the home and the school (McQuillan & Tse, 1995). Also, when there are visitors to the house, such as sellers and traders, religious persuasionists and local officials, a parent may call a child to the door to help translate what is being said. The child interprets for both parties (e.g. the parent and the caller). Similarly, at stores, hospitals, the doctor's, dentist's, optician's, school and many other places where parents visit, the child may be taken to help interpret (Valdés, 2003). Interpretation may be needed in more informal places: on the street, when a parent is phoned, watching the television or listening to the radio, reading a local newspaper or working on the computer.

Pressure is placed on children in language brokering: linguistic, emotional, social and attitudinal pressure. First, children may find an exact translation difficult to achieve as their language is still developing. Second, children may be hearing information (e.g. medical troubles, financial problems, arguments and conflicts) that is the preserve of adults rather than children. Third, children may be expected to be adult-like when interpreting and child-like at all other times; to mix with adults when interpreting and 'be seen and not heard' with adults on other occasions. Fourth, seeing their parents in an inferior position may lead to children despising their minority language. Children may quickly realize when language brokering that the language of power, prestige and purse is the majority language. Negative attitudes to the minority language may result. Fifth, bilinguals are not necessarily good interpreters. Interpretation assumes an identical vocabulary in both languages. Since bilinguals tend to use their two languages in different places with different people, an identical lexicon may not be present. Also, proficiency in two or more languages is not enough. Some reflection on language (in chapter 7 discussed as metalinguistic awareness), such as an awareness of the linguistic nature of the message may also be required (Malakoff, 1992).

Language brokering also has many **positive outcomes**. **First**, it can bring parental praise, reward and status within the family for playing a valuable role. The research of Malakoff (1992) found that this ability is widely distributed among bilingual children who are quite expert as early as the 3rd or 4th grade. Such ability may gain both esteem from others and raise self-esteem. **Second**, the child learns adult information quickly and learns to act with some authority and trust. Early maturity has its own rewards in the teenage peer group. **Third**, Kaur and Mills (1993) found that children accustomed to acting as interpreters learnt to take the initiative. For example, a child may give the answer to a question rather than relaying the question to the parent. This puts children in a position of some power, even of censorship.

Fourth, when parents become dependent on their children for language brokering, it may make the family more close, trusting and integrated. Such language brokering is a lifeline for the many parents who have to hand over much power to their children. Yet it may make parents aware of their own language inadequacies, resulting in feelings of frustration and resentment, particularly in language minority cultures where children are expected to stay in a subordinate position for a long time.

Fifth, the cognitive outcomes for child language brokers may be valuable. Children who are regular interpreters for their parents may realize early on the problems and possibilities of translation of words, figures of speech and ideas. For example, such children may learn early on that one language never fully parallels another, and that it is hard to translate exactly the inner meaning of words and metaphors. This may lead such children to be more introspective about their languages. This is termed metalinguistic awareness and is considered in chapter 7. Thus, interpretation may both require and stimulate metalinguistic awareness (Tse, 1996a).

Sixth, another advantage for the child language broker is in character formation, for example, possibly gaining more empathy. The children are negotiating between two different social and cultural worlds, trying to understand both, and provide bridges between these two worlds. Their understanding of different cultures may be deepened by the responsibility. This handling of dialogue may lead to increased maturity, astuteness, independence and higher self-esteem. Being expected to carry an adult role early on may lead to a positive self-concept, and to feeling responsible like an adult.

CONCLUSION

This chapter has discussed bilingual development in early childhood through themes of differentiating between languages, and dual language storage. Parental influence start at the fetal stage with language difference being apparent at babbling stage. Children of two and three raised in two languages form birth will know 'what language to speak to whom'.

The one-parent-one language is a well-documented and successful route to bilingualism in children, but there are many other successful pathways. Some parents both use two languages with their children. Some bilingual children are raised in one language but become bilingual early via influences outside the home (e.g. carers, nurseries, extended family). One-parent families can be as successful as nuclear and extended families. However, language loss can occur when political contexts are particularly unfavorable to minority language maintenance. Other families succeed in raising trilingual children, although it is not usual for all three languages to become equally proficient.

Codeswitching is a frequent behavior among bilinguals with a variety of valuable purposes and benefits. Interpreting is a similarly frequent expectation of bilinguals – including young children in immigrant families.

KEY POINTS IN THE CHAPTER

- Children are born ready to become bilinguals, trilinguals, multilinguals.
- There is a difference between simultaneous (acquire two languages together) and sequential (acquire one language later than the other) childhood bilingualism.
- Dual language acquisition starts at the fetal stage, extends into babbling and can be operating successfully at two and three years of age.
- Young children learn to differentiate between two languages and can effectively store those languages.
- Early studies of bilingual children revealed that if each parent speaks a different language to the child, dual language competence can occur, although the balance shifts throughout an individual's language history.
- The 'one person, one language' parental approach in a family is a well documented and often successful route to bilingualism. Many other routes are equally successful including when both parents speak both languages to the child.
- Trilingualism and multilingualism can also be successfully achieved in young children, although the languages may not become equally strong.
- Bilingualism typically favors the acquisition of a further language. Bilinguals tend to have an advantage in learning a new language.
- Codeswitching is typical in bilinguals and has many valuable purposes in relationships and relaying messages, as well as expressing roles, norms and values.
- Codeswitching varies according to who is in the conversation, what is the topic, and in what kind of context the conversation occurs.
- Children may act as language brokers for parents when their proficiency in the majority language is ahead of their parents. This has many advantages and disadvantages for the child.

SUGGESTED FURTHER READING

CENOZ, J., 2003, The additive effect of bilingualism on third language acquisition: A review. *International Journal of Bilingualism*, 7, 1, 71–87.

CENOZ, J. & HOFFMANN, C., 2003, Acquiring a third language: What role does bilingualism play? *International Journal of Bilingualism*, 7, 1, 1–5.

DEUCHAR, M. & QUAY, S., 2000, *Bilingual Acquisition: Theoretical Implications of a Case Study*. Oxford: Oxford University Press.

GENESEE, F., 2001, Bilingual first language acquisition: Exploring the limits of the language faculty. *Annual Review of Applied Linguistics*, 21, 153–168.

GENESEE, F., 2003, Rethinking Bilingual Acquisition. In J-M. DEWAELE, A. HOUSEN & LI WEI (eds), *Bilingualism: Beyond Basic Principles*. Clevedon: Multilingual Matters.

GENESEE, F., PARADIS, J. & CRAGO, M.B., 2004, *Dual Language Development & Disorders: A Handbook on Bilingualism and Second Language Learning*. Baltimore: Paul H. Brookes.

MEISEL, J.M., 2004, The bilingual child. In T.K. BHATIA & W.C. RITCHIE (eds), *The Handbook of Bilingualism*. Malden, MA: Blackwell.

VALDÉS, G., 2003, *Expanding Definitions of Giftedness: The Case of Young Interpreters from Immigrant Communities*. Mahwah, NJ: Lawrence Erlbaum.

See also journals for the most recent research in this area: (a) *International Journal of Bilingualism* and (b) *International Journal of Multilingualism*.

STUDY ACTIVITIES

(1) Create a case study of one person's bilingual development. This may be yourself or someone you know. By interviewing that person, or self-reflection, make a recording or a written case study of the factors which seem personally important to that person in their bilingual development. This may be developed as a project. A project may include the following stages. First, look in the library for case studies of bilinguals. Books by Arnberg (1987), Barron-Hauwaert (2004), Döpke (1992), Cunningham-Andersson & Andersson (2004), Harding-Esch and Riley (2003) and Lyon (1996) provide examples. Deuchar & Quay (2000) provide an excellent guide to conducting such a case study (especially chapters 1 and 2). Second, prepare an interview guide. Write down (as an aide memoire) the topics and kinds of questions you would like to ask in an interview. Third, try to use a tape recorder, or write down when the respondent is talking to record the interview. If you make a tape, transcribe the key quotes or all of the interview. Fourth, write out a case study of the bilingual development of that person. Are there particular stages or periods in the development? Or was the development more smooth with gradual changes?

(2) Interview a mother or father who is learning a second language at the same time as their child. Ask about the progress each is making. What differences are there? Ask about why there are qualitative and quantitative differences in progress? What attitudes and motivations do the language learners have? If there are differences of attitude, try to work out an explanation.

(3) By observation or recording, gather samples of codeswitching. Try to find illustrations of different purposes of codeswitching. Ask the people in your sample (after completing the observation/recording) how conscious they are of codeswitching. What are their explanations for codeswitching? What particular purposes for codeswitching were most found in your samples? How regular was codeswitching in the conversation? What was the personal history of those you observed or recorded that helps explain such codeswitching?

(4) Examine between three and six of the 120 'questions about bilingualism most asked by parents' in Baker (2000a) or from web sites that provide advice to bilingual parents. Discuss in a group whether the advice given in the answers (a) matches the group's experience and (b) seems relevant. Compose a poster presentation giving the group's advice to any one question or issue.

(5) Watch and write a short review of the video 'Growing up with English Plus'

(1999). ISBN: 1 875578 90 0. This 45 minute video derives from Monash University's Language and Society Centre. The main contributors are typical parents talking about their experience of bringing up children bilingually with expert contributions from Professor Michael Clyne, Dr Heather Lotherington and Dr Suzanne Döpke. The video presents a number of ways of raising children bilingually through the presentation of typical family situations and experiences, confronting the anxieties and fears that parents typically experience when bringing up bilingual children. The video is available from: Language Australia, GPO Box 372F, Melbourne, 3001, Australia.

CHAPTER 6

The Later Development of Bilingualism

CHAPTER 6

The Later Development of Bilingualism

INTRODUCTION

Sequential acquisition of bilingualism refers to the situation where a child or adult acquires a first language, and later becomes proficient in the second language and sometimes further languages. The sequential acquisition of bilingualism takes us into the field of **second language acquisition**. Such acquisition may be through formal or informal means; informally through street, nursery school and community, or formally through school, adult classes and language courses. There is no single 'best' route by which learners, young or old, become competent in a second language. There are a variety of informal and formal educational means of acquiring proficiency in a second language.

Many children become competent bilinguals through the process of simultaneous bilingualism. The track record of bilingualism achieved through sequential routes (e.g. foreign language learning) is not always so positive. In the US and Britain, despite extensive foreign language learning in school (and the extensive research on second language acquisition), only a small proportion of children learning a foreign language become functionally and fluently bilingual. In the US, fewer than one in 20 children become bilingual following foreign language instruction. There are various popular reasons for such **failure**: the emphasis on reading and writing rather than on authentic communication; having a low aptitude to learn a second language; a lack of motivation and interest, and a lack of opportunity to practice second language skills. Another popular explanation is attempting to learn a language too late; that is, believing that it is easier to learn a language when someone is younger rather than older. The issue of age in learning a language is considered later.

In certain western countries (e.g. the Netherlands, Switzerland, Sweden, Belgium) and eastern countries (e.g. Israel, Singapore), foreign language learning has been relatively more successful. Such international comparisons highlight the need to bring political, cultural and economic factors into second language learning discussions. No language learner or language program is an island. Surrounding the shores of the individual psychology of effective second language acquisition lie the seas of social, cultural and political context. Any map of sequential bilingualism needs to include all these features.

REASONS FOR SECOND LANGUAGE LEARNING

The various overlapping reasons why second or third language are taught can be clustered under two headings: **societal and individual**. Such reasons include external (out of the classroom) goals and internal (classroom) goals (Cook, 2002b). Such purposes may clash. For example, national politics may insist on the teaching of a national language for unity and social cohesion, while individuals may prefer instruction through the regional language. Basque separatists in Spain, and Eastern Europeans rejecting Russian as the language of Communism, are two examples of difference between societal and individual wishes. Some reasons are for learning a language, others for teaching a language, and there may be variance between the two.

Societal Reasons

For language minority children, the aim of second language instruction may be **assimilationist** and subtractive. For example, the teaching of English as a second language in the United States and the UK often aims at rapidly assimilating minority language groups into mainstream society. Assimilationist ideology (see chapter 18) tends to work for the dominance of the second language, even the repression of the home, minority language.

In contrast, children are sometimes taught minority languages in order to **preserve** or restore a language that is being or has been lost. Learning the national language as a second language may be a step towards economic, social and political freedom. In Ireland, English-speaking children are taught Irish for this reason; the same is true of English-speaking Māori children in New Zealand and Spanish-speaking Basque children in the Basque autonomous region; in each case, the aim is to revive or regenerate a threatened indigenous language. Such maintenance may not only exist in indigenous language 'territory'. Where first language English children in the US learn to speak Spanish as a second language (e.g. in dual language schools), there may be an attempt to preserve the language within a particular social and cultural network (e.g. Miami). This provides an additive situation: a second language is added at no cost to the first language.

A different societal reason for second language acquisition other than assimilationist or preservationist is to reduce conflict and obtain increased **harmony** between language groups through bilingualism. In Canada, French speaking children learning English, and English speaking children learning French may help parents and politicians produce a more dual language, integrated Canadian society.

The assimilationist, preservationist and harmony viewpoints all argue for the importance of a second language for careers, access to further and higher education, access to information and communications technology and for travel. However, it is important to distinguish whether the second language is to replace the first language or to be added to that first language.

While teachers may be relatively powerless to change the basic societal aims and reasons in second language teaching, understanding the role they play in such teaching is important. Second language teaching does not exist in a political vacuum. Nor is language teaching a neutral, value-free activity.

Second and third language learning is often encouraged for **economic and trade** reasons (e.g. in Singapore, Scandinavia). Given notions such as globalization, common markets, open access to trade, the free market economy, the importance of international trade to developing nations, then facility with languages is seen as opening doors to economic activity. Selling to the Japanese, for example, may be quite difficult through English or German. Speaking Japanese and having a sympathetic understanding of Japanese culture, manners, values and thinking may be the essential foundation for successful economic activity (see chapter 19). There is a growing realization that speaking foreign languages is important in increasingly competitive international **trade**, even as a matter of long-range economic self-interest. Translating jobs in the US tend to be filled by foreign-born individuals because there are relatively few US students and adults who are proficient in the second languages required for such posts.

Second and third language learning is also encouraged for its potential value in **interaction across continents**. For many mainland Europeans, for example, to speak two, three or four languages is not uncommon. Such language facility enables time to be spent in neighboring European countries or in North, Central or South America. In the attempted unification of Europe, traveling across frontiers is becoming more common, encouraging a person to acquire a repertoire of languages. However, English is growing as a 'common denominator' language, not only in Europe but internationally. Therefore learning English as a second or foreign language is growing (see chapter 4).

Languages provide access to **information and hence power**. Whether the information is in technical journals, on large computer databases, on the Internet, on satellite television or in international e-mail lists, a repertoire of languages gives wider access to social, cultural, political, economic and educational information. For the business person and the bureaucrat, for the scholar and the sports person, access to multilingual international information opens doors to new knowledge, new skills and new understanding.

Language learning is also ideally a means of promoting **intercultural understanding and peace** (Cook, 2002b). Such ideals have become more focused following a new wave of terrorism across the world, but interact uncomfortably with defense and intelligence needs. For example, following the **September 11** 2001 terrorist attacks in New York, the lack of foreign language proficiency in US intelligence was much criticized (Morrison, 2001; Brecht & Ingold, 2002). Since 9/11, it is

The European Union's (2001) Eurobarometer Survey of 15,900 people through-out Europe found that:

- 53% of Europeans report speaking another European language apart from their mother tongue.
- 26% of Europeans report speaking two European languages apart from their mother tongue.
- 93% of parents say it is important for their children to learn one or more European languages other than the mother tongue. This was endorsed by 98% of parents from Greece and 96% of parents from Spain. Improving job opportunities is given as the main reason (by 74% of parents).
- The second/foreign language most often known in Europe is English (40.5%) followed by French (19.2%), German (10.3%), Spanish (6.6%) and Italian (3.0%).
- In Sweden, 88% believe their English is 'good' or 'very good' compared with the Netherlands (72.3%) and Denmark (71.6%).
- The most effective way of learning a language is seen as long or frequent visits to a country where the languages are spoken (94% agreement), followed by talking informally to a native speaker (92%) and one-to-one lessons with a teacher (90%).

more apparent that English cannot be the only language of international diplomacy or the telescope to view the world. Languages identify, symbolize and embody their cultures. Ideally, to create coalitions, foster friendships, and to produce peace, requires the use of languages other than English. To heal long-standing wounds from the past requires bridges built through the languages of old opponents and recent rivals. Yet, in contrast, the more basic need is often to search out intelligence, which requires both ground operatives, interpreters and translators. A supply line of both operatives and translators is possible not only via language learning in school and at college, but also via heritage language speakers (e.g. Arabic, Farsi, Pashto). In contrast, however, current US ideology tends to prefer the assimilation of heritage language speakers, for example by the sole use of English at school (as witnessed in the US 'No Child Left Behind' Act of 2001)' (see chapter 9). As Brecht & Ingold (2002, p. 1) suggest:

> The United States has an unprecedented need for individuals with highly developed language competencies not only in English, our societal language, but also in many other languages. In fact, the need for individuals with profi-ciency in languages other than English for use in social, economic, diplomatic, and geopolitical arenas has never been higher. Even before the events of September 11, 2001, congressional hearings had begun to document a shortage of professionals with the language proficiencies required to carry out a wide range of federal government activities. More than 70 government agencies reported a need for individuals with foreign language expertise.

Such shortages of staff with **foreign language expertise** were hindering US military, law enforcement, intelligence, counter terrorism, and diplomatic efforts. Brecht & Ingold (2002, p. 1) indicate that there is already a reservoir of language talent currently being ignored:

> There exists, however, a largely untapped reservoir of linguistic competence in this country, namely heritage language speakers – the millions of indigenous, immigrant, and refugee individuals who are proficient in English and also have skills in other languages that are developed at home, in schools, in their countries of origin, or in language programs provided by their communities in the United State.

Individual Reasons

There are many reasons why the individual child or adult can benefit by being taught a second or third language. A center for languages at Southampton University (UK) lists 700 reasons (http://www.lang.ltsn.ac.uk/700reasons/700reasons.aspx).

One reason is for **cultural awareness**. To break down national, ethnic and language stereotypes, one motive in second language learning has become intercultural sensitivity and awareness. Increasing individual cultural sensitivity is seen as important as the world becomes more of a global village, with more sharing of experience and mutual understanding.

Cultural awareness in the classroom may be achieved at one level by discussing ethnic variations in eating and drinking, rituals of birth, death and marriage, religious practices among Aborigines, Arabs and Jews, or comparing shopping rituals in Malaysian markets, San Francisco superstores or all-purpose village stores in Venezuela (but see chapter 19 for a critique). Such activity widens human understanding and attempts to encourage sensitivity towards other cultures and creeds. While cultural awareness may be conveyed in the first language, the inseparability of culture and language means that such awareness may best be achieved through simultaneous language learning.

The second 'individual' reason for second language teaching has traditionally been for **cognitive development**. The learning of foreign languages has been for general educational and academic value. Just as history and geography, physics and chemistry, mathematics and music have traditionally been taught to increase intellectual fitness and stamina, so modern language learning has been defended as a way of sharpening the mind and developing the intellect (Cook, 2002b). Given the memorization, analysis (e.g. of grammar and sentence structure) and the need to negotiate in communication, language learning has been regarded as a valuable academic activity in itself.

The third reason for an individual to acquire a language is for social, emotional and moral development, self-awareness, self-confidence, and social and ethical values. Such **affective** goals include the possibility of incipient bilinguals being able to create more effective relationships with target language speakers. Bilinguals can potentially build social bridges with those who speak the second language.

Self-confidence and enhanced self-esteem may result from being able to operate socially or vocationally with those who speak the second or third language. The addition of a second language skill can boost an individual's self-confidence as a learner, a linguist and a cultural broker.

The fourth 'individual' reason for acquiring a language is for **careers and employment**. For language minority and language majority children, being able to speak a second or third or fourth language may mean avoiding unemployment, opening up possibilities of a wider variety of careers or gaining promotion in a career (see chapter 19). Potential individual careers include becoming translators and interpreters, buying and selling goods and services, exchanging information with local, regional, national and international organizations, migrating across national frontiers to find work, gaining promotion in neighboring countries, becoming part of an international team or company, as well as working from home or from the local village and using multilingual telecommunications to spread a product (e.g. US and UK telephone answering services that are located in India).

Bourdieu (1977, 1991) argued that language learning takes place in competitive and political dynamics in society. Inequality, dominance and social hierarchicization shape language learning such that the individual engaged in such learning is also to negotiating their social worth and wealth. Languages operate in a **marketplace**, such that languages have different currency values. The ability to 'command the listener' is unequal for different speakers due to the power relations between them (e.g. a minority language person learning English). Norton (2000) has applied this perspective to language learning, suggesting that such learners **invest** in additional languages to enrich their social, cultural and economic capital, and their symbolic and material resources. It is an investment that may yield a return (e.g. US immigrant learning English; employment and promotion for being a multilingual, evolving a multiple identity) or not (e.g. marginalization by the target language community).

FORMAL SECOND LANGUAGE LEARNING

Where a second language is not acquired in the community, **the school** has been the major institution expected to produce second language learning (for both elective and circumstantial bilinguals but for different reasons – see chapter 1). Through second language and foreign language lessons, via language laboratories and computer-assisted language learning, drill and practice routines, immersion classes, drama and dance, the initial stages of monolingualism to bilingualism may occur.

The routes to bilingualism are not solely in early childhood and in formal education. **Voluntary language classes** sometimes exist for school-age children. When the school does not support immigrant languages, reproduction of those languages in the family may be not enough for language maintenance. Therefore, local community groups have developed extra schooling for their children. In England and Canada, for example, evening classes, vacation classes, Saturday schools and

Sunday schools are organized by various communities for children to learn the heritage language of their parents and grandparents. Children of second, third or fourth generation immigrants may have learnt English as their first or dominant language. If parents have chosen to speak English to their children, even if their own first language is not English, the heritage language may be learnt in voluntary classes. Where English is the dominant language of the community and the only language of the school, such voluntary classes may be important in attaining bilingualism rather than moving children towards majority language monolingualism (V. Edwards, 1995a, 1996, 2004; Dosanjh & Ghuman, 1996).

Such **voluntary provision** may be for religious, cultural, social, integrative and ethnic minority vitality reasons. Thus the providers are often religious institutions such as synagogues, mosques, temples and Orthodox churches. Jewish families attending a local synagogue are often enthusiastic for Hebrew to be taught to their children to maintain a Jewish identity and for religious observance. Moslems have often been keen for Qur'anic Arabic to be transmitted for worship in the mosque, just as *gurdwaras* have been instrumental in the acquisition of Panjabi. The Roman Catholic Church also has promoted the community language teaching of Polish, Ukrainian and Lithuanian.

In the United Kingdom, there have been such **community language classes** in Finnish, Spanish, Italian, Portuguese, Greek, Turkish, Urdu, Hindi, Panjabi and Bengali, for example. In the case of some European languages, High Commissions and Embassies in London have often lent support. In other communities, particularly among the British Asians, the providers are groups of enthusiastic parents and local community organizations who rent premises such as schools and halls to teach a heritage language. Another example comes from Belgium where the Polish government supports accredited Polish classes that pupils attend in addition to their classes in mainstream Belgium schools.

Apart from voluntary classes for children, another well traveled route to developing bilingualism and multilingualism is **adult provision** (see Baker & Jones, 1998; Spolsky & Shohamy, 1999; Harnisch & Swanton, 2004). Such provision takes varying forms in different geographical areas:

- **Evening classes**. Sometimes called night schools or classes, a second or foreign language is taught on a once or twice weekly basis for several weeks to several years. Such classes have often traditionally aimed at securing formal qualifications in the language (e.g. passing exams in a second majority language) or at gaining proficiency in the majority language. One example is 'English as a Second Language' classes established for immigrants into the US and UK. Recently, the growth has also been in acquiring communicative competence in a heritage language (e.g. Hebrew, Basque, Welsh).
- **Ulpan courses**. Perhaps the most notable example of a mass movement of adult language learning has been the case of Hebrew in Israel. After the establishment of the State of Israel in 1948, the steady flow of immigration became a flood. Emergency measures were needed to teach Hebrew in a short time to large numbers of people as a living, spoken language. The idea of creating an

intensive Hebrew language course was born and called an *Ulpan*. The word 'Ulpan' is derived from an Aramaic root meaning 'custom, training, instruction, law'. There were originally about 25 students in the class, and they met for six hours each day apart from the Sabbath. From the beginning, the emphasis was on equipping the learners for everyday communication in the spoken language. Cultural activities such as singing and field trips were part of the course. Over the years different kinds of *Ulpanim* have been established in Israel (Baker & Jones, 1998).

Like Israel, the Basque and Welsh *Ulpanim* vary in intensity from five days a week courses to two mornings or two evenings a week (Baker & Jones, 1998). Some vocational courses are held for teachers, hospital workers, administrators and workers in industry. Other courses have a bias towards the needs of particular groups like parents. As in Israel, the emphasis is on developing competence in the spoken language.

- **Distance learning methods.** A variety of media-based courses for learning a second language are often available to adults. Radio and television series, use of satellite television, DVDs, CDs, videos, self-teach books, computer programs (computer-assisted language learning) and correspondence courses are all well tried approaches in second language acquisition. Evaluation studies of the relative effectiveness of these different approaches tend to be lacking.

In early childhood, becoming bilingual is often a subconscious event, as natural as learning to walk or to ride a bicycle. In a school situation, a child is not usually the one who has made a decision about the language(s) of the classroom. Second language acquisition at school is often imposed by teachers and a local or national educational policy. For migrant workers, refugees and immigrants, adult language learning also may be essential for work and adaptation to new institutions and bureaucracy. However, for other adults, second language acquisition sometimes becomes more voluntary, more open to choice. This raises the issue of whether it is preferable to learn a new language as a child or as an adult?

Apart from formal language learning, bilingualism is often achieved through the informal acquisition processes of the street and screen, friends and siblings. A child sometimes acquires a second or third language rapidly in addition to that of the home without planning or intent by parents. Peers in the playgroup or street, cartoons and shows on television are two examples of language influences that may informally lead to bilingualism in the child. Little researched, the almost incidental addition of a second or third language via the street and screen may be as influential as formal education, and sometimes more potent than language classes. This particularly tends to be the case with acquiring the majority language of the neighborhood (see the discussion of circumstantial bilinguals in chapter 1).

THE AGE FACTOR

A much debated theme in second language acquisition is the relationship of **age in learning a second language** and success in gaining language proficiency. One argument is that the lower the age at which a second language is learnt, the greater the long-term proficiency in that language. According to this viewpoint, young children learn a language more easily and successfully. For young children, a new language is caught rather than taught; acquired rather than learned. Others tend to argue that older children and young adults learn a language more efficiently and quickly than young children. For example, a 14-year-old learning Spanish as a second language has superior intellectual processing skills than the five-year-old learning Spanish. Therefore, it is thought that less time is required in the teenage years to learn a second language than in the younger years due to older children's cognitive superiority. However, the use of two or more languages changes across the years, so exact comparability is difficult.

Reviews of this area are provided by Marinova-Todd *et al.* (2000), Singleton (2003), Singleton and Ryan (2004). Their analyses may be briefly summarized as follows:

(1)   Younger second language learners are neither globally more nor less efficient and successful than older learners in second language acquisition. There are many factors that intervene and make simple statements about age and language learning simplistic and untenable.

(2)   Children who learn a second language in childhood do tend to achieve higher levels of **proficiency** than those who begin after childhood. This difference found between younger and older learners reflects typical outcomes rather than potential. Thus a finding favoring the young does not contradict the idea that someone can become proficient in learning a second language after childhood. This may be related to social contexts in which language is acquired and maintained or lost (e.g. kindergarten), as well as to the psychology of individual learning (e.g. motivation, opportunity). As Marinova-Todd *et al.* (2000) suggest, older learners tend in practice not to master a second language as well as young learners, but that 'age differences reflect differences in the situation of learning rather than in the capacity to learn' (p. 9).

(3)   In a formal classroom language learning situation, older learners tend initially to learn quicker than younger learners. However, the **length of exposure** (e.g. the number of years of second language instruction) is an important factor in second language success. Those children who begin to learn a second language in the elementary school and continue throughout schooling, tend to show higher proficiency than those who start to learn the second language later in their schooling. In absolute rather than comparative terms, this still includes the possibility of late learners becoming highly proficient, particularly when they are strongly motivated or have strong needs (e.g. immigrants) or excellent opportunities (e.g. extensive immersion across many months). Adults can learn to a native-like level of competence in a second language.

(4)   Support for foreign language instruction at an early age in school can find its **rationale** from areas other than second language research. For example, teaching a foreign language early in the elementary school may be defended in

terms of general intellectual stimulation, the general curriculum value of teaching a modern language, the benefits of biculturalism and the benefits of learning a language for as long as possible rather than as quickly as possible. Second language instruction in the elementary school rests on the suitable provision of language teachers, suitable materials and resources, favorable attitudes of the teachers and parents, and the need to make the learning experience enjoyable.

(5) There is some research and much public discussion about the large numbers of high school students and adults who **fail** to learn a second language (Marinova-Todd *et al.*, 2000). In comparison, there is a lack of research on adults who are successful learners of second and third languages. Research itself is in danger or perpetuating a 'younger is better' belief about age and language learning.

(6) In the **United States**, one pressure is for immigrant children to learn English as soon as possible, particularly since the No Child Left Behind Act of 2001 (see chapter 9). Some claim that the optimal time to learn a language is from age three to seven, and because of supposed biological constraints, such learning should occur before the onset of puberty. In a review of this area, Hakuta (2001, pp. 11–12) argues that:

> The evidence for a critical period for second language acquisition is scanty, especially when analyzed in terms of its key assumptions. There is no empirically definable end point, there are no qualitative differences between child and adult learners, and there are large environmental effects on the outcomes. . . . The view of a biologically constrained and specialized language acquisition device that is turned off at puberty is not correct.

Similarly, Marinova-Todd *et al.* (2000) conclude that 'Age does influence language learning, but primarily because it is associated with social, psychological, educational and other factors that can affect L2 proficiency, not because of any critical period that limits the possibility of language learning by adults' (p. 28). While there are no critical periods of language learning, there are advantageous periods. Early childhood and elementary and secondary school days seem two advantageous periods.

How **successful** have adults been in becoming bilingual? There is a distinction between answering this question in an absolute and a relative manner. The 'absolute' answer simply is that adults do learn a second language to varying degrees of fluency. Some fall by the wayside, others reach a basic, simple level of communication, yet others become operationally bilingual. In Israel, Wales and the Basque country, the adult route to bilingualism has many success stories.

The 'relative' answer involves comparing children and adults of varying ages. In this sense, the question becomes 'Who is more likely to become proficient in a second language, children or adults?' A specific example of adult success provides an illustration of a typical pattern. This example focuses on language usage rather than acquisition.

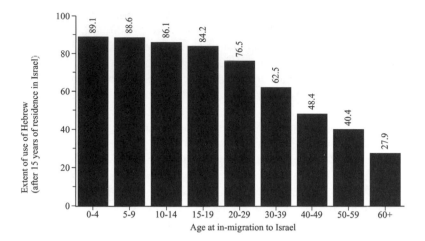

From 1950s Israeli census data, it is possible to examine whether older or younger adults become functional in **Hebrew**. For example, do young immigrants become more or less functional in Hebrew as a second language compared with older immigrants? The results follow a clear pattern (Bachi, 1956; Braine, 1987). As the figure above illustrates (based on Bachi, 1956), the extent of the everyday use of Hebrew varies with age of in-migration. The younger the child, the more likely he or she will be to use Hebrew. Between 30 and 40 years of age, a notable drop occurs. Is this due to a loss of learning ability, less exposure to Hebrew, less motivation or decreasing social pressure? From age 40 onwards, the likelihood of being functional in Hebrew falls again.

Language Loss in Children

Apart from children learning a second or third language, it is important to mention that **language loss** occurs in bilingual children. Children from language minorities (indigenous and particularly immigrant children) are sometimes at risk of losing their minority language, even when very young. With a higher status majority language ever present on the screen, in the street, at school and in shops, children quickly learn which language has prestige, power and preference. They soon understand that they are differences in language, behavior, ethnicity and culture, and some children, and particularly teenagers, may come to perceive their minority language and culture as undesirable. Students quickly perceive what helps them belong and become accepted in mainstream society.

Language loss in children is a particular reality in the **United States**. Research by Hakuta and D'Andrea (1992), Wong Fillmore (1991) and Valdés (2004) indicates the strength of the dominance of English in US society that places considerable pressure on language minority students not only to acquire English at a young age, but also to replace their minority language with English. In such subtractive situations, the ideal of early bilingualism meets a challenge due to a societal ethos that frequently does not favor bilingualism. Hakuta and D'Andrea (1992) found in the United States that early exposure to English (e.g. in the home) can lead to a shift from Spanish to English and the potential loss of Spanish. Such early exposure to English in the US may also decrease the chances of placement in a dual education program where Spanish is used.

This is not to warn against early bilingualism, but rather to suggest that the minority language needs care and attention, status and much usage in the young child. This is not a limitation of early bilingualism, but rather a caution that minority language development needs particular nurturing in political situations where another language is ever-dominant. For example, when **English** is introduced very early and dominantly into a US language minority child's life, the minority language may be insufficiently stable and developed, and may therefore be replaced by the majority language. A loss of the minority language may have social, emotional, cognitive and educational consequences for the child, as later chapters (e.g. chapter 17) will examine. As Wong Fillmore (1991a, p. 343) argued: 'What is lost is no less than the means by which parents socialize their children: When parents are unable to talk to their children, they cannot easily convey to them their values, beliefs, understandings, or wisdom about how to cope with their experiences'.

The **immigrant, refugee and asylum seeker** context and its affect on family language patterns is under-researched, with most of the studies on early childhood bilingualism being located in middle class, majority language and geographically stable families. Tannenbaum and Howie (2002) argue that immigration often potentially means loss of the extended family and significant people, a loss of familiarity, family cohesion, family 'atmosphere' and secure attachment. Uprooting may affect not only the act of parenting but also the cultural and linguistic development of young children and the language patterns of the immigrant family. Tannenbaum and Howie's (2002) research on Chinese immigrant families in Australia suggests that family relations affect language maintenance or loss. Families that are more cohesive, more positive in relationships and with secure attachment patterns tend to foster language maintenance in young immigrant children.

The dialogue that takes place between parents and children is an important contributor to the child's cognitive development. As children interact with parents, they are introduced to new features of language. When the child loses the home language, the parent can no longer offer this language education to the child in that language. Important cognitive scaffolding is dismantled. Thus minority language loss is an issue not just of geographical regions and language communities but also for individual children. **Family language planning** is needed to initiate, establish and maintain childhood bilingualism.

INDIVIDUAL DIFFERENCES: ATTITUDES AND MOTIVATION

A popular explanation for success or failure to learn a second language (or of success in learning) is attitudes and motivation (Baker, 1992; Dörnyei, 2001a, 2001b; Garrett et al., 2003). As Dörnyei (1998, p. 117) suggests:

Motivation provides the primary impetus to initiate learning in the L2 and later the driving force to sustain the long and often tedious learning process . . . Without sufficient motivation, even individuals with the most remarkable abilities cannot accomplish long-term goals, and neither are appropriate curricula and good teaching enough on their own to ensure student achievement.

What are the **motives** for learning a second language? Are the motives economic, cultural, social, vocational, integrative or for self-esteem and self-actualization? Reasons for learning a second (minority or majority) language tend to fall into two major groups:

Group 1: A wish to identify with or join another language group
Learners sometimes want to affiliate with a different language community. Such learners wish to join in and identify with the minority or majority language's cultural activities, and consequently find their roots or form friend-ships. This is termed **integrative motivation**.
Group 2: Learning a language for useful purposes
The second reason is utilitarian in nature. Learners may acquire a second language to find a job and earn money, further career prospects, pass exams, help fulfill the demands of their job, or assist their children in bilingual schooling. This is termed **instrumental motivation**.

Considerable research on this area was conducted by Gardner and associates (Gardner, 1985; see Chambers (1999) for a review). Gardner argued that integra-tive and instrumental attitudes are independent of 'intelligence' and aptitude. Integrative motivation may be particularly strong in an additive bilingual environment.

Much of the research in this area, but not all, links **integrative motivation** rather than **instrumental motivation** with the greater likelihood of achieving proficiency in the second language. Gardner and Lambert (1972) originally considered that integrative motivation was more powerful in language learning than instrumental motivation. The reason was that integrative motivation concerns personal relation-ships that may be long lasting. On the other hand, instrumental motivation may be purely self-oriented and short term. When employment has been obtained or finan-cial gain has accrued, instrumental motivation may wane. An integrative motive was thought to be a more sustained motive than an instrumental motive due to the relative endurance of personal relationships.

Research has subsequently suggested that there may be occasions when the **instrumental motive** is stronger than the integrative motive in learning a language. Lukmani (1972) found that Bombay female school students gave instrumental rather than integrative reasons for learning English. In the research by Yatim (1988), the language motivations of student teachers in Malaysia appeared to combine instru-mental and integrative motives into an integrated entity. A person's motives may be a subtle mix of instrumental and integrative motives, without clear discrimination between the two. Such research relates motivation not only to the desire to learn a language but also to predicting language retention and language loss in individuals over time.

Pavlenko (2002a) provides a critique of these socio-psychological studies. In a **post-structuralist** approach, language attitudes are partly replaced by language ideologies that are seen as more socially and culturally derived, ever-developing and not static, and capable of being criticized and changed (Pavlenko, 2002a). For example, saying that someone has an integrative attitude to Irish may imply a relatively stable trait that is individually derived and owned. Instead, it is possible to depict that person's language identity as related to political, cultural, social and economic ideologies surrounding Irish that are ever changing and fluid but open to challenge and conflict. Language attitudes thus become part of larger societal processes and ideologies that can be examined for bias, racism, discrimination and oppression. The psychological is merged into the political. A relatively stable and separate variable (attitude) is a part of a multiple and dynamic scenario (identity construction) that allows second language acquisition to have individual, group and societal dimensions.

Pavlenko (2002a) suggests that such research tends to be: reductionist and static in its approach; not offering insight into the social and political origins of attitudes; assuming that cause-effect is stable and in one direction whereas social contexts and attitudes/motivation constantly shape and influence each other; individual differences are socially constructed with variations across communities and cultures; and a tendency of such research to relate to wholesome, agreeable contexts whereas 'In reality, no amount of motivation can counteract racism and discrimination, just as no amount of positive attitude can substitute for access to linguistic resources such as educational establishments' (Pavlenko, 2002a, p. 281).

Teachers are still left with the question: 'How can I motivate learners?' What interventions and strategies are possible to motivate language learners? From a small number of research studies, Dörnyei (1998) offers the following **motivational advice** to teachers:

(1) Set a personal example with your own language behavior.
(2) Create a pleasant, relaxed atmosphere in the classroom, reduce anxiety.
(3) Present language tasks thoughtfully and carefully.
(4) Develop a friendly relationship with learners.
(5) Increase the second language self-confidence of the learner.
(6) Make language classes lively and interesting.
(7) Promote learner autonomy.
(8) Personalize the learning process.
(9) Increase each learner's goal-orientation.
(10) Familiarize learners with the culture attached to the language being learnt.

This is elaborated in the accompanying textboxes.

Dörnyei (1994) provides a list of overlapping and interacting strategies for teachers to use to motivate their students (see also Dörnyei & Scott, 1997; Dörnyei & Csizer, 1998).

Language
(1) Include a sociocultural component in the syllabus (e.g. television programs, inviting native speakers).
(2) Develop learners' cross-cultural awareness systematically, focusing on cross-cultural similarities rather than differences.
(3) Promote student contact with second language speakers (e.g. exchange programs, pen pals, trips).
(4) Develop learners' instrumental motivation by highlighting the usefulness of second language study

Learner
(1) Develop students' self-confidence in use of the language (e.g. realizable short-term goals, praise and encouragement, a regular experience of success, using confidence building tasks).
(2) Promote students' self-efficacy with regard to achieving learning goals (e.g. teaching useful communication strategies, developing realistic expectations).
(3) Promote favorable self-perceptions of competence in the second language (e.g. highlighting what students can do rather than what they cannot do, students not worrying about making mistakes).
(4) Decrease student anxiety in learning a second language.
(5) Promote motivation-enhancing attributions (e.g. students recognize the link between effort and outcome, attribute past failures to factors that can be changed).
(6) Encourage students to set attainable sub-goals for themselves (e.g. by a personal learning plan).

Situational
(1) Make the syllabus of the course relevant (e.g. based on a student 'needs analysis').
(2) Increase the attractiveness of course content (e.g. use of more authentic materials, audio-visual aids, multimedia technology).
(3) Discuss the choice of teaching materials with students (e.g. type of text-books, computer-assisted language learning programs).
(4) Arouse and sustain curiosity and attention (e.g. introduce the unexpected and novel; break-up tedious or repetitious routines).
(5) Increase students' interest and involvement in language learning tasks (e.g. selecting varied and challenging activities, including students' interests, problem-solving, engaging students' emotions, personalizing tasks, using pair work and group activities).

(6) Match the difficulty of the students' language learning tasks with students' abilities.
(7) Increase student expectancy of task fulfillment (e.g. by creating realistic students' expectations, explanations of content and process, giving ongoing guidance about how to succeed, and making the criteria of success clear and transparent).
(8) Facilitate student satisfaction (e.g. allowing students to complete tasks that they can display or perform, celebrating student success).

Teachers
(1) Try to be empathic (sensitive to students' needs), congruent (behave in honest and true-to-self manner) and accepting of students' strengths and weaknesses.
(2) Adopt the role of a facilitator rather than that of an authority figure.
(3) Promote learner autonomy by allowing students real choices in learning, minimize external pressure, with students sharing tasks and responsibility for their own learning, using peer-teaching and project work.
(4) Act as a role model, sharing personal interests and perspectives, transmit personal positive values about second language, sharing personal commitment to the second language.
(5) Introduce language learning tasks to stimulate intrinsic motivation and help internalize *extrinsic* motivation, showing the purpose (and its integration into a whole) of each language learning task.
(6) Use motivating feedback, give feedback that is informative, and not over-react to errors.

Learning Group
(1) Establish goals with which the group agree and feel they own so as to establish a clear sense of direction.
(2) From the beginning, promote the internalization of classroom norms of behavior.
(3) Maintain classroom norms of acceptable behavior in a consistent manner, not letting misbehaviors go unnoticed, and maintaining professional standards of personal behavior.
(4) Minimize any detrimental effects of assessment on intrinsic motivation by focusing on improvement and progress, avoiding comparison of one student with another, making student assessment private rather than public, not encouraging a focus on competition in achievement outcomes, with personal interviews to consider the individual assessment of language proficiency.
(5) Promote the development of group cohesion and enhance inter-member relations by promoting friendships and effective working relationships, organizing outings and extra-curricular activities.
(6) Use cooperative learning techniques by plenty of groupwork where the evaluation of success is appropriate to the group rather than a focus on individual success.

IDENTITY AND SECOND LANGUAGE ACQUISITION

'All the world's a stage,
And all the men and women merely players.
They have their exits and their entrances;
And one man in his time plays many parts.'
(William Shakespeare from 'As You Like It', Act 2, Scene 7)

This drama metaphor suggests that we are like actors. We play different roles that vary according to the scenery, the audience, our fellow actors and the expected lines of the play. As scenery, co-actors, audience and the play changes, so do our many identities in life's drama. We construct our identities yet are also created and confined by other players, situations and the unfolding play. Second language acquisition is such a play and it relates to **identity formation** (Blackledge & Pavlenko, 2001; Pavlenko, 2003b).

Social Identity and Second Language Learning

While psychometric tests attempt to profile us as individuals (e.g. extravert, creative, 110 IQ), we are also simultaneously members of different **groups** (e.g. woman, young parent, teacher, Moslem, Democrat, Californian, bilingual). Such membership helps form our **social identity**. Our multiple social identities are thus created dynamically by us, by our interactions and negotiations with other group actors, the expectations of each group, and the varying social environments in which we play. Second language acquisition is affected by, and affects our membership of groups (e.g. majority and minority language networks and groups). Acquiring a second language is not just about gaining vocabulary, grammar and pronunciation. When we use a second language, it is a social event with particular others. It is also often about joining a **social grouping** (e.g. a target language community or networks) and finding an accepted voice. Bourdieu (1977, 1991) argued that finding such an accepted voice is about the value given to people who are speaking (e.g. a newly learnt language). A speaker wants to be understood but there is also a social dimension to this: being believed, respected and valued as a speaker.

Language learning is partly about becoming **socialized** through interaction with other language speakers in particular social contexts (Pavlenko, 2002a). **Classrooms**, in this perspective, have major limitations. They tend not to provide spontaneous interaction. Outside the classroom, target language speakers may be reluctant or refuse to interact with learners (e.g. too low level of conversation, or due to gender, race, ethnicity, heritage language, social class, age, sexuality or creed). Opportunities for participation in the second language may be rare – a limitation of bilingual education that often produces competent bilinguals who only use one language outside the school. Authentic language situations may be restricted by target language speakers 'gate-keeping', or suitable opportunities not being available for new speakers to internalize the 'voices' of target language speakers. A sense of vulnerability and powerlessness may decrease a learner's investment in language learning (Norton, 2000).

Constructing Meaning in Second Language Learning

While language has shared sounds, signs and symbols, there are often different and sometimes contested **meanings and values** attached to such language. "When I use a word,' Humpty Dumpty said, in rather a scornful tone, 'it means just what I choose it to mean – neither more nor less" (Lewis Carroll, 1872). Words don't have fixed or ideal meanings.

Humpty Dumpty apart, words are constructed by people in dialogue with others to find shared or contested meanings. Such discourse takes place in changing situations (contexts) with differences of power and status between people affecting whose meaning is ascendant or dominant, and with such meanings being open to change, even conflict. Thus there is no correct or true definition of a 'bilingual' or 'bilingual education'. Meanings of these terms vary across people, time and place, with dominance at any one time being about who has status, prestige and power. **Meaning** and the importance of an utterance is thus determined in part by the status and value attributed to the second language speaker.

> When a language learner interacts with a member of the target language group, he is not only searching for words, phrases, and idiomatic expressions; he is asking to what extent he will be able to impose reception on his interlocutor. When a language learner write a poem, a letter, or an academic essay, she considers not only the demands of the task but how much of her history will be considered relevant to this literary act (Norton & Toohey, 2002, p. 115)

Language and Power

Interacting in a second language both uses and shapes our identity, and this relationship needs to be understood in terms of differential **power and prestige** between people and language groups. In this post-structuralist tradition, learning a second language is not just about language. It is also about who we are, what we want to become, and what we are allowed (e.g. by first language speakers) to become.

On all language stages, there are underlying dimensions of control and influence, domination and subordination (see chapter 18). Gaining belief, respect and social value from dialogue with others is not straightforward as there is **unequal dominance, status and power** in relationships. There may be sensitive listeners, empathic conversationalists in the target language community, and much faith in second language learning. However, many immigrants have experiences of obstruction, ridicule or rejection when using the majority language of the adopted country. Thus **power relationships** and social structures in the target language community are an important component in the extent to which a second language learner (including those exiting from bilingual education) will be accepted as a speaker of that language. Opportunities for practicing and participating in that new language, access to the usual utterances of native speakers, acceptance of errors when using of that language, and acceptance as 'non-native speakers' by the target community will affect a learner's acceptance, identity and language life.

Multiple Identities and Second Language Acquisition

The identity of second language learners has hitherto sometimes been seen as relatively stable and enduring, essential to a coherent 'core' in an individual's psyche. Just like IQ and personality traits, identity was seen as fairly fixed. A contemporary view is that identity is multiple, complex, context contingent, varied, overlapping, sometimes fragmented and even contradictory across different contexts. Our identities constantly **develop and change**, across time and across situations. We are made and remade in our conversations across time, place and person.

Acquiring a second language may, for example, **change our identity** from an 'immigrant' to a 'Californian'. Pavlenko (2003b) suggests that early and late immigrants into the US differed in their negotiation of a new or changed language identity. At the turn of the 20th century, immigrants learning English was more positive as it connected with individual achievement and the American dream. More recent immigrants tend toward more hybrid, hyphenated, transnational or cosmopolitan identities, with relatively more themes in autobiography of the second language learning of English as connected with language loss, loss of primary identity, and not least with linguistic discrimination and intolerance (see chapter 18). Since not all languages are equal in power and status, learning a prestigious language may (or may not) lead to employment, social mobility, new friends, and access to good quality education. Learning a minority language may also affect identity, for example increasing the chances of acceptance into a local community.

Acquiring a language affects individual identity, but this **interacts with other dimensions** (e.g. gender, socioeconomic class, race, ethnicity, creed) that mediate the outcomes of such acquisition (Pavlenko, 2002a). The success of language learning may be affected by the wealth or restriction of opportunities for identity development in new networks (e.g. acceptance, rejection). Identity conflict may sometimes occur, for example, when our preferred self-identity (e.g. as a Latino) is different from other people's attempts to label us (e.g. as an American). This is sometimes found in immigrants (see chapter 17) where second language learners of a majority language are regarded as incompetent workers or uneducated parents or social oddities. They may find resistance from majority language speakers to them having a new identity via second language acquisition, with subsequent effects on the extent of second language acquisition and reconstruction of identities. Surrounding ideologies may work against the best of language acquisition intentions. Or language minority speakers may resist the symbolic domination of them as a people that is attempted by the majority language power and politics.

Language learning may **change** how we think of ourselves, how others see us, and importantly (in turn) how we then confirm their expectations in our behavior. Acquiring a second language goes beyond linguistic competence to having the potential to be heard in that language, the means to address an audience in that language on chosen stages, and to mix with other actors using that language. Language learning is not just a cognitive activity operating in the mind, but is also about becoming part of a new language community and **developing multiple identities** (see chapter 18).

An important component in being accepted as a speaker is our **other identities** (e.g. gender, race, religion) that interact with being a second language learner. A second language learners' identity is multiple and goes well beyond language to gender, social class, ethnicity, sexuality, age, creed, lifestyle, networks and many other constantly changing scenarios. Sometimes, despite achieving linguistic proficiency in a second language, access to a language community is difficult, as **other dimensions of identity** (e.g. race, gender, social class) bar easy (or any) access.

Imagined Communities

Language learners, negotiating meanings and identity also come together in the recent concept of '**imagined communities**' (see *Journal of Language, Identity, and Education*, 2003, volume 2, no. 4). For example, when students in second language classrooms are learning French in the US, they commence as beginners. The teacher is introducing them to the language practices of a community of French speakers. What language practices? What is the 'imagined community' for such learners? Or are such communities 'imagined' for them in a controlled manner? Desirable imaginings may motivate learners; less desirable and low status imaginings may de-motivate learners; hidden or controlled imaginings from outside may remove understanding and alienate. For example, a second language learner imagines obtaining well-paid employment; another imagines returning to the land of her ancestors and extended family.

Some further examples from research demonstrate the powerfulness of 'imagined communities'. Dagenais (2003) found that parents with Asian background children attending immersion bilingual education in Canada (see chapter 11) were investing in such education to prepare their children for imagined multilingual, transnational, multiple communities of the future. In Japan, Kanno (2003) found that schools have visions of 'imagined communities' for which they are preparing their students: the least privileged children for impoverished bilingual communities; the most privileged children for elite international bilingualism. Pavlenko (2003a) found that teaching TESOL students about bilingualism and second language acquisition opened up **new imagined communities** for them, as bilingual or multilingual multi-competent speakers. The low expectation of becoming two competent monolinguals in one person and belonging to two separate imagined communities was replaced by feeling part of an imagined community of worthy multilingual speakers.

CONCLUSIONS

There are both **societal and individual** reasons for a person learning a second language later in life. This mirrors the opening chapters of this book that engaged bilinguals as individuals and as groups, and communities. Once societal reasons are present, then politics is not far away. Such reasons are varied, even paradoxical: assimilation but also harmony between different language communities; trade and profit but also intercultural understanding; security and defense yet also diplomacy. Individual reasons for language learning are not separate from societal reasons. Languages for career enhancement and employment have become more important motives as international trade and globalism have risen. Schools and communities influence language learning, such that societal and individual reasons interconnect and merge.

Sequential bilingualism occurs through a variety of routes with school a major source of formal learning. Such schools may be state-funded and mainstream with long histories of language teaching. But also there are many schools run by religious organizations, language communities and Embassies that teach new languages on Saturdays and Sundays, for example. For adults, language learning can be by classes at work and for leisure, self-study or an intensive Ulpan experience. The vehicles of voluntary classes and adult courses provide the opportunity for a second or foreign language to be learnt and developed. Also, playing in the street and watching the screen can be informal means to bilingualism and multilingualism.

Such 'later' routes to bilingualism and multilingualism allow individuals of all ages to become bilingual and multilingual. While younger learners tend to achieve higher levels of **proficiency** in practice, older learners tend to learn faster. While there may be no critical periods for language learning, there are times when there will be greater opportunities (e.g. in school) and varying levels and types of motivation. Surrounding societal ideologies (e.g. for immigrants) and individual differences may interact to make language learning more or less successful.

There are outcomes from language learning that go further than bilingualism and multilingualism. For immigrants, this may relate to assimilation or integration into the host society. For students, this may mean employment and career progression. For adults, it may mean moving closer to desired imagined communities. For all these groups, language learning affects **identity**. Such learners are socialized into new meanings and values as well as new language. They enter into new relationships that involve different status and power, acceptance or rejection. Learning a language means changes to our multiple identities. Language learning is so much more than learning a language.

KEY POINTS IN THE CHAPTER

- Reasons for second language learning include ideological (e.g. assimilation), international (e.g. trade, peace) and individual (e.g. cultural awareness, employment) reasons.
- Voluntary language learning classes, community classes, Saturday schools, classes in the mosque, synagogue, temple or church and Ulpan adult language learning schemes are routes to sequential bilingualism and minority language maintenance in individuals.
- While there are no critical periods of language learning, there are advantageous periods. Early childhood and school days are two advantageous periods. Many successful adult second language learners show that increasing age is not a disadvantage.

- Individuals differ in their language learning histories due to societal and personal factors. Among immigrants, language loss is often present as assimilation can be a dominant influence. Among individuals, differences in integrative and instrumental motives is regarded as influencing success.
- Second language learning affects social identity. Language learning is partly about socialization into a new group. We learn the meaning, values and power relationships of a new group, and changing our multiple identities.

SUGGESTED FURTHER READING

MARINOVA-TODD, S.H., MARSHALL, D.B. & SNOW, C.E., 2000, Three misconceptions about age and L2 learning. *TESOL Quarterly*, 34, 1, 9–34.

MITCHELL, R. & MYLES, F., 1998, *Second-Language Learning Theories*. London: Arnold.

PAVLENKO A. & BLACKLEDGE, A. (eds), 2004, *Negotiation of Identities in Multilingual Contexts*. Clevedon: Multilingual Matters.

RICHARDS, J. & ROGERS, T., 2001, *Approaches and Methods in Language Teaching* (2nd edition). Cambridge: Cambridge University Press.

SINGLETON, D. & RYAN, L., 2004, *Language Acquisition: The Age Factor* (2nd edition). Clevedon: Multilingual Matters.

STUDY ACTIVITIES

(1) Locate a teacher, parent or a friend who has learnt a second language in school or in adult life. Ask them about the importance of school, classroom and learning factors in their second language acquisition. Discuss with them how they see their current ability, identity and usage of their second language.

(2) In a small group of students, discuss different experiences of learning a second language. From the experiences of the group, what dimensions seem most important? How did societal pressures, local politics and school policies affect language learning?

(3) Visit a school where students are learning a foreign language. By interviewing the teachers and observing classroom sessions, describe the overt and latent reasons for second (or third) language acquisition. Ask the teachers and the students their purposes in learning a foreign language. If there are differences in aim between teachers and students, examine whether you think these can be made compatible or are in conflict.

(4) Locate one or more immigrants who have learnt a language as an adult. What were their reasons and motives for learning a language? What is their perception of any pressures, politics, and opportunities surrounding learning that language?

(5) Imagine you are in a classroom 20 years hence. In that futuristic classroom, describe how language acquisition might take place. What kind of technology might be used? Will there be more or less emphasis on learning minority and majority languages? What motivations might the students have in the futuristic classroom? For what purposes are languages being learnt? What forms of assessment are being used?

CHAPTER 7

Bilingualism and Cognition

CHAPTER 7

Bilingualism and Cognition

INTRODUCTION

There is one piece of advice that parents sometimes receive from well-meaning teachers, doctors, speech therapists, school psychologists and other professionals: *Don't raise your child bilingually or problems will result*. Predicted problems ranged from bilingualism as a burden on the brain, mental confusion, inhibition of the acquisition of the majority language, identity conflicts, split loyalties, even schizophrenia. Parents and teachers are sometimes still advised by professionals to use only one language with individual children.

In the last decade or so, such prejudiced and unfounded advice has decreased. Better advice based on a wealth of research is slowly spreading. Yet historically, anti-bilingualism advice has frequently predominated. For example, when Welsh children persisted in speaking two languages in school, having their mouths washed with soap and water (Isaacs, 1976) and being beaten with a cane for speaking Welsh were once offered as remedies.

A quotation from a professor at Cambridge University in 1890 portrays this historical (and hysterical) **deficit viewpoint**:

> If it were possible for a child to live in two languages at once equally well, so much the worse. His intellectual and spiritual growth would not thereby be doubled, but halved. Unity of mind and character would have great difficulty in asserting itself in such circumstances. (Laurie, 1890: 15)

Such anxieties about bilingualism and thinking remain among some members of the public. The anxiety that two languages may have a negative effect on an individual's thinking skills tends to be expressed in two different ways. First, some tend to believe that the more someone learns and uses a second language, the less skill a person will have in their first language. Rather like weighing scales or a **balance**, the more one increases, the more the other decreases. Second, concern is sometimes expressed that the ability to speak two languages may be at the cost of **efficiency** in thinking. The intuitive belief is sometimes that two languages residing inside the thinking quarters will mean less room to store other areas of learning. By comparison, the monolingual is pictured as having one language in residence and therefore maximal storage space for other information.

Does the ownership of two languages interfere with efficient thinking? Do monolinguals have more effective thinking quarters? Is a bilingual less intelligent than a monolingual because of a dual language system? This chapter examines these typically negatively phrased questions and evaluates the evidence on bilingualism and thinking. We start by considering the relationship between intelligence and bilingualism. 'Intelligence' has been a major concept in psychology and sometimes related to bilingualism. It is also a term often used by members of the public in phrasing questions about bilingualism.

The chapter then moves on to consider recent research that focuses on a wider sample of products and processes of a bilingual's cognition. Do bilinguals and monolinguals differ in thinking styles? Are there differences in the processing of information? Does owning two languages create differences in thinking about language? These types of question are examined in this chapter.

BILINGUALISM AND 'INTELLIGENCE'

The Period of Detrimental Effects

From the early 19th century to approximately the 1960s, the dominant belief amongst academics was that bilingualism had a detrimental effect on thinking. The early research on bilingualism and cognition tended to confirm this negative viewpoint, finding that monolinguals were superior to bilinguals on mental tests. Research up to the 1960s looked at this issue through one concept – 'intelligence'. A typical piece of research gave bilinguals and monolinguals an 'intelligence' test. When bilinguals and monolinguals were compared on their **IQ scores**, particularly on verbal IQ, the usual result was that bilinguals were behind monolinguals. An example of this early research is by a Welsh researcher, D.J. Saer (1923). He gathered a sample of 1400 children aged 7 to 14 from bilingual and monolingual backgrounds. A 10-point difference in IQ was found between bilinguals and monolingual English speakers from the rural areas of Wales. Saer (1923) concluded that bilinguals were mentally confused and at a disadvantage in thinking compared with monolinguals. Further research by Saer *et al.* (1924) suggested that university student monolinguals were superior to bilinguals: 'the difference in mental ability as revealed by intelligence tests is of a permanent nature since it persists in students throughout their University career' (p. 53).

While it is possible that situations exist where bilinguals will perform on such tests at a lower level than monolinguals (this is considered in chapter 8), the early research that pointed to detrimental effects has a series of weaknesses that tend to invalidate the research in terms of individual studies and cumulatively across studies. These limitations may be listed as follows.

Definition
The concept of 'intelligence' and the use of intelligence tests is controversial and

hotly debated. One part of the controversy lies in the **problems of defining and measuring intelligence**. The underlying questions are: What is intelligence and who is intelligent? A thief who cracks a bank vault? A famous football coach? Someone poor who becomes a billionaire? Don Juan? Is there social intelligence, musical intelligence, military intelligence, marketing intelligence, motoring intelligence, political intelligence? Are all or indeed any of these forms of intelligence measurable by a simple pencil and paper IQ test which requires a single, acceptable, correct solution to each question? Howard Gardner's (2003) typology of intelligence includes logical-mathematical, verbal-linguistic, visual-spatial, musical-rhythmical, bodily-kinesthetic, naturalist, interpersonal, intrapersonal and existentialist 'multiple intelligences'. A further recent interest is in emotional intelligence both as a personality trait and as a component in performance (Goleman, 1995). Emotional intelligence may have facets related to bilingualism and multiculturalism such as: adaptability, perception and communication of feelings, relationship skills, self-esteem, social competence and empathy (Petrides *et al.*, 2004).

A subjective value judgment is required about what constitutes intelligent behavior or not, as well as about the kind of person regarded as of more worth. This stance may affect how language minorities are seen. A simple view of intelligence can be comfortable for language majorities if they believe social inequalities are based on lack of 'intelligence' in an ethnic or linguistic minority. Such a view 'releases one from an obligation to entertain the uncomfortable view that inequalities are created by ourselves, and are neither natural nor inevitable' (Howe, 1997, p. 139). IQ tests also tend to relate to a middle class, white, Western view of intelligence. The cultural boundedness or relativity of IQ tests suggests that cross-cultural generalizations are dangerous and limited (Valdés & Figueroa, 1994).

Language of Testing

The second problem is the **language of the IQ test** given to bilinguals. It is preferable to test the IQ of bilinguals in their stronger language or in both languages. In the early research, many verbal IQ tests were administered in English only (Valdés & Figueroa, 1994). This tended to be to the disadvantage of bilinguals in that they were tested in their weaker language and thus under-performed in the IQ test. Even testing bilinguals in their stronger language may be less than fair. Tests that cater holistically and sensitively for the dual language capabilities of bilinguals may be preferable.

Analysis

The early research tended to use simple averages when comparing monolingual and bilingual groups. **Statistical tests** were often not performed to see whether the differences between the average scores were real or due to chance factors. Thus, for example, when W.R. Jones (1966) re-analyzed Saer's (1923) research, he found that there was no statistically significant difference between the monolingual and bilingual groups.

Classification

As has been shown in chapter 1, the classification of people into bilingual and monolingual groups is fraught with difficulty. It is too simplistic to place people into a monolingual or a bilingual group. We need to ask what language competences are being used for classification (Bialystok, 2001a). Are all four basic language abilities being used? What is the **degree of fluency** in each language? Were bilinguals classified by their use of languages (functional bilingualism) or by their ability in language? As chapter 1 revealed, who is or is not bilingual is a complex issue. The earlier research on bilingualism and cognition tended to regard classification as non-problematic. This means that the research results are simplistic and ambiguous, having classified bilinguals in an imprecise manner.

Generalization

A fifth problem concerns sampling and the generalization of research results to the population of bilinguals. With all research, the findings should be restricted to the population that the **sample** exactly represents. In particular, research using a non-random sample of a population, merely a convenience sample, should theoretically have no generalization beyond that sample. Much of the research on bilingualism and cognition is based on convenience samples. Thus research on 11-year-olds cannot be generalized to other age groups. Findings in the US cannot be generalized to bilinguals in the rest of the world. In much of the early research on bilingualism and cognition, the sampling is both small and inadequate, making generalization dangerous.

Context

The **language and cultural environment** of the research sample needs to be considered. This relates to the notion of subtractive and additive environments (see chapter 4). Negative, detrimental cognitive findings may be more associated with minority language groups in subtractive environments. Subtractive environments are where the child's first language is in danger of being replaced by a more prestigious second language. Where bilingualism has high prestige in an additive environment, a different pattern of results may be more likely.

Also, IQ and similar tests are presented as context-free circumstances. In reality, 'intelligent' responses will be affected by the particular context in which a task is completed. 'Intelligent' responses are relative to situations (e.g. car driving, money-making, musical composition, classroom learning).

Matched Groups

The final problem is particularly important. To compare a group of bilingual children with monolinguals on IQ, or on any other measure of cognitive ability, requires that the two groups be equal in all other respects. The only difference between the two groups should be in their bilingualism and monolingualism. If such control does not occur, then the results of the research may be due to the other factor or factors on which the groups differ (rather than their monolingualism or bilingualism). Take the example of a monolingual group being mostly of higher socioeconomic status, and the bilingual group being mostly of a lower socioeconomic status. A result (e.g. showing monolinguals to be ahead of bilinguals) may be due to social class rather than, or as well as, bilingualism. The great majority of research on bilingualism and 'intelligence' failed to match the groups on other factors that might explain the results. It is necessary to match the groups on variables such as sociocultural class, gender, age, type of school attended and urban/ rural and subtractive/additive environments.

However, as Bialystok (2001a) notes, exact equivalency of groups is impossible. Bilingual children are never exactly the same as monolinguals: socially (e.g. mixing in varying language communities, family (e.g. learning a language from the extended family), travel (e.g. to the 'homeland'), attending classes at weekends or evenings to acquire a heritage language. Therefore, cognitive differences between bilinguals and monolinguals may have explanations other than language.

Conclusion

The period where research accented detrimental effects lasted from approximately the 1920s to the 1960s. While the dominant result was that bilinguals were inferior to monolinguals, particularly on verbal IQ, these early studies share many serious **methodological weaknesses**. Singly and cumulatively, the early research on bilingualism and IQ has so many limitations and methodological flaws that its conclusion of detrimental effects cannot be accepted.

Modern research does not suggest that bilinguals have no cognitive disadvantages when compared with monolinguals. There are researches that locate differences that favor monolinguals in language specific processing (e.g. reaction times, an initial developmental lag in vocabulary knowledge specific to a language). For example, Gollan *et al.* (2002) suggest that a monolingual's semantic fluency is a little faster than bilingual. (e.g. as bilinguals need to ensure the correct word is chosen from their two languages) and that bilinguals are more likely to report a 'tip of the tongue' state (unable to immediately retrieve a word) possibly because they use some words in each language less often (Gollan & Acenas, 2004).

However, none of these studies suggest that bilinguals have a mental overload, process inefficiently or in everyday thinking have weaknesses compared with monolinguals. In areas such as speed of reaction in retrieving words, the milliseconds difference is of little or no importance in everyday functioning.

The Period of Neutral Effects

There are a series of studies that reported **no difference** between bilinguals and monolinguals in IQ. For example, research in the United States by Pintner and Arsenian (1937) found a zero correlation (no relationship) between verbal (and non-verbal) IQ and Yiddish–English bilingualism/monolingualism. While the number of studies with a 'no difference' conclusion is small in number, the period of neutral effects is important because it highlighted the inadequacies of the early detrimental effect research. An example is the research by W.R. Jones (1959) in

Wales. Using 2500 children aged 10 and 11, Jones (1959) initially found that bilinguals were inferior to monolinguals on IQ. A re-analysis showed that this conclusion was invalid. After taking into account the varying socioeconomic class of bilinguals and monolinguals, Jones (1959) concluded that monolinguals and bilinguals did not differ significantly in non-verbal IQ so long as parental occupation was taken into account. He also concluded that socioeconomic class largely accounted for previous research that had reported the inferiority of bilinguals on non-verbal IQ. Therefore, his conclusion was that bilingualism is not necessarily a source of intellectual disadvantage.

While the period of neutral effects overlaps chronologically with the detrimental and additive periods, there was a period when (in Wales, for example) such neutral effects were taught and publicized. Such a 'neutral' conclusion was historically important as it gave a boost to parents who wished to support bilingualism in the home and in the school. As a **transitional period**, it both helped to question a fashionable belief of bilingualism as a source of cerebral confusion, and became a herald for the modern and current additive effects period.

The Period of Additive Effects

A major turning point in the history of the relationship between bilingualism and cognition was reached in Canadian research by Peal and Lambert (1962). This research broke new territory in three respects, each setting the pattern for future research.

First, the research overcame many of the methodological deficiencies of the period of detrimental effects. Second, the research found evidence that bilingualism need not have detrimental or even neutral consequences. Rather, there is the possibility that bilingualism leads to **cognitive advantages** over monolingualism. Peal and Lambert's (1962) finding has been widely quoted to support bilingual policies in various educational contexts. The political implication of the study was that bilingualism within a country was not a source of national intellectual inferiority (Reynolds, 1991). Third, the research by Peal and Lambert (1962), while using IQ tests, moved research towards a **broader look at cognition** (e.g. thinking styles and strategies). Other areas of mental activity apart from IQ were placed firmly on the agenda for research into bilingualism and cognitive functioning.

Peal and Lambert (1962) commenced with a sample of 364 children aged 10 years old drawn from middle-class French schools in Montreal, Canada. The original sample of 364 children was reduced to 110 children for two reasons. First, to create a group of balanced bilinguals (see chapter 1) and a group of monolinguals. Second, to ensure that the bilingual and monolingual groups were matched on socioeconomic class.

Bilinguals performed significantly higher on 15 out of the 18 variables measuring IQ. On the other three variables, there was no difference between balanced bilinguals and monolinguals. Peal and Lambert (1962) concluded that bilingualism provides: greater mental flexibility; the ability to think more abstractly, more independently of words, providing superiority in concept formation; that a more enriched bilingual and bicultural environment benefits the development of IQ; and that there is a positive transfer between a bilingual's two languages, facilitating the development of verbal IQ. These results provided the stimulus for further research and debate.

The study by Peal and Lambert (1962), while being pivotal in research on bilingualism and cognitive functioning, has four basic methodological weaknesses that need to be briefly considered before accepting the research at its face value. **First**, the results concern 110 children 10 years of age and of middle-class, Montreal extraction. This is not a sample that can be generalized to the population of bilinguals either in Canada or throughout the world. This is particularly so since the results concern 110 children selected from an original sample of 364. An unanswered question is how the other 254 children performed across the broad range of tests given by Peal and Lambert (1962).

Second, children in the bilingual group were 'balanced' bilinguals (see chapter 1). While the term 'bilingual' includes balanced bilinguals, there are many other groups of children 'less balanced'. We cannot assume that the results from this study apply to such 'less balanced' bilinguals. Are balanced bilinguals a special group with their own characteristics in terms of their motivation, aptitude for languages, cognitive abilities and attitudes? Are balanced bilinguals a special group of children who have a higher IQ that is due not only to owning two languages, but due to other factors as well (e.g. parental values and expectations)?

The **third** problem with Peal and Lambert's (1962) research is the chicken and egg problem – which comes first? What is the cause and what is the effect? Is it bilingualism that enhances IQ? Or does a higher IQ increase the chances of becoming bilingual? When research suggests that IQ and bilingualism are positively related, we cannot conclude the order of cause and effect. It may be that bilingualism enhances IQ. It may be that those with a higher IQ are more likely to become bilingual. The relationship may also be such that one is both the cause and the effect of the other. Research by Diaz (1985) suggests that, if there is a particular direction in the relationship, it is more likely to be bilingualism positively affecting 'intelligence', rather than 'intelligence' affecting bilingualism.

The **fourth** problem concerns socioeconomic status. While Peal and Lambert (1962) tried to equate their bilingual and monolingual groups for socioeconomic class by exclusion of some children, there are residual problems. Equating socioeconomic class does not control for all the differences in a child's home environment. Socioeconomic class is only a simple and very partial measure of a child's home and environmental background. This is true of monolingual children. It is even more so with children who are bilingual and bicultural where there may be an even more complicated home and family background regarding sociocultural factors. Parental occupation of bilingual children is likely to summarize differences between children very inadequately.

In the following example, notice how the sociocultural element is very different, yet the socioeconomic class is the same. Take two Latino children of the same age and gender living in the same street in New York. Their fathers both have the same job – taxi drivers. One family regularly attends church services in Spanish and belongs to a Latino/Latina organization with cultural activities in Spanish. This taxi driver and his wife send their children to a Spanish–English dual language school. The child is bilingual. In the second family, the child speaks English only. There is no interest in sending their children to a dual-language school. Neither does the family attend a church or another organization where Spanish is spoken and valued. The Latin-American roots are neither discussed nor appreciated. While the families are matched on socioeconomic status, the sociocultural differences between them are considerable. In this example, the first child is bilingual and the second child is monolingual, with the bilingual child having a higher IQ. The child's bilingualism may not be the only explanation of a higher IQ. Rather the alternative or additional explanation may be in the different social and cultural environment of these children. Thus, with Peal and Lambert's (1962) study, socioeconomic class may have been controlled, but not sociocultural class.

This completes the examination of Peal and Lambert's (1962) historically important and **pivotal** study. Since their research, the dominant approach to bilingualism and cognitive functioning has moved away from IQ testing to a range of thinking styles, strategies and skills. As an overview, studies since the 1960s mostly confirm Peal and Lambert's (1962) positive findings (see later).

A related area of research concerns the **mental representation** of a bilingual's two languages and the processing emanating from such representation (Fabbro, 1999, 2002). A principal issue has been the extent to which a bilingual's two languages function **independently or interdependently**. The early research attempted to show that early bilinguals (compound bilinguals) were more likely to show interconnections and inter-relatedness in their two languages than late (coordinate) bilinguals. In the 1960s, Kolers (1963) re-defined the issue in terms of memory storage. A **separate storage** hypothesis stated that bilinguals have two independent language storage and retrieval systems with the only channel of communication being a translation process between the two separate systems. A **shared storage** hypothesis stated that the two languages are kept in a single memory store with two different language input channels and two different language output channels. Evidence exists for both independence and interdependence (Bialystok, 2001a). Recent theories and research have therefore emphasized both the separate and connected aspects of bilingual's mental representations by integrating the topic with general cognitive processing theories. For example, Kroll and De Groot (1997) suggest that the lexical representations for each language are separately stored by a bilingual, while the conceptual representations are shared. This is further considered in the next chapter. However, there is general agreement that (1) both languages are active when just one of them is being used, and (2) that even if there are shared conceptual representations and both languages are active in bilinguals, functionally the languages are independent (e.g. when speaking, reading, writing). 'Adults are not confused by the fact that two linguistic systems share processing space for knowledge and communication' (Bialystok, 2001a, p. 104).

BILINGUALISM AND THE BRAIN

Just as members of the public ask basic questions about 'intelligence' and bilingualism, so questions often arise about bilinguals' brains. A frequently asked question is whether a bilingual's brain functions differently compared with that of a monolingual's brain? The issue becomes whether language is differently organized and processed in the brain of a bilingual compared with that of the monolingual (Fabbro, 1999). As Paradis (2000, 2004) and Goral *et al.* (2002) outline, many 'neurolinguistics of bilingualism' questions remain unanswered (e.g. differences in brain organization depending on how many languages are known).

One topic in the study of bilingualism and the brain has been **lateralization** (Paradis, 2004). In the majority of right-handed adults, the left hemisphere of the brain is dominant for language processing (Vaid, 2002). The question has naturally arisen as to whether bilinguals are different from monolinguals in this left lateralization? Using a quantitative procedure called **meta-analysis** to review previous research in this area, Vaid and Hull (2001) found that the left hemisphere dominated language processing for monolinguals while bilateral involvement was pronounced in early fluent bilinguals compared with late fluent bilinguals. Thus bilinguals appear to be less left lateralized than monolinguals.

The expectation has been that images of relevant areas of the brain would add much to our understanding of bilingualism in terms of language storage and processing. Advances in **neuroimaging** have led to bilinguals being studied by (1) event-related potential (ERP) (2) positron emission tomography (PET) and (3) functional magnetic resonance imaging (fMRI). Basically, each approach tries to take a snapshot of which part of the brain is doing what when we are thinking.

One recent area of such research on bilinguals is how their two languages are stored and used in the brain. For example, if someone learns two languages from birth, are the two languages stored differently in the brain from someone who learns a second language at school or in adult life? One much publicized piece of research by Mechelli *et al.* (2004) suggested that learning a second language increases the density of gray matter. When comparing 25 monolinguals, 25 early bilinguals and 33 late bilinguals, gray matter density was greater in bilinguals than monolinguals, with early bilinguals having increased density than late bilinguals. Thus such density of gray matter 'increases with second language proficiency but decreases as the age of acquisition increases' (p. 757) such that 'the structure of the brain is altered by the experience of acquiring a second language' (p. 757). However, the implications of such early findings for everyday thinking and performance are not clear.

Kim *et al.* (1997) appeared to show a difference between early bilinguals (e.g. both languages learnt before three years of age) and late bilinguals. Using fMRI in Broca's area, a finding was that in early bilinguals, the two languages are found in distinct but adjacent sites. This suggests that similar or identical regions of the brain serve both languages. In comparison, among late bilinguals, the native and second languages are stored more separately.

The research, published in *Nature*, received much attention in the press. Like many pieces of innovative research, replication and extension is needed. (1) Only 12 people were used in this study, of whom six were early bilinguals and six late bilinguals. The first and second languages included English, Korean, Spanish, German, Turkish, Hebrew, Croatian, Italian and Chinese. Twelve people is not a large enough sample from which to generalize to millions of bilingual worldwide. (2) These bilinguals were shown pictures of morning, noon and night. They were then asked to think in one or the other of their two languages about what they had done during those times in the previous day. Thus the brain scans were restricted to someone purportedly thinking in one language rather than speaking a language. (3) Most of the data did not show any difference between early and late bilinguals. (4) Other research has not replicated these results and there existing conflicting results using ERP and PET (Bialystok, 2001a; Goral *et al.*, 2002).

There is a danger of believing that brain images represent thought. Such snap-shot brain images are a visible consequence of thinking but do not reveal the complex operation of the mind. The correspondence between these images of the brain and thought processes is futuristic.

BILINGUALISM AND DIVERGENT AND CREATIVE THINKING

One problem with IQ tests is that they restrict children to finding the one correct answer to each question. This is often termed convergent thinking. Children have to converge onto the sole acceptable answer. An alternative style is called divergent or creative thinking. A child regarded as a diverger is more creative, imaginative, elastic, open ended and free in thinking. Instead of finding the one correct answer, divergent thinkers prefer to provide a variety of answers, all of which can be valid. In the British tradition, the term used for this area is divergent thinking (Hudson, 1966, 1968).

Divergent thinking is investigated by asking questions such as: 'How many uses can you think of for a brick?'; 'How many interesting and unusual uses can you think of for tin cans?'; 'How many different uses can you think of for car tires?'. On this kind of question, the student has to diverge and find as many answers as possible. For example, on the 'uses of a brick' question, a convergent thinker would tend to produce a few rather obvious answers to the question: to build a house, to build a barbecue, to build a wall. The divergent thinker will tend to produce not only many different answers, but also some that may be fairly original: for blocking up a rabbit hole, for propping up a wobbly table, as a foot wiper, breaking a window, making a bird bath.

In the North American tradition, it is more usual to talk about **Creative Thinking**. In this tradition, Torrance (1974a, 1974b) analyzes answers to the 'Uses of an Object' test (e.g. unusual uses of cardboard boxes, unusual uses of tin cans) by four categories. This test may be adapted into any language, with a culturally appropriate use of objects. Also, there are figural tests where a person is given a sheet of 40 circles or 40 squares and asked to draw pictures using these individual circles or squares, and subsequently place a label underneath.

A person's **fluency** score in creative thinking is the number of different acceptable answers that are given. A **flexibility** score is the number of different categories (listed in the Test Manual) into which answers can be placed. **Originality** is measured by reference to the Test Manual that gives scores of 0, 1, or 2 for the originality (statistical infrequency) of each response. **Elaboration** refers to the extent of the extra detail that a person gives beyond the basic use of an object.

The underlying hypothesis concerning creative thinking and bilingualism is that the ownership of two or more languages may increase fluency, flexibility, originality and elaboration in thinking. Bilinguals will have two or more words for a single object or idea. For example, in Welsh, the word *ysgol* not only means a school but also a ladder. Thus having the word 'ysgol' in Welsh and 'school' in English may provide the bilingual with added associations – the idea of the school as a ladder (e.g. the steps as going through the grades). Similarly, having words for 'folk dancing' or 'square dancing' in different languages may give a **wider variety of associations** than having a label in just one language.

Does having two or more words for the one object or idea allow a person more freedom of association and richness of thought? Research has compared bilinguals and monolinguals on a variety of measures of divergent thinking (Ricciardelli, 1992). The research is international and cross cultural: from Ireland, Malaysia, Eastern Europe, Canada, Singapore, Mexico and the US, sampling bilinguals using English plus Chinese, Bahasa Melayu, Tamil, Polish, German, Greek, Spanish, French, Ukrainian, Yoruba, Welsh, Italian or Kannada. As Laurén (1991) notes, such research has mostly occurred in additive bilingual contexts. The research findings largely suggest that **bilinguals are superior** to monolinguals on divergent thinking tests. An example will illustrate that links with an explanation of which bilinguals may have advantages.

Cummins (1975, 1977) found that **balanced bilinguals** (see chapter 1) were superior to 'matched' non-balanced bilinguals on the fluency and flexibility scales of verbal divergence, and marginally on originality. The 'matched' monolingual group obtained similar scores to the balanced bilingual group on verbal fluency and flexibility but scored substantially higher than the non-balanced group. On originality, monolinguals scored at a similar level to the non-balanced bilinguals and substantially lower than the balanced group. Probably due to the small numbers involved, the results did not quite attain customary levels of statistical significance. That there are differences between matched groups of balanced bilinguals and non-balanced bilinguals suggests that bilingualism and superior divergent thinking skills are not simply related. Thus Cummins (1977) proposed that:

> there may be a threshold level of linguistic competence which a bilingual child must attain both in order to avoid cognitive deficits and allow the potentially beneficial aspects of becoming bilingual to influence his cognitive growth. (p. 10)

The difference between balanced and non-balanced bilinguals is thus explained by a **threshold**. Once children have obtained a certain level of competence in their second language, positive cognitive consequences can result. However, competence in a second language below a certain threshold level may fail to give any cognitive benefits. This is the basic notion of the threshold theory that is examined further in chapter 8.

The evidence suggests that balanced bilinguals have superior divergent thinking skills compared with other less balanced bilinguals and monolinguals. In a review of 24 studies, Ricciardelli (1992) found that in 20 of these studies, bilinguals performed higher than monolinguals. Studies not supporting bilingual superiority sampled less proficient bilinguals, a result consistent with the Threshold Theory.

However, some care must be taken in reaching too firm a conclusion. For example, Laurén (1991) found that linguistic creativity differences were found in Grades 3, 6 and 9. Older bilinguals were ahead on only one of the four measures (use of compound nouns). Also, the term 'creativity' is defined in different ways. As Laurén (1991) reveals, there are interpretations by psychologists (e.g. cognitive flexibility, fluency, originality and elaboration; tolerance of ambiguity); by linguists (e.g. the ability to create new meanings in different contexts); child development researchers (e.g. transforming the language input of parents and teachers); and creative writing proponents. Do bilinguals show advantages on psychological rather than the purely linguistic creativity measures?

Does bilingualism bestow cognitive advantages of a **permanent nature**? If there are positive cognitive advantages linked with bilingualism, it is important to ask whether these are temporary, or cumulative and everlasting? Research studies tend to use children aged 4 to 17. What happens into the twenties or middle age or older age? Does bilingualism accelerate cognitive growth in the early years, with monolinguals catching up in later years?

BILINGUALISM AND METALINGUISTIC AWARENESS: INITIAL RESEARCH

The research on bilingualism and divergent thinking suggests that bilinguals may have some advantage over matched monolinguals. For many bilingual children, the size of their total vocabulary across both languages is likely to be greater than that of a monolingual child in a single language. Does a larger overall vocabulary allow a bilingual to be more free and open, more flexible and original particularly in meanings attached to words? Is a bilingual person therefore less bound by words, more elastic in thinking due to owning two languages? For example, Doyle *et al.* (1978) found that bilinguals tend to be superior in their ability to relate stories and to express concepts within those stories when compared with monolinguals.

Leopold's (1939–1949) famous case study (see chapter 5) of the German–English development of his daughter, Hildegard, noted the looseness of the link between word and meaning – an effect apparently due to bilingualism. Favorite stories were not repeated with stereotyped wording; vocabulary substitutions were made freely in memorized songs and rhymes. Word sound and word meaning were separated.

The name of an object or concept was separated from the object or concept itself. Hildegard is a single case. What has research revealed about samples of bilinguals?

Ianco-Worrall (1972) tested the sound and meaning separation idea on 30 Afrikaans–English bilinguals aged four to nine. The bilingual group was matched with monolinguals on IQ, age, sex, school grade and social class. In the first experiment, a typical question was: 'I have three words: CAP, CAN and HAT. Which is more like CAP, CAN or HAT?' A child who says that CAN is more like CAP would appear to be making a choice determined by the **sound** of the word. That is, CAP and CAN have two out of three letters in common. A child who chooses HAT would appear to be making a choice based on the **meaning** of the word. That is, HAT and CAP refer to similar objects.

Ianco-Worrall (1972) showed that, by seven years of age, there was no difference between bilinguals and monolinguals in their choices. Both groups chose HAT, their answer being governed by the meaning of the word. However, with four- to six-year-olds, she found that bilinguals tended to respond to word meaning, monolinguals more to the sound of the word. This led Ianco-Worrall (1972) to conclude that bilinguals:

> reach a stage of semantic development, as measured by our test, some two–three years earlier than their monolingual peers. (p. 1398)

In a further experiment, Ianco-Worrall (1972) asked the following type of question: 'Suppose you were making up names for things, could you call a cow 'dog' and a dog 'cow'?' Bilinguals mostly felt that names could be interchangeable. Monolinguals, in comparison, more often said that names for objects such as cow and dog could not be interchanged. Another way of describing this is to say that monolinguals tend to be bound by words, bilinguals tend to believe that language is more arbitrary. For bilinguals, **names and objects are separate**. This seems to be a result of owning two languages, giving the bilingual child awareness of the free, non-fixed relationship between objects and their labels.

Other early research in this area, for example, by Ben-Zeev (1977a, 1977b), suggested that the ability of bilinguals to analyze and inspect their languages stems from the necessity of avoiding 'interference' between the two languages. That is, the process of separating two languages and avoiding codemixing may give bilinguals superiority over monolinguals through an increased analytical orientation to language. One of Ben-Zeev's (1977a) tests, called the Symbol Substitution Test, asked children to substitute one word for another in a sentence. For example, they had to use the word 'macaroni' instead of 'I' in a sentence. The sentence to say becomes 'Macaroni am warm', thus avoiding saying 'I am warm'. Respondents have to ignore word meaning, avoid framing a correct sentence and evade the interference of word substitution in order to respond to the task correctly. Bilinguals were found by Ben-Zeev (1977a) to be superior on this kind of test, not only with regard to meaning, but also with regard to sentence construction.

Ben-Zeev (1977a), using Hebrew–English bilinguals from Israel and the United States aged 5–8, argued that bilinguals have advantages because they experience two language systems with two different sets of construction rules. Therefore bilinguals appear to be more flexible and analytical in language skills.

BILINGUALISM AND METALINGUISTIC AWARENESS: RECENT RESEARCH

Much of the older research on bilingualism and cognitive functioning has concentrated on cognitive style (e.g. divergent and creative thinking). The focus of research tended to be on the person and on the product. It attempted to locate dimensions of thinking where bilinguals perform better than monolinguals. The recent trend has been to look at the **process** of thinking rather than the **products** of thinking, working within the information processing, memorization and language processing approaches in psychology (e.g. Bialystok, 2001a; Pavlenko, 1999). Not all such studies are 'favorable to bilinguals' (Bialystok, 2001a). For example, Nick Ellis (1992) and Geary *et al.*, (1993) found bilinguals slower on the processing of numbers. However, while bilinguals may be slower in calculations in their weaker language, they may be equally as good at problem solving and getting correct mathematical solutions (Bialystok, 2001a). McLeay (2003) found advantages for adult 'balanced' bilinguals in dealing with complex mathematical spatial problems while Kessler and Quinn (1980, 1982) found bilinguals were superior on scientific problem solving.

There is another limitation to research on bilinguals and cognition. Research on memorization, language recall, reaction times and processing times tends to use bilinguals to help describe and explain cognitive processing and language processing. Comparisons with monolinguals aim to aid psychological understanding of cognitive processes rather than to focus on bilinguals per se. Pavlenko (1999, 2000) provides a review that is both critical of research in this area, but places the bilingual at the forefront.

Research that has focused on bilinguals has particularly studied the **metalinguistic awareness of bilingual children** (Bialystok, 2001a, 2001b). Metalinguistic awareness (also metalinguistic knowledge and metalinguistic ability – see Bialystok, 2001a for the differences) may loosely be defined as thinking about and reflecting upon the nature and functions of language:

> Metalinguistic awareness may be defined as the ability to reflect upon and manipulate the structural features of spoken language, treating language itself as an object of thought, as opposed to simply using the language system to comprehend and produce sentences. (Tunmer & Herriman, 1984, p. 12)

An example of metalinguistic knowledge is second language learners who do not have to relearn the fundamentals of **language structure**. They arrive that metalinguistic knowledge from first language acquisition. A language template is available for second language learning that enables selective attention to new and different information.

Early research suggested a relationship favoring bilinguals in terms of increased metalinguistic awareness (e.g. Ianco-Worrall, 1972; Ben-Zeev, 1977a, 1977b; see Tunmer & Myhill, 1984 for a review). It appeared that bilingual children develop a more analytical orientation to language through organizing their two language systems. Phonological awareness and the cognitive skills of symbolic representation are needed to read and write. Letters are symbols without inherent meaning and do not resemble the sounds they represent. Bilinguals may comprehend such symbolic representation earlier than monolinguals as they see words written in two different ways.

In research that directly engages bilingualism and metalinguistic awareness, Bialystok (1987a, 1987b, 1997, 2001a, 2001b) found that bilingual children were superior to monolingual children on measures of the **cognitive control of linguistic processes**. Bialystok (1987a) conducted three studies each involving around 120 children aged five to nine. In the experiments, children were asked to judge or correct sentences for their syntactic acceptability irrespective of meaningfulness. Sentences could be meaningfully grammatical (e.g. why is the dog barking so loudly?), meaningful but not grammatical (e.g. why the dog is barking so loudly?); anomalous and grammatical (e.g. why is the cat barking so loudly?); or anomalous and ungrammatical (e.g. why the cat is barking so loudly?). These sentences test the level of analysis of a child's linguistic knowledge. The instructions requested that the children focus on whether a given sentence was grammatically correct or not. It did not matter that the sentence was silly or anomalous. Bialystok (1987a) found that bilingual children in all three studies consistently judged grammaticality more accurately than did monolingual children at all the ages tested.

Bialystok (1987b) also examined the difference between bilinguals and monolinguals in their **processing of words** and the **development of the concept of a word**. She found in three studies that bilingual children showed more advanced understanding of some aspects of the idea of words than did monolingual children. A procedure for testing children's awareness of 'What is a word?' is to ask children to determine the number of words in a sentence. It can be surprisingly difficult for young children to count how many words there are in a sentence. Until children are about six to seven years of age and learning to read, they do not appear to have this processing ability.

To be able to count how many words there are in a sentence depends on two things: first, a knowledge of the boundaries of words; second, a knowledge of the relationship between word meaning and sentence meaning. At around seven years of age, children learn that words can be isolated from the sentences in which they are contained, having their own individual meaning. Bialystok (1987b) found that bilingual children were ahead of monolingual children on counting words in sentences because (1) they were more clear about the criteria that determined the identity of words; and (2) they were more capable of attending to the units of speech they considered relevant.

> Bilingual children were most notably advanced when required to separate out individual words from meaningful sentences, focus on only the form or meaning of a word under highly distracting conditions, and re-assign a familiar name to a different object. (Bialystok, 1987b, p. 138)

A **conclusion** based on an overview of research can be summarized as follows (Bialystok, 2001a, 2001b). A bilingual does not have across-the-board metalinguistic advantages or universally superior metalinguistic abilities. Relatively balanced bilinguals have increased metalinguistic abilities particularly in those tasks that require **selective attention** to information (e.g. when there is competing or misleading information). Such selective attention relates to two components: bilinguals' enhanced analyzing of their knowledge of language; and their greater control of attention in internal language processing. Bialystok (2001a) suggests that the overall research evidence gives bilinguals superiority in control but not necessarily in analysis, 'a formidable advantage in cognitive processing' (Bialystok, 2001b, p. 179). This may be due to bilinguals needing to differentiate between their two languages. Since both languages remain active during language processing (rather than a switch mechanism occurring), there is inhibition of the one language when in conversation so as to avoid intrusions (Bialystok, 2001a).

Implications and Explanations

Bilinguals appear to understand the symbolic representation of words in print earlier than monolinguals as they see words printed in two separate ways. In turn, this may facilitate earlier acquisition of reading. Such metalinguistic awareness is regarded by Bialystok (2001a) as a key factor in the **development of reading** in young children. This hints that bilinguals may be ready slightly earlier than monolinguals to learn to read. In a review of this area, Bialystok and Herman (1999) analyze the effects that early bilingualism has on children's early literacy development but urge caution. Three areas of early literacy development are analyzed: experience with stories and book reading, concepts of print, and phonological awareness. These three areas cover the social, cognitive and linguistic aspects of literacy learning. The authors argue that each of these three areas of competence will have a different link to bilingualism.

However, there are many intervening variables that make simple statements currently impossible. The child's experience and level of proficiency in each language, the relationship between the two languages, and the type of writing systems employed by each language are examples of intervening factors that alters the nature of the bilingual experience. A similar cautious approach is taken by Green (1998) who suggests that current research is often simplistic in just connecting bilingualism and cognitive performance.

Apart from literacy, Bialystok and Codd (1997) found that four- and five-year-old bilinguals were ahead of monolinguals in developing concepts of **number** (cardinality of number) due to their higher levels of attentional control. Bilingual children need to be attentive to which language is being spoken, by whom, where and when. This attentiveness appears to give advantages in early number work, when attention to the symbolic nature of number is needed.

The research of Galambos and Hakuta (1988) provides further refinement of the reasons for differences between bilinguals and monolinguals on cognitive processes. In two studies with low income Spanish–English bilingual children in the US, Galambos and Hakuta (1988) used a series of tests that examined children's ability to spot various errors in Spanish sentences. Such errors might be in terms of gender, word order, singular and plural, verb tense and time. For example, on a grammatically oriented test item, a child had to correct the following: 'La perro es grande'. The correction would be 'El perro es grande'. In a content oriented test item, 'La perro es grande' would become 'El perro es pequeño'. In the experiment, children were read the sentences, asked to judge whether it had been said in the right way, and then correct the error.

The effect of bilingualism on the processing of the test items was found to vary depending on the level of bilingualism and the difficulty level of the items. The more bilingual the child was, that is where both languages were relatively well developed, the better he or she performed on the test items:

> The information-processing approach successfully accounts for our findings that bilingualism by and large enhances the metalinguistic abilities to note errors and correct errors . . . The bilingual experience requires that the form of the two languages being learned be attended to on a routine basis. Experience at attending to form would be predicted to facilitate any task that required the child to focus on form upon demand. (Galambos & Hakuta, 1988, p. 153)

Galambos and Hakuta (1988) concluded that metalinguistic awareness is most developed when a child's two languages are developed to their highest level. Galambos and Hakuta (1988) agreed with Cummins (1976) that a certain level of proficiency in both languages must be attained before the positive effects of bilingualism on metalinguistic awareness can occur. This is usually termed the **thresholds** theory and is considered in chapter 8.

Carlisle et al. (1999) also found that the **degree of bilingualism** constrains or enhances metalinguistic performance. Those in the early stages of bilingualism do not share the benefits until sufficient vocabulary development, in both languages, has occurred. Similarly, Bialystok and Majumder's (1999) research showed that balanced bilinguals in Grade 3 were superior to partial bilinguals on non-linguistic problem-solving tasks requiring selective attention. However, a reservation is expressed by Nicoladis and Genesee (1996) who did not find this effect with pre-literate children

Age Effects

Are these metalinguistic advantages of balanced bilinguals temporary and located with certain younger children (e.g. those already embarked on the initial stages of reading)? Do they give a child an initial advantage that soon disappears with growing cognitive competence? Are the effects in any way permanent? Are these early benefits for bilinguals cumulative and additive?

Older bilingual adults may have some advantages. De Bot and Makoni (2005) analyze the relationship between aging (in its physical, psychological and social dimensions) and language. One suggestion of these authors is that being bilingual may allow access to additional cognitive processes and storage as memory functions decline with age. Bialystok et al. (2004) provide evidence across a series of experiments that a metalinguistic advantage persists into adulthood, and further-more helps lessens some of the negative cognitive effects of aging in adults.

Bialystok *et al.* (2004) used the **Simon Task** to compare groups of younger and older bilinguals and monolinguals. In the Simon Task colored stimuli are presented on either the left or the right side of a computer screen. Each of two colors (or two pairs of colors) are associated with a response key on the two sides of the keyboard underneath the stimuli. A person in the experiment has to press the key on the correct side. For example, a correct 'congruent' response occurs when the person presses the left key when red is presented on the left side of the screen. A correct 'incongruent' response is when the subject presses the left key when red is presented on the right side of the screen. An incorrect response is when red is presented on the right side and the person press the right key. The time taken to respond is an important measure-ment (i.e. 'incongruent' trials have longer reaction times and this is termed the Simon effect). Longer reaction times tend to occur with aging.

Across a series of experiments, Bialystok *et al.* (2004) found that performance on the Simon task was **superior in bilinguals** than monolinguals and that this result was evident in younger and older bilinguals. Balanced bilinguals tended to perform the Simon Task quicker than 'matched' monolinguals, irrespective of age, and showed less interference in the 'incongruent' trials. However, bilingualism signifi-cantly reduced the age-related lower performance. Older bilinguals performed significantly better than older monolinguals. This implies that 'the lifelong experi-ence of managing two languages attenuates the age-related decline in the efficiency of inhibitory processing' (Bialystok *et al.*, 2004, p. 301).

Abilities that depend on executive cognitive control show a decline in efficiency with aging. For example, older people (e.g. 60 to 88 in these experiments) tend to be less able to attend to the most important aspects in a situation or ignore irrelevant stimuli, as in the Simon task. Thus lifelong bilingualism may provide a partial defense against the normal decline in cognitive control associated with aging.

The Simon effect is similar to advantages found in bilingual children (discussed previously) who appear to be superior in **selective attention** to problems, inhibition of attention to misleading information, and switching quickly between competing alternatives. From these experiments, such inhibitory control appears to last a life-time (Bialystok *et al.*, 2004). This advantage may be due to bilinguals using one language while both their languages are constantly active. 'The joint activity of the two systems requires a mechanism for keeping the languages separate so that fluent performance can be achieved without intrusions from the unwanted language' (Bialystok *et al.*, 2004, p. 291).

So the conclusion of Bialystok *et al.* (2004) is that metalinguistic advantages for bilinguals appear to be sustained into adulthood with some defense effects on cognitive processing decline as aging occurs. The bilingual advantage appears to be in complex cognitive processing that requires **executive control**. 'The simple expe-rience of bilingualism that relies on some aspect of these processes to control the production of the relevant language appears to yield widespread benefits across a range of complex cognitive tasks' (Bialystok *et al.*, 2004, p. 302).

BILINGUALISM AND COMMUNICATIVE SENSITIVITY

In Ben-Zeev's research (1977b) on the comparative performance of bilingual and monolingual children on Piagetian tests, she found that bilinguals were more responsive to hints and clues given in the experimental situation (see Baker & Jones, 1998, for a review of Piagetian research and bilingualism). That is, bilinguals seemed more sensitive in an experimental situation, and corrected their errors faster compared to monolinguals. Ben-Zeev's (1977b) research gave the first clue that bilinguals may have cognitive advantages regarding 'communicative sensitivity'.

What is **communicative sensitivity**? Bilinguals need to be aware of which language to speak in which situation. They need constantly to monitor the appropriate language in which to respond or in which to initiate a conversation (e.g. on the telephone, in a shop, speaking to a superior). Not only do bilinguals often attempt to avoid interference between their two languages, they also have to pick up clues and cues as to when to switch languages. The literature suggests that this may give a bilingual increased sensitivity to the social nature and communicative functions of language.

An interesting experiment on sensitivity to communication, deserving replication, was undertaken by Genesee *et al.* (1975). They compared children in bilingual and monolingual education on their performance on a game. In this simple but ingenious research, students aged 5 to 8 were asked to explain a board and dice game to two listeners. One listener was blindfolded, the other not. The listeners were classmates and not allowed to ask any questions after the explanation. The classmates then attempted to play the game with a person giving the explanation. It was found that children in a bilingual education program (total immersion – see chapter 11) were more sensitive to the needs of listeners. This bilingual education group gave more information to the blindfolded children than to the sighted listener compared with children in the monolingual education comparison group. The authors concluded that children in bilingual education 'may have been better able than the control children to take the role of others experiencing communicational difficulties, to perceive their needs, and consequently to respond appropriately to these needs' (p. 1013).

This implies that bilingual children may be more **sensitive** than monolingual children in a social situation that requires careful communication. A bilingual child may be more aware of the needs of the listener. In a variety of cognitive tests with bilingual and monolingual samples among the Konds (Kandhas) in Orissa, India, Mohanty (1994) found an increased sensitivity to messages among bilinguals. This links with sociolinguistic competence (see chapter 1) and suggests a heightened social awareness among bilinguals of verbal and non-verbal message cues and clues in communication.

More research is needed to define precisely the characteristics and the extent of the sensitivity to communication that bilinguals may share. Research in this area is important because it connects cognition with interpersonal relationships. It moves from questions about skills of the bilingual mind to a bilingual's social skills.

THINKING IMPLICATIONS OF SPEAKING SPECIFIC LANGUAGES

Is it the case that different languages, or combinations of languages, influence the thinking of individuals? For example, does the structure, concepts (e.g. of time, number, space) and discourses of a particular language affect thinking (the neo Whorfian hypothesis, see Pavlenko, 2005a)? Does someone who learns a second language also acquire new meanings, concepts and enhanced perspectives? Do they transform the thinking of the individual? And do such new insights become only partially translatable across a bilingual or multilingual's languages?

Pavlenko (2005a) reviews studies on the concepts of color, shape, number, motion, space, time, emotions, personhood (e.g. egocentric, sociocentric), discourse and autobiographical memory. For example, while a monolingual Hindi has no term for 'gray', an English-Hindi bilingual is likely to have the concept of gray. She shows that a **specific language** will sensitize and socialize speakers to particular aspects of a concept. That sensitization will vary from language to language. It will also vary between bicultural simultaneous (early) bilinguals, late bilinguals and incipient language learners (e.g. in a 'foreign' context).

LIMITATIONS OF THE FINDINGS

Researchers who find cognitive advantages mostly focus on **balanced bilinguals**. Do balanced bilinguals represent all bilinguals? MacNab (1979) argued that bilinguals are a special, idiosyncratic group in society. Because they have learnt a second language and are often bicultural, bilinguals are different in major ways from monolinguals. For example, parents who want their children to be bicultural and bilingual may emphasize divergent thinking skills, encourage creative thinking in their children and foster metalinguistic skills. The parents of bilingual children may be the ones who want to accelerate their children's language skills. Such parents may give high priority to the development of languages within their children compared with monolingual parents. While this does not detract from the possibility that bilinguals do share some cognitive advantages, it does suggest a need to take care about a decision as to what are the determining factors. It may be that it is not only language that is important. Other non-language factors may be influential as well (e.g. the immigrant experience, political pressures, subtractive and additive contexts).

We also need to ask **which types of children share the benefits of bilingualism**? This concerns whether children of all abilities share the cognitive advantages of bilingualism. Is it just 'elective' bilinguals (see chapter 1) upon whom much of the research is based, or do the results extend to circumstantial bilinguals (Valdés & Figueroa, 1994)? Do children below average in cognitive abilities also gain the advantages of bilingualism? There is a tendency in research to use children from the middle classes, particularly those of above average ability. However Rueda (1983), using analytical orientation to language tests (see earlier in this chapter), found that bilingual, less able children (51–69 IQ level) tended to have cognitive advantages over 'matched' monolinguals. Rueda's (1983) research in Canada, which needs thorough replication, hints that cognitive advantages may be shared by below average ability children and not just the average and above average ability children.

In addition, when reviewing all research we need to consider the hopes and the ideologies of the researcher. Rosenthal (1966) has shown that **experimenters' expectations** can affect the outcomes and results of human and animal studies. As Hakuta (1986, p. 43) suggests: 'a full account of the relationship between bilingualism and intelligence, of why negative effects suddenly turn in to positive effects, will have to examine the motivations of the researcher as well as more traditional considerations at the level of methodology.' Have the assumptions and political preferences of authors crept unintentionally into their research and affected both the results and the interpretations of the results? In the choice of psychological tests and the choice of a sample, has there recently been a built-in bias towards finding positive results on bilingualism and cognitive functioning?

As Pavlenko (2005a) argues, the dominant research on bilingualism and cognition is about the implications of bilingualism for individual cognition. This assumes that such cognitive effects of bilingualism are universal. But do **different languages and cultures** (and their multilingual combinations) have specific cognitive effects? The contested Sapir-Whorf hypothesis has been that different languages may give their speakers different views of the world (linguistic relativity). Learning a second language is thus partly a socialization into new understandings, perspectives and ways of speaking. Recent neo-Whorfian views suggest that different languages may variedly influence individual's thought contents (e.g. concepts) and processes (e.g. selectively attending, remembering, reasoning). Evidence for this can be located in the experiences of color, number, space, motion, time, autobiographical memory, personhood and the Self in different languages (Pavlenko, 2005a). Such evidence is also present in cross-linguistic differences in terms and understandings about **emotion**. Pavlenko (2002b) showed that in English, emotions are relayed through adjectives as emotional states, while in Russian the tendency is to convey emotions more via verbs as actions and processes, with for example, more attention to body language. Bilinguals may therefore have access to different conceptual representations, experience different imagery and index more varied discourses and identities (Pavlenko, 2005a, 2005b). She concludes that bilingualism can be advantageous for enriching a person's linguistic repertoire. Bilingualism can provide varied and alternative conceptualizations which enable flexible and critical thinking (Pavlenko, 2005a).

CONCLUSION

This chapter has reviewed the traditional expectation that bilingualism and intelligence are linked negatively. The conception has been that bilingualism leads to lower intelligence. Research from the 1920s to the 1960s supported that conception.

Recent research has shown that a simple negative relationship is a misconception. The narrow view of intelligence contained in IQ tests and severe flaws in the design of early research combine with other limitations to cast doubts on this negative link.

Rather, the need is to specify the language ability levels of bilinguals (see chapter 1) and to ensure like is compared with like. Since 1960, the indication has been that a more positive relationship between bilingualism and cognitive functioning can be expected, particularly in 'balanced' bilinguals.

A review of research on cognitive functioning and bilingualism suggests that two extreme conclusions may both be untenable. To conclude that bilingualism gives undoubted cognitive advantage fails to consider the various criticisms and limitations of research in this area. It also fails to recognize that there are studies where bilinguals may sometimes be at a disadvantage compared with monolinguals. However, to conclude that all the research is invalid fails to acknowledge that the judgment of the clear majority of researchers tends to be that there are many positive links between bilingualism and cognitive functioning with bilinguals having some distinct cognitive advantages over monolinguals. Such advantages are not just individual but societal and global: 'those who envision a future world speaking only one tongue . . . hold a misguided ideal and would do the evolution of the human mind the greatest disservice' (Whorf, 1956, p. 244).

KEY POINTS IN THE CHAPTER

- Historically, bilinguals were regarded as having a relatively lower IQ than monolinguals.
- Research on the relationship between intelligence and bilingualism has moved from a period of investigating 'detrimental effects' to a current focus on the additive effects given by bilingualism.
- The ownership of two languages does not interfere with efficient thinking. On the contrary bilinguals who have two well developed languages tend to share cognitive advantages.
- Bilinguals have advantages on certain thinking dimensions, particularly in divergent thinking, creativity, early metalinguistic awareness and communicative sensitivity. There are likely to be many other cognitive skills on which there are no real differences between bilinguals and monolinguals
- Research on the metalinguistic advantages of bilinguals is strong, and suggests bilinguals are aware of their languages at an early age, separating form from meaning, and having reading readiness earlier than monolinguals.

SUGGESTED FURTHER READING

BAKER, C. & JONES, S.P., 1998, *The Encyclopedia of Bilingualism and Bilingual Education*. Clevedon: Multilingual Matters.
BIALYSTOK, E., 2001, *Bilingualism in Development: Language, Literacy and Cognition*. Cambridge: Cambridge University Press.

BIALYSTOK, E., CRAIK, F.I., KLEIN, R. & VISWANATHAN, M., 2004, Bilingualism, aging, and cognitive control: Evidence from the Simon Task. *Psychology and Aging*, 19, 2, 290–303.

PARADIS, M., 2004, *A Neurolinguistic Theory of Bilingualism*. Amsterdam/Philadelphia: John Benjamins.

PAVLENKO, A., 2005, Bilingualism and thought. In A. DE GROOT & J. KROLL (eds), *Handbook of Bilingualism: Psycholinguistic Approaches*. Oxford: Oxford University Press.

See also two journals for the most recent research in this area: (a) *International Journal of Bilingualism* and (b) *Bilingualism: Language and Cognition*.

STUDY ACTIVITIES

(1)   Find one or more examples of an IQ test. Examine the content of the test and locate any items which you think will be unfair to bilinguals in your region. Examine both the language and the cultural content of the IQ test.

(2)   Find a student or a teacher who you consider to be bilingual. Ask them to talk about the relationship between their bilingualism and thinking. Ask them if they feel it gives them any advantages and any disadvantages. Collect from them examples and illustrations.

(3)   Using one of the tests or experiments mentioned in this chapter, select a student (or a group of students) and give them that test. For example, ask them how many uses they can think of for a brick or for a cardboard box. Compare the answers of those who are more and less bilingual and see if there are differences in quality and quantity of answers.

Cognitive Theories of Bilingualism and the Curriculum

CHAPTER 8

Cognitive Theories of Bilingualism and the Curriculum

INTRODUCTION

The previous chapter examined the relationship between bilingualism and cognition. The discussion was primarily based on research findings and culminated in explanations of the likely positive relationship between bilingualism and thinking processes and products. This chapter extends that discussion of explanations by firstly considering a 'naive' theory of language and cognitive functioning; then, secondly, examining the development of a major and dominating theory of bilingualism and cognition. The culmination of the chapter is a discussion of how this evolved theory has direct curriculum implications.

THE BALANCE THEORY

The previous chapter noted that initial research into bilingualism and cognitive functioning and into bilingualism and educational attainment often found bilinguals to be inferior to monolinguals. This connects with a naive theory of bilingualism that represents the two languages as existing together in **balance**. The picture is of weighing scales, with a second language increasing at the expense of the first language. An alternative naive picture-theory attached to the early research is of **two language balloons** inside the head. The picture portrays the monolingual as having one well filled balloon. The bilingual is pictured as having two less filled or half filled balloons. As the second language balloon is pumped higher (e.g. English in the US), so the first language balloon (e.g. Spanish) diminishes in size, leading to confusion, frustration and failure.

The balance and balloon picture theories of bilingualism and cognition appear to be held intuitively by many people. Many parents and teachers, politicians and

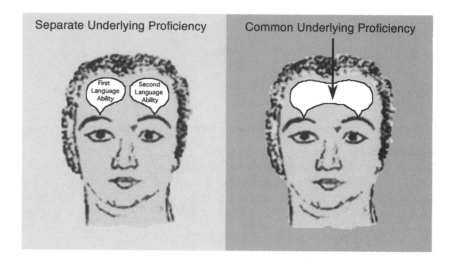

large sections of the public appear to latently, subconsciously take the balloon picture as the one that best represents bilingual functioning. Cummins (1980a) termed this the **Separate Underlying Proficiency Model of Bilingualism**. This model conceives of the two languages operating separately without transfer and with a restricted amount of 'room' for languages. As Bialystok (2001a, p. 59) argues: 'nothing we know about memory substantiates these fears. Indeed, the fact that millions of children routinely grow up with more than one language in their environment and appear to suffer no obvious trauma should allay the concerns of most parents'.

What appears logical is not always psychologically valid. While both the balance or balloon ideas are plausible, neither fits the evidence. As the previous chapter concluded, when children become relatively balanced bilinguals, the evidence suggests that there are cognitive advantages rather than disadvantages for being bilingual. Similarly, chapters 11 and 12 will show that certain types of bilingual education (e.g. early total immersion and heritage language bilingual education) appear to result in performance advantages (e.g. in two languages and in general curriculum performance) compared with submersion or monolingual education.

Research has also suggested that it is wrong to assume that the brain has only a limited amount of room for language skills, such that monolingualism is preferable (see chapter 7). There appears to be enough cerebral living quarters not only for two languages, but for other languages as well. The picture of the weighing scales, of one language increasing at the expense the second language, does not fit the data. Other pictures, provided later in this chapter, better encapsulate research findings.

There is another fallacy with the balance or balloon theory. The assumption of this theory is that the first and second language are kept apart in two 'balloons' inside the head. The evidence suggests the opposite – that language attributes are not separated in the cognitive system, but transfer readily and are interactive. For example, when school lessons are through the medium of Spanish, they do not solely feed a Spanish part of the brain. Or when other lessons are in English, they do not only feed the English part of the brain. Rather concepts learnt in one language can readily transfer into the other language. Teaching a child to multiply numbers in Spanish or use a dictionary in English easily transfers to multiplication or dictionary use in the other language. A child does not have to be re-taught to multiply numbers in English. A mathematical concept can be easily and immediately used in English or Spanish if those languages are sufficiently well developed. Such easy exchange leads to an alternative idea called **Common Underlying Proficiency** (Cummins, 1980a, 1981a).

THE ICEBERG ANALOGY

Cummins' (1980a, 1981a) **Common Underlying Proficiency model** of bilingualism can be pictorially represented in the form of two icebergs (see below). The two icebergs are separate above the surface. That is, two languages are visibly different in outward conversation. Underneath the surface, the two icebergs are fused so that the two languages do not function separately. Both languages operate through the same central processing system.

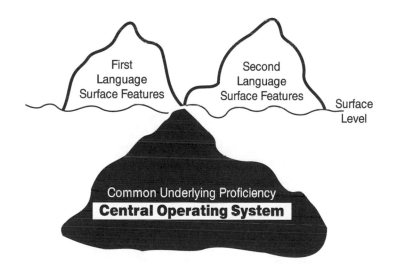

The **Common Underlying Proficiency** model of bilingualism may be summarized in six parts:

(1) Irrespective of the language in which a person is operating, the thoughts that accompany talking, reading, writing and listening come from the **same central engine**. When a person owns two or more languages, there is one integrated source of thought.

(2) Bilingualism and multilingualism are possible because people have the **capacity to store** two or more languages. People can also function in two or more languages with ease.

(3) Information processing skills and educational attainment may be developed through **two languages** as well as through one language. Cognitive functioning and school achievement may be fed through one monolingual channel or equally successfully through two well developed language channels. Both channels feed the same central processor.

(4) The language the child is using in the classroom needs to be sufficiently **well developed** to be able to process the cognitive challenges of the classroom.

(5) Speaking, listening, reading or writing in the first or the second language helps the whole cognitive system to develop. However, if children are made to operate in an **insufficiently developed** second language (e.g. in a 'submersion' classroom – see chapter 10), the system will not function at its best. If children are made to operate in the classroom in a poorly developed second language, the quality and quantity of what they learn from complex curriculum materials and produce in oral and written form may be relatively weak and impoverished. This was the experience of some Finns in Swedish schools operating in Swedish (Skutnabb-Kangas & Toukomaa, 1976). Such children tended to perform poorly in the curriculum in both Finnish and Swedish because both languages were insufficiently developed to cope with relatively complex curriculum material.

(6) When one or both languages are **not functioning fully** (e.g. because of pressure to replace the home language with the majority language), cognitive functioning and academic performance may be negatively affected.

The distinction between Separate Underlying Proficiency (SUP) and Common Underlying Proficiency models of bilingualism (CUP) does not fully sum up the findings from research on cognitive functioning and bilingualism. For example, the continuing debate on the Sapir-Whorf hypothesis (e.g. that different languages intrinsically lead to different views of the world) challenges the idea that bilinguals have one integrated source of thought (Pavlenko, 2005a). Language influences both the content and process of thinking. Thus varied languages can influence thought differently through their structure and particularly through their customary discourse, concepts and meanings. If this is so, second language learning may augment and enhance a person's understandings, views and ideas. It may offer alternative and extra meanings. The extent to which bilinguals change their thinking when changing languages is complex without a simple 'black or white' answer (see Pavlenko, 2005a). Translation of meaning can occur across languages, yet some enduring **relativity** within a language seems also to occur.

THE THRESHOLDS THEORY

Many studies have suggested that the further the child moves towards balanced bilingualism, the greater the likelihood of cognitive advantages (e.g. Cummins &

Mulcahy, 1978; Duncan & de Avila, 1979; Kessler & Quinn, 1982; Dawe, 1982, 1983; Clarkson, 1992; Cummins, 2000b; Bialystok, 2001a). Thus the question has become 'Under what conditions does bilingualism have positive, neutral and negative effects on cognition?' How far does someone have to travel up the two language ladders to obtain cognitive advantages from bilingualism?

One theory that partially summarizes the relationship between cognition and degree of bilingualism is called the **Thresholds Theory**. This was first postulated by Toukomaa and Skutnabb-Kangas (1977) and by Cummins (1976). They suggested that the research on cognition and bilingualism is best explained by the idea of two thresholds. Each threshold is a level of language competence that has consequences for a child. The first threshold is a level for a child to reach to avoid the negative consequences of bilingualism. The second threshold is a level required to experience the possible positive benefits of bilingualism. Such a theory therefore limits which children will be likely to obtain cognitive benefits from bilingualism. It also suggests that there are children who may derive detrimental consequences from their bilingualism.

The Thresholds Theory may be portrayed in terms of a house with three floors (see the following diagram). Up the sides of the house are placed two language ladders, indicating that a bilingual child will usually be moving upward and will not usually be stationary on a floor. On the **bottom floor** of the house will be those whose current competence in both their languages is insufficiently or relatively inadequately developed, especially compared with their age group. When there is a low level of competence in both languages, there may be negative or detrimental cognitive effects. For example, a child who is unable to cope in the classroom in either language may suffer educationally. At the **middle level**, the second floor of the house, will be those with age-appropriate competence in one of their languages but not in both. For example, children who can operate in the classroom in one of their languages but not in their second language may reside in this second level. At this level, a partly-bilingual child will be little different in cognition from the monolingual child and is unlikely to have any significant positive or negative cognitive differences compared with a monolingual. At the top of the house, the **third floor**, there resides children who approximate 'balanced' bilinguals. At this level, children will have age-appropriate competence in two or more languages. For example, they can cope with curriculum material in either of their languages. It is at this level that the positive cognitive advantages of bilingualism may appear. When a child has age-appropriate ability in both their languages, they may have cognitive advantages over monolinguals.

Research support for the **Thresholds Theory** comes, for example, from Bialystok (1988), Clarkson and Galbraith (1992), Clarkson (1992), Dawe (1983) and Cummins (2000b). Dawe's (1983) study examined bilingual Panjabi, Mirpuri and Jamaican children aged 11 to 13. On tests of deductive mathematical reasoning, Dawe (1983) found evidence for both the lower and the higher threshold. As competency in two languages increased, so did deductive reasoning skills in mathematics. Limited competence in both languages appeared to result in negative cognitive outcomes.

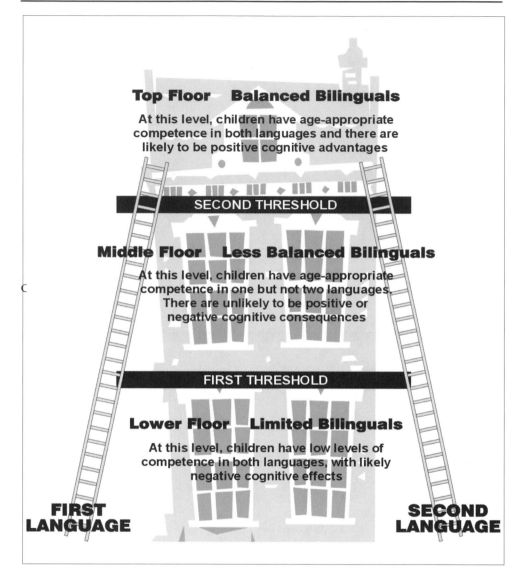

Bialystok (1988) examined two aspects of metalinguistic awareness (analysis of linguistic knowledge and control of linguistic processing) in six- to seven-year-old monolingual, partial bilingual and fluently French–English children. She found that 'the level of bilingualism is decisive in determining the effect it will have on development' (p. 567).

The Thresholds Theory relates not only to cognition but also to **education**. With children in Immersion Education (e.g. in Canada – see chapters 11 and 12), there is usually a temporary lag in achievement when the curriculum is taught through the second language. Until the second language (e.g. French) has developed well enough to cope with curriculum material, a temporary delay may be expected. Once French is developed sufficiently to cope with the conceptual tasks of the classroom, Immersion Education is unlikely to have detrimental achievement consequences for children. Indeed, such an immersion experience seems to enable children to reach the third floor of the house, with resulting positive cognitive advantages (Cummins, 2000b).

The Thresholds Theory also helps to summarize why minority language children taught through a second language (e.g. immigrants in the US) sometimes fail to develop sufficient competency in their second language (e.g. English) and fail to benefit from 'weak' forms of bilingual education (see chapter 10). Their **low level of proficiency** in English, for example, limits their ability to cope with the curriculum. Therefore Dual Language programs, that allow a child to operate in their more developed home language, can result in superior performance compared with submersion and transitional bilingual education (see chapter 10).

A **problem** with the Thresholds Theory is in precisely defining the level of language proficiency a child must obtain in order, firstly to avoid the negative effects of bilingualism, and secondly, to obtain the positive advantages of bilingualism. At what language 'height' the ceilings become floors is not clear. Indeed, the danger may be in constructing artificial 'critical stages' or levels, when transition is gradual and smooth. This point is returned to in the following section.

THE EVOLUTION OF THE THRESHOLDS THEORY

From out of the Thresholds Theory developed a succession of more refined theories of bilingualism. The first evolution of the Thresholds Theory considered the relationship between a bilingual's two languages. To this end, Cummins (1978, 2000a, 2000b) outlined the language **Developmental Interdependence hypothesis**.

This hypothesis suggests that a child's second language competence is partly dependent on the level of competence already achieved in the first language. The more developed the first language, the easier it will be to develop the second language. When the first language is at a low stage of evolution, it is more difficult to achieve bilingualism. Huguet *et al.* (2000) found that the Linguistic Developmental Interdependence hypothesis was supported in research on the language competence of Spanish/Catalan speakers of varying balance. For example, those 12-year-old students who knew more Catalan also knew more Spanish, and vice versa. Similarly, in research on 952 Miami, Florida, students in Dual Language and English Immersion schools, it was found that this hypothesis helped explain the reading and writing results (see Oller & Eilers, 2002). For example, 'children did not tend to excel in one language at the expense of the other' (Cobo-Lewis *et al.*, 2002, p. 120) and there appeared to be a positive transfer of skills and concepts from one language to another. Proctor's (2003) sophisticated analysis of data Spanish / English 4th grade data from Boston, Chicago and El Paso showed that students with well-developed Spanish and English vocabularies outperformed their less bilingual (e.g. Spanish dominant, English dominant) counterparts in English reading achievement. Such findings also appear to hold for learning a third language (Errasti, 2003; Cenoz, 2003).

Alongside this, there developed a distinction between surface fluency and the more evolved language skills required to benefit from the education process (Cummins, 1984a). This was partly a reaction against Oller (1979) who claimed that language proficiency differences between individuals were located on just one dimension (see chapter 1). Cummins (1979) found that everyday conversational language could be acquired in two years while the more complex language abilities needed to cope with the curriculum could take five to seven or more years to develop. In California, Hakuta *et al.* (2000) found that English oral proficiency takes three to five years to develop, while academic English proficiency can take **four to seven years**. This makes calls for English immersion schooling for immigrants (see chapters 9 to 13), where children are expected to acquire English in just one year, unrealistic and damaging.

Simple communication skills (e.g. holding a simple conversation with a shop-keeper) may hide a child's relative inadequacy in the language proficiency necessary to meet the cognitive and academic demands of the classroom. The language used when playing with a ball in the school playground is very different from 'calculate, using a protractor, the obtuse angle of the parallelogram and then construct a diagonal line between the two obtuse angles and investigate if this creates congruent triangles'. Teaching **mathematics**, for example, in multilingual classrooms requires particular care with language (Adler, 2001; Barwell, 2002, 2005a, 2005b; Frederickson & Cline, 2002; Leung, 2005). The mathematical use of words such as adjacent, difference, mean, opposite, base, chord, even, odd, angle, parallel, power, product, prime, root, similar, solid, table, takeaway, times and value all differ from vernacular usage. mathematics problems are often word problems. Children may need to negotiate each other's mathematics language (e.g. altogether, share, each, disappear, joined, extra, times, left – see Barwell, 2002). Frederickson and Cline (2002) also suggest that, particularly for those being taught in their second language (e.g. English), it is 'not just the vocabulary of maths that causes difficulty. The syntax in which mathematical ideas are expressed is often more complex than children are accustomed to in other areas of the curriculum' (p. 347).

Cummins (1984a, 1984b, 2000b) expressed this distinction in terms of **basic interpersonal communicative skills (BICS)** and **cognitive/academic language proficiency (CALP)**. BICS is said to occur when there are contextual supports and props for language delivery. Face-to-face '**context embedded**' situations provide, for example, non-verbal support to secure understanding. Actions with eyes and hands, instant feedback, cues and clues support verbal language. CALP, on the other hand, is said to occur in **context reduced** academic situations. Where higher order thinking skills (e.g. analysis, synthesis, evaluation) are required in the curriculum, language is '**disembedded**' from a meaningful, supportive context. Where language is 'disembedded', the situation is often referred to as '**context reduced**'.

The distinction between BICS and CALP is aided by an image of an iceberg (see

Cummins, 1984b). Above the surface are BICS language skills such as comprehension and speaking. Underneath the surface are the CALP skills of analysis and synthesis. Thus, above the surface are the basic language skills of pronunciation, vocabulary and grammar. Below the surface are the deeper, subtle language skills of meanings and creative composition.

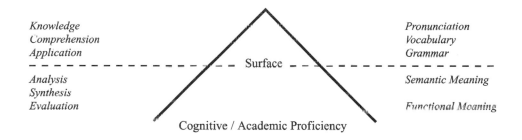

Knowledge		Pronunciation
Comprehension		Vocabulary
Application		Grammar

‑ ‑ ‑ ‑ ‑ ‑ ‑ ‑ ‑ ‑ ‑ ‑ ‑ Surface ‑ ‑ ‑ ‑ ‑ ‑ ‑ ‑ ‑ ‑ ‑ ‑ ‑ ‑ ‑

Analysis — *Semantic Meaning*
Synthesis
Evaluation — *Functional Meaning*

Cognitive / Academic Proficiency

The BICS/CALP distinction has been influential and valuable for policy and practice. It was never intended as contextually universal, a complete theory, or to indicate when second language reading (e.g. English in the US) or cognitively challenging content instruction in English should be introduced. Indeed, the conceptual distinction has been unfairly criticized for the absence of many components it was never intended to contain (see Cummins, 2000a, 2000b). However, before leaving this BICS/CALP distinction, it is important to declare its boundaries and limitations (see Wiley, 1996a, 2005c; MacSwan & Rolstad, 2003).

(1) The distinction between BICS and CALP has intuitive appeal and does appear to fit the case of children who are seemingly fluent in their second language, yet cannot cope in the curriculum in that language. However, it only paints a two-stage idea. A large number of dimensions of language competences exist (see chapter 1). Children and adults may move forward on language dimensions in terms of sliding scales rather than in big jumps. Such development is like gradually increasing in language competence analogous to increasing gradually the volume on a television set. A bilingual's language competences are evolving, dynamic, interacting and intricate. They are not simple dichotomies, easily compartmentalized and static.

(2) The BICS/CALP distinction enabled an understanding and explanation of previous research (e.g. Wong Fillmore, 1979; Snow & Hoefnagel-Höhle, 1978; Cummins, 1984b, 2000b). However, Martin-Jones and Romaine (1986) express doubts about testing the distinction. The distinction between BICS and CALP does not indicate how the two ideas may be precisely defined and accurately tested. Thus the distinction becomes difficult to operationalize in research.

(3) Terms such as BICS and CALP tend to be imprecise and become over-compartmentalized, simplified and misused. These hypothetical terms may

unwittingly be regarded as real entities. Such terms may be used to label and stereotype students, especially if BICS is seen as inferior to CALP (Wiley, 1996a, 2005c).

(4) The relationship between language development and cognitive development is not unequivocal or simple. It is not simply a case of one growing as a direct result of the other. Cognitive and linguistic acquisition exist in a relationship that is influenced by various other factors (e.g. politics, power relationships, social practices, culture, context, motivation, school, home and community effects). Language proficiency relates to an individual's total environment, not just to cognitive skills.

(5) The sequential nature of BICS first and then CALP is a typical route for immigrant children learning a second language. However, the order is not absolute. Occasionally there will be exceptions (e.g. a scholar who reads a language for research purposes but does not speak that language).

(6) CALP may relate to an ability to perform well on school tests (test-wisdom). This relates to specific, traditional, school-based literacy practices. Such practices favor the middle-class groups that control institutions. Such tests favor 'standard' academic language with a bias against speakers of dialects, Creoles and non-standard language (e.g. Black English). MacSwan and Rolstad (2003) argue that the theory gives special status to educated, middle class language styles and hence belittles working class oral language styles. This hides a deficit view of language that stigmatizes non-academic language. This was certainly not Cummins' intention (Baker & Hornberger, 2001) and given that this theory has persuaded many educators not to prematurely mainstream English language learners especially in the US, the theory has not had this effect. However, MacSwan & Rolstad (2003) introduce the term SLIC: second language instructional competence that refines terminology.

(7) Oral language and interpersonal communication is not necessarily less cognitively demanding than literate academic language. For example, careful logic, metaphor and other abstract aspects of language occur in face-to-face communication and not just in written language.

(8) School-based academic/cognitive language does not represent universal higher-order cognitive skills nor all forms of literacy practice. Different sociocultural contexts have different expectations and perceived patterns of appropriateness in language and thinking such that a school is only one specific context for 'higher order' language production.

The distinction between BICS and CALP helps explain the relative failure within the educational system of many minority language children. For example, in the United States, various programs (see chapter 10) aim to give language minority students sufficient English language skills to enable them to converse with peers and teachers and to operate in the curriculum. Having achieved surface fluency, they may be transferred to regular classes. The transfer occurs because children appear to have sufficient language competence (BICS) to cope in mainstream education. Cummins' (1984a) distinction between BICS and CALP explains why such children tend to fail when mainstreamed. Their cognitive academic language proficiency is not developed enough to cope with the demands of the curriculum. What Cummins (1984a) regards as essential in the bilingual education of children is that the 'common underlying proficiency' be well developed. That is, a child's language-cognitive abilities need to be sufficiently well developed to cope with the curriculum processes of the classroom. This underlying ability could be developed in the first or the second language, but also in both languages simultaneously.

Cummins (2000a, 2000b) has extended the instructional implications of CALP in terms of three components: Cognitive, Academic and Language.

Cognitive: instruction should be cognitively challenging using higher order thinking skills such as evaluating, inferring, generalizing and classifying.

Academic: curriculum content should be integrated with language instruction so that students learn the language of specific academic areas.

Language: critical language awareness should be developed both linguistically (e.g. conventions of each language) and socioculturally/sociopolitically (e.g. different status and power with languages, language use).

A further development of this theory proposed two dimensions (Cummins, 1981b, 1983b, 1984b). This theory is represented in the diagram below:

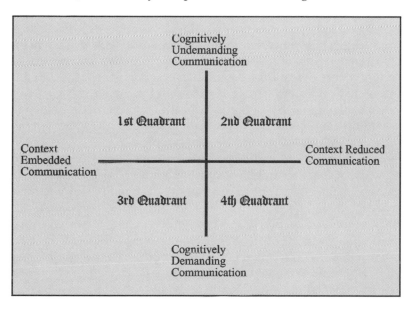

Both dimensions concern communicative proficiency. The **first dimension** refers to the amount of contextual support available to a student. **Context embedded communication** exists when there is a good degree of support in communication, particularly via body language. For example, by pointing to objects, using the eyes, head nods, hand gestures and intonation, people give and receive plenty of clues and cues to help the content of the message to be understood.

An example of context embedded communication would be when two children who are hardly able to use each other's languages seem able to communicate quite well by gestures, non-verbal reinforcements and bodily movements. It is not infrequent to see two young children of different languages playing together without difficulty. In **context reduced communication** there will be very few cues to the meaning that is being transmitted. The words of the sentence exist almost alone in conveying the meaning. An example of context reduced communication is often the classroom where the meaning is restricted to words, with a subtlety and precision of meanings in the vocabulary of the teacher or the book.

The **second dimension** is the level of cognitive demands required in communication. **Cognitively demanding communication** may occur in a classroom where much information at a challenging level needs processing quickly. **Cognitively undemanding communication** is where a person has the mastery of language skills sufficient to enable easy communication. An example would be having a conversation in the street, shop, or stadium, where the processing of information is relatively simple and straightforward.

Surface fluency or basic interpersonal communication skills will fit into the first quadrant (see diagram). That is, BICS (basic interpersonal communication skills) is context embedded, cognitively undemanding use of a language. Language that is cognitively and academically more advanced (CALP) fits into the fourth quadrant (context reduced and cognitively demanding). Cummins' (1981b) theory suggests that second language competency in the first quadrant (surface fluency) develops relatively independently of *first* language surface fluency. In comparison, context reduced, cognitively demanding communication develops inter-dependently and can be promoted by either language or by both languages in an interactive way. Thus, the theory suggests that bilingual education will be successful when children have enough first or second language proficiency to work in the context reduced, cognitively demanding situation of the classroom.

The quadrants can act as a guide for **instructional planning**. A teacher valuably takes into account students' linguistic development and experience, as well as their understanding of the topic. Then the teacher can create activities or experiences that are cognitively challenging and contextually supported as needed. This will be exemplified in the next section of this chapter.

For Cummins (1981b, 2000b) it often takes one or more years for a child to acquire context-embedded second language fluency, but five to seven years or more to acquire context-reduced fluency. This is illustrated in the graphs on the following page. Research by Hakuta and D'Andrea (1992) with Mexican-Americans found that 'English proficiency reaches asymptotic performance after about eight years. This corresponds quite well with the figures of five to seven years required for attainment of the full range of second language acquisition as estimated by Cummins (1984a) based on a heterogeneous L1 population in Canada' (p. 96). In the San Francisco Bay Area, Hakuta *et al.* (2000) found that social English takes three to five years to develop, while academic English can take four to seven years. Collier (1989, 1992) suggests that as many as ten years are needed to catch–up on academic

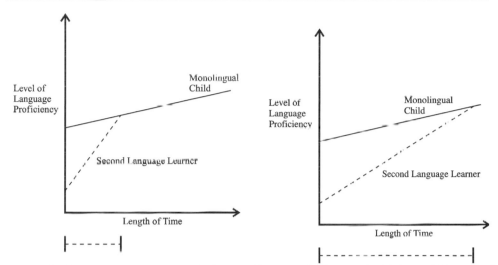

It takes approximately **two years** for the second language learner to reach the same level of proficiency as a monolingual in **context embedded** language proficiency

It takes approximately **five to eight years** for the second language learner to reach the same level of proficiency as the monolingual in **context reduced** language proficiency

language abilities. Shohamy (1999) found that seven to nine years are needed for heterogeneous immigrant students in Israel to catch-up with native speakers in Hebrew literacy. Such native-speakers are not standing still in language development. The immigrants are chasing a moving target.

Spada and Lightbown (2002) found failure among Inuit students in northern Quebec because they experience a transition from their home language (used in Kindergarten to Grade 2) to education almost solely in French or English. This results in many students working in classrooms where the cognitively demanding language is beyond their grasp. This was continued from elementary to secondary school, with particularly severe problems at High school level with its needs for more abstract academic language. The lack of **age-appropriate** French language ability is regarded as the principal cause of academic failure.

Children with some conversational ability in their second language may falsely appear ready to be taught through their second language in a classroom. Cummins's (1981b) theory suggests that children operating at the context embedded level in the language of the classroom may fail to understand the content of the curriculum and fail to engage in the higher order cognitive processes of the classroom, such as synthesis, discussion, analysis, evaluation and interpretation.

This two-dimensional model helps explain various research findings:

(1) In the **United States**, language minority children sometimes move from being classified as LEP (Limited English Proficiency) or EL (English Learners) to FEP (Fluent English Proficient) as soon as their conversational ability in English seems sufficient (Linquanti, 2001). Such students then frequently perform

poorly. The theory suggests that this is due to their not having the developed ability in 'curriculum' or 'grade level' English (or their home language) to operate in an environment that is more cognitively and academically demanding. Linquanti (2001) suggests that a common notion among US politicians, policymakers and educators is that ' students only need to learn English and their academic achievement will naturally follow' (p. 6). Reclassification too quickly and prematurely to FEP may put language minority students at academic risk as language supports are withdrawn.

(2)   Immersion students in **Canada** tend to lag behind their monolingual peers for a short period. Once they acquire second language proficiency sufficient to operate in a cognitively demanding and context reduced environment, they usually catch up with their peers.

(3)   Experiments in the United States, Canada and Europe with minority language children who are allowed to use their minority language for part or much of their elementary schooling show that such children do not experience retardation in school achievement or in majority language proficiency. Through their minority language, they develop the ability to be relatively successful in the cognitively demanding and context reduced classroom environment (Secada, 1991). This ability then **transfers** to the majority language when that language is sufficiently well developed. Children learning to read in their home language are not just developing home language skills. They are also developing higher order cognitive and linguistic skills that will help with the future development of reading in the majority language as well as with general intellectual development. As Cummins (1984a) noted, 'transfer is much more likely to occur from minority to majority language because of the greater exposure to literacy in the majority language and the strong social pressure to learn it' (p. 143).

CURRICULUM RELEVANCE

What a student brings to the classroom in terms of previous learning is a crucial starting point for the teacher. A student's reservoir of knowledge, understanding and experience can provide a meaningful context on which the teacher can build (Robson, 1995). For example, there will be occasions when a student will learn more from a story read by the teacher than listening to a language tape. When the teacher dramatizes a story by adding gestures, pictures, facial expressions and other acting skills, the story becomes more context-embedded than listening to a tape cassette. Getting a student to talk about something familiar will be cognitively less demanding than talking about something culturally or academically unfamiliar. This means that any curriculum task presented to the student needs considering for the following points:

- what the task requires of the child; the cognitive demands inherent in the task (as found by an individual child); the 'entry skills' that a task necessitates. This is illustrated below;

- form of presentation to the child (degree of context embeddedness or context reduction); what form of presentation will be meaningful to the child; use of visual aids, demonstration, modeling, computers, oral and written instructions; amount of teacher assistance. This is extended in Mohan's (2001) Knowledge Framework and exemplified in Tang (2001);
- the child's language proficiencies;
- the child's previous cultural and educational experience and knowledge, individual learning style and learning strategies; expectations and attitudes, confidence and initiative; the child's familiarity with the type of task;
- what is acceptable as evidence that learning has successfully occurred; what constitutes mastery or a sufficient approximation; an appropriate form of 'formative' and 'summative' assessment (see chapters 2 and 15) that may be gestural, action (e.g. building a model), drawing, oral or written (Robson, 1995);

Cognitively undemanding

Context embedded	Greeting someone	Recites nursery rhymes	Context reduced
	Talking about today's weather	Listens to a story or poem	
	Tells their own stories	Describes a story on TV	
	Describes what they have just seen	Copies information from a screen or text	
	Compares and contrasts	Reflects on feelings	
	Summarizes	Argues a case	
	Recalls and reviews	Sustains and justifies an opinion	
	Solution seeking to problems		
	Explains and justifies	Evaluates and analyzes critically	
	Role play	Interprets evidence	
		Applies principles to a new situation	

Cognitively demanding

A simple example of using the two dimensions to produce an appropriate **teaching strategy** is now presented (see Frederickson & Cline, 1990, 2002; Cline & Frederickson, 1995, 1996; Hall *et al.*, 2001, plus Sjöholm, 2004, for an example in a trilingual context).

A teacher wants a group to learn how to measure height and to understand the concept of height. Listed below are a few of the teaching strategies for teaching about height. Following the list is a diagram placing the four strategies on the two dimensions:

- One-to-one, individual teaching using various objects to measure height (1).
- A demonstration from the front of the room by the teacher using various objects (2).
- Teacher giving oral instructions without objects (3).
- Reading instructions from a work card without pictures (4).

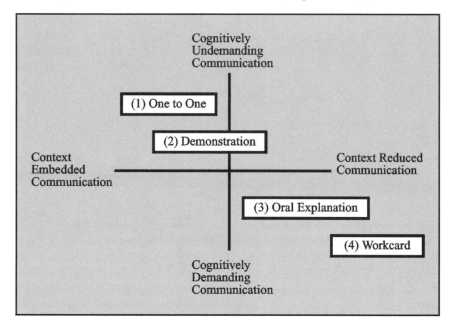

As the diagram indicates, the example of teaching height can be analyzed in terms of the two dimensions. One-to-one individual teaching will fit somewhere in the context embedded, cognitively undemanding quadrant. Using work cards may be closer to the context reduced, cognitively demanding area. Demonstrations and oral explanations appear on the diagonal from 'top left' to 'bottom right', in-between individual teaching and work cards. The exact location of teaching approaches on the graph will vary according to teacher, topic, learner and lesson. The example illustrates that the two dimensions can be a valuable way of examining teaching approaches with bilingual children. The dimensions are also useful for analyzing appropriate methods of **classroom assessment**. The dimensions may help focus on task-related curriculum assessment that is more fair and appropriate to bilingual children than norm referenced testing. A teacher wanting to check progress on measuring height has a choice, for example:

- **observing** a child measure the height of a new object (1);
- asking the child to give a **commentary** while measuring a new object (2);
- asking the child to provide a **write-up** of the process (3);
- **discussing** in an abstract way the concept of height (4).

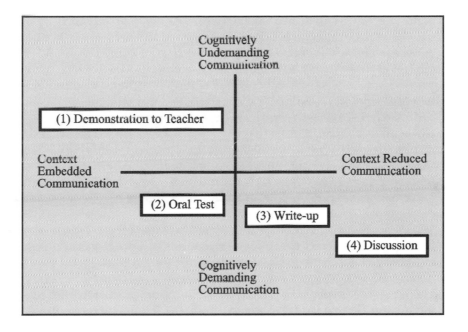

In plotting these four methods of assessment (see diagram), placement on the graph will vary with different kinds of tasks and testing procedures. All four quadrants can be 'filled' depending on the student, teacher, topic and test. There is also value in comparing the two graphs presented here. The teaching and learning approach taken may well influence the form of assessment. That is, if a context embedded, cognitively undemanding learning strategy is used with a child, assessment may be on similar lines (e.g. observation of child activity). Equally, a context reduced, cognitively demanding learning strategy suggests a 'matched' method of assessment (e.g. discussion).

CRITICISMS

There are criticisms of Cummins' (1981b) theory of the relationship between language and cognition (Edelsky *et al.*, 1983; Edelsky, 1991; Martin-Jones & Romaine, 1986; Rivera, 1984; Frederickson & Cline, 1990, 2002; Robson, 1995; Wiley,

1996a; MacSwan & Rolstad, 2003). A detailed rebuttal can be found can be found in Cummins (2000a, 2000b). The criticisms can be briefly summarized as follows:

(1)   Cummins's (1981b) early theory may artificially isolate certain ingredients in a bilingual's cognitive or classroom experience. The attainment of bilingualism or the relationship between bilingual education and school achievement rests on many other factors than are presented in this theory. The early theory was essentially individual and psychological. Socioeconomic class or socio-cultural differences as variables are not a element in the theory. Bilingualism and bilingual education need to consider other variables: cultural, social, political, community, teacher expectations and home factors. Each and all of these variables help explain bilingualism as an individual and societal phenomenon. Cummins (1986, 2000b) addressed these issues in further theoretical formulations.

(2)   Cummins's (1981b) criterion of educational success tended to center on dominant, middle-class indices of achievement. Thus language skills, literacy and formal educational achievement are highlighted. Alternative outcomes of schooling such as self-esteem, social and emotional development, divergent and creative thinking, long-term attitude to learning, employment and moral development were not initially considered.

(3)   The theory has been produced as a *post hoc* explanation of a variety of research findings. The theoretical framework requires direct empirical investigation and confirmation with replication across culture and country, time and educational tradition.

(4)   The labels used may create an over-simplification and a stereotyping of individual functioning and classroom processes. Essentially hypothetical and abstract, the labels may be adopted as concrete and real (see earlier in this chapter).

(5)   The two dimensions are not necessarily distinct, and may not best be represented by two maximally separated (90 degrees apart) axes. When applying Cummins' two dimensions to curriculum tasks, Frederickson and Cline (1990) found it . . .

> difficult to disentangle the 'cognitive' from the 'contextual'. In some cases, movement along the contextual dimensions has actually been represented on the model as a diagonal shift [on the diagram from top left to bottom right], as it was found in practice that making tasks or instructions more context embedded also made them somewhat less cognitively demanding. Similarly, changes in cognitive demand may result in tasks actually being presented with greater context embeddedness. (p. 26)

(6)   The dichotomy between de-contextualized and contextualized communication may be too simple as all communication appears in some kind of context. For example, teachers' use of the language in mathematics is classroom-based within a mathematics lesson.

(7)   When bilingual children appear to have learning difficulties, a teacher may decide to simplify tasks into smaller and more isolated steps. Such a strategy is

part of the behavioral objectives approach or a task analysis approach to the curriculum. It may sometimes result in a non-meaningful context to a curriculum task. By making the task context-reduced, the learning may become more difficult rather than easier.

(8)   Attempting to achieve context embeddedness in any curriculum situation requires empathic understanding of a child's cultural background which itself is dynamic and ever evolving. A danger lies in the teacher developing self-defeating stereotyped assumptions about a child's ethnic experience which may transmit low expectations.

(9)   The theory does not make allowances for a child's cognitive strategies in learning, nor their learning style.

CONCLUSION

Early and now discredited ideas of two languages within an individual are represented by two pictures. First, two languages as a balance; second, two languages operating as two separate balloons in the head. Such misconceptions can be replaced by pictures such as the dual iceberg and the three tiered house. Depending on language development in both languages, the cognitive functioning of an individual can be viewed as integrated, with easy transfer of concepts and knowledge between languages. Understanding and thinking will be affected by the contextual support that exists and the degree of cognitive demands in a task. Successful cognitive operations in the classroom will depend on matching curriculum tasks with language competences. Sensitivity to the need for contextual support and the cognitive demands of a classroom are important if an individual is to maximize learning in the curriculum.

KEY POINTS IN THE CHAPTER

- Two languages acting like a balance in the thinking quarters of a bilingual is incorrect. Instead the Common Underlying Proficiency model suggests that languages operate from the same central operating system.
- The Thresholds Theory suggests that bilinguals who have age-appropriate competence in both languages share cognitive advantages over monolinguals.
- There is a distinction between Basic Interpersonal Communicative Skills (BICS) that concern everyday, straightforward communication skills that are helped by contextual supports, and Cognitive/Academic Language Proficiency (CALP). CALP is the level of language required to understand academically demanding subject matter in a classroom. Such language is often abstract, without contextual supports such as gestures and the viewing of objects.
- On average, it takes about two years for a new immigrant to acquire Basic Interpersonal Communicative Skills in a second language, but five to eight

years to achieve Cognitive/Academic Language Proficiency in that second language.

SUGGESTED FURTHER READING

BAKER, C. & HORNBEGER, N.H. (eds), 2001, *Introductory Reader to the Writings of Jim Cummins*. Clevedon: Multilingual Matters.

CLINE, T. & FREDERICKSON, N. (eds), 1996, *Curriculum Related Assessment, Cummins and Bilingual Children*. Clevedon: Multilingual Matters.

CUMMINS, J., 2000, *Language, Power and Pedagogy: Bilingual Children in the Crossfire*. Clevedon: Multilingual Matters.

FREDERICKSON, N. & CLINE, T., 2002, *Special Educational Needs, Inclusion and Diversity: A Textbook*. Buckingham (UK): Open University Press.

VALDÉS, G., 2004, Between support and marginalisation: The development of academic language in linguistic minority children. *International Journal of Bilingual Education and Bilingualism*, 7, 2&3, 102–132.

WILEY, T.G., 2005, *Literacy and Language Diversity in the United States* (2nd edn). Center for Applied Linguistics and Delta Systems, McHenry, Illinois.

STUDY ACTIVITIES

(1) Observe a classroom with bilingual children. Make a 10 minute cassette tape of the discourse between the teacher and various students, and/or between students themselves. Use the concepts and ideas of this chapter to describe and discuss the language used.

(2) Collect some language samples of the same student when working academically and when holding a simpler conversation (e.g. in the playground). What differences are noticeable? Does the student have any problems in understanding the language of the classroom? What does the teacher do to help students whose language proficiency may hinder them full understanding in the classroom?

(3) Visit a mathematics lesson where bilingual students are present. Listen and record math terms that may be difficult for the students (e.g. words such as adjacent, opposite, base, chord, even, odd, angle, power, prime, root, similar, table, takeaway and times, that differ from vernacular usage). Talk to the students and locate those terms that they find difficult to understand. Estimate if misunderstandings relate in any way to a difference between conversational and academic language.

CHAPTER 9

Historical Introduction to Bilingual Education: The United States

Introduction

A Short History of Bilingual Education in the United States

California and Proposition 227

The 'No Child Left Behind' 2001 Legislation

Current Statistics

The Achievement Gap Issue

Explanations of Underachievement in Bilinguals

Conclusion

CHAPTER 9

Historical Introduction to Bilingual Education: the United States

INTRODUCTION

One of the **illusions** about bilingual education is that it was a 20th century phenomenon. In the US it may appear that bilingual education was born in the 1960s. The Canadian bilingual education movement is often charted from an experimental kindergarten class set up in St Lambert, Montreal, in 1965. In Ireland, bilingual education is sometimes presented as a child of the Irish Free State of 1922. The story of bilingual education in Wales often starts in 1939 with the establishment of the first Welsh-medium elementary school. Despite these events, the historical origins of bilingual education lie well before the 20th century.

The illusion of bilingual education as a modern phenomenon is dangerous on two counts. **First**, it fails to recognize that bilingual education has existed in one form or another for 5000 years or more (Mackey, 1978). Bilingualism and multilingualism are 'a very early characteristic of human societies, and monolingualism a limitation induced by some forms of social change, cultural and ethnocentric developments' (E. Lewis, 1977, p. 22). E. Lewis (1977, 1981) discusses the history of bilingualism and bilingual education from the Ancient World through the Renaissance to the modern world. Second, there is a danger in isolating current bilingual education from its **historical roots**. In many countries (e.g. the US, Canada, England and Sweden), bilingual education must be linked to the historical context of immigration as well as political movements such as civil rights, equality of educational opportunity, affirmative action and melting pot (integrationist, assimilationist) policies. Bilingual education in Ireland and Wales can only be properly analyzed by the rise of nationalist demands for self-government and language rights movements (Jones & Martin-Jones, 2004). In Japan, language education policy has to be examined through movements from monolingual ideology to internationalism (Maher, 1997). McCarty (2004) provides an analysis of the history of language education policies in the US.

Bilingual education relates to debates about the fundamental purposes and aims of education in general: for individuals, communities, regions and nations. Bilingual education, while isolated as a concept in this chapter, is one component inside a wider social, economic, educational, cultural and political framework. As Paulston (1992, p. 80) observes: 'unless we try in some way to account for the socio-historical, cultural, and economic–political factors which lead to certain forms of bilingual education, we will never understand the consequences of that education'. The political context of bilingual education is considered in chapters 17 and 18. The history of bilingual education in the United States is now considered, with a particular emphasis on the dynamic and ever developing nature of bilingual education policy.

A SHORT HISTORY OF BILINGUAL EDUCATION IN THE UNITED STATES

In the United States, bilingual education has been determined partly by federal government and partly by state government, partly by local initiatives and partly by individuals (e.g. Proposition 227 in California – see later). There has been neither total centralization nor full devolution to states in bilingual education. Whilst states engage in much planning and policy-making, the federal government has exerted a powerful influence through funding, legislation and law.

Bilingual education in the United States has moved through constant change in the perspectives of politicians, administrators and educationalists that indicate underlying shifts in ideology, preference and practice (Andersson & Boyer, 1970; Crawford, 2004; E. Garcia, 2002; Kloss, 1977, 1998; Lyons, 1990; McCarty, 2004; Miguel, 2004; Ovando, 2003; Perlmann, 1990; Schlossman, 1983; Schmidt, 2000; Wiley, 2002).

Long before European immigrants arrived in the United States, the land contained many **native** (indigenous) languages. When the Italian, German, Dutch, French, Polish, Czech, Irish, Welsh and other immigrant groups arrived, there were already more than 300 separate (Native Indian) languages in the United States. The indigenous languages were not immediately colonized. Often led by Jesuits and Franciscans, the Catholic church sometimes taught through Spanish (also French and English) but often through a native language. Other missionaries (e.g. Dutch Reform, German Moravian) also instrumentally used indigenous languages to secure conversion to Christianity and for teaching (McCarty, 2004).

Immigrants brought with them a wide variety of languages and initially there was linguistic tolerance (McCarty, 2004). In the 18th and 19th centuries in the United States, up until the first World War, linguistic diversity was often accepted and the presence of different languages was frequently encouraged through religion, newspapers in different languages, and in both private and public schools.

There were exceptions to the acceptance of language diversity in this early period, such as Benjamin Franklin's anti-German stance in the 1750s, the Californian legislature mandating English-only instruction in 1855 and the ruthless language suppression policies of the Bureau of Indian Affairs in the 1880s (Crawford, 2004). The concepts of 'bilingualism' and 'language minorities' were not part of a major national consciousness about language in the 18th and 19th centuries. A high-profile and much-debated US language policy has not been present until recent years.

However, there were early, pioneering public and private examples of bilingual education in the United States as in the **German–English** schools in the mid 19th century. Set up by German communities in Ohio, Pennsylvania, Missouri, Minnesota, North and South Dakota and Wisconsin, bilingual as well as monolingual German education was accepted. Also, Scandinavian languages (e.g. Dutch, Danish), Italian and Polish were among the languages of instruction within ethnic based schools. This was not just a 19th century phenomenon as German-speaking Americans started schools using their mother tongue as early as 1694 in Philadelphia (Crawford, 2004).

This **openness to immigrant languages** in the latter half of the 19th century was partly motivated by competition for students between public and private schools. Other factors such as benevolent (or uninterested) school administrators, the isolation of schools in rural areas, and ethnic homogeneity within an area also enabled a permissive attitude to mother tongue and bilingual education before World War I.

In most large cities in the latter half of the 19th century, English monolingual education was the dominant pattern. However, in cities such as Cincinnati, Baltimore, Denver and San Francisco, dual language education was present. In some schools in Cincinnati, for example, half the day was spent learning through German and the other half of the curriculum was delivered through English.

At the turn of the 20th century, Italian and Jewish immigrants were mostly placed in English-medium mainstream schools. However, examples of **bilingual education** existed and were permitted. For example, some Polish immigrants in Chicago attended Catholic schools where a small amount of teaching was through the mother tongue. So long as policy was within the jurisdiction of local towns and districts, the language of instruction did not become an issue in educational provision.

In the first two decades of the 20th century, a **change** in attitude to bilingualism and bilingual education occurred in the United States. A variety of factors are linked to this change and a subsequent restriction of bilingual education.

- The **number of immigrants** increased dramatically around the turn of the 20th century. Classrooms in many public schools were filled with immigrants. This gave rise to fears of new foreigners, and a call for the integration, harmonization and assimilation of immigrants. Immigrants' lack of English language and English literacy was a source of social, political and economic concern. A demand for Americanization was made, with competence in English becoming associated with loyalty to the United States. The Nationality Act (1906) required immigrants to speak English to become naturalized Americans. The call for child literacy in English rather than child labor, socialization into a unified America rather than ethnic separation, along with increased centralized control, led to a belief in a common language for compulsory schooling.

- In 1919, the Americanization Department of the United States Bureau of Education adopted a resolution recommending 'all states to prescribe that all schools, private and public, be conducted in the English language and that instruction in the elementary classes of all schools be in English' (quoted in O. García, 1992). By 1923, 34 states had decreed that **English** must be the sole language of instruction in all elementary schools, public and private.
- A major influence on bilingual education in the United States came with the entry of the United States into the **First World War** in 1917. Anti-German feeling in the United States spread, with a consequent extra pressure for English monolingualism and a melting pot policy achieved through monolingual education. The German language was portrayed as a threat to the unity of Americanization. Linguistic diversity was replaced by linguistic intolerance. Schools became the tool for the socialization, assimilation and integration of diverse languages and cultures. Becoming an American meant the elimination of languages and cultures other than English from schools. An interest in learning foreign languages declined.

This period was not totally restrictive. In 1923, the US Supreme Court declared that a Nebraska state law prohibiting the teaching of a foreign language to elementary school students was unconstitutional under the Fourteenth Amendment. This case, known as *Meyer* v. *Nebraska* concerned a case against a teacher for teaching a Bible story in German to a 10-year-old child. The original Nebraska ruling was that such mother-tongue teaching cultivated ideas and attachments that were foreign to the best interests of the country. The Supreme Court, in overturning the Nebraska ruling, found that proficiency in a foreign language was 'not injurious to the health, morals, or understanding of the ordinary child'.

This **Supreme Court** finding did not, in essence, support bilingualism or bilingual education. The Court observed that the desire of a state legislature to foster a homogeneous people was 'easy to appreciate'. This theme is considered further in chapter 18 when integration and assimilation is considered.

In 1957, the Russians launched their Sputnik into space. For United States politicians and public, a period of soul-searching led to debates about the quality of US education, US scientific creativity and US competence to compete in an increasingly international world. Doubts arose about the hitherto over-riding concern with English as the melting-pot language, and a new consciousness was aroused about the need for foreign language instruction. In 1958, the **National Defense and Education Act** was passed, promoting foreign language learning in elementary schools, high schools and universities. This, in turn, helped to create a slightly more soul-searching attitude to languages other than English spoken among ethnic groups in the US.

In the United States in the 1960s, various other factors allowed a few opportunities to bring back bilingual education, albeit in a disparate, semi-isolated manner. This needs to be understood in the wider perspective of the **Civil Rights movement**, the struggle for the rights of African-Americans, and the call to establish general equality of opportunity (and equality of educational opportunity) for all people, irrespective of race, color or creed. The 1964 Civil Rights Act prohibited discrimination on the basis of color, race or national origin, and led to the establishment of the Office of Civil Rights. This Act symbolized a less negative attitude to ethnic groups, and possibilities for increased tolerance of ethnic languages, at least at the Federal level.

The restoration of bilingual education in the US in the second half of the 20th century is often regarded as starting in 1963, in one school in Florida. In 1963, **Cuban exiles** established the first modern dual language school (Coral Way Elementary School) in Dade County in South Florida. Believing they were only in exile for a short period, the educated, middle-class Cubans set up this Spanish–English bilingual school. The need to maintain their mother tongue of Spanish was aided by (1) highly trained professional teachers being ready to work in such schools, (2) the Cubans' plight as victims of a harsh Communist state, and (3) their expected temporary stay in the United States. Their unquestioned loyalty to United States' policies and democratic politics gained sympathy for the Cubans. Bilingual education in Dade County received both political support and funding (see chapter 11, also Baker & Jones, 1998).

While the re-establishment of bilingual schools in the US has benefited from the example and success of Coral Way Elementary School (Pellerano & Fradd, 1998), an understanding of bilingual education in the United States requires a grasp of legislation and lawsuits (Crawford, 2004; Hornberger *et al.*, 1999; Wiese & Garcia, 2001).

In 1967, a Texas Senator, Ralph Yarborough, introduced a **Bilingual Education Act** as an **amendment** of the **1965 Elementary and Secondary Education Act**. The legislation was designed to help mother tongue Spanish speakers who were seen as failing in the school system. **Enacted in 1968** as **Title VII of the Elementary and Secondary Education Act**, the Bilingual Education Act indicated that bilingual education programs were to be seen as part of federal educational policy (Wiese & Garcia, 2001). It authorized the use of federal funds for the education of speakers of languages other than English. It also undermined the English-only legislation still lawful in many states. The 1968 Bilingual Education Act also allocated funds for such minority language speakers while they shifted to working through English in the classroom. Since 1968, the Act was re-authorized in 1974,1978,1984,1988,1994 and 2001 (see Miguel, 2004, for details).

A landmark in United States' bilingual education was a lawsuit. A court case was brought on behalf of Chinese students against the San Francisco School District in 1970. The case concerned whether or not non-English speaking students received equal educational opportunities when instructed in a language they could not understand. The failure to provide bilingual education was alleged to violate both the equal protection clause of the 14th Amendment and Title VI of the Civil Rights Act of 1964. The case, known as *Lau versus Nichols*, was rejected by the federal district court and a court of appeals, but was accepted by the Supreme Court in 1974. The verdict outlawed English mainstreaming (often called 'submersion') programs for language minority children and resulted in nationwide 'Lau remedies'. The Supreme Court ruled that 'There is no equality of treatment merely by providing students with the same facilities, textbooks, teachers and curriculum; for students who do not understand English are effectively foreclosed from any meaningful education.'

The **Lau remedies** acknowledged that students not proficient in English needed help. Such remedies included classes in English as a Second Language, English tutoring and some form of bilingual education. The Lau remedies created some expansion in the use of minority languages in schools. However, the accent nationally was still on a temporary, transitional use of the home language for English language learners.

The Lau court case is symbolic of the dynamic and continuing contest to establish language rights in the US particularly through testing the law in the courtroom (Crawford, 2004; Lyons, 1990; Schmidt, 2000). However, the kind of bilingual education needed to achieve equality of educational opportunity for language minority children was not defined. Although the right to equal opportunity for language minorities was asserted, the means of achieving that right was not declared. Nevertheless, during this era, there was a modest growth in developmental maintenance bilingual education and ethnic community mother tongue schools (Fishman, 2006).

From the 1980s, there were moves against an emergence of a strong version of bilingual education in the US, particularly found in the rise of pressure groups such as English First and US English that sought to establish English monolingualism and cultural assimilation (consideration of such political movements is found in chapter 18). In recent decades in the US, bilingual education has become contentious, as will now be illustrated by examining recent legislative changes with respect to bilingual education in the United States.

We return to the 1968 Bilingual Education Act (Title VII and part of the Elementary and Secondary Education Act). This provided a compensatory 'poverty program' for the educationally disadvantaged among language minorities. It did not require schools to use a child's home language other than English. However, it did allow a few educators to bring 'home languages' into the classroom rather than exclude them. The **1974 amendments** to this **Bilingual Education Act** (see the chronology table on pp. 201 & 202) required schools receiving grants to include teaching in a student's home language and culture so as to allow the child to progress effectively through the educational system (Wiese & Garcia, 2001). Effective progress in student achievement could occur via the home language or via English. However, this gave rise to fierce debates about how much a student's native language should be used in school (Rhee, 1999). Some argued that it was essential to develop a child's speaking and literacy skills in their native language before English was introduced in a major way. Others argued that educational equality of opportunity could best be realized by teaching English as early as possible and assimilating language minority children into mainstream culture.

In **1978**, the United States Congress reauthorized Transitional Bilingual Education, allowing the native language to be used only to the extent necessary for a child to achieve competence in the English language. **Title VII funds** could not be used for Maintenance Bilingual Education programs. The **1984 and 1988 amendments** allowed increasing percentages of the funds available to be allocated to programs where a students' first language was not used (Wiese & Garcia, 2001).

The **Reagan administration** was generally hostile to bilingual education. In the *New York Times* on the 3rd March 1981, President Reagan is quoted as saying that 'It is absolutely wrong and against the American concept to have a bilingual education program that is now openly, admittedly, dedicated to preserving their native language and never getting them adequate in English so they can go out into the job market'. Reagan believed that preservation of the native language meant neglect of English language acquisition. Bilingual education programs were seen as serving to neglect English language competence in students. Reagan dismissed bilingual education in favor of mainstreaming/submersion and transitional programs.

In 1985, **William Bennett**, as Secretary of Education, suggested that there was no evidence that children from language minorities (whom the Bilingual Education Act had sought to help), had benefited from this Act. Some 25% of funds were made available for English monolingual, alternative instructional programs (e.g. Structured English programs; Sheltered English programs). This represented a further political dismissal of education through the minority language and a dismissal of 'strong' forms of bilingual education.

The Lau remedies were withdrawn by the Reagan government and no longer had the force of law. The federal government left **local politicians** to create their own policies. Further changes in the rights to bilingual education in the US are given in the table below. This reveals that legislation and litigation mostly led to 'weak' forms of bilingual education (e.g. transitional bilingual education) and the eradication of bilingual education. During the Reagan and George H.W. Bush (senior) Presidencies in the United States, the accent was more on mainstreaming/submersion and transitional bilingual education. The right to early education through a minority language failed to blossom in those years (Crawford, 2004). However, in the early 1990s, the election of Bill Clinton brought some hope as he 'had campaigned in support of bilingual education and promised to strengthen it' (Miguel, 2004, p. 79.)

In 1994, the 103rd Congress undertook a major reform of education through legislation entitled **Goals 2000; Educate America Act**, and also by the **Improving America's Schools Act**. This extensive reform included an acknowledgement that students for whom English was a second language ('Limited English Proficient' students) should be expected to achieve high academic standards. Such legislation aimed to provide children with an enriched educational program, improving instructional strategies and making the curriculum more challenging. The Improving America's Schools Act of 1994 reauthorized Title VII, strengthening the state role by requiring state educational authorities to review Title VII appropriations and provide additional funds for specific groups such as immigrants (Wiese & Garcia, 2001). Thus the reauthorization of Title VII in 1994 continued limited federal support for bilingual education programs. From 1994, the issue about bilingual education moved partly from being narrowly focused on the language of instruction to a broader range of questions being asked about the quality and standards of education being given to language minority students. The **Clinton administration** tended to a more 'language as a resource' (see chapter 18) stance but also tended to lessen federal influence on bilingual education (Crawford, 2004).

Opponents of bilingual education in the United States do not generally oppose **foreign language programs** for English speakers. Such programs are regarded as important in educating students for the global economy (see chapter 6). Some forms of bilingualism (e.g. English–Japanese, English–German) are seen to be of value for US economic prosperity. One of the goals of the National Education Goals Panel of 1994 was thus that the percentage of students who are competent in more than one language should substantially increase. The 1994 Amendments to the Bilingual Education Act meant that proficient bilingualism became a desirable goal when it brought economic benefits to individuals and particularly to the nation. Hence the Amendments resulted in funding for a larger number of dual language programs.

However, the 1994 reauthorization of Title VII came under attack both by politicians and the US Press. Congress considered legislation to repeal the law and eliminate its funding. Whilst this did not succeed, it nevertheless pointed to many politicians and much of the mass media being against bilingual education. Title VII appropriations were reduced by 38% between 1994 and 1996 leading to cuts in bilingual programs, in teacher training and reducing the budgets for research, evaluation and support of bilingual education in the United States.

CALIFORNIA AND PROPOSITION 227

Between 1978 and 2000, the number of students designated as limited English proficiency (LEP) in California rose from approximately a 250,000 to 1.4 million with significant populations of Vietnamese, Hmong, Cantonese, Tagalog, Khmer, Korean, Armenian, Mandarin, Russian, Ukrainian, Serbo Croatian, Urdu, Hindi and Panjabi students, for example. With a multilingual population, California had become a state where both experimentation and experience with bilingual education had blossomed.

In early 1996, the *Los Angeles Times* gave extensive coverage to the political activism of a small group of Spanish-speaking parents pulling their children out of the Ninth Street Elementary School. A Silicon Valley businessman called **Ron Unz** saw this as his political opportunity, having failed to win a Republican nomination three years earlier. Based on a personal philosophy of assimilation of immigrants, he criticized bilingual education, multiculturalism and ethnicity. But rather than talk about the English language and unifying American identity, his arguments were targeted at the supposed educational ineffectiveness of bilingual schools in California (Ovando *et al.*, 2003). The press were delighted to add heat to the debate with mostly one-sided, personality-based, controversy-cultivating reports (Crawford, 2000, 2004).

Proposition 227 in California was posed as an effort to improve English language instruction for children who needed to learn English for economic and employment opportunities. It aimed at outlawing bilingual education in that state. 'Therefore' says the text of Proposition 227 'it is resolved that: all children in California public schools shall be taught English as rapidly and effectively as possible' and such children 'shall be taught English by being taught in English'. Bilingual education was virtually eliminated; sheltered (or structured) English-immersion programs were put in their place (Orellana *et al.*, 1999; Quezada *et al.*, 1999; Crawford, 2004; see also Bilingual Research Journal, 2000, volume 24, numbers 1&2 for a variety of articles on Proposition 227: (http://brj.asu.edu/).

In a public ballot, Proposition 227 was passed on 2nd June 1998 by a margin of 61% to 39%. Analysis of the voting and subsequent surveys found that many Latinos were clearly against the Proposition, but nevertheless, bilingual education had become virtually illegal (Attinasi, 1998). With the sweet scent of victory in California, Ron Unz proceeded elsewhere across the United States with success in Arizona (Proposition 203 passed by a 63% vote) and Massachusetts (passed by a 68% vote). In these two states, parental choices were more severely limited than in California and with increased ease of suing. However, Ron Unz was defeated in Colorado (44% vote) – see Crawford (2004) and James Crawford's WWW site: http://ourworld.compuserve.com/homepages/jwcrawford/home.htm.

Those teachers and administrators who willfully and repeatedly violate Proposition 227 are left open to being sued by parents and are personally liable for financial damages and legal fees. However, there is a provision for parental waivers and exceptions. The student numbers in Californian bilingual education fell from 498,879 in 1997–98 to 167,163 in 2000–01 (Valdés *et al.*, 2006) and to around 141,000 students (9% of LEPs) in 2002–03 (Crawford, 2004). This provision has preserved some bilingual education in school districts where there is strong parental support and a history of effective bilingual programs. Wiley & Wright (2004) indicate variations across California in the extent to which parents were informed of their right to waivers from English-only programs, and the continuation of some quality bilingual programs.

The evidence for the success or failure of Proposition 227 is not yet agreed (but see Bali, 2001; Gándara *et al.*, 2000; Stritikus, 2001; Parrish *et al.*, 2002; Thompson *et al.*, 2002; Rumberger *et al.*, 2003; Stritikus & Garcia, 2003; Crawford, 2004, Wright, 2004; Wiley & Wright, 2004; Stritikus, 2003; Valdés *et al.*, 2006). There is danger is using one research study to support a particular belief (see chapter 12). Instead, well controlled, large-scale research plus detached and critical overviews of a number of studies will be needed to suggest success or failure.

The attempted outlawing of bilingual education in California, Arizona and Massachusetts indicates:

(1)   the need to disseminate research findings on bilingual education (see chapters 11 &12). **Dissemination** of research is needed not just to teachers but also to parents and the public. The public image of bilingual education is preferably based on fact rather than fiction, on evidence rather than on prejudice.

Parents and community leaders need to be informed, involved and active, not just treated as passive recipients of expertise from professional educators.

(2) Bilingual education is not simply about provision, practice, and pedagogy but is unavoidably about **politics**. Despite the call for the depoliticizing of bilingual education (August & Hakuta, 1997), the reality is that opponents of bilingual education would win more ground if supporters stopped arguing for bilingual education.

To survive, bilingual education needs to demonstrate it works for the national interest. Bilingualism is often seen as producing opponents to monolingual and monocultural politics (see chapters 17 and 18). Instead, bilingual education can be a more secure route to English language fluency. In the US, that is in the national interest. Bilingual education can also create students who are fully competent in another language. In the wake of 9/11, that is also in the national interest.

(3) Secure **evidence** is needed, not just from individual case studies, studies of outstanding schools or examples of effective practice. In a culture of high stakes testing, monitoring standards and accountability, raising the achievement of all students in all schools is needed. Bilingual education needs to provide evidence for high standards, high achievements and those outputs and outcomes of schooling that parents, public and politicians regard as important. This includes helping children acquire a thorough competence in English. Such outcomes go beyond language to other curriculum areas (e.g. mathematics, science), affective outcomes (e.g. self esteem) and employment and vocational success.

(4) Evidence is not enough. There is a propaganda battle that goes beyond the dissemination of research. The media (e.g. newspapers, magazines, television) are influential and can be utilized to support bilingual education. McQuillan and Tse (1996) found that in the period 1984 to 1994, 82% of research studies reported favorably on the effectiveness of bilingual education. However, only 45 percent of United States newspaper articles took a similar favorable position on bilingual education. Less than half of all newspaper articles made any mention of research findings, while nearly a third of such articles relied on personal or anecdotal accounts. This implies that research may need to become more accessible as well as disseminated through influential mass media channels. **Promotion and marketing** of research and reviews may be necessary in such a politicized climate, targeted at policy-makers and politicians, parents and the press. The alternative is that prejudice and ignorance will be dominant.

THE 'NO CHILD LEFT BEHIND' 2001 LEGISLATION

On 28th April 1998, the **US Secretary of Education**, Richard W. Riley, declared his non-support for Proposition 227. He stated that the Unz initiative 'would lead to fewer children learning English and would leave many children lagging behind in their academic studies'. In arguing that the initiative will be counter-productive, Secretary Riley (1998) asserted that a one-size-fits-all approach to learning English 'is not supported by years of research', deprofessionalizes teachers, 'is punitive and threatening' as it allows liability in litigation (see below), and is a direct attack on local control of education. Instead, he affirmed 'the economic, cultural, and political importance of being bilingual in our global culture'.

In direct contrast, in 2001, the Bilingual Education Act was replaced by new federal legislation entitled **No Child Left Behind** (NCLB). The reasons behind the public and political support for NCLB are many, varied and interacting, but include the following perceptions that vary in substance and motivation (Crawford, 2004; Wiley & Wright, 2004):

- Language minority students underachieving especially in English language test scores.
- Higher Hispanic drop-out rates.
- The need to raise the expectations of language minority children.
- Need for standardization of treatment of all language minority children.
- Many poor quality and under-resourced bilingual programs.
- The implementation of bilingual schools following a transitional or compensatory model.
- A shortage of qualified bilingual teachers.
- Variability and insufficient accountability in bilingual programs across states. The need for emphasis on measuring success, that is outputs rather than inputs or process, with less excuses for contextual differences.
- The centrality of competence in English at an early age as possible so as to succeed in school, society and employment.
- The need for language minority children to be annually measured and monitored for English language progress, with rewards and punishments based on achieving (or not) that goal.
- Fears about ethnic segregation, national disunity, and potential community divisiveness when perpetuating immigrant languages. The need for integration and assimilation.

No Child Left Behind (NCLB) was approved on Thursday December 13th, 2001 by an overwhelming vote of 381 to 41 in the House of Congress. President George Bush signed it into law on the 8th January 2002. It reauthorized the Bilingual Education Act for six years.

NCLB is radical in its requirements for the treatment of English language learners. This partly reflects the general support for the legislation among both the public and politicians, plus careful deal-making. Opposition to NCLB tended to be small and afterward. Symbolically demonstrating a break with the past, the numbering of the section regarding English language learners changed from Title VII to Title III (Crawford, 2004).

In essence, NCLB makes states, districts and schools accountable for the performance of LEP students. The requirement is to (1) identify languages other than English in the student population; (2) develop academic assessments (3) use English language (oral, reading, writing) proficiency assessment with LEP students on an annual basis; (4) include LEP Grade 3 to Grade 8 students in the assessment of reading and mathematics with appropriate accommodations; (5) administer reading assessment in English to students who have been in US schools for at least three years; but (6) in 2004, states were allowed to exempt LEP students for one year from reading assessment during their first year of enrollment in a US school and (7) were allowed some flexibility in including former LEP students for Adequate Yearly Progress calculations (Batt *et al.*, 2005).

Any mention of bilingualism or developing native language competences is missing from this federal law (Wiley & Wright, 2004). While bilingual education (e.g. dual language schools) can still apply for funding, the thrust of the legislation is for English-only instruction. The rule of law is joined by the heavy influence of **high-stakes assessment**. Since there is almost no more powerful way to transform a curriculum than via compulsory and focused assessment, No Child Left Behind (2001) requires the testing of English language skills for LEP students. Such tests expect standard English with sophisticated use of decontextualized language skills. An example is New York (state) where school districts are required to identify LEP students and test them through the use of the Language Assessment Battery-Revised (LAB-R) and the New York State English as a Second Language Test (Education Commission of the States, 2004).

As Crawford (2004) wryly comments, the legislation could be named 'No Child Left Untested'. Such testing makes schools highly accountable, thus placing pressure on teachers to ensure the rapid learning of test-driven English language skills. Annual student testing of reading and mathematics (and English for LEP students) means raising test outcomes, otherwise there will be sanctions. English learners must be assessed for English proficiency each year. Each state must have a timeline for ensuring yearly progress with all students proficient by 2013–14. The National Clearinghouse for English Language Acquisition and Language Instruction Educational Programs (http://www.ncela.gwu.edu/) was set up to collect, analyze, synthesize and disseminate information on effective programs for ELL / LEP students.

'High-stakes tests increasingly determine who gets promoted, who graduates from high school, who enters college, who teaches' (O. García & Traugh, 2002, p. 311). Thus teachers of bilingual students are powerfully pressed into teaching only through English, fearful of parents, managers and their own perceived failure. Schools and teachers may try to avoid language minority students who they fear will lower their school's test results and hence its reputation. Garcia and Traugh (2002) suggest a Catch 22 situation: colleges closing their doors on language minority students who are the ones who could be the most committed (and linguistically and culturally competent) to educate such children in the future.

Title III of the **No Child Left Behind** law entitled 'Language Instruction for Limited English Proficient and Immigrant Students' (2001) eliminated a direct federal role in supporting bilingual education. Instead, the US government requires **states** to have accountability plans that particularly focus on measurable outcomes, and closely monitors implementation. Schools must meet test performance targets, including in subgroups, and schools can be labeled as 'failing schools' if targets are not reached. Such subgroups include major ethnic groups and limited English proficient students. Adequate Yearly Progress (AYP) for limited English proficient children (not defined, and therefore variably interpreted across states) is required for immigrant children who have been in the US for three consecutive years. Where there is assessment failure, then the blame is likely to be placed (often unfairly) on the school and on the teacher (and not the system e.g. lack of support for a child's bilingualism). Underachievement on tests is therefore seen as an education management problem, not a societal issue.

The UK experience is that test achievement becomes a dominant aim in itself, with teachers 'teaching for the test', spending much time preparing students to perform well, with students practicing on similar tests and becoming test-wise. Assessment rather than education may become the focus, with a narrowing of the curriculum for the very students who most need an empowering curriculum. High stakes testing may improve assessment results; this is different from improving the quality of learning. Wiley & Wright (2004) and Batt *et al.* (2005) suggest other potential outcomes: drop-out rates increase, elimination of students from testing, less time for curriculum areas other than mathematics and English, failure to rectify human and material resource inequalities between schools, measurement of an instable and inconsistently defined LEP subgroup producing inaccurate results and loss of fluent bilingual teachers and native-speaker aides as insufficiently qualified.

All states have to set English proficiency standards (including for English language learners) and provide high quality teachers by 2005 to ensure such English language learners become fluent in English and achieve well in other curriculum areas. However, the legislation does not dictate a particular strategy or method of instruction for such students (e.g. mainstreaming, transitional bilingual education), other than this should be scientifically based on research. **No Child Left Behind** (Public Law 107–110, section 9101) requires decisions about suitable programs for English language learners to be based on scientific, empirical, systematic and objective research that involves replicated and well designed experiments, reliable and valid measurement, and rigorous data analysis. As Wiley & Wright (2004) suggest,

> it is possible that educational officials could select a single study, no matter how dubious or flawed, which supports agendas. In Arizona, for example, the superintendent of public instruction touts the Guzman (2002) study – which experts in the field have found flawed – as 'scientific' evidence that bilingual education is ineffective. (p. 157)

The following chapters examine previous 'scientific' research. Suffice to add at this point that the research evidence tends to support 'strong' forms of bilingual education. These forms appear, paradoxically, to have been discouraged by the No Child Left Behind (2001) legislation. However, Title VII authorizes programs for Indian, native Hawaiian and native Alaska Education.

A summary of major events affecting the history of United States bilingual education is given in the table on the following two pages.

Year	US Legislation / Litigation affecting Bilingual Education	Implication
1906	Nationality Act passed	First legislation requiring in-migrants to speak English to become naturalized.
1923	*Meyer v Nebraska* ruling by the US Supreme Court	The ruling outlawed, as an unconstitutional infringement of individual liberties, arbitrary restrictions on the teaching languages other than English. Proficiency in a foreign language was also constitutional.
1950	Amendments to the Nationality Act	English literacy required for naturalization.
1954	*Brown v Board of Education*	Segregated education based on race made unconstitutional.
1958	National Defense Education Act	The first federal legislation to promote foreign language learning.
1965	Immigration and Nationality Act	The Act eliminated racial criteria for admission expanding immigration especially from Asia and Latin America. The Act also emphasized the goal of 'family unification' over occupational skills. This encouraged increased immigration by Mexicans in particular.
1965	Elementary and Secondary Education Act (ESEA)	Funds granted to meet the needs of 'educationally deprived children'.
1968	Elementary and Secondary Education Act (ESEA) amendment: The Bilingual Education Act, Title VII	Provided funding to establish bilingual programs for students who did not speak English and who were economically poor.
1974	*Lau v Nichols*	Established that language programs for language minorities not proficient in English were necessary to provide equal educational opportunities.
1974	Equal Educational Opportunity Act (EEOA)	Codified the *Lau v. Nichols* decision, requiring every school district to take appropriate action to overcome language barriers that impede equal participation by its students in its instructional programs.
1974	Reauthorization of Bilingual Education Act Title VII of ESEA	Native-language instruction was required for the first time as a condition for receiving bilingual education grants. Bilingual Education was defined as transitional (TBE).
1975	Lau Remedies	Informal guideline on schools' obligations toward LEP students. This required the provision of bilingual education in districts where the civil rights of such students had been violated.
1976	*Keyes v School District no. 1, Denver, Colorado*	Established bilingual education as compatible with desegregation.

1978	Reauthorization of Bilingual Education Act Title VII of ESEA	A new restriction was introduced. Grants could support native-language instruction only to the extent necessary to allow a child to achieve competence in the English language. Funding was thus restricted to TBE; maintenance programs were now ineligible for funding. The term 'Limited English Proficient' (LEP) introduced, replacing LES (Limited English Speaking).
1980-81	Lau Regulations	The Carter Administration attempted to formalize the Lau Remedies, requiring bilingual instruction for LEP students where feasible. The Reagan Administration subsequently withdrew the proposal, leaving uncertainty about schools' obligations in this area.
1981	*Castañeda v. Pickard*	An Appeals court decision established a three-part test to determine whether schools were taking "appropriate action" under the 1974 Equal Educational Opportunity Act. Programs for LEP students (bilingual or otherwise) must be: (1) based on sound educational theory, (2) implemented with adequate resources, and (3) evaluated and proven effective.
1983	US English Movement launched	Debates about the dominant place of English in law, society and education became more prominent.
1984	Reauthorization of Bilingual Education Act Title VII of ESEA	While most funding was reserved for TBE, monies for maintenance programs were once again permitted, along with 'special alternative' English-only programs.
1988	Reauthorization of Bilingual Education Act Title VII of ESEA	Same as in 1984, but 25% of funding given for English-only Special Alternative Instructional (SAIP) programs.
1994	Reauthorization of Bilingual Education Act Title VII of ESEA	Full bilingual proficiency recognized as a lawful educational goal. Funded dual language programs that included English speakers and programs to support Native American languages. The quota for funding SAIP programs was lifted. The new law sought to bring LEP students into mainstream school reform efforts, making it more difficult for their particular needs to be ignored in policymaking.
1998	Proposition 227 passed in California	The 'Unz initiative' sought to impose severe restrictions on native-language instruction for English learners in California. Most bilingual programs dismantled, with similar measures in Arizona (2000) and Massachusetts (2002).
2002	No Child Left Behind legislation as a reauthorization of the Elementary and Secondary Act of 1965 and a repeal of the Bilingual Education Act	Schools and states encouraged to move to English-only education through mandatory high-stakes testing in English. Measures of Adequate Yearly Progress (AYP) reported for schools, school districts and states including English proficiency.

CURRENT STATISTICS

The estimated number of 'English Language Learners' (ELL), also termed 'Limited English Proficient' students (LEP), in US states and DC is close to 5 million (or 11.4% of all Kindergarten to Grade 12 students), showing considerable growth since 1989 when there were 2.7 million such students (a 84.4% increase: National Clearing-house for English Language Acquisition, 2005, http://www.ncela.gwu.edu/). The growth in ELLs over the last decade is given in the table below.

Year	Total Kindergarten to Grade 12 Enrolment	English Language Learner (ELL) Enrolment	ELL Growth since 1992
1992–1993	44,444,939	2,735,952	
1993–1994	45,443,389	3,037,922	11.0%
1994–1995	47,745,835	3,184,696	16.4%
1995–1996	47,502,665	3,228,799	18.0%
1996–1997	46,714,980	3,452,073	26.2%
1997–1998	46,023,969	3,470,268	26.8%
1998–1999	46,153,266	3,540,673	29.4%
1999–2000	47,356,089	4,416,580	61.4%
2000–2001	47,877,577	4,584,946	67.6%
2001–2002	48,296,777	4,747,763	73.5%
2002–2003	49,509,923	5,044,361	84.4%

Source: National Clearinghouse for English Language Acquisition, 2005, http://www.ncela.gwu.edu/)

Most growth (1997 to 2003) in percentage terms is found in Arkansas (121%), Georgia (186%), Indiana (148%), North Carolina (110%), South Carolina (168%), Virginia (100%) and West Virginia (230%), with the highest English Language Learner (ELL) populations found in California (1.6 million, 25.6% of the total enroll-ment), Texas (630 thousand, 14.8%), Arizona (149 thousand, 15.3%), Florida (292 thousand, 13.1%) New York (303 thousand, 7.9%) and Illinois (169 thousand, 8.4%) (NCELA, 2005, http://www.ncela.gwu.edu/). Estimates from state-wide research by Kindler (2002) of the home languages of ELLs includes Spanish (76.6%), Viet-namese (2.3%), Hmong (2.2%), Haitian Creole (1.1%), Korean (1.1%) and Cantonese (1.0%), with other languages below 1%, for example, Arabic (0.9%) and Navajo (0.9%). The grade variations (Kinder, 2002) are shown in the graph overleaf.

THE ACHIEVEMENT GAP ISSUE

In almost every country there are achievement gaps between the economically rich and poor, different ethnic groups and not least among language minorities and language majorities. Closing the **achievement gap** has become a political and public issue. This involves both improving school success for all children, but

United States 'English Language Leaner' Enrolment by Grade 1999-2000

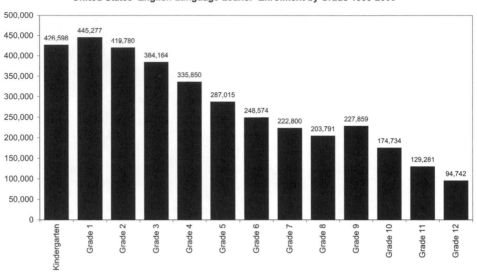

Adapted from Kindler (2002)

particularly raising the achievement levels of under-achieving groups, and improving these levels to that of mainstream students.

The growth in ELLs (English language learners) in the United States has led to claims that many such students are underachieving in the US education system. The 'achievement gap' of language minority children, especially if they are classed as immigrants, is often a popular feature among the United States press and politicians with claims of lower achievement among ELLs especially compared with native English speakers. For example, Thomas and Collier (1997, 2002a) found that students in 'weak' bilingual education (ESL withdrawal, Content ESL and Transitional Bilingual Education – see chapter 10) typically finish school well below average English reading achievement (at the 11th to 32nd percentile). Bilingual education is thus popularly blamed for the low achievement. Yet, 'strong' bilingual education (such as the Dual Language model – see chapter 11) in the Thomas and Collier studies (2002a), showed promising outcomes for ELLs. Students enrolled in such Dual Language programs scored at or above the average. Such programs were found to be more influential in achievement than student background variables such as socioeconomic status.

Nevertheless, bilinguals in the US do tend to perform below the norm. Using reports from 41 US states, Kindler (2002) suggests that only 18.7% of ELL students met state norms for reading in English. Other claims are for relatively higher drop-out rates and more frequent placement in lower ability groups for ELLs (Genesee *et al.*, 2005). Freeman *et al.* (2002) suggest that, among refugees to the US, 'the English language learners who experience the highest rate of academic failure are those who have lived in the United States all their lives' (p. x). They typify such longer-term English language learners as performing below grade level, with low test scores and as having a mis-perception of their academic achievement. Low school performance is attributed to schools and instruction, including bilingual programs. Freeman *et al.* (2002) suggests that it is classroom learning strategies and practices that will close the achievement gap. Is it the case that both the cause and remedy of achievement gap is the school? What kind of school and language policies? Are there explanations of the achievement gap outside school? This section examines the varying explanations, particularly whether bilingualism is a cause of such underachievement. Chapters 10 and 11 will then examine different models of education for ELLs, and show how the achievement gap is related to a choice between 'weak' and 'strong' models of bilingual education.

EXPLANATIONS OF UNDERACHIEVEMENT IN BILINGUALS

There are frequent occasions when language minorities (in the US and in other countries where there is much immigration) are found to underachieve or show high drop-out rates. Sometimes this is analyzed in research but it is also a frequent topic of debate among teachers, educational psychologists, speech therapists, parents, students themselves and not least politicians (see chapter 17).

When language minority children appear to exhibit underachievement in the classroom, what is the **explanation**? When first, second or third generation immigrant language minority children appear to fail in the classroom, where is the 'blame' typically placed? When refugee children, indigenous minorities and distinct ethnic groups are shown statistically to have high drop-out rates, achieve less in examinations and tests or receive lower grades and averages, what is the cause?

Explanations are likely to be multiple, complex, about associations that are not necessarily causal, and may include the following (EALAW, 2003): majority language competence, socioeconomic background, poverty and material home conditions, racism, gender, school attendance, parental encouragement and assistance (e.g. with homework), peer influence, and the quality of teachers and school. The most typical explanations are now considered.

First, the blame may be attributed to the child **being bilingual**. Bilingualism itself is often popularly seen as causing cognitive confusion. The explanation given is a picture of the bilingual brain with two engines working at half throttle, while the monolingual has one well tuned engine at full throttle. As chapter 8 revealed, such an explanation is usually incorrect. Where two languages are well developed, then bilingualism is more likely to lead to cognitive advantages than disadvantages (see the 'three level house' diagram in chapter 8). Only when both languages are insufficiently developed to cope in the curriculum can 'blame' be attributed to bilingualism itself. Even then, the blame should not go to the victim, but to the home, neighborhood or societal circumstances that create under-developed languages.

Second, where underachievement exists, the reason may be given as **lack of exposure to the majority language**. In the US and the UK, a typical explanation for the underachievement of some language minorities is insufficient exposure to English. Failure or below average performance is attributed to students having insufficiently developed English language competence to cope in English-medium instruction. Those who use Spanish or Bengali at home and in the neighborhood are perceived to struggle at school due to a lack of competence in the dominant, mainstream language. Thus mainstreaming and transitional (TBE) forms of education attempt to ensure a fast conversion to the majority language.

Attempting a fast conversion to the majority language stands the chance of doing more harm than good. It denies the child's skills in the home language, denies the cognitive and academic competence already available through that home language, and often denies the identity and self-respect of the child itself. Instead of building upon existing language proficiency and knowledge, the 'sink or swim' approach attempts to replace such language abilities (see chapter 10). When a child doesn't quickly acquire sufficient 'academic' English and shows underachievement, there are frequent demands for more of the same medicine (more English language lessons).

In the context of the **Ebonics** debate in the US, Wiley *et al.* (2005, p. xi) express the issue thus:

> we continue to impose language standards and expectations on children, *at the point of their entry into the educational system*, which methodically privileges some children, while disadvantaging others. Under NCLB, annual testing reinforces the importance of meeting these language standards. All children enter school with knowledge of the language of their parents, homes, and communities. When we ignore the knowledge that some children bring in favor of the knowledge that others have, we impose a criterion that renders a socially constructed minority being *deficient, at risk, remedial, nonstandard*, or *failing*.

Bilingual education, when effectively implemented, is not the cause of underachievement; rather it is the **cure**. Underachievement in majority language education (e.g. mainstreaming and transitional bilingual education) may be combated by providing education through the medium of the minority language (e.g. dual language, heritage language programs). When language minority students are allowed to operate in their heritage language in the curriculum, the evidence (see chapter 11) suggests that success rather than failure results. Such success includes becoming fluent in the majority language (e.g. English). In the US, Krashen's (1999) overview of US research concludes that 'well-designed bilingual programs produce better academic English . . . because they supply subject matter knowledge in the students' primary language, which makes the English the students hear and read much more comprehensible' (p. 7). Thus lack of exposure to English is a popular but inappropriate explanation of underachievement. This explanation fails to note the advantages of education in the minority language for achievement. It inappropriately seeks an answer in increased majority language tuition rather than increased minority language education.

Third, when bilingual children exhibit underachievement, the attributed reason is sometimes a **mismatch between home and school**. For example, advice by some educational psychologists and speech therapists has been for language minority parents to raise their children in the majority, school language. Such a mismatch is seen as not just about language differences but also about dissimilarities in culture, values and beliefs. As an extreme, this tends to reflect a majority viewpoint that is assimilationist, imperialist and even oppressive. The child and family is expected to adjust to a uniform mainstream system, not that the system should be pluralist and incorporate variety. For such an assimilationist viewpoint, the solution is in the home adjusting to mainstream language and culture to prepare the child for school.

The alternative view is that, where practicable, the school system should be flexible enough to incorporate the home language and culture. A mismatch between home and school can be positively addressed by 'strong' forms of bilingual education for language minorities (see chapter 11). By dual language and heritage language programs, through the inclusion of parents in the operation of the school, by involving parents as partners and participants in their child's education (e.g. paired reading schemes), the mismatch can become a merger. An additive and not subtractive outcome is then probable: bilingualism, biliteracy and biculturalism.

Fourth, underachievement may be attributed to **socioeconomic factors** that surround a language minority group. Some typical circumstances are described by Trueba (1991, p. 53):

> Many immigrant and refugee children have a life of poverty and rural isolation in crowded dwellings where they lack privacy, toilet and shower facilities, comfort, and basic medical attention. In some cases migrant life for children means abuse, malnutrition, poor health, ignorance and neglect.

Krashen (1999) reviewed **drop-out rates** in the US among Hispanic young adults. He concluded that such young adults are more likely to drop-out (e.g. 1 in 12 non-Hispanic whites compared with one in five Hispanics). However, when Hispanic young adults have received bilingual education, there are lower drop-out rates. Drop-out seems connected with socioeconomic factors such as relative material poverty and the home literacy environment. When such factors are taken into account, Hispanic young adults have the same, or nearly the same drop-out rates as other groups.

Socioeconomic status is a broad umbrella term that rightly points to a definite cause of language minority underachievement. It provides an example of the importance of not blaming the victim, but analyzing societal features that contribute to underachievement. Such features may be relative economic deprivation, material circumstances and living conditions as well as psychological and social features such as discrimination, racial prejudice, depression and immobilizing inferiority.

While **socioeconomic factors** are a strong explanation of language minority underachievement, two cautions must be expressed. Socioeconomic status does not explain why different language minorities of similar socioeconomic status may perform differently at school. Different ideologies or orientations may vary between and within language minority groups. Sociocultural factors within and between ethnic groups and not simply socioeconomic status are needed to begin to work out the equation of language minority achievement and underachievement.

This raises another issue. Underachievement cannot be simply related to one cause. Nothing is so simple. The equation of underachievement is going to be complex, involving a number of factors. Those factors will interact together and not be simple 'standalone' effects. For example, umbrella labels such as socioeconomic status need to be deconstructed into more definable predictors of underachievement (e.g. parents' attitude to education, literacy environments, material and emotional home conditions). Home factors will then interact with school factors providing an enormous number of different routes that may lead to school success or failure. The recipes of success and failure are many, with varying ingredients that interact together in complex ways. However, socioeconomic and sociocultural features are important ingredients in most equations of underachievement. And instead of being static explanations or political criticism, actions must result to change and enhance. After the elucidation of cause must come transformation.

Fifth, part of the language minority underachievement equation is the **type of school** a child attends. Chapters 10 and 11 highlight the different outcomes for language minority children in 'strong' compared with 'weak' forms of bilingual education. The same child will tend to attain more if placed in programs that use the heritage language as a medium of instruction than in programs that seek to replace the home language as quickly as possible. Therefore, when underachievement occurs in a language minority child or within a language minority group, the system of schooling needs scrutiny. A system that suppresses the home language is likely to be part of the explanation of individual and ethnic group underachievement where such problems exist (Cummins, 2000a).

Sixth, 'type of school' is a broad heading under which there can exist superior and inferior mainstream schools, outstanding and mediocre dual language, and high-quality and sub-standard heritage language schools. Where underachievement exists, it is sometimes too simple to blame the type of school rather than digging deeper and locating more specific causes. Chapter 13 considers some of the attributes that need examining to establish the **quality of education** for language minority children (e.g. the supply, ethnic origins and bilingualism of teachers, the commitment of teachers to bilingual education, the balance of language minority and language majority students in the classroom, the use and sequencing of the two languages across the curriculum over different grades, reward systems for enriching the minority language and culture, appropriate curriculum resources and the engagement of parents). 'Strong' forms of bilingual education are not an instant guarantee of quality education. Diminishing and eradicating underachievement depends on the process of classroom activity, not just on a style of education.

Seventh, underachievement may be due to **real learning difficulties** and the need for some form of special education. It is important to make a distinction between real and apparent learning difficulties. Too often, bilingual children are labeled as having learning difficulties that are attributed to their bilingualism (Baca & Cervantes, 1998). As we have discussed in this section, the causes of apparent learning problems may be much less in the child and much more in the school or in the education system. The child is perceived as having learning difficulties when the problem may lie in the subtractive, assimilative system which itself creates negative attitudes and low motivation. In the 'sink or swim' mainstreaming approach, 'sinking' can be attributed to an unsympathetic system and to insensitive teaching methods rather than individual learning problems. However, apart from system-generated and school-generated learning problems, there will be bilinguals with genuine learning difficulties (Cummins, 2000a). The essential beginning is to distinguish between real, genuine individual learning difficulties and problems that are caused by factors outside the individual.

Such a **distinction between the real and the apparent**, the system-generated and the remediable problems of the individual, focuses attention on alternatives. When underachievement exists, do we blame the victim, blame the teacher and the school, or blame the education system? Blaming the bilingual student is typically about poor language, poor motivation, culturally unacceptable behavior, low personal and parental expectations, poor parental support, material deprivation at home and lack of community support. In contrast, blaming the school is often about inadequate diagnosis, inappropriate curriculum, low teacher expectations of bilingual students, untrained or non-specialist teachers, large classes of students, poor resources, failing ethos and poor leadership.

When assessment, tests and examinations occur and show relatively low performance among language minority individuals and groups, will prejudices about bilingual children and ethnic groups be confirmed? Or can we use such assessment to reveal deficiencies in the architecture of the school system and the design of the curriculum and not blame the child? As this section has revealed, underachievement tends to be blamed on the child and the language minority group. Yet often the explanation lies in factors outside of the individual. This discussion is now extended by examining bilinguals with special needs and bilingual special education.

CONCLUSION

Three conclusions. First, there is sometimes a perception that educational policy is fairly static, conservative and slow to change. The history of bilingual education in the United States tends to falsify and contradict such beliefs. Such history shows that there is constant change, a constant movement in ideas and ideology. One conclusion is that change will always occur in bilingual education policy and provision. Nothing is static. While there will be periods when bilingual education is criticized, forbidden and rejected, there will be reactions, with the possibility of more positive, accepting periods ahead. Uncertainty and constant change provide occasional opportunities for bilingual education to progress.

Second, the conclusion must not be that bilingual education only moves in one direction: from more positive 'golden' times to being dismissed and rejected. The history of bilingual education in the Basque Country and Wales follows a different sequence to the US. In these countries, bilingual education has moved from being dismissed and suppressed to considerable expansion. From a time when Basque and Welsh were banned in the classroom, there is currently a widespread acceptance and provision of bilingual education in these countries.

A current international issue is the underachievement of many language minority students. The blame for this is easily but wrongly attributed to bilingualism or to insufficient experience in learning a majority language. Instead, the achievement gap is often related to failing to use a child's ability and achievements that are available in their home language. Sometimes the achievement gap is blamed on language, when the real roots are situated in the relatively impoverished economic, social and educational environments that immigrants, of example, experience. For such students, bilingual education, utilizing the home language, becomes the cure and not the cause of underachievement.

KEY POINTS IN THE CHAPTER

- Bilingual education has a history spanning 5000 or more years and current movements need understanding within the historical context of the last century.
- Bilingual education in the United States has a rapidly changing history where permissiveness towards bilingual education was initially present. In recent decades, a more dismissive and restrictive climate has been experienced (e.g. the No Child Left Behind (2001) legislation). However, dual language schools currently provide a window of opportunity.
- Underachievement in school is typically unfairly blamed on bilingualism. Lack of exposure to the majority language and a mismatch between the languages of home and school are often cited as causes of underachievement.
- The real causes of underachievement tend to lie in relative social and economic deprivation and exclusion, a school which rejects the home language and culture of the child, and occasionally real learning difficulties.

SUGGESTED FURTHER READING

CRAWFORD, J., 2004, *Educating English Learners: Language Diversity in the Classroom*. Los Angeles: Bilingual Education Services.
CRAWFORD, J., 2000, *At War With Diversity*. Clevedon: Multilingual Matters.
MIGUEL, G.S., 2004, *Contested Policy: The Rise and Fall of Federal Bilingual Education in the United States 1960–2001*. Denton, Texas: University of North Texas Press.
VALDÉS, G., 2001, *Learning and Not Learning English: Latino Students in American Schools*. New York: Teachers College Press.

See also the *International Journal of Bilingualism and Bilingual Education* for the most recent articles on this topic.

STUDY ACTIVITIES

(1) Visit one or more schools and ask about the history of a bilingual education program or language program within that school. What have been the aims of the school with regard to languages? Have these aims changed over the last 10 or 20 years? How do the teachers perceive the first and second language of children being ignored or used over the last decade or more? Are there issue about the 'achievement gap' in the school? If so, what explanations do teachers give for under-achievement?

(2) By using documents, interviews, visits to schools and visits to administrators, try to sketch the history of language and bilingual education within a specific community. Also observe what signs and symbols there are of language within the community. For example, on posters, in newspapers, mass media and community activity, is there more than one language in use?

(3) Retrieve the transcript of the debate between Ron Unz and Catherine Snow at the Harvard Graduate School of Education, October 15, 2001. The document is entitled 'Bilingual Education: A Necessary Help or a Failed Hindrance?' and is found in the Harvard Education Letter, January / February 2002. (http:// www.edletter.org/past/issues/2002-jf/forum.shtml). Create a poster to summarize briefly the main arguments of each person. Add your own verdict at the bottom of the poster regarding who you think was more ascendant in the outcome of the debate.

Types of Bilingual Education

CHAPTER 10

Types of Bilingual Education

INTRODUCTION

So far in this book, the term bilingual education has been used as if its meaning is unambiguous and self-evident. The opposite is the case. Bilingual education is a **simplistic label for a complex phenomenon**. At the outset, a distinction is needed between (1) education that uses and promotes two languages and (2) relatively monolingual education for language minority children. This is a difference between (1) a classroom where formal instruction fosters bilingualism and (2) a classroom where bilingual children are present, but bilingualism is not fostered in the curriculum. The umbrella term, bilingual education, has been used to refer to both situations leaving the term ambiguous and imprecise. Precision can be attempted by specifying the major types of bilingual education.

One early and highly detailed classification of bilingual education was by Mackey (1970). This account of 90 different patterns of bilingual schooling considers: the languages of the home; the languages of the curriculum; the languages of the community in which the school is located and the international and regional status of the languages. A different approach to categorizing types of bilingual education is to examine the aims of such education. A useful distinction in aims is between transitional and maintenance bilingual education.

Transitional bilingual education aims to shift the child from the home, minority language to the dominant, majority language. Social and cultural **assimilation** into the language majority is the underlying aim. **Maintenance** bilingual education attempts to foster the minority language in the child, strengthening the child's sense of cultural identity and affirming the rights of an ethnic minority group in a nation. Otheguy and Otto (1980) make a distinction between the different aims of **static maintenance** and **developmental maintenance**. Static maintenance aims to maintain language skills at the level of the child entering a school. Developmental maintenance seeks to develop a student's home language skills to full proficiency and full biliteracy. This is sometimes referred to as **Enrichment Bilingual Education** for language minority children. (The term 'Enrichment Bilingual Education' is also used for language majority children who are adding a second language in school). Static maintenance attempts to prevent home language loss but not to increase skills in that first language. Enrichment bilingual education aims to extend the individual and group use of minority languages, leading to **cultural pluralism** and linguistic diversity.

Ferguson *et al.* (1977) widened these distinctions and provided 10 examples of the varying aims of bilingual education:

(1) To **assimilate** individuals or groups into the mainstream of society; to socialize people for full participation in the community.
(2) To **unify** a multilingual society; to bring unity to a multi-ethnic, multi-tribal, or multi-national linguistically diverse state.
(3) To enable people to **communicate** with the outside world.
(4) To provide language skills which are marketable, aiding **employment** and status.
(5) To preserve ethnic and religious **identity**.
(6) To **reconcile** and mediate between different linguistic and political communities.
(7) To spread the use of a colonial language, socializing an entire population to a **colonial existence**.
(8) To strengthen elite groups and preserve their **privileged position** in society.
(9) To give equal **status** in law to languages of unequal status in daily life.
(10) To deepen an **understanding** of language and culture.

This list shows that behind bilingual education are varying and conflicting philosophies and politics about the aims of bilingual education. Baker (2002) suggests that bilingual education has four major contemporary perspectives: as part of language planning (see chapter 3), politics (see chapters 17 & 18), economics and cost-efficiency (see chapter 19) and as pedagogy. Bilingual education is not just about education. There are sociocultural, political and economic issues ever present in the debate over the provision of bilingual education.

A TYPOLOGY OF BILINGUAL EDUCATION

A typology of bilingual education helps illustrate that multi-dimensionality and is presented in the following table. Ten types of language education are portrayed. Skutnabb-Kangas (2000) provides many detailed international examples of these different types. The 10 different types of program have **multitudinous sub-varieties**, as Mackey's (1970) 90 varieties of bilingual education indicate. However, one of the intrinsic limitations of typologies is that not all real-life examples will fit easily into the classification. For example, elite 'finishing schools' in

Switzerland, and classrooms in Wales where first language Welsh speakers are taught alongside 'immersion' English first language speakers make classification simplistic, although necessary for discussion and understanding (Mejía, 2002). Thus typologies have value for conceptual clarity but they have **limitations**: (1) models suggest static systems whereas bilingual schools and classrooms constantly develop and evolve (as the short history of bilingual education in the US revealed); (2) there are wide and numerous variations within a model; (3) models address 'inputs' and 'outputs' of the education system, but rarely address the classroom process; (4) models do not explain the successes or failures or the relative effectiveness of different types of bilingual education; (5) models are non-theoretical, reductionalist, essentialist and compared to complex individual schools, tend to simplify unsympathetically.

Each of 10 broad types of program will now be briefly considered in this chapter and the next.

MONOLINGUAL FORMS OF EDUCATION FOR BILINGUALS				
Type of Program	Typical Type of Child	Language of the Classroom	Societal and Educational Aim	Aim in Language Outcome
MAINSTREAMING /SUBMERSION (Structured Immersion)	Language Minority	Majority Language	Assimilation /Subtractive	Monolingualism
MAINSTREAMING /SUBMERSION with Withdrawal Classes / Sheltered English / Content-based ESL	Language Minority	Majority Language with 'Pull-out' L2 lessons	Assimilation / Subtractive	Monolingualism
SEGREGATIONIST	Language Minority	Minority Language (forced, no choice)	Apartheid	Monolingualism
WEAK FORMS OF BILINGUAL EDUCATION FOR BILINGUALS				
Type of Program	Typical Type of Child	Language of the Classroom	Societal and Educational Aim	Aim in Language Outcome
TRANSITIONAL	Language Minority	Moves from minority to majority language	Assimilation /Subtractive	Relative Monolingualism
MAINSTREAM with Foreign Language Teaching	Language Majority	Majority Language with L2/FL lessons	Limited Enrichment	Limited Bilingualism
SEPARATIST	Language Minority	Minority Language (out of choice)	Detachment / Autonomy	Limited Bilingualism

STRONG FORMS OF BILINGUAL EDUCATION FOR BILINGUALISM AND BILITERACY				
Type of Program	Typical Type of Child	Language of the Classroom	Societal and Educational Aim	Aim in Language Outcome
IMMERSION	Language Majority	Bilingual with initial emphasis on L2	Pluralism and Enrichment. Additive	Bilingualism & Biliteracy
MAINTENANCE/ HERITAGE LANGUAGE	Language Minority	Bilingual with emphasis on L1	Maintenance, Pluralism and Enrichment. Additive	Bilingualism & Biliteracy
TWO WAY/DUAL LANGUAGE	Mixed Language Minority & Majority	Minority and Majority	Maintenance, Pluralism and Enrichment. Additive	Bilingualism & Biliteracy
MAINSTREAM BILINGUAL	Language Majority	Two Majority Languages Pluralism	Maintenance, & Biliteracy and Enrichment. Additive	Bilingualism

Notes:
(1) L2 = Second Language; L1 = First Language; FL = Foreign Language.
(2) This table is based on discussions with Ofelia García who extends this to 14 types in García (1997, p. 410).
(3) See Mangubhai (2002) for how such a typology can be used in educational language planning.

MAINSTREAMING/SUBMERSION EDUCATION

When language minority students are placed in mainstream schools, the 'nickname' term often used to describe this is submersion. Submersion Education is a label to describe education for language minority children who are placed in mainstream education. However, no school calls itself a submersion school.

Submersion contains the idea of a language minority student thrown into the deep end and expected to learn to swim as quickly as possible without the help of floats or special swimming lessons. The language of the pool will be the majority language (e.g. English in the US) and not the home language of the child (e.g. Spanish). The language minority student will be taught all day in the majority language, typically alongside fluent speakers of the majority language. Both teachers and students will be expected to use only the majority language in the classroom, not the home language. Students will either sink, struggle or swim.

In the US, such an experience is also found in '**Structured Immersion**' programs (Brisk, 1998). Structured Immersion programs contain only language minority children and no language majority children. As will be apparent later in this book, the language experience in a Structured Immersion program is 'submersion' rather than 'immersion'. Structured Immersion programs are thus for minority language speakers conducted in the majority language. The first language is not developed but is replaced by the majority language. Different from submersion, the Structured Immersion teacher will use a simplified form of the majority language, and may initially accept contributions from children in their home language (Brisk, 1998; Hornberger, 1991). However, typically there is no native language support (August & Hakuta, 1997). In the US, there are also '**Sheltered English**' programs, an alternative to ESL (English as a Second Language) programs. Since such programs can be 'pull-out' with special content and curriculum materials, they are discussed in the next section.

Within US mainstreaming, there is typically **ESL provision**. Most ESL programs aim to develop English language skills (grammar, vocabulary and communication) for curriculum and communication purposes. In **Content-based ESL**, students are taught parts of the curriculum through English and not just English as a language. Typically, such content instruction will be 'sheltered' by simplifying the language used (and often the content). 'Sheltered' or comprehensible input in English requires increased non-verbal communication (e.g. visual aids, gestures), simple syntax, repetitions and summaries, speaking slowly and clearly, and frequently checking for understanding.

Guadalupe Valdés (1998, p. 7) found that in such programs 'English-language learners interacted only with each other and with teachers who taught their classes' with few opportunities to hear English from native-speaking peers. She also found that questioning, critical thinking and collaboration became impossible in 'sheltered' classes. The students understood too little English to move to higher-order thinking despite having the cognitive capacity that was available through their home language. The **outcome** of this can be frustration, non-participation, even dropping-out, such that these children become educationally, economically and politically disempowered. This then replicates the inequality and injustice that exists for many language minority children outside the classroom (Valdés, 1998).

In an intensive two-year research, Valdés (2001) provides exemplification of the **paradox** of English language learning policies enacted in such US schools that can deny access to the language and knowledge that could empower immigrant children. She shows that, separately and cumulatively, there are complex interacting classroom factors that frequently work against a student's English language development, achievement, employment, citizen rights and opportunities and self-esteem. Such factors include: impoverished second language interactions due to a teacher-student ratio of over 1:30, passive learning and 'tight discipline' strategies, mixed language competence classes working to a low common denominator, subject matter kept simplistic as the second language is insufficiently developed, and teachers' concerns with 'flawed language' forms rather than communication. Valdés (2001) engages multi-level explanations: '*Placing blame is not simple. Structures of dominance in society interact with educational structures and educational ideologies as well as with teachers' expectations and with students' perspectives about options and opportunities*' (p. 4).

There are various other **criticisms** of a mainstreaming/submersion form of education, including its variants. Language minority children, especially in their first months of schooling, often have little or no idea what the teacher is saying. Because such teachers are infrequently trained in ESL methodology, they may have little expertise in modifying instruction to accommodate such children. Carra-squillo & Rodríguez (2002, p. 3) comment that

> Many LEP students do not receive any specialized language services, and are assigned to regular classrooms where they are mainstreamed with English speaking students, in spite of their limitations in understanding instruction presented in English. This means that LEP students may be taught by regular classroom teachers who may or may not have the support of a language specialist. Consequently, the majority of LEP students receive most, if not all, of their instruction from classroom teachers, many of whom have had no specialized training in this area.

The basic **aim** of such mainstreaming is **assimilation** of language minority speakers, particularly where there has been immigration (e.g. US, UK). Also, where indigenous language minorities are perceived as 'outside' the common good, mainstreaming becomes a tool of integration. The school becomes a melting pot to help create common social, political and economic ideals. As Theodore Roosevelt urged in 1917:

> We must have but one flag. We must have but one language. That must be the language of the Declaration of Independence, of Washington's Farewell Address, of Lincoln's Gettysburg Speech and Second Inaugural. We cannot tolerate any attempt to oppose or supplant the language and culture that has come down to us from the builders of the republic with the language and culture of any European country. The greatness of this nation depends on the swift assimilation of the aliens she welcomes to her shores. Any force which attempts to retard that assimilative process is a force hostile to the highest interests of our country. (quoted in Wagner, 1980, p. 32).

Such a sentiment is still strong in the US (and UK) almost 100 years later.

Language diversity has often been discouraged in the US. It was (and still is) argued, that linguistic harmony hastens a healthy and homogeneous nation. A common language provides, according to some, common attitudes, aims and values. A common language and culture cements society. A God-blest-English speaking America is preferable to the threat of Babel. Language uniformity, some suggest, is required for unity.

Considerable variations in student language ability in a mainstream classroom may often create **challenges** in teaching and class management for the teacher. If the classroom contains students who range from fluent majority language speakers to those who can understand little classroom talk, the task of the teacher may be onerous. In formal 'context-reduced' classrooms, there is no reason to assume that children will quickly and effortlessly acquire the majority language skills necessary to cope in the curriculum. The formal and complex language of the classroom typically takes five to seven or more years to develop.

Alongside problems of language, there may be problems of social and emotional **adjustment** for mainstreamed language minority children that have connections with later drop-out rates from high school. It is not just the child's home language that is deprecated. The identity of the child, the parents, the home, community and culture appear to be deprecated, disparaged and discounted. It is not only the students' language that is denied. It also denies or denounces what they hold most sacred: self esteem, relationships, roots and sometimes race. McKay (1988, p. 341) quotes from a student in a submersion classroom:

> School was a nightmare. I dreaded going to school and facing my classmates and teacher. Every activity the class engaged in meant another exhibition of my incompetence. Each activity was another incidence for my peers to laugh and ridicule me with and for my teacher to stare hopelessly disappointed at me. My self-image was a serious inferiority complex. I became frustrated at not being able to do anything right. I felt like giving up the entire mess.

Skutnabb-Kangas (1981, 2000) indicates the **stresses** of learning through an undeveloped language in mainstreaming. Listening to a new language demands high concentration. It is tiring, with a constant pressure to think about the form of the language and less time to think about curriculum content. A child has to take in information from different curriculum areas and learn a language at the same time. Stress, lack of self-confidence, 'opting-out', disaffection and alienation may occur.

The reality is that many mainstream schools in the US contain children for whom English is a second language, and mainstream teachers are expected to provide effective and challenging education for such children. Such teachers are required to develop both the English language proficiency of their students and to teach subject content (see Carrasquillo & Rodríguez, 2002; Echevarría & Graves, 1998; Echevarría *et al.*, 2000; Faltis, 1997 for teaching approaches in such situations). Given this reality, Carrasquillo & Rodriguez (2002) discuss inter-linked elements of effective teacher practice that include: eliminating social and racial barriers and maximizing equality of opportunity, enabling students to interact purposively with English proficient speakers, and such teachers being sensitive to the language needs of the students.

MAINSTREAMING WITH PULL-OUT CLASSES

Mainstream education may occur with or without the addition of **withdrawal classes** or '**pull-out' classes** to teach the majority language. Language minority children in mainstream schools may be withdrawn for 'compensatory' lessons in the majority language (e.g. English as a second language (**ESL**) pull-out programs in the US and UK). Such **ESL pull-out** programs are provided as a way of keeping language minority children in mainstream schooling and are in preference to no English language support. For many US students and schools, the choice is mainstreaming with or without ESL support. The latter may therefore be valuable, giving students not only English language learning provision, but also the chance to build self-esteem and acquire the only language medium of the subject curriculum.

However, 'withdrawn' children may fall behind on curriculum content delivered to others not in withdrawal classes. There may also be a stigma for absence. A withdrawal child may be seen by peers as 'remedial', 'disabled' or 'backward in English'. ESL classes tend to be frequent in the US, but Ovando *et al.* (2003) suggest they are often not particularly effective:

> Problems with this model are lost time in students' access to the full curriculum, lack of curriculum articulation with grade-level (mainstream) classroom teachers, and no access to primary language schooling to keep up with grade-level academic work while learning English. The social assumption is that the language the child speaks is a problem to be remediated, and students often feel that they are stigmatized by attending what is perceived as a remedial class (p. 73)

A variation under this heading is **Sheltered English or Sheltered Content Instruction** or **SDAIE** (specially designed academic instruction in English), where US minority language students are taught the curriculum with a simplified vocabulary but also purpose-made materials and methods (such as cooperative learning, use of non-verbal communication, visual aids, demonstrations, hands-on experience, and frequent checks for understanding so that learning 'makes sense') – but only through the medium of English (Faltis, 1997; Faltis & Hudelson, 1998; Echevarría & Graves, 1998). In Sheltered English or Sheltered Content Instruction, content and curriculum materials are developed and pitched to match the English proficiency of the students (comprehensible input). Sheltered English or Sheltered Content English is distinct from ESL (English as a Second Language), as in ESL English is taught as a language, with a focus on learning that language (Faltis, 1997; Faltis & Hudelson, 1998; Echevarría & Graves, 1998; Echevarría *et al.*, 2000). In comparison, Sheltered Content Instruction has curriculum content knowledge, understanding and skills as the goals. Echevarría *et al.* (2000) present a model of sheltered instruction with the Sheltered Instruction Observation Protocol (SIOP), that provides a tool for observing and quantifying a teacher's implementation of quality sheltered instruction that teaches content material to English language learners.

Sheltered Content Teaching may involve temporary segregation from first language English speakers (Echevarría & Graves, 1998; Ovando *et al.*, 2003). There can be positive features to temporary withdrawal. Such segregation may produce: (1) greater opportunity for participation among students (they may be less inhibited due to no competition or comparisons with first language speakers of English); (2) greater sensitivity among teachers to the linguistic, cultural and educational needs of a homogeneous group of students; and (3) a collective identity among students in a similar situation (Faltis, 1993a, 1993b). However, such language segregation removes first language role models; may produce social isolation with overtones of stigmatization and reinforce negative stereotypes; may encourage the labeling of segregated students as linguistically and educationally inferior, deprived and in need of remedial attention; and may generate inequality in treatment (e.g. in curriculum materials and the lack of relevant training of teachers).

SEGREGATIONIST EDUCATION

A form of 'minority language only' education is segregationist language education (Skutnabb-Kangas, 1981, 2000; Mangubhai, 2002). Segregationist education occurs where minority language speakers are denied access to those programs or schools attended by majority language speakers. Such separation can be through law (*de jure*) or practice (*de facto*).

Monolingual education through the medium of the minority language can be for **apartheid** (e.g. educating a colonial people only in their native language). The ruling elite prescribes education solely in the minority language to maintain subservience and segregation. Such language minorities 'do not learn enough of the power language to be able to influence the society or, especially, to acquire a common language with the other subordinated groups, a shared medium of communication and analysis' (Skutnabb-Kangas, 1981, p. 128). Segregationist education forces a monolingual language policy on the relatively powerless.

TRANSITIONAL BILINGUAL EDUCATION

Transitional bilingual education has been a frequent type of bilingual education in the United States and the form that was most supported by Title VII funds. The aim of transitional bilingual education is **assimilationist**. It differs from submersion education in that language minority students are temporarily allowed to use their home language. Such students are taught briefly through their home language until they are thought to be proficient enough in the majority language to cope in mainstream education (Cummins, 1980b). Thus, transitional education is a brief, temporary swim in one pool until the child is perceived as capable of moving to the mainstream pool. The aim is to increase use of the majority language in the classroom while proportionately decreasing the use of the home language in the classroom (Villarreal, 1999).

The educational rationale is based on perceived priorities: children need to function in the majority language in society. The argument used is that if competency in the majority language is not quickly established, such children may fall behind their majority language peers (Mitchell *et al.*, 1999). Thus, arguments about equality of opportunity and maximizing student performance are used to justify such transitional programs. The extent to which such justifications are valid or invalid is considered later (see chapter 12).

Transitional bilingual education (TBE) can be split into two major types: **early exit** and **late exit** (Ramírez & Merino, 1990). Early-exit TBE refers to two years maximum help using the mother tongue. Late-exit TBE allows around 40% of classroom teaching in the mother tongue until the 6th grade. Historically (e.g. 1980s and 1990s in the US), early-exit TBE was predominant. Some programs are for older students (e.g. middle and high schools) who have received education through their native language, immigrated, and require a transition to mainstream classes (August, 2002).

Ovando *et al.* (2003) criticize this TBE model for being remedial, compensatory and segregated, perpetuating the status quo by separating language minority students from the mainstream and thus reproducing differences in power and progress for those with lower class status. Also, a TBE program needs much time to teach English such that the academic content and cognitive complexity of the remainder of the curriculum is weakened.

While majority language monolingualism is the aim of transitional bilingual education, teachers or their assistants need to be bilingual. The temporary home language swim requires, for example, a Spanish speaking teacher who may be more sensitive and successful in teaching English to Spanish speaking children than English-only teachers. The former can switch from one language to another and be more sympathetic to the language of the children. However, a **bilingual teacher** can become the unwitting promoter of transition from one language to another, and assimilation into the majority culture. Such teachers can promote the transition from home to school language from within their own cultural group. An Anglo teacher is thus not imposed on the Hispanic language minority; the conversion job is achieved by a bilingual teacher.

Similarly, in US schools with transitional programs, there is sometimes a hidden message in the **staffing**. People with power and prestige, such as principals and assistant principals, are often English monolinguals (O. García, 1993). The people with the least power and status are cooks, lunch monitors, cleaners and janitors, who, for example, speak a minority language such as Spanish. The language of formal announcements is English; the language used by those who serve may be Spanish. The language to learn is the language of power and prestige. The language to forget is the language of servitude, stigma and shame.

However, such Hispanic teachers may alternatively recognize the needs and wishes of their own communities. Such communities may desire their young to speak English early in schooling, but differ from administrators in wanting to preserve Spanish (García, 1991). Hispanic teachers may continue to teach English in transitional bilingual education, but also try to preserve Spanish in the children, becoming allies of the community and not just allies of politicians and bureaucrats.

The transitional model is not just found in the United States. Where there is a majority language and much immigration, then education is often expected to provide a linguistic and cultural transition. In **England**, for example, languages other than English are used in the classroom only while there is a quick transition to the majority language (Creese, 2004). The argument for this is pragmatic. In a class of 30 children, there may be many different heritage languages. There are so many immigrant languages (e.g. over 300 in London) that, it is claimed, bilingual education is impossible. Instead, UK ethnic communities are expected to engage in mother tongue maintenance and not mainstream schools.

In the UK, bilingual 'English as an additional language' (EAL) support teachers are found in some primary (elementary) and secondary (high) schools to aid the transition. Such EAL teachers provide individual support, translate where needed, team-teach with the class teacher, and may occasionally manage the whole class for bilingual story-telling sessions (Bourne, 2001b). However, EAL teachers may feel use of a language other than English is inappropriate or embarrassing and therefore mostly use English. They are also typically poorly paid, low status and subordinate to the classroom teacher (Bourne, 2001b).

In both majority language and minority language contexts, there are sometimes transitional **Newcomer Centers**. For example, in the US recent immigrants and refugees may be placed in a newcomer program particularly if they arrive in the US as older than younger students (e.g. High school level). In Welsh language regions in Wales, English speakers will often be placed in **Latecomer Centers** so as to learn Welsh rapidly before moving to bilingual elementary or high mainstream schools. Coelho (1998) provides Canadian examples with much expert advice. Such Centers offer a 'shock-absorber' transitional experience, culturally, educationally and linguistically. In a sheltered, welcoming and supportive environment, newcomers can adjust to a new language, provide an orientation to the new society, adapt to a new culture over one or two semesters, or one to two years. A student with low-level literacy skills may stay in such a Center for longer.

Sale *et al.* (2003) provide a detailed, elementary **school-based** example of 'shock absorbing' in Mississauga (Ontario, Canada). With many immigrants, the school developed a detailed reception protocol (e.g. to discover the child's learning history), orientation activities (e.g. ESL teacher arranges a buddy, explains the school's curriculum to the parents, answers parents' and students' questions), plus assessment of the child's prior learning to design a learning program and integration into the school.

This case study reflects Guadalupe Valdés' (2001) recommendations for the treatment of immigrants in ESL programs in the US: developing academic English (and interpersonal English) so that students can succeed in school and society, building on their existing academic strengths; all teachers in a school to share responsibility for immigrant students, not just ESL teachers; and integrating rather than isolating immigrant students in school.

MAINSTREAM EDUCATION (WITH FOREIGN LANGUAGE TEACHING)

In the US, Australia, Canada and parts of Europe, most language majority school-children take their education through their home language. For example, children whose parents are English speaking monolinguals attend school where English is the sole teaching medium (often with some second (foreign) language teaching). In Canada, this would be called a core program. In Wales and elsewhere, it is sometimes called a 'drip-feed' language program. The term 'drip-feed' highlights the kind of language element in mainstream schooling. Second (foreign) language lessons of half an hour per day may constitute the sole 'other' language diet. Drip-feeding Arabic, French, German, Mandarin, Japanese or Spanish makes the language a subject in the curriculum similar to science and mathematics. This is distinct from teaching through the medium of a second language where curriculum content is the main focus rather than language learning (the latter is sometimes called embedding or content instruction).

In the US, a nation-wide survey (Branaman & Rhodes, 1998) found that 31% of elementary schools reported **teaching a foreign language** (22% in 1987) compared to 86% of secondary schools (87% in 1987). Spanish and French were the most popular foreign languages, with Spanish increasing and French decreasing (Branaman & Rhodes, 1998). Spanish for Spanish speakers rose considerably over a decade: from 1% to 9% in elementary schools, and from 1% to 10% in secondary schools.

The problem in some countries (e.g. US, England) is that relatively few second language students become competent in that second language. Where children receive a half an hour second language lesson per day for between five and 12 years, few students become functionally fluent in the second language. LeBlanc (1992, p. 35) poses the critical question:

> We all know how much our country [Canada] invests in second-language training. We are talking in terms of millions and millions of dollars. All these students are taking second-language courses and, once they have finished, should normally be able to function in the second language. But what happens in reality?

The Canadians found that after 12 years of French drip-feed language teaching, many English-background students were not fluent enough to communicate in French with French Canadians. Similarly in the UK, five years of French or German or Spanish in secondary school (age 11 to 16) results in only a few sufficiently competent to use that second language. For the great majority, the second language quickly shrivels and dies. **Mainstream education** rarely produces functionally bilingual children. A very limited knowledge of a foreign language tends to be the typical outcome for the mass of the language majority.

This is not the only outcome of second and foreign language teaching. The learning of English in Scandinavia does not fit this pattern, with many learners becoming fluent in, for example, English. When motivation is high, when economic and vocational circumstances encourage the acquisition of a trading language, then foreign language teaching may be more fruitful. Learning a foreign language in the elementary school has become increasingly favored in mainland Europe.

SEPARATIST EDUCATION

A more narrow view of language minority education would be to choose to foster monolingualism in the minority language. The aims are minority language monolingualism and monoculturalism in a context where such choice is self-determined. Schermerhorn (1970) called this a **secessionist** movement where a language minority aims to detach itself from the language majority to pursue an independent existence. As a way of trying to protect a minority language from being over-run by the language majority, or for political, religious or cultural reasons, separatist minority language education may be promoted. This type of education may be organized by the language community for its own survival and for self-protection.

It is unlikely that a school would formally state its aims in a linguistic separatist fashion. Rather, in the implicit functioning of isolationist religious schools and the political rhetoric of extreme language activists, the 'separatist' idea of such schools exists. Small in number, the importance of this category is that it highlights that language minority education is capable of moving from the goal of pluralism to separatism.

CONCLUSION

Having considered some of the history of bilingual education and 'weak' types of such education, the next chapter moves onto 'strong' forms of bilingual education where bilingualism and biliteracy are part of the aims. What can then be examined (in chapter 12) is the relative success and effectiveness of these different forms of 'weak' and 'strong' bilingual education.

KEY POINTS IN THE CHAPTER

- Ten varieties of bilingual education are suggested with a particular contrast between 'strong' and 'weak' forms of bilingual education. In the latter, bilingual pupils are present but bilingualism and biliteracy is rarely the outcome.
- The basic aim of 'weak' forms of bilingual education is assimilation of language minorities rather than maintenance of their home languages and cultural pluralism.
- Language minority students in mainstream schools may be helped by pull-out classes and sheltered content instruction.
- Transitional bilingual education allows a student temporary use of their home language for content learning. The basic aim remains assimilation and not bilingualism or biliteracy.

SUGGESTED FURTHER READING

CARRASQUILLO, A.L. & RODRIGUEZ, V., 2001, *Language Minority Students in the Mainstream Classroom* (2nd edition). Clevedon: Multilingual Matters.

CRAWFORD, J., 2004, *Educating English Learners: Language Diversity in the Classroom*. Los Angeles: Bilingual Education Services.

CUMMINS, J. & CORSON, D. (eds), 1997, *Bilingual Education. Volume 5 of the Encyclopedia of Language and Education*. Dordrecht: Kluwer.

GARCÍA, O. & BAKER, C. (eds), 2006, *Bilingual Education: An Introductory Reader*. Clevedon: Multilingual Matters.

GENESEE, F. (ed.), 1999, *Program Alternatives for Linguistically Diverse Students*. University of California, Santa Cruz: Center for Research on Education, Diversity and Excellence.

OVANDO, C.J., COLLIER, V.P. & COMBS, M.C., 2003, *Bilingual and ESL Classrooms: Teaching in Multicultural Contexts* (3rd edition). New York: McGraw Hill.

SKUTNABB-KANGAS, T., 2000, *Linguistic Genocide in Education – or Worldwide Diversity and Human Rights*. Mahwah, NJ: Erlbaum.

VALDÉS, G., 2001, *Learning and Not Learning English: Latino Students in American Schools.* New York: Teachers College Press.

See also the *International Journal of Bilingualism and Bilingual Education* for the most recent articles on this topic.

STUDY ACTIVITIES

(1) Write a personal account of one type of language education which you have experienced or with which you are most familiar. Present this in a small group seminar to find out differences and similarities of experience.

(2) There is a distinction between (a) teaching a new language (e.g. foreign language learning) (b) teaching about a language (e.g. language awareness) and (c) teaching through a language (content teaching). What approach does your region favor, for which groups of students, and for what reasons?

(3) Create a photographic display of the linguistic landscape of one or more schools (e.g. classroom walls, school signs and notices, class literacy materials). What do the images reveal about the language aims of the schools?

CHAPTER 11

Education for Bilingualism and Biliteracy

CHAPTER 11

Education for Bilingualism and Biliteracy

INTRODUCTION

The two previous chapters provided a historical background to bilingual education and an introduction to 'weak' forms of bilingual education. This chapter examines the **'strong'** forms of bilingual education introduced in the ten-fold typology outlined in chapter 10. Both US and international models are examined, with an initial consideration of dual language education that has grown in the United States from one school in the 1960s to a movement that has both educational and political support.

'Strong' forms of bilingual education have bilingualism, biliteracy and biculturalism as intended outcomes. Some schools aim for multilingualism, multiliteracies and multiculturalism. This chapter particularly examines (1) dual language education that has grown in the US and is expanding elsewhere in the world, (2) Heritage Language bilingual education that is concerned with teaching content through a minority language and exists worldwide, (3) immersion bilingual education that originated in Canada and has been exported successfully to many countries, and (4) mainstream bilingual education through two or more majority languages. Each of these models is well established, favorably evaluated and flourishing.

DUAL LANGUAGE BILINGUAL EDUCATION

Dual language (or two way) bilingual education in the United States typically occurs when approximately equal numbers of language minority and language majority students are in the same classroom and both languages are used for instruction. For example, approximately half the children may be from Spanish speaking homes, the other half from English monolingual homes, and they work together in the classroom. Since both languages are used for learning, the aim is to

228

produce relatively balanced bilinguals (Lindholm-Leary, 2001). Biliteracy is as much an aim as full bilingualism, with literacy being acquired sequentially (occasionally simultaneously) in both languages (see chapter 14).

There has been a variety of **terms** used to describe such schools: two way schools, two way immersion, two way bilingual education, developmental bilingual education, dual language education, bilingual immersion, Spanish immersion, double immersion and interlocking education.

The **growth** of these programs has been considerable, with the oldest dating back to 1963 in Dade County, Florida, developed by a US Cuban community (see O. García & Otheguy, 1985, 1988; Baker & Jones, 1998). There are currently about 300 programs (http://www.cal.org/twi/directory/). US dual language programs tend to share the following features (Genesee & Gándara, 1999; Lindholm-Leary, 2001):

(1)   A non-English language (i.e. a minority language) is used for at least 50% of instruction that lasts for up to six years.
(2)   In each period of instruction, only one language is normally used. Instruction must be adjusted to the student's language level, but must also be challenging, empowering and enabling. Language is learned primarily through content.
(3)   Both English and non-English speakers are present in approximately balanced numbers and integrated for most content instruction. The English and non-English speakers are integrated in all lessons.

A **language balance** among students close to 50%–50% is attempted because if one language becomes dominant (e.g. due to much larger numbers of one language group), the aim of bilingualism and biliteracy may be at risk. The reality of such schools is often different, with an imbalance towards larger numbers of language minority students being more common.

An **imbalance** in the two languages among students may result in one language being used to the exclusion of the other (e.g. Spanish speaking children having to switch to English to work cooperatively). Alternatively, one language group may become sidelined (e.g. Spanish speakers become excluded from English speaking groups). Segregation rather than integration may occur. In the creation of a dual language school or classroom, careful student selection decisions have to be made to ensure a psychological **language balance** that goes beyond a balance of numbers. Differences in minority and majority language status, and power relations between English and other languages, make language balance decisions crucial in a school. However, numerical balance does not necessarily lead to language balance. The large-scale study of dual language education in Miami by Oller & Eilers (2002) suggested that regardless of school type and school age, dual language children tended to speak predominantly in English, even in the first semester of kindergarten. Perceptions of the power of each language and linguistic assimilation can negate neat dual language education mathematical balances among children.

When an **imbalance** does exist, it may thus be preferable to have more language minority children. Where there is a preponderance of language majority children, the tendency is for language minority children to switch to the higher status, majority language. In most language contexts, the majority language is well represented outside school (e.g. in the media and for employment). Therefore, the balance towards the majority language outside school can be complemented by an imbalance towards the minority language in school (among student enrollment and in curriculum delivery). However, if the school enrolls a particularly high number of language minority children, the prestige of the school can sometimes suffer (both among language majority and language minority parents).

In **dual language magnet schools** in the US, **students** may be drawn from a wide geographical area. For example, if a magnet school focuses on environmental arts and sciences, parents throughout a district may be eager to gain a place for their children. Ensuring a language balance in each classroom then becomes a key **selection** feature.

There are situations in which **attracting language majority students** to a dual language bilingual school is difficult. Where the monolingual mainstream school is as (or more) attractive to prospective parents, recruitment to dual language bilingual schools may be an initial challenge. For parents, allocation of their children to dual language bilingual programs will be voluntary and not enforced. Hence, the good **reputation**, perceived effectiveness and curriculum success of dual language bilingual schools become crucial to their continuation. Evidence from the US suggests that language minority parents may be supportive of such a program (e.g. Hornberger, 1991). Majority language parents may need more persuading. Community backing and community involvement in the school may also be important in long-term success.

The **development** of dual language bilingual schools often starts with the creation of a dual language kindergarten class rather than with implementation throughout a school. As the kindergarten students move through the grades, a new dual language class is created each year. As Wiese (2004) demonstrates, the reality can be different as new dual language schools go through a period of evolution and construction rather than holistic and full implementation. Teachers do not passively implement a model but interpret it in terms of the instructional context and students (e.g. presence of African-American students, the means to appreciate and celebrate linguistic and cultural diversity, and the treatment of African-American Vernacular English).

Apart from elementary dual language bilingual schools, there is also dual language secondary education in the US and, with different names, in many other countries of the world (e.g. Wales, Spain, India). A dual language bilingual school may be a whole school in itself (for examples see McCarty, 2003). Also, there may be a dual language strand within a 'mainstream' school. For example, there may be one dual language classroom in each grade.

Lindholm-Leary (2000) and Howard & Christian (2002) indicate the major **goals** of dual language programs:

- High levels of proficiency in students' first language and a second language.
- Reading and writing at grade level in both languages.

- Academic achievement at, or above, grade level (e.g. mathematics, science, social studies).
- Positive intercultural (multicultural) attitudes and behaviors.
- Communities and society to benefit from having citizens who are bilingual and biliterate, who are positive towards people of different cultural backgrounds, and who can meet national needs for language competence and a more peaceful co-existence with peoples of other nations.

The **aim** of dual language bilingual schools is thus not simply to produce bilingual and biliterate children. Genesee and Gándara (1999) suggest that such schools enhance inter-group communicative competence and cultural awareness. They produce children who, in terms of inter-group relations, are likely to be more tolerant, sensitive and equalized in status. 'Contact between members of different groups leads to increased liking and respect for members of the outgroup, including presumably reductions in stereotyping, prejudice, and discrimination' (Genesee & Gándara, 1999, p. 667). Positive interactions between students can be facilitated by strategies such as cooperative learning (Howard & Christian, 2002), but this goal also requires suitably trained teachers.

To gain status and to flourish, dual language schools need to aim to show success throughout the curriculum (Lindholm-Leary, 2001). On high-stakes state testing, on attainment compared with other schools in the locality, and in specialisms (e.g. music, sport, science), dual language bilingual schools will strive to show relative success. A narrow focus on proficiency in two languages will be insufficient.

Similarly, Lindholm-Leary (2000) suggests that dual language schools promote the 'competencies necessary for the new global business job market' (p. 5). Students graduating in Spanish and English, for example, should be well placed to operate in international markets, transnational businesses and global operations (e.g. national defense), as these two languages are spoken across different continents and in many countries outside the US (see chapter 19). However, this has drawn some criticism. For example, it may be that native English speakers becoming fluent in Spanish may benefit most. It may be that this reduces Latinos' natural advantage as bilinguals in such employment and promotion opportunities.

The **mission** of dual language bilingual schools may also be couched in terms such as 'equality of educational opportunity for children from different language backgrounds', 'child-centered education building on the child's existing language competence', 'a positive self-image for each child', 'a community dedicated to the integration of all its children', 'enrichment not compensatory education', 'a family-like experience to produce multicultural children', and 'supporting bilingual proficiency not limited English proficiency'.

The mission of all dual language bilingual schools (compared with mainstreaming) is to produce **bilingual, biliterate and multicultural children**. Language minority students are expected to become literate in their native language as well as in the majority language. At the same time, majority language students should make 'normal' progress in their first language and in all content areas of the curriculum. To achieve these aims, a variety of practices are implemented in dual language bilingual schools (Christian *et al.*, 1997; Cloud *et al.*, 2000; Lindholm-Leary, 2001, 2005; Soltero, 2004; Gómez *et al.*, 2005; also Howard *et al.* (2005) http://www.cal.org/twi/guidingprinciples.htm).

(1) The two **languages** of the school (e.g. Spanish and English, Japanese and English) have **equal status**. Both languages will be used as a medium of instruction, with an integration of language and content learning. Math, science and social studies, for example, may be taught in both languages. However, care has to be taken not to be repetitive, not to teach the same content in both languages.

(2) The **school ethos** will be bilingual. Such an ethos is created by classroom and corridor displays, notice boards, curriculum resources, cultural events, lunch-time and extra-curricular activity using both languages in a relatively balanced way. Announcements across the school address system will be bilingual. Letters to parents will also be in two languages. While playground conversations and student-to-student talk in the classroom are difficult to influence or manipulate, the school environment aims to be transparently bilingual.

(3) In some dual language bilingual schools, the two **languages** are **taught** as languages (sometimes called language arts instruction). Here, aspects of spelling, grammar, metaphors and communicative skills may be directly taught. In other two way bilingual schools, use of both languages as media of instruction is regarded as sufficient to ensure bilingual development. In such schools, children are expected to **acquire proficiency** in language informally throughout the curriculum as well as through interaction with children who are effective first language role models. In both cases, reading and writing in both languages are likely to receive direct attention in the curriculum. Biliteracy is as much an aim as full bilingualism. Literacy will be acquired in both languages either simultaneously or with an initial emphasis on native language literacy (see chapter 14).

(4) **Staff** in the dual language classrooms are often bilingual. Some **teachers** use both languages on different occasions with their students. Where this is difficult (e.g. due to teacher supply or selection), teachers may be paired and work together closely as a team. A teacher's aide, paraprofessionals, secretaries, custodial staff, and/or parents offering or invited to help the teacher may also be bilingual. Language minority **parents** can be valuable 'teacher auxiliaries' in the classroom (Soltero, 2004). For example, when a wide variety of Spanish cultures from many regions is brought to the classroom, parents and grandparents may describe and provide the most authentic stories, dances, recipes, folklore and festivals. This underlines the importance of the culture of language minorities being shared in the classroom to create an additive bilingual and multicultural environment.

(5) The **length of the dual language bilingual program** needs to be longer rather than shorter. Such a program for two or three grades is insufficient. A

minimum of four or five years, or extending as far as possible through the grades is more effective (see chapter 8 on the time required to achieve academic proficiency in a second language). A relatively longer experience of a dual language bilingual program is important to ensure a fuller and deeper development of language skills, and biliteracy in particular. Where a US dual language bilingual program exists across more years, there is a tendency for the curriculum to be increasingly taught in English.

A central idea in dual language bilingual schools is **language separation and compartmentalization**. In each period of instruction, only one language is used. **Language boundaries** are established in terms of time, curriculum content and teaching.

First, a decision is made about **when** to teach through each language. One frequent preference is for each language to be used on **alternate days**. On the door of the classroom may be a message about which language is to be used that day. For example, Spanish is used one day, English the next, in a strict sequence. Alternately, **different lessons** may use **different languages** with a regular change over to ensure both languages are used in all curricula areas. For example, Spanish may be used to teach mathematics on Monday and Wednesday and Friday; English to teach mathematics on Tuesday and Thursday. During the next week, the languages are reversed, with mathematics taught in Spanish on Tuesday and Thursday. There are other possibilities. The division of time may be in half days, alternate weeks, alternate half semesters. The essential element is a careful distribution of time to achieve bilingual and biliterate students.

The amount of **time** spent learning through each language varies from school to school. The two main models in the US are 50:50 and 90:10. In the 90:10 model, 90% of instruction is in the minority language in the kindergarten and 1st grade, with 10% to develop English oral language proficiency and pre-literacy skills. Over the remaining elementary grades this ratio changes to 50:50 (e.g. by the 4th to 6th grade). Students often begin formal English reading in the 3rd grade. But from the 1st grade, they are exposed to English literacy more informally.

In the 50:50 model, a 50%–50% balance in use of languages is attempted in both early and later grades. Variations between 90:10 and 50:50 are possible where the minority language will be given more time (60%, 75%, 80%), especially in the first two or three years. In the middle and later years of schooling, there is sometimes a preference for a 50%–50% balance, or occasionally more accent on the majority language.

Gómez *et al.* (2005) portray a '50:50 content model' that allocates different languages for different content areas. That is, it divides languages by subject and not time (although overall, English and Spanish are approximately equally used). Mathematics is taught through the English language, science and social studies through Spanish. In such a model, the balance of students is often not 50:50 (e.g. there being a predominance of Latino students). This is justified on the basis that the balance needs to be between languages of instruction rather than a balance of students.

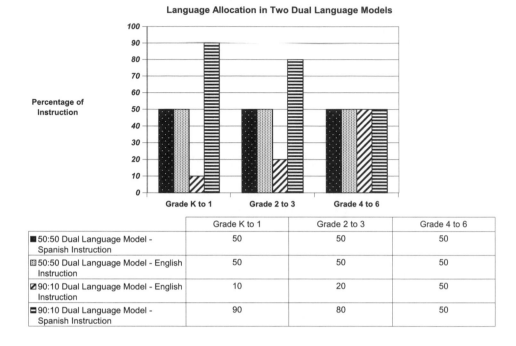

Language Allocation in Two Dual Language Models

	Grade K to 1	Grade 2 to 3	Grade 4 to 6
■ 50:50 Dual Language Model - Spanish Instruction	50	50	50
▦ 50:50 Dual Language Model - English Instruction	50	50	50
◪ 90:10 Dual Language Model - English Instruction	10	20	50
◩ 90:10 Dual Language Model - Spanish Instruction	90	80	50

In addition to these two main models there is a less common 'differentiated' model (Howard *et al.*, 2004). In this model, language minority and language majority students are separated for native language instruction in the morning (kindergarten to Grade 2). In the afternoon, students are integrated for instruction using both languages. From Grade 3, the two language groups are integrated for all instruction throughout the day becoming a 50:50 model.

Whatever the division of time, instruction in a dual language bilingual school will attempt to keep **boundaries** between the languages. Switching languages within a lesson is not considered helpful (see chapter 13). If language mixing by the teacher occurs, students may wait until there is delivery in their stronger language, and become uninvolved at other times. When there is clear separation, the Spanish speakers, for example, may help the English-speakers on Spanish days, and the English speakers help the Spanish speakers on English days. Interdependence may stimulate cooperation and friendship, as well as learning and achievement. The potential problems of segregation and racial hostility may thus be reduced.

However, the two languages will, in reality, sometimes be **switched** or mixed in the classroom (e.g. in private conversations, in further explanations by a teacher, and internal use of the dominant language). Use of languages by children, especially when young, is not usually consciously controlled. Switching often has both communication value (see chapter 5) and pedagogic value (see chapter 13). Switching language can be as natural as smiling.

Second, **bilingual teachers** usually try to ensure they do not switch languages. Children hear them using one language (during a lesson period or during a whole day) and are expected to respond in that same language. When, as in many forms of 'strong' bilingual education, there is a shortage of bilingual teachers, a **pairing of teachers** may ensure language separation. A teacher using only Spanish will work in close association with a teacher who uses only English with the same class.

Third, language boundaries may be established in the **curriculum**. This may occur according to which 'language day' it is. Alternatively, in some schools, different parts of the curriculum are taught in different languages. For example, social studies and environmental studies may be taught in Spanish, science and math in English. Such a policy establishes separate occasions where each language is to be used, and keeps the two languages apart. Christian *et al.* (1997) found in research in two-way (dual language) schools that the separation of languages differed in the schools studied. Schools varied in how strict or flexible they were about language separation. For example, when a student did not understand curriculum content or instructions, a teacher might naturally move into the child's stronger language to explain. However, the danger is that students learn that they do not need to understand the second language because the teacher or peers will translate for them.

One danger in language separation is when the allocation of languages is by content (e.g. the majority language is used for science and technology and the minority language is used for social studies). In this example, the majority language becomes aligned with modern technology and science, while the minority language becomes associated with tradition and culture. This may affect the **status** of the language in the eyes of the child, parents and society. The relationship of each school language to employment prospects, economic advantage and power also needs to be considered. Valdés (1997) cautions that power relations between, for example, Spanish and English speakers in dual language schools are important, especially where programs contain white middle class English speakers and low income Spanish speakers. Opportunities for both groups to reach high levels of achievement are important. Otherwise native Spanish speakers may be exploited as a language resource, and English speakers become the bilinguals with high achievement and the economic/employment advantages of bilingualism and biliteracy.

Origins and Development

Dual language bilingual schools in the US date from 1963 in Dade County, Florida, and were developed by the US Cuban community in that area (see Lindholm, 1987; O. García & Otheguy, 1985, 1988; Baker & Jones, 1998). In September 1963, the **Coral Way Elementary School** started a bilingual program that embraced both Spanish and English speaking students. During the 1960s, another 14 such bilingual schools were set up in Dade County. This is related to the fact that many Cubans expected to return to Cuba, believing the Castro regime would not survive. Local people supported the maintenance of Spanish among the 'soon-to-leave' Cubans. Local English speaking children from middle class families were enrolled in the school.

The Rise of Dual Language Schools in the United States

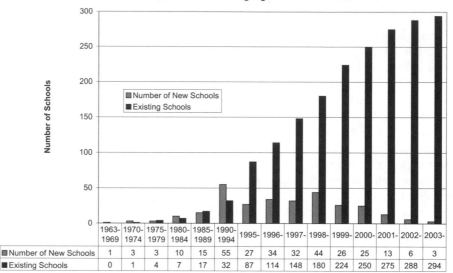

	1963-1969	1970-1974	1975-1979	1980-1984	1985-1989	1990-1994	1995-	1996-	1997-	1998-	1999-	2000-	2001-	2002-	2003-
■ Number of New Schools	1	3	3	10	15	55	27	34	32	44	26	25	13	6	3
■ Existing Schools	0	1	4	7	17	32	87	114	148	180	224	250	275	288	294

This reflected a wish among parents for foreign language instruction following Russia's initial triumph over the US in the space race. (In 1958, the Russian Sputnik was launched.)

Since that era, there has been a steady **rise** in the number of Dual Language bilingual schools in the US, particularly since 1989 – as the graph illustrates (adapted from http://www.cal.org/twi/directory/). Some 25 states (plus the District of Columbia) have 297 dual language bilingual schools (e.g. Arizona, New Mexico, Illinois, Massachusetts, Oregon and Florida). Approximately 60% of these schools are located in Texas, California and New York. Most dual language schools are Elementary, although there are also 32 Middle schools and eight High schools (http://www.cal.org/twi/directory). The languages of instruction in US dual language bilingual programs are predominantly Spanish/English (in 94% of schools) but with the following combinations also represented: French/English; Chinese/English; Korean/English and Navajo/English. However, their future under both federal (e.g. 'No Child Left Behind', 2001) and state (e.g. ballots and Propositions in California and Arizona) policies and politics is not assured. While Dual Language school philosophy favors an equal balance between two languages, the current US political preference is for a balanced tilted strongly towards English.

Specific **examples** of Dual Language schools are documented by Morison (1990) for New York, Senesac (2002) for Chicago, and Jong (2002) for Framingham (Massachusetts). One example of a dual language bilingual school is the James F. Oyster Bilingual Elementary School in Washington DC which has a two-way Spanish / English program that commenced in 1971 (Freeman, 1998, 2004). The initiative was taken by the local community (by parents and local politicians) to produce a school that crossed language, cultural, ethnic and social class lines. Parents are active in the running of the school. In 1998, Freeman reported an ethnic mix of students (from kindergarten to 6th grade) of around 60% Hispanic, 20% White; 15% Black and 5% Asian and other language minorities (Freeman, 1995, 1998). Approximately two in every five children came from low-income families (e.g. they were eligible for the free-lunch program under federal guidelines). In 2002, when 30 new enrollment slots became available in the kindergarten, many English-speaking parents camped out in the snow for up to five days hoping to gain a place for their child (Crawford, 2004).

The **Oyster** program is distinctive because it has two teachers in each classroom: one teacher speaks only Spanish to the students; the other teacher speaks only English. In this relatively expensive approach, the students experience Spanish and English medium instruction for approximately equal amounts of time. Strong equality dimensions pervade the curriculum (ethnic, multicultural, linguistic, social class), with the contributions of different children encouraged and respected. The notion of language equality permeates the ethos of the school (Freeman, 1995, 1998, 2004) which is reflected in the school's mission statement:

> Oyster Bilingual School's focus is on the development of bilingualism, biliteracy, and biculturalism for every student through the mastery of academic skills, the acquisition of language and communicative fluency, the appreciation of differences in racial and ethnic backgrounds, and the building of a positive self-concept and pride in one's heritage.

Freeman (2004) summarizes the delivery of the mission:

> it is considered successful because Spanish-speaking students maintain and develop expertise in their native language, English-speaking students acquire Spanish as a second language, all students achieve academically through two languages, and everyone develops positive intergroup understanding and relations. (p. 67)

As Dicker (2003) notes about English language children learning through Spanish, Oyster students learn that the gift of bilingualism is not reserved for Latinos. Oyster students graduate from the school fluent in two world languages such that they can communicate proficiently in many countries on different continents.

Dual Language Schools and Peace

Dual language schools exist outside the United States. In Macedonia (Tankersley, 2001), China (Zhou, 2001), the United States (Wiese & Garcia, 2001), and the South Pacific (Lotherington, 1998), bilingual education is located within attempts to effect social, cultural, economic or political change, particularly in strengthening the weak, empowering the powerless, and working for peace and humanity in the midst of war and terror. Two particular examples (Macedonia and Israel) link such schools with current **peace initiatives**. The role of dual language schools in bringing peace is well illustrated by Tankersley (2001) in her article aptly entitled 'Bombs or Bilingual Programmes?'. Contextualized within the recent ethnic conflict in the Balkans, she examines a Macedonian/Albanian dual language program. The program demonstrated success in aiding community re-building after the war and the growth of cross-ethnic friendships. The research shows the potential for bilingual education programs to develop students' respect for different languages and cultures, and help to resolve ethnic conflict. However, since the Macedonian language was connected with greater power and prestige, obtaining an equal balance of languages in the classroom was complex.

A similar dual language (Arabic/Hebrew) program with the aim of breaking down barriers of mistrust and building peace is portrayed by Feuerverger (2001) in an ethnography of a village (Neve Shalom/Wahat Al-Salam) in Israel where **Jews and Palestinians** attempt to live together harmoniously and cooperatively, maintaining respect for the culture, identity and languages of each group. This social engineering is attempted by two schools: an elementary school and the 'School for Peace', that create bilingual Hebrew–Arabic bilinguals, biculturals and students sensitive to each others' traditions, religions and customs. Jewish children learning through Arabic, and Palestinian children learning through Hebrew is a means of increasing inter-group sensitivity, respect and integration.

Bekerman (2003, 2005) and Bekerman and Shhadi (2003) also analyze initiatives in Palestinian-Jewish bilingual education to 'keep the dream alive under extremely difficult circumstances', which is a 'daring enterprise' Bekerman, 2005, p. 5). Two schools in Jerusalem and the Upper Galilee aim to build cooperation based on equality and mutual respect, such that 'bilingual education is an empowering pedagogy which helps increase the self esteem' (Bekerman, 2005, p. 6). Yet such schools cannot be islands, and 'bottom-up' rather than 'top-down' initiatives are not always easy to sustain. **Peace schools** are inevitably part of a wider society, such that equality of languages and resoluteness of purpose and mission can be difficult to deliver. Parents also have other dreams, such as English language fluency, high educational achievement and social mobility for their children, that make language and political ideology just one component in a complex whole. Yet such initiatives symbolize that bilingual education can include a vision that goes beyond languages, and beyond a troubled present and past.

HERITAGE LANGUAGE BILINGUAL EDUCATION

Another '**strong form**' of bilingual education occurs where language minority children use their native, ethnic, home or heritage language in the school as a medium of instruction with the goal of full bilingualism. Examples include education through, or more often partly through, the medium of Navajo and Spanish in the US (Krashen *et al.* 1998; House, 2002; Francis & Reyhner, 2002; McCarty, 2002a, 2002b, 2003; Benally & Viri, 2005; Valdés *et al.*, 2006) Hawai'ian indigenous immersion (Hinton, 1998; Hinton & Hale, 2001; Warner, 1999, 2001; Wilson, 1998; Wilson & Kamana, 2001; McCarty, 2002b, 2003); community and heritage languages in Australia (see Hornberger, 2005) Basque (N. Gardner, 2000; Lasagabaster, 2001), and Welsh (Baker, 1993, 2000c; Baker & Jones, 2000; I.W. Williams, 2003; W.G.

Lewis, 2004). The native language is protected and cultivated alongside development in the majority language.

In New Zealand, the Māori language has been promoted in schools with indications of positive outcomes in achievement (Jacques & Hamlin, 1992) and expansion (May *et al.*, 2004; May & Hill, 2004; May, 2004). The full immersion pre-school programs (called *Te Kohanga Reo* language nests) were first established in 1982 and have become internationally famous for their early language success with Māori speakers. An early start to bilingual education can create a 'domino effect', producing a demand for bilingual education beyond pre-school to elementary, secondary and higher education, helping to legitimize the language minority, and transforming its power and status (May, 2004).

A similar promotion of Aboriginal languages occurs in heritage language education in Australia (Caldwell & Berthold, 1995; Hartman & Henderson, 1994; de Courcy, 2002; Nicholls, 2005) as well as in community languages such as Maltese (Borland, 2005; Baldauf, 2005). In Ireland, Irish medium education is often available for children from Irish language backgrounds (Ó Murchú, 2003; Harris & Murtagh, 1999). Children become fluent in English and Irish and possibly other European languages. In China there are 55 ethnic minority groups plus the Han who are in a majority (92% of the 1.2 billion population). Since 1979, minority language education has been provided for over 20 minority groups, partly as a way of improving ethnic minority relationships with central government (Blachford, 1997; J. Lin, 1997; Zhou, 2001; Geary & Pan, 2003). Similar movements are reported in Papua New Guinea and elsewhere in the South Pacific (Siegel, 1996, 1997) and for American Indians (Cantoni, 1996; Hinton & Hale, 2001).

In its more inclusive usage, **heritage language education** is found in schools and classes for established and recent immigrant language groups and community-based language initiatives (Wiley, 2001; Valdés *et al.*, 2006). For example, in the early 1980s in the US, Joshua Fishman located 6553 heritage language schools (mostly private), with an impression that there were 1000 more he had not located (Fishman, 2006). These schools were using 145 different mother tongues of various communities: Arabs, Africans, Asians, French, German, Greek, Haitian, Italian, Jewish, Polish, Japanese, Latin American, Armenian, Dutch, Bulgarian, Irish, Russian, Rumanian, Serbian, Turkish, Ukrainian and Yiddish (Fishman, 2001a). Maintained by those who had lost or were losing their 'native' language, the schools mostly taught that native language and used it as a medium of instruction (Fishman, 1989, 2001a, 2006). Such schools have been supported by foreign governments and religious institutions (churches, mosques, temples, synagogues). Some community-based organizations also foster after-school programs, Saturday schools, weekend schools and religion-based programs. These supplemental schools have grown, especially among the Chinese and Korean communities. Such efforts are grass-roots based and therefore often have much vibrancy and an enthusiasm to succeed. Currently, these schools are poorly documented (Fishman, 2006). There is no recent national or local survey (e.g. of the rise of US Moslem schools using Arabic).

Day schools are typically fee-paying, private establishments. Hence the students tend to come from middle-class or relatively more affluent working-class backgrounds. These schools achieve biliteracy and biculturalism with some success (O. García, 1988). For example, there have been over 130 Yiddish day schools in New York alone, 'successful in teaching children to read and write English, Hebrew, and many times Yiddish' (García, 1988, p. 22). This kind of school, mostly attended by the Jewish Hassidic Orthodox Community, has increased in New York in recent years with its own association of Yiddish teachers and schools. In contrast, non-religious day schools organized by ethnic groups have tended to become more English-focused. For example, many Greek schools in New York are now teaching in English, with a Greek taught as a second language class every day (García, personal communication).

While US bilingual education has not received much federal or state support in recent years, there are positive signs of hope for indigenous languages (Peyton *et al.*, 2001). For example, Hawai'ian now shares official language status with English in Hawaii and is used in some schools for content teaching (McCarty, 2003). Also, when the US Heritage Language Initiative commenced in 1998, it provided the opportunity for heritage language planning on a nation-wide basis (Peyton *et al.*, 2001; see also Hornberger (ed.), 2005).

In the US, this form of bilingual education is sometimes called **maintenance bilingual education** or **developmental maintenance bilingual education**. These programs are relatively few in number with Navajo education being one major example (Holm & Holm, 1990, 1995; Reyhner & Tennant, 1995; McLaughlin & McLaughlin, 2000; House, 2002; Francis & Reyhner, 2002; McCarty, 2003; Benally & Viri, 2005). The term most used internationally to describe this education is **heritage language education**. In Canada, there is a distinction between heritage language lessons and heritage language bilingual education. (1) Heritage language programs provide about two and a half hours per week **language teaching**, currently in more than 60 languages. These lessons often occur during lunch hours, after school and at weekends. (2) In provinces such as Manitoba, British Columbia, Saskatchewan and Alberta, there are heritage language bilingual education programs (e.g. see Benyon & Toohey (1991) on programs in British Columbia; Feuerverger (1997) on Toronto). The heritage language is the **medium of instruction** for about 50% of the day (e.g. Ukrainian, Italian, German, Hebrew, Yiddish, Mandarin Chinese, Arabic and Polish; see Cummins, 1992a). In essence, heritage language education refers to the education of **language minority** children through their minority and majority language. In most cases, the majority language will be present in the curriculum, ranging from second language lessons to a varying proportion (e.g. 10% to 50%) of the curriculum being taught in the majority language.

While the term 'heritage language' is used internationally for indigenous peoples as a language minority, it can also include 'foreign born', colonial (e.g. German in Pennsylvania – see Baker & Jones, 1998) and African American Vernacular English in the US (Baugh, 1999). Wiley (2001) and Deusen-Scholl (2003) carefully examine the definitional issues of 'heritage language' in terms of educational programs, community and the language itself. In the US, the term encompasses those raised in a non-English language home who understand and may speak a language other than English (Valdés, 2001; Wiley, 2005a). However, heritage language education programs will teach (and typically teach through) a heritage language, and not just include heritage language children. Such a program may include other native language children as well.

The term 'heritage language' may also be called 'native language', 'ethnic language', 'minority language', 'ancestral language', aboriginal language, or, in French, *'langues d'origine'*. A **danger** of the term 'heritage' is that it points to the past and not to the future, to traditions rather than the contemporary. Partly for this reason, the UK and Australian term tends to be 'community language' or 'where English is an additional language'. The heritage language may or may not be an indigenous language. Both Navajo and Spanish can be perceived as heritage languages in the US depending on an *individual's* perception of what constitutes their heritage language.

Heritage language programs in the US (see Krashen *et al.*, 1998; McCarty, 2003) and elsewhere vary in structure and content, and overlap with the 90:10 model of dual language education (see later). Some of the likely features of heritage language programs are as follows:

(1) Most, but not necessarily all of the children will come from **language minority homes**. At the same time, the minority language may be the majority language of a local community. In certain areas of the US, Spanish speakers are in a majority in their neighborhood or community. In Gwynedd (Wales, UK) where the minority language (Welsh) is often the majority language of the community, heritage language programs are prevalent (I.W. Williams, 2003). The children are frequently joined in these programs by a smaller number of majority language children.

(2) **Parents** will often have the choice of sending their children to mainstream schools or to heritage language programs. Ukrainian, Jewish and Mohawkian heritage language programs in Canada, for example, have given parents freedom of choice in selecting schools.

(3) The language minority student's home language will often be used for approximately half or more of the **curriculum time**. The Ukrainian programs in Manitoba have allotted half the time to Ukrainian, half to English. Mathematics and science, for example, has been taught in English; music, art and social studies in Ukrainian. There is a tendency to teach technological, scientific studies through the majority language. Other models use the student's home language for between 50% to almost 100% of curriculum time. Changes across grades usually move from much early use of the student's home language to approximately equal use of the two languages (e.g. by Grade 6).

(4) Where a minority language is used for a majority of classroom time (e.g. 80% to almost 100%), the justification is that children easily transfer ideas, concepts, skills and knowledge into the majority language. Having taught a child multi-

plication in Spanish, this mathematical concept does not have to be retaught in English. Classroom teaching **transfers** relatively easily between languages when such languages are sufficiently developed to cope with concepts, content and curriculum materials.

(5) The **justification** given for heritage language programs is also that a minority language is easily lost, while a majority language is easily gained. Children tend to be surrounded by the majority language. Television and town advertisements, shops and signs, videos and visits often provide or induce bilingual proficiency. Thus bilingualism is achieved by an initial concentration on the minority language at school. In the later stages of elementary schooling, increasing attention may be given to majority language development, ensuring that full bilingualism occurs. Heritage language programs will quickly be seen to fail if students do not become fully competent in the majority language.

(6) Heritage language **schools** are mostly elementary schools. This need not be the case. In Wales, for example, such schools are available to the end of secondary education and the heritage language can be used as a medium of vocational and academic study at College and University (Baker & Jones, 2000). Another example is a Hawaiian heritage language program that operates from kindergarten through to Grade 12 (Wilson & Kamana, 2001).

Key Differences between Models

Immersion bilingual education differs from **Dual Language** bilingual schools in the language backgrounds of the students. Immersion schools usually contain only language majority children learning much or part of the curriculum through a second language (e.g. English speaking children learning through the medium of French in Canadian schools). Dual language bilingual schools aim to contain a balanced mixture of children from two (or more) different language backgrounds (e.g. from Spanish speaking and English speaking homes in the US). **Dual Language** bilingual schools differ from **Heritage Language** (developmental maintenance) schools in aiming for more of a balance of majority and minority language children. Heritage Language education is comparatively more concerned with preservation of the ethnic language, ethnic culture and, in many cases, has a large preponderance of language minority children. The type of school possible in a neighborhood is often determined by the demographic and sociolinguistic character of the school population (e.g. the size of one or more language minority groups, the presence of recent or more established immigrants, the numbers of majority language speakers).

Indigenous Education in the United States

An important example of heritage language bilingual education is provision for indigenous **American Indians**, Alaskan Natives and Native Hawai'ians. Approximately 300 or more American Indian languages were once spoken in the US (McCarty, 2002b). McCarty and Watahomigie (1999) indicate that currently approximately two million American Indians, Alaska Natives and Native Hawaiians reside in the United States representing some 550 nations and 175 distinct languages. Krauss (2000) and McCarty (2002b) predict that as few as 20 of those languages will survive (e.g. Navajo, Ojibwa, Dakota, Choctaw, Apache, Cherokee, Tohono O'odham, Yup'ik). Only about 20 American Indian languages are spoken in the home by younger generations – language transmission in the family being highly important for language survival (Fishman, 1991, 2001a; Reyhner & Tennant, 1995; Krauss, 2000). All of California's 50+ native American Indian languages may be dying as they are only spoken by small numbers of elders.

A history of American Indian education is a record of attempts to **eradicate** the heritage languages and cultures (Cantoni, 1996; Crawford, 1999; McLaughlin & McLaughlin, 2000; Spack, 2002; Reyhner & Eder, 2004; Benally & Viri, 2005). Forced assimilation has been prevalent for over a hundred years, symbolized in a phrase from the Commissioner of Indian Affairs, J.D.C. Adkins, in 1887: 'Teaching an Indian youth in his own barbarous dialect is a positive detriment to him' (Krauss, 2000; McCarty & Watahomigie, 1999; McCarty & Bia, 2002; McCarty, 2002b). One technique was to remove children from their tribes and send them to distant boarding schools. Stories abound of children being kidnapped from their homes and taken on horseback to boarding schools, many of which were located at former military forts. Such children were given an English-only curriculum, military-style discipline with resulting physical and psychological scars. There was severe punishment (e.g. use of belts and hoses) for speaking their native language and a manual labor system which required them to work half days in kitchens and boiler rooms to minimize school costs (McCarty, 1998; McCarty & Bia, 2002; McCarty, 2003). As one of House's (2002) interviewees commented: 'I think it was outright really abusing students, wiping away another culture, another language . . . It was very clear our language, our religion, our custom, was not something that we should practice or carry on with' (p.62).

In the 1970s, Congress approved the Indian Education Act (1972) and the Indian Self-Determination and Educational Assistance Act (1975). In 1990, with the passage of the Native American Languages Act (authorized for funding in 1992), a further effort was made to preserve, protect and promote the rights and freedoms of Native Americans to use and develop their own indigenous languages (Reyhner & Eder, 2004). Also, the No Child Left Behind (2001) legislation authorizes programs for Indian, Native Hawaiian and Native Alaska education. However, this legislation emphasizes English language acquisition, the high stakes testing of English, threats of school closure or other interventions where there is insufficient progress in English, and bilingual teaching assistants acquiring a college qualification. Such a policy, joined with the English-only ballots in Arizona and California, leaves indigenous bilingual education with an uncertain, if not perilous, future.

An example of a Native American language maintenance program is the **Rock Point Community School** in Arizona, which was established in the mid-1930s, and has been famous since the early 1970s for its role in maintaining the **Navajo** language (Holm & Holm, 1990, 1995). Rock Point is a reservation-interior community on the middle reaches of Chinle Wash in northern Arizona. Enrolling 99% Navajo children, the languages used in this kindergarten to Grade 12 bilingual education program are Navajo and English. The three program aims are defined as: (1) students to become proficient speakers, readers, and writers of the Navajo and English languages; (2) students to acquire cultural knowledge of at least two cultures: Navajo and Anglo-American; (3) students to develop critical thinking skills in Navajo and English. In Kindergarten to Grade 5, Navajo is used for 50% of class time; in Grade 6 for 25%, and in Grades 7 to 12 for 15% of total class time. In Kindergarten to Grade 5, reading, language arts, math, science, social studies and health are taught through both Navajo and English, with separation of languages by differing blocks of time. In Grades 6 to 12, teaching through Navajo occurs for literacy, social science, electives and science (one semester in Grade 6) with teaching in English for reading, language arts, math, science, social studies, health, home economics and physical education. The language of initial reading in instruction for Navajo speakers is Navajo and for English speakers it is English. All program teachers are proficient in both languages. Over 90% of the teaching staff are members of the Navajo ethnic group and provide bilingual role models (McCarty, 1997, 2003). A similar Navajo case study (of Rough Rock) is effectively portrayed in words and pictures by McCarty & Bia (2002) and (of Fort Defiance) by McCarty (2003) and Arviso & Holm (2001).

These interventions show that bilingual education can be successful in raising language awareness, raising standards of education, and preserving the indigenous languages of the United States. Such bilingual education gives a sense of identity and pride in their origins to American Indian children, preserving not just their languages but also their rich cultures (Cantoni, 1996; Hinton & Hale, 2001; McLaughlin & McLaughlin, 2000; Benally & Viri, 2005). This reflects the growing US awareness of historical brutal assimilation and the current need to preserve the deep repository of history, customs, values, religions and oral traditions that belong to American Indians but which can be valuably shared far beyond the Reservations to enrich all people.

Yet language rights and bilingual education programs do not guarantee language maintenance for American Indians. Parents have sometimes made choices against language maintenance, sometimes based on their own indoctrination that 'white and English is best' (McCarty & Bia, 2002; McCarty, 2003). Also, it is dangerous to expect too much from heritage language education in saving a language and culture (see chapter 3). This form of education can produce new speakers and ensure deeper language and cultural roots for native speakers. Without these kind of initiatives, a minority language can quickly die. When schools do nothing, it is not only the minority language that is not being produced in children. Such a policy also signals the low value, economic worthlessness and stigmatization of a language, affecting the decisions of both parents and students, and not least the fate of the language.

Heritage language schooling is a language and cultural **supply line** that creates potential. But supply is dependent on demand. Also, potential has to be turned into everyday language usage, outside the school and for the life-span. Parents and students expect bilingual education to have purpose and value beyond schooling. It needs to lead to economic and employment, social and cultural opportunities, or heritage language education can create a fine product without much future use.

IMMERSION BILINGUAL EDUCATION

When applied to language, 'immersion' was first used to describe intensive language programs for US troops about to go abroad in the Second World War. In the 1960s, 'immersion education' was coined in Canada to describe a new form of bilingual education. **Immersion bilingual education** derives from a Canadian educational experiment in the 1960s. The modern immersion movement has been dated to an experiment in the Montreal suburb of St Lambert in 1965 (Lambert & Tucker, 1972) although Rebuffot (1993) suggests that École Cedar Park in West Island Quebéc (started in 1958) and the Toronto French school (dating from 1962) were already in existence. A few English speaking, middle-class parents persuaded school district administrators to set up an experimental kindergarten class of 26 children. The stated aims were for students (1) to become competent to speak, read and write in French; (2) to reach normal achievement levels throughout the curriculum including the English language; (3) to appreciate the traditions and culture of French speaking Canadians as well as English speaking Canadians. In short, the aims were for children to become bilingual and bicultural without loss of achievement. Subconsciously or consciously, the economic and employment advantages to be gained from bilingualism, biliteracy and biculturalism may also have been motivations (see later).

Types of Immersion Bilingual Education

Immersion education is an umbrella term. Within the concept of immersion experience are various programs (in Canada and countries such as Finland, Spain and Ireland) differing in terms of the following aspects:

- **Age** at which a child commences the experience. This may be at the kindergarten or infant stage (**early** immersion); at nine to ten years old (delayed or **middle** immersion), or at secondary level (**late** immersion);
- amount of **time** spent in immersion. **Total** immersion usually commences with 100% immersion in the second language, reducing after two or three years to 80% per week for the next three or four years, finishing junior schooling with approximately 50% immersion in the second language per week. **Partial** immersion provides close to 50% immersion in the second language throughout infant and junior schooling.

Early Total Immersion has been the most popular entry-level program in Canada, followed by late and then middle immersion. The histograms on the following page illustrate several possibilities, with many other variations around these.

The **St Lambert** experiment was a success. Evaluations suggested that the educational aims were met. Attitudes and achievement were not hindered by the immersion experience. Tucker and d'Anglejan (1972, p. 19), summarized the outcomes as follows:

> the experimental students appear to be able to read, write, speak, understand, and use English as well as youngsters instructed in English in the conventional manner. In addition and at no cost they can also read, write, speak and understand French in a way that English students who follow a traditional program of French as a second language never do.

Since 1965, immersion bilingual education has spread rapidly in Canada (Rebuffot, 1993) and in parts of Europe. There are currently around 357,000 English speaking Canadian children (7.3% of the total school population) in some 2133 French immersion schools (Centre for Education Statistics, Statistics Canada; Canadian Heritage Official Languages, 2004, personal communication). In the 2001 Canadian Census, 17.5 million people reported their mother tongue as English, with 6.8 million as French, and 5.3 million as other languages. 17.7% of the population reported speaking both French and English, with bilingualism strongest in Quebec (40.8%). Immersion education, as well as language reproduction in the home, is a key to maintaining Canada's bilingualism.

From one school started in 1965, immersion education spread rapidly in Canada. What are the essential features of this speedy educational growth? **First**, immersion in Canada aims at bilingualism in two prestigious, majority languages (French and English). This relates to an additive bilingual situation. Such a situation is different from the incorrectly termed 'immersion' or 'structured immersion' of children from language minority backgrounds in the majority language (e.g. Spanish speakers in the US). Use of the term 'immersion' in a subtractive, assimilationist situation is best avoided. Submersion is a more appropriate term.

Second, immersion bilingual education has been optional not compulsory. Parents choose to send their children to these schools. The cultural and economic convictions of parents plus the commitment of the teachers may aid the motivation of students. Immersion thrives on conviction, not on conformity. **Third**, children in early immersion are often allowed to use their home language for up to one and a half years for classroom communication. There is no compulsion to speak the second (school) language in the playground or dining hall. The child's home language is appreciated and not belittled. **Fourth**, the teachers are competent bilinguals. They initially appear to the children as able to speak French but only understand (and not speak) English.

Fifth, classroom language communication aims to be meaningful, authentic and relevant to the child's needs; not contrived, tightly controlled or repetitive. The content of the curriculum becomes the focus for the language. Perpetual insistence

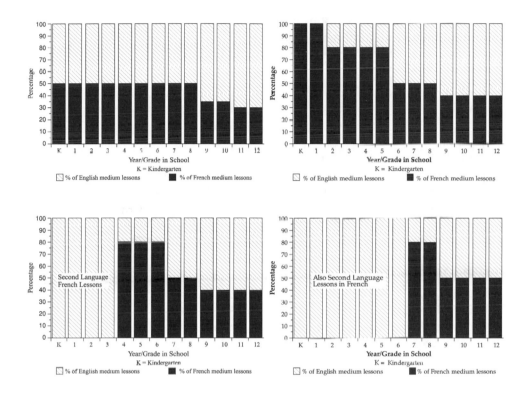

on correct communication is avoided. Learning a second language in early immersion becomes incidental and subconscious, similar to the way a first language is acquired. Emphasis is placed on understanding before speaking. Later on, formal instruction (e.g. French grammar) may occur (see chapter 13).

Sixth, the students start immersion education with a similar lack of experience of the second language. Most are monolingual. Students commencing schooling with relatively homogeneous language skills not only simplifies the teacher's task, it also means that students' self-esteem and classroom motivation are not at risk due to some students being linguistically more expert. **Seventh**, students in immersion education experience the same curriculum as mainstream 'core' students. **Eighth**, immersion is not simply an educational initiative. There is also a societal, political and sometimes economic rationale that will differ from country to country. In Canada, immersion matches a French / English dual language history and differentiates Canada from its larger neighbor, the United States (Johnstone, 2002). In Wales and Ireland, immersion is partly about establishing a Celtic identity separate from England (D.V. Jones & Martin-Jones, 2004). Unification of a country with varying languages, economic advantage in global trade, international communications and increasing peace, harmony and integration may also be elements of a wider rationale than education.

To summarize, Swain and Johnson (1997) provide a list of the core features and variable features of immersion programs

Core Features

(1) The second language is the medium of instruction.
(2) The immersion curriculum is the same as the local first language curriculum.
(3) The school supports first language development.
(4) Additive bilingualism occurs.
(5) Exposure to the second language is largely confined to the classroom.
(6) Students enter with similar (limited or nonexistent) levels of second language proficiency.
(7) All the teachers are bilingual.
(8) The classroom culture is that of the first language community.

Variable Features

(1) The grade level of which immersion is introduced.
(2) The extent of immersion, full or partial.
(3) The ratio given to the first and second language in content-based teaching at different grade levels.
(4) Whether there is continuity from elementary to secondary education, and occasionally from secondary to further and higher education.
(5) The amount of language support given to students moving from their first to their second language, including the training that teachers need so as to give bridging support.
(6) The amount of resources that are available in the first and second language and the teacher training to use these.
(7) The commitment of teachers and students, administrators and politicians to immersion.
(8) The attitudes of students particularly towards the second language culture.
(9) The status of the second language.
(10) What counts as success in an immersion program.

By today, immersion schooling occurs internationally: Australia, the Basque Country, Catalonia, Finland, Hungary, Hong Kong, Ireland, New Zealand, Singapore, South Africa and Wales, for example. With over a 1000 research studies, immersion bilingual education has been an educational experiment of unusual success and growth (see Johnstone, (2002) for an overview of the international research and chapter 12 of this book). It has influenced bilingual education throughout the world. With variations to suit regional and national contexts,

Some of the Differences between Canadian Immersion and US Structured Immersion (Submersion) Approaches

	US Structured Immersion	Canadian Immersion
Use of first (home) language in classroom	No	Yes
Bilingualism as an outcome	No	Yes
Biliteracy as an outcome	No	Yes
Cultural diversity promoted	Unlikely	Yes
Teacher operates bilingually	No	Likely
Bilingual (certified) teacher	No	Likely
Home language of the Student	Minority	Majority
Underlying Ideology	Assimilation	Pluralism

research in the following countries suggests similar success to Canada: **Catalans and Basques** (Artigal, 1991, 1993, 1997; Bel, 1993; Cenoz & Perales, 1997; N. Gardner, 2000; Lasagabaster, 2001) **Finnish** (C. Laurén, 1994; Manzer, 1993; Mejía, 2002), **Japanese** (Oka, 1994; Maher, 1997), **Australians** (Berthold, 1992, 1995; Caldwell & Berthold, 1995; de Courcy, 2002; Mejía, 2002), **Colombians** (Mejía, 2002), the Gaelic speakers in **Scotland** (MacNeil, 1994; Johnstone, 2002), **South Africans** (Brown, 1997; O. Martin, 1997), **Swiss** (Stotz & Andres, 1990; Brohy, 2005) and the **Welsh and Irish** (Baker, 1988, 1993, 2000c; Baker & Jones, 2000; D.V. Jones & Martin-Jones, 2004; W.G. Lewis, 2004; D. Reynolds *et al.*, 1998; I.W. Williams, 2003).

The **Finnish** implementation of immersion derived not from parents but from a politically active women's group at Vaasa (Finland), which quickly gained political credibility for integrating Swedish and Finnish speaking children, and high academic credibility from the research of Christer Laurén and his team at the University of Vaasa (Laurén, 1994; Mejía, 2002). The Finnish implementation is also noted for (1) evolving into having third and fourth languages (e.g. English and German) producing fluent multilinguals, and (2) providing high quality teacher preparation courses (including by distance learning) that include immersion teaching methodology.

In **Catalonia**, research indicates that Spanish speaking children who follow an immersion program not only become fluent in Catalan, but also that their Spanish does not suffer. Throughout the curriculum, Catalan immersion children 'perform as well and sometimes better than their Hispanophone peers who do not' [follow an immersion program] (Artigal, 1993, pp. 40–41). Similarly, research studies in the **Basque** Country show that their Model B immersion program (50% Basque and

50% Spanish) has successful outcomes in bilingual proficiency (Sierra & Olaziregi, 1989; N. Gardner, 2000; Lasagabaster, 2001).

In **Canada**, a new initiative commenced in 2003 partly due to Core (mainstream) 'drip feed' language teaching not producing fluent French speakers, partly because immersion student numbers have declined slightly, and partly as a political scheme to radically increase the number of young Canadians who can use French in their lives. Called **Intensive French**, this program aims to provide intensive exposure in French as a second language (Netten & Germain, 2004). By achieving rapid language learning in this program, it is hoped that students will become motivated to continue towards French fluency.

Intensive French was piloted in Newfoundland and Labrador from 1998 to 2001 and has since spread to other Canadian provinces and territories (and to Wales, UK). In contrast to 1000 hours of 'drip feed' French from Grade 4 to Grade 12 in Core programs, and in contrast to 6000 to 7000 hours of French instruction in early immersion, Intensive French operates in Grade 5 or Grade 6 for a five month intensive period of language learning (Netten & Germain, 2004). In one school year, the first five months may be devoted to the concentrated learning of French; the following five months are devoted to achieving necessary learning outcomes in the regular curriculum. Sometimes, the final five months of the school year are devoted to intensive French. Either way, the overall aim is produce fluent speakers who can communicate spontaneously in French.

In this program, between 50% and 80% of each school day is devoted to learning French. Although no subjects are taught in French (as in immersion), the time allotted to some other subjects is reduced (e.g. social studies, health, science and particularly English). The time allocation to mathematics is not normally reduced. Early findings show linguistic and educational success (Netten & Germain, 2004) and expectations of expansion in the future.

BILINGUAL EDUCATION IN MAJORITY LANGUAGES

Bilingual education in majority languages comprises the joint use of two (or more) **majority languages** in a school. The aims of these schools usually include bilingualism or multilingualism, biliteracy and cultural pluralism (Mejía, 2002). Such schools are in societies where much of the population is already bilingual or multilingual (e.g. Singapore, Luxembourg) or where there are significant numbers of natives or expatriates wanting to become bilingual (e.g. learning through English and Japanese in Japan). **Asian** examples of bilingual education in majority languages include Arabic–English, Bahasa Melayu–English, Mandarin Chinese–English and Japanese–English. In Africa and India there are also schools where a 'majority' regional language and an international language coexist as teaching media in a school. Bilingualism in that regional language and an international language (e.g. French, English) is the aim and outcome of formal education. Generally, these schools will contain majority language children, with variations in the language heterogeneity or language homogeneity of the classes.

In the Asian examples, a country (e.g. Brunei, Taiwan) or a region may have one dominant indigenous language with a desire to introduce a second international language (especially English) into the school. The international language will be used as a medium of instruction alongside the native language. The aim is for fully bilingual and biliterate students through an enrichment bilingual education program. For example, the *Dwibahasa* (two language) school system in Brunei operates through Malay (Bahasa Melayu) and English (G.M. Jones *et al.*, 1993, 1997; Baetens Beardsmore, 1999). In Nigeria, bilingual education is present, particularly at the secondary school level, in English plus one of the national languages of Nigeria: Hausa, Ibo or Yoruba (Afolayan, 1995). In Singapore, English plus Mandarin, Malay or Tamil (the four official languages of the country) create bilingual education (Pakir, 1994). In Germany, German is paired with French, English, Spanish and Dutch to create a 'German model' of European multicultural and bilingual education (Mäsch, 1994).

Bilingual education in majority languages means that some curriculum content is learnt through a student's second language. In Europe, this is often called Content and Language Integrated Learning (CLIL – see http://www.clilcompendium. com/).

Davison & Williams (2001) provide the rationale for teaching and learning content through a second language. First, learning a language is quicker when it is via an integration of language and content, and much slower if just learnt as a language. Second, CLIL ensures a student gains language competence in academic domains and not just in social communication. Third, such an integration of language and content is efficient. Two outcomes can be achieved at the same time: learning a language and subject matter learning. Fourth, Met (1998) argues that a communicative approach to second language teaching emphasizes **meaningful and authentic communication** where the purpose of using language is to interpret, express and negotiate meaning. Thus integrating second language and content provides a purpose for using that second language reflecting real curriculum needs and purposeful learning for success in the curriculum.

Constructivist theory also stresses that learning best takes place in a holistic sense with the parts making a unified whole in a meaningful way. Traditional learning tends to rely on teachers transmitting small chunks of information which students are expected eventually to integrate into an understanding of the whole. Given that the brain stores information in networks, and the greater the number of connections and the stronger the connections among chunks of information the deeper and more powerful the learning, the more valuable it is to tie language and content together. Thus vocabulary and grammar should not be taught in isolation but in a context of authentic holistic learning. In **content-based second language instruction**, meaning and understanding is the focus, and second language learning a valuable by-product.

Two examples of bilingual education in majority languages will now be considered, commencing with the International School Movement and continuing with the European School Movement. Mejía (2002) provides many further international examples including Finishing Schools in Switzerland and elite bilingual provision in Morocco, Tanzania, Brazil, Argentina, Columbia, Japan, Hong Kong, Brunei Darussalam, Finland, Sweden, Belgium, Catalonia, and Australia.

International Schools

International Schools are a diverse collection of schools throughout the world. Numbering over 830 schools, they are found in over 80 countries of the world, mostly in large cities (European Council of International Schools (ECIS), 1998; Sears, 1998; Mejía, 2002). Mainly for the affluent, parents pay fees for mostly **private, selective, independent education** but there are also scholarships and bursaries. Children in these schools often have parents in the diplomatic service, multinational organizations, or in international businesses and who are geographically and vocationally mobile. Other children in an International School come from the locality, with parents who want their children to have an internationally flavored education (Sears, 1998). One **language** of the school is frequently English. International Schools that have English as the sole medium of transmitting the curriculum cannot be included under the heading of Bilingual Education in Majority Languages. Such schools become bilingual when a national or international language is incorporated in the curriculum (Mejía, 2002). Sometimes the second language taught (for up to 12 years) is only taught as a language. In other schools, the second language is used as a medium to teach part of the curriculum. Some schools enable their students to acquire third and fourth languages. Generally, the languages of International Schools are majority languages with international prestige. Minority languages are rarely found in these schools.

The primary and secondary **curriculum** of **International Schools** tends to reflect US, British as well as the local curriculum tradition. The teachers are from various countries, usually with a plentiful supply of British and American trained staff. Sometimes preparing children for the International Baccalaureate, United States tests or British examinations, most prepare their clientele for universities in Europe and North America. Sears (1998) in particular, but also Baker and Jones (1998) and Mejía (2002) provide a further discussion of the International Schools Movement.

European Schools Movement

Another European example of bilingual education in majority languages is the **European Schools movement** (Baetens Beardsmore, 1993a; Baetens Beardsmore & Swain, 1985; Baker & Jones, 1998; Bulwer, 1995; Hoffmann, 1998; Housen, 2002; Housen & Baetens Beardsmore, 1987; Mejía, 2002; Swan, 1996). Mostly for the relatively elite workers of the European Community (EC), such schools are multilingual and cater for some 15,000 children from the different EC nations. The first school was opened in Luxembourg in 1953, with schools now sited in Belgium, Italy, Germany, the Netherlands and England (Swan, 1996). European Schools have up to 11 different language sections reflecting the first language of the students (and this may increase as other countries join the European Community). Younger children use their native language as the medium of learning but also receive second language instruction (English, French, or German) in the primary school years. Older children take part of their schooling in their native language and part through the medium of a '**vehicular**' or 'working' language. The 'vehicular' language will usually be a 'majority' second language for the child selected from English, French or German. This language will be taught by native speakers. Native student speakers of that language will also be present in the school as language models. The **vehicular language** is used to teach mixed language groups of students history, geography and economics from the third year of secondary education. In addition, students are taught a **third language** for a minimum of 360 hours.

The outcome of such schooling tends to be functionally bilingual and often multilingual students with a sense of European multiculturalism and European identity (Swan, 1996). Integration and harmonization of students from different nationalities is formally achieved in the '**European Hours**' lessons using the vehicular language. 'European Hours' are an important curriculum component from Grade 3 in primary education. In classes of 20 to 25 students for three lessons a week, children from different language backgrounds work cooperatively together. A small group project with a realistic, attainable goal (e.g. making puppets) provides the focus for a context embedded and cognitively undemanding 'European Hour'. Deliberately and explicitly, students are encouraged to respect each person's native language. Games and physical education are also occasions for a cooperative mixing of students from the different language sections. Students are linguistically mixed to avoid stereotypes and prejudices, and to build a supranational European identity (Baetens Beardsmore, 1993a; Swan, 1996).

A major difference between the European schools movement and immersion programs is that the second language is taught as a subject before being used as a medium of instruction. The second language also continues to be taught as a subject (language learning), leading to a high level of grammatical accuracy (Baetens Beardsmore, 1993a).

According to Housen and Baetens Beardsmore's (1987) research in one European School: 'This strong language commitment has no detrimental effects on academic achievement as can be gauged from results on the final European Baccalaureate examination, on which 90% of students have been successful' (p. 85). However, bilingualism, biliteracy and multiculturalism are not only due to the effects of schooling. The parents may also be bilingual or multilingual, and the children are more likely to come from literacy-oriented, middle class bureaucrat homes, with a positive view of bilingualism. Playgrounds are multilingual, satellite TV in Europe is multilingual and the growing notion of Europeanisation creates privileged European schoolchildren who are 'educated bilinguals, equally at ease with two languages, with their own national culture and the supranational European identity' (Tosi, 1991, p. 33).

Research by Housen (2002) suggests multiple positive program outcomes from the European Schools model. He found that L2 proficiency is close to native speaker levels by the end of secondary schooling at no cost to either L1 proficiency or academic achievement. Pupils also gain high levels of proficiency in a third, and sometimes fourth language, becoming multilinguals. Housen (2002) suggests that European School students tend to

> produce their own independent, grammatically accurate, and lexically precise sustained discourse in an L2, even in contexts where additional, out-of-school support for L2 learning is absent (e.g., English-L2 in the ES in Brussels). This is one of the most impressive achievements of the ES program and stands in sharp contrast to many Canadian immersion programs. (Housen, 2002, p. 6)

In **Europe**, there are other schools (apart from the European School Movement) that use two or more prestigious languages in the curriculum (Baetens Beardsmore, 1993b; Cenoz, 1998, 2004; Genesee, 1998; Cenoz & Jessner, 2000; Mejía, 2002). In the Basque Country, bilingual schools have effectively provided content teaching in Basque and Spanish (N. Gardner, 2000; Lasagabaster, 2001). A recent interest (e.g. by parents) in English language learning means that about 95% of Basque children now learn English starting at kindergarten or in Grade 3 for about three hours per week (Cenoz, 1998; Lasagabaster, 2000, 2001). Early evaluations revealed that 'learning English from such an early age does not adversely affect the students' acquisition of Basque or Spanish or their overall cognitive development' (Cenoz, 1998, p. 181). **Trilingual education** is thus being evaluated.

In **Luxembourg,** children who speak Luxembourgish (Lëtzebuergesch) after birth become trilingual (Luxembourgish, French and German) through schooling (Hoffmann, 1998; Lebrun & Baetens Beardsmore, 1993). Children start their formal education at age five through the medium of Luxembourgish (a variety of German). German is initially a subject in the curriculum, then introduced as the main teaching medium. By the end of Grade 6, children function in much of the curriculum in German. French is introduced as a subject in Grade 2, and is increasingly used as a teaching medium in secondary education. Most students have a working knowledge of three languages by the conclusion of schooling (Hoffmann, 1998; Lebrun & Baetens Beardsmore, 1993). Through emphasis on the home tongue in the early years, emphasis on German in the primary school and emphasis on French in the secondary school, children become **trilingual and biliterate** (French and German literacy).

In **Switzerland**, there are four national languages (German, French, Italian and Rumansch) although, contrary to popular expectation, 'the majority of Swiss citizens are not multilingual' (Grin *et al.*, 2003, p. 86). Each of the 26 Swiss cantons has control over language, culture and education without central rule. English is on the increase as a student favored language, and central guidelines favor children becoming trilingual. Brohy (2000, 2005) portrays the many and varied optional and compulsory models of bilingual and trilingual education in Switzerland. She finds that the optional or compulsory component of such bilingual education has political rather than pedagogic justifications (Brohy, 2001).

CONCLUSION

Support for bilingual education tends to circle around eight interacting advantages of bilingual education that are claimed for students. There are also societal benefits that have already been alluded to and will be considered in chapter 17.

First, bilingual education typically enables a student's two languages to attain higher levels of competency. This potentially enables children to engage in wider **communication** across generations, regions and cultural groups (Cummins, 2000a). Second, bilingual education ideally develops a broader **enculturation**, a more sensitive view of different creeds and cultures. Bilingual education will usually deepen an engagement with the cultures associated with the languages, fostering a sympathetic understanding of differences. Third, 'strong' forms of bilingual education frequently lead to **biliteracy** (see chapter 14). Accessing literacy practices in two or more languages adds more functions to a language (e.g. using it in employment), widening the choice of literature for enjoyment, giving more opportunities for understanding different perspectives and viewpoints, and leading to a deeper understanding of history and heritage, traditions and territory (Tse, 2001).

Fourth, research on Dual Language schools, Canadian immersion education and heritage language education suggest that classroom **achievement** is increased through content learning occurring via dual language curriculum strategies (Cummins, 2000a; Tse, 2001). This is considered later in the next chapter. Fifth, plentiful research suggests that children with two well-developed languages share **cognitive** benefits (see chapter 7). Sixth, children's **self-esteem** may be raised in bilingual education for minority language students (Cummins, 2000a). The opposite occurs when a child's home language is replaced by the majority language. Then, the child itself, the parents and relatives, and not least the child's community may appear as inadequate and disparaged by the school system. When the home language is used in school, children may feel themselves, their home, family and community to be accepted, thus maintaining or elevating their self-esteem.

Seventh, bilingual education can aid the establishment of a more secure **identity** at a local, regional and national level. Sharing Welsh, Māori or Native American Indian identities may be enhanced by the heritage language and culture being celebrated and honored in the classroom. Developing a Korean–American, Bengali–British or Greek–Australian identity can be much aided by 'strong' forms of bilingual education, and challenged or even negated by 'weak' forms. Eighth, in some regions (e.g. Catalonia, Scandinavia) there are **economic** advantages for having experienced bilingual (or trilingual) education. Being bilingual can be important to secure employment in many public services (see chapter 19), particularly when there is a customer interface requiring switching effortlessly between two or more languages. To secure a job as a teacher, to work in the mass media, to work in local government and increasingly in the civil service in countries such as Canada, Wales and the Basque Country, bilingualism has become important. Thus, bilingual education is increasingly seen as delivering relatively more marketable employees than monolingual education (Dutcher, 2004; Tse, 2001).

To this list may be added the potential **societal**, ethnic group or community **benefits of bilingual education** (May, 2001; Peyton *et al.*, 2001; Stroud, 2001; Tse, 2001; Batibo, 2005) such as: continuity of heritage, cultural transmission, cultural vitality, empowered and informed citizenship, raising school and State achievement standards, social and economic inclusion, socialization, social relationships and networking, ethnic identity, ethnic group self-determination and distinctiveness.

Having considered 10 types of bilingual education in this and the previous chapter, the natural question to ask is whether one type is more effective than another. For Spanish speaking children in the US, is it better for them to be placed in mainstream, transitional, developmental maintenance or dual language schooling? For a monolingual English speaker, is it detrimental to enter immersion schooling compared with mainstream schooling? Such questions will be examined in the next chapter by 'effectiveness' research.

KEY POINTS IN THE CHAPTER

- Ten varieties of bilingual education include different forms of 'strong' bilingual education where the use of both languages in the curriculum is fostered.
- 'Strong' forms of bilingual education aim for students to become bilingual, biliterate and bicultural, and sometimes multilingual, multicultural with multiliteracies.
- Immersion, Heritage Language and Dual Language education are the most well known forms of strong bilingual education.
- Dual Language education has recently grown in the United States mixing majority and minority language students.
- In Heritage Language programs, the revitalization of home languages and cultures is a key aim.
- Immersion bilingual education started in Canada and has spread to many countries of the world. It caters for majority language children learning through a second language.
- Content teaching can occur through two or more majority languages as in the European schools movement.
- The varieties of 'strong' bilingual education differ in the amount of time given to the minority and majority languages in the classroom but full bilingualism and biliteracy is expected as outcomes.

SUGGESTED FURTHER READING

BAETENS BEARDSMORE, H. (ed.), 1993, *European Models of Bilingual Education*. Clevedon: Multilingual Matters.
CUMMINS, J. & CORSON, D. (eds), 1997, *Bilingual Education. Volume 5 of the Encyclopedia of Language and Education*. Dordrecht: Kluwer.
FREEMAN, R., 2004, *Building on Community Bilingualism*. Philadelphia: Caslon Publishing.
GARCÍA, O. & BAKER, C. (eds) 2006, *Bilingual Education: An Introductory Reader*. Clevedon: Multilingual Matters.
GENESEE, F. (ed.), 1999, *Program Alternatives for Linguistically Diverse Students*. University of California, Santa Cruz: Center for Research on Education, Diversity and Excellence.

JOHNSON, R.K. & SWAIN, M., 1997, *Immersion Education: International Perspectives*. Cambridge: Cambridge University Press.

JOHNSTONE, R., 2002, *Immersion in a Second or Additional Language at School: A Review of the International Research*. Stirling (Scotland): Scottish Centre for Information on Language Teaching. http://www.scilt.stir.ac.uk/pubs.htm

LINDHOLM-LEARY, K.J., 2001, *Dual Language Education*. Clevedon: Multilingual Matters.

MCCARTY, T.L. & BIA, F., 2002, *A Place To Be Navajo: Rough Rock and the Struggle for Self-Determination in Indigenous Schooling*. Mahwah, NJ: Lawrence Erlbaum.

McCARTY, T.L. & WATAHOMIGIE, L.J., 1999, Indigenous community-based language education in the USA. In S. MAY (ed.), *Indigenous Community-Based Education*. Clevedon: Multilingual Matters.

MEJÍA, A-M. de, 2002, *Power, Prestige and Bilingualism: International Perspectives on Elite Bilingual Education*. Clevedon. Multilingual Matters.

PEYTON, J.K., RANARD, D.A. & MCGINNIS, S. (eds.), 2001, *Heritage Languages in America: Preserving a National Resource*. McHenry, IL: Delta Systems.

SEARS, C., 1998, *Second Language Students in Mainstream Classrooms*. Clevedon: Multilingual Matters.

See also the *International Journal of Bilingualism and Bilingual Education* for the most recent articles on this topic.

STUDY ACTIVITIES

(1) Imagine you are a parent or teacher and are required to make a public speech about changing a school from a 'weak' form of bilingual education to a 'strong' form. Start by considering the needs of the local community (e.g. languages used, preferences for bilingualism in children). Prepare, and then deliver in front of the class, a speech of about five minutes to persuade the administration.

(2) Visit a school, and by interview and observation decide the extent to which that school fits one or more of the types of bilingual education in this and the previous chapter.

(3) Using some of the following World Wide Web addresses and search engines, create a short information pack or booklet on an aspect of bilingual education that is relevant in your district.

1. ERIC Clearinghouse on Languages and Linguistics

http://www.cal.org/ericcll/

2. The National Clearinghouse for English Language Acquisition and Language Instruction Educational Programs

http://www.ncela.gwu.edu/

3. University of Birmingham, (UK) School of Education Bilingualism Database

http://www.edu.bham.ac.uk/bilingualism/database/biweb.htm

4. Yahoo – Bilingual Education

http://dir.yahoo.com/Education/Bilingual/

5. Center for Applied Linguistics (US)

http://www.cal.org/

6. James Crawford's Language Policy Web Site and Emporium

http://ourworld.compuserve.com/homepages/JWCRAWFORD/

7. National Association for Bilingual Education

http://www.nabe.org/

8. Language Policy Research Unit
http://www.asu.edu/educ/epsl/lpru.htm
9. OISE, University of Toronto, Second Language Education on the Web
http://www.oise.utoronto.ca/~aweinrib/sle/
10. CAIT (Canadian Association of Immersion Teachers)
http://www.educ.sfu.ca/acpi/

CHAPTER 12

The Effectiveness of Bilingual Education

CHAPTER 12

The Effectiveness of Bilingual Education

INTRODUCTION

Having considered 10 types of bilingual education, this chapter turns to considering research on the major types of bilingual education. Is there a 'best model'? How effective are these major models for which types of children? What are the successes and limitations of different models?

From early research in the 1920s in Wales (Saer, 1922) and Malherbe's (1946) evaluation of bilingual education in South Africa, there have been many evaluations of bilingual projects, programs and interventions. The research has been international (see Baker & Jones, 1998). A report from the World Bank (Dutcher, 2004) provides one of the few comparative international studies, covering bilingual education in the Philippines, Ireland, Canada, Mexico, Nigeria, Sweden and the United States.

It is possible to find historical research **support** for most of the different forms of bilingual education by selecting and emphasizing a particular study. For example, Danoff *et al.* (1977, 1978) found mainstreaming to be superior to transitional bilingual education with a large US sample of almost 9000 children. In contrast, McConnell (1980) found US transitional bilingual education to be better than mainstreaming, while Matthews (1979), also in the USA, found no difference between these two forms of bilingual education.

KEY THEMES IN SCHOOL AND CLASSROOM EFFECTIVENESS

Articles by Carter and Chatfield (1986), Lucas *et al.* (1990), Baker (1990) and Cziko (1992) and overviews by August and Hakuta (1997, 1998) and Cummins (2000b) have suggested that the effectiveness of bilingual education can be addressed from different perspectives. First, there is the effectiveness at the level of the **individual child**. Within the same classroom, children may respond and perform differently. Second, there is effectiveness at the **classroom** level. Within the same

260

school and type of bilingual education program, classrooms may vary considerably. Third, effectiveness is often analyzed at the **school** level. What makes some schools more effective than others even within the same **type of bilingual education program** and with similar student characteristics? Fourth, beyond the school level there can be aggregations of schools into different types of **program** (e.g. transitional compared with heritage language programs) or into different geographical regions.

It is possible to look at effective bilingual education at each and all of these levels, and at the inter-relationship between these four levels. For example, at the individual level we need to know how bilingual education can best be effective for children of different levels of ability and special needs. How do children with learning difficulties and specific language disorders fare in bilingual education? At the classroom level, we need to know what teaching methods and classroom characteristics create optimally effective bilingual education. At the school level, the characteristics of staffing, the size of groups and the language composition of the school all affect 'whether, where, when and how' bilingual education is successful. In all these levels, there are frequently issues about human, material and physical **resources**. The demands are for an adequate supply of well trained bilingual teachers, curriculum materials in all content areas, buildings and facilities).

Apart from individual classroom and school characteristics, the effectiveness of bilingual education is influenced by the **social, economic, political and cultural context** of such education. For example, the differences between being in a subtractive or additive context may affect the outcomes of bilingual education. The willingness of teachers to involve parents, and good relationships between the school and its community may be important in effective bilingual education (Smyth, 2003). Also, the **local economics** of schooling play an important part. Where the funding of schools is based on a local tax, then 'per student' expenditure in more affluent areas will be considerably greater than in the less affluent areas. In the US for example, language minority students from an economically poor district will typically have considerably less **expenditure** on them (per student) than those in more wealthy suburbs. It is difficult to advance the effectiveness of bilingual education with very limited financial and material resources.

It is also important in bilingual education effectiveness research to examine a wide variety of **outcomes** from such education. Such outcomes may derive from high stakes testing, measures of basic skills (e.g. oracy, literacy, numeracy), or the broadest range of curriculum areas (e.g. science and technology, humanities, mathematics, languages, arts, physical, practical and theoretical pursuits, skills as well as knowledge). Non-cognitive outcomes are also important to include in an assessment of effectiveness (Rolstad *et al.*, 2005). Such non-cognitive outcomes may include: attendance at school, attitudes, self-concept and self-esteem, tolerance, social and emotional adjustment, employment and moral development.

For example, Stephen Krashen (1999) provides evidence to show that bilingual education is not the cause of **dropping-out** in United States schools – but it may be the cure. Latino students do have higher drop-out rates (e.g. 30% of Latino students classified as drop-outs compared to 8.6% of non-Latino whites and 12.1% of non-Latino Blacks). Krashen's (1999) review of the evidence suggests that those who had experienced bilingual education were significantly less likely to drop-out. There are factors other than bilingual education, related to dropping-out such as socioeconomic class, recency of immigration, family environment, and the presence of print at home. It is estimated that 40% of Latino children live in poverty compared with 15% of white non-Latino children. Latino children are more likely to have parents who did not complete High School. When these factors are controlled statistically, the drop-out rate among Latinos is the same (or virtually the same) as for other groups (Krashen, 1999). Since 'strong' forms of bilingual schooling tend to produce higher standards of academic English and performance across the curriculum, then such schools become part of the cure.

Effective bilingual education is not a simple or automatic consequence of using a child's home language in school (as in heritage language education) or a second language (as in immersion education). Various home and parental, community, teacher, school and society effects may act and interact to make bilingual education more or less effective.

THE EFFECTIVENESS OF BILINGUAL EDUCATION: THE UNITED STATES DEBATE

This section centers on the United States debate about the effectiveness of bilingual education. After a substantial number of individual research studies on bilingual education had accumulated in the US, various reviews and overviews appeared. A reviewer will assemble as many individual studies as possible and attempt to find a systematic pattern and an orderliness in the findings. Is there a **consensus** in the findings? Is it possible to make some generalizations about the effectiveness of different forms of bilingual education? Rarely, if ever, will all the individual researches agree. Therefore, the reviewer's task is to detect reasons for variations. For example, different age groups, different socioeconomic class backgrounds, varying types of measurement device, different experimental designs and varying research methodologies may explain variations in results.

Early Research

The **initial reviews** of bilingual education effectiveness were published in the late 1970s. Zappert and Cruz (1977), Troike (1978) and Dulay and Burt (1978, 1979) each concluded that bilingual education in the US effectively promoted bilingualism with language minority children and was preferable to monolingual English programs. Since the late 1970s, many individual studies have been added and more recent reviews have emerged (e.g. Cummins & Corson, 1997; Dutcher, 1995; August & Hakuta, 1997, 1998).

While in the 1960s and 1970s bilingual education slowly evolved in the United States, from the late 1970s to the present, politicians have not tended to favor such evolution. One branch of political opinion in the United States sees bilingual education as failing to foster integration and producing **underachievement**. Such opinion regards bilingual education as leading to both a lack of proficiency in English and to social and economic divisions in society along language grounds. Minority language groups are sometimes portrayed as using bilingual education for political and economic self-interest, even separatism. In this kind of political context, the federal government commissioned a **major review** of bilingual education in the early 1980s.

K.A. Baker and de Kanter (1983) posed two narrow questions to focus their review. These two questions were: (1) Does Transitional Bilingual Education lead to better performance in English? (2) Does Transitional Bilingual Education lead to better performance in non-language subject areas? Only English language and non-language subject areas were regarded as the desirable outcome of schooling. Other outcomes such as self-esteem, employment, preservation of minority languages, the value of different cultures, moral development, identity, social adjustment and personality development were not considered.

Baker and de Kanter (1981, 1983) located 300 pieces of bilingual education research from North America and the rest of the bilingual world, rejected 261 studies as irrelevant or poor quality and contentiously used 39 studies. Canadian French immersion (an additive program for majority language speakers) was incorrectly classified as the same as US Structured English Immersion (which is a subtractive program for minority language speakers – see Rolstad *et al.*, 2005). The **conclusion** of Baker and de Kanter's (1983) review is that no particular education program should be legislated for or preferred by the US Federal Government. The review therefore came out in support of English-only and transitional bilingual education. Assimilation and integration appeared as the social and political preference behind the conclusions.

There was considerable **criticism** of the Baker and de Kanter (1983) review (e.g. Willig, 1981/82; American Psychological Association, 1982; Rolstad *et al.*, 2005). The main criticisms may be summarized as follows: a narrow range of outcome measures was considered, although this is often the fault of the original research rather than the review; focusing on transitional bilingual education implicitly valued assimilation and integration and devalued aims such as the preservation of a child's home language and culture; and the criteria used for selecting only 39 out of 300 studies were narrow and rigid.

Baker and de Kanter's (1983) approach is **narrative integration**. This is essentially a biased, subjective and unsystematic process, and the methods of procedure tend to be variable from reviewer to reviewer. A comparison of the reviews of Baker and de Kanter (1983) with the earlier reviews by Zappert and Cruz (1977); Troike (1978) and Dulay and Burt (1978, 1979), shows that reviews of similar studies can result in differing conclusions. That is, different reviewers use the same research reports to support contrary conclusions.

An alternative and more rule-bound strategy is to use **meta-analysis** (Rolstad *et al.*, 2005). The technique mathematically examines the amount of effect or differences in the research studies. For example, how much difference is there in outcome between transitional and immersion bilingual education? There is no need to exclude studies from the meta-analysis that the reviewer finds marginal or doubtful in terms of methodology. The quality of the evaluations can be allowed for statistically.

Willig (1985) adopted a statistical meta-analysis approach to reviewing bilingual education. She selected 23 studies from the Baker and de Kanter (1981, 1983) review. All of her 23 studies concerned United States bilingual education evaluations and excluded Canadian immersion education evaluations. As a result of the meta-analysis, Willig (1985) concluded that bilingual education programs that supported the minority language were consistently superior in various outcomes. Small to moderate advantages were found for bilingual education students in reading, language skills, mathematics and overall achievement when the tests were in the students' second language (English). Similar advantages were found for these curriculum areas and for writing, listening, social studies and self-concept when non-English language tests were used.

A **criticism** of Willig's (1985) meta-analysis is that it only included 23 studies. An international review of the bilingual educational effectiveness studies could have included many more studies and provided more generalizable conclusions. Further criticisms of Willig (1985) are given by August and Hakuta (1997) and Keith Baker (1987).

An eight-year, congressionally mandated, 4.5 million dollar **longitudinal study of bilingual education** in the US compared Structured English 'Immersion', Early Exit and Late Exit Bilingual Education Programs (Ramírez *et al.*, 1991; Ramírez, 1992). (The term 'Immersion' is not used in the original Canadian sense – English Submersion or mainstreaming is more accurate.) Over 2300 Spanish speaking students from 554 Kindergarten to 6th grade classrooms in New York, New Jersey, Florida, Texas and California were studied.

As a generalization, the outcomes were different for the three types of bilingual education. By the end of the 3rd grade, mathematics, language and English reading skills were not particularly different between the three programs. By the 6th grade, **Late Exit Transitional Bilingual Education** students were performing higher at mathematics, English language and English reading than students on other programs. Parental involvement appeared to be greatest in the late exit transitional programs. One **conclusion** reached by Ramírez *et al.* (1991) was that Spanish speaking students 'can be provided with substantial amounts of primary language instruction without impeding their acquisition of English language and reading skills' (p. 39). When language minority students are given instruction in their home language, this

> does not interfere with or delay their acquisition of English language skills, but helps them to 'catch-up' to their English speaking peers in English language arts, English reading and math. In contrast, providing LEP students with almost exclusive instruction in English does not accelerate their acquisition of English language arts, reading or math, i.e., they do not appear to be 'catch-ing-up.' The data suggest that by Grade 6, students provided with

English-only instruction may actually fall further behind their English speaking peers. Data also document that learning a second language will take six or more years. (Ramírez, 1992, p. 1)

The results also showed little difference between early exit and the English Immersion (Submersion) students. Opponents of bilingual education have used this result to argue for the relative administrative ease and less expensive mainstreaming (Submersion) of language minority students (e.g. K. Baker, 1992).

A series of reviews and **criticisms** of the Ramírez *et al.* (1991) research followed (e.g. Cazden, 1992; Meyer & Fienberg, 1992; Thomas, 1992) with particular emphasis on the following:

- The benefits of 'strong' forms of bilingual education programs are not considered (e.g. Two Way bilingual education; Heritage Language education). This makes statements about bilingual education based on an incomplete range of possibilities (Cummins, 1992b). Mainstream classrooms with English Second Language (ESL) pull-out (withdrawal) classes – widely implemented in the United States – were also not included in the study (Rossell, 1992).

- The range of variables used to measure 'success' is narrow. For example, language minority parents may expect attitudinal, self-esteem, cultural and ethnic heritage goals to be examined as a measure of successful outcomes (Dolson & Meyer, 1992).

- The considerable differences that exist within bilingual education programs (let alone differing types of bilingual education program) makes comparisons and conclusions most difficult (Meyer & Fienberg, 1992). Also, the complexity of organization within a school, the ethos and varying classroom practices makes categorization of schools into watertight bilingual education programs formidable (Willig & Ramírez, 1993).

- The National Academy of Sciences reviewed this (and other) studies and concluded that the design of the study was ill-suited to answer key policy questions (Meyer & Fienberg, 1992; US Department of Education, 1992). More clarity in the aims and goals of bilingual education in the US is needed before research can be appropriately focused. The goals for bilingual education in the US are typically more implicit than explicit.

- There is a lack of data to support the long-term benefits of late exit transitional programs over other programs (K. Baker, 1992).

In 1996, Rossell and Keith Baker reviewed 75 studies they regarded as methodologically acceptable. They concluded that there was no evidence to show that bilingual programs were superior to English-only options. **Greene (1998)** re-analyzed the Rossell and Baker (1996) studies using a rigorous statistical technique – meta-analysis (echoing Willig's (1985) re-analysis of Baker and de Kanter (1983)). Greene (1998) indicates that classification of 'weak' forms of bilingual education into transitional bilingual education (TBE), ESL and developmental maintenance is fraught with difficulty. What is called TBE in one district could be ESL in the next. Crucially, Greene (1998) controlled for background characteristics between 'treatment' and control groups (e.g. socioeconomic class, parents' level of education); thus a third of the 75 research studies were ruled out of analysis. (Other studies were excluded due to the need for legitimate control groups, unpublished and unavailable, duplicated reporting of the same program, and not being an evaluation study of bilingual education.) From the 11 remaining studies, it was found that the **use of native language instruction helps achievement in English**. That is, use of the home language in school tends to relate to higher achievement than English-only instruction. The numerical 'effect size' of home language programs on English reading, mathematics and a non-English language were almost an exact mirror of Willig's (1985) findings, although only four studies were in common (Krashen, 1999).

A recent meta-analysis of Arizonian research by Rolstad *et al.* (2005) using four studies matches previous meta-analysis conclusions by Willig (1985) and Greene (1998). They found that Dual Language bilingual education was superior in terms of English language reading achievement and mathematics. They conclude that 'The evaluation literature has been remarkably clear in demonstrating that bilingual education is not only as effective as English-only alternatives, but that it tends to be *more effective*' (p. 62).

Public Opinion and the Effectiveness of Bilingual Education

Apart from effectiveness studies, research on bilingual education research needs to include **public opinion** surveys (Krashen, 1996). The amount of parental and public support that exists for different forms of bilingual education is important in participative democratic societies as bilingual education is both an educational and political key topic (Crawford, 2004).

Krashen (1999) provides a wide-ranging review of US public opinion polls regarding bilingual education. In polls that attempted to ask a representative sample of people, approximately two thirds of the public are in favor of bilingual education. However, considerable differences in public opinion polls occur because questions differ considerably. How bilingual education is defined differs widely. Leading questions that hint at the preferred or desirable answer, and the ambiguity of what respondents perceive as bilingual education, clearly has an effect on results.

Certainly there is little support in the United States for a separatist form of bilingual education in which only the home language is used. There is a high degree of support for English language proficiency for all children. When questions are phrased so that bilingual education includes proficiency in both languages, then generally there is a **consensus support for bilingual education**.

Expert Overviews of the Effectiveness of Bilingual Education

While public opinion surveys are infrequent, **expert opinion** is more likely to be privately or publicly sought. The United States Committee on Education and Labor asked the General Accounting Office (1987) to conduct a study on whether or not the research evidence on bilingual education supported the current government preference for assimilationist, transitional bilingual education. The General Accounting Office (1987) therefore decided to conduct a survey of experts on bilingual education. Ten experts were assembled, mostly professors of education, selected from prestigious institutions throughout the US.

In terms of learning English, eight out of ten experts favored using the native or heritage language in the classroom. They believed that progress in the native language aided children in learning English because it strengthened literacy skills which easily transferred to operating in the second language. On the learning of other subjects in the curriculum, six experts supported the use of heritage languages in such teaching. However, it was suggested that learning English is important in making academic progress (General Accounting Office, 1987).

Another high profile review was by an **expert panel of the US National Research Council** – The Committee on Developing a Research Agenda on the Education of Limited-English-Proficient and Bilingual Students. It declared that (1) all children in the US should be educated to be become fully functional in the English language; (2) the expectations of, and academic opportunities given to, such students must equal that of other students; and (3) 'in an increasingly global economic and political world, proficiency in language other than English and an understanding of different cultures are valuable in their own right, and should be among the major goals for schools' (August & Hakuta, 1997, p. 17).

This expert panel concluded that use of a child's native language in school does not impede the acquisition of English, but there is 'little value in conducting evaluations to determine which type of program is best. First, the key issue is not finding a program that works for all children and all localities, but rather finding a set of program components that works for the children in the community of interest, given the goals, demographics, and resources of that community' (August & Hakuta, 1997, p. 147). That is, a developmental maintenance program or a submersion program can both be successful in particular local contexts.

Also, many LEP children come from materially poor and disadvantaged homes, schools and communities. While bilingual programs academically benefit such children, the effect of these programs does not close the gap between disadvantaged and middle-class populations. These bilingual students face many issues beyond language, at home and at school, which affect their achievement (Valdés, 1997). Simply introducing bilingual programs will not by itself solve all the educational problems such children face – although they are one important part of the package.

The conclusion from the expert panel of the US National Research Council was that the effectiveness debate was too **simple and polarized** (August & Hakuta, 1997). All programs could be effective (e.g. transitional, mainstreaming, dual language, developmental maintenance) depending on the subtle chemistry of interacting ingredients, environments and processes. Attempts to prove the superiority of a particular model are pointless and unproductive. Theory based research and interventions which predicted the effects of components on the 'growth' of children in different environments were needed.

As Crawford (1999) notes, being even-handed, wanting to depoliticize the issue and injecting scientific detachment into research is an academic vision that has little

Brisk (1998) provides a comprehensive examination of the **situational factors** that affect both the standards reached by bilingual students and the effectiveness of bilingual schools. Her model suggests that there are five situational areas that can promote or otherwise such effectiveness:

(1) **Linguistic**, e.g. amount of language use in the community, media, technology, home.
(2) **Cultural**, e.g. parental participation in classroom, curriculum content and the assumptions about background knowledge of students.
(3) **Economic**, e.g. the economic viability of the languages, career opportunities, educational costs.
(4) **Political**, e.g. the treatment of immigrants, attitudes to language diversity.
(5) **Social**, e.g. size and cohesiveness of the language community, race and gender relationships, attitudes to language and ethnic groups.

or no impact on journalists and politicians. The 487-page expert review was seized by opponents and proponents of bilingual education as justification of their quite different positions (Crawford, 1999). The report thus became a tool used by opposing political groups to support their position.

This chapter now examines recent reviews and major research on dual language, immersion education and heritage language education. Each of these three models has a relatively large collection of literature allowing some overview of findings. In comparison, there are relatively few and sufficiently rigorous evaluations of other types of bilingual education preventing consideration here.

THE EFFECTIVENESS OF DUAL LANGUAGE EDUCATION

Evaluations of the **effectiveness** of Dual language schools and recent overviews indicate relative success (Cazabon *et al.*, 1993; Lambert & Cazabon, 1994; Lindholm, 1991; Lindholm & Aclan, 1991; Lindholm, 1994; Lindholm-Leary, 2001, 2005; Thomas *et al.*, 1993; Oller & Eilers, 2002; Howard *et al.*, 2004; Krashen, 2004; Lindholm-Leary & Borsato, 2006). As Christian (1994, overview page) summarizes:

> Emerging results of studies of two way bilingual programs point to their effectiveness in educating non-native English speaking students, their promise of expanding our nation's language resources by conserving the native language skills of minority students and developing second language skills in English speaking students, and their hope of improving relationships between majority and minority groups by enhancing cross-cultural understanding and appreciation.

However, as Krashen (2004) indicates, many individual studies have small sample sizes, are short-term rather than longitudinal, inadequately control variables such as social class and initial language differences, and ignore variations in design and program. Students in dual language education are not a random selection of the population of students. They are self-selecting. Hence, it is difficult to know if the successes of dual language schools are due to the program, the characteristics of the students, or both these, or other factors such as the quality of the teachers.

One of the most rigorous and comprehensive **evaluations** of dual language schools is by Kathryn Lindholm-Leary (2001). With wide-ranging and well documented data from 18 schools, she analyzed teacher attitudes and characteristics, teacher talk, parental involvement and satisfaction, as well as student outcomes (using 4854 students) in different program types. These programs included Transitional Bilingual Education, English-Only, the 90:10 Dual Language Model and the 50:50 Dual Language Model. The measured outcomes included Spanish and English language proficiency, academic achievement and attitudes of the students. socioeconomic background and other student characteristics were taken into account in reporting results. Among a wealth of findings, Lindholm-Leary (2001) found that:

- students who had 10% or 20% of their instruction in English scored as well on English proficiency as those in English-Only programs and as well as those in 50:50 Dual Language (DL) programs;
- Spanish proficiency was higher in 90:10 than 50:50 Dual Language (DL) programs. Students tended to develop higher levels of bilingual proficiency in the 90:10 than the 50:50 DL program;
- for Spanish-speaking students, no difference in English language proficiency was found between the 90:10 and 50:50 DL programs. However, DL students outperformed Transitional Bilingual Education (TBE) students in English by Grade 6;
- students in both the 90:10 and 50:50 DL programs were performing about 10 points higher in reading achievement than the Californian state average for English-speaking students educated in English-Only programs;
- higher levels of bilingual proficiency were associated with higher levels of reading achievement;
- on mathematics tests, DL students performed on average 10 points higher on Californian norms for English-speaking students educated only in English. There was a lack of difference in the scores of 90:10 and 50:50 DL students;
- DL students tended to reveal very positive attitudes towards their DL programs, teachers, classroom environment and the learning process.

Lindholm-Leary (2001) concludes that DL programs are effective in promoting high levels of language proficiency, academic achievement and positive attitudes to learning in students. Parents and teachers involved in such programs are both enthusiastic and recommend the expansion of such programs to raise the achievements of other majority and minority language children.

Oller and Eilers (2002) carefully document quasi-experimental research in Miami, Florida using 952 bilingual and monolingual students from Kindergarten to Grade 5. Dual language education is compared with English immersion, and by the

5th grade, students' English language outcomes were largely comparable with the gap narrowing from Kindergarten to Grade 5. While there is a lag for dual language students in English test performance, by the 5th grade this is minimal.

Thomas and Collier (2002a) compared the performance of dual language students with those in other programs. Their conclusion is that **two-way bilingual education** at the elementary school level is the **optimal program** for the long-term academic success of language minority students. Such students maintain their first language skills and cognitive/academic development while developing in a second language. In such a model, students develop deep academic proficiency and cognitive understanding through their first language to compete successfully with native speakers of the second language.

> 90–10 and 50–50 one-way and two-way developmental bilingual education (DBE) programs (or dual language, bilingual immersion) are the only programs we have found to date that assist students to fully reach the 50th percentile in both L 1 and L2 in all subjects and to maintain that level of high achievement, or reach even higher levels through the end of schooling. The fewest dropouts come from these programs. (Thomas & Collier, 2002a, p. 333).

Thomas and Collier (1995, 1997, 2002a, 2000b) produce a growth pattern of language minority English language achievement in different types of bilingual education programs. This is summarized below (see also the graphs).

- In kindergarten through to Grade 2, there is little difference between language minority children in ESL 'pull-out', transitional and two-way (dual language) programs in the United States. On a 'English language achievement' scale of 0–100 (with 50 as the average performance of native English language speakers), language minority children score around the 20 mark.
- ESL 'pull-out' children initially (Grades 1 and 2) progress faster in English language achievement than children in transitional and dual language programs. This might be expected as they have more intensive English-medium activity.
- By Grade 6, students in dual language programs and late-exit transitional programs are ahead on English language performance compared with early-exit and ESL pull-out students. Dual language and late-exit transitional students achievements in English language tests are close to those of native English speakers (i.e. around the 50th percentile). Early-exit and ESL pull-out students tend to perform around the 30th percentile on such tests.
- By Grade 11, the order of performance in the English language is:
    (1) Two-way bilingual education (*highest performance*);
    (2) Late-exit transitional bilingual education;
    (3) Early-exit transitional bilingual education;
    (4) ESL pull-out programs (*lowest performance*).
- By Grade 11, two-way bilingual education students are performing above the average levels of native English speakers on English language tests. On a 'English language achievement' scale of 0–100, two-Way bilingual education

students average around 60, late-exit students about the same as native English speakers around 50, early-exit students around 30 to 40, and ESL pull-out students around 20.

Student Achievement in English Language

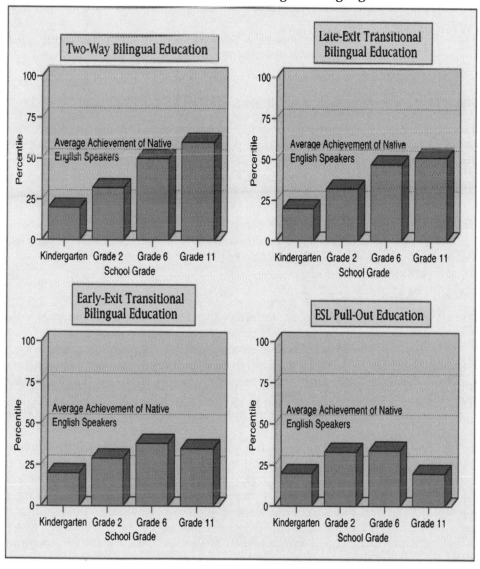

Criticisms of Thomas and Collier's (1995, 1997) growth trajectories of language minority English language achievement in different types of bilingual education programs include:

(1) their aggregation is based on selective individual research studies and well-implemented and mature programs;

(2) little information is presented on how the growth trajectories were determined;

(3) the effects of student geographical mobility (e.g. leaving a district) are not clear and may produce biased results (e.g. when such students are excluded from longitudinal data);

(4) few details are provided about the 700,000 language minority students on which the growth trajectories are based and which date from 1982–1996.

THE EFFECTIVENESS OF IMMERSION BILINGUAL EDUCATION

The various reviews of immersion tend to paint a relatively uniform picture. The 1980s overviews of Swain and Lapkin (1982), the California State Department of Education (1984), and Genesee (1983, 1984, 1987) highlighted four major outcomes of immersion bilingual education that are still found in recent reviews (Swain & Johnson, 1997; Swain, 1997; G.M. Jones, 1997; C. Laurén, 1997; Arnau, 1997; Genesee & Gándara, 1999; de Courcy, 2002; Johnstone, 2002). The vast majority of these studies concern Canadian immersion education, but there are a growing number of studies outside Canada (see Johnson & Swain, 1997; Hickey, 1997; Johnstone, 2002; Laurén, 1997; Lasagabaster, 2001; de Courcy, 2002).

Second Language Learning

It is easy to predict that immersion students will surpass those in mainstream (core) programs given 'drip-feed' second language lessons for 30 minutes a day. Most students in **early total immersion** programs approach native-like performance in the second language around 11 years old in receptive language skills (listening and reading). Such levels are not so well attained in the productive skills of speaking and writing (Swain & Johnson, 1997).

The reviews confirm that immersion students mostly succeed in gaining competence in two languages (Johnstone, 2002). However, as chapter 1 revealed, bilingual ability is not the same as being functionally bilingual. One of the **limitations** of immersion bilingual education is that for many students, the second language can become a school phenomenon. Outside the school walls, immersion students tend not to use the second language any more than 'drip feed' students (Swain & Johnson, 1997). Such students are competent in a second language, but tend not to communicate in that language in the target community. Potential does not necessarily lead to production; skill does not ensure street speech. Lack of spontaneous or contrived second language opportunity and a dearth of cultural occasions to actively and purposefully use the second language may partly be the explanation (other explanations will be considered later). Ideally, immersion programs not only create bilinguals, but also widen students' cultural horizons and sensitize them to second language culture and values.

First Language Learning

If immersion education provides the route to near-native fluency in a second language, is it at the cost of attainment in the first language? Does bilingualism result in lesser achievement in the first language compared with 'mainstream' students? Like a balance, as one goes up, does the other go down?

For three or four years of **early total immersion**, students tend not to progress in the first language to the same extent as monolingual students in mainstream classes. This first language development relates more to school language measured by tests rather than a vernacular first language. Reading, spelling and punctuation, for example, are not as developed and there is a temporary lag. Since such children are usually not given first language instruction for one, two or three years after starting school, these results are to be expected. However, the initial pattern does not last. After approximately six years of schooling, early total immersion children have typically caught up with their monolingual peers in first language skills. By the end of elementary schooling, the early total immersion experience has generally not affected first language speaking and writing development. Parents of these children tend to believe the same as the attainment tests reveal.

Indeed, when occasional differences in first language achievement between immersion and mainstream children have been located by research, it tends to be in favor of immersion students (Swain & Lapkin, 1982, 1991; Johnstone, 2002). This finding links with chapters 7 and 8 that discussed the possible cognitive advantages consequential from bilingualism. If bilingualism permits increased linguistic awareness, more flexibility in thought, more internal inspection of language, such cognitive advantages may help to explain the favorable first language progress of early immersion students.

Early partial immersion students also tend to lag behind for three or four years in their first language skills. Their performance is little different from that of total early immersion students, which is surprising since early partial immersion education has more first language content. By the end of elementary schooling, partial early immersion children typically catch up with mainstream peers in first language attainment. Unlike early total immersion students, partial immersion children do not tend to surpass mainstream comparison groups in first language achievement. Similarly, **late immersion** has no detrimental effect on first language skills (Genesee, 1983).

The evidence suggests that immersion children learn a second language at no cost to their first language. Rather than acting like a weighing balance, early total immersion, in particular, seems more analogous to cooking. The ingredients, when mixed and baked, react together in additive ways. The product becomes more than the sum of its parts.

Other Curriculum Areas

If immersion education results in children becoming bilingual, the question is whether this is at the cost of achievement in other curriculum areas. Compared with children in mainstream education how do immersion children progress in curriculum areas such as mathematics and science, history and geography? The reviews of research suggest that **early total immersion** students generally perform as well in these subjects as do mainstream children. That is, achievement in the curriculum is typically not adversely affected by early total immersion bilingual education.

The evaluations of **early partial immersion education** are not quite so positive. When children in early partial immersion learn mathematics and science through the medium of a second language, they tend to lag behind comparable mainstream children, at least initially. This may be because their second language skills are insufficiently developed to be able to think mathematically and scientifically in that second language.

The results for **late immersion** are similar. The important factor appears to be whether second language skills are sufficiently developed to cope with fairly complex curriculum material. Johnson and Swain (1994) argue that there is a gap in second language proficiency that needs bridging when students move from learning a language as a subject to learning through that second language. The more demanding the curriculum area, the higher the level of learning expected, and the later the switch to learning through a second language, the more important it is to provide 'bridging' programs. Such 'bridging programs' ease the discrepancy between second language proficiency and the language proficiency required to understand the curriculum. A 'bridging program' may require a language teacher and a content teacher (e.g. of mathematics) to operate together.

The overall results suggest that bilingual education by an immersion experience need not have negative effects on curriculum performance, particularly in early total immersion programs. Indeed, most children **gain** a second language without cost to their performance in the curriculum (Johnstone, 2002). However, the key factor seems to be whether their language skills have evolved sufficiently in order to work in the curriculum in their second language (see chapter 8).

There is also some evidence to suggest that immersion programs are suitable for almost all children, including those in the **lower ability** ranges. De Courcy *et al.* (2002) found that, in Australia, such children were successful in immersion education (e.g. in mathematics). Indeed, in immersion classes they appear to fare better, partly due to 'the attention to language the teachers need to have' (p. 117). There is care with vocabulary, sensitivity to language form and not just to subject content. This parallels Bruck's (1978,1982) research in Canada where 'language impaired' children were not found to suffer but gain some second language proficiency from the immersion experience. Canadian research also suggests that there are no adverse effects from immersion on below average IQ students compared with such students being in a monolingual program. Rather, some degree of bilingualism is attained (Genesee, 1992). De Courcy *et al.* (2002, p. 125) found that

> The research identified in the literature review and our own data leads us to conclude that children from diverse backgrounds should not be forced out of immersion programmes, as they would do no better in the English mainstream, but would lose the benefit of learning an additional language, at a cost to their self-esteem.

Attitudes and Social Adjustment

Apart from performance throughout the curriculum, evaluations of immersion education have examined whether immersion has positive or negative effects on students' motivation, attitude and study skills. The most positive results in this area have been found with **early total immersion students**. Parents of such students tend to express satisfaction with their offspring's learning as well as their personal and social behavior (e.g. Hickey (1997) in Ireland). Early immersion students also tend to have more positive attitudes towards themselves, their education and, in Canada to French Canadians (in comparison, for example, with late immersion students). However the danger here lies in attributing the positive attitudes to schooling. The cause may alternatively be parental values and beliefs, home culture and environment. This is further discussed in the next section.

Problems and Limitations

Various authors have recently highlighted possible limitations in immersion education that were not present in the early evaluations (e.g. Hammerly, 1988; reply by Allen *et al.*, 1989). **First**, Rebuffot (1993) suggests that Canadian immersion students do not always become grammatically accurate in their French. Immersion students also tend to lack the social and stylistic sense of appropriate language use which the native speaker possesses. For example, the restricted use of verb tenses other than the present, and the sometimes inappropriate use of 'tu' and 'vous', appear to be related to the functionally restricted language of the classroom. Certain forms of language do not naturally nor regularly occur in the classroom (e.g. because of the focus on learning and adult–student relationships). This communication difficulty may be due to students communicating only among themselves and with the teacher. This is a restricted social environment where understanding each other is possible without grammatical accuracy (Netten & Germain, 2004). Sometimes, the motivation to increase accuracy may not be present as the focus is on content and curriculum achievement. The teacher may concentrate on subject performance rather than grammatically accurate performance.

One solution is to investigate problematic areas of vocabulary and grammar, provide increased opportunities for receptive and particularly productive language in such weak areas, integrate a focus on the form of language used with meaningful content teaching, and give systematic and consistent feedback on language development to the student. Increasing group and collaborative learning is also seen as important in developing the productive language proficiency of students towards the standards of native French-Canadian speakers (Swain, 1993). Also, students need to be exposed to authentic uses of a second language outside the school (e.g. in Wales such children attend enjoyable youth camps for weekend leisure activities and mix with native speakers). This links with another potential limitation of immersion education.

Second, surveys of graduates of Canadian immersion programs tend to find that relatively few students make much use of French after leaving school (Harley, 1994; Wesche, 1993). This partly reflects opportunity, partly a lack of confidence in their competence in speaking French, and partly a preference for English use. Also, immersion students do not tend to interact significantly more with francophones than students in mainstream (core) programs. Such students do not actively seek out situations where French is used (e.g. French language television). Their usage of French in **out-of-school-contexts** is relatively negligible compared with their use of English (Genesee & Gándara, 1999). Ability in French is not often translated into use of French outside the school gates, except, for example, where employment and personal economics become a focus. In most immersion programs, exposure to the second language is largely confined to the classroom. As de Courcy's (2002) Australian research suggests 'students in these immersion programs do not feel that they have acquired any part of the language until they have had the opportunity to use it in a real, communicative situation. When they can make somebody else understand them, then they know that they know' (p.149).

Many immersion programs occur in geographical areas where the first language is dominant. While it is hoped that student will use the second language in the community, the reality is that the second language is used in the classroom, less so in playground, and very little in the wider community. Thus the culture of the classroom and school may aim to strengthen and support the second language. But the latent peer culture is often that of the first language community and may be dominant (Swain & Johnson, 1997).

Third, there is difficulty in pinpointing the **crucial interacting factors** that create an effective immersion experience. There are, for example, intervening variables such as teaching techniques that may change the pattern of results. Genesee (1983) argued that individualized, activity based teaching techniques may be more effective than traditional whole class techniques. Genesee (1983) also argued that the intensity of language learning, for example, how many hours per day, is likely to be more important than the length of language learning (e.g. the number of years of second language learning). This is connected with the finding that older students tend to learn a second language more quickly than younger learners. Is it immersion as a system that leads to relatively successful outcomes or do factors such as 'student motivation, teachers' preparation, home culture, parental attitude, ethnolinguistic vitality, amount of time studying different curricula' (Carey, 1991, p. 953) play a part as well?

Fourth, immersion programs can have **effects on mainstream schools**. For example, effects may include: a redistribution of classroom teachers and leaders, a change in the linguistic and ability profile of mainstream classes, discrepancies in class size with increasing numbers of mixed aged classes.

Fifth, Heller (1994, 1999b) has argued that Canadian immersion schools provide anglophones with the linguistic and cultural capital for increased social and economic mobility and for political power. Immersion education is thus, in this perspective, about ulterior motives and vested interests. Such education is about gaining **advantages** in Canadian society: educational, cultural, linguistic, social, power, wealth and dominance advantages. Dagenais (2003) argues that French immersion parents see bilingualism as accumulating economic and symbolic capital. They invest in immersion as a means of securing their offspring's access to imagined prestigious communities both in Canada and internationally in an increasingly mobile and multilingual world. Hence, immersion education may produce conflict with the minority francophone community (e.g. in Ontario) rather than the harmonious unity and 'bridge building' that bilingualism aims to achieve in Canadian society. French immersion may produce upwardly mobile students who are seen as competition and a threat by those from a minority francophone community whose bilingualism has hitherto been a major asset and advantage. This issue is considered further in chapter 18.

In contrast, but not necessarily in contradiction, the 2001 Census figures in Canada showed that, outside Quebec, bilingualism in teenage groups had dropped between 1996 and 2001 (from 12.9% to 11.5% in 10 to 14 year olds; from 16.3% to 14.7% in 15 to 19 year olds). An increasingly English-speaking world is one explanation for the downward trend. Increasing competition for students among schools is another. Also, in political contrast is the immersion method being suspended in Breton language Diwan schools in France in 2001. The argument has been that such immersion undermines the French Republic's principle of equality and unity, as it 'imposes' a language other than French.

Sixth, the volume of research has concentrated on the outcomes of immersion education. As de Courcy (2002) suggests, 'we still know little about students' immersion learning processes from the perspective of the learner' (p. 3). Students' views of their experiences and perspectives on the processes of immersion are relatively little sought. In contrast, de Courcy (2002) in the Australian context, shows how crucial internal or private speech is in the immersion language learning experience. Creating new sentences, for example, when speaking to oneself, 'plays a crucial role in language acquisition. It is in this turning inwards that students start to make sense of the new language; the internalizing is a signal that they are starting to make sense of the world through the new language' (p. 148).

One danger of the immersion classroom is that language minority students may learn to understand a second language well (comprehensible input), but not to produce well (**comprehensible output**). This particularly occurs if the classroom emphasis is on correctness rather than on everyday communicative language skills. When a student has opportunities to use his or her spoken language outside the classroom (e.g. in the street), language skills (e.g. grammar, syntax and communication of meaning) may be considerably enhanced (Housen & Baetens Beardsmore, 1987; Baetens Beardsmore & Swain, 1985). Immersion schools may need to build in opportunities for such out-of-school use (e.g. during vacations).

Seventh, there is a danger in generalizing from the successful Canadian experience to elsewhere in the world. In Canada, immersion concerns two major high status international languages: French and English. In many countries where bilingualism is present or fostered, the situation is different. Often the context is one of a majority and a minority language (or languages) co-existing. This links with **additive and subtractive** bilingual situations. Canada is regarded as an additive bilingual context. Many countries across the world contain subtractive bilingual contexts.

If immersion education is thought worthy of **generalizing from Canada to other countries**, there are certain conditions which need to be kept in mind:

(1)   Immersion bilingual education as practiced in Canada is **optional** not enforced. The convictions of teachers and parents and of the children themselves affect the ethos of the school and the motivation and achievement of the children. Immersion education will work best when there is conviction and not enforced conformity.

(2)   Immersion education in Canada starts with children who are at a similar level in their language skills. Such a **homogeneous** grouping of children may make the language classroom more efficient. Where there are wide variations in ability in a second language, teachers may have problems in providing an efficient and well-structured curriculum with equality of provision and opportunity.

(3)   The Canadian immersion experience ensures that there is **respect** for the child's home language and culture. This relates to an additive bilingual situation. Parents have generally been seen as partners in the immersion movement and some dialogue has existed with administrators, teachers and researchers (Hickey, 1999).

(4)   Immersion **teachers** in Canada tend to be committed to such immersion education. Research in Wales has pointed to the crucial importance of teacher commitment to bilingual education in effecting achievement in school (C. Roberts, 1985).

(5)   It is important not to view immersion education in Canada in purely educational terms. Behind immersion education is political, social and cultural **ideology**. Immersion education is not just immersion in a second language (French). Such bilingual education has aims and assumptions, beliefs and values that sometimes differ from and, at other times, are additional to mainstream education. It is important to see immersion education not just as a means to promote bilingualism, but also as a move to a different kind of society (see chapter 18). By promoting bilingualism in English speakers, immersion education in Canada may support French language communities, increase the opportunities for francophones outside Quebec and help promote bilingualism in the public sector (and debatably in the private sector). However, immersion education is seen as a Trojan horse of further English assimilation by some francophones. 'Francophones question whether an increase in bilingual anglophones will simply act to deprive them of their historical advantage in occupying bilingual jobs' (Lapkin *et al.*, 1990, p. 649). This is linked to the finding that children from higher socioeconomic backgrounds tend to be over-represented in immersion programs. Thus immersion education may act to reproduce elite groups, giving anglophone children with bilingual abilities an advantage in the jobs market (Heller, 1994, 1999a).

THE EFFECTIVENESS OF HERITAGE LANGUAGE EDUCATION

Major **reviews** of heritage language education are provided by Cummins (1983a, 1993), Cummins and Danesi (1990), Dutcher (1995) plus Demmert (2001, who provides a detailed annotated bibliography) and McCarty (2002b) for indigenous American schooling (e.g. Hawaiian, Navajo). Apart from looking at individual international educational interventions, the reviews also look at the pattern that can be found in the results of evaluations of heritage language education, thus attempting to derive international generalizations.

The results of such evaluations suggest that heritage language programs can be effective in four different ways. **First**, the students maintain their **home language**. This is especially in comparison with language minority children who are placed in mainstream or transitional education. Such mainstreamed children tend partly to lose and sometimes avoid using their heritage language. **Second**, such children tend to perform as well as comparable mainstream children in curriculum areas such as mathematics, science, history and geography. That is, there is no loss in **curriculum performance** for such children taking their education in their home language. Indeed the evaluations suggest that they perform better than comparable children in mainstream education. To illustrate: take two 'equal' children from a language minority background. One attends a mainstream program, the other attends heritage language education. The chances are that the child in heritage language education will achieve more highly, all other factors being equal.

One 'cognitive' explanation is that heritage language education commences at the level of linguistic–cognitive competence reached on entry to school. (The cognitive reasons for this increased performance are considered in chapter 8). In comparison, mainstreaming such language minority students has negative cognitive implications. It seemingly rejects a child's level of cognitive competence. It entails re-developing sufficient language capability in order for them to cope with the curriculum. If the analogy will stand, it is like someone with a basic level of skill in salmon fishing (with a fishing rod) who is made to learn big game sea fishing instead. The instructor ignores skills already attained with a rod. The student is made to practice casting on dry land, instead of building on existing skills with the fishing rod.

Third, studies suggest that children's **attitudes** are particularly positive when placed in heritage language education. When the home language is used in school, there is the possibility that a child's sense of identity, self-esteem and self-concept will be enhanced (Duquette, 1999; Johnstone *et al.*, 1999; Rolstad *et al.*, 2005). The child may perceive that the home language, the home and community culture, parents and relations are accepted by the school when the home language is used. In comparison, a language minority child who is mainstreamed is vulnerable to a loss of self-esteem and status. The home language and culture may seem disparaged. The school system and the teachers may seem latently or manifestly to be rejecting the child's home language and values. This may affect the child's motivation and interest in school work and thereby affect performance. A student whose skills are recognized and encouraged may feel encouraged and motivated; a student whose skills are ignored may feel discouraged and rejected.

The **fourth** finding of heritage language evaluations is perhaps the most unexpected. Indeed, it tends to go against 'common sense'. When testing children's **English language performance** (or whatever the second language is for that child), performance is generally comparable with mainstreamed children (see Cummins, 2000a). To explain this, take the previous example of two children from identical heritage language backgrounds with the same 'IQ', gender, socioeconomic class and age. One is placed in heritage language education, the other in mainstream schooling. It might be expected that the child placed in mainstream English language education would perform far better in English language tests than the child in a heritage language education program. The prediction might be that the greater the exposure to English in mainstream education, the higher the English language test performance will be. Evaluations of heritage language education suggest something different. The child in heritage language education is likely to perform at least as well as the child in mainstream education. The explanation seems to lie in self-esteem being enhanced, and language and intellectual skills better promoted by education in the home language. Such skills appear to transfer easily into second language (majority language) areas, although some subject areas 'may lend themselves more easily to the transfer of knowledge across languages, depending on the structure of knowledge within the domain' (August & Hakuta, 1997, p. 52).

While evaluations of heritage language education are positive, not all Canadians are agreed on the issue. For some, empowerment of heritage language groups is perceived as a major societal challenge – a challenge to existing power and political arrangements (Taylor *et al.*, 1993). Official Canadian policy has been supportive of multiculturalism, especially of the two 'solitudes' – French language and English language cultures. Extending multiculturalism to other 'heritage' languages has been more contentious (Cummins, 1992a). Ethnocultural communities (e.g. Ukrainian, German, Hebrew, Yiddish, Mandarin Chinese, Arabic and Polish) tend to support heritage language education. Anglophone and francophone Canadians tend to have a tolerance and goodwill towards such communities. Lukewarm support for heritage language communities tends to stop short if public monies are to be used to support heritage language education. The **anxieties** of sections of public opinion and of government include: the disruption of mainstream schools (e.g. falling rolls), problems of staffing, minimal communication between heritage language teachers and mainstream teachers, segregation of school communities, the financial costs of the absorption of immigrants into a bilingual education system, loss of time for core curriculum subjects, social tensions, and effects on the integration and stability of Canadian society (Cummins & Danesi, 1990; Cummins, 1992a; V. Edwards & Redfern, 1992).

Such **anxieties** have increased with the high levels of Canadian immigrants since the mid 1980s onwards. Due to low birth rates and a rapidly aging population in Canada, the population has been increased by in-migration policies. Hence language diversity in Canada has increased. In Toronto and Vancouver, for example, more than half the school population comes from a non-English speaking background (Cummins, 1992a).

Gupta (1997) also voices concerns about heritage language education. She suggests that such education can be impractical when a child has multiple mother tongues, and is unprincipled as the maintenance of social cohesiveness in a multi-cultural, cosmopolitan environment is of more importance than mother tongue education. Sometimes ethnic privilege and socioeconomic status can be reproduced by heritage language education at the expense of other ethnic minority groups.

If the focus switches from public political opinion to the educational opinion of teachers, parents and students, there is general satisfaction with Canadian Heritage Language programs. While such programs may present administrative challenges (e.g. shortage of teachers, availability of pre-service and in-service teacher education and a lack of curriculum materials), the **advantages** may be summarized as follows (Canadian Education Association, 1991):

- positive self-concept and pride in one's background;
- better integration of child into school and society;
- more tolerance of other people and different cultures;
- increased cognitive, social and emotional development;
- ease in learning of new languages;
- increased probability of employment;
- fostering stronger relationships between home and school;
- responding to the needs and wishes of community.

The overall **conclusions** from Cummins' (1983a, 1993), Danesi *et al.* (1993) and Cummins and Danesi's (1990) reviews of heritage language education suggest that such education is not likely to have detrimental effects on a child's performance in the subject curriculum. Indeed, the indication from research is that language minority children tend to prosper more in such education than when placed in mainstream education. They maintain and enrich their home language and culture. Their performance throughout the curriculum does not suffer. This notably includes performance in the second language (majority language). Cognitive enhancement can also occur (Cummins, 1993; Danesi, 1991).

An important perspective comes from Dutcher (1995) who includes an **economic analysis** of heritage language education. In a World Bank paper on the use of first and second languages in elementary education, she examines international evidence from Haiti, Nigeria, the Philippines, Guatemala, Canada, New Zealand, United States (Navajo), Fiji, the Solomon Islands, Vanuatu and Western Samoa. She concludes that development of the mother tongue is critical for cognitive development and as a foundation for learning the second language. That is, mainstreaming and transitional models of bilingual education are internationally less effective in developing a child's thinking abilities. When such development is slowed considerably by learning in a second language (e.g. submersion), then the second language will in itself be learnt more slowly. Dutcher (1995) also found that parental support and community involvement were essential for successful bilingual education programs.

What is particularly important about Dutcher's (1995) review is the **economics of bilingual education**. She concludes that the recurrent costs for bilingual education are approximately the same as for traditional programs. Bilingual education is not an expensive option and has similar costs to mainstream programs. However, the most important conclusion is that strong forms of bilingual education create cost savings for the education system and for society. For example, such bilingual education provides higher levels of achievement in fewer years of study. Student progress is faster, and higher achievement benefits society by less unemployment and a more skilled work force.

When there are 'weak' forms of bilingual education, or language minority children are mainstreamed, there may be costs to a national economy due to slower rates of progress at school, lower levels of final achievement, and sometimes the need for special or compensatory education. Higher drop-out rates mean lower potential for the employment market, and the economy suffers with a lower level of skills among the work force and higher unemployment rates. In economic terms, students need to gain productive characteristics through education and Dutcher (1995) indicates that this is through early use of the native language.

For example, a World Bank **cost-effectiveness study** on Guatemala found that bilingual education was an economically prudent policy (World Bank, 1997; Dutcher, 2004). Repetition and drop-out rates were decreased through a bilingual education intervention program, and standards of achievement rose (including in Spanish). It was estimated that education cost savings due to bilingual education were 5.6 million US dollars per year, while cost benefits were in the order of 33.8 million US dollars per year. Also, individual earnings rose by approximately 50%. In Guatemala, a strong form of bilingual education made economic sense as it produced a more skilled, highly trained and employable work force. Weak forms of bilingual education in comparison tend to have higher dropout rates and lower levels of achievement, and thus have less chance of serving and stimulating the economy through a skilled work force.

RESEARCH LIMITATIONS

So far in this chapter, we have examined research on specific models of bilingual education (dual language, heritage language, immersion). Underneath such bilingual education, irrespective of which model is being discussed, is **politics**. Bilingual education is, and will continue to be, a political issue. For some pluralism, biculturalism and multilingualism are a **desirable outcome**. For others the assimilation of minority languages, the integration of minorities within the overall society are the important outputs. This suggests that a definitive statement on whether bilingual education is more or less successful than, for example, mainstream education is impossible due to the variety of underlying values and beliefs that different interest groups have about education and the future society they envisage.

This chapter has also assumed that research reviews can directly inform policy-making. Cummins sees this as naive due to the 'myriad human, administrative, and political influences that impact the implementation of programs over time' (Cummins, 1999a, p. 26). There are hundreds of variables that affect program outcomes such that research cannot, by itself, directly advise policy, provision and practice. Rather, Cummins (1999a, 2000b) argues that it is tested theory that should drive policy-making.

> In complex educational and other human organizational contexts, data or 'facts' become relevant for policy purposes only in the context of a coherent theory. It is the *theory* rather than the individual research findings that permits the generation of predictions about program outcomes under different conditions. (Cummins, 1999a, p. 26)

That is, research should commence from theoretical propositions, testing, refining and sometimes refuting those propositions. When theory is firmly supported by research and it accounts for findings from a variety of contexts, theory will explicitly inform policy-making. Thus Cummins (1999a, 2000b) is critical of the US National Research Council report (August & Hakuta, 1997) as it comprehensively summarizes research but virtually ignores theories that address policy-relevant issues. Cummins (1999a, 2000b) asserts that theories such as Thresholds, Interdependence, Conversational and Academic Language Proficiency (see chapter 8) are supported by research and answer a range of policy issues. Such theories are a more important focus than reviews of research.

However, policy makers (e.g. politicians, local and national civil servants, political advisors) rarely base their decisions solely on theory or research. The reason is that the researcher/policy-maker relationship is not one of 'truth speaking to power', or 'science providing evidence-based decisions'. That is too simplistic. Policy in bilingual education is shaped by a myriad of influences other than research and theory (e.g. political ideology, pragmatism, conflicting interests and varied stakeholders). When research does have an influence, it can be through 'cherry-picking' the most convenient and supportive findings for a particular viewpoint. Evidence from research and theory can inform policy and be a part of the shaping of that policy. Its effects will be partial and modest, and be part of a continuous shared search for worthwhile education.

Research cannot provide evidence-based policy, only evidence-informed policy. No research on bilingual education is perfect, even totally objective. This section now provides the critical lens to assess such research.

The Sample of Children

The results of one study are limited to that sample of children at the time of the study. If there is some form of probability sampling (e.g. a random sample of a defined population is chosen), then these results may generalize to that specific population. Such **sampling** rarely occurs in bilingual education evaluations. Instead, many studies have small and unrepresentative samples. It is usually ethically questionable and practically impossible to allocate children randomly into experimental and control groups that contain perfect mirrors of a large population of schoolchildren.

Given the wide variety of samples of children used in bilingual education effectiveness research, it is not surprising that differences in findings emerge. Samples of children include urban and rural schools, various socioeconomic class backgrounds, different ages and varying profiles of teachers (e.g. teacher training). The international research includes a mixture of bilingual groups: indigenous language minority groups, immigrants, and majority language children in minority language education. **Generalization** of results from one group to another is rarely valid. Such children may be in a subtractive or additive environment in the home, school, community and nation.

Unlike the physical world, simple laws of behavior that govern large groups of people are not likely. The immense variety of individual differences and contextual differences makes clear-cut, simple research results intrinsically elusive. Such results also say something about what has been, not what will always be. They do not guarantee that results will be stable across time as educational practices are always changing and developing.

Interacting Factors

Various factors, other than the sample of children, may have a variable effect on bilingual education. Parental interest, parental involvement in their children's education and parental cooperation with teachers is one intervening factor. Another factor is likely to be the enthusiasm and commitment of teachers to the education program. With a novel experiment in bilingual education, there may be extra enthusiasm and interest. The level of resource support (e.g. books, curriculum guidelines, computers, science equipment) may also produce variable outcomes. Mackey (1976) suggested that up to 3000 input, contextual, process and outcome variables could individually, and interactively, create a bilingual classroom (see Baetens Beardsmore (1997) and Baker (1988) for major categories of such variables). In contrast, policy makers deal in general scenarios and trends and prefer a broad-brush canvas (Hakuta, 2002).

There can be as much **variation** in outcomes inside a particular bilingual education program (e.g. achievement in different curriculum areas) as between different types of program (e.g. transitional, immersion or heritage language). The crucial point is this. The language policy and language practice in schooling are only one element among many that make a school more or less successful. A recipe for success is unlikely to result from one ingredient (e.g. the language of the classroom). A great variety of factors act and interact to determine whether bilingual education is successful or not. It makes more sense to consider the wide variety of conditions which make bilingual education more or less successful. We need to specify all the ingredients in different recipes to fully understand the success or failure of forms of bilingual education. Bilingual education, whatever type or model, is no guarantee of effective schooling (Baker, 2003b).

Laosa (2000) indicates that **program characteristics** such as the type and number of instructors per student, the instructor's qualifications, and fragmentation of instruction are potentially influential on student achievement. That is, particular models of bilingual education interact with a host of student, teacher, curriculum and contextual variables in complex ways to influence student outcomes. This suggests that there is no single best practice; multiple best practices are more likely, if elusive.

Definitions of particular programs can be vague such that classification into a 'model' may not be accurate of easy. For example, the provision of specialized language services is not always clear or included in categorizing a school. Labels can hide many differences.

Measures of Success

An important question is: what tests or other sources of evidence are used to determine whether a form of bilingual education is successful (Torres-Guzmán et al., 2002)? Should the sole **outcomes** be competence in one or two languages? What aspects of language should be assessed (see chapters 1 and 2)? Should the measure of success be performance across the whole curriculum? Who defines what are the important outcomes of the curriculum (e.g. computational versus conceptual emphasis in mathematics; religious knowledge versus moral development; nuggets of knowledge or critical thinking)? Preferred learning outcomes are not 'correct' or 'right'. Instead, desired learning outcomes are a subjective belief in what is of worth and important. A value judgment is made that will change over time and vary across educationalists and not least politicians.

How important is it to include non-cognitive outcomes such as self-esteem, moral development, school attendance, social and emotional adjustment, integration into society, identity and gaining employment? What are the long-term effects of bilingual schooling (e.g. economic advantage, students later becoming parents who raise their children in the minority language)? These questions suggest that there will be debates and disputes over what are the valuable outcomes of schooling. Research on the effectiveness of bilingual education has varied in the choice of measures of outcome. Such a choice reflects a particular emphasis, ideology or conviction. It is not a neutral or value-free judgment.

The Style of the Research

A particular problem is that measures of success have often been restricted to what is **measurable**. Quantitative outcomes (e.g. test scores) are used; qualitative evidence has rarely been gathered. Can a play be judged only on an applause meter reading? Do a drama critic's notes add a vigorous, insightful interpretation to the performance? While critics will differ in their evaluations, they may add flesh and life to the statistical bones of educational tests.

In the United States, the 2001 **No Child Left Behind** legislation (see chapter 9) requires decisions about the best programs for English language learners to be based on scientific, empirical, systematic and objective research. This implies a particular research method: replicated, controlled and well designed **experiments**, with valid and reliable measurement plus rigorous statistical analysis. The ideal is children randomly assigned to two or more models. Such students are then tested at the beginning and at the end of the program (or at the end of a school year). Random assignment to a model attempts to remove other differences between children that could explain the results. For example, if dual language schools had middle class children and Sheltered English had working class students, the results could be as much about social class differences as a model of education.

However, there are considerable limitations to such experiments.

- A new program approach to bilingual children may exaggerate its effectiveness (**novelty effect**). There may be extra enthusiasm and motivation to succeed (and better materials) in a new approach. A comparison of new and old can be unfair as the effect is temporary.

- Being in an experiment can change a schools' or teachers' behavior (**Hawthorne effect**). Being 'under the spotlight' can make a difference (positive or negative) to customary performance in teachers and students.

- It is impossible to **match teachers**, so differential gains may be due to teachers rather than a particular model of bilingual education. Even when (unusually) the same teachers are used in different models, their motivation may be different in each, this not controlling this important variable.

- An experiment measures success on a very narrow range of outcomes. It does not usually measure **side-effects** (e.g. less enthusiasm, less time for leisure activities). There is a distinction between program effectiveness (e.g. attaining learning outcomes) and effects (i.e. any consequence, intended or not).

- An experiment does not investigate **process** e.g. how a teacher interprets and operates within a program. When there are programs and schemes, teachers interpret and adapt in the light of their own experience and the type of students to be instructed, such that the process can vary considerably across classrooms within the same program.

- An experiment is thus a '**black box model**' of research. It can be run by researchers without ever visiting a school. They need to send pre-tests and post-tests to the school and then analyze the returned results. (Engaging the process of classrooms is called a glass box model of research, whereby the detail of classroom activity is open to viewing.) Experiments take snapshots. A glass box model (e.g. observation) takes a film.

- Attention is focused on program aggregation and averages. Outstanding individual schools that may be **atypical** are lost in an overall result.

- The assumption is that there is an **objective scientific truth**, experimentally demonstrable that allows a trustworthy prediction of outcomes. This can sometimes be linked to the desire to impose uniformity and political control. Instead, educational outcomes will always be debated and contested, being changeable across time and ideology.

The Researchers

Research on bilingual education is rarely neutral. Often the researchers have hypotheses that hide their **expectations**. No educational research can be totally value-free, neutral or objective. The questions asked, the methodological tools chosen, decisions in analysis and manner of reporting usually reveal ideological and political preferences (August & Hakuta, 1997, 1998). Many researchers will be supporters of bilingual education, ethnic diversity, minority language rights and cultural pluralism (Hakuta, 2002). Such supporters may be convinced of the correctness of their beliefs. This is definitely not to argue that all evaluation research on bilingual education is invalid. Rather, it cannot be assumed that results are not affected by researchers, their beliefs, opinions and preferences. Some of the research on bilingual education is committed, prescriptive in nature, with interests, idealism and ideology mixed with investigation and intelligent discussion. As Hakuta (2002) argues:

> The education of language-minority students has a long history rooted solidly in the civil-rights era of the 1960s. It has never been a knowledge-based movement. Members of the research establishment who are visible in it . . . have all been recruited as legitimating devices and defense mechanisms for the movement. Stellar as these researchers might be, anything they say would be immediately suspect by the very fact that they work in an area that flows directly from civil rights . . . plus the fact that university faculty, especially in education and social sciences, are seen as ideologically in the 'politically correct' camp by the ideological right. (pp. 134–5)

There is a fine line between research and advocacy some attempt not to cross; others cross very quickly.

CONCLUSION

This chapter has examined the development of studies which have investigated whether bilingual education is more or less effective than monolingual education. It has also examined studies which look at the relative effectiveness of different forms of bilingual education. The initial studies examined individual programs and schools. A wide variety of different outcomes and conclusions resulted.

The evaluations of immersion bilingual education and heritage language education tend to favor '**strong**' forms of bilingual education. Such studies indicate that such bilingual education not only results in bilingualism and biliteracy but also tends to heighten achievement across the curriculum. Strong forms of bilingual education tend to raise the standards and performance of children. However, these results do not stop at individual achievement. In societal terms, there are benefits for the economy in strong forms of bilingual education.

The chapter has revealed a paradox. US research on bilingual education has clearly tended to favor more years rather than less in bilingual education. Yet there has been little US government support for bilingual education. **Politics** has proved stronger than research, selectively using the evidence, and marching on regardless. This is because there is a contest about whose definition of a US citizen is dominant. Bilingual education, as practiced in the United States, has tended to be more about politics than pedagogy, 'mythology' more than effective methodology, and prejudice rather than preferable practice.

However, another conclusion is that simple questions give simplistic answers. We cannot expect a simple answer to the question of whether or not bilingual education is more (or less) effective than mainstream education. The question itself needs to be more refined. It needs to look at the **conditions** under which different forms of bilingual education become more or less successful. This means departing from simple studies and simple results to broad investigations that include a wide variety of conditions and situations. The scales of justice of bilingual education cannot give a simple verdict. The evidence needs to be wide-ranging and complex; witnesses have complex accounts and arguments. There is no simple right or wrong, good or bad; no simple orthodoxy of approach that can guarantee success.

The effectiveness of bilingual education needs to consider children, teachers, the community, the school itself and the type of program. One particular factor cannot be isolated from another. Children have a wide variety of characteristics which also need investigation. Children cannot be isolated from the classroom characteristics within which they work. Within the classroom there are a variety of factors which may make for effective education. Outside the classroom the different attributes of schools may, in their turn, interact with children and their classrooms to make education for language minority children more or less effective. Outside the school is the important role played by the family and the community. The social, cultural and political environment in which a school works will affect the education of language minority children at all levels.

The key issue becomes 'what are the optimal conditions for children who are either bilingual, becoming bilingual or wish to be bilingual?' The following chapters address this issue.

KEY POINTS IN THE CHAPTER

- Immersion, Heritage Language and Dual Language bilingual education generally promote both first and second languages for academic purposes with no lowering of performance elsewhere in the curriculum and typically increased achievement.
- Research generally supports 'strong' forms of bilingual education where a student's home language is cultivated by the school. 'Weak' forms of bilingual education where the student's second language is replaced for educational purposes by a second majority language tend to show less effectiveness.
- Strong forms of bilingual education can be an economically valuable policy. Repetition and drop-out rates are decreased, and a more skilled, highly trained and employable work force is produced.

- Individual researches, meta-analyses, expert reviews and public opinion polls do not provide an agreed belief in the effectiveness of bilingual education. This is explained partly by the varying political aims of those who either support or oppose bilingual education.
- However, academic empirical research generally supports 'strong' forms of bilingual education where a student's home language is cultivated by the school. 'Weak' forms of bilingual education where the student's second language is replaced for educational purposes by a second majority language tend to be less effective.
- Experts fail to agree about the value of bilingual education because their political beliefs differ. Reliance on tested theory is one answer to differing opinions.

SUGGESTED FURTHER READING

AUGUST, D. & HAKUTA, K., 1998, *Educating Language-Minority Children.* Washington, DC: National Academy Press.
BAETENS BEARDSMORE, H. (ed.), 1993, *European Models of Bilingual Education.* Clevedon: Multilingual Matters.
CUMMINS, J. & CORSON, D. (eds), 1997, *Bilingual Education. Volume 5 of the Encyclopedia of Language and Education.* Dordrecht: Kluwer.
CUMMINS, J. & DANESI, M., 1990, *Heritage Languages: The Development and Denial of Canada's Linguistic Resources.* Toronto: Our Schools/Ourselves Education Foundation and Garamond Press.
DUTCHER, N., 1995, *The Use of First and Second Languages in Education: a Review of International Experience.* Washington, DC: World Bank.
HELLER, M., 1994, *Crosswords: Language, Education and Ethnicity in French.* Ontario and New York: Mouton de Gruyter.
JOHNSON, R.K. & SWAIN, M., 1997, *Immersion Education: International Perspectives.* Cambridge: Cambridge University Press.
JOHNSTONE, R., 2002, *Immersion in a Second or Additional Language at School: A Review of the International Research.* Stirling (Scotland): Scottish Centre for Information on Language Teaching. http://www.scilt.stir.ac.uk/pubs.htm
LINDHOLM-LEARY, K.J., 2001, *Dual Language Education.* Clevedon: Multilingual Matters.
THOMAS, W.P., & COLLIER, V.P., 2002, *A National Study of School Effectiveness for Language Minority Students' Long-Term Academic Achievement. Final report.* Washington, DC: Center for Research on Education, Diversity & Excellence.

STUDY ACTIVITIES

(1) Arrange a debate among students where two people support 'weak' forms of bilingual education, and two support 'strong' forms. Present the arguments for two major kinds of bilingual education, highlighting those which are most important in your region. Allow other students to ask questions of the four presenters.

(2) In local schools, what are the beliefs about the effectiveness of education for language minority children, and especially the achievement levels of these children? Is their a concern about under-achievement, and if so, what reasons are given for this? Do you think the beliefs and reasons are valid or not?

(3) Collect together newspaper clippings about language in schools within your

area. Try to find different attitudes in these clippings. Different newspapers may report the same story in different ways. Collect together these different interpretations and try to give an explanation of the variation.

(4) With a partner or in a small group, prepare a two minute television interview sequence on bilingual education. Locate questions which are important and likely to be of concern to the public. Prepare short punchy answers to these questions.

(5) Sit with a group of children or in a formal class of children, and attempt to measure the time the children and teacher spend using each language in the classroom. Try to work out over two or three sessions how much time is spent in either language. When recording, try to locate which language is being used for what purpose. For example, what language is used for classroom instructions, classroom management, discipline, questions, on-task and off-task talk among children, greetings, rewards and reinforcement.

CHAPTER 13

Effective Schools and Classrooms for Bilingual Students

Effective Schools and Classrooms for Bilingual Students

INTRODUCTION

The aim of this chapter is to outline some of the foundational elements of effective and **successful** bilingual schools and classrooms for their students. When a school adopts a particular model (e.g., submersion/mainstreaming, immersion, dual language, heritage language), there is an implementation that entails interpretation, adjustments and occasional compromises to meet local traditions and realities. The idealized model is translated from academic and administrative concepts into the intricate actualities of local school and classroom life (Wiese, 2004).

Schools and classrooms are highly **complex organizations**. They are sites where a multitude of actions and reactions, inputs and processes, variable and changing environments, and differing local and regional expected learning outcomes. The formula for **success** is never simple, partly as success is diversely defined and understood, and partly as perceived effectiveness varies across person, administration, region and time. Partly also, the mixture of factors affecting effectiveness is so complex that simple recipes are impossible. Effectiveness inevitably goes far beyond language medium and language outcomes to embrace the full education of a student. Ultimately, effectiveness concerns what is deemed best for the child and not just a language. However, there is sufficient international research, grounded wisdom and accumulated expertise that it is possible to suggest key factors that need discussion in effective bilingual schools and classrooms. This chapter attempts to provide a menu for that dialogue.

Two introductory points: first, it is important to repeat the distinction between teaching a language and teaching through a language. Language acquisition in the immersion, heritage and dual programs is mostly through a second language being used as a medium of instruction (see chapter 11). In the US, this is sometimes called **content-based second language instruction**. In Europe, it is referred to as **CLIL** (content and language integrated learning). This chapter is about such an approach, and not about teaching a language for its own sake, as in second language lessons.

Second, close to the idea of two or more languages being used for instruction is the concept of **language across the curriculum**. In all curriculum areas, students learn skills, knowledge, concepts and attitudes mostly through language. Thus, every curriculum area develops language competence. All subject areas, from music to mathematics, science to sport, contribute to the growth of a child's language or languages. At the same time, achievement in a particular curriculum area is partly dependent on proficiency in the language of that area. Obtaining fluency in the language of chemistry, psychology or mathematics, for example, is important to understanding that subject.

The chapter now proceeds to consider those classroom contexts where the first (heritage) language of students is developed.

FIRST LANGUAGE DEVELOPMENT AT SCHOOL

For language minority bilingual children, the **school** is usually an **essential agent** in developing the home language. When a child enters kindergarten or elementary school, first language development needs to be formally addressed, irrespective of whether or not that child has age-appropriate competency in the home language. While first language development throughout schooling is important for majority and minority language children, the minority context places extra reasons for careful nurturance of a minority language (Dutcher, 2004). (The immersion approach for majority language children is considered later).

Two quotes from a historically influential report by **UNESCO** (1953) entitled *'The Use of Vernacular Languages in Education'* provide the basis for the use of the home language in school, where pragmatically possible:

> It is axiomatic that the best medium for teaching a child is his mother tongue. Psychologically, it is the system of meaningful signs that in his mind works automatically for expression and understanding. Sociologically, it is a means of identification among the members of the community to which he belongs. Educationally, he learns more quickly through it than through an unfamiliar linguistic medium. (p. 11)

> It is important that every effort should be made to provide education in the mother tongue . . . On educational grounds we recommend that the use of the mother tongue be extended to as late a stage in education as possible. In particular, pupils should begin their schooling through the medium of the mother tongue, because they understand it best and because to begin their school life in the mother tongue will make the break between home and school as small as possible. (pp. 47–48)

The Center for Applied Linguistics (2001) estimates that some 221 million school-age children of lesser-used languages live in non-industrialized countries of the world. Many never go to school. Others drop out early. The remainder are often struggling to learn in a majority language they hardly understand. Therefore, **use of the mother tongue** in education is important for children's achievement, self-esteem, and not least for learning the majority language (see chapter 8). 'When the mother tongue is not used, they are made to feel backward, inferior, and stupid. Their culture is denigrated, and the children are scared, confused, and traumatized. This can have long-term effects' (Center for Applied Linguistics, 2001, p. 19).

When some minority language children start school, teachers do not always believe they are fully fluent in their mother tongue. For example, a teacher may consider that the child has a dialect that needs developing into a more standard variety. Or a teacher may hear the child speak a 'limited', nativized or a 'non-standard' variety of English, and therefore wrongly deduce that a child's native language is under-developed. In such cases, securing the minority (and majority) language can become a classroom aim.

Securing the Minority Language

The typically lower status of the minority language, the anglophone nature of most mass media, and the dominance of 'common denominator' majority languages outside the school requires that special attention be paid to the continual evolution and progression of the minority language in **heritage language education** and **dual language schools**. Such bilingual schools can considerably develop the minority language learnt at home so that it has more uses and potentially can be used in more domains (e.g. reading, writing, preparation for employment). The school will widen vocabulary, teach conventional syntax, and help standardization of the minority language (e.g. new terminology in Information Technology). The school also gives the minority language status, esteem and market value to its students.

To preserve and reproduce the minority language in the young, a 'strong' form of bilingual education (one that supports the heritage language) needs to include a 'first language' program with explicit language development aims and goals. Such a program may involve lessons devoted to that language (e.g. Spanish listening, speaking, writing and reading development in the US). It may also valuably involve a strategy for first **language development across the curriculum** through **content based language approaches** (Wesche & Skehan, 2002; Met, 1998). Where children take lessons (e.g. social studies, science) through the medium of their home language, language development in those curriculum areas can be overtly and consciously fostered. A child's home language develops when it is cultivated, encouraged and promoted in a purposeful way in many or all curriculum areas (e.g. humanities, sciences, mathematics). Such content areas shape the language that is learnt, although language proficiency may constrain the content that can be learnt (Met, 1998).

The **learning methodologies** and teaching strategies used to support language minority children in school are also important. Mainstream classrooms often assume a homogeneous student population, with similar linguistic and cultural characteristics, delivering a standardized 'transmission' or 'banking' curriculum with individual competition symbolized in regular standardized tests (Cummins, 2000a). Mainstream classrooms are often organized in ways that do not fully support minority language children's linguistic and cultural development.

In contrast, language minority students may thrive in an atmosphere where linguistic and cultural diversity is assumed, sharing a bicultural or multicultural curriculum with multiple perspectives and linguistic equality of opportunity (Freeman, 1995, 1998). Supportive and non-threatening **cooperative learning** techniques that stress teamwork, interdependence, social interaction and teamwork have been successfully used with culturally and linguistically diverse students (Holt, 1993). For example, small groups of around four students work together to complete a given task, especially in classes that are numerically large. Active learning, the amalgamation of language and content, and the integration of linguistically diverse students can be engineered in such cooperative learning (Ovando *et al.*, 2003).

Cummins (2000b) argues for a 'transformative pedagogy' that sees knowledge as fluid and not fixed, collaboratively constructed rather than memorized, where the sharing of experiences affirms students' identity, but essentially also involves critical enquiry to understand power, inequality, justice, and local social and economic realities (see the critical literacy approach, chapter 14).

The benefits inherent in a well-developed home (minority) language spread to the learning of a second language. As Swain and Lapkin (1991) found in research, those students **literate in their heritage language** progressed significantly more in written and oral second language French than those without such skills. First language literacy, in particular, enables relative ease of learning (and learning through) a second language by the transfer of knowledge, language abilities (e.g. literacy strategies, communication skills) and learning processes (see chapters 8, 11, 12 and 14).

Codeswitching in the Classroom

Codeswitching is frequent in many bilingual classrooms. Ferguson (2003) suggests that codeswitching:

> is not only very prevalent across a wide range of educational settings but also seems to arise naturally, perhaps inevitably, as a pragmatic response to the difficulties of teaching content in a language medium over which pupils have imperfect control. Moreover, because teaching is an adrenalin-fuelled activity, making numerous competing demands on one's attentional resources, much switching takes place below the level of consciousness. Teachers are often simply not aware of when they switch languages, or indeed if they switch at all. (p. 46)

Yet A.M. Lin (1996) has shown that the patterns of codeswitching in Hong Kong classrooms are highly ordered and patterned (e.g. using Cantonese to explain or annotate English key terms) and also have pedagogic and social functions (e.g. increased communication of meaning, decreasing distance, saving face, emphasis; see Man & Lu, 2006).

Martin-Jones (2000) and Simon (2001) survey three decades of research on such interactions between students, and between students and teachers. They observe that bilingual classroom talk is best understood within the context and traditions of that school and class. Such **situations** provided clues and cues for expected and allowable patterns of talk. For example, **codeswitching** by the teacher may be used to signal the start of a lesson or a transition in the lesson, to specify an interaction with a particular student, or to move from teaching content to classroom management. Such codeswitching may occur simultaneously with body communication such as gestures and eye-contact.

Choice of 'which language to use and when' tends to be patterned and will reflect (1) the teacher's strong preference and lead (2) a student's proficiency or preference or (3) a negotiation between teacher and child. A teacher's **language choice** tends to be more child-centered in the early years of schooling, for example when explanations, clarifications and checks on understanding are needed with young children (e.g. language minority children in mainstream, language majority classes). Facilitating understanding by moving between two or more languages tends to underlie much classroom codeswitching. But such codeswitching in classrooms varies among teachers, schools and countries in terms of its prohibition, discouragement, allowance or encouragement (Martin-Jones, 2000). For example, the Education Department of Hong Kong has decreed that 'mixed-code teaching should not be used in [secondary] schools' (Education Department of Hong Kong, 1997, p. 2). Even when there is discouragement, students may privately move from the teacher's language to their own preferred language, for example to help each other understand (Man & Lu, 2006). Thus there is often a difference between formal policy and the informal practice of codeswitching, with 'center stage' and 'back stage' choices.

Research has examined the patterns of language choice and codeswitching in classrooms (Simon, 2001). Behind such patterns are often histories of dual or multiple language use, latent and stated pedagogies from different models of bilingual education (e.g. immersion, dual language), and the pressures of regional or national politics. There is also the typical preference of a teacher to 'exploit all the potential means available to facilitate the learning process' (Simon, 2001, p. 338), which includes codeswitching even when it is discouraged.

The use of two languages in the classroom is also about which language is relatively valued, **privileged**, how use of two languages are synchronized and sequenced, negotiated and switched, how meanings and understandings are constructed. Such bilingual talk occurs in the classroom, yet can often only be understood and explained beyond the school through the lens of community, economic, historic and especially political contexts.

For example, there is a tendency in classrooms for minority language children, even when very young, to move towards the majority high status language. The Oller and Eilers (2002) research in Miami found that regardless of school type (e.g. dual language education), and regardless of age, students from Spanish language home spoke predominantly in English. Even in the first semester of kindergarten, the Miami children seemed to be aware that English was the prestigious language and used English for conversations.

Translanguaging and Transliteracy

An example of the use of both languages in a lesson highlights a potential problem. The teacher introduces a topic in English, making some remarks in Spanish. Hand-outs and work sheets are in English. Class activities (e.g. teamwork) are carried out in the students' preferred language. The teacher interacts with the small groups and individual students in a mixture of Spanish and English. The students complete the work sheet in English. This type of situation is unlikely to develop students' literacy in Spanish. The languages have an unequal status and use. To allow students to make progress in both languages, there needs to be **strategic classroom language planning**.

Cen Williams' (1994, 1996) research suggests that there are strategies that develop both languages successfully and also result in effective content learning. In particular he found 'translanguaging' to work well in High schools in Wales. In 'translanguaging', the **input** (reading or listening) tends to be in one language, and the **output** (speaking or writing) in the other language, and this is systematically varied. For instance, a science worksheet in English is read by students. The teacher then initiates a discussion on the subject matter in Spanish, switching to English to highlight particular science terms. The students then do their written work in Spanish. Next lesson, the roles of the languages are reversed. In this example, the students need to understand the work to use the information successfully in another language.

Translanguaging and transliteracy (Baker, 2004) has **four potential advantages**. Firstly, it may promote a deeper and **fuller understanding** of the subject matter. If the students have understood it in two languages, they have really understood it. It is possible, in a monolingual teaching situation, for students to answer questions or write an essay about a subject without fully understanding it. Processing for meaning may not have occurred. Whole sentences or paragraphs can be copied or adapted out of a text book, from the WWW or from dictation by the teacher without real understanding. It is less easy to do this with 'translanguaging'. To read and discuss a topic in one language, and then to write about it in another language, means that the subject matter has to be processed and 'digested'.

Secondly, 'translanguaging' may help students **develop literacy in their weaker language**. Students might otherwise attempt the main part of the work in their stronger language and then undertake less challenging, related tasks in their weaker language. 'Translanguaging' attempts to develop academic language skills in both languages leading to **full bilingualism and biliteracy**.

Thirdly, the dual use of languages can facilitate **home–school cooperation**. If a child can communicate to a minority language parent in their usual medium, the parent can support the child in their school work.

Fourth, the integration of fluent English speakers and English learners (e.g. in US schools) of various levels of attainment is helped by 'translanguaging'. If English learners are integrated with first language English speakers, and if sensitive and strategic use is made of both languages in class, then the learners can **develop their second language ability concurrently with content learning**.

There are potential problems in the complexity of managing, allocating and organizing such a use of two languages (Jacobson, 1990; Ferguson, 2003). However, the value of the idea is that the teacher plans the **strategic use** of two languages, thinks consciously about the allocation of two languages in the classroom, reflects and reviews what is happening, and attempts to cognitively stimulate students by a 'language provocative' and 'language diversified' lesson.

Cultural Awareness

'It is possible to become bilingual and not bicultural or multicultural' is an oft repeated caution to teachers. A language divorced from its culture is like a body without a soul. Therefore, **developing heritage cultural awareness** alongside first language teaching is an important element in minority language education. Similarly, in two majority language bilingual education situations, developing intercultural competence is important (Byram, 1998).

Classroom activities to foster minority language cultural awareness can include: enacting social conventions; cultural rituals and traditions using authentic visual and written materials; discussing cultural variations (e.g. the colorful kaleidoscope of Latin American dances, festivals, customs and traditions); identifying the varying experiences and perspectives of the particular language variety (e.g. of French Canadians, of the French majority in France, of bilinguals in France (e.g. Bretons, Provencal); classroom visits by native speakers of the language for 'question and answer' sessions.

In Wales, **developing a cultural awareness** about Wales is contained in a central curriculum concept called the '*Curriculum Cymreig*' (Welsh Cultural Curriculum) that endeavors to reflect the whole range of historical, social, economic, cultural, political and environmental influences that have shaped contemporary Wales. This involves giving students a sense of place, distinctiveness and heritage, of belonging to the local and a wider community with its own traditions, a strong Welsh identity, access to the literature of Wales, differences and traditions in the use of the Welsh and English languages in Wales, and the distinctive nature of Welsh music, arts, crafts, technology, religious beliefs and practices (Estyn, 2001; ACAC, 1993). Such activity is directly related to students' experiences, contexts and interests, and is therefore seen as important and relevant. Homework can involve active discovery and personal research. Fieldwork, visits and extra-curricular activities may be integral to such an approach. It uses teachers' local knowledge, enabling teachers to be creative and original, hopefully firing their enthusiasm.

There can also be an emphasis on developing heritage cultural awareness in mathematics, science and technology and not just in humanities and aesthetic areas. For example, in Wales students study mathematicians William Jones (1675–1749) who first used the 'pi' (π) symbol and Robert Recorde (16th century) who devised the 'equals' (=) symbol. In science, children discuss local soil samples and how they connect with local farming and agriculture, the coal and slate mining that have been important to the Welsh economy, local small industries, and working from home via computer and communication networks. Some of this involves cross-curricular activity.

It is sometimes argued that a minority language must be fostered to **preserve the attendant culture**. The opposite is also tenable. The attendant culture must be fostered in the classroom to preserve the minority language. While separation of culture and language is false, minority language culture can be weakly or strongly represented in the classroom and in the whole ethos of the school. Such culture may be incidentally taught with little intent or rationale. Alternatively, such culture may be consciously included in language teaching and the overall physical and psychological environment of the school. This is particularly valuable in encouraging participation by children in their heritage language culture. Language skills in the minority language are no guarantee of continued use of that language into teens and adulthood. Enculturation therefore becomes essential if that language is to be useful and used.

Not all language minority children are allowed to develop their home language at school. Many such students are mainstreamed, where all content teaching is through the majority language. The chapter now considers this context.

MONOLINGUAL SCHOOLS AND CLASSES

Majority Language Development in Monolingual Schools

When language minority children are placed in mainstream schools, then the emphasis will be on securing proficiency in the second (majority) language (e.g. English in the US). This section examines the issue of how long this takes, and then how 'scaffolding' is important to ensure a sensitive and sympathetic transition into the second language.

If a child is required to work through a second language in school, a deep level of language proficiency is required and this has to be developed throughout schooling. Collier (1995) argues that it is difficult for second language students to develop **proficiency levels in their second language** to compete with native speakers. One reason is that native speakers are not sitting around waiting for non-native speakers to catch up. During the school years, native speakers' first language development continues at a rapid rate, such that the goal of proficiency equal to a native speaker is a moving target for the language learner (Thomas & Collier, 2002a). Such students in mainstreaming or transitional forms of education 'must make fifteen months of progress for each ten months of progress that the native-English speaker is making each year of school, and they must do this for six consecutive years to eventually reach the 50th percentile – a dramatic accomplishment!' (Thomas & Collier, 2002b, pp. 19–20).

In the US, how quickly ELLs (English Language Learners) reach a level of **English proficiency** to work successfully in the mainstream is important in funding decisions (e.g. special services to teach English). A review of research by Genesee *et al.* (2005) suggests that such an advanced level of oral English proficiency is reached within three to five years. Progress at the beginning is rapid, but is slower from middle to higher levels of oral language proficiency. As higher levels of oral proficiency develop, reading achievement and academic uses of language both increase. ELL students with well developed English oral skills (especially phonological awareness) achieve greater success in English literacy than those with less well developed skills. However, if a student has literacy skills in their first language, these transfer easily to reading in English (e.g. inferencing, phonological awareness, self-monitoring of comprehension – see chapter 14).

The review by Genesee *et al.* (2005) also indicates that oral proficiency increases with: (1) use of English outside school (which increases with proficiency), (2) friendships with fluent or native English speakers (which also increase with proficiency), and (3) paired work with native or fluent speakers so long as the task is well designed.

Collier's (1995) **longitudinal studies** suggest that, in US schools where all the instruction is given through the second language (submersion schooling), second language speakers of English with no schooling in their first language take between **seven and ten years** or more to reach the language proficiency of native English speaking peers. Some never reach native levels of language proficiency. Where students have had two or three years of first language schooling in their home country before emigrating to the United States, they take between five and seven years to reach native speaker performance. Collier (1995) found this pattern among different home language groups, different ethnic groups and different socio-economic groups of students.

The most significant variable in becoming proficient in the second language (English in the US) is the amount of formal schooling students have received in their **first language** (Collier, 1995). Those students who are schooled solely in their second language, particularly from the 4th grade onwards, when the academic and cognitive demands of the curriculum increase rapidly, tend to progress relatively slowly and show less academic achievement. Thus one essential feature for students to develop academic language proficiency is that there is strong development through the first language of academic-cognitive thinking skills. Thinking abilities, literacy development, concept formation, subject knowledge and learning strategies developed in the first language transfer to the second language. As students expand their vocabulary and literacy skills in their first language, they can increasingly demonstrate the knowledge that they have gained in the second language.

Teachers and Bilingual Support Assistants

In many mainstream schools where there are bilingual students, there is a frequent shortfall of teachers who are either trained to work with such children, or who come form the same language communities, or both of these. This is an world-wide experience. In the US following the No Child Left Behind Act of 2001, it is estimated that between 2 and 3.5 million new teachers are required for bilingual and ESL education (Menken & Barron, 2002).

One solution to a lack of suitable teachers has been to hire **bilingual support**

assistants who work, especially in the early grades, under the guidance of the mainstream teacher and typically can speak the home language of some or most of the bilingual students. In the UK, such support workers help the very young, newly arrived and slower learners, often working with small groups (Bourne, 2001b, 2001c). They may translate, interpret, create classroom materials (e.g. dual language texts), sometimes also assisting the mainstream teacher in assessment. The assistant may also be the link between teacher and home, enabling parents to collaborate in their children's education.

At its best, this creates a bilingual resource that enables the student to learn in their home and stronger language while they are acquiring English. This discussion will be extended in terms of 'scaffolding' (see the next section). In the UK experience, one danger is that the bilingual assistant uses English rather than the home language because English is the dominant and prestige language of a mainstream school. As Bourne (2001b, 2001c) warns, another danger is that the mother tongue is used by the bilingual assistant for discipline and control, sending the wrong message about language use and functions. The **asymmetry of power** between a qualified monolingual teacher and a lower paid bilingual assistant may also send the wrong language status message to students.

Scaffolding Language

Many bilingual children are required to attend mainstream schools and operate as quickly as possible in a **second language** (e.g. ESL students in the United States). They are expected to learn a new language, engage in subject learning, and develop thinking skills at the same time. Content instruction will be in that new language and will increasingly become more complex, abstract and require a different register from informal conversation. Within a short period, such students are expected to have developed a second language so that they can operate in the subject curriculum and show success (e.g. on tests, grade transfer).

Taking the US as an example, it is unlikely that such students will learn English solely through content instruction. Their level of understanding of English is often too rudimentary to comprehend mathematics or social studies. Irrespective of whether a 'transmission of knowledge' (pouring nuggets of knowledge into empty heads) approach or a progressive 'discovery learning' approach is taken by the teacher, the language level of the child may be insufficient to assimilate content and engage in the process of learning.

Hence, such students need **language support** if they are to succeed in the classroom. Rather than instruction being teacher-directed or student-centered, teacher–student cooperation appears important for these students. In such a social collaboration, the key issue is how that teacher supports the student by a careful pitching of comprehensible language. This is termed **'scaffolding'** (Gibbons, 2002) and originates from the Russian psychologist, **Vygotsky** (1962). He argued that student learning occurs when the present level of understanding of a child is understood and is moved to a further level that is within the child's capability.

The Transition of Refugee and Immigrant Children into a New Classroom

Elizabeth Coelho (1998) provides advice regarding the transition of immigrant and refugee children into the classroom. A few of her wealth of ideas are listed below:

- Create welcome signs in the children's languages.
- Use an interpreter where possible, to facilitate transition. Interview parents with the interpreter present, to provide basic information and begin a relationship with parents in a friendly and facilitative manner.
- Provide children with a welcome booklet of basic school information, in their own language. Include the day-to-day life, special events, role of parents.
- Encourage the home use of the first language and explain to the parents that first language development will help the child in acquisition of the majority language.
- Appoint friendly and sensitive children as official student ambassadors or student friends, to nurture newcomers and help them adjust.
- Introduce newcomers positively, showing the country of origin with the aid of a world map, ensuring that all children learn to pronounce and spell new names. Make it clear the new child speaks a different language at home and is learning the majority language, avoiding the negative 'So-and-so doesn't speak English.' Display photographs of all the children to show they all belong equally to the classroom. Provide a resource corner for newcomers and ensure they understand via translation or paralinguistic language the daily activities and announcements. Communicate positive attitudes about the linguistic and cultural diversity of the classroom.
- A second (host) language program for adult learners, that encourages immigrant parents to attend, helps both parents and children. Such a program in the school can also provide information about the area and about survival and success in the new culture and employment system.
- Announce events in the different school languages, to spread information and raise the status of heritage languages.
- Select classroom and library materials with a multicultural and multiracial approach, as well as books in heritage languages.

During the decade 1924–1934, Vygotsky outlined the ways that teachers can intervene and arrange effective learning by challenging and extending the child's current level of understanding. This is achieved by the teacher moving from the present level of understanding of a child to a further level that is within the child's capability. This 'stretching' of the child is by locating the **zone of proximal development**. Vygotsky (1962) saw this zone of proximal development as the distance between a student's level of current understanding as revealed when problem

Villarreal (1999), August (2002), Breen (2002) and Smyth (2003) suggest that when bilingual children are not in 'strong' forms of bilingual education (e.g. they are mainstreamed), the following school attributes are important:

- Teachers build on the prior knowledge and experience of children that has often built through the minority and not just concentrate on developing the majority language.
- Peer support systems are used in the classroom so that language shepherding and support is possible through friends.
- Language minority students are well integrated into the mainstream operation including with majority language native speakers.
- Student linguistic and cultural diversity is valued and celebrated.
- High expectations are communicated to language minority students.
- The curriculum is carefully paced so that children comprehend, but is ever challenging and enriching, not compensatory or remedial.
- Linguistic competence and conceptual understanding are not confused. For example, a student's proficiency in second language English is not a measure of the quality of their thinking.
- Language and content is comprehensible to the student.
- Transition from a language minority home and community to a majority language mainstream school is sensitive, sympathetic and successful.
- Literacy and oral language development is integrated.
- Higher order thinking skills are developed (e.g. in a literacy program).
- Assessment needs to be fair and valid especially when not conducted in a child's stronger language, and avoid using monolinguals for unfavorable comparisons.
- Teachers relate instruction to meaningful student experiences, including experiences from their language minority homes and networks.
- Local language minority communities and parents are seen as partners and included in delivering successful outcomes.
- Teachers are carefully selected, trained and consistently developed to teach language minority students.
- Schools are advocates of children's rights and work with families to secure needed welfare and social services.

solving without adult help, and the level of potential development as determined by a student problem solving in collaboration with peers or teachers. The zone of proximal development is where new understandings are possible through collaborative interaction and inquiry.

Rather than simplifying a task, the teacher provides the 'scaffolding' so that the student is working within their 'zone of proximal development'. **Scaffolding** is thus a temporary device to enable understanding of content. When learning is successful, that support is removed as the child can then complete the same task independently.

Gibbons (2002) and Smyth (2003) provide a wealth of illustrations for the scaffolding of listening, speaking, reading and writing. An example of scaffolding in learning to write will illustrate this idea. Scaffolding occurs when a teacher ensures: (1) that a student has enough prior experience or prior knowledge to make a task understandable and personally relevant. This may be achieved by reading, listening to the teacher, in a group of peers, gathering information from parents and others. (2) The student is made familiar with the purpose, structure and linguistic features of the kind of text that they will write. Help is given with the particular form and function of some text they will produce. (3) The teacher and the student write the text together, with advice on the process, content and form. (4) Students should then be able to write their own text with the scaffold being removed, often gradually. They have moved from the familiar to being stretched, from **guidance to independence**.

Such scaffolding can be provided by strategies other than teacher mediated support (Santamaría *et al.*, 2002). Task scaffolds may give directions (e.g. on cue cards) as to steps through a task. Materials scaffolds are advanced organizers or prompts for students (e.g. story maps) regarding content.

LANGUAGE TEACHING AND LEARNING IN IMMERSION CLASSROOMS

This section considers the approach to language learning often taken in immersion education programs. What are the main classroom features of successful immersion programs in Canada, Finland, Australia, the Basque Country, Catalonia and Wales and elsewhere?

Main Classroom Features of Immersion Classrooms

First, the minimum time the second language needs to be used as a medium to ensure customary achievement levels is four to six years. Around the end of elementary schooling, immersion students show equal or higher performance in the curriculum compared with their mainstream peers. **Second**, the curriculum tends to be the same for immersion children as for their mainstream peers. Thus immersion children can easily be compared with mainstream children for levels of achievement. Immersion students compared with mainstream students are neither more advantaged nor more disadvantaged by studying a common curriculum.

While immersion attempts to cultivate empathy for a student's **second language culture**, the immersion curriculum has hitherto tended not to have major distinctive components, which differ from mainstream education, to develop such empathy and participation. For example in Canada, a known challenge is that French becomes the language of school, and English the language of the playground, street and vocational success. The anglophone North American cultural influence is often so strong and persuasive that French immersion children are in danger of becoming passive rather than active bilinguals outside the school gates. The same occurs in immersion schools in many other countries, where the minority language is a language of the classroom, but the majority language is the peer 'prestige' language in the school yard and on the streets. Engineering formal language use inside an immersion classroom is possible; outside the classroom walls is very difficult to influence.

Third, it has often been thought preferable to **separate languages in instruction** rather than to mix them arbitrarily during a single lesson. Thus immersion typically uses one language for one set of subjects; the other language for a separate set. Sustained periods of monolingual instruction will require students to attend to the language of instruction, thereby both improving their language competence and confidence, and acquiring subject matter simultaneously.

One residual problem is the language in which particular subjects are taught. For example, if mathematics and science, technology and computing are taught in the English language, will the hidden message be that English is of more value for scientific communication, for industrial and scientific vocations? Will English latently receive a special, reserved status? If the minority or second language is used for humanities, social studies, sport and art, is the hidden message that minority languages are only of value in such human and aesthetic pursuits? The choice of language medium for particular subjects may relegate or promote both the functions and the status of minority languages.

This raises the **fourth** issue. How much **time** should be devoted to the two languages within the curriculum? The typical recommendation is that a minimum of 50% of instruction should be in the second language. Thus, in French immersion in Canada, French medium teaching and learning may occur from 50% to 100% of the school week. As the graphs in chapter 11 reveal, the amount of instruction in the English language may increase as children become older. One factor in such a decision can be the amount of exposure to English a child receives outside school. Where a child's environment, home and street, media and community are English medium, for example, such saturation may imply that a smaller proportion of time needs to be spent on English in the school.

At the same time, the public will usually require bilingual schools to show that children's majority language competences, particularly literacy, are not affected by bilingual education. Bilingual schools need to ensure that, through school instruction and school learning experiences, majority language proficiency and literacy is monitored and promoted (Rebuffot, 1993). Such majority language instruction may range from a minimum of 10% for seven-year-olds and older, to 70% or more for those in secondary level schooling.

Fifth, immersion education has historically enjoyed the synergy of teacher enthusiasm and parental commitment. Immersion **parents** have tended to be middle class, involved in teacher–parent committees, and take a sustained interest in their children's progress (see Holobow *et al.* (1991) for evidence that foreign language immersion in the US is also successful with working-class children). For example, immersion education in Canada has, from its beginnings in Montreal in 1965 to the present, been powerfully promoted by parents (Baker & Jones, 1998). The first immersion classroom in 1965 owed much to parent initiation. Since then, the Canadian Parents for French organization has been a powerful pressure group for the recognition and dissemination, evolution and dispersion of immersion education. Such parents are frequently English-only speakers wanting bilingualism for their children. Parents have also been powerful advocates at the grassroots level for other 'strong' forms of bilingual education (e.g. through localized pressure groups).

Teachers in immersion classrooms tend to have native or native-like proficiency in both the languages of the school. Such teachers are fully able to understand children speaking in their home language but speak to the children almost entirely in the immersion language. Teachers are thus important language models through their status and power role, identifying the immersion language with something of value and importance. Immersion teachers also provide the child with a model of pronunciation and style in the immersion language.

Immersion teachers are typically enthusiastic about bilingualism in society, acting as bicultural and multicultural crusaders. Teacher commitment in immersion education is a crucial element to success. This commitment exists beyond teachers' interest in the education of children. In the equation of a successful bilingual school, such enthusiasm and commitment for language by headteachers and principals, teachers and auxiliary workers may be an important and often underestimated factor in success.

Sixth, the immersion approach implies a relatively **homogeneous language classroom**. For example, in early total immersion, all children are beginners without second language proficiency. This makes the task of the teacher less complex than in bilingual classes where there is a mixture of first and second language speakers. Initially, there will be no disparity of status due to some children being more proficient than others in the second language.

In Finland and Canada, children are typically linguistically homogeneous at the start of schooling in not speaking the immersion language of the school. However, in other countries using the immersion approach, there is sometimes a **mixture** of those who are fluent and those who are less fluent in the classroom language. For example, in an Irish immersion school, the classroom may be composed both of children whose home language is Irish and those whose home language is English but whose parents are keen for their children to be taught through the medium of Irish. The Irish and Welsh experiences tend to suggest that most children whose home language is English will cope successfully in minority language immersion classrooms. For such children, the language context is additive rather than subtractive. The danger is that the majority language of English, being the common denominator, will be the language used between students in the classroom, in the playground and certainly out of school. We lack research on the optimal classroom composition of majority and minority language students for successful bilingual education. A balance towards a greater proportion of minority language speakers may help to ensure that the 'common denominator' majority language does not always dominate in informal classroom and playground talk.

Seventh, immersion provides an **additive bilingual environment**. Students acquire a second language at no cost to their home language and culture. Such enrichment may be contrasted to subtractive bilingual environments where the home language is replaced by the second language. For example, where the home language is Spanish and the submersion approach is to replace Spanish by English, negative rather than positive effects may occur in school performance and self-esteem. This underlines that the term immersion education is best reserved for additive rather than subtractive environments. The term 'immersion education' is appropriate only when the home language is a majority language and the school is adding a second minority or majority language.

Eighth, most immersion teachers have to 'wear two hats': promoting achievement throughout the curriculum and ensuring second language proficiency. Such a dual task requires **immersion teacher training** (Bernhardt & Schrier, 1992; Björklund, 1997; Met & Lorenz, 1997). This has tended to be a weakness in some countries using the immersion approach or a version of it. Both at the pre-service and professional development levels of education of teachers, the special needs of immersion teachers should be addressed. Methods in immersion classroom require induction into skills and techniques beyond those required in ordinary mainstream classrooms. Immersion teaching (and teacher training) methods are still evolving.

In Finland, general teacher-training includes an introduction to the societal and individual features of bilingualism and bilingual education and centers such as the University of Vaasa have evolved a continuing education program for immersion teachers (Björklund, 1997). In the US, the expertise is often found among teacher-training consultants rather than in colleges, with mentoring programs and videotapes also aiding professional development (Met & Lorenz, 1997).

Language Strategies in Immersion Classrooms

Immersion education is based on the idea that a first language is acquired relatively subconsciously. Children are unaware that they are learning a language in the home. Immersion attempts to replicate this process in the early years of schooling. The focus is on the content and not the form of the language. It is the task at hand that is central, not conscious language learning. In the early stages, there are no formal language learning classes, although simple elements of grammar such as verb endings may be taught informally.

In the latter years of elementary schooling, formal consideration may be given to the rules of the language (e.g. grammar and syntax). The early stages of immersion tend to mirror the **subconscious acquisition** of learning of the first language. Later will a child be made conscious of language as a system, to reinforce and promote communication. If there is an absence of emphasis on syntax and analysis of the immersion language, then the danger is that this second language reaches 'a plateau ('fossilization') with recurrent problems in gender, syntax and morphology, rather than continuing to develop' (Johnstone, 2002, p. 5). Thus immersion tends to focus on the form of language and not just on meanings in later grades.

Immersion also tends to assume that the earlier a language is taught the better. While teenagers and adults may learn a second language fluently and proficiently (see chapter 5), research evidence tends to suggest that, for example, young children acquire authentic pronunciation better than adults (De Houwer, 1995). The argument for immersion schooling tends to be 'the earlier the better'.

In the first stages in Early Immersion classrooms, a teacher typically concentrates on listening and speaking skills. Students are not made to speak the immersion language with their teacher or with their peers in the initial stages. Children will initially speak their first language to each other and to their teacher (sometimes called 'the **silent period**'), without any objection or reprimand. Immersion teachers do not force children to use the immersion language until they are naturally willing to do so. Early insistence on the immersion language may inhibit children and develop negative attitudes to that language and to education in general. Over the first two years, immersion children gradually develop an understanding of the immersion language and begin to speak that language, particularly to the teacher.

In Canada, the most frequent grade in which English becomes part of the formal curriculum in Early Total French Immersion is Grade 3. Other practices include introducing English at an earlier grade or kindergarten and at Grade 4 (Canadian Education Association, 1992). While initially students will **lag** behind mainstream 'English' students in English language achievement, by Grade 5 or 6 Early Immersion students catch up and perform as well (Rebuffot, 1993).

In these early stages of Early Immersion, it is crucial that the teacher is **comprehensible** to the children. The teacher needs to be sympathetically aware of the level of a child's vocabulary and grammar, to deliver in the immersion language at a level the child can understand, and simultaneously be constantly pushing forward a child's competence in that language. The teacher will aim to push back the frontiers of a child's immersion language by ensuring that messages are both comprehensible and are slightly ahead of the learner's current level of language competence.

The language used to communicate with the child at these early stages is sometimes called **caretaker speech**. For the first year or two in immersion education, the vocabulary will be deliberately limited with a simplified presentation of grammar and syntax. The teacher may be repetitive in the words used and the ideas presented, with the same idea presented in two or more different ways. The teacher will deliberately speak slowly, giving the child more time to process the language input and understand the meaning. This tends to parallel the talk of mother to child (**motherese**) and **foreigner talk** (a person deliberately simplifying and slowing down so a foreigner can understand). During this caretaker stage, the teacher may be constantly questioning the child to ensure that understanding has occurred.

A teacher may also advise on the language to be used before a lesson topic is presented. When new words and new concepts are being introduced into a lesson, the teacher may spend some time in introducing the words and clarifying the concepts so that the language learner is prepared. Such teachers may also be sensitive to **non-verbal feedback** from students: questioning looks, losing concentration and glazed attention. Students will be encouraged to question the teacher for clarification and simplification when a misunderstanding has occurred.

Such teaching strategies thus cover two different areas: the importance of **comprehensible input** and the importance of **negotiating meaning**. The worst case is when neither the teacher nor the student is aware that misunderstanding (or no understanding) has taken place. A more effective classroom is when students and teachers are negotiating meaning, ensuring that mutual understanding has occurred. Not only is the negotiation of meaning important in language development and in maximizing achievement throughout the curriculum, it is also important in aiding motivation of children within the classroom. Patronizing such children and oversimplifying are two of the dangers in this process. Therefore, constantly presenting students with ever challenging and advancing learning situations is important in fostering classroom achievement.

Immersion classrooms need to have a particular view about **language errors**. Language errors are a usual and frequent part of the language learning process. Errors are not a symptom of failure. Errors are not permanent. They are a natural part of learning. With time and practice, they disappear. Therefore, immersion teachers are often discouraged from over-correcting children's attempts to speak the immersion language. Just as parents are more likely to correct children's factual errors than their language errors, the immersion teacher will tend to avoid constant correction of errors. Constant error correction may be self-defeating, even penalizing second language acquisition. Language accuracy tends to develop over time and with experience. Constant correction of error disrupts communication and content learning in the classroom (Met & Lorenz, 1997). When a child or several children constantly make the same errors, then appropriate but positive intervention may be of value.

In the early stages of immersion, there will be a natural **interlanguage** among children. A child may change the correct order in a sentence yet produce a perfectly comprehensible message. For example, faulty syntax may occur due to the influence of the first language on the second language. A child may put the pronoun or a preposition in the wrong order: as in 'go you and get it'. Interlanguage is not to be seen as 'error'. Rather it indicates the linguistic creativity of students who are using their latent understanding of the first language to construct meaningful communication in the second language. Interlanguage is thus an intermediate, approximate and temporary system. It is a worthwhile attempt to communicate and therefore needs acceptance rather than condemnation. Seen as a halfway stage in-between monolingualism and being proficient in a second language, interlanguage becomes a stage in the journey and not a permanent rest point.

However, Kowal and Swain (1997) indicate that a danger of immersion is that students reach native-like levels in reading and listening but not in writing and speaking. Once students are able to communicate their meaning to teachers and peers, there can be a lack of incentive for achieving native-like accuracy. Therefore, at later stages, intervention in error correction and more focus on form and not just content may be valuable. Encouraging students to be more analytical of the accuracy of their speech may be important if native-like performance is targeted.

Proficiency in the first language will contribute to proficiency in the second language. Concepts already attached to words in the first language will easily be

M. A. Snow (1990) provides a list of 10 specific techniques that tend to be used by experienced and effective immersion teachers. This is a valuable summary of the discussion in this section.

(1) Providing plenty of contextual support for the language being used (e.g. by body language – plenty of gestures, facial expressions and acting).
(2) Deliberately giving more classroom directions and organizational advice to immersion students. For example, signaling the start and the end of different routines, more explicit directions with homework and assignments.
(3) Understanding where a child is at, thereby connecting the unfamiliar with the familiar, the known with the unknown. New material is linked directly and explicitly with the child's present knowledge and understanding.
(4) Extensive use of visual material. Using concrete objects to illustrate lessons, using pictures and audio-visual aids, giving the child plenty of hands-on manipulative activities to ensure all senses are used in the educational experience.
(5) Obtaining constant feedback as to the level of a student's understanding. Diagnosing the level of a student's language.
(6) Using plenty of repetition, summaries, restatement to ensure that students understand the directions of the teacher.
(7) The teacher being a role model for language emulation by the student.
(8) Indirect error correction rather than constantly faulting students. Teachers ensure that the corrections are built in to their language to make a quick and immediate impact.
(9) Using plenty of variety in both general learning tasks and in language learning tasks.
(10) Using frequent and varied methods to check the child's level of understanding.

transferred into the second language. The acquisition of literacy skills in the first language tends to facilitate the acquisition of literacy skills in the second language. However, not all aspects of a language will transfer. Rules of syntax and spelling may not lend themselves to transfer. The closer a language structure is to the second language structure, the greater the transfer there is likely to be between the two languages. For example, the transfer between English and Spanish is likely to be more than Arabic to English due to differences in syntax, symbols and direction of writing. However, the system of meanings, the conceptual map, and skills that a person owns may be readily transferable between languages.

The focus of immersion classrooms is typically on **real, authentic communication**, tasks, curriculum content and creative processes (e.g. Bernhardt, 1992; Dicks, 1992; K. Hall, 1993). Willingness to communicate is particularly aided when there are authentic uses for the language (MacIntyre *et al.*, 2001). However, as Harley

(1991) has indicated, there is also a place for an analytical approach to the second and the first language in the classroom. An immersion classroom will not just enable children to acquire the second language in a subconscious, almost incidental manner. Towards the end of elementary education, the experiential approach may be joined by a meaning-based focus on the form of language. A child may at this point be encouraged to analyze their vocabulary and grammar. At this later stage, some lessons may have progress in the second language as their sole aim. After early sheltering with language, the development of vocabulary and grammar may be dealt with in a direct and systematic manner.

THIRD LANGUAGE ACQUISITION IN SCHOOL

With respect to **learning a third language**, there is a current belief that bilinguals are relatively better at learning a new language in school than monolinguals. This belief is usually expressed as (1) bilinguals being more linguistically attuned to language learning and (2) that there is positive transfer from already having learnt a second language to learning another (e.g. in learning strategies, vocabulary, sensitivity to grammatical differences). The studies that exist mostly, but not universally, tend to support this belief (see Cenoz, 2003 for a review, and chapter 5).

Cenoz and Valencia (1994) conducted a relatively sophisticated study in the Basque country of 320 17- to 19-year-old students. They found that the English language achievement of bilingual students (Spanish and Basque) was higher than monolingual Spanish speakers. This result was found when other influential factors (intelligence, motivation, age and length of exposure to English) were taken into account. Bilingualism, in and by itself, appears to give an **advantage in learning a third language**.

One explanation for this is the greater metalinguistic awareness of bilinguals and their possible greater sensitivity to communication (see chapter 7). Another explanation may be in the transfer between languages of phonological (sound system) and pragmatic (communication) abilities (Verhoeven, 1994). This is predicted in Cummins' (1986) interdependence hypothesis that suggests such a transfer between languages. Confidence in learning a new language may be another explanation. A bilingual may find learning a new language less daunting than a monolingual, and sometimes more attractive. Related to this is that third language learners are relatively expert language learners when compared to relatively novice second language learners (e.g. expertise in strategies of language learning).

A current conclusion is that 'Studies on the effect of bilingualism on third language acquisition tend to confirm the advantages of bilinguals over monolinguals in language learning' (Cenoz, 2003, p. 82). This particularly occurs in additive language contexts and when there are literacy skills in both languages. 'This effect can be explained as related to learning strategies, metalinguistic awareness and communicative ability but it can also be linked to the fact that bilinguals have a wider linguistic repertoire that can be used as a basis in third language acquisition' (Cenoz, 2003, p. 83).

KEY TOPICS IN EFFECTIVE BILINGUAL SCHOOLS

There are elements that make all types and models of bilingual education more or less effective. While dual language policies, provision and practices are a keystone of such schools, effectiveness reaches far beyond language. For a bilingual school to become a beacon of success, the following themes may need addressing, albeit not in separation but as an entity and as part of a process of continuous enhancement and school development:

Intake of Students and Language Balance: The ingredients of bilingual schooling commence with the students. Their life history (e.g. as immigrants or refugees), identity, community background (e.g. isolation or saturation in their community of their home language), proficiency in languages on entry to the school, cultural knowledge, language aptitude, motivation and self-esteem all affect the process of classroom interaction and learning outcomes. A key issue has been the **balance of majority and minority language students** in a school so that the majority language does not increasingly dominate (Lindholm-Leary, 2000, 2005). This is an issue both in dual language schools and in heritage language schools (Hickey, 2001a; W.G. Lewis, 2004). Where the balance is weighted too much to majority language speakers, informal classroom language may turn to the majority language. What is officially about minority language development can become unofficial immersion in the majority language.

Particularly in rural language minority areas, bilingual classrooms may have a **mixture** of majority language speakers who are learning through the minority language (e.g. Irish) and native speakers of that minority language. This can mean two different language agendas: minority language children speedily acquiring the majority language; majority language children being applauded for acquiring the minority language.

In Ireland, Hickey (2001a) found that in pre-school **mixed language classes**, Irish first language speakers may not be achieving sufficient enrichment in their language development as the emphasis is on second language learners of Irish. Teachers tended to tailor their language to accommodate second language learners, asking fewer questions, giving less feedback and more repetition for understanding by L2 children. Even at the pre-school level, children appear aware of the different status, power and intergroup relationship between the two languages (Hickey, 2001a). Their language preference can thus be affected by the saturation of majority language speakers in a mixed language classroom (Hickey & O. Cainín, 2001).

Wong Fillmore (1982) found that in US classrooms where there were large numbers of second language learners, effective organization tended to occur by teacher-direction rather than having an open, informal classroom. In contrast, where the classes comprised second language learners *and* native speaking children, open classroom organization rather than teacher direction seemed to constitute an optimal learning environment. This may be explained as follows:

(1) In classes where there were large numbers of second language learners, the teacher was most effective by herself controlling the input. In such classes

where there was more open organization, students tended to talk to each other in their **first** language, thus not obtaining practice in the second language.

(2)   In classes of mixed second language learners and native speaking children, the optimal environment was a more open organization where second language learners received input from the teacher and from native speaking children. In such mixed classes, where the teacher tended to control the input, this tended to be at the level of **native** speakers and did not necessarily provide comprehensible input for second language learners.

The language of **teachers** is likely to be affected by the balance of native speakers and learners in such mixed language classrooms. Ramírez & Merino (1990) found that teachers ask fewer questions in mixed language groups compared with more homogeneous language groups. Teachers may also use more simplified language to accommodate the second language learners. Native speakers may thus not be receiving the native language enrichment they need. What is a language opportunity is also a language challenge for the teacher.

While native speakers of a minority language provide a language role model for second language speakers in speaking that minority language, the danger is that second language speakers overly influence minority language speakers (W.G. Lewis, 2004). Hickey (2001a) aptly entitles this 'mixing beginners and native speakers in minority language immersion: who is immersing whom?' Researching in Ireland, she found that in such mixed home language classrooms, children from minority language homes tended to switch to English. Such children had less language effect on majority language speakers than those English-only speakers had on Irish speakers. Even at pre-school level, the **majority language was pervasive** and was eroding the minority language. Majority language students immerse native speakers in the majority language.

This suggests that the numerical balance of native speakers and learners of a minority language is important, possibly tilted to a predominance of minority language speakers. Also, supporting and enriching the first language competences of **native speakers** of a minority language is crucial in such schools. This implies the possible separation of children of different language abilities for 'language lesson' sessions while avoiding language group separation and discrimination (W.G. Lewis, 2004). Baker and Jones (1998) and Hickey (2001a) recommend that the small-group composition of students needs care and consideration by teachers. Such teachers need training to become aware of cross-language influence, and of the need to raise the status and increase the use of the minority language in the classroom by well-designed activities and reward systems. It is important that language minority students are empowered by having positions of responsibility in the class and school, and are actively involved in school activities (e.g. sports teams, societies).

Muller and Baetens Beardsmore (2004) provide illustrations of teacher accommodation from the European School experience of mixed language students in European Hours sessions (see chapter 11). Discrimination, exclusion, ghettoization and separation of languages are avoided by rewarding the plurality of (majority) languages and language use. Codeswitching is used strategically by the teacher, and accepted, so as to integrate languages and their native speakers. Bilingualism is celebrated.

Staffing: Without staff, no bilingual school can commence, continue or achieve. With untrained or poor quality staff, the best bilingual model program will fail. Teacher training and developing teacher effectiveness is a foundation to the sustainability of any bilingual program. Thus a foundational ingredient into a bilingual school is the characteristics and language proficiency of the teachers and other support staff, their own biculturalism or multiculturalism, attitudes to minority languages and minority students, and their professional and personal identity (Morgan, 2004; Varghese, 2004; Varghese, Morgan *et al.*, 2005; Howard *et al.*, 2005, http://www.cal.org/twi/guidingprinciples.htm).

It is paramount that such teachers are positive towards students' language and cultural backgrounds, sensitive to their home and community contexts, respond to children's language and cultural needs, celebrate diversity and recognize the talents of such children. Teachers in bilingual classrooms may sometimes find barriers to success in: large and overcrowded classes of under-nourished students, inadequate teacher training, a lack of teaching resources, poor pay and promotion prospects, the stigma of working with lowly regarded bilinguals, and limited funding (Benson, 2004; Yeh *et al.*, 2002).

As Benson (2004) reminds us in the context of developing countries, bilingual teaching is often more **challenging** than monolingual teaching, frequently occurring in contexts with inequality between urban and rural areas, elite and subordinate power and status divisions, between language/ethnic groups, and between gender. Teachers are expected to address such inequalities, provide cultural and linguistic capital, meet high stakes test standards of student achievement in literacy and numeracy, bridge the home and school gap, become respected members of the community, and campaign for educational reform and innovation. The roles include: 'pedagogue, linguist, innovator, intercultural communicator, community member, and even advocate of bilingual programmes' (Benson, 2004, p. 207–8).

Teaching in such bilingual contexts therefore requires much professionalism, **commitment** and support. School staff need to be committed to the empowerment of language minority students through education. Such commitment is not just realized in the classroom but also in staff involvement in extra-curricular activities, participation in community events, interest in developing their pedagogic skills, and even cooperation in the political process of improving the lot of language minority students.

Shared Vision, Mission and Goals among Staff: A consensus in the goals of the school is needed among staff, with consistency across staff in the treatment of language minority students, and effective collaboration across staff. Value and status should be given to the language minority students' language and culture. Native language skills need to be celebrated and encouraged inside and outside the formal curriculum and flagged as an advantage rather than a liability. While clear and agreed aims, goals and mission are important, an effective bilingual school has a system for constant improvement and development, and is always seeking to increase its effectiveness – a continuous upward spiral of enhancement (Lindholm-Leary, 2005).

Staff Professional Development and Training: Staff professional development can be designed to help all staff effectively serve language minority students. For example, staff development programs can sensitize teachers to students' language and cultural backgrounds, increase their knowledge of second language acquisition and help develop effective curriculum approaches in teaching language minority students. All teachers can be trained to recognize themselves as teachers of language irrespective of their subject area. The mentoring of new teachers by more expert and experienced teachers can be valuable (see Howard *et al.*, 2005, http://www.cal.org/twi/guidingprinciples.htm).

Such initial and in-service **staff development** may include an individual person, community and wider societal awareness program, models and curriculum approaches to bilingual education, cultural diversity, and the politics that surround local and regional implementation of education for bilinguals (Schwartz, 2001). Wong Fillmore and Snow (2000) indicate particular teacher competencies that bilingual teachers need, based on their multiple roles as classroom communicators, educators, evaluators, citizens and socializers. They suggest that such teachers need to know the basics of language form (e.g. phonemes, morphemes, regularity, lexicon, structure, dialects, academic English, spelling) and not just language functions and uses.

Leadership: The leadership of the school is a crucial factor, and ideally the appointee has an excellent knowledge of curriculum approaches to language minority children and communicating this to the staff (Shaw, 2003). Strong leadership, the willingness to hire bilingual teachers and high expectations of bilingual students tend to be part of the repertoire of effective leaders. Effectiveness research tends to suggest that such leaders should demonstrate a strength of purpose and proactive management while engaging the professionalism of teachers and empowering all staff in decision-making processes. Not only do they inspire, motivate, support and communicate well with staff, they also identify, secure and mobilize human, financial and material resources (Montecel & Cortez, 2002). Open to change and innovation, they are not only politically informed but also developing themselves as educationalists and leaders.

Excellent leaders also project their leadership beyond the school into the neighborhood, and liaise with homes and families. Such leaders are likely to be well known, highly respected and easily accessible in their communities. They are likely to work in partnership with community leaders.

Curriculum: A subject curriculum needs to provide intellectually challenging, active and meaningful lessons that have coherence, balance, breadth, relevance, progression and continuity. This entails a focus on basic skills but crucially also on developing higher-order thinking skills. Effective curriculum planning also tends to include: language and literacy development across the curriculum, smooth language transitions between grades, systematic, equitable and authentic assessment integrated with learning goals, a bilingual and bi/multicultural hidden curriculum and ethos throughout the school, a safe and orderly school environment, and a supportive, constructive classroom atmosphere.

Supportive Ethos and Environment: The student may experience prejudice and discrimination, the subordinate status of their language minority group and assimilation influences. Such external influences may effect internal psychological workings such as self-esteem, anxiety, integration with peers and achievement in school. A socioculturally supportive environment for language minority students is therefore important. Also vital is a safe and orderly school and classroom environment where students feel they belong, are cared for as well as educated, and that values cultural, ethnic and racial diversity (Montecel & Cortez, 2002).

High Expectations: High expectations among teachers and peers are important for all students, but no more so than for 'at risk' minority students. When bilingual students come from materially impoverished homes, with low aspirations present in the family and community, then low expectations may too easily and implicitly be embedded in a schools' ethos. Instead, a positive 'can do' atmosphere for the 'have nots' will attempt to reverse a self-perpetuating pattern of low expectation and consequent failure.

High expectations need to be **clearly communicated** to such students, with the school responsive to a student's individual needs and to varying community profiles (e.g. culture, newcomers). High expectations are conveyed, for example, by providing opportunities for student-directed activities, involving students in decisions and building their competences, trust and self-esteem, with positive and regular feedback based on careful monitoring.

Apart from strategies to motivate students and recognize their achievement, the provision of **individualized support** for language minority students is often needed. The provision of counseling, cooperation with parents and the hiring of language minority staff in leadership positions to act as role models are some of the ploys used to raise expectations of success at school.

Parents: plenty of parental involvement, with home–school collaboration that is reciprocal is typically a major dimension of school effectiveness. Parents of language minority children can be encouraged to become involved in their children's education, including in governance. This includes participation in parents' meetings, contact with teachers and counselors, telephone contact and neighborhood meetings. Parents and their children can be perceived as stakeholders, customers and partners whose satisfaction levels are valued and with whom there is regular two-way communication (see chapter 14).

CONCLUSION

In schools and classrooms, there are myriads of decisions to make daily, hourly, second by second. Bilingual classrooms and schools add a language dimension to such decision-making. The allocation of languages and support for growing languages mixes with decisions about grouping, curriculum materials, styles of learning and use of support assistants and parents. The relationship between language, culture and literacies interacts with overall curriculum decisions about intake, ethos and expectations.

In such complexity, teacher training and continuous professional development of the staff is crucial. Without teachers there can be no bilingual school or classroom provision. With effective leadership and well-trained staff, the effectiveness of any bilingual school is greatly enhanced.

KEY POINTS IN THE CHAPTER

- Heritage language classrooms integrate minority language maintenance, majority language development, biliteracy and cultural awareness.
- Minority language bilinguals in mainstream classrooms often take seven or more years to reach the language proficiency in the majority language.
- Mainstream classrooms sometimes use Bilingual Support Assistants to help the teacher with minority language students in a transition phase.
- Language scaffolding is often needed to support minority language students in the early stages of using the majority language in a mainstream classroom.
- 'Translanguaging' involves varying the language of input and output in a lesson.
- Bilingual school effectiveness includes attention to: intake of students, staffing and staff professional development, vision, aims and goals, leadership, a challenging curriculum, supportive ethos, high expectations and home–school collaboration.
- Immersion methodology attempts to ensure high levels of academic proficient language development in both languages, empathy for two or more cultures, and thus an additive experience.
- Language separation is preferred to the concurrent uses of language.
- Teacher enthusiasm and parental commitment are important ingredients in effective immersion approaches.
- Policies for when to introduce formal attention to the home language, comprehensible communication in the immersion language, plentiful feedback, attitude to language errors and interlanguage are needed in effective immersion classrooms.

SUGGESTED FURTHER READING

CLOUD, N., GENESEE, F. & HAMAYAN, E.V., 2000, *Dual Language Instruction: A Handbook for Enriched Education.* Boston: Heinle and Heinle.
GIBBONS, P., 2002, *Scaffolding Language, Scaffolding Learning: Teaching Second Language Learners in the Mainstream Classroom.* Portsmouth, NH: Heinemann.
HOWARD, E.R., SUGARMAN, J., CHRISTIAN, D., LINDHOLM-LEARY, K. & ROGERS, D., 2005, *Guiding Principles for Dual Language Education.* Washington, DC: Center for Applied Lingusitics. http://www.cal.org/twi/guidingprinciples.htm

JOHNSON, R.K. & SWAIN, M., 1997, *Immersion Education: International Perspectives*. Cambridge: Cambridge University Press.

LINDHOLM-LEARY, K., 2005, *Review of Research and Best Practices on Effective Features of Dual Language Education Programs*. http://www.lindholm-leary.com/resources/review_research.pdf

MARTIN-JONES, M., 2000, Bilingual classroom interaction: A review of recent research. *Language Teaching*, 33, 1, 1–9.

SCHECTER. S.R. & CUMMINS, J. (eds), 2003, *Multilingual Education in Practice: Using Diversity as a Resource*. Portsmouth, NH: Heinemann.

SMYTH, G., 2003, *Helping Bilingual Pupils to Access the Curriculum*. London: David Fulton.

VILLARREAL, A., 1999, Rethinking the education of English language learners: Transitional bilingual education programs. *Bilingual Research Journal*, 23, 1, 11–45. (http://brj.asu.edu/v231/articles/ar4.html)

WILLIAMS, C., 2000, Welsh-medium and bilingual teaching in the further education sector. *International Journal of Bilingual Education and Bilingualism*, 3, 2, 129–148.

STUDY ACTIVITIES

(1) List those effectiveness factors which you think are part of any form of education, and list separately those which you think are solely concerned with the language part of bilingual education. Discuss in a group what are the priorities in producing bilingual children through formal education.

(2) Make a list of 'classroom effectiveness factors' from your reading. Following observation in one or more classrooms, consider the effectiveness of these classrooms against this list. What factors seem, as the result of your classroom observation, to be more and less important?

(3) Using the same list of 'effectiveness factors', study one program in your area (e.g. transitional bilingual education). What features of that program are effective and which are less than effective due to the aims and nature of that program?

(4) Visit a classroom, and by diagrams, sketches or photographs, portray the bilingual displays of the classroom. Capture in picture form the wall displays, project work, activity corners, and other forms of display that attempt to provide a bilingual classroom.

CHAPTER 14

Literacy, Biliteracy and Multiliteracies for Bilinguals

CHAPTER 14

Literacy, Biliteracy and Multiliteracies for Bilinguals

INTRODUCTION

Different bilingual classrooms and schools, different languages and cultures, tend to have different views about the purposes of reading and writing for bilingual children. Politicians and parents often vary in their **viewpoints**; educationalists passionately debate methods and strategies. Some think that, for immigrant bilinguals and multilinguals, literacy should be about enculturation and assimilation into a new language and culture. For indigenous minority language bilinguals, literacy may be aimed at reading and writing fluently in two or more languages. In some 'prestigious bilingual' contexts, biliteracy is about promoting a wider rationality, critical thinking, balanced and detached awareness, empathy and sensitivity to varied cultures. Some scholars define basic skills in learning to read (e.g. phonemic awareness, phonics, fluency, vocabulary and comprehension; see the (US) National Reading Panel, 2000). Other academics from the New Literacy Studies camp (e.g. Street, 2000, 2003) talk about multilingual literacies and multiliteracies among bilingual and multilingual children.

Thus the nature of being a bilingual (e.g. immigrant, indigenous, elite) interacts with the type of literacy that is offered and experienced. It is not just the school that delivers this. For some language minority **parents**, literacy is about memorization, transmission of life stories revealing their heritage, values and morality. In some religions, literacy concerns the transmission of rules of religious and moral behavior. A Moslem for example, will be expected to read aloud from the *Qur'an* but will not necessarily be expected to understand what they read, this being provided in their mother tongue. In some cultures, the mother is expected to read to her children and help them develop literacy skills, but she is not expected to read national newspapers or complete bureaucratic forms herself. Older siblings may also be expected to help develop the skills of reading and writing in younger siblings. So while school is important in developing literacy, a bilingual also develops literacies in the family, community and religion, for example.

Where language minority members are labeled as immigrants, under-achievers or as a potentially dissident minority, literacy can be variously regarded as a key to economic self-advancement, personal empowerment or as social control. Such literacy may be encouraged at school only in the **majority language** and not in two or more languages (e.g. English language literacy in the US; English in parts of Africa as an 'official' or international language). In the US, access to English literacy is certainly essential for higher education, employment and voca-tional mobility. 'The pinnacle of young children's educational development is the acquisition of literacy. Literacy is the ticket of entry into our society, it is the currency by which social and economic positions are waged, and it is the central purpose of schooling' (Bialystok, 2001a, p. 152). Thus, all US students need English language literacy. However, many have tended to exit with 'survival' levels of English literacy that channels them into low paid jobs (Valdés, 2001). Only a relatively small percentage of US students exit with well developed literacy in more than one language.

In contrast, where language minorities have access to 'strong' forms of bilingual education, literacy may be introduced in the home/minority language. Whether language minority children should first become literate in the majority language or in their minority language will be discussed later. Before engaging in such discus-sions, it is important to explore the kind of literacy that language minority students may be given. We start by considering **contrasting viewpoints on literacy**. This provides an instant flavor of the debate about the nature and value of different kinds of literacy for bilingual and particularly language minority students (Wiley, 2005c; Street, 1995, 2002).

DIFFERING VIEWPOINTS ON LITERACY FOR MINORITY LANGUAGE STUDENTS

The Skills Approach

The US No Child Left Behind Act of 2001 mandated that literacy in English from kindergarten to the 3rd grade should contain explicit instruction in phonemic awareness, phonics, vocabulary development, reading fluency (including oral reading skills) and reading comprehension strategies (Section 1208 (3) of Title 1). This is a **skills approach** to literacy. It assumes that literacy is the ability to decode symbols on a page into sounds, followed by making meaning from those sounds. Reading is about saying the words on the page. Writing is about being able to spell correctly, and write in correct grammatical sentences. This approach is also found in the National Curriculum and the National Literacy Strategy in the UK (Street, 2002).

The US research backing for this approach derives from the National Reading Panel (2000) with their evidence-based assessment of the scientific research litera-ture on reading and its implications for reading instruction (see also Center for the

Improvement of Early Reading Achievement, 2003). The key to literacy in any language is regarded as developing skills in phonemic awareness, phonics, fluency, vocabulary and text comprehension. For many teachers, these skills are an essential foundation for learning to read and write, and do not preclude other approaches that are considered below. Closing the achievement gap for language minority students may require such foundations, but may also need approaches to literacy that are much more than just skill acquisition.

For example, the **assessment** of success in such a skills approach is measured by standardized tests of reading and writing. Such tests tend to assess decomposed and decontextualized language skills, eliciting skills comprehension rather than deeper language thinking and understanding. These tests tend to be used as templates for instruction. Measurement-led instruction promotes 'teaching to the test' and possibly decreases the importance of developing higher order language and thinking skills.

A skills approach cannot be simply dismissed. Research suggests that the direct instruction of phonological skills is an important ingredient of early literacy programs (National Reading Panel, 2000). US federal and state policy has moved towards an increasingly phonics-based program. However, other in the US argue that, for English language learners, an over-emphasis on literacy skills in the early grades will fail to **incorporate students' language and cultural backgrounds**. This will limit their ability to construct meaning.

While there is unlikely to be a simple formula or universal 'best bet' to acquiring reading and writing skills (Snow *et al.*, 1998), a review by Genesee *et al.* (2005) of literacy approaches for ELLs (English language learners) in the US suggests that **explicit instruction** of reading and writing skills and **interactive instruction** (e.g. interaction with teachers and competent readers and writers) are both effective approaches, as is a combination of the two. In contrast, solely using process approaches that emphasize authentic uses and de-emphasize skills, is less effective. It appears insufficient just to expose students to literacy-rich environments for reading and writing skills to evolve. However, there are differences in defining 'effectiveness' as the remainder of this chapter demonstrates.

Such a skills approach to literacy has implications for the conception **language minority children**. It can connect with, for example, the assimilation of immigrants and subservience of language minorities. Underneath the skills approach to literacy can be a belief that children only need functional or 'useful' literacy. Effective functioning implies that the student or adult will contribute in a collaborative, constructive and non-critical manner to the smooth running of the local and national community. Such **functional literacy** implies accepting the status quo, understanding and maintaining one's place in society, and being a faithful, contented citizen. Functional literacy implies operating at a low level: for example being able to read labels on food packaging and road signs, and finding a number in a telephone directory.

The Construction of Meaning Approach

In contrast to the skills approach, there is a 'constructivist' view of literacy that is particularly relevant to classrooms where there are bilinguals and multilinguals. It emphasizes that readers bring their own meanings to text, and therefore that reading and writing is essentially a construction and reconstruction of meaning. This implies that the meaning individuals give to a text depends on their language(s), culture, personal experiences and histories, personal understandings of the themes and tone of text, and the particular social context where reading occurs.

Within Vygotskian theory, students are viewed as active constructors of meaning from text. Learning is mediated by the social interaction between the child and an experienced teacher or parent, for example, or peer modeling and coaching, scaffolding, and instruction that is directed toward the child's 'zone of proximal development'.

Teachers using a meaning construction approach will typically attempt to help language learners (e.g. ELLs in the US) bridge any cultural mismatch through explicitly teaching them the culture, understandings and values of the dominant culture, as well as by providing with vocabulary and strategies needed to construct meaning.

For language minority students, initial understandings will partly or mainly derive from their minority language culture. Different students of varying backgrounds will make **different interpretations** of the text. When there is a mismatch between the reader's knowledge and that which is assumed by the school, the construction of meaning will be affected. Language minority children, in particular, can be trapped in this situation. Trying to make sense out of texts from a different culture, with different cultural assumptions, makes predicting the storyline and understanding the text more difficult. One role for teachers therefore is to **mediate** in the construction of meaning, helping students to construct meaning from text.

The Sociocultural Literacy Approach

A related view about the needs of language minority students is found in the ideas of **sociocultural** literacy. Wells and Chang-Wells (1992) suggest that 'To be literate is to have the disposition to engage appropriately with texts of different types in order to empower action, thinking, and feeling in the context of purposeful social activity' (p. 147). This definition allows for the possibility that different language minority communities attach a different value to **different types of literacies or multi-literacies**. The social nature of literacy encourages many authors to use the term 'literacies' and 'multiliteracies' (Martin-Jones & Jones, 2000). The use of the plural 'literacies' suggests that reading and writing is not autonomous or independent.

> Literacies are social practices: ways of reading and writing and using written texts that are bound up in social processes which locate individual action within social and cultural processes. . . . Focusing on the plurality of literacies means recognizing the diversity of reading and writing practices and the different recognizing the diversity of reading and writing practices and the different genres, styles and types of texts associated with various activities, domains or social identities. (Martin-Jones & Jones, 2000, pp. 4–5)

Street (2000) provides an examination of terms in this area.

Sociocultural literacy approaches use the idea of '**discourses**' that do not just include reading and writing but also different ways of talking, listening, interacting, believing, valuing, and feeling, and which cannot be explicitly taught. Many language minority children enter school with discourses that differ from the dominant school discourse, leading to difficulties in students achieving well.

Sociocultural literacy is the ability to construct appropriate cultural meaning when reading (Díaz & Flores, 2001). In theory, a person can be functionally literate but culturally illiterate (e.g. reading without meaning). In reading and writing, we bring not only previous experience, but also our values and beliefs enabling us to create meaning from what we read and insert understanding into what we write. A **cultural heritage** is discovered and internalized in reading. For example, a language minority literacy program may be enthusiastic to ensure the child is fully socialized and enlightened in the heritage culture.

For some people, such cultural literacy may lead to **assimilation** of language minority immigrants (e.g. accepting the values and norms embedded in English language classics). Assimilationists may argue for a common literacy, transmitting the majority language culture to ensure assimilation of language minority groups within the wider society. In contrast, a cultural pluralist viewpoint will argue that national unity is not sacrificed by cultural literacy in the minority language or by multicultural literacy. Multicultural literacy is likely to give a wider view of the world, more windows on the world, a more colorful and diverse view of human history and custom, and a less narrow view of science and society.

Where there is much variety of language cultures within a region, issues about 'local literacies' arise. Street (1994, 2002) regards **local literacies** as literacy practices identified with local and regional cultures (as different from national culture). Such local literacies may be forgotten by international and national literacy campaigns (Hornberger, 1994) or there may be tensions between local and national/international literacy practice. Local literacies (see Street, 1994, 2002) avoid the impoverishment of uniformity in literacy that is created by the dominance of English, for example. They make literacy relevant to people's lives, their local culture and community relationships.

The Critical Literacy Approach

Literacy can work to maintain the status quo, to ensure that those with power and dominance in society influence, even control what language minorities read and think. Propaganda, political pamphlets and newspapers and books can all be used to attempt to control the thinking and minds of the masses. Literacy can be conceived as an attempt through schooling and other formal and informal means of education to produce **hegemony** in society. Thus, those in power maintain control over those who could be subversive to social order, or democratically challenge their power base. Literacy can be used to instill certain centrally preferred attitudes, beliefs and thoughts. Similarly, some religious traditions have deliberately used literacy to ensure that their members were, at the least, influenced by writings, at the worst, brainwashed. Careful selection by religious leaders and parents over what their children read is an attempt to use literacy to control and contain the mind.

Those with power and dominance in society also maintain their position by their view of what is '**correct language**'. Language minorities with little political and economic power are often taught that their patterns of speech and writing are inferior and deficient, and such language varieties are connected with their economic social and cultural deprivation. Such groups are expected to adopt standard majority language use (e.g. to speak 'proper' or 'correct' or 'standard' English).

A philosophical basis of critical literacy is that all cultures are attempts to discover meanings and understandings. No one culture (including the umbrella idea of Western culture) has the monopoly of understanding, knowledge or wisdom. The **Postmodernist** view is that there is little or no transcendent truth, no ultimate reality or wisdom outside of culture, no unalterable or fundamental qualities of women, ethnic groups or language minorities. All meaning is socially constructed. In Postmodernism, all meanings are unstable, and none are neutral, but change through continuous negotiation and reconstruction. There is value in the meanings of those in a subordinate position (e.g. language minorities) just as there is in language majorities. The voices of the poor are as meaningful as the privileged; the understandings of the oppressed becomes as valid as the oppressor.

Literacy can be a tool of oppression; it can also be a **liberator** for language minorities (Hornberger, 1994). It can be bar to opportunity; or a means of opening a door to empowerment. One way of attempting to **empower** people is through **critical literacy**. Freire (1970, 1973, 1985) and Freire and Macedo (1987) argued for a literacy that makes oppressed communities socially and politically conscious about their subservient role and lowly status in society. The argument is that literacy must go well beyond the skills of reading and writing. It must make people aware of their sociocultural context and their political environment. This may occur through mother tongue literacy and local/national/international **multiliteracies**.

For language minority speakers, literacy for empowerment can be about stimulating language activism, the demand for language rights, self-determination and an equitable share of power. Freire's literacy education in Brazil's peasant communities (and with other oppressed groups around the world) assumes that when people become conscious about their subordinate role and inferior position in their community and society, they then become empowered to change their own lives, situations and communities.

What alternative is posed by the critical literacy movement? At school level, the critical literacy approach is that language minority students should not just be invited to retell a story. They should be encouraged to offer their **own interpretation and evaluation of text**. Who is the writer? What is their perspective and bias? What kind of moral interpretation is made? What alternative interpretations and viewpoints are possible? Children will be encouraged not just to seek answers to such questions, but to look critically and take on multiple viewpoints. Multicultural and multilingual children may be given diverse pieces of writing that reflect different cultural knowledge and attitudes. Differences in interpretation, and differences in experience and knowledge children bring to the text can be contrasted and compared (Goldstein, 2002). Diversity of understanding can be celebrated.

Alma Flor Ada (1988a, 1988b) presents a critical literacy approach for US bilingual students based on Paulo Freire's work. She distinguishes four phases in the creative reading act.

The Descriptive Phase
In the descriptive phase, teachers will ask questions about text such as: What happened in a story? Who did what and why? This kind of phase exists in many classrooms, but in critical literacy, it must be extended beyond this stage. If reading stays at this phase, it tends to be passive, receptive and domesticating.

The Personal Interpretive Phase
Children will be asked if they have ever seen or experienced something like that portrayed in the story. What did you feel when you read the story? Did you like it? What kinds of emotion did you have? Does your family and community have similar experiences or stories? Ada points out that this process of personalization of stories may raise children's self-esteem. They are made to feel that their experiences and feelings are valued by the teacher and other students. It also enables children to learn that 'true learning occurs only when the information received is analyzed in the light of one's own experiences and emotions' (Ada, 1988a, p. 104).

The Critical Analysis Phase
The text is used to bring out broader social issues and generalizations. Students are asked: Is the text valid? What kind of experience or person is promoted by the story? Are there other ways in which the story could have been constructed? How and why would people of different cultures, social classes and gender have acted differently in the story? Students are invited to analyze, reflect and expand on the experiences of the story. Social implications are engaged and analyzed.

Creative Action Phase
Students are then challenged as to how their learning can be used to improve their lives or resolve issues and problems they face. Here the critical approach is transformed into constructive action. For example, students may decide to write letters to political figures, to those in their locality who have power, status and authority, or create a poster to try to persuade friends and neighbors. Students may compile a class newsletter or booklet that is given to other students in their school, or other schools, to sensitize people to the issues. They may write and circulate a petition in their neighborhood, write a play, or create poetry that tries to both analyze, and inform others, leading ultimately to empowerment and raised consciousness among language minorities. Goldstein (2002) provides many further ideas, including in the inclusive context of the education of special education needs students.

To conclude this section, the following table lists some of the practical contrasting characteristics of the transmission and critical classrooms.

Functional Literacy/Transmission Classrooms
(1)   Literacy is getting the correct answers on worksheets, filling in blanks, circling appropriate answers.
(2)   Literacy is answering closed questions having read a story.
(3)   Literacy is reading words, sometimes without understanding their meaning.
(4)   Literacy is reading aloud to the teacher and the rest of the class, being perfect in pronunciation, intonation and accent.
(5)   Literacy is spelling words correctly, and writing in correct grammar.
(6)   Literacy is mechanically going through exercises, practicing skills, and giving correct answers on tests.
(7)   Literacy is learning to do but not necessarily to think.

Critical Literacy Classrooms
(1)   Literacy is seeing oneself as an active reader and writer.
(2)   Literacy involves enjoying reading, developing independent thoughts and judgments about reading and writing.
(3)   Literacy is sharing ideas, reflections, experiences and reactions with others in the classroom, both peers and teachers.
(4)   Literacy is gaining insights into oneself, one's life in the family and the community, into social and political control, the use of print and other mass media to inform, persuade and influence so as to maintain the status quo.
(5)   Literacy is about understanding the power relationships that lie behind reading and writing.
(6)   Literacy is about constructing and reconstructing meaning, critically examining the range of meanings in the story and outside the story.
(7)   Literacy is active writing for various purposes and audiences, often to influence and assert.
(8)   Literacy is about developing consciousness, increased self-reflection, increased reflection about status, power, wealth and privilege in society.
(9)   Literacy is about developing critical thinking habits, creative imagination, and posing alternatives, some of which may be radical.
(10) Literacy is about learning and interpreting the world, explaining, analyzing, arguing about and acting upon the world in which a person lives.

BILITERACY

Introduction

This section examines biliteracy and strategies that promote biliteracy in the home and classroom. The notion of biliteracy adopted in this chapter is that of 'any or all instances in which communication occurs in two (or more) languages in or around writing' (Hornberger, 2003, p. xii).

Literacy in two or more languages is **advantageous** at the individual and societal levels. For individuals, biliteracy reinforces and develops both oral languages in terms of, for example, vocabulary, automatic decoding, fluency and positive attitudes (Hickey, 2001b). There are also reasons why biliteracy is societally important, especially in language revitalization. In chapters 3 and 4, we briefly discussed the importance of minority language literacy in the survival, reversal and enhancement of that language. At both the individual and the group level, minority language literacy gives that language increased functions, usage and status. It also helps standardize a minority language. A minority language has a greater chance of survival when bureaucracy and books, newspapers and magazines, adverts and signposts are in that language. This may help to avoid the colonial situation where the majority language is used for all literacy purposes and the vernacular language is used for oral communication. Where oral communication is in the minority language and literacy is in the majority language, that minority language will have lower prestige and may have less chance of survival.

More positively, literacy in the minority language enables the attendant traditions and the culture to be accessed and reproduced. Reading literature in the minority language may be both for education and recreation, for instruction and for enjoyment. Whether minority language literature is regarded as aiding moral or religious teaching, of value as an art form, or as a form of vicarious experience, literacy is both an emancipator and an educator. As the UK Bullock Report (1975) stated:

> Literature brings the child into an encounter with language in its most complex and varied forms. Through these complexities are presented the thoughts, experiences, and feelings of people who exist outside and beyond the reader's awareness . . . It provides imaginative insights into what another person is feeling; it allows the contemplation of possible human experiences which the reader himself has not met. (p. 125)

This quotation illustrates that literacy in the minority language is of **value** because it recreates the past in the present. It may both reinforce and extend the oral transmission of a minority culture. Minority language oracy without literacy can disempower the student. Literacy in the minority language not only provides a greater chance of survival at an individual and group level for that language. It also may encourage rootedness, self-esteem, the vision and world-view of one's heritage culture, self-identity and intellectual empathy.

Literacy enables access to language minority practices that help make sense of the world and hence affect the structure of human cognition (Wells, 1986). Biliteracy gives access to different and varied social and cultural worlds. Does this in turn lead to more diversified cognitive abilities, an increased ability to process and manipulate ideas and symbols? The research by Swain and Lapkin (1991a) points to first language literacy and then biliteracy as a strong source of cognitive and curriculum **advantage** for bilinguals.

However, **mother tongue literacy**, while often culturally advantageous, is sometimes not without practical problems nor protests. Some languages lack a grammar or an alphabet, have few educational materials for teaching purposes, plus a shortage of appropriate teachers and teacher training. Political objections include native language literacy being an impediment to national unity and immigrant assimilation, and the cost of maintaining a variety of indigenous and 'immigrant' languages in a region.

The Development of Biliteracy

Given that literacy empowers, emancipates, enculturates, educates and can be an inherently enjoyable activity, there seems to be a strong argument for biliteracy. Pragmatically, most students from a minority language need to **function in the minority and majority language society**. This requires biliteracy rather than literacy only in the minority language.

In different minority language situations, the same question is often asked by parents and teachers. Is it better to be thoroughly literate in one language rather than attempt to be literate (or semi-literate) in two languages? Does literacy in one language interfere with becoming literate in a second language? Questions typically tend to be phrased in this negative way. The positive questions must also be asked. Does literacy in one language aid rather than impede literacy in a second language? Do the skills learnt in reading and writing one language transfer to reading and writing in a second language?

From key **reviews** (Hornberger, 1989; Krashen, 1996, 2002; P. McKay *et al.*, 1997; V. Edwards, 1998), the evidence tends to support the positive rather than the negative positions.

Bialystok (1997, 2001a, 2001c) has shown that children who learn to read in two languages early on have an initial **advantage** over their monolingual peers. Her experiment is to show 4 to 5 year old monolingual and bilingual children two pictures: a picture of a dog and a separate picture of a tree. She then shows children a card with the word 'tree' written on it. She firstly places that word 'tree' under the picture of the tree. This is seen to be correct. Then, when the children are distracted, she moves the word 'tree' to underneath the picture of the dog. When the children are asked what the card said with the word on it, only a third of the monolingual children got it correct. Two thirds of such monolingual children said that the word 'tree' referred to the picture of the dog. The bilingual children got it correct.

Bialystok (1997, 2001a, 2001c) suggests that children who are familiar with print and story books in two languages (e.g. French and English, or English and Chinese), more quickly develop an understanding that words are symbols that correspond to specific meanings. When bilingual children are shown a picture accompanied by a word, they understand early on that the word contains the meaning as well as the picture.

> Across all the studies, the bilingual children outperformed the monolingual children by a large margin, often revealing more than a year advantage in understanding this principle. On average, the monolinguals were correct about 40% of the time and the bilinguals, about 80%. . . . Just being exposed to two writing systems, or two kinds of storybooks, enabled bilingual children to appreciate that the written forms are the symbolic system from which the story emerges. (Bialystok, 2001c, p. 22)

Research has also suggested that academic and linguistic skills in a minority language **transfer** relatively easily to the second language. Simply stated, a child who learns to read in Spanish at home or in school, does not have to start from the beginning when learning to read in English.

When biliteracy is encouraged in minority language children, literacy skills and strategies from the first language appear to **transfer** to the second language (if using a similar writing system). While the vocabulary, grammar and orthography may be different, generalizable skills in decoding and reading strategies may easily transfer from first language literacy to second language literacy. Concepts and strategies easily transfer from first to second language literacy (e.g. scanning, skimming, contextual guessing of words, skipping unknown words, tolerating ambiguity, reading for meaning, making inferences, monitoring, recognizing the structure of text, using previous learning, using background knowledge about the text). So does self-confidence as being literate (Calero-Breckheimer & Goetz, 1993; Jiménez *et al.*, 1995). This is the idea found in the Common Underlying Proficiency or Dual Iceberg idea of Cummins and his Interdependence principle (see chapter 8).

A view that reading ability in a second language is purely a function of proficiency in that second language is not generally supported by research (Calero-Breckheimer & Goetz, 1993). While the sounds of letters and decoding of words have a **separation** in learning to read in each language, the higher cognitive abilities and strategies required in making meaning from text are common to both languages. Overall, reading competence in two languages does not operate separately.

When two languages have **different writing systems** (e.g. English, Chinese), 'general strategies, habits and attitudes, knowledge of text structure, rhetorical devices, sensorimotor skills, visual-perceptual training, cognitive functions, and many reading readiness skills transfer from L1 to L2 reading' (Ovando *et al.*, 2003, p. 175). However, Bialystok (2001c) notes that progress in biliteracy is more affected by the close or distant relationship of the two languages (orally, graphemically and orthographically, e.g. comparing English–French, English–Hebrew and English–Chinese) than by bilingualism.

> For concepts of print, exposure to two writing systems that looked different but were both alphabetic was the most beneficial background; for phonological awareness, exposure to two spoken languages that were different from each other but drew on a common set of sounds led to highest levels of awareness; and for fluent reading, two alphabetic writing systems encouraged the transfer of known strategies. (Bialystok, 2001c, p. 30)

Transfer from first language to second language literacy is not unconditional and is likely to be contingent on the context of learning and the characteristics of the learner. The following factors may play an intervening role: (1) differences in the facilitating nature of the school, home and community environment (P. McKay *et al.*, 1997); (2) individual differences in language ability, language aptitude and language learning strategies; (3) individual differences in the analysis of their language (metalinguistic abilities); and (4) the inter-relationship between pairs of languages (e.g. Portuguese and Spanish compared with English and Chinese) – see McKay *et al.* (1997) and Bialystok (2001c). (5) Reading ability in a second language is also partly dependent on the degree of proficiency in that second language (Lee & Schallert, 1997). Children literate in their first language still need to acquire the differences found in the second language (e.g. different sounds, vocabulary, grammatical structures), and these may need explicit instruction.

In contrast, Kenner (2004a) proposes that some bilingual children experience their biliteracies **simultaneously** and not as the separate entities that a 'transfer' idea may suggest. Her 6 year olds in London were learning to write in Chinese, Arabic or Spanish as well as English and sought connections between different writing systems. In drawing on experiences from different social and linguistic worlds, these children combined, integrated creatively and synthesized imaginatively. Such children may learn to understand diverse perspectives of people from different cultures and languages, including beyond their own, in a **synchronized** manner.

This 'transfer' rather than 'separation' viewpoint has implications for the teaching of reading among language minority students. A '**separation**' view is that reading in the second language (e.g. English for language minority students in the US) depends on the level of proficiency in the second language and not on first language reading ability. Therefore, students should be swiftly moved to education through the second language; maximal exposure to literacy is needed in the second (majority) language. Time spent reading in the minority language is time lost in learning to read in the majority language. In contrast, a '**transfer**' view argues for initial mastery of literacy in the minority language so that the cognitive skills and strategies needed for reading can be fully developed. Once well developed, these literacy skills and strategies transfer easily and readily to the second language. It is this latter view that receives research support (Krashen, 2002).

One implication for teachers of the 'transfer' viewpoint is that repetition is to be avoided. For example, there is little point introducing the concept of metaphors in English lessons and then repeating exactly the same subject matter in Spanish lessons. Coordination, integration and synchronization are needed to ensure learning is cumulative and not repetitive.

Additive and Subtractive Contexts

An important intermediate factor is the **context** in which such language and literacy acquisition occurs. Strategies and advice for developing biliteracy are not universal, but context bound. In Canadian immersion programs, for example, the context is additive. That is, the child's home language of English is not being replaced but is being added to by the acquisition of French. Evaluations of such immersion programs (see chapter 12) show that literacy in French is acquired at no cost to literacy in English. In this additive, majority language context, a child may acquire literacy through the second language at no cost to literacy in the first language. In contrast, in a **subtractive environment** (e.g. 'weak' forms of bilingual education), the transfer of literacy skills between the two languages may be impeded. In such subtractive situations, literacy may more efficiently be acquired through the home, heritage, minority language. Literacy can be built up via the higher level of language skills in the home language rather than through the weaker majority language of English. When literacy is attempted through the second, majority language in the US, the child's oracy skills in English may be insufficiently developed for such literacy acquisition to occur.

For teachers, this leaves the question of **when** to encourage biliteracy, given that there is some degree of literacy in one language. One model will be the **simultaneous** acquisition of biliteracy as well as bilingualism. This tends to be the approach in the 50:50 Dual Language model (see chapter 11) where both minority and majority language children remain integrated all day (Howard & Christian, 2002; Howard *et al.*, 2004).

Other children will learn to read in their second language **before** they learn to read in their first (majority) language. An example is immersion education in Canada, where children learn to read in French before learning to read in English. This approach tends to result in successful biliteracy but note that it takes place in an additive language context. The first language, a majority language, is not threatened, and literacy in both languages will follow.

The third approach is where children acquire literacy in their first language, a minority language, and then **later** develop literacy skills in the majority language. In the 90:10 Dual Language Model (see chapter 11) and Heritage language education all children typically receive literacy instruction in the minority language first. The research of Howard *et al.* (2004) in US Dual Language schools suggests that by the end of 5th grade, dual language students had reached expected levels of mastery in Spanish and English reading and writing, demonstrating 'impressive levels of performance on oral language, reading and writing measures in English and Spanish (p. 32). Their conclusion is that 'students can continue to develop language and literacy skills in their first language while simultaneously developing language and literacy skills in a second language' (p. 33).

However, in a **subtractive** context, minority (first) language literacy may quickly become neglected. In Transitional Bilingual Education, for example, majority language literacy is promoted at the cost of minority language literacy.

In the United States, Krashen (2002, p. 143) neatly sums up the argument for language minority children **developing literacy in their first language early** in order to facilitate strong literacy development in English:

> There is very good reason to believe that learning to read in the primary language is a shortcut to reading in the second language. The argument in

favor of this consists of three stages:
1. we learn to read by reading, by understanding what is on the page;
2. it is easier to understand text in a language you already know;
3. once you can read, you can read; reading ability transfers across languages.

Simple answers about when to promote literacy in the second language are made difficult by other factors such as the educational and societal **context**, but also the age and ability of the child. Contrast the six-year-old just beginning to acquire pre-reading and pre-writing skills in the first language with an 18-year-old student, fluent in a first language. In the first case, biliteracy may be delayed. In the latter case, oracy and literacy in the second language may be mutually reinforcing. Contexts will vary. When a language minority child is constantly bombarded with majority language written material, from adverts to comics, computers to supermarkets, basic biliteracy may occur relatively easily. The accent in school can be on minority language literacy, but not exclusively. The preference with younger children may be to ensure first language literacy is relatively well established before introducing literacy in a second language. Such second language literacy may develop in the middle years of elementary schooling (e.g. from seven years of age to 12 years of age depending on the level of literacy achieved in the first language).

The Continua of Biliteracy

The literacy that is developed in classrooms varies considerably, and escapes neat classification into transmission and critical literacy orientations. Such classification is best achieved by reference to Hornberger (2003, 2004) and Hornberger and Skilton-Sylvester (2003) who provide a comprehensive set of dimensions to understand and elaborate the nature of biliteracy at classroom practice and regional policy levels. The ecological Continua of Biliteracy has four nested and intersecting components (each of which has three sub-dimensions) labeled Contexts, Development, Content and Media. (1) The Contexts of Biliteracy has three sub-dimensions from micro to macro, oral to literate and bi(multi)lingual to monolingual. (2) The Development of Biliteracy also has three sub-dimensions: reception to production, oral to written, and first language to second language. (3) The Content of Biliteracy has sub-dimensions of: minority to majority language, vernacular to literary, and contextualized to decontextualized. (4) The Media of Biliteracy's sub-dimensions are: simultaneous to successive exposure, dissimilar to similar structures, and divergent to convergent scripts. This Continua provides a wide-ranging yet unifying conceptual framework for biliteracy in society and school.

MULTILITERACIES IN THE CLASSROOM

Introduction

From the New Literacy Studies movement derives the contemporary concepts of **multilingual literacies and multiliteracies** (Martin-Jones & Jones, 2000). Such terms refer to different languages, different varieties of a particular language, and different regional uses of a language. Since literacy is formed in varied social, cultural and religious contexts, there are diverse reading and writing practices with 'different genres, styles and types of texts associated with various activities, domains or social identities' (Martin-Jones & Jones, 2000, p. 5). For example, a person may speak Sylheti (a regional language of Bangladesh), read and write in Bengali (the standard language of Bangladesh) as well as English, be fluent in English but also use a local variety of east London English. Such a person may exhibit **multiple literacies** that have varied and different: specific uses, levels of expertise, degrees of prestige, which contain different symbols of social and linguistic identity, have different opportunities for use (e.g. according to the speaker's gender), which change over time with experience and opportunity, and are often not used separately but in combinations with innovative blending (syncretism). Such multilingual children do not remain in separate language and literacy worlds but acquire their multilingualism and multiliteracies simultaneously (Gregory *et al.*, 2004).

This is not just an academic point, but it has definite implications for literacy in the **classroom**. The concept of multiliteracies and multilingual literacies, for example, suggests that teachers have choices about what to develop and how. For example, should a classroom concentrate on literacy in 'standard English' or include local regional varieties of English? Is just majority language literacy developed or are multilingual literacies developed as well? What value does the teacher give to literacy practices outside the school, including in the early stages of reading and writing? Are such home and community multiliteracies incorporated in the school and classroom, for example by help from parents, grandparents and siblings (Ada, 1995, 1997; Ada & Smith 1998; Gregory *et al.*, 2004)? Bourne's (2001a) research suggests that teachers may not be aware of home literacies, with incorporation missing and much potential lost. She contrasts the mismatch in perceptions between children and teachers as a 'difference between the way these bilingual children perceive their languages and cultures as a normal part of daily life, and the ways in which the dominant culture perceives bilingualism as exotic and extraordinary' (p. 112).

This section initially focuses on the more practical aspects of multiliteracies in bilingual and multicultural classrooms. Teachers often adopt a varied and eclectic approach to literacies and multiculturalism with bilinguals. Hence different classroom strategies are examined. A strategic approach by a teacher includes decisions about the grouping of children, resources to aid literacy and multicultural development, and the key nature of community, home and school relationships.

School Resources

Where multilingual classes exist, then learning, motivation and self-esteem may be raised by celebrating multiliteracies. For example, Kenner (2004b) recommends **displays** in a classroom that celebrate the different scripts of children (e.g. photos of the children with text about their languages and literacies; text on community and religious schools attended to learn to read other languages). In whole class or school events, children reading in their **heritage language** may give them both recognition and pride, and also be educative for other children.

Culturally relevant books for children are valuable to engage and excite. Such books will be more understandable (and supportively predictable) as they connect with their personal histories, cultural backgrounds and communities. Motivation to read, to read independently and enjoyably, will be enhanced when the student meets text that has a friendly **cultural meaning**. This can be achieved by (a) characterizations that are similar to the student's family and language community, (b) themes and contexts that are comprehensible within their life experiences, and (c) language and discourse that are familiar to the student (Freeman *et al.*, 2003).

As computers (and mobile phones) increasingly become a part of children's lives, representing their varied language worlds and multiliteracies on screen and printer builds status and use for multilingualism. Such **electronic literacies** build international (e.g. with a 'heritage' country) and well as local networks of multilinguals. Such literacies then become more multimodal: scripts, pictures, moving images and sounds. Children (and parents) telling stories about their homes and family lives which values their home and community culture, can be stored and relayed to other children beyond the classroom via the internet (Skourtou, 2002).

As far as possible, the language resources of the classroom need to be multilingual partly to reflect the mother tongues of the children in the classroom, but also for the multilingual awareness of all children (V. Edwards, 1998). Sometimes it is difficult to find the quantity, quality and variety of reading materials in the mother tongues of children in bilingual classrooms. There are often problems importing books from other countries and problems in purchasing expensive books. Yet some schools do manage to collect excellent libraries of books in different languages (and multicultural books) via help from language communities, parents of children in the school and using minority language organizations who have contacts and a commitment to literacy development in children's mother tongues. Partnership with parents in literacy events is important, especially in multilingual classrooms, and is discussed later.

Resources include not just materials and literacy strategies but also people. Apart from parents (discussed later), teacher support staff may be able to help literacy development in another language. Similarly, peer teaching and peer support can be utilized (Kenner, 2004a) to introduce different scripts, listen to someone reading in a language the teacher does not understand, comparing the script that used predominantly in the classroom (e.g. directionality, accents), and sometimes providing a model to emulate.

Combinations of whole classwork, individual tasks, partner activity, small group discussion, word processing, and individual self-directed learning are common (Toohey, 2000). In contexts where bilingual students come from language minorities, August and Hakuta (1998) suggest that cooperative learning can effec-

Dual Language Books

Dual language books contain a story, folk tale, myth or information in two languages. Such languages may have a similar script (as in French and English, or Spanish and English) or different scripts (for example Chinese and English, Urdu and English, Bengali and English). Often the two languages are on the same page or on opposite sides of the page, sharing the same pictures.

Some dual language books are professionally produced and published. Also, teachers may work with children (and their parents) to produce these texts. Such books help children, both bilinguals and monolinguals, become aware that other languages have value and functions. 'The best dual-text books are often written from the perspective of the home culture and translated into English, rather than vice-versa, making them more culturally relevant than books written from an Anglo-centric perspective and translated into the community language' (Blackledge, 2000a, p. 86).

For children whose first language is not the majority language of the country, dual language books may serve as a bridge to literacy in English. Such children will read the story in Greek or Korean, Russian or Spanish first of all. Subsequently, they may read the other language (e.g. English version) and, having already understood the storyline, be able to make sense of English words.

Dual language books act as an important bridge between parents and children, and between the home and the school. Parents and other members of the extended family may be able to read to their children in their home language. Such books can enable small groups or pairs of students to work collaboratively on the book. If one child can read in Arabic and the other in English, they can work together, discuss the story and complete activities set by the teacher around that story.

Dual language books are not without controversy. Firstly, some teachers and parents argue that children only read one language in the book, and ignore the other. Having understood the story in one language, it may be tiresome and pointless reading the story in another language. Children may thus concentrate on just one half of the book. Secondly, teachers and children sometimes observe that the presence of the majority language such as English tends to remove the desire to read in the home, minority language. The different status of the two languages may mean that the child will only wish to read in the higher status language (V. Edwards, 1995b).

tively increase intergroup friendships and increase the achievement of such students, raising their motivation, self esteem, and empathy for others (see chapter 12). Datta (2000) places emphasis on multiliteracy strategies and activities that utilize the child's experience in both private and **interactive social activity**: for example discussing experiences of the home as well as the 'home country', of trips and television, religion and family rituals, anecdotes and achievements, imaginations and shared incidents. Teachers, older siblings, grandparents, aunts and uncles, and parents can help provide multilingual classroom displays (and video recordings of multiliteracies, for example in community or religious language classes) celebrating a diversity of script (e.g. Arabic, Chinese, Cyrillic, Greek, Urdu, Hebrew as well as English).

Such a multilingual approach also means avoiding narrow standardized tests that purely reflect a skills approach to a dominant language literacy. As Genesee and Hamayan (1994) argue, classroom based **assessment** needs to go much further than tests of inauthentic, decontextualized language skills (see chapter 2). Student portfolios, for example, are one important way that a teacher may gather information about the performance of their bilingual children in a classroom; they may give a much fuller understanding of the strengths and weaknesses of, and therefore the diagnostic attention needed to improve and develop, a child's literacies (see chapters 2 and 15).

COMMUNITY RELATIONSHIPS

The social and cultural context of literacy importantly includes the relationship between an **ethnic community** and literacy acquisition (see Martin-Jones & Jones (2000) for case studies). What constitutes 'reading' differs between cultures, sub-cultures and ethnic groups. As Gregory (1993, 1994, 1996) demonstrates in studies of UK Asian and Chinese families, the purposes of reading, the resources provided by the home, and the process of parents helping their children to read may differ from the purposes, resources and processes for literacy in the school. The school may teach reading for recreation and enjoyment; a language minority group wants literacy for utilitarian purposes (e.g. avoiding unemployment and poverty, for trading and business transactions). The school literacy policy may aim for a child-centered, individualized approach, with the teacher as facilitator, partner and guide, allowing a wide choice of colorful attractive books. An ethnic group may, in contrast, provide literacy classes in Saturday schools, at the mosque or temple, sometimes with large numbers being tutored in the same class.

In such out-of-school classes, the teacher may act as an authority and director. Learning the will of Allah, for example, may be the valued outcome. A treasured *Bible*, the *Qur'an* or other holy or highly valued book may be the focus of reading. At its best, the biliterate child comes to appreciate and understand different cultures, differing traditions and viewpoints, leading to greater cultural sensitivity and inter-group tolerance.

Gregory (1993, 1994, 1996) further compares the style of literacy teaching in the community and the school. In the schools she researched, the child was socialized gently into the 'literary club' via 'playing' with books in a relaxed atmosphere with little correction of mistakes. In ethnic Saturday schools, for example, children learn by rote, repeating letters, syllables and phrases until perfect. There is continuous practice, testing and correction of mistakes in a fairly strict and disciplined regime. Children may be given books only after they have proved their reading skills are worthy of such esteemed treasures.

> To have immediate access to books devalues both the book and the principle of hard work. Children must work their way towards knowledge slowly and the book is a reward for a child's conscious achievements. A love of books, therefore, comes after reading is learned and not as a necessary prerequisite for it. (Gregory, 1993, p. 57)

The **difference between school and ethnic group** literacy expectations and practices may be challenging for the child. The child is exposed to two literacy worlds, two versions of appropriate literacy behavior. The school, in particular, has a responsibility to defuse tension, create a fusion and a harmony between the differences, such that both approaches are respected, prized and celebrated. If this is achieved, the bilingual student becomes not just biliterate but more deeply bicultural, with an expanded vision of literacy practices. Too often, schools take little or no account of the community literacies that children bring to school. This will be discussed in the next section.

Alternatively, schools disparage such ethnic group literacies and infer that parents and their children are illiterate if they do not function in English, and exclude parents as literacy partners (Blackledge, 2000a; Gregory & Williams, 2000). When children come from economically poor, minority language culture homes, there is a tendency to assume they derive from less effective language and literacy environments than those from middle-class majority language backgrounds (Blackledge, 2000a, 2000b).

Literacy is not a separate cultural event, but mirrors in its form and function general **socialization** practices. For particular cultural and ethnic groups, this may make the transition from home to school a relatively more challenging and strange experience. Edwards and Nwenmely (2000) discuss the disadvantage of fundamentalist religious children in mainstream schools where discussion and questions are expected rather than giving 'correct' formulaic answers. Yet it is the school that has the responsibility to effect harmonization, transition or preferably celebration of different literacy practices.

HOME AND SCHOOL RELATIONSHIPS

Many multilingual children often move seamlessly between different literacies. For example, Arabic may be used for reading the Qur'an, Urdu for family talk, and English for classroom activities. This is portrayed by Kenner (2004a) in young biliterates in Chinese and English, Arabic and English, and Spanish and English. The families in her research saw biliteracy as creating deep links with the extended family and a local networks, the child's heritage and cultural identity, and broadening the curriculum of the school.

Parents and siblings are typically important in a student's multiliteracy development. They often provided a literacy 'eco-system' where there is mutual support (e.g. the children help with the parents' English writing), adaptability, and linguistic survival and spread. Different languages may mean differing roles (Kenner, 2004a). For example, **older siblings** may help with school homework, father may help with a religious literacy, with mother listening to her younger children reading story books in one or more languages.

The literacy practices of the school may be different from that of the home, as the research by Gregory (1993, 1994, 1996) illustrates. Parents may be educated by the school about 'good reading habits' in their children, mirroring school literacy practices and school culture. This **assumes a deficit** in family literacy practices that may be unwarranted. Parents are seen as failing to provide school-style literacy experiences and therefore contributing to underachievement in their children (Daniel-White, 2002; Edwards & Nwenmely, 2000). 'Followers of cultural deficit explanations for minority failure assert that minority home environments do not provide sufficient intellectual stimulation for the normal development of their children' (Daniel-White, 2002, p. 31).

No home is without literacy, and multilingual literacy knowledge tends to be invisible in an English-dominant neighbourhood (Kenner, 2000). Teachers visiting such homes may find no classroom-type storybooks, but miss newspapers, religious texts, shopping lists, airletters, calendars, flashcards, videos and WWW use that provides a different but rich literacy background. When children commence elementary school, their literacy worlds may be ignored (Bourne, 2001a), with an accent on one literacy only (e.g. school English). For a biliterate child and parent, this may feel like a language-deprived environment (Kenner, 2000).

Instead, language minority parents may, in reality, be highly motivated towards literacy in their children and valued it as a key to vocational and economic mobility. Marginalized immigrant groups may 'see literacy and schooling as the key to mobility, to changing their status and preventing their children from suffering as they did' (Blackledge, 2000a, p. 4).

Huss-Keeler (1997) found in research in the north of England that parents' interest in their child's literacy and helpfulness at home may not be apparent to the teacher who sees non-attendance at parent–teacher meetings as indicative of parental disinterest. Similarly, in a Gujerati Moslem community in London, Sneddon (2000a, 2000b) and Sneddon and Patel (2003) found a positive parental attitude to education, including to English literacy: 'The data on literacy practices in the home revealed that both groups were aware of the need to support their children's learning to read in English and that most did this on a regular basis' (Sneddon, 2000b, p. 124). Children themselves engage in much hidden self-initiated literacy activity, as classroom observation, waste bins and their drawers and cupboards at home reveal (Kenner, 2000).

Children can be encouraged to bring **texts from the home** into the classroom. Kenner (2000) found in such a project that, when encouraged, children will bring calendars, newspapers, textbooks, airletters, videos and posters in their homes languages. Also, when encouraged, their parents will **create material** that can be displayed, discussed and exploited in literacy learning (e.g. letters, cards, posters, booklets, travel brochures, photos with captions, alphabet charts). 'Literacy materials brought into school by families can be a resource for this work, acting as "home pages" for children in the classroom' (Kenner, 2000, p. x). One stage further is

inviting parents into the classroom to help the teacher and students create multi-lingual texts (e.g. creating a multilingual newspaper; a workshop on collaborative writing – see Kenner, 2000).

Delgado-Gaitan (1990) suggests **three models** of **parental involvement** in children's education. Other relevant typologies of parental role are Epstein's (1992) six types of partnership between family, community and school, and Frederickson & Cline's (2002) typology of teachers as sole experts, professionals directing passive parents, and parents as key decision makers.

In the first, the **Family Influence Model**, the family is seen as a direct recipient of the school's influence, and the school–family collaboration establishes maximally effective environments for school learning. Where 'strong' types of bilingual education are present, bilingualism and biliteracy may thrive in such cooperation. In 'weak' versions of bilingual education, the chances of biliteracy are decreased as teachers and parents join to emphasize the majority language. Jeynes's (2003) meta-analysis of the effects of parental involvement in minority student's academic achievement attests to the value and power of this model.

Blackledge (2000a, 2000b) suggests that this model contains a deficit view of minority language parents as it assumes that there are 'correct' literacy practices. Teachers will need to teach parents as well as students what counts as literacy as home literacy is deficient. He also indicates that schools can themselves exclude students and parents from collaboration as the only legitimate literacy activities are those that require majority language understandings. This can isolate minority language students and parents who do not understand the school's expectations, operations or priorities.

The **School Reform Model** operates where parents try to change schools and make them more responsive to parents. This is well portrayed by Mejía (2002) in terms of the varying roles of parents in Japanese 'returners', and Canadian, Colombian and Australian Immersion students. A national collective example is the Canadian Parents for French organization that commenced in 1977 and has over 17,000 members (Baker & Jones, 1998; Canadian Heritage Official Languages, 2004). Language minority groups, however, may relatively infrequently become activist and assertive, even though their voice is often much needed to secure bilingualism and bilingual education for their children. This is not 'blaming the victim' but is often due to such language minorities having a perceived subordinate status and inferior economic situation that leaves them feeling powerless.

In the **Cooperative Systems Model** parents see the home, school and community as interrelated, cooperative, and functioning as a whole. Parents play the roles of volunteer, paid part-time employee, teacher at home, adult learner and helper. Especially in 'weak' forms of bilingual education, language minority parents have a valuable role in representing the literacies of their home and community.

Blackledge (2000a) extends this model to the ideal of full reciprocation between home and school. 'By involving parents and other family and community members in the teaching and learning of literacy, and by building on the existing literacies of family and community, schools can act as a catalyst in a process of empowerment for children, their families and their teachers' (Blackledge, 2000a, p. 1).

An important explication of processes in teacher–parent relationships is given by Moll (2001). Luis Moll and his colleagues at the University of Arizona have used ethnographic studies of student communities to identify skills, knowledge, expertise and interests that Mexican **households** possess that can be used for the benefit of all in the classroom. For many language minority children and their families, the relationship between school and parents is limited and often non-existent. However, Moll shows how parents and other community members have much to offer children in Latino classrooms. Such people can supplement the teacher, providing what Moll calls '**funds of knowledge**' that are 'cultural practices and bodies of knowledge and information that households use to survive, to get ahead or to thrive' (Moll, 1992, p. 21). Examples of funds of knowledge that could be used by schools include information about flowers, plants and trees, seeds, agriculture, water distribution and management, animal care and veterinary medicine, ranch economy, car and bike mechanics, carpentry, masonry, electrical wiring and appliances, fencing, folk remedies, herbal cures and natural medicines, midwifery, archaeology, biology and mathematics. With the demise of so many of the world's languages and cultures (see chapter 3), retaining and transforming funds of knowledge has become essential for preserving diversity and color in the world. The concept of 'funds of knowledge' also serves 'to debunk the prevalent idea of working-class households as devoid of intellect or of worthwhile resources' (Moll, 2001, p. 23). Martin-Jones and Saxena (2003) provide a valuable analytical UK illustration of Panjabi–English bilingual teaching assistants utilizing 'funds of knowledge' in three multi-ethnic classrooms.

Alternatively, the teacher may visit parents not for 'top-down' conveying of educational information and enlisting support for the school, but rather to understand and learn about the parents' culture and 'funds of knowledge' (Moll, 2001). Teachers ask questions; **parents supply stored wisdom**. Such questions may be about family history and heritage, social networks, childrearing, religion, language use and educational expectations. Teachers are the learners; the parents the teachers.

As Moll (2001, p.17) also suggests: 'it is particularly important to document how households function as part of a wider economy, both in the formal and informal sectors of the economy'. Creating good social relationships is also part of the agenda. Sometimes, teachers become a part of the parents' social networks (e.g. attending weddings, birthdays) signaling mutual trust and confidence. Teachers may develop and change their curriculum content as a result of such visits.

However, there is also a scenario where parent-teacher relationships are a concern or a challenge. There are many possible reasons that some parent–teacher relationships show non-cooperation, a **lack of understanding**, a distance and even an antagonism between home and school cultures. Understanding such reasons helps explain why many language minority children fail in the system, have high drop-out rates and exhibit relatively low achievement.

The research of Blackledge (2000a, 2000b) on Bangladeshi families in central England found that mothers felt 'largely unsupported by the school in their efforts to help their children to read the books they brought home from school. School books were sent home with young children without any explicit advice or instructions about how best to use them . . . so parents felt frustrated and "disempowered"' (p. 84).

Such language minority families may be socially, culturally, economically and educationally **isolated** from the school. For example, an information gap between such families and the school may need bridging (Pérez & Torres-Guzmán, 1996). If language minority parents are unable to speak the majority language of the teachers in the school, there may be an increased sense of helplessness and isolation. Such parents are reluctant or unable to discuss their children's progress with the teacher, unable or unwilling to go to parent–teacher meetings and other school events. While such parents may discuss problems about their children's schooling with one another, the issues and worries do not become resolved because there is a gulf between the school and the home. Some parents may be intimidated by high status schools, authoritative teachers and principals, or feel that schools know best and it should therefore act unilaterally in dealing with their children.

In an attempt to show what can constructively be accomplished to empower such parents and resolve this problem, Delgado-Gaitan (1990) explains via an ethnographic study how parents were encouraged to organize themselves into a leadership group, and teach each other about how to communicate with schools. Through building awareness, followed by mobilization, motivation, and commitment, the attitudes and actions of a group of parents were changed. Over time, **parents** became convinced that they had the right, responsibility and power to deal with their children's academic and social concerns, and to foster strong relationships with the school for their children's greater achievement. Individual parents also began to realize that they had something to offer other parents, their children and the school. As parents became more involved, they felt more in control of their lives. They became empowered. 'Feelings of incompetence create isolation for parents. Those feelings must be replaced with a recognition of the ability to collaborate with others before active participation can occur' (Delgado-Gaitan, 1990, p. 158).

In this research study, the pre-school teacher included Mexican family activities in the classroom, and taught parents to be more conscious of their own interactions with their children. This teacher organized a parent committee that involved parents in decision-making activities in the kindergarten. She also incorporated the students' culture into the daily school curriculum. Therefore, she produced a culturally and educationally congruent education experience between the home and the school. Such a teacher became an important advocate of the power of parent–teacher cooperation.

CONCLUSION

This chapter has revealed that different approaches to literacy have different **expectations** about bilingual children that pervade national and school literacy policies, curriculum provision and classroom practices. One recent contrast is literacy only in a majority language (e.g. English) compared with an accent on local, regional literacies perhaps leading to 'multiple literacies' with different uses of literacy in different contexts.

Schools are a powerful provider of literacy and help dictate what counts as proper language, correct ideas and appropriate knowledge to be transmitted though literacy practices. Superior forms of literacy, and the kinds of literacy required for success in education are school transmitted; other literacies are often devalued (except religious literacies). Therefore, the self-esteem and identity of language minority children may be affected by which literacies are legitimated by the school, and which are ignored or despised.

One expectation of education is that children acquire literacy skills so they can function as 'good citizens' in a stable society. A contrasting expectation is that children should become empowered, even politically activated by becoming literate. Language minority children should be able to read, for example, to understand propaganda, and write to defend their community's interests or protest about injustice, discrimination and racism. They need to **read the world and not just the word** (Freire & Macedo, 1987).

The importance of different literacy and multiliteracy approaches lies in their varying proposals for the role, status and self-enhancement of bilingual children and adults. Does literacy produce cogs who aid the smooth running of a well oiled wheel? Does literacy produce bilingual students who are activated into asserting their rights to equality of power, purse and opportunity? A fundamental issue of literacy, biliteracy and multiliteracy is thus political. When clarity is achieved in defining the intended uses of literacy for bilingual students, educational considerations such as approaches, methods and strategies become more rational.

This chapter has suggested the importance of literacy and biliteracy in the empowerment of bilingual students and their communities. Classroom practicalities are not divorced from educational and political policies; that education provision cannot be separated from issues of **power** that affect the lives of bilinguals.

KEY POINTS IN THE CHAPTER

- Literacy has many uses in bilingual, multicultural societies: for learning, citizenship, pleasure and employment for example.
- Cultures, sub-cultures and localities differ in their uses of literacy (e.g. religious groups, transmission of heritage values and beliefs).
- Approaches to literacy include: the skills approach (functional literacy), construction of meaning, sociocultural literacy and critical literacy.
- A transmission style to classroom literacy is contrasted to a critical approach

where issues of power, status, equity and justice are addressed through a language minority perspective.

- Strategies in the classroom to promote biliteracy require cross-curriculum, collaborative and personalized approaches.
- Parents as partners in biliteracy development is important, including when local and family 'funds of knowledge' are utilized.
- When biliteracy is encouraged in minority language children, specific skills and strategies from the first language transfer to the second language.
- Some bilingual children simultaneously learn to read and write in both languages. Other children will learn to read in their first language before they learn to read in their second (majority) language. In immersion education this order is reversed. Both these approaches will tend to result in successful biliteracy. Contexts become important in the decision.

SUGGESTED FURTHER READING

BLACKLEDGE, A., 2000, *Literacy, Power and Social Justice*. Stoke on Trent: Trentham.

CUMMINS, J., 2000, *Language, Power and Pedagogy: Bilingual Children in the Crossfire*. Clevedon: Multilingual Matters.

EDWARDS, V., 1998, *The Power of Babel: Teaching and Learning in Multilingual Classrooms*. Stoke-on-Trent (UK): Trentham.

HORNBERGER, N.H. (ed.), 2003, *Continua of Biliteracy: An Ecological Framework for Educational Policy, Research, and Practice in Multilingual Settings*. Clevedon: Multilingual Matters.

MARTIN-JONES, M. & JONES, K. (eds), 2000, *Multilingual Literacies: Reading and Writing Different Worlds*. Amsterdam / Philadelphia: John Benjamins.

MEJÍA, A-M. de, 2002, *Power, Prestige and Bilingualism: International Perspectives on Elite Bilingual Education*. Clevedon: Multilingual Matters.

REYES, M. & HALCON, J., (eds), 2001, *The Best for Our Children: Critical Perspectives on Literacy for Latino Students*. New York: Teachers College Press.

WILEY, T.G., 2005, *Literacy and Language Diversity in the United States* (2nd edn). Center for Applied Linguistics and Delta Systems, McHenry, Illinois.

STUDY ACTIVITIES

(1)   Visit a school where there is some attention to biliteracy. Make a case study (or a written or oral report) of one or more of the following:

   (a)   Discuss with the teacher the aims of such biliteracy. Does the teacher feel that biliteracy is possible or that literacy in one language is more important?

   (b)   What provision of reading matter in two languages is available in the classroom? How many books are there in different languages? Do any of the books have two or more languages within them? What is the style and content (e.g. type of stories) of the books? Are there differences (e.g. color, datedness, level of language) between books in the two languages?

   (c)   Observe and record how much time is spent on reading in classrooms in a school. How much time is allotted to each language?

   (d)   Ask teachers at what stage and ages reading in each language is introduced in their classrooms? What variations are there between teachers?

To what level does oral and reading achievement in one language need to develop before the introduction of biliteracy? Does a child's interest and attitude have an influence on literacy and biliteracy?

(e) Ask a number of students their views on being able to read in two languages. Ask the students how much reading they do after school, and in what language or languages? What are their favorite books and what language is preferred?

(f) By interviewing, find examples of parent–teacher collaboration in the reading process. What kind of collaboration exists? How well do you feel it works? What improvements might be made? How are literacy practices different and similar in the home and school?

(2) Working with the students of a particular classroom, create one or more of the following (see Blackledge, 2000a, pp. 120–123):

(a) posters to be placed on the walls of the classroom that use different languages of the students and have personal meaning to them;

(b) a classroom newspaper using different languages;

(c) a booklet or brochure about the school for parents in their heritage language;

(d) translations of letters from the school to parents that use the parents' preferred language;

(e) picture books for children in their home language;

(f) a short drama for students to present that uses more than one language.

(3) Observe two classrooms with different literacy programs for language minority children. How do the classrooms differ? What are the different beliefs and assumptions about literacy in the two classrooms?

(4) Design a short program to illustrate how critical literacy could be introduced to language minority students in Grades 5, 6 or 7.

(5) Reflect on occasions when you (or friends) have received input in one language (e.g. in a classroom, religious location) but have worked or responded (output) in a different language. What kind of processing seemed to occur? How subconscious or conscious was the movement between languages? What were the possible benefits and concerns?

(6) Examine some dual language books (e.g. Spanish on one page, English on the opposite page). Ask some teachers and students their opinions about such books. Make a list of the pros and cons. Provide your own reasoned conclusion.

(7) Visit a home where two or more literacies are used. What literacy resources are used in the home? Do the children read and write in different languages? Who helps each child at home with what language, what activities and when. Describe the 'eco-system' of multiliteracies in that family by investigating if parents are also helped by their children, and the role of siblings and the extended family. What relationships are there with the school in mutually understanding multiple literacies?

The Assessment and Special Educational Needs of Bilinguals

CHAPTER 15

The Assessment and Special Educational Needs of Bilinguals

INTRODUCTION

This chapter considers bilingual children with special needs, and the purpose and effectiveness of bilingual special education. The role of assessment in the identification, and particularly the mis-identification of bilingual children follows.

It is initially important to define who are the children with special needs possibly requiring special education provision. **Categories of special need** that may be thought to affect language vary in definition from country to country but are likely to include the following areas: communication disorders, learning disabilities (e.g. dyslexia and developmental aphasia), severe subnormality in cognitive development, behavioral and emotional problems. As Frederickson and Cline (2002) note, there is a distinction between special needs that can be assessed by objective criteria (e.g. visual impairment, hearing and deafness) and those where a more subjective, value judgment is required (e.g. emotional and behavioral difficulties). The risk of an assessment bias against those who are refugees, immigrants, live in material poverty and speak a minority language at home will be greater in the latter category. For example, the placement of immigrants into special education may increase where there is a subjective judgment about their perceived language deficit.

Certainly, some bilingual children do have special needs, and this includes children from 'elite' bilingual families (e.g. English–German) as well as from language minorities. However, none of these is caused by bilingualism. As Frederickson and Cline (2002, p. 292) comment: 'The only language difficulties experienced by most bilingual children arise simply because they are living in a mainly monolingual society'. **Bilingualism** is not a direct cause of speech or language impairment, autism, dyslexia, developmental aphasia, severe subnormality in cognitive development, serious emotional disturbance or behavioral problems (e.g. see Cline & Frederickson (1999) and Peer & Reid (2000) on dyslexia in bilinguals). Being a member of a language minority may co-exist with such conditions, but is **not a cause** as will be illustrated later. Bilinguals with such special needs would have equally experienced these problems had they been raised as a monolingual. But a bilingual special needs child may have increased needs for support (e.g. if working in school in their second language).

GIFTED MULTILINGUAL AND BILINGUAL CHILDREN

Special needs includes those with exceptional gifted abilities (e.g. high IQ, very creative, outstanding musical or mathematical talent, artistic, and students who excel in leadership or in specific performance areas such as sports). Such **gifted multilinguals and bilinguals** are rarely discussed in the literature, and often much under-represented in acceleration programs for the gifted (Valdés, 2003). While the discussion of 'children with special needs' more often revolves around those students with problems, it is valuable to recognize that many bilinguals are **high-achievers**, and research on immersion students (see chapter 11) suggests that bilingualism has been linked with enhanced achievement. Similarly, chapters 7 and 8 have portrayed the **cognitive giftedness** that many bilinguals share (e.g. metalinguistic abilities, creative thinking). This examples suggests a distinction between bilinguals who share language gifts due to their multilingualism or bilingualism, and those bilinguals whose academic, artistic, scientific or musical gifts are less related to their bilingualism, although not necessarily irrelevant to their success.

Valdés (2003) portrays by research a particular **language giftedness** of many bilingual students who act as **gifted interpreters**, especially in immigrant families (see chapter 5). A collection by Castellano and Díaz (2002) examines the identification, assessment and classroom education of gifted bilinguals in the US, including the foundational nature of the recruitment and training of teachers for such students. Such recent attention to gifted multilinguals and bilinguals helps to reconstruct the negative 'remedial' and 'deficit' labels that have surrounded bilinguals in past decades.

THE FREQUENCY OF SPECIAL NEEDS IN BILINGUAL CHILDREN

There is evidence in the US that **bilingual children are over-represented** among those in need of special education (Harry, 1992; Gersten & Woodward, 1994; Baca & Cervantes, 1998). For example, Mercer's (1973) pioneering study found that Mexican-Americans were 10 times more likely to be in special education than white Americans. In the US, around 1 in 10 students are identified for special education services, with approximately 6% of students deemed to have learning disabilities (Donovan & Cross, 2002). However, there have been variations across and within US states (Artiles & Ortiz, 2002). For example, English language learners in Special

Education have varied from over 25% in Massachusetts and South Dakota to less than 1% in Maryland and South Carolina.

The US National Research Council's study of minority students in special education suggested that American Indians were disproportionally over-represented as having learning disabilities (Donovan & Cross, 2002). Such over-representation is often due to biased assessment practices (see later). Over-representation is not the only scenario. **Under-representation** also occurs, particularly in states and districts where language minority students are a relatively small percentage of the population (Artiles, 2003). In the UK, Cline and Frederickson (1999) have shown that the identification of dyslexics who are also bilinguals is often overlooked. If bilinguals are ignored or unobserved by teachers, for example, then they may not be allocated the usual assessment or treatment process.

The US Department of Education (2004) estimated that 9% of all English Language Learners (ELLs) have learning disabilities. Of all children in US Special Education, 8% are ELLS with a learning disability – some 357,000 children. 24% of ELLS with a learning disability were classified as having a speech/language impairment. This raises questions as to why language minority children may need special education. Why do bilingual children have special needs? Does bilingualism in some students lead to language and communication disorders (e.g. language delay)?

One incorrect assumption is that bilingualism leads to language and communication disorders (e.g. language delay). Research does not attribute such disorders to bilingualism (Li Wei *et al.*, 1997). Rather, such beliefs derive from prejudice and ignorance of linguistic and cognitive research.

The communicative **differences** of bilingual children must be **distinguished from** communicative **disorders**. The failure to make this important distinction partly occurs because basic mistakes in assessment and categorization are sometimes made. A bilingual child is often assessed in their weaker, second language. Hence, both language development and general cognitive development are measured inaccurately. For example, in the US and the UK, immigrant children are sometimes assessed through the medium of English and on their English proficiency. Their level of language competence in Spanish, Vietnamese, Hmong, Korean, Cantonese, Turkish, Talagog, Bengali or Panjabi, for example, is ignored.

The result is that such children can be classed as having a 'language disability' and perhaps a 'learning disability'. Instead of being seen as developing bilinguals (i.e. children with a good command of their first language who are in the process of acquiring a second, majority language), they may be classed as of 'limited English proficiency' (LEP in the US), or even as having general difficulties with learning. Their below-average test scores in the second language (e.g. English) are wrongly defined as a 'deficit' or 'disability' that can be remedied by some form of special education.

One particular language condition (language delay) has been particularly associated with bilingualism and illustrates how prejudice and misunderstanding can arise.

LANGUAGE DELAY

A particular pathology in children, 'language delay,' is often erroneously attributed to bilingualism. Language delay occurs when a child is very late in beginning to talk, or lags well behind peers in language development. Estimates of young children experiencing language delay vary from 1 in 20 to 1 in 5 of the child population. Such varying estimates partly reflect that some delays are brief and hardly noticeable, while others are more severe.

Language delay has a **variety of causes** (e.g. autism, severe subnormality, cerebral palsy, physical problems [e.g. cleft palate], psychological disturbance, emotional difficulties). However, in approximately two-thirds of all cases, the precise reason for language delay is not known (Li Wei *et al.*, 1997). Children who are medically normal, with no hearing loss, of normal IQ and memory, who are not socially deprived or emotionally disturbed, can be delayed in starting to speak, slow in development or have problems in expressing themselves well. In such cases, specialist, professional help should be sought. Speech therapists, clinical psychologists, educational psychologists, counselors or doctors may be able to give an expert diagnosis and suggest possible treatment of the problem. It is crucial that such professionals have an understanding of the nature of bilingualism in the clients they advise and treat.

Occasionally, well-meaning professionals make the diagnosis that bilingualism is the cause of language delay. If the causes are unknown, bilingualism might seem a likely cause. Raising children bilingually is widely believed to produce language delayed children. The evidence does not support this erroneous belief (Li Wei *et al.*, 1997).

For the teacher, psychologist, speech therapist, counselor and parent, a decision needs to be made in respect of severely language delayed bilingual children. Will the removal of one language improve, worsen or have no effect on such a child's language development? Given that the cause of the problem may be partially unknown, intuition and guesswork rather than 'science' often occurs. Research in this area is still developing.

Let us assume the professional advice is to move from bilingualism to monolingualism. One issue immediately becomes **which language** to concentrate on if there is major diagnosed language delay. The danger is that parents, teachers and other professionals will want to accent the perceived importance of the majority language. In the US, the advice is often that the child should have a solid diet of English (at home and particularly at school). The perceived language of school and success, employment and opportunity is the majority language. The advice often given is that the home, minority language should be replaced by the majority language.

Even when professionals accept that bilingualism is not the cause of a child's problem, moving from bilingualism to monolingualism is seen by some as a way to help improve the problem. The reasoning is usually that the 'extra demands' of bilingualism, if removed, will lighten the burden for the child. For example, if the child has an emotional problem or a language delay condition, for whatever cause, simplifying the language demands on the child may be seen as one way of solving or reducing the problem. The apparent complexity of a two language life is relieved by monolingualism. Is this the rational and suitable solution?

There are many occasions when changing from bilingualism to monolingualism will have no effect on language delay. For example, if the child seems slow to speak without an obvious cause, or seems low in self-esteem, dropping one language is unlikely to have any effect. On the contrary, the sudden change in schooling or family life may exacerbate the problem. The child may be further confused, even upset, if there is a dramatic change in the language of the school or family. If someone who has loved, cared for, or educated the child in one language (e.g. a minority language) suddenly only uses another language (e.g. the majority language), the emotional well-being of the child may well be negatively affected. Simultaneously, and by association, the child may feel that the love and care has changed. Such an overnight switch may well have painful outcomes for the language delayed child. The mother tongue is denied, the language of the family is implicitly derided, and the communicative medium of the community is disparaged. **The solution in itself may exacerbate the problem**.

An alternative is that the **home language** is retained. Even if the child is slow in developing in that language, with progress delayed, it is the vehicle best known to the child. Being forced to switch to the majority language will not make the journey faster or less problematic. Thus, in most cases, it is inappropriate to move from bilingualism to monolingualism. However, it is dangerous to make this suggestion absolute and unequivocal. When there is language delay, there may be a few situations where maximal experience in one language is preferable. For example, where one language of a child is much securer and more well developed than another, it may be sensible to concentrate on developing the stronger language.

This does not mean that the chance of bilingualism is lost forever. If, or when, language delay disappears, the other language can be **reintroduced**. If a child with language delay really dislikes using (or even being spoken to) in a particular language, as part of a solution, the family may sensibly decide to accede to the child's preference. Again, once behavioral and language problems have been resolved, the 'dropped' language can be reintroduced, so long as it is immediately and consistently associated with pleasurable experiences.

Any temporary move from bilingualism to monolingualism need not be seen as the only solution needed. A focus on such a language change as the sole remedy to the child's problem is naive and dangerous. For example, emotional problems causing language delay may require other rearrangements in the school or family's pattern of behavior. Language delay may require visits to a speech therapist for advice about language interaction between the child and significant adults. Temporary monolingualism is one component in a package of attempted changes to solve the child's language problem. However, it is important to reiterate that, in the majority of cases, language delay will not be affected by retaining a bilingual approach.

THE ASSESSMENT AND PLACEMENT OF BILINGUAL CHILDREN

Bilingual children are often over-represented in special needs education, and this is much due to biased assessment practices. Assessment can result in both cultural and linguistic bias, in the testing and the tester, in interpretation, discounting and omission (Usmani, 1999).

When bilingual children are assessed, it is important to keep three different aspects of their development distinct: (1) first language proficiency; (2) second language proficiency; and (3) the existence (or not) of a physical, learning or behavioral difficulty. This three-fold distinction enables a more accurate and fair assessment to be made with regard to special education. The student's level of functioning in a second language must not be seen as representing the child's level of language development. The child's development in the **first language** needs to be assessed (e.g. by observation if psychological and educational tests are not available) so as to paint a picture of proficiency rather than deficiency, of potential rather than deficit. The child's language proficiency is different from potential problems in an individual's capacities that require specialist treatment (e.g. hearing impairment, severely subnormal in 'IQ'). Neither the language and culture of the home, nor socioeconomic and ethnic differences should be considered as handicapping conditions in themselves. Social, cultural, family, educational and personal information needs to be collected to make a valid and reliable assessment and to make an accurate placement of the child in mainstream or special education. This is considered separately in the following section on the assessment of bilingual children.

A key element of assessment with language minority children is that there is **early identification, assessment and intervention** (Ortiz, 2002). This leads to earlier, and therefore more effective **prevention** or **intervention** (Artiles & Ortiz, 2002; Donovan & Cross, 2002). Yet assessment systems often wait until the child fails before there is assessment and intervention. The 'wait to fail' principle means that highly effective early supports are missing, and later support may have decreased effectiveness. This problem is exacerbated when students come from disadvantaged communities and attend poorly resourced schools. Early screening is therefore important where disadvantaged language minority children exist.

THE EXAMPLE OF THE UNITED STATES

In the US, Public Law (94–142) gives a **right** to assessment that is not culturally discriminatory, to tests in the child's native language, to multi-dimensional 'all areas' assessment for all 'handicapped' students. The misdiagnosis of bilingual students for special education has led to court cases. Such court cases revealed how bilingual students were wrongly assessed as in need of special education (Maldonado, 1994). In some cases, teachers were unsure how to cope with a child whose English was relatively 'weak'. On this basis only, the teacher wanted special education for the 'Limited English Proficient' child.

In the US, there is **legislation** to govern appropriate processes of assessment of those for whom English is an additional language. For example, the 1970 Californian case of *Diana* v. *The California State Board of Education* was based on nine Mexican-American parents who protested that their children (who were dominant in Spanish) were given an English language IQ test. The IQ test revealed 'normal' non-verbal IQ scores, but very low verbal IQ scores (as low as 30 for one child). As a result of using this linguistically and culturally inappropriate IQ test, the Mexican-American children were placed in classes for the 'mentally retarded'. In a preliminary settlement, it established that testing should be conducted in a child's native language (and in English), and that non-verbal IQ tests were usually a fairer measurement of IQ than verbal tests (Valdés & Figueroa, 1994). As a result of this case, the collection of broader data on language minority children was required (rather than simple test data) to justify placement of such children in Special Education.

In 1975, Public Law 94–142, the Education for All Handicapped Children Act, federally mandated that all testing and assessment procedures should be non-discriminatory. 'Non-discriminatory' means using tests that are culturally and linguistically appropriate. Such testing procedures were only to be used by trained members of a **multidisciplinary** team. Apart from tests, teacher recommendations, observations of a child and other relevant information should create a multi-source file (portfolio) of evidence (Barona & Barona, 1992).

Such multidisciplinary teams are not always pragmatically possible, but remain a most effective practice. Such a team may be drawn from a school/educational psychologist, a speech pathologist/therapist, a social worker, an ESL leader, and the students' teacher(s). The involvement, and not exclusion, of parents in such a team process is important, as is collecting **evidence** other than test scores about the student's family and home, learning history and community/cultural lifestyle.

Such litigation and law has shown the importance of separating bilinguals with real learning difficulties from those bilinguals whose second language (e.g. English) proficiency is below 'native' average. The latter group should not be assessed as having learning difficulties and therefore in need of special education. The litigation also showed the wrongs done to bilingual students: **mis-identification**, (as well as under-identification and over-identification), misplacement, misuse of tests and resulting failure when allocated to special education.

The fear of litigation by school districts can lead to an **over-referral** of bilingual students with a real need of special education. In the early 1980s, the trend in California, for example, was to assume that too many language minority students were in need of special education. When students did not appear to be benefiting from instruction in 'regular' classrooms, special education classes became the easy answer. Or, if teachers were unsure how to deal with a behavioral or learning problem, transfer to special education provision became an instant solution.

Towards the end of the 1980s, this was reversed. The tendency moved to **under-estimating** the special needs of language minority children (Gersten & Woodward, 1994; Baca & Cervantes, 1998). Wrongful placement of children in special education (over-referral) made various administrators cautious of special education placement. A fear of legal action by parents, and a realization that assessment devices often had low validity, led administrators to be hesitant to place bilingual children in Special Education.

The see-saw between over- and under-referral to special education makes accurate assessment a key focus. However, accurate assessment and placement in different schools is not enough. The development of **effective instruction strategies** and an appropriate curriculum for such students is crucial. So is the need to train teachers for bilingual students in special education. Educating the parents of special needs children is also a high priority.

Assessment will sometimes locate those who are bilingual *and* have a physical, neurological, learning, emotional, cognitive or behavioral difficulty. Such children may need some kind of special education or intervention. What form of Special Education should such children receive? Should such education be in their home language, where feasible, or in the majority language of the region? Or should such children be provided with education that uses both home and majority languages?

BILINGUAL SPECIAL EDUCATION

Special Education bilingual children can be served by a **variety** of institutional arrangements (Cloud, 1994). These include: Special Education schools (resident and non-resident), hospital-based education, residential homes, Special Education Units attached to mainstream schools, specially resourced classes in mainstream schools, withdrawal and pull-out programs (e.g. for extra speech and language help, behavioral management) and special help given by teachers, paraprofessionals or support staff in 'regular' classes. The extent to which such provision will be bilingual or monolingual will vary within and across regional and institutional arrangements. Such bilingual or monolingual provision will depend on the availability of provision (material, human and financial), the type and degree of special education need or condition, the degree of proficiency in both languages, learning capacity, age, social and emotional maturity, degree of success in any previous education placements, and not least, the wishes of the parents and child.

When bilingual or language minority children have been assessed as having special needs, some educators argue that education is needed solely in the dominant, majority language. In the US, the advice given is sometimes that Latino and other language minority children with special needs should be educated in monolingual, English language special schools. The argument is that such children are going to live in an English speaking society. When there is severe cognitive disability, it may seem that a child should be educated monolingually, in the minority or majority language. This is especially the case when such a child develops very slowly in one language. However, this may not advantage the child.

Many special needs bilingual children will benefit from **bilingual provision** rather than monolingual education, where this is practicable (Baca & Cervantes, 1998; Carrasquillo, 1990). One example is the recently arrived (immigrant) special needs child. Placing such a child in a class where he or she doesn't speak the language of the classroom (e.g. English in the US) will only increase failure and lower self esteem. To be educated, the child preferably needs initial instruction mostly in the first language, with the chance of becoming as bilingual as possible.

Many children with special needs are capable of developing in two languages (e.g. Down's Syndrome). Most children do not reach levels of proficiency in either language compared with their peers in mainstream classrooms. Nevertheless, they reach functional levels of **proficiency in two languages according to their abilities**. Becoming bilingual does not detract from achievement in other areas of the curriculum (e.g. mathematics and the creative arts). Canadian research tends to show that less able bilingual children share some of the cognitive advantages of bilingualism (Rueda, 1983). Just as their mathematical ability, literacy and scientific development may occur at a slower pace, so the two languages will develop with less speed. The size of vocabulary and accuracy of syntax may be less in both languages than the average bilingual child. Nevertheless, such children, acquiring two languages early, will usually be able to communicate in both languages, usually as well as they would communicate in one language.

The movement of a bilingual student into special education occurs after a conclusion is reached that the child's needs cannot be met by inclusion in a regular (i.e. non-special) classroom. If children are placed in bilingual special education, it is important that they gain the benefits of those in other forms of bilingual education: dual language competence, biculturalism and multiculturalism, and other educational, cultural, self-identity and self-esteem benefits. These benefits have been discussed previously in this book.

However, **inclusion** has increasingly been regarded as preferable to the stigmatization of segregation (Frederickson & Cline, 2002). Segregation can restrict access to educational opportunities. In the UK, children who failed an English language screening test were sometimes cut-off from a mainstream school environment, with a restricted subject curriculum, and subsequent stereotyping as failures and outcasts. Inclusion tries to combat the intolerance of language and cultural difference and perpetuating inequalities by severance from mainstream education. Thus UNESCO (1994) adopted the 'principle of inclusive education, enrolling all children in regular schools unless there are compelling reasons for doing otherwise' (p. 44). Such inclusion means special needs bilinguals attending a mainstream classroom and fully participating in the curriculum. Special Needs teachers, paraprofessionals and teacher assistants will work with such children in that school and in an inclusive philosophy. Apart from locational integration of bilingual special needs students, inclusion attempts social (peer) integration and curriculum integration. Social inclusion and matching the mainstream curriculum to the special needs of the child require well trained teachers, high quality material support, parental involvement and constant monitoring (Frederickson & Cline, 2002).

The concept of **inclusion** is an important comparison to the historical view of bilingual special needs children The belief has been that such students have a 'disease' that needs to be 'cured' by 'treatment' (Artiles & Ortiz, 2002). The inclusion movement holds that all children can learn successfully within integrated education that is adapted to their particular needs. Inclusive education may increase positive expectations of special needs students by their teachers, peers and themselves. In contrast, the current accountability ideology and high-stakes testing systems tend to exclude or negatively label culturally and linguistically diverse students in a mainstream system. Escamilla *et al.* (2005) argue that it is often automatically assumed with high stakes testing scores that Latinos and Spanish speakers will under-achieve, and that their language and cultural difference is the explanation.

One example not discussed so far is when children **fail** in a mainstream school due to their language proficiency not being sufficient to operate in the curriculum. For example, in the US, some Spanish speaking children are in mainstream schools (a 'submersion' experience) and, although of normal ability, fail in the system (e.g. drop out of school, repeat grades, leave high school without a diploma) because their English proficiency is insufficiently developed to comprehend the increasingly complex curriculum.

This situation creates an apparent dilemma. By being placed in some form of **special education**, the child is possibly stigmatized as having a 'deficiency' and a 'language deficit'. Such special education may be a separate school (or a special unit within a larger school) that provides special ('remedial') education for bilingual children. Such schools and units may not foster bilingualism. Often, they will emphasize children becoming competent in the majority language (e.g. English in the US). Such segregation may allow more attention to the second language but result in ghettoization of language minorities. While giving some sanctuary from sinking in second language submersion in a mainstream school, special education can be a retreat, marginalizing the child. Will such children in special education realize their potential across the curriculum? Will they have increased access to employment? Will the perception of failure be increased because they are associated with a remedial institution? Will there be decreased opportunities for success in school achievement, employment and self-enhancement?

The **ideal** for children in this dilemma may be neither mainstreaming nor special education. It is education that allows them to start and continue learning in their first language. The second language is nurtured as well, so as to ensure the development of bilinguals who can operate in mainstream society. In such schools, both languages are developed and used in the curriculum. Such schools avoid the 'remedial' or 'compensatory' associations of special education. Such schools celebrate the cultural and linguistic diversity of their students. The inclusion of special needs students can mean that they are placed in bilingual education along with their 'non special needs' peers.

Yet such mainstream bilingual education is sometimes in danger of being seen as a form of special education. Even when the 'language delayed' are separated from those who are in the early stages of learning the majority language (e.g. English in the US), the danger is that the latter will still be assessed as in need of compensatory, remedial special education.

It is also the case that a bilingual student with special needs may be placed in monolingual special education due to no bilingual special education provision being viable. Where particular language minority special needs students are isolated and unique, then pragmatism typically predominates.

ALTERNATIVE CAUSES OF SPECIAL NEEDS AND LEARNING DIFFICULTIES IN CHILDREN

Six examples of **causes outside the child** and his or her bilingualism follow. This list, which is not exhaustive nor comprehensive, will indicate that bilingualism has nothing directly to do with many learning problems, either as a secondary or a primary cause.

(1) Poverty and deprivation, child neglect and abuse, feelings of pessimism, help-lessness and desperation in the home, extended family and community may create personality, attitudinal and learning conditions that make assessment of learning difficulties more probable. Sometimes, such assessment will reflect prejudice, misjudgments and misperceptions about the child's home experiences. The learning problem may thus be in a **mismatch** between the culture, attitudes, expectations about education and values of the home and school. In chapter 14, this variation is discussed with reference to local literacy and variations in ethnic group and social class uses of literacy. Different beliefs, culture, knowledge and cognitive approaches may be devalued with the child immediately labeled as of inferior intelligence, academically incompetent and of low potential.

(2) The problem may be in the **standard of education**. A child may be struggling in the classroom due to poor instruction methods, a non-motivating, culturally alien classroom environment, a dearth of suitable teaching materials, or clashes with the teacher.

(3) The **school** may be inhibiting or obstructing learning progress. If a child is being taught in a second language and the home language is ignored, then failure and perceived learning difficulties may result. One example is that of some Spanish speaking children in the US. Such children are often placed in English-only classrooms on entry to school. They must sink or swim in English. Some swim; others sink and may be deemed to have a deficiency. By being assessed in their weaker second language (English) rather than in their stronger home language (Spanish), such children are labeled as in need of special or remedial education. Thus the monolingual school system is itself responsible for learning failure. A school that promoted bilingualism would probably ensure learning success for the same child.

(4) Another set of causes of learning difficulties are a lack of self-confidence, **low self-esteem**, a fear of failure and high anxiety in the classroom.

(5) A fifth possibility is failure caused partly by **interactions among children** in the classroom. For example, where a group of children encourage each other to misbehave, have a low motivation to succeed, or where there is bullying,

hostility, social division, rather than cohesion among children in a classroom, the learning ethos may hinder the child's development.

(6) Another case is where there is a mismatch between the **gradient of learning** expected and the ability level of the child. Some children learn to read more slowly than others, still learning to read well, but after a longer period of time. Less able children can learn two languages within the (unknowable) limits of their ability. Other children experience specific learning difficulties (for example, dyslexia, neurological dysfunction, 'short-term memory' problems, poor physical coordination, problems in attention span or motivation). None of these specific learning difficulties or other language disorders are caused by bilingualism. At the same time, bilingual children will not escape from being included in this group. Bilingual families are no less likely to be affected than other families.

Almost the only occasion when a learning difficulty of a bilingual child is attached to bilingualism is the case when a child enters the classroom with neither language sufficiently developed to cope with the particular language skills demanded by the curriculum. In such cases where a child has simple conversational skills in two languages but cannot cope in the curriculum in either language, language may be related to learning difficulties.

ASSESSMENT AND BILINGUAL CHILDREN

The allocation of bilinguals to Special Education and the attribution of learning difficulties usually depends on some form of assessment. It is essential for any psychological and educational assessment of bilingual children to be fair, accurate and broad. Too often, tests given to bilingual children only serve to suggest their 'disabilities', supposed 'deficits' or lack of proficiency in a second language (Figueroa, 2002). Assessment can too easily legitimize the disabling of language minority students. Such students may come to be stigmatized by such tests, for example, because tests locate apparent weaknesses in the majority language and use monolingual scores as points of comparison. English language tests and IQ tests administered in the second language to US children are particular examples.

Despite advice in legislation, discussions in academic literature and in research, bilinguals tend in many countries to be discriminated against in testing and assessment (Figueroa, 2002; Hall *et al.*, 2001). Therefore, it is important to review the components of such bias, and more constructively, to suggest desirable practice. Overlapping and interacting issues in the assessment of bilingual children are now considered.

(1) The **temporary difficulties** faced by bilinguals must be distinguished from relatively more permanent difficulties that impede everyday functioning and learning. Brief language delays, temporary adjustment problems of immigrants and short-term stammering (stuttering) are examples of transient difficulties (Baker, 2000b). Dyslexia, hearing loss and high neuroticism are

examples where longer term problems will need treatment. This simple distinction hides different and complex dimensions. The means for distinguishing temporary and longer term problems follows.

(2)   Diagnosis needs to go beyond a few, simple tests and engage a wide diversity of measurement and observation devices. Diagnosis needs to be extended over a time period and to avoid an instant conclusion and instantaneous remedy. **Observing** the child in different contexts (and not just in the classroom) will provide a more valid profile (language and behavior) of that child. The family and educational history of the child needs assembling. Parents and teachers need to be consulted, sometimes psychologists, doctors, counselors, speech therapists and social workers (e.g. in multidisciplinary teams) as well. Samples of a child's natural communication need gathering, with the child in different roles and different situations. Figueroa (2002, p. 57) argues for much less testing, and much more observation of the student.

> Determining why an English language learner is not progressing can best be done by observing the child in an enriched, effective classroom. There, it is possible to distinguish learning problems that can be attributed to a deficiency in the teaching and learning environment from problems that can be attributed to disabilities.

An awareness or basic knowledge of a child's ethnic, cultural and linguistic background is important in fair assessment, but it may not be enough. To interpret test scores and classifications meaningfully and wisely and, in particular, to make decisions on the basis of assessment, requires a sensitive and sympathetic **understanding of a child's community, culture, family life and individual characteristics**. Children come to school with very differing home experiences, where different kinds of competences are cultivated and stressed. Such abilities prized by parents may be different from the abilities learnt at school.

For example, discovery learning and learning through play is not a part of all cultures. An investigative, questioning mode of thinking may not be encouraged within a culture. Instead, adults provide authoritative knowledge that must be accepted and enacted by the child. Parents may teach literacy in a 'respectful' style, where a child is expected to memorize much or all of the Holy Book and repeat it without comprehension. Such family and community socialization practices have implications (1) for the type of assessment that reveals the strengths and weaknesses of the child; (2) for the importance of acquiring evidence about the culture of the child; and (3) for the process of assessment by the teacher, psychologist, speech therapist, counselor or other professional.

Test scores (e.g. on educational and psychometric tests) tend to be decontextualized and attenuated (Resnick & Resnick, 1992). An analogy helps to illustrate this important point. Test scores are like latitude and longitude. They provide points of reference on a map of human characteristics. As a standard measurement usable on all maps, they provide initial, rapid and instantly comparable information. But imagine the most beautiful place you know (e.g.

a flower-enfolded, azure-colored lake set amid tall, green-sloped, ice-capped mountains). Does the expression of the latitude and longitude of that scene do justice to characterizing the personality and distinctiveness of that location? The attempted precision of the sextant needs to be joined by the full empathic exploration and evaluation of the character and qualities of the child.

Authentic language in each language needs assessing rather than just decomposed and decontextualized language skills. Such dual language assessment should be kept separate from the assessment of behavioral or cognitive difficulties. The levels of thinking and understanding of a child through each language need assessing rather than cursory comprehension gleaned from a 'scientific' test (e.g. with high test–retest reliability, and high correlations with similar tests). 'Inauthentic language' tests relate too often to a transmission style curriculum where obtaining the correct answer and 'teaching to the test' dominates teacher thinking and classroom activity. Such tests do not capture the quality of the communication abilities of the child, as for example, occur in the playground, on the street, at the family meal-table and in internal conversations when alone.

(3) The choice of **assessors** for the child will affect the assessment (Ortiz & Yates, 2002). Whether the assessors are trained professionals, perceived to be from the same language group as the child will affect the child's performance (and possibly the diagnosis). The perceived age, social class, powerfulness and gender of the assessor(s) will affect how the child responds and possibly the assessment outcomes. The assessment process is not neutral. Who assesses, using what devices, under what conditions, all contribute to the judgment being made. An inappropriate assessor creates an increased risk of making two common, opposite judgmental errors concerning bilingual children: (1) generating a 'false positive', that is, diagnosing a problem when none is present; and (2) generating a 'false negative', that is, failing to locate a problem when one exists.

(4) Children need assessing in their **stronger language**. Ideally children need assessing as bilinguals – in both their languages. The tests and assessment devices applied, and the language of communication used in assessment, should ideally be in the child's stronger language. An assessment based on tests of (and in) the child's weaker language may lead to a misdiagnosis, a false impression of the abilities of the child and a partial and biased picture of the child. This sometimes occurs in the UK and the US where bilingual children are tested in English, partly because of the availability of well regarded psycho-metric tests.

(5) Parents and educators need to make sure the **language used** in the test is **appropriate** to the child. For example, a translation of the test (e.g. from English to Spanish) may produce inappropriate, stilted language. Kester & Peña (2002) indicate that item difficulty and validity can change as word frequency, word order cues, uses of language in different domains and grammar (e.g. gender marking) vary across a bilingual's two languages. Also,

the different varieties of Spanish, for example, may not be that used by the student. Chicano Spanish speaking parents will want the tests in Chicano or at least Mexican Spanish rather than the Cuban, Puerto Rican or Castilian variety of Spanish. Once Spanish speaking children have been in the US for a time, their Spanish changes. English influences their way of speaking Spanish. So a test in 'standard' Spanish is often inappropriate. A Spanish test may accept only one right answer, penalizing children for their bilingualism and their US Spanish. A monolingual standard of Spanish is inappropriate to such bilingual children.

Since there are language problems with tests (as outlined above and continued below), it is important to distinguish between a child's language profile and **performance profile** (Cummins, 1984a). The performance profile is more important as it attempts to portray a child's underlying cognitive abilities rather than just language abilities. A performance profile seeks to understand the overall potential of the child, not just their language proficiency. Cummins (1984a) demonstrated this **distinction between a language profile and a performance** profile on one frequently used IQ test in individual assessment – the Wechsler Intelligence Scale for Children: Revised (WISC-R). Bilingual children tend to score significantly higher on the Performance than the Verbal subtests.

(6) There are times when a test or assessment device cannot be given in the child's stronger language. For example, appropriate bilingual professionals may not be available to join the assessment team, tests may not be available in the child's home language, and **translations** of tests may make those tests invalid and unreliable.

Therefore, **interpreters** are sometimes necessary and have a valuable function. If trained in the linguistic, professional and rapport-making competences needed, they can make assessment more fair and accurate. Interpreters can also bring a possible bias into the assessment (i.e. 'heightening' or 'lowering' the assessment results through the interpretation they provide).

(7) The US '**No Child Left Behind Act**' (NCLB) of 2001 (see chapter 9) halted the exclusion of English language learners (ELLs) from large-scale assessments and mandated their inclusion in state-wide testing (Abedi, 2004). NCLB shapes schooling for such learners from enrollment until they are no longer classified as ELL. States are held accountable for ELL's yearly progress by the use of tests of, for example, English language proficiency (oracy and literacy). Technical problems in such assessment (e.g. inconsistency across states, quality of assessment tests) are discussed by Abedi (2004).

The NCBL Act requires that such students be 'assessed in a valid and reliable manner and provided reasonable accommodations on assessments'. When English language learners are tested in English in the US, support or '**accommodations**' are often given (Abedi *et al.*, 2004). Examples of accommodations are: simpler English in the instructions without changing the content, use of a dictionary and glossary, extra time to complete, oral administration, and oral response. The test may be explained to students in an easier form of language and they may be given longer to complete, for example, so that use of a second language becomes less of an influence and performance is more accurate. Ideally, this produces a more level playing field for ELLs. A translation into the student's home language may not always help as the instruction and hence 'curriculum language' will have been in English. The use of accommodations is a much debated topic (Abedi *et al.*, 2004). They question the influence of accommodations on the validity of the test result, which students are eligible for accommodations and on what criteria, plus the amount of advantage (even unfair advantage) resulting from different accommodations. However, the performance gap between English learners and others has been narrowed by such accommodations (Abedi *et al.*, 2004).

(8)   In the US, standardized, norm-referenced (see later) English language assessment tests are used to redesignate and reclassify students from being LEPs or ELLs to FEP (fluent English proficient). **Reclassification** rates are used to assess the effectiveness of a district or school in helping ELLs (Linquanti, 2001). Such tests perpetuate the illusion that such students only need to learn English to succeed in the curriculum and that academic success will then follow (Linquanti, 2001). As chapter 8 discussed, mastery of 'curriculum English' is needed. If such tests reclassify students as fluent English proficient too quickly, needed curriculum support may be removed and the tests may contribute to educational inequity and failure.

(9)   There is a danger of focusing the assessment solely on the child. If the child is tested, the assumption is that the 'problem' lies within the child. At the same time, and sometimes instead, the **focus** needs to shift to **causes outside the child**. Is the problem in the school? Is the school failing the child by denying abilities in the first language and focusing on failure in the second (school) language? Is the school system denying a child's culture and ethnic character, thereby affecting the child's academic success and self-esteem? Is the curriculum delivered at a level that is beyond the child's comprehension or is culturally foreign to the child? The remedy may be in a change in the school and not to the child.

(10) The danger of assessment is that it will lead to the disablement rather than the **empowerment** of bilingual children (Cummins, 1984a, 1986, 2000a). If the assessment separates children from powerful, dominant, mainstream groups in society, the child may become disempowered. The assessment may lead to categorization in an inferior group of society and marginalization. Instead, assessment should work in the best, long-term interests of the child. 'Best interests' does not only mean short-term educational remedies, but also long-term employment and wealth-sharing opportunities. The assessment should **advocate** for the child, and not against the child.

(11) It is important to use the understanding of a child's **teachers** who have observed that child in a variety of learning environments over time. What do the child's teachers think is the root problem? What solutions and interven-

tions do teachers suggest? Have the child's teachers a plan of action? A team of teachers, meeting regularly to discuss children with problems, is a valuable first attempt to assess and treat the child. Such a team can also be the school decision-maker for referral to other professionals (e.g. speech therapist, psychologist, counselor).

(12) Norm referenced **tests** are often used to assess the child (e.g. for entry into, or exit from a bilingual program). This means that the assessor can compare the child with other so called 'normal' children. The assessor can indicate how different the child is from the average. Many such tests are based on scores from 'native' language majority children. Thus, comparisons can be unfair for bilingual children. For example, tests of English language proficiency may have 'norms' (averages, and scores around the average) based on native speakers of English (see chapter 2). This makes them biased against bilinguals and leads to the stereotyping of particular language and ethnic groups.

The **testing of bilinguals** has developed from the practice of testing **monolinguals**. Bilinguals are not the simple sum of two monolinguals but are a unique combination and integration of languages. The language configuration of bilinguals means that, for example, a bilingual's English language performance should not be compared with a monolingual's English language competence. A decathlete should not be compared with a 100 meter sprinter solely for speed of running. Monolingual norms are simply inappropriate for bilinguals (see chapter 1). One example helps illustrate this point. Bilinguals use their languages in different contexts (domains). Thus they may have linguistic competence in varying curriculum areas, on different curriculum topics and on different language functions. Equal language facility in both languages is rare. Comparison on monolingual norms assumes such equal language facility across all domains, language functions and curriculum areas. This is unfair and inequitable.

Such norm referenced tests are often written by white, middle-class Anglo test producers. The test items often reflect their language style and **culture**. For example, the words used such as 'tennis racquet', 'snowman' and 'credit cards' may be unfamiliar to some immigrants who have never seen a snowman, played or watched tennis, or do not yet know about the culture of plastic money. Assessment items that reflect the unique learning experiences of language minority children will be excluded from a test for majority language or mainstream children. Such items will be highlighted by item analysis of an early draft of the test as 'unconnected' with the majority of the test items.

Such norm referenced tests are often 'pencil and paper' tests, sometimes involving multiple choice answers (one answer is chosen from a set of given answers). Such tests do not measure all the different aspects of language. Spoken, conversational language, for example, cannot be adequately measured by a simple pencil and paper test.

Some norm referenced tests report the results in **percentiles** (especially in the US). Percentiles refer to the percentage of children below (and above) the child being tested. For example, being in the 40th percentile means that 39% of children score lower than the child being tested. Sixty percent of children of an age group score above the 40th percentile child. The child is in the 40th group from the bottom, all children being assumed to be divided into 100 equally sized groups. Percentiles have often been used for the entry (and exit) of students into bilingual programs in the US. For example, a student may need to reach the 40th percentile on an English language test to be exited to a mainstream class. What 'percentile threshold' (e.g. 40th percentile) is used for entry or exit is essentially arbitrary, and liable to political as well as educationally derived decisions.

Norm referenced tests essentially compare one person against others. Is this important? Or is the more important measurement about what a bilingual child can and cannot do in each curriculum subject? To say a child is in the 40th percentile in English doesn't tell the parent or the teacher what are a child's strengths and weaknesses, capabilities and needs in English. The alternative is assessment related directly to progress in each curriculum area.

Such **curriculum based assessment** is called **criterion referenced testing,** and seeks to establish the relative mastery of a child in a curriculum area (Baker, 1995). It seeks to establish what a child can do, and what is the next area of a curriculum (e.g. reading) where progress can be made. A diagnosis may also be made, not necessarily of a fundamental psychological or learning problem, but of weaknesses that need remedial treatment to enable conceptual understanding (e.g. if a child has a problem in reading certain consonantal blends). Such criterion referenced assessment of bilingual students gives parents and teachers more usable and important information. It profiles for parents and teachers what a child can do in a subject (e.g. mathematics) and where development, or accelerated learning, should occur next. Such assessment enables an individualized program to be set for the child.

However, the sequences of learning that underpin a criterion referenced test may still reflect a **cultural mismatch** for the child. Criterion referenced assessment (usually, but not necessarily) assumes there is a relatively linear, step-by-step progression in a curriculum area (e.g. in learning to read, in number skills, in science). Such a progression may be culturally relative and culturally determined. As Cline (1993, p. 63) notes 'because of their different prior experiences, their learning hierarchy for a particular task may follow different steps or a different sequence (e.g. in relation to phonology and orthography in learning to read)'. Therefore, it is important to use curriculum assessment contexts and processes that are appropriate, comprehensible and meaningful to the bilingual child.

ASSESSMENT SOLUTIONS

Three solutions to the problems of testing bilinguals are provided by Valdés and Figueroa (1994). Their **first** solution is to attempt to minimize the potential harm of existing tests when given to bilingual individuals, by applying some of the guidelines given above. Their **second** solution is, temporarily, to ban all testing of bilinguals until more valid tests can be produced for bilingual populations. Their **third** alternative is that alternative approaches to testing and development be developed. This third option may be the one most favored by many teachers, educationalists and parents. It would, for example, bring in bilingual norms, more curriculum based assessment and portfolio type assessment, and a greater cultural and linguistic awareness of bilinguals.

Portfolio assessment that is developmental and which has width, linguistically and contextually, has become particularly popular. This is a collection over time of a sample of a child's unique growth (e.g. in both their languages). A student's portfolio will reveal advancing accomplishments in the form of authentic activities (possibly with staff observations included). A sense of ownership of the portfolio by the student is important to raise awareness of evolving accomplishments and a personal possession of progress. Frederickson and Cline (2002) argue for the child's perspective to be part of this assessment (e.g. self perceptions of the school, special needs, friends, home, feelings and the future). Parents' and family collaboration and viewpoints add a further important dimension to assessment and to solutions (S. García, 2002).

However, this third solution is probably a new beginning but it is not enough. A **more radical solution** places change in assessment within (and not separate from) a change in expectations about the nature and behavior of bilingual students. This entails a shift in the politics and policy dimensions of the assessment of bilinguals. Merely changing tests may alleviate the symptoms of a problem, but not change the root cause. The root cause tends to be a bias against language minorities that is endemic in many societies and is substantiated by unfair tests. By being biased against bilinguals in a cultural and linguistic form, and by a failure to incorporate an understanding of the cognitive constitution of bilinguals, assessment confirms and perpetuates various discriminatory perceptions about language minority children.

Assessment thus sometimes serves by its nature and purpose, its form, use and outcomes to provide the evidence for **discrimination** and **prejudice** against language minorities (e.g. in the US and UK) to be perpetuated. Assessment results serve to marginalize and demotivate, to reveal underachievement and lower performance in language minority children. These results are often a reflection of the low status, inequitable treatment and poverty found among many language minorities. Assessment provides the data to make expectations about language minority students self-fulfilling and self-perpetuating. Changing assessment does not necessarily break into that cycle, unless it is a component of a wider reform movement.

Assessment must not in itself be blamed for bias against bilinguals. It is a conveyer and not a root cause of language minority discrimination and bias. Until there is authentic and genuine acceptance of cultural pluralism in a region, a more widespread agreement for multiculturalism, a minimizing of racism and prejudice against ethnic minorities, minor modifications in the assessment of bilinguals stand the chance of merely confirming the lower status and perceived 'deficiencies' of language minority children.

Too often the focus in assessing bilinguals is on their language competence (or on their 'limited proficiencies' as in the test-designated 'Limited English Proficient' students in the US via tests such as the English Language Assessment Battery (LAB)). Rarely does the assessment of bilinguals in the education system focus on other important competences of a bilingual.

In the US, the 1991 Secretary's Commission on Achieving Necessary Skills (SCANS) recommended that attention be given in high schools to work-related **competences**. For example, performance standards were called for in: interpersonal skills (e.g. working in a team, negotiating, working well with people from culturally diverse backgrounds), interpreting and communicating information, thinking creatively, taking responsibility, sociability, self-management and integrity. These important 'life-skills' are regarded as 'essential accomplishments' for employment, self-respect and building a better world.

On some of these attributes, there is evidence to suggest that bilinguals may have advantages over monolinguals (e.g. negotiating, working well with people from culturally diverse backgrounds, interpreting and communicating information, thinking creatively). If the assessment of bilinguals focused more on these 'outside world' attributes and less on classroom linguistic skills in the majority language, a more affirmative and favorable, productive and constructive view of bilinguals might be promoted.

CONCLUSION

The chapter has indicated that placement in special education is not caused by bilingualism. The reasons for special needs tend to reside in factors that surround bilinguals (e.g. their social and economic conditions) and are not an inevitable component of bilingualism. Traditional assessment in education often serves to misplace and misdiagnose bilinguals. Apparent rather than real difficulties are identified, with a depreciation of bilinguals' language and potential curriculum performance.

KEY POINTS IN THE CHAPTER

- Bilingual children are often over-represented in Special Education, being seen as having a language deficit. Paradoxically, they can also be under-represented when there is a fear of legal action for wrongful placement.
- Bilingualism has been associated with language and communication disorders (e.g. language delay). This is not supported by research.
- Special Education bilingual children are served by a variety of institutional arrangements including Special Education schools, Special Education Units attached to mainstream schools, specially resourced classes in mainstream schools, withdrawal and pull-out programs and special help given by teachers, paraprofessionals or support staff in 'regular' classes. Most special

needs children will benefit from bilingual special education rather than mono-lingual special education.
- Assessment of bilingual children is enhanced when there is observation (in and out of the classroom) and not just testing, curriculum based assessment, a cultural and linguistic awareness of bilinguals, using appropriately trained assessors who seek to empower such children.

SUGGESTED FURTHER READING

ARTILES, A.J. & ORTIZ, A.A. (eds), 2002, *English Language learners with Special Educational Needs.* Washington DC & McHenry, IL: Center for Applied Linguistics & Delta Systems Co..

BACA, L.M. & CERVANTES, H.T., 1998, *The Bilingual Special Education Interface* (3rd edn). Upper Saddle River, NJ: Prentice Hall.

CLINE, T. & FREDERICKSON, N., 1995, *Progress in Curriculum Related Assessment with Bilingual Pupils.* Clevedon: Multilingual Matters.

CUMMINS, J., 2000, *Language, Power and Pedagogy: Bilingual Children in the Crossfire.* Clevedon: Multilingual Matters.

FREDERICKSON, N. & CLINE, T., 2002, *Special Educational Needs, Inclusion and Diversity: A Textbook.* Buckingham (UK): Open University Press.

GENESEE, F., PARADIS, J. & CRAGO, M.B., 2004, *Dual Language Development & Disorders: A Handbook on Bilingualism and Second Language Learning.* Baltimore: Paul H. Brookes.

LI WEI, MILLER, N. & DODD, B., 1997, Distinguishing communicative difference from language disorder in bilingual children. *Bilingual Family Newsletter* 14 (1), 3–4.

STUDY ACTIVITIES

(1) Interview some parents or teachers with a bilingual student who has special needs (preferably gathering a variety of different viewpoints). Define the exact nature of those special needs. Find out the history of that student's education. Ask the parents or teachers what their preferences are for the use of languages in school and if they want their children to be bilingual as a result of schooling. Inquire about the value and use they see in languages for special needs children.

(2) Locate two students who are considered to have 'special needs'. Write a case study of each student, with contrasts and comparisons, to show the history of assessment and school placement. Evaluate the decisions made, indicating particular issues of practical importance.

(3) Find out about assessment practices in schools in your neighborhood. What practices exist at district or school level? What tests are used? What other evidence is gathered? Which individual or team assesses? How do assessment practices impact on bilingual students?

(4) Researching on two or three bilingual students, administer one or more assessment tests, tasks or other devices as allocated by your instructor. Analyze the results and profile the students (a) purely in terms of the test results, then (b) relating the test results to other qualitative information available on the students (e.g. interview the students).

(5) Locate students who could be called 'gifted multilinguals / bilinguals'. What form of giftedness does each person exhibit? (for help with identification see:

http://www.teachstudents.com/product.cfm). Are these students receiving special tuition or in programs for the gifted? What is the link between their language abilities and the use and their giftedness?

Deaf People, Bilingualism and Bilingual Education

CHAPTER 16

Deaf People, Bilingualism and Bilingual Education

INTRODUCTION

The chapter concerns a special group of bilinguals who form their own language minority: Deaf people. Often a neglected language minority, it will be demonstrated that many of the attributes of hearing bilinguals are shared by Deaf bilinguals. Different views about Deaf bilinguals are presented, followed by the debate about which kind of bilingual education is valuable for Deaf students.

DEAF PEOPLE

About 1 in a 1000 people are born each year with varying degrees of deafness and they form a distinct minority. While Deaf people form a numeric minority of the total population, being a minority group refers to dimensions of power and status. Generally, Deaf people have much less power and prestige, lower recognition and leverage than majority groups in society. Deaf people have historically often been regarded as 'problems' within the education system, the social welfare system, among doctors and psychologists, and in the employment market. This is similar to most ethnic minority groups in the world.

The theme of this section is symbolized in the **spelling** of 'deaf' as preferred by Deaf groups. In the above paragraph, the word 'deaf' has been spelt with a lower case 'd'; other times with a capital 'D'. Why? Just as it is accepted that we use a 'U' for Ukrainian and a 'L' for Latino, so a Deaf community, or someone who culturally identifies as a Deaf person, requires a 'D'. A lower case 'd' is reserved to refer to the audiological (non-hearing) condition. As James and Woll (2004) succinctly state: 'To be deaf is to have a hearing loss; to be Deaf is to belong to a community with its own language and culture' (p. 125). Also, rather than talking about 'the deaf', the use of 'Deaf people' is usually preferred. This moves from using an audiological condition solely to define the person, to accenting the humanity of Deaf people. These recent

370

changes mirror a movement in the identity of Deaf people that derives from their 'ethnic revival' (Baker, 1999).

Those who are deaf or have partial hearing are already, or can become, **bilinguals**. There is also a current campaign for Deaf people to become bilingual through learning to sign first of all, followed by literacy in the language of the non-deaf (e.g. English in the US, French in France). The aim of this section is to examine the relationship between bilingualism and Deaf people (Baker, 1999; Cline, 1997). We will find that there are many similarities between hearing bilinguals and current interests in the languages of Deaf communities throughout the world (Brelje, 1999).

DEAF PEOPLE AS BILINGUALS

Deaf individuals can become bilingual through learning to sign first of all, followed by literacy in a language of the non deaf. There are other forms of bilingualism among Deaf people (see Froude (2003) for a case study): for example, those who learn to speak from hearing parents, followed by learning to sign. Others learn to sign first and then learn an oral form of the hearing language. Others learn to communicate by different means, by signs, speaking and writing – a Total Communication approach. Some Deaf people sign when in face-to-face communication, and use a written form (e.g. English) to communicate with members of the Deaf community via fax, textphone, email and letters. The path from signing to majority language literacy is discussed later in this section.

For the moment, it is important to recognize that Deaf people (like many hearing bilinguals) form relatively **disadvantaged language minorities** and have certain things in common with hearing, language minority individuals and groups. Deaf people often have their own language **community** (e.g. Deaf clubs) and will typically wish to identify with that Deaf cultural community (Burch, 2000; Ladd, 2003; James & Woll, 2004). Sometimes, they have been required to attempt to assimilate into the hearing community (Jankowski, 1997; Wrigley, 1996). Those with a hearing loss vary in their identification, sometimes identifying with Deaf people, other times with hearing people, sometimes with both groups with many possible variations.

Ladd's (2003) ground-breaking book defines how deaf communities can create a positive, collective version of 'deafhood' by their own construction and counter-narrative of being a Deaf person. This means being in control of their own destiny rather than being controlled by the colonizing non-Deaf who are in power and 'know best'. Such liberation from 'mission control' requires recognition for sign languages as being official minority languages and of 'Deaf wellness'.

Like many hearing bilinguals, Deaf people tend to use their two languages for **different functions and purposes**. For example, signing may be used to communicate with the Deaf community, while a spoken language or literacy in a majority language is used to communicate with the hearing community. Deaf people have too often been placed in **deficit types of education** that submerge them in the language and culture of hearers rather than an enrichment model where signing is encouraged as the primary language.

TWO VIEWPOINTS ABOUT DEAF PEOPLE

The **first viewpoint** is the **medical view** of deafness. Here deafness is defined as a defect or a handicap that distinguishes 'abnormal' Deaf people from 'normal' hearing persons. Deafness is seen as a condition that needs to be remedied or cured as much as possible. Viewed as a disability, hearing aids and other devices that enhance hearing or the understanding of speech are recommended. Deaf people are expected to become as 'normal' as possible by avoiding purely visual methods of communication such as sign language, and learning spoken language (as much as is viable) to integrate into mainstream society.

One historical conception of Deaf people is that they live in a silent and therefore deprived world. The following poem from William Wordsworth (1770–1850 – extracted from *The Excursion*, Book VII) sums up how hearing people have often conceived of deafness: a world that is silent, tragic and empty, unable to experience the stimulating and wonderful sounds of nature.

> . . . there, beneath
> A plain blue stone, a gentle Dalesman lies,
> From whom, in early childhood, was withdrawn
> The precious gift of hearing. He grew up
> From year to year in loneliness of soul;
> And this deep mountain-valley was to him
> Soundless, with all its streams. The bird of dawn
> Did never rouse this Cottager from sleep
> With startling summons; not for his delight
> The vernal cuckoo shouted; not for him
> Murmured the labouring bee.

This view that Deaf people inhabit a world that is silent and hollow is not a view shared by Deaf people themselves. Sound, or the lack of sound, is not an issue for Deaf people unless they are told by hearing people that it is a problem. Sign language provides a natural form of communication.

To less aware people, **sign language** may seem primitive, rudimentary, and just a simple picture language whereas the spoken language is seen as the natural language for all in the community, including Deaf people. A central aim of education for the Deaf deriving from this viewpoint therefore becomes a mastery of spoken and eventually written language. Such education, and social pressures within the community, aim for the integration or **assimilation** of Deaf people with hearing people. Deaf people existing in separate communities, miming to each other, using sign-speech or having a Deaf culture is not entertained as wholesome or desirable. Thus such educators, professionals and policy-makers see themselves as helping Deaf people to overcome their 'handicap' and to live in the hearing world.

A **second viewpoint** is more in line with that increasingly expressed about hearing bilinguals: one of bilingualism, vitality as a linguistic and cultural minority community, and the need for an enriching dual language education (Baker, 1999; Cline, 1997). Such a viewpoint commences with the assertion that Deaf people can do everything except hear. While there are differences between Deaf and hearing people, these are natural cultural differences, not deviations from a hearing norm. Thomas Gallaudet, the founder of the first Deaf school in the US, argued that Deaf children cannot learn to speak or 'speech-read' well enough to use it as their primary means of communication and education. Signing for Deaf people is natural. As Veditz expressed in 1913, sign language is 'the noblest gift God has given to Deaf people' (quoted in Jankowski, 1997).

Thus, in this second viewpoint, deafness is regarded as a difference, a characteristic that distinguishes 'normal' Deaf people from 'normal' hearing people. Deaf people are regarded as owning sign language which is a full language in itself, grammatically complex and capable of expressing as much as any spoken language. Deaf people are regarded as a linguistic and cultural minority that needs preservation, enrichment and celebration. They **add diversity** and **much color** to the languages of the world

Instead of emphasizing the deficiencies of Deaf people, their **abilities are emphasized**. A strong emphasis is placed on the use of vision as a positive, efficient and full communicative alternative to audible speaking and hearing. Sign language is thus not only equal to spoken language, but also the most natural language for people who are born deaf.

In Deaf children's **education**, the focus is increasingly on language development through signing, and later on bilingualism through literacy in the majority language. It is felt important that maximal language development occurs early on through signing. Early signing enables a focus on the subject matter of the curriculum (rather than learning to speak a majority language). Early use of signing in the classroom can enable Deaf people to perform relatively well in the curriculum. While there tends to be a lack of teachers fluent in sign, ideas about the importance of signing in education are gradually evolving.

In this viewpoint, Deaf people should form, where possible, a **cultural community** of their own. The Deaf have a common language in signing, a culture (see Ladd, 2003) and a set of needs that are distinct from the hearing community (Adams, 1997; James & Woll, 2004). The Deaf community is an important vehicle for the socialization of Deaf and partially hearing people. Deaf adults can provide important role models for Deaf children, either as teachers or in the community. Thus, this second viewpoint supports bilingualism, a Deaf culture and the bilingual education of Deaf people.

Among Deaf people and the partially hearing, there are not only different sub-groupings but also differences of opinion about the appropriate language of the Deaf, the education of the Deaf and their integration into mainstream speaking society. Such differences will now be briefly represented.

Hagemeyer (1992) suggests that there are **nine sub-populations among the deaf** in the United States. Such sub-dimensions refer to deaf culture and not to whether a person is also a member of Hispanic, native American, Asian or any other ethnic group that exists alongside being deaf. The nine groupings are as follows:

(1) Those who use sign language (e.g. American Sign Language – often represented as ASL) as their primary language.
(2) Those who can communicate both in ASL and English.
(3) Those mostly from the hearing impaired group who can communicate primarily through speech.
(4) Adults who became deaf later in life, who were not born deaf and may have acquired speech before deafness. Such people have the experience of hearing normally for a shorter or a longer period and may have speech patterns relatively well embedded before deafness occurred.
(5) The elderly who became hearing impaired or deaf later in life as the result of the aging process.
(6) Those who do not know either ASL nor English, but communicate through gestures, mime and their own signing system. Such people may have been denied access to a Deaf culture, to ASL and to education at an early age.
(7) Those who have residual hearing, perhaps describing themselves as hard of hearing, and who can hear with the use of various aids.
(8) Those people who are deaf and blind. An example is Helen Keller.
(9) Those people who have normal hearing, but because their parents, children, or other members of the family are deaf, they understand signing, or are fully conversant with Deaf culture and integrate with the Deaf community.

DEAF PEOPLE AND SIGN LANGUAGE

Deaf people share a common mode of language. Sign language can be a major marker in defining Deaf community membership. Through sign language, there is the possibility of establishing community culture, a sense of identity, shared meanings and understandings, and a way of life that is owned by the Deaf community (Ladd, 2003). Sign language, once a symbol of oppression, has become transformed into a **symbol of unity**.

> Sign language became the distinction that gave dignity to the Deaf community and transformed the 'abnormal' into the 'distinguished' by creating a reversal of the hierarchy . . . and to define normality on their own terms. (Jankowski, 1997, p. 44)

There are over **200 sign languages** in the world, almost all with no official status or recognition (Ladd, 2003). Sign languages have allowed Deaf people to match the skills and abilities of hearing people: in communication, cognition and having an empowering community. Sign language has enabled Deaf people to create their own sense of 'normality'. Despite the promises of genetic engineering, Paddy Ladd (2003) argues for the 200-plus sign languages as 'a valid and valuable part of creation ... Deaf people have also started to realize that their beliefs in themselves as "beings of Nature" intersects with the newly emerging ecological thinking about bio-diversity' (p. 456). Ladd (2003) argues for sign languages being retained as they are a delightfully visible and beautiful creation.

Sign language is a fully developed, authentic language which allows its users to communicate the same, complete meaning as a spoken language. Sign language is not gesturing. Gesturing is relatively unsystematic, and is used in an *ad hoc* way to express a small number of basic expressions (e.g. pointing to something that is wanted). We all use non-verbal communication to add emphasis to our speech.

In contrast, **signing** is a very extensive, structurally complex, rule-bound, complete means of communication. Sign language can perform the same range of functions as a spoken language, and can be used to teach any aspect of the curriculum. As part of an ethnic awakening, sign language has increasingly been seen as the natural language of Deaf people (Baker, 1999).

There are a wide variety of sign systems in existence. To name but a few: American Sign Language, British Sign Language, Chinese Sign Language, Danish Sign Language, French Sign Language, Russian Sign Language and Thai Sign Language. However, many Deaf people do not use Sign Language. In the US, for example, some have not learnt ASL because their parents were hearing people. Others have been to schools that taught them oralist (speaking) approaches (see later in this chapter). Other Deaf people prefer to use speech rather than sign language in their communities.

A breakthrough occurred in 1983 when the Swedish Government officially recognized Swedish Sign Language as a native language of Sweden. This was a crucial world precedent and a goal for Deaf communities in other countries to achieve political recognition as a distinct social group, rather than, as is sometimes the case, a scattering of individuals.

THE EDUCATION OF DEAF STUDENTS

There are a variety of approaches to the education of Deaf students and those who are hearing impaired (Powers *et al.*, 1999). These approaches range from minimal help to specially designed programs. At its worst, in mainstream 'hearing' education, the deaf may be regarded as having a serious intellectual as well as an auditory 'defect' and classified as remedial. In the history of schooling in most countries, there are plentiful examples of such an insensitive and uncivilized treatment (Deaf Ex-Mainstreamers Group, 2003, 2004).

In contrast, there are **Special Schools and Units** for Deaf students where, for example, the children are taught to thoroughly learn signing first of all, are given a full curriculum mostly through signing, and develop written and/or oral skills in the majority spoken language. Strong (1995) provides a review of nine programs in North America that use American Sign Language (ASL) and English in the classroom, and aim to promote a 'strong' version of bilingualism and biculturalism among Deaf people. English is usually taught as a second language (ESL) with varying emphasis on oracy and literacy in English (Ochse, 2001).

There is considerable discussion, **debate** and development occurring in Deaf education (Knight & Swanwick, 1999; Powers *et al.*, 1999; Powers & Gregory, 1998). There is not total agreement as to preferred methods of approach: for example, using signing and literacy in the spoken language, a **Total Communication approach**, using Sign Supported English or Signed Exact English, the kind of sign language to use, whether to develop oral and/or written skills in the spoken majority language, policies of integration with hearing children and the development of relatively segregated Deaf communities.

[handwritten margin note: not bilingual]

One traditional approach has been to develop any residual hearing with the assistance of hearing aids and to develop speech reading skills and speech production among those deaf and hearing impaired. For most of this century until the 1970s, this was the approach that dominated the education of Deaf students in North America and Europe. Such an approach was based on a belief:

- that Deaf children should integrate into mainstream society;
- that the curriculum could not be taught through sign language but required majority language proficiency;
- that signing as a language was insufficient for full intellectual development;
- that sign language was only a temporary crutch for those for whom the majority spoken language was essential;
- that achievement in the curriculum requires oracy and literacy in the majority language (e.g. English).

A **second approach** developed since the 1970s has been based on the philosophy of Total Communication. All modes of communication are regarded as appropriate for those who are deaf or partially hearing. Simultaneous communication is used that combines auditory input plus visual information, for example, via the use of signed English. However, a Total Communication approach is often assimilationist, aiming to enable Deaf people to communicate with hearing people.

A **third approach** concerns bilingualism for Deaf children through bilingual education (Knight & Swanwick, 1999). This recent initiative is contained in 12 suggestions that are mirrored in spoken bilingual education:

(1) That sign language should be the first language of all Deaf children and be regarded as their primary language.
(2) That sign language should be used to teach curriculum subjects such as science, humanities, social studies and mathematics.
(3) Sign language can be used to teach English or another majority language as a second language. Usually this will be to teach reading and writing skills in English rather than English oracy.
(4) The culture and language of the Deaf community are recognized and validated, with children learning that they belong to the culture of the Deaf. This approach tends to be favored by most but not all the Deaf community, but has

not been favored by many politicians and education professionals who formulate policy and provision.

(5) Such bilingual education for Deaf students is partly based on the research and arguments for an enrichment form of bilingual education for hearing children:

- bilingual education builds on a child's existing linguistic and intellectual resources;
- concepts and knowledge developed in the first language transfer easily to the second language;
- use of a children's heritage language gives pride and confidence in their culture and community;
- a child's self-esteem and self-identity are boosted and not threatened by use of their first language;
- school performance and curriculum attainment is raised when the first language is celebrated rather than devalued;
- the lower achievement of minority language students and Deaf students needs to be addressed by enrichment forms (or 'strong forms') of bilingual education.

(6) Deaf children cannot acquire a spoken language easily or quickly because they have limited hearing abilities. If the curriculum is transmitted in the spoken language, they are expected to learn the content of the curriculum using a level of language not yet acquired. This is analogous to minority language children being expected to operate in submersion education in the language of the majority they have yet to master.

But those students at least have access to the language.

(7) English or another majority language is developed through sign language. Often native sign language teachers will be employed in schools, where possible, to teach and to act as role models.

(8) The acquisition of a sign language should begin as early as possible, ideally soon after birth. Since about nine out of every ten Deaf children are born to hearing parents, this is often difficult, but with such parents being increasingly willing to learn signing, the first language of such Deaf children can be sign language. Current thinking among the Deaf tends to suggest that early signing is preferable in most cases. Parents of Deaf children need to be aware of Deaf communities, of bilingual education for Deaf children to enhance their child's curriculum achievement, and to expect signing as the medium of curriculum delivery plus literacy in the majority language.

(9) It is important to avoid language-delay in Deaf children, as has been found to occur when using auditory approaches and sometimes the Total Communication approach. Curriculum achievement will suffer if there is language delay.

(10) The supply of trained personnel in Deaf bilingual education, staff pre-service education programs, in-service education and certification and funding are often current challenges that are being faced by Deaf educators. These are practical problems to be overcome rather than problems of principles that are insurmountable.

(11) The parents of Deaf children need considerable social and emotional support, information and guidance to help their children become bilingual. In order for cognitive, linguistic, social and emotional development to occur among Deaf children, there needs to be a partnership between school and parents, and between school and community. While there is a considerable debate about the integration of Deaf children into a hearing society, (and their first loyalty being to the Deaf community – see Ladd, 2003), hearing parents of Deaf children need considerable support and sensitivity.

(12) A bilingual Deaf education system may involve team teaching. The Deaf teacher may be a natural model for the acquisition of sign language with a hearing teacher acting as a model for the acquisition of proficiency in a majority language such as English or Spanish. Ideally, both teachers should be bilingual models, being able to communicate in both sign language and the 'hearing' language. Also, both teachers in the team should have a knowledge of Deaf culture, Deaf differences and all the possibilities for Deaf children and adults.

In conclusion, this section on Deaf bilinguals has shown that there are considerable **similarities between hearing bilinguals and Deaf bilinguals**. Many of the justifications for retaining a minority language child's first language and for a 'strong' form of bilingual education for such children also hold for Deaf children. The argument that children from language minorities should become bicultural and culturally pluralistic also tends to hold for Deaf bilinguals. Language minorities are often the poor, low status, low power relations of majority language speakers. Even more so are Deaf people. Deaf bilinguals are often the poor relations of language minority bilinguals. A spoken minority language is often disdained and derided. Even more so is sign language. Achievement and status among Deaf children and adults are often only recognized and granted when speech monolingualism occurs.

When Deaf people come from **language minority communities** they form a minority of a minority (Frederickson & Cline, 2002). The examples of a Latino Deaf person in the US, a Deaf Turk in Germany and a Deaf Bengali in England all represent individuals who are a minority within a minority. They are often the doubly underprivileged and the doubly despised. Where being a member of a language minority is joined by being Deaf, disempowerment, low status, discrimination and low self-esteem may be compounded. Diagnosis may be difficult, delayed or distrusted (Frederickson & Cline, 2002). If many groups of bilinguals are underprivileged, even more so are Deaf bilinguals.

CONCLUSION

This chapter has portrayed the many parallels between Deaf bilinguals and hearing bilinguals. Views about Deaf people vary, with the medical view and a 'competent bilingual' view contrasted in this chapter. Both views link to different beliefs about the education of Deaf students. The discussion of different forms of bilingual education for Deaf students highlight this topic as an important area for discussion and debate.

KEY POINTS IN THE CHAPTER

- Deaf people are frequently bilinguals, with sign language being a natural first language, plus literacy (and oracy) in a second 'hearing' language.
- The medical view of deafness as a problem and the need for assimilation of Deaf people into mainstream society is contrasted to a bilingual/bicultural viewpoint which emphasizes their abilities, community and culture.
- Bilingual education for Deaf students mirrors this bilingual/bicultural viewpoint and reveals that many of the arguments for a 'strong' version of bilingual education hold for Deaf students.

SUGGESTED FURTHER READING

BAKER, C., 1999, Sign language and the deaf community. In J.A. FISHMAN (ed.), *Handbook of Language and Ethnic Identity*. New York: Oxford University Press.

CLINE, T, 1997, Educating for bilingualism in different contexts: Teaching the deaf and teaching children with English as an additional language. *Educational Review* 49 (2), 151–158.

KNIGHT P. & SWANWICK, R., 1999, *The Care and Education of a Deaf Child*. Clevedon: Multilingual Matters.

LADD, P., 2003, *Understanding Deaf Culture: In Search of Deafhood*. Clevedon: Multilingual Matters.

MASHIE, S.N., 1995, *Educating Deaf Children Bilingually*. Washington, DC: Gallaudet University.

STUDY ACTIVITIES

(1) Visit a family with a deaf student and/or a school where there are deaf students. What are the goals in language development? What form of bilingualism exists? What are the attitudes and aspirations of the student and parents/teachers regarding language.

(2) Examine the differences between the education of Deaf people before and after the ethnic revival (see Baker, 1999). Discuss whether a 'Total Communication' approach is justified? Examine this from the viewpoints of the Hearing Community and the Deaf Community. Do you support the full integration of Deaf people into mainstream society or separate Deaf communities, and what part should education play in this preference?

(3) Examine the William Wordsworth poem (see early in the chapter). What experiences does it consider 'normal' and essential, and what characterization of Deaf people does it make? What does the following poem 'My Sign' by Kate Wheat convey in contrast? How does this viewpoint differ from Wordsworth?

> **My Sign**
> The silent hand moves slowly with grace
> then bursts with excitement and quickens the pace
> Images drawn with precision in air

with energetic passion, beauty and flair
Saying so much more than the spoken word
A language of generations, never to be heard
The magnet just drew me, it all seemed to fit
Sparking powerful emotions – the flame had been lit
Just like the return to a well loved home
no longer on the outside feeling alone
No more incomprehension, struggling to see
What people are saying – I've now found the key
I've unlocked the door and found what I'd lost
I'm staying right here whatever the cost!
A new freedom of speech to express what I feel
With meaning and depth, in a language that's real
This is what matters, now I feel I can shine
As I show to the world my language, my sign . . .

Poem by Kate Wheat from 'Between a Rock and a Hard Place' (2003) edited and published by the Deaf EX-Mainstreamers' Group, Ossett, West Yorkshire, WF5 9JN, UK. (http://www.dex.org.uk/). Reprinted with the kind permission of Kate Wheat and the Deaf EX-Mainstreamers' Group.

CHAPTER 17

Bilingualism and Bilingual Education as a Problem, Right and Resource

Introduction

Three Perspectives on Languages
Language as a Problem
Language as a Right
Language as a Resource
United States Language Orientations
The Advance of English in the
United States

Conclusion

CHAPTER 17

Bilingualism and Bilingual Education as a Problem, Right and Resource

INTRODUCTION

Bilingualism is not only studied linguistically, psychologically and sociologically, it is also studied in relationship to **power** and **political systems** in society. The basis of this and the next chapter is that bilingualism and bilingual education, whatever form it takes, cannot be properly understood unless connected to ideologies and politics in society. The activity of a bilingual classroom, and decisions about how to teach minority language children, are not based purely on educational preferences. Rather, calls for and against bilingual education are surrounded and underpinned by basic beliefs about minority languages and cultures, linguistic and cultural diversity, immigration and immigrants, equality of opportunity and equality of outcomes, empowerment, affirmative action, the rights of individuals and the rights of language minority groups, assimilation and integration, desegregation and discrimination, pluralism and multiculturalism, diversity and discord, equality of recognition for minority groups and social cohesion.

For some people, bilingual education will facilitate national cohesion, cultural integration and enable different language communities inside a country to communicate with each other (e.g. Singapore). For other people, bilingual education will create language factions, national disunity, and cultural, economic and political disintegration. Education has thus been conceived alternatively as part of the **solution** and part of the **problem** of achieving national unity, achieving diversity or unity in diversity.

Teachers and education administrators are not only affected by political decisions and processes, they also deliver and implement those decisions and processes. Teachers are part of **language paradoxes** that are daily enacted and temporarily resolved in the classroom: ensuring equality of opportunity for all while celebrating distinctiveness and difference; ensuring that diversity does not become discord; encouraging students to share a common purpose while encouraging colorful variety; developing the dignity of ethnicity while aiding national stability. In multilingual classrooms, teachers have overt and covert beliefs about languages ranging from prohibition to tolerance, limited permission to promotion.

THREE PERSPECTIVES ON LANGUAGES

We begin by considering different assumptions and varying perspectives that are at the root of the politics of bilingualism and bilingual education. Ruiz (1984) proposed three basic perspectives about language around which people and groups vary: **language as a problem, language as a right and language as a resource**. These three different dispositions may be conscious but they are also embedded in the subconscious assumptions of teachers, planners and politicians. Such orientations are regarded as fundamental and related to a basic philosophy or ideology held by an individual.

Language as a Problem

Public discussions of bilingual education and languages in society often commence with the idea of language as causing complications and difficulties. This is well illustrated in the historical debates about the supposed **cognitive problems** of operating in two languages (see chapters 7 and 8). Perceived problems are not limited to thinking. **Personality and social problems** such as split-identity, cultural dislocation, a poor self-image, low self-esteem, alienation, emotional vulnerability and anomie have also sometimes been attributed to bilinguals (Pavlenko, 2005b). David Blunkett, once a UK Home Secretary, suggested that speaking English among Asian immigrants 'helps overcome the schizophrenia which bedevils generational relationships' (reported in the Observer, 15 September, 2002). Bilinguals sometimes have a language anxiety ('schizoglossia') because they feel their language does not compare well with the supposed monolingual standard, and in extreme cases this has led to psychoanalysis and therapy (Pavlenko, 2005b).

The positioning of **bilingual women** has been connected to a deficit framework (Pavlenko, 2001a; Pavlenko & Piller, 2001). For example, women have been posed as less bilingual than men and also more connected to the minority language: 'in many language contact communities, the dominant language, perceived as a power code, is associated with masculinity, and the minority language with domestic values and femininity' (Pavlenko, 2001a, p. 128). This serves as an important reminder that **gender** and languages interact in ways that make bilingualism have different meanings to different groups, including more of a problem for one, more of a benefit for another. For example, in some communities, women may be given less access to a second prestigious language (e.g. English), restricting their bilingualism, access to education, employment or economic advancement. The opposite can also occur.

> **Ngugi wa Thiong'o** spoke Gikuyu as a child, in the fields, in the home, and in the community. However, he was sent to a colonial school that taught solely through the medium of English. The language of education was at variance with the language of his culture. Gikuyu was suppressed, as he vividly recalls: 'In Kenya, English became much more than a language: it was *the* language, and all others had to bow before it in deference. Thus one of the most humiliating experiences was to be caught speaking Gikuyu in the vicinity of the school. The culprit was given corporal punishment – three to five strokes of the cane on bare buttocks – or was made to carry a metal plate around the neck with the inscription: I AM STUPID or I AM A DONKEY. Sometimes the culprits were fined money they could hardly afford' (Ngugi wa Thiong'o, 1985, pp. 114–115).

'Where bilingualism is associated with inequality and social disadvantage, ideologies of language and gender may conspire to put more pressure to be bilingual on the less powerful group, often women' (Pavlenko, 2001a, p. 131).

At a group rather than an individual level, bilingualism is sometimes connected with the potential of national or regional disunity and inter-group conflict. Language is thus viewed by some people as a **political problem**. Part of the 'language-as-problem' orientation is that perpetuating language minorities and language diversity may cause less integration, less cohesiveness, more antagonism and more conflict in society (Parrillo, 1996). This is to be **solved by assimilation** into the majority language (see chapter 18). Such an argument holds that the majority language (e.g. English) unifies the diversity. The ability of every citizen to communicate with ease in the nation's majority language is regarded as the common leveler. Unity within a nation is seen as synonymous with uniformity and similarity. The opposing argument is that it is possible to have national unity without uniformity. Diversity of languages and national unity can co-exist (e.g. Singapore, Luxembourg, Switzerland).

The co-existence of two or more languages is rarely a cause of tension, disunity, conflict or strife. Rather, the history of war suggests that economic, political and religious differences are typically the causes. **Language, in and by itself, is seldom the cause of conflict**. Religious crusades and *jihads*, rivalries between different religions, rivalries between different political parties and economic aggression tend to be the instigators of strife (Otheguy, 1982).

In an internationally comparative research study on causes of civil strife, Fishman (1989) found that language was not a cause of such discord. His analysis involved 130 countries with one outcome (dependent) variable, namely civil strife (defined as the frequency, duration and intensity of conspiracy, internal war and turmoil). Predictor variables concerned measures of linguistic homogeneity / heterogeneity, social cultural, economic, demographic, geographic, historical and political measures. 'The widespread journalistic and popular political wisdom that linguistic heterogeneity *per se* is necessarily conducive to civil strife, has been shown, by our analysis, to be more myth than reality' (Fishman, 1989, p. 622).

Rather, the causes of strife were found to be deprivation, authoritarian regimes and modernization.

Romaine (2000, p. 14) concludes:

> Because languages and dialects are often potent symbols of class, gender, ethnic and other kinds of differentiation, it is easy to think that language underlies conflict. Yet disputes involving language are really not about language, but instead about fundamental inequalities between groups who happen to speak different languages.

In the United States, 'becoming American' has historically been associated with being English-speaking. And that is English-speaking monolingualism and not bilingualism. Bilingualism is seen as a characteristic of the poor, the disadvantaged, and the unassimilated immigrant. **Speaking English** is valued for its perceived link with liberty, freedom, justice and wealth. In consequence, other languages in the US are sometimes seen as linked to terror, injustice, poverty and other societal problems. American ideals are learnt through English. A belief of some is that other languages teach un-American ideas, and therefore must be discouraged in schools (Valdés *et al.*, 2006). Bilingualism, in this US 'problem' viewpoint, will lower the GNP, increase civil strife, foster political and social unrest, and endanger US stability.

A minority language is often connected with the **problems** of poverty, underachievement in school, minimal social and vocational mobility and with a lack of integration into the majority culture. In this perspective, the minority language is perceived as a partial cause of social, economic and educational problems, rather than an effect of such problems. This 'language is an obstacle' attitude is illustrated in the phrase, 'If only they would speak English, their problems would be solved'. The minority language is thus seen as a handicap to be overcome by the school system. One resolution of the problem is regarded as the increased teaching of a majority language (e.g. English) at the expense of the home language. Thus, mainstreaming and transitional bilingual education aim to develop competent English language skills in minority language children as quickly as possible so they are on a par with English first language speakers in the mainstream classroom. In the US, the rise of high stakes testing has suggested that language is a problem since Spanish-speakers have relatively lower test scores. The group label (e.g. Hispanics, Spanish speakers) becomes the perceived cause (Escamilla *et al.*, 2005) such that, for example, Hispanics are immediately associated with lower test performance. Language is wrongly attributed as the origin of under-achievement rather than, for example, the relatively poor economic conditions that surround many such bilinguals.

A **language problem** is sometimes perceived as caused by 'strong' forms of **bilingual education**. Such education, it is sometimes argued, will cause social unrest or disintegration in society. Fostering the minority language and ethnic differences might provoke conflict and disharmony. The response is generally that 'strong' forms of bilingual education will lead to better integration, harmony and social peace. Otheguy (1982, p. 314) replies from the US experience:

> Critics of bilingual education with a concern for civil order and social dishar-
> mony should also concern themselves with issues of poverty, unemployment,
> and racial discrimination . . . In pledges of allegiance, it is liberty and justice –
> not English – for all, that is to keep us indivisible.

'Strong' forms of bilingual education do not create a language problem. Rather, the evidence suggests that developing bilingualism and biliteracy within 'strong' bilingual education leads to higher achievement across the curriculum and therefore a better usage of human resources in a country's economy and less wastage of talent. Fostering self-esteem, self-identity and a more positive attitude to schooling through such bilingual education may also relate to increased social harmony and peace.

Within this 'problem' orientation, there not only exists the desire to remove differences between groups to achieve a common culture. There can be the desire for **intervention** to improve the position of language minorities. 'Whether the orientation is represented by malicious attitudes resolving to eradicate, invalidate, quarantine or inoculate, or comparatively benign ones concerned with remediation and 'improvement', the central activity remains that of problem-solving' (Ruiz, 1984, p. 21).

Language as a Right

A different orientation to that of 'language as a problem' is thinking of language as a **basic, human right**. Just as there are often individual rights in choice of religion, so it is argued, there should be an individual right to choice of language, and to bilingual education (Cummins, 1999b). Just as there are attempts to eradicate discrimination based on color and creed, so people within this orientation will argue that language prejudice and discrimination need to be eradicated in a democratic society by establishing language rights (May, 2001; Skutnabb-Kangas & Phillipson, 1994; Skutnabb-Kangas, 1999b, Skutnabb-Kangas, 2000).

At one level, language rights concern **protection from discrimination**. Many language minorities (e.g. Māori, Native Americans) have suffered considerable discrimination. Skutnabb-Kangas (2000) vividly portrays the oppression of the Kurdish language by torture, imprisonment, confiscation of books, dismissal from jobs, even execution. Ngugi wa Thiong'o (1985) depicts the discrimination that African people have suffered economically, politically, culturally and linguistically from a European colonialist attitude and Americanization. For Ngugi wa Thiong'o, African language rights concern self-regulation and self-determination, and not just non-discrimination.

Kloss (1977, 1998) makes a distinction between **tolerance-oriented rights** and **promotion-oriented rights**. At a promotion-oriented level, language rights are more positive and constructive, asserting the right to use a minority language freely, including in all official contexts. Such rights flourish particularly where there is relatively greater individual and group **self-determination** (Kibbee, 1998; Moses, 2000). However, language rights can sometimes be idealistic rather than realistic. For example, if all majority and minority European languages were used in the

European Parliament, translation and interpretation would be cost prohibitive. In South Africa, it is costly to produce the full range of educational resources (for different ages, curriculum areas, and ability levels) for the 11 official languages. Yet to privilege one or more languages over the others will be at cost to the speakers (e.g. less educational success) and the languages themselves (e.g. language shift).

A 'non-rights', *laissez-faire* approach to minority languages serves to strengthen the already powerful and prestigious languages. Therefore, some form of linguistic rights becomes important for protection and preservation of minority languages, particularly in public domains. Governments typically have less power in economic activities, making rights in government-controlled areas (e.g. law, local government, education) more possible.

Such language rights may be derived from **personal**, human, legal and constitutional rights. Personal language rights will draw on individual liberties and the right to freedom of individual expression (May, 2001). It has also been argued that there may be language rights in **group** rather than individual terms. Languages are rarely spoken in solitude but in pairs, groups and networks. The rights of language groups may be expressed in terms of the importance of preservation of heritage language and culture communities and expressed as 'rights to protection' and 'rights to participation'. This includes rights to some form of self-determination and social justice (May, 2000). May (2001) argues the case for greater ethnocultural and ethnolinguistic self-determination and democracy as nation-states fragment.

Group rights are likely to be contested. What constitutes a group (or identity with a group) for collective linguistic human rights, and defining who is, or is not, a member of a language community is problematic (May, 2000). Also, nation states, and liberalism as a political ideology are both built on the notion of individual citizenship rights and not group rights (May, 2000). Such collective rights may at times clash with individual rights and freedoms (e.g. to bilingual education or not; local employment when a person has the professional but not bilingual competence). Hoffmann (2000) cites the case of Catalonia (Spain) where 'access to white-collar jobs has become increasingly restricted to those with fluency in Catalan . . . amid claims that this situation pushes disproportionately high numbers of non-Catalan speakers into low-status occupations' (p. 435).

A further level of language rights is **international** (Del Valle, 2003). For example, the 1993 United Nations Draft Declaration on the Rights of Indigenous Peoples states in Article 3 that 'Indigenous peoples have the right to self-determination. By virtue of that right they freely determine, their political status and freely pursue their economic, social and cultural development'. Such peoples are also accorded the 'right to establish and control their educational systems and institutions providing education in their own languages (Article 15). The European Charter for Regional or Minority Languages (1992) tends to be more about standards than rights with options (e.g. use of a minority language in pre-school education) from which states can choose (Grin *et al.*, 2003). Education is one of the domains in which the Contracting States undertake to protect and promote minority languages in their territories. Such education can range from being exclusively in the minority language (heritage language education) to dual language education, to bilingual education where there is a demand and sufficient numbers. However, individual countries have often ignored such international declarations or violated the agreements (Skutnabb-Kangas, 2000). Nevertheless, a struggle over language rights is important as it 'constitutes efforts to legitimize the minority group itself and to alter its relationship to the state' (Tollefson, 1991, p. 202). Non-recognition of language human rights (as often occurs among immigrant language minorities) is in itself a form of oppression, domination and injustice (K. Hall, 2002).

The kind of **rights**, apart from language rights, that ethnic groups may claim include: protection, membership of their ethnic group and separate existence, non-discrimination and equal treatment, education and information in their ethnic language, freedom to worship, freedom of belief, freedom of movement, employment, peaceful assembly and association, political representation and involvement, and administrative autonomy. Thus language rights are a component in a wider constellation of rights for minorities.

In the **US**, the rights of the individual are a major part of democracy (Del Valle, 1998). From the expert perspective of a civil rights lawyer, Sandra Del Valle (2003) analyzes how language rights advocates in the US can take much heart from an early history of tolerance, from the absence of a history of monolingualism in the US, the growth and uses of the Fourteenth Amendment of the US Constitution (e.g. equal protection clause), and supportive court cases (e.g. *Meyer vs Nebraska*). Del Valle shows that English-only laws tend to be 'more symbolic than restrictive' (p. 79) but that there has been a 'proliferation of English-only workplace rules enforced by employers of bilingual employees. Unlike state-wide or public English-only laws, these rules can be easily passed, explicitly, consciously, and in writing by an employer without company-wide discussion. . . . that may be challenged in court. (p. 118). Del Valle's (2003) wide-ranging examination of language rights in the US includes interrogation, searches, interpreters, document translation, unfairly removing bilingual jurors and commercial labeling, and serves to demonstrate that linguistic human rights goes much deeper than national and international laws and charters, as such rights are enacted at a local level, in courts, workplaces and not least classrooms

In the US, language rights have a history of being tested in US courtrooms. This is significantly different from European experience where language rights have rarely been tried in law. From the early 1920s to the present, there has been a continuous debate in **US courts of law** regarding the legal status of language minority rights (Del Valle, 2003). To gain short-term protection and a medium-term guarantee for minority languages, legal challenges have become an important part of the language rights movement in the US. The legal battles are not just couched in minority language versus majority language contests. The test cases also concern children versus schools, parents versus school boards, state versus the federal authority (Del Valle, 2003). Whereas minority language activists among the Basques in Spain and the Welsh in Britain have been taken to court by the central government for their actions, US minority language activists have taken the central and regional government to court. Two connected examples will illustrate.

A crucial Supreme Court case in the US was *Brown v. Board of Education* in 1954. Black children were deliberately segregated in southern schools. The Supreme Court ruled that equality in the US educational system was denied to such Black children due to segregation from their peers. Segregation denied equal educational opportunity through a crucial element in classroom learning: peer interaction. The Court decided that education must be made available to all children on equal terms, as guaranteed by the 14th Amendment. A segregationist doctrine of separate but equal education was inherently unequal.

A landmark in US bilingual education was a lawsuit. A court case was brought on behalf of Chinese students against the San Francisco School District in 1970. The case concerned whether or not non-English speaking students received equal educational opportunity when instructed in a language they could not understand. The failure to provide bilingual education was alleged to violate both the equal protection clause of the 14th Amendment and Title VI of the Civil Rights Act of 1964. The case, known as *Lau versus Nichols*, was rejected by the federal district court and a court of appeals, but was accepted by the Supreme Court in 1974. The verdict prohibited English submersion programs and resulted in nationwide 'Lau remedies'. Such remedies reflected a broadening of the goals of bilingual education to include the possible maintenance of minority language and culture. The Lau remedies created some expansion in the use of minority languages in schools, although they rarely resulted in true heritage language, enrichment or maintenance programs. For the purposes of this chapter, the Lau court case is symbolic of the dynamic and continuing contest to establish language rights in the US particularly through testing the law in the courtroom (Crawford, 2004; Del Valle, 2003; Dicker, 2003).

Language rights are not only expressed in lawsuits. Language rights are often expressed at the **grassroots level** by protests and pressure groups, by local action and argument. For example, by such means the *Kohanga Reo* (language nests) movement in New Zealand provides a grassroots-instituted immersion pre-school experience for the Māori people (May, 1996). One example of grass-roots expression of 'language as a right' is the recent Celtic (Ireland, Scotland and Wales) experience. In these countries, it is bottom-up (rather than top-down) 'grassroots' movements that created pre-school playgroups, 'mother and toddler' groups and adult language learning classes for heritage language preservation (I.W. Williams, 2003). Strong activism and non-violent but insistent demands led to the establishment of heritage language elementary schools, particularly in urban areas. Not without struggle, opposition and antagonistic bureaucracy, parents obtained the right for education in the indigenous tongue. Such pressure groups have contained parents who speak the indigenous language, and those who speak only English, yet wish their children to be taught in the heritage language of the area and become thoroughly bilingual.

In North American and British society, no formal recognition is usually made in politics or the legal system to categories or groups of people based on their culture, language or race. Rather the focus is on **individual rights**. The accent is on individual equality of opportunity, individual rewards based on individual merit. Policies of non-discrimination, for example, tend to be based on individual rather than group rights. Language minority groups will nevertheless argue for rewards and justice based on their existence as a definable group in society. Sometimes based on territorial rights, often based on ethnic identity, such **language group rights** have been regarded as a way of redressing injustices to language minorities. This may be a temporary step on the way to full individual citizenship rights as participative democracy tends to favor the equality of each individual rather than group privilege (C.H. Williams, 1998). Alternatively, language minorities may claim the right to some independent power, some measure of decision-making and some guarantee of self-determination. This is typically seen by the majority language group as a step on the road to self-determination, even apartheid (May, 1996).

When language group rights are obtained, 'what limited autonomy that is granted them is usually viewed with a great deal of suspicion, and often with outright opposition, because it may infringe on the individual rights of majority group members' (May, 1996, p. 153). An example is when English monolinguals cannot obtain teaching or local government posts in a bilingual community, and the feel their rights to employment have been infringed.

A note of caution about language rights needs sounding. Liberal words about individual rights can hide preferences for coercion and conformity (Skutnabb-Kangas, 1991). Stubbs (1991) talks of the experience in England with language minorities where government reports

> use a rhetoric of language entitlement and language rights, and of freedom and democracy . . . [which] makes the correct moral noises, but it has no legislative basis, and is therefore empty. There is talk of entitlement, but not of the discrimination which many children face; and talk of equality of opportunity, but not of equality of outcome. (pp. 220–221)

Similarly in the US, when some school administrators express a 'language as right' orientation, they tend to provide the legal minimum in support services for languages minority students.

Language as a Resource

An alternative perspective to 'language as a problem' and 'language as a right', is the idea of language as a **personal, community and regional resource**. Bilingualism can provide an intellectual (see chapter 7), cultural, economic (see chapter 19), social, communication (see chapter 19) and citizenship resource (Lo Bianco, 2001). Bilingualism is seen as an asset, both for communities and for individuals. Languages aid individual participation in public, leisure and private lives. For example, public participation is aided when a person can operate in the different languages of varying groups, fostering inclusion by being able to debate and persuade in the language of the group.

The movement in mainland Europe for increased multilingualism (e.g. in Spain,

Scandinavia, Slovenia) fits into this orientation. Under the general heading of 'language as a resource' also comes regarding minority and lesser used languages as a cultural and social resource. While languages may be viewed in terms of their economic bridge building potential (e.g. foreign trade), languages may also be supported for their ability to build social bridges across different groups (e.g. where there is religious conflict), and bridges for increasing inter-cultural understanding post 9/11.

The recent trend in Europe and North America, for example, has been to attempt to expand **foreign language education**. Second language study is increasingly viewed as an essential resource to promote foreign trade, world influence, even peace. The paradox is that while bilingual education to support minority languages has tended to be undervalued in the US, the current trend is to appreciate English speakers who learn a second language to ensure a continued major role for the US in world politics and the world economy. There is a tendency to value the acquisition of languages while devaluing the language minorities who have them (e.g. Spanish, Arabic, Mandarin and Korean speakers). While integration and assimilation is still the dominant ideology in US internal politics, external politics increasingly demand bilingual citizens.

> On the one hand we encourage and promote the study of foreign languages for English monolinguals, at great cost and with great inefficiency. At the same time we destroy the linguistic gifts that children from non-English language backgrounds bring to our schools. (Ovando, 1990, p. 354)

It is ironic that many US and UK students spend time in school learning some of the very languages that children of immigrants are pressurized to forget. The politics of immigration serve to deny bilingualism; the politics of global trade serve increasingly to demand bilingualism. One result is that, along with the United Kingdom, the 'United States is a veritable cemetery of foreign languages, in that knowledge of mother tongues of hundreds of immigrant groups has rarely lasted past the third generation' (Portes & Hao, 1998, p. 269).

In the US, the idea of language as a resource not only refers to the development of a second language in monolingual speakers. It also refers to the **preservation of languages** other than English. For example, children whose home language is Spanish or German, Italian or Mandarin, Greek or Japanese, Hmong or French have a home language that can be utilized as a resource. One case is the Spanish speakers in the US who together make the US the fourth largest Spanish speaking country in the world. Just as water in the reservoir and oil in the oil field are preserved as basic resources and commodities, so a language such as Spanish, despite being difficult to measure and define as a resource, may be preserved for the common economic, social and cultural good. Suppression of language minorities, particularly by the school system, may be seen as economic, social and cultural wastage. Instead, such languages are a **natural resource** that can be exploited for cultural, spiritual and educational growth as well as for economic, commercial and political gain.

Within the 'language as a resource' orientation, there tends to be the assumption that linguistic diversity does not cause separation nor less integration in society. Rather, it is possible that **national unity and linguistic diversity can co-exist**. Unity and diversity are not necessarily incompatible. Tolerance and cooperation between groups may be as possible *with* linguistic diversity as they would be *unlikely* when such linguistic diversity is repressed.

A frequent debate concerns **which languages** are a resource? The favored languages tend to be those that are both international and particularly valuable in international trade. A lower place is given in the status rankings to minority languages that are small, regional and of less perceived value in the international marketplace. For example, in England, French has traditionally been placed in schools at the top of the first division. German, Spanish, Danish, Dutch, Modern Greek, Italian and Portuguese are the major European languages placed into the second division. Despite large numbers of mother tongue Bengali, Panjabi, Urdu, Gujerati, Hindi and Turkish speakers, the politics of English education had relegated these languages to a lowly position in the school curriculum. Thus a caste system of languages can be created. In the UK, such a caste system is Eurocentric, culturally discriminatory and economically shortsighted, 'allowing languages already spoken in the home and community to be eroded, whilst starting from scratch to teach other languages in schools and colleges' (Stubbs, 1991, p. 225).

To **conclude**: while the three orientations have differences, they also share certain common aims: of national unity, of individual rights, and of fluency in the majority language (e.g. English) being important to economic opportunities. The basic difference tends to be whether monolingualism in the majority language or full bilingualism should be encouraged as a means to achieving those ends. All three orientations connect language with politics, economics, society and culture. Each orientation recognizes that language is not simply a means of communication but is also connected with socialization into the local and wider society, as well as a powerful symbol of heritage and identity. The differences between the three orientations lie in the socialization and identity to be fostered: assimilation or pluralism, integration or separatism, monoculturalism or multiculturalism.

UNITED STATES LANGUAGE ORIENTATIONS

That the three orientations have common aims as well as vital differences is illustrated in the case of the US. The US has long been a willing receptacle of peoples of many languages: German, French, Yiddish, Polish, Italian, Irish, Greek, Russian, Welsh, Arabic, Mandarin and Cantonese Chinese, Korean, Japanese and particularly Spanish to name just a few examples. Bull *et al.* (1992) portrayed the situation as follows:

> Cultural and linguistic differences have been a source of strength and controversy in the USA since its founding. Indeed, this country's founding and much subsequent US history can be seen as a continuing search for unity in diversity, for *e pluribus unum*, especially among its residents of European extraction. What could unite the New York Dutch, the Pennsylvania German, and the Virginia English; the Massachusetts Puritan, the Pennsylvania Quaker, the

Maryland Catholic, and the Virginia Anglican; the Yankee trader, the northern farmer, and the southern plantation owner? How could the USA assimilate and capitalize upon its Norwegian, Irish, Russian, Italian, Polish, and Jewish immigrants? And more recently, what relationship could white Anglo majorities establish with formerly disenfranchised and economically marginalized African-American, Chinese, Japanese, Native American, and Latino minorities? (Bull *et al.*, 1992, p. 1)

The receptacle of in-migration was transformed into a **melting pot** to assimilate and unify. The dream became an integrated United States with shared social, political and economic ideals. Quotes from two US Presidents illustrate this 'melting pot' attitude. Roosevelt in 1917 urged all immigrants to adopt the English language:

It would be not merely a misfortune but a crime to perpetuate differences of language in this country . . . We should provide for every immigrant by day schools for the young, and night schools for the adult, the chance to learn English; and if after say five years he has not learned English, he should be sent back to the land from whence he came. (quoted in Gonzalez, 1979)

President Reagan's view in the late 1980s was that it is 'absolutely wrong and against American concepts to have a bilingual education program that is now openly, admittedly dedicated to preserving their native language and never getting them adequate in English so they can go out into the job market and participate' (quoted in Crawford, 2004, p. 120; from the *Democrat Chronicle*, Rochester, 3 March, 1981, p. 2a). This melting pot attitude has continued (e.g. the No Child Left Behind legislation of 2001).

The Advance of English in the United States

Within the US, basic differences in 'language orientation' are especially exemplified in the movement to make English the official rather than the *de facto* national language (Crawford, 2000, 2004; Dicker, 2000, 2003; Wiley & Lukes, 1996; McGroarty, 1997; Schmidt, 2000; Del Valle, 2003). The political debate over the place of English in the US illustrates how languages can be alternatively seen as a problem, right or resource.

At the federal level, there is no reference to language in either the 1776 Declaration of Independence or the 1789 United States Constitution, the two founding documents of the US. However, in the last 25 years, there have been proposals to add amendments to the Constitution that would name English as the official language. Considerable debate about Official English or English-only legislation has occurred (Dicker, 2003).

In April 1981, Senator S.I. Hayakawa, a Californian Republican, proposed an English Language Amendment to the US Constitution. This aimed at making English the official language of the US so, he said, to develop further participative democracy and unification. The Amendment failed but it helped spawn the 'English-Only' or 'Official English' movement in the US (which includes the 'US English' and the 'English First' organizations). US English was founded in 1983 by Senator Hayakawa and John Tanton who was particularly interested in restrictions on immigration and population control. In 1987, a more militant group – **English First** – joined US English in lobbying for the total supremacy of English in education, voting and administration.

The English-only movement argues that **English** is the social glue that bonds diverse Americans and overcomes differences. English is therefore best learnt early (e.g. by mainstreaming) to counteract the tendency for immigrants to refuse to learn English. If heritage languages are allowed to flourish, there will be conflict, separatism and inter-group hostility (Crawford, 2000).

As Barker and Giles (2002) found in one of the few empirical studies of the English-only movement, Anglo-Americans supporting the English-only position believe that Latino vitality (e.g. economic and political power and status) is growing in the US as Anglo vitality is decreasing. In this research, attachment to a traditional conceptualization of 'good Americans' was connected to an English-only position. Less contact with the Spanish language was associated with greater support for the English-only position. Those with lower levels of education were more likely to support such a position as were those who were blue-collar or unemployed. Such groups may perceive Latinos as more of a **threat** to their chances of enhancement and improvement. This suggests that the roots of English-only may lie not only in personal **insecurity** and intolerance of difference but also in perceived threats to power, position and privilege, plus a fear of difference and competition for perceived scare resources (Barker *et al.*, 2001).

For English-only advocates, **bilingual education** is seen as promoting separatist language communities, a division in US society, an indifference to English, and making English speakers strangers in their own localities (Crawford, 2003). Instead, the English language should unite and harmonize. Learning English early in school, learning curriculum content through English would produce, it is claimed, integrated neighborhoods. Thus, US English's preferred immigrant is someone who learns English quickly as well as acquiring US customs and culture, acquires skills that are useful in the economic prosperity of the country, works hard and achieves the US dream. For Imoff (1990), bilingual education only serves to destroy rather than deliver that dream.

The movement for English as the proclaimed US national language has not been purely about English and national unity. Racism, bigotry, paranoia, xenophobia, white superiority and dominance have also been present. A Memorandum by Dr John Tanton, when Chairman of US English, revealed the darker side: 'As Whites see their power and control over their lives declining, will they simply go quietly into the night? Or will there be an explosion?' (quoted in Crawford, 2004, p. 136). This Memorandum went on further to pose perceived threats from Latinos: bribery as an accepted culture, Roman Catholicism as cultivating church authority rather than national authority, the non-use of birth control and fast population growth of Latinos, high drop-out rates in school and low educability. This hints at **scapegoating**, the displacement of fears about social, political and economic positioning onto language, and using English as a means of asserting cultural and economic superiority (Dicker, 2000, 2003).

While the debate about integration and pluralism will be examined in the next chapter, there is little disagreement about certain desirable outcomes between the positions of the English-only group and the '**English-plus**' pro-bilingual response in the US (e.g. both agree about children becoming fluent in English). The difference is in the route to its achievement. For the English-only group, English language skills are best acquired through English monolingual education. For the English-plus group, skills in the English language can be successfully fostered through 'strong' forms of bilingual education (Feinberg, 2002). Both groups appear to acknowledge that full English proficiency is important in opening doors to higher education, the economy and the occupational market. Full proficiency in the majority language is usually equated with a route to equality of educational and vocational opportunity.

However, as Crawford (2003, p. 7) suggests, the danger of English-plus is 'plus what'? If 'plus what' means 'the priority of bilingual education was not to teach English but to maintain other languages', it fails to capture the aspirations of children and parents, and is a red rag to the political English-only bull. The goal of bilingualism must be strongly identified as meaning high competence in English and not just in a heritage language. Strong forms of bilingual education can deliver that agenda.

As chapter 12 shows, there is considerable evidence to support 'strong' versions of **bilingual education** and hence for the 'English plus' position. Such evidence supports the use of the home minority language in the classroom at no cost to majority language competence. Achievement across the curriculum, achievement in subjects as diverse as science and social studies, mathematics and foreign language learning would not seem to suffer but be enhanced by 'strong' forms of bilingual education. Research on the cognitive effects of bilingualism supports the ownership of two languages to enhance rather than impoverish intellectual functioning.

However, the dominant majority often see bilingual education as creating national disunity rather than unity, disintegration rather than integration. The frequent **criticism of bilingual education** is that it serves to promote differences rather than similarities, to separate rather than integrate. In the US, the expressed public viewpoint tends to be for unity, integration and assimilation of immigrant, language minority communities. Indeed, the strongest arguments for bilingual education on cognitive and educational grounds may well fail unless a strong argument can be advanced for linguistic and cultural pluralism.

CONCLUSION

For schools, whether the surrounding community and society sees language as a problem, right or resource affects the role of languages in the school. When a language as a problem attitude is dominant, bilingual education is likely to be discouraged. Language rights may give bilingual education a protected entitlement to exist. The language as a resource orientation may more maximally allow bilingual education to flourish. Thus these three orientations have different outcomes for bilinguals and bilingual education.

But political debates about bilingual education go deeper into politics and personal arguments. Does bilingual education lead to greater or lesser tolerance, a common or a separate identity, a sense of anomie or an ability to belong to two cultures simultaneously? Are language minority children taught (rightly or wrongly) to be in conflict or at peace with the majority? Is bilingual education the arena for a power struggle between majority and minority? These questions are examined in the next chapter through the central debate on assimilation and pluralism.

KEY POINTS IN THE CHAPTER

- Three perspectives on languages depict variations among people: language as a problem, right or resource.
- The 'language as a problem' is currently a prevalent political and mass media viewpoint in the US where the cultural assimilation of immigrants is sought, but not necessarily the economic assimilation.
- Language rights can be individual, group and international. In the US, rights are tested in law courts.
- The place of English in the US is frequently contested, with English-only groups asking for English as the sole official language and the removal of bilingual education.

SUGGESTED FURTHER READING

CRAWFORD, J., 2000, *At War With Diversity*. Clevedon: Multilingual Matters.
CRAWFORD, J., 2004, *Educating English Learners: Language Diversity in the Classroom*. Los Angeles: Bilingual Education Services.
DEL VALLE, S., 2003, *Language Rights and the Law in the United States: Finding Our Voices*. Clevedon: Multilingual Matters.
DICKER, S.J., 2003, *Languages in America: A Pluralist View* (2nd edn). Clevedon: Multilingual Matters.
HALL, J.K. & EGGINGTON, W.G. (eds), 2000, *The Sociopolitics of English Language Teaching*. Clevedon: Multilingual Matters.
MAY, S., 2001, *Language and Minority Rights: Ethnicity, Nationalism and the Politics of Language*. London: Longman.
SKUTNABB-KANGAS, T., 2000, *Linguistic Genocide in Education – or Worldwide Diversity and Human Rights*. Mahwah, NJ: Erlbaum.

STUDY ACTIVITIES

(1) Among student groups, teachers in schools or in language communities, find out about different political viewpoints on language. Are there differences between different groups? Or are there more differences within those groups than between those groups?

(2) Follow one particular event regarding language in education. If possible,

examine how that event is treated in two different languages (e.g. a Spanish newspaper and in an English language newspaper). What differences are there of interpretation and perception?

(3) Within a specific community, locate different interest groups and different sociocultural or socioeconomic groups of people. For example, compare working-class and middle-class viewpoints on bilingual education. How much do you think these varying viewpoints, if they exist, relate to home, social, economic, political and educational differences between the groups? Are there similarities as well as differences?

Bilingualism and Bilingual Education: Ideology, Identity and Empowerment

CHAPTER 18

Bilingualism and Bilingual Education: Ideology, Identity and Empowerment

INTRODUCTION

Politicians, policy-makers and the public have varying agendas about languages. Some wish to assimilate different language groups to a homogeneous society of monolinguals, others are keen to retain linguistic diversity and pluralism. Some language minorities dream of self-sustainability and self-determination. Others aspire to internationalism (e.g. Europeanization) and globalism. Bourhis (2001b) proposes four ideologies on a continuum from pluralism, civic, assimilation to ethnist. These four ideologies will be briefly introduced and then assimilation and pluralism will be explored in more detail.

IDEOLOGY AND BILINGUALISM

Pluralist ideology tends to assert an individual's liberty to own, learn and use two or more languages (e.g. in school, work). This right is then supported by those in power by promotion-oriented language policies (Wiley, 2002). Given that a language minority pays taxes, then 'it is equitable that state funds be distributed to support the cultural and linguistic activities of both the majority and the minority group' (Bourhis, 2001b, p. 11). Schools, the judiciary and civil administration will expect to operate bilingually, where reasonable, and not in opposition to national coherence and unity. Canada's Official Languages Act (1969, 1988) and Multiculturalism Act (1988) reflect such a pluralism ideology.

    Civic ideology expects language minorities to adopt the public values of the politically dominant majority while allowing freedom in the private values of individuals (e.g. to a minority language and culture). But no public funding of the language minority is expected. Instead civic ideology 'is characterized by an official state policy of non-intervention and non-support of the minority languages and cultures' (Bourhis, 2001b, p.12). This is considered as a tolerance-oriented language policy (Wiley, 2002).

Assimilation ideology tends to argue that there may be some areas of private values where the state has a right to intervene. Language is such an area. Immigrants are expected to abandon their heritage language. This may be voluntarily and gradually across generations, or speedily by state regulation in public domains (e.g. exclusion of minority languages in schools). The politically and economically dominant group often has a vested interest in preserving its privileged position by asserting that its majority language is a symbol and creator of a unified and integrated nation. In contrast, minority languages and cultures are seen as potentially divisive and conflictive, working against national loyalty and allegiance by producing factions.

Ethnist ideology encourages or forces language minorities to give up their language and culture and adopt that of the dominant group. It also attempts to prevent or exclude such minorities from assimilating legally or socially even when such individuals seek cultural, linguistic and economic assimilation. The ideology is exclusive and defines who can be a rightful member of the dominant group or a legitimate citizen. For example, only certain racial groups are given full legal status as determined by 'blood', birth and kinship. Political, economic and social marginalization may result. Wiley (2002) terms this a repression-oriented language policy. As an extreme, ethnist ideology results in a policy of exclusion, expulsion, apartheid, ethnic cleansing, even genocide.

This chapter now considers assimilation as a dominant ideology in many countries, especially where there has been immigration.

ASSIMILATION

The social and political questions surrounding bilingual education tend to revolve around two contrasting ideological positions. **Assimilation** is a belief that cultural groups should give up their heritage cultures and take on the host society's way of life. In contrast, pluralism believes that these groups should maintain their heritage cultures in combination with the host culture. In the US example, Schmidt (2000, p. 4) argues that 'Pluralists favor using the state to enhance the presence and status of minority languages in the United States, while assimilationists seek state policies that will ensure the status of English as the country's sole public language.'

Assimilation has been a favored response to the considerable **immigration** in the US. Currently, some 28.4 million (10%) of US residents were born outside the US (2000 Census). The immigration population in the US is thus large, but compared to 42% in Israel, 41% in Hong Kong and 16% in Canada (Feinberg, 2002), it is not the highest proportion in the world. The United States bargain with immigrants has been: come to the economically prosperous land, start a new and better life, but assimilate and become 'American'. Assimilation means giving up the native tongue and 'swat the hyphenated' dual identity. Cultural unity and national solidarity are seen as achieved through assimilation. Three generation shift from native language to English (see chapter 4) among immigrant families delivers this. The transition to English monolingualism and loss of bilingualism is swift and successful (Portes & Hao, 2002).

The assimilationist viewpoint is pictured in the idea of a **melting pot** (Dicker, 2003). Zangwill's play '*The Melting Pot*' (1914) introduced the idea of diverse immigrant elements being merged to make a new homogenized whole. 'Into the Crucible with you all! God is making the American'. The idea of the melting pot immediately throws up two different perspectives. First, there is the idea that the final product, for example the US American, is made up by a contribution of all the cultural groups that enter the pot. The cultural groups melt together until the final product is a unique combination. No one ingredient dominates. Each cultural group makes its own contribution to the final product. However, this is not the usual view associated with the melting pot. So second, the melting pot often means cultural groups giving up their heritage culture and adopting that of the host culture.

A strong assimilationist ideology is particularly created when it is believed that: immigrants have no or few employment skills, need welfare and are a tax burden; that immigrant labor depresses wages and makes residents unemployed; immigrants increase crime and inter-group hostility; and they constitute a security hazard as they may be terrorists (Feinberg, 2002).

An assimilationist perspective is based on equality of opportunity and a meritocracy that enables each **individual** to have a fair chance of economic prosperity. Such a view argues that the separate existence of different racial and cultural groups prevents such equality occurring. When the emphasis is on individuality in terms of rights, freedom, effort and affluence, the argument for assimilation is that language **groups** should not have separate privileges and rights from the rest of society. Advantage and disadvantage associated with language minority groups must be avoided so individual equality of opportunity can prevail.

> The assimilationist vision yearns for and insists upon a national community that is monolingual and monocultural, in which linguistic diversity does not threaten to engulf us in a babel of discordant sounds signifying a shredded social fabric. The pluralist vision, in contrast, understands the United States as an ethnically diverse and multilingual society with a tragic past of racialized ethnocultural domination, but standing now at a point of historic opportunity to realize – through a policy of multicultural and linguistic pluralism – the promise of its ongoing project of democratic equality. (Schmidt, 2000, p. 183)

Assimilationist ideology is an umbrella term under which a variety of types of assimilation may occur: cultural, structural, marital, identificational, attitudinal, behavioral, social and civic (Gordon, 1964). Linguistic assimilation has two broad goals: deculturation to achieve subordination and acculturation to promote absorption (Wiley & Wright, 2004). An important distinction is between **economic-structural assimilation and cultural assimilation** (Skutnabb-Kangas, 1977). Some immigrant and minority group members may wish to assimilate culturally into the mainstream society. Cultural assimilation refers to giving up a distinct cultural identity, adopting the mainstream language and culture. Many immigrant and indigenous language minorities wish to avoid such cultural assimilation. However, economic-structural assimilation may be sought by such language minorities. Such assimilation refers to equality of access, opportunities and treatment. For example, equal access to jobs, goods and services, equality in voting rights and privileges, equal opportunities and treatment in education, health care and social security, law and protection, may be desired by language minorities. Therefore, structural incorporation tends to be more desired and cultural assimilation more resisted (Schermerhorn, 1970; Paulston, 1992).

Assimilation may be explicit, implied or concealed (Tosi, 1988). For example, **explicit assimilation** occurs when language minority children are required to take monolingual education solely in the majority language (e.g. mainstream education in the US). The coercive assimilation of Native Americans by taking tribal lands and forcefully placing children in English-only boarding schools is another example (Wiley & Wright, 2004). **Implied assimilation** is when such children are diagnosed as having 'special needs' and are offered compensatory forms of education (e.g. Sheltered English and Transitional Bilingual Education in the US). **Concealed assimilation** may be found, for example, in some types of multicultural education program where language minorities may be instructed in racial harmony, national unity, and individual achievement using majority language criteria to gauge success. Such a program is designed to achieve hegemony and ethnic harmony (Tosi, 1988).

Since there are a **variety of forms of assimilation**, measuring the extent to which assimilation has occurred is going to be difficult. Is assimilation measured by segregation and integration in terms of housing of immigrants, by their positions within the economic order, by the extent of intermarriage between different cultural groups or by the attitudes they exhibit? Assimilation is thus multidimensional and complex (Skutnabb-Kangas, 2000). Assimilation is neither easily defined nor easily quantified. Assimilationists may also have differing views. One example will illustrate. A few assimilationists may accept that school students should maintain their home language and culture. However, they would argue that this is the **responsibility of the home** or the local language community and not the school. Other assimilationists desire the abandonment of the minority language and culture.

In longitudinal (10 year) **research on assimilation**, Portes and Hao (2002) found that only 27% of 5000 second generation immigrant students in South Florida and Southern California remained fluent bilinguals. The march to English as the dominant or only language was apparent. Using measures of family solidarity, intergenerational conflict, ambition and self-esteem, their careful statistical analyses show that fluent bilinguals had the most positive profiles. For example, those fluent in English and their parents' native language were 8% more likely to hold higher educational aspirations. Those children who retained their native language without learning English showed high family solidarity, but had much lower self-esteem and ambition. Portes and Hao's (2002) conclusion is that such second generation immigrants who do not become fluent bilinguals are deprived of 'a key social resource at a critical juncture in their lives' (Portes & Hao, 2002, p. 23). Indeed, a complete transition to English monolingualism in the US is not the most desirable outcome. Assimilation that produces English language monolingualism has hidden costs for family relationships, personality development and adaptation.

PLURALISM

With an increased accent on **ethnicity** since the 1960s, the assumptions of assimilation have been challenged and a 'new ethnicity' born (see Fishman, 1999). Ideologies that surround the terms **'integration'**, **'ethnic diversity'**, **'pluralism'** and **'multiculturalism'** challenged the assimilationist philosophy. The picture of the melting pot has been contrasted with alternative images: the patchwork quilt, the tossed salad, the linguistic mosaic and the language garden. One popular metaphor is the salad bowl, with each ingredient separate and distinguishable, but contributing in a valuable and unique way to the whole. A different 'integration' metaphor, favored in Canada, is the linguistic mosaic, with different pieces joined together in one holistic arrangement. But such pictures are too simplistic.

A pluralist approach assumes that different language groups can live together in the same territory in relative harmony and without the unjust domination of one group by another. An atmosphere of mutual understanding and tolerance is the ideal (Parrillo, 1996).

> 'Pluralists also argue that individual bilingualism is not only possible but desirable in that it facilitates cultural enrichment and cross-cultural understanding. By combating distrust and intolerance toward linguistic diversity, pluralists hope to create a climate of acceptance that will promote greater status equality between ethnolinguistic groups and therefore a higher level of national unity.' (Schmidt, 2000, p. 62/63)

Assimilationists argue that linguistic pluralism, rather than promoting harmony, leads to ethnic enclaves that cause inequalities between groups and particularly create ethnic conflict. For such people, linguistic assimilation provides the social, political, and economic integration necessary for equality of opportunity and political harmony.

In reality, there are often large status differences between languages in a society. Where one language is associated with power, wealth and prestige, the tendency of individuals is to choose the language of economic and social mobility. The economic dice is often so loaded against pluralism such that forced assimilation is a superfluous idea. Assimilation often happens without external pressure.

Schmidt (2000) argues that the root of the assimilation/pluralism issue is not language but **identity** (see later), of which language is one component: 'ultimately the language policy debate in the United States is not about language as such but about what kind of political community we are and wish to be. It is, in short, centered in identity politics' (p. 183).

Schmidt (2000) also suggests that apart from assimilation and pluralism, there are two other approaches to language policy: total domination by the language majority group and the exclusion of minority language (e.g. apartheid in the old South Africa), and confederation (as in Switzerland, Belgium and India – see Baker & Jones, 1998).

LANGUAGE POLICY ALTERNATIVES

In the context of the US, Schmidt (2000) considers three language policy alternatives. He rejects the assimilationist argument as it ignores the legacy of racialized ethnic injustice and misconstrues the nature of relationships between individual identity, culture, the state, and equality of opportunity. He argues that the assimilationist argument also serves to maintain the privileged position of white, native English speakers.

While favoring a **pluralist alternative**, Schmidt (2000) finds obstacles to its complete acceptance. He argues that the kind of social integration that is envisioned by pluralism (i.e. individualist and voluntarist) is likely to perpetuate the very social inequalities between language groups that it seeks to overcome. He argues that a policy of linguistic pluralism is insufficient to achieve social and economic justice for language minority communities. Pluralists argue for individual choice in language and culture, but there is no equal choice as there is no equal starting point or level playing field. Without an equal starting point, the context of choice for individuals is constrained by numerous unequal circumstances for which language minorities bear no responsibility. Thus Schmidt (2000) is pessimistic about the reality of outcomes for a pluralist position when there is free choice. The language of power in the US is English, so individuals will typically choose English in pursuit of their own advantage. Social mobility and economic advance are pragmatically unlikely from a pluralist position, however strong the intellectual arguments.

> Assimilationists are unrealistic because their ideology posits a monocultural and monolingual country that does not exist in the real world; more importantly, a consequence of its unrealistic assumptions is the continued unjust subordination of language minority groups by the privileged Anglo, European-origin majority. Pluralists too are unrealistic in that they assume that an egalitarian society of multiple cultural communities can be achieved through a combination of individualistic rights-based free choice measures and moral exhortations to Anglos to respect linguistic and cultural diversity. (Schmidt, 2000, p. 209)

In Quebec, one political answer has been to seek to establish a separate French language community. This is an unlikely alternative for the US, that is the establishment of non-English-dominant territories to reproduce themselves and flourish. Such language communities require territory of their own to withstand the strong pressure to shift to English in North America. Such a linguistic territory might give a minority language status and avoid marginalization and stigmatization. The US already has such linguistic territories in the island commonwealth of Puerto Rico and in the American Indian reservations on the mainland. If this option was followed, it would give regional autonomy to areas such as southern California, northern New Mexico and south Texas.

The establishing of non-English-dominant territories in the US is seemingly not a politically viable option partly because most urbanized US areas have multiple groups of language minorities and thus a complex linguistic mosaic. Another alternative is an enhanced pluralist language policy in the US that aims for pluralistic integration – Schmidt's (2000) first-choice option that is also supported by May (2001) who argues for language minority group rights that retain within them the protection of individual liberties.

The two positions of assimilation and pluralism differ in such fundamental ideological ways that simple solutions and **resolutions** are virtually impossible. When evidence for the maintenance of minority languages and cultures is produced, assimilationists are likely to argue that attitudes and behavior are still in the process of change. That is, assimilationists will argue that, over time, people will move away from minority cultural maintenance and prefer the majority language and culture. Assimilationists tend to believe that bilingualism and biculturalism are temporary and transient, and lead eventually to a preferable unifying monolingualism.

When evidence favors assimilation having taken place in society (e.g. by the second or third generation after in-migration), pluralists will tend to argue in two different ways. First, that the change towards assimilation has only occurred on certain dimensions (e.g. language rather than economic assimilation). Second, that sometimes the wheel turns full circle. Revival and resurrection in future generations may occur in response to repression and renouncement by previous generations.

The **difference between assimilationists and pluralists** is rooted in basic human ideologies and motives, making resolution all the more difficult. Any such resolution of the assimilation versus pluralism debate is strongly affected by the **economic reward system**. Both assimilation and pluralism can be promoted and defended as ideas by the need to earn a living and the desire to acquire or increase affluence. Assimilation may be chosen to secure a job, to be vocationally successful and to achieve affluence. The minority language and culture may be left behind in order to prosper in the majority language community. At the same time, language planning can be used to ensure that there are jobs and promotion within the minority language community, as discussed in chapter 3.

Resolution of assimilation versus pluralism is sometimes avoided. The dominant group in society may, at times, not prefer the assimilation of minority groups. Such minority groups may not be permitted to assimilate, thus keeping their members in poorly paid employment. Such a minority group is then exploited by the dominant group. The economic interests of the majority group can be served by **internal colonialism** rather than assimilation (e.g. economically isolating or manipulating an indigenous minority language group for majority group advantages).

Resolution is often **pragmatic** rather than philosophical. Often, being fluent in the majority language is an employment necessity, and this can promote assimilation. To obtain work and compete with members of the majority group, a minority language person typically has to function in the majority language. Bilinguals may also perceive that they can function economically both in their minority group and with the dominant group. That is, they have the ability to be economically viable in either language community and form a bridge between those two communities.

However, becoming bilingual by learning the majority language is no guarantee of economic improvement. Otheguy (1982, p. 306) provides a salutary warning from the US experience.

> English monolingualism has meant little in terms of economic advantages to most blacks and to the masses of poor descendants of poor European immigrants. Hispanics who now speak only English can often be found in as poor a state as when they first came. English monolingualism among immigrants tends to follow economic integration rather than cause it.

Two opposing views – assimilation and pluralism – have so far been discussed. John Edwards (1985) indicates that **other positions** are possible. It is possible to participate in mainstream society and maintain one's minority language and culture. For many individuals, there will be both a degree of assimilation and a degree of preservation of one's heritage. Total assimilation and total isolation may be less likely than some accommodation of the majority ideology within an overall ideology of pluralism; cultural maintenance within partial assimilation. Within multiculturalism and pluralism, an aggressive, militant pluralism may be seen as a threat to the social harmony of society. Instead, a more liberal pluralistic viewpoint may allow both membership of the wider community and an identification with the heritage cultural community.

ASSIMILATION AND IMMIGRANTS

The **political debate** over assimilation and pluralism is fundamental to understanding language minorities and is ever-present in language debates (J. Edwards, 1994b; Takaki, 1993; Fishman (ed.), 1999; McKay & Wong, 2000). A re-emphasis on personal endeavor, individual striving for success, a lessening of reliance on welfare has been joined by ethnic conflicts (e.g. in Bosnia, Croatia, Serbia, Chechnya). This has led to increased arguments and disputes about the merits of assimilation and pluralism. But such debates need placing in their historical context, particularly where immigrants are concerned.

The expectation was that **immigrants** into the US, Australia, Canada, Germany and the UK, for example, would be pleased to have escaped political oppression or economic disadvantage and be jubilant to embrace equality of opportunity and personal freedom. The expectation was that an individual would be pleased to give up their past identity and make a commitment to a new national identity. Yet heritage culture and cultural identity have persisted, resisted and insisted. Assimilation has not always occurred. Is this deliberate or unintended, desired or unwelcome?

Assimilation may be sought by immigrants. Many wish to assimilate, but come to reside in segregated neighborhoods and segregated schools. Thus desired assimilation can be prevented by social and economic factors outside the wishes of the immigrants. Some groups of immigrants may wish to be categorized as US citizens, but are categorized and treated by mainstream society as different, separate, 'foreigners', immigrants and non-US. The conditions under which immigrants live may create the negative labels and social barriers that enforce non-integration. The result may be the prevention of assimilation and integration with a consequent need to embrace some form of multiculturalism for survival, security, status and self-enhancement.

Veltman (2000) has shown empirically from US census data that US immigrants **learn English** quite rapidly, many adopting English as their primary and preferred language, even abandoning use of their mother tongue (e.g. Scandinavians, Germans), and rearing their children solely in English. All language minorities want to learn English, although Spanish, Chinese and Greek immigrants are relatively more likely to maintain bilingualism. Thus repressive measures to assimilate immigrants or initiatives to promote English assimilation in schools are not needed. There is an intrinsic motive in immigrants to learn English rapidly and well. Immigration does not pose a threat to the dominance of English in the US or UK.

> The desire of immigrants in all minority language groups to learn English and make this language their own is sufficiently high to produce the kind of outcome that most Americans cherish, that is, that immigrants become English-speaking people. I unequivocally demonstrate that rates of language shift to English are so high that all minority languages are routinely abandoned, depriving the USA of one type of human resource that may be economically and politically desirable both to maintain and develop. (Veltman, 2000, p. 58)

If the linguistic assimilation of immigrants occurs so easily, what happens to their identity? To begin to answer this, the nature of identity needs exploring.

IDENTITY

Our individual identity is **not fixed**, given or unitary. Identity is socially created and claimed through language, through an intentional negotiation of meanings and understandings. We speak a language or languages and it often identifies our origins, history, membership and culture. But that identity is daily authored, imagined, re-constructed and displayed as we translate social experiences and take on multiple roles and identities (Norton, 2000). For Heller (1999b), 'language has become the principal characteristic differentiating groups which clearly think of themselves as distinct' (p. 144). Our identity is conveyed in our language, in our expressions and engagements, predilections and preferences. **Language** is a symbol of our identity, conveying our preferred distinctiveness and allegiance (e.g. Irish). However, language does not by itself define us. It is one feature or marker amongst many that makes up our constructed, shifting and hybrid identity (May, 2000).

We do not own an identity so much as hybrid and **multiple identities**. Our social constructions of our gender, age, ethnicity, race, dress, nationality, region (e.g. county, state), locality, group membership (e.g. religion, politics), socioeconomic class, for example, provide us with a host of complementary, diverse, interacting, ever-changing, negotiated identities. A girl can speak English and Spanish, be a Moslem, Democrat, see herself as American, San Francisco Californian and Mexican, with identity as a teenager and trombonist, a school drop-out and lesbian. As situations change, so our identities are re-framed, developed, sometimes challenged, sometimes in conflict. We do not establish our identities by ourselves but through social comparison, labeling by others, dialogue within ourselves and with others, and through the experience of ever-varying contexts.

No one is purely their labels. To share identity as a woman, white and Welsh-speaking is just a temporary starter and is left behind as distinctiveness, connections and complexity become apparent. Labels are sometimes fleeting as situations and contexts change. This is particularly the case with ethnic labels (or national identities) that are too reductionist. Being a Jew or Arab does not immediately correspond with other fixed religious, economic or personality attributes. Young people in particular re-construct their 'language' and 'culture' with new mixtures and situated translations (K. Hall, 2002). Rampton (1995) noted the **'language crossing'** of teenagers in London who shared expressions in each other's languages, a multiethnic form of talking. Such a friendly crossing of languages created a new set of multilingual identities. But multiple identities may involve a challenge to establishing a coherent sense of Self, which is not always achieved as inherent tensions may remain (Mills, 2004).

A context that affects how language and identity interact is **immigration** (Dicker, 2003; Pavlenko, 2004a). A 13 year old immigrant to Canada, Eva Hoffman, expresses it thus:

> I wait for the spontaneous flow of inner language which used to be my night-time talk with myself . . . Nothing comes. Polish, in a short time, has atrophied, shriveled from sheer uselessness. Its words don't apply to my new experiences . . . In English, words have not penetrated to those layers of my psyche from which a private conversation could proceed. (Hoffman, 1989, p. 107)

When writing a teenage diary, Eva Hoffman finds that her Polish is now connected with the past, so she writes in impersonal, school English, the language of the present, but not the language of the Self. In contrast, Bourne (2001a) shows how children in classrooms are active participants in constructing their identity, not passive recipients, and that heritage languages play a part in this, even in English-dominant classrooms.

Immigrants often produce vibrant, volatile, commodified, new ethnic identities and are not easily classified into existing cultural, ethnic or linguistic groups. Young people growing up in multilingual urban settings (e.g. Utrecht, London, New York) are simplistically considered as Turkish–Dutch, Somali–British or Cuban–American. They may be seen by others as Dutch, British or American, but the self perception of identity may be of a new, dynamic, multiple, overlapping and situationally-changing nature. Language and ethnic dimensions of identity interact with other attributes such that we have simultaneous, fluid and complex multiple classifications. Stereotyping, prejudice and distance is reduced when we see others across multiple classifications rather than just by, for example, ethnicity or language.

Identity is more or less imposed, assumed and negotiated (Blackledge & Pavlenko, 2001; Pavlenko, 2003b). For some, being called a member of a language minority is imposed and negative as 'minority' suggests a stigma of being marginal, non-mainstream and unusual. Hence, **labels** such as 'linguistically diverse' try to create an identity that is more positive. Such labels can be ascribed rather than chosen. For example, an individual may not describe themselves as a 'Bengali speaker' or 'Cantonese bilingual' as these may hint at negative, unwanted differences in a homogeneous society. Instead of 'native speaker' and 'heritage language' to describe the language of a child, 'language expertise' and 'language affiliation' may be more positive. Similarly, the label 'Hispanic' for some is a derogatory term. Just as 'Negro' became 'Black person' to signal an identity based on freedom rather than slavery, so language-based identity labels are sometimes renewed to attempt more positive associations and expectations. Hence, some have a preference for 'Latina' and 'Latino' instead of Hispanic. Sometimes identities can be negotiated (e.g. being American and bilingual – see Pavlenko, 2001b), other times not (e.g. Jews in Nazi Germany and middle class 'enemies of the people' in Stalinist Russia – see Blackledge & Pavlenko, 2001).

However, such group labels are never static. In Europe, ethnic and linguistic identity is dynamic as mass immigration, technology (e.g. air travel, satellite, internet), religion, post-colonialism, mythologizing the past, ongoing enlargement of the European Union, feminism, inter-cultural marriage are some of the interacting modern trends that create ever changing, hybrid language identities (Gubbins & Holt, 2002). This is witnessed in the adaptation of English in Europe. In Germany, Germans want to sound like Germans when they speak English, not like North Americans or the British. Native speakers of English are decreasingly the norm for English. New varieties of English are heard in multilingual communities in England, especially in the multiple identities found in **youth culture** (Cheshire, 2002). These differ from their family identities, and allow different strengths of membership of different networks, plus shared (not divided) loyalties. Wray *et al.* (2003) outline a process of 'turfing' (knowledge, practice and subjective experiencing) whereby a new identity is adopted by individuals with no 'grass roots' affinity to that identity.

Another debate accenting the negative, sometimes voiced by politicians and members of the public is whether multilingualism leads to being caught in-between two languages, with a resulting **conflict of identity**, social disorientation, even isolation and split personality. An old Irish poem talks of the struggle to express Irish identity in the language of the English oppressor: Who ever heard / Such a sight unsung / As a severed head / With a grafted tongue. Li Wei *et al.* (2002)

suggest that there is much variety in multilingual identity (e.g. among asylum seekers, refugees, immigrants): switching to a majority language identity, retaining the minority identity, bridging and combining, and rootlessness.

In contrast, the **South African** ambition (with nine indigenous languages plus English and Afrikaans) is for multilingualism at individual and not just national level to be a defining characteristic of a South African, 'an identity that is dynamic, overlapping, inclusive and egalitarian' (Chick, 2002, p. 466). This is partly achieved in schools where students learn through more than one language, where additional languages are taught, as well as through language immersion and language maintenance programs.

However, if there are anxieties and struggles, bilingualism is unlikely to be the cause: 'it is not language *per se* that causes the identity crisis; rather, it is often the social, economic and political conditions surrounding the development of bilingualism (Li Wei *et al.*, 2002, p. 4). Such conditions tend to be economic (e.g. material poverty), political oppression, racism, social exclusion, discrimination, hostility and powerlessness. For example, Blackledge (2001) shows how Bangladeshi women in England who did not have the linguistic capital (English) to gain access to crucial information on their children's schooling were marginalized in helping their children. Such marginalization is blamed on the power structures of schools that operate only in English, not on the women's linguistic capital. The consumption of goods and services, and the processes and magnitude of consumerism, provide greatly varying conditions that increasingly affect social identities rather than bilingualism and multilingualism.

Pavlenko and Lantolf (2000) suggest that there is a process of **reconstruction of identity** (e.g. in adults following immigration). After (1) an initial loss of linguistic identity, the inner voice and first language attrition comes (2) a period of recovery and transformation that goes through stages of: appropriation of others' voices, emergence of a new voice (e.g. in writing), reconstructing one's past, and continuous growth into new understandings and subjectivities. In terms of language, there is transformation or 're-narratization' rather than replacement, with an outcome that represents an identity in motion that is not exclusively anchored in one language or another.

MAINTAINING MINORITY IDENTITY

Where an ethnic group wishes to maintain its cultural identity and a degree of enclosure (Schermerhorn, 1970), **boundaries** between it and the dominant majority may be essential to continued ethnic identity (Barth, 1966). Boundaries between the language minority group and the dominant group will help to preserve ethnic identity and the heritage language. Establishing boundaries and ethnic identity rest on several criteria (Allardt, 1979; Allardt & Starck, 1981):

(1)   Self-categorization as a distinct ethnic group.
(2)   Common descent and ancestry, be it real or imagined.

(3) Exhibiting relatively distinctive cultural patterns, of which language may be the strongest example.
(4) Well established networking patterns for interacting within the group and separately with 'outsiders'.

Some of the members of an ethnic group will fulfill all these four criteria; every member must fulfill at least one of the four criteria to be a member of that ethnic group (Allardt & Starck, 1981). These criteria highlight the difference between **self-categorization** and **categorization by others**, particularly categorization by the dominant group. Barth (1966) argued that such categorizations essentially define an ethnic group.

Ethnic identity can occur by imposed categorization from without, or by invoked categorization from within. Self-categorization can be achieved through promoting ethnic social institutions (e.g. law, mass media, religious units, entertainment, sport and cultural associations working in the heritage language). Ethnic community schools (heritage language education) plus the careful planning of the ethnic language in the curriculum may be a major component in self-categorization. Mobilizing ethnic group members to agitate for language legitimacy and reform, and working towards a defined vision of the status of the language may also aid self-categorization (C.H. Williams, 1991b). This raises a fundamental debate of how to achieve ethnic identity and language rights: persuasion or agitation; reform or revolt? This debate is now considered.

Should minority language groups always be in a cooperative functional relationship with the majority language? Does non-violent conflict sometimes need to be present to achieve rights for a language community? The achievements of the Basques and the Welsh would both seem to suggest that non-violent conflict with the majority is one mechanism of achieving language rights. Such a conflict viewpoint will place more emphasis on group rights than on individual rights. To be Basque may conflict with being Spanish. To be Welsh can conflict with being British. To be Quebecois may conflict with being Canadian. In these circumstances, cultural pluralism may not always lead to order and the maintenance of majority language rules in society. Should language minority groups pursue equilibrium or conflict?

ACHIEVING CHANGE: FUNCTIONAL OR CONFLICT?

Two contrasting theories can be used to interpret language minority rights, identity and bilingual education (Paulston, 1992; Chick, 2002). In **functional theory**, society is in a state of equilibrium and this equilibrium should be maintained as a first principle. The school, the economic order, social mobility and social processes interlock and work relatively harmoniously and normatively together. Change in society occurs by gradual, slow and smooth evolution. Conflict and disharmony are to be avoided because they lead to a breakdown in a smooth clockwork mechanism. Radically new components will cause the system to stop functioning smoothly. Individual components in the mechanism are relatively unimportant in themselves. It is the overall clockwork mechanism that is important.

When the clock goes wrong, the fault is not within the **system**. One or more components must be a problem and will need to be adjusted. With language minority groups and bilingual education, any apparent failure will not be due to the system, but will be due to problems that lie with the minority language groups and within the form of bilingual education. Any failure in language minority students may be attributed to their poor English proficiency rather than to the educational system. Individuals will be blamed – not the system. For example, since the US system works through English language instruction, more English language instruction is needed with the language minorities if there is a perceived problem. In turn, any disadvantage or poverty that exists in such groups can be solved by improving their achievement at school via greater competence in the majority language. Since the oil of the clockwork mechanism is English language proficiency, once this is in place, language minority students will have equality of opportunity in the educational and economic systems. Bilingual education must maintain equilibrium in society and not upset clockwork correctness.

Genesee (1987) analyses the **Canadian immersion programs** through this equilibrium approach. Such immersion programs are regarded as giving the majority group in society – the English speaking Canadian children – the bilingual proficiency to maintain their socioeconomic dominance in Canada. Set against the protests from French Quebec about the status of the French language in Canada, immersion education may be seen as aiding the stability of the bilingual situation in Canada. More French–English bilinguals created by the immersion schools seems to answer some of the protests of the Quebec people. (This is not necessarily the view of Quebec people, who sometimes believe that their right to French speaking jobs is threatened by such immersion students.) Thus Canadian immersion programs are seen to produce equilibrium in the Canadian language situation.

A different viewpoint to the 'clockwork mechanism' equilibrium perspective is **conflict theory** (Paulston, 1992; Chick, 2002). Such a theory holds that conflict is a natural and expected part of the relationship between unequal power groups in a complex society. Given differences in culture, values, the unequal allocation of resources, and variations in power within society, conflict, radical views and disruption can be expected. Dominant groups seek to maintain their power and high status, while subordinate groups seek to wrest power from them. Dominant groups will tend to exercise power coercively, control (if possible) communication (e.g. in the mass media), and subconsciously or deliberately belittle and stigmatize the discourse of subordinate groups. In the education of tomorrow's citizens, schools are prime sites where such contests of dominant discourse are fought.

Conflict theory argues that real change occurs more by protest, non-violent and sometimes non-peaceful action, and less through the mending of minor problems within a system. Formal education tends to reproduce the dominance of the ruling elite over the masses, reproduces economic, social and political inequalities, inequality of opportunity and inequality of outcome in society. Change can only come by struggle and dispute.

The picture of a clockwork mechanism is replaced by a picture of an operation on an unhealthy body. The removal of an organ, a painful injection, the replacement or addition of tissue by grafting or plastic **surgery** may be radical and initially disruptive, but is perceived as important if the health of the whole body is to improve. Minority language groups may be allotted too little power, too few rewards, and be disadvantaged in resources and rights. Since schools may perpetuate that disadvantage and subordinate power position, such linguistic, cultural and educational discrimination will need radical surgery.

'Weak' forms of bilingual education tend to perpetuate inequalities experienced by language minorities (Skutnabb-Kangas, 1999a). In consequence, within the conflict perspective, **bilingual education** should attempt to remedy such inequality and injustice by positive action. Bilingual education should be interventionist, even clashing with dominant viewpoints. Bilingual education can serve to encourage social, economic and educational change and cultural pluralism. 'Strong' forms of bilingual education can aid the status of minority languages and cultures, reduce the pulls and pushes towards assimilation, and aid the empowerment of minorities (Skutnabb-Kangas, 1999a).

The **Canadian immersion** program, a 'strong' form of bilingual education, can be analyzed through a conflict perspective and not just through the equilibrium approach (e.g. Heller, 1994, 1999b). There are language tensions and conflicts in Canada. For example, some French first language speakers feel economically and politically threatened by those bilinguals for whom French is a second language. 'The anglophones have taken everything from us; now they want to take our language' (Franco-Ontarian teenager quoted in Heller (1999b)). Bilingual anglophones are seen to be accessing power, prestige and privilege that have hitherto been the preserve of bilingual francophones (e.g. by gaining positions in high status professions). With immersion schools, anglophones can gain the linguistic and cultural capital for increased social and economic mobility and for political power.

> Education is currently a major site of the struggle waged between anglophones and francophones, and within each group as well, over whether or not bilingualism should be valuable; and if so, whose property it should be. As such, it represents a struggle over the distribution of wealth and power. (Heller, 1994, p. 7)

Bilingual education is thus not about unity or integration, in this perspective, nor is it neutral. Bilingual education is about gaining advantages, cultural, linguistic and social wealth, and dominance in Canadian society. As such, it can produce conflict with the minority francophone community (e.g. in Ontario).

Heller and Martin-Jones (2001) argue that conflict is often necessary for change and to achieve equality. Language policies and practices in education are ultimately struggles over power and authority, equity and marginalization, legitimacy and social order, symbolic domination and identities, social categorization and social hierarchization. Any consideration about who should speak what language, how, when and where, is essentially about what counts as legitimate language and who has dominance and control. Those in power legitimate the current social order by regulating access to language norms and linguistic resources to preserve their power and position.

For Heller and Martin-Jones (2001), education is a central arena where language-related power struggles and political episodes are enacted. This is illustrated by various classroom behaviors that reproduce marginalization and result in relative academic failure: teacher dominated classroom talk, the use of closed and convergent questioning, recitation and chorus responses by pupils, lesson routines that are safe, going through the motions of a lesson with minimal cognitive gain, using a prestigious colonial language that is remote from the child's home and community experience, the use of 'safetalk' and 'safetime' (Hornberger & Chick, 2001), and the paucity of classroom materials in a minority language, reinforcing the dominance of a majority language. Another example is the role played by bilingual teaching assistants (see chapter 14) who are made marginal to the 'main action' of the classroom by monolingual (majority language) teachers, thus reproducing the **symbolic dominance** of (for example) English and the perceived inferiority of minority languages and language minorities.

Teachers and education administrators, policy-makers and college professors may sometimes be faced with a choice: oil the wheels of the system or be radical and attempt to change the system. Heller and Martin-Jones (2001) regard the choice as **collusion or contestation**: supporting and maintaining the language-power relations of the dominant group, or challenging and contesting. Often, compromises are made by professionals: seeking evolution within relative stability, and development within dominant perspectives. Within an overall desire for equilibrium, small conflicts about policy and provision among school staff, for example, may regularly occur.

ACHIEVING CHANGE FOR MINORITY STUDENTS

This chapter has suggested that bilingualism and bilingual education can only be properly understood through the lens of power, ideology and politics. Cummins (1996, 2000b) argues that relations of power are at the heart of bilingual schooling. This is no more so than for minority language children who often suffer devaluation of identity, added subordination and disempowerment in their schooling experience. He argues that much restructuring of schools in the last two decades has had little impact on the achievement levels of minority language students. The reason is that we have failed to engage the core, essential issues such as securing a very positive student identity, creating strong school–parental partnerships and empowering children and raising their expectations. A new political agenda is needed for such children.

Cummins' (1986, 1996, 2000b) has developed a theoretical framework that directly relates to politics, policy, provision and practice with language minority students. Behind the theory are two ideas that have been discussed in this book already. First, 'language minority students instructed through the minority language (for example, Spanish) for all or part of the school day perform as well in English academic skills as comparable students instructed totally through English'

(Cummins, 1986, p. 20). Teaching children through a second or minority language usually leads to the satisfactory development of English academic skills.

Instead, bilingual children in the US, for example, are taught English with the covert aim being to create a socially cohesive society. There is a simultaneous rejection of the home language and culture. Such 'language replacement' creates failure followed by 'blaming the victim' and more intense efforts to eradicate language diversity in children (Cummins, 1996). A vicious circle is produced whereby the method (submersion education) of reducing the perceived threat of social disruption and division in itself produces outcomes (low achievement) that reinforce the myth of bilingual children as culturally and linguistically deprived.

The second idea is the **'interdependence hypothesis'**. This proposed that 'to the extent that instruction through a minority language is effective in developing academic proficiency in the minority language, transfer of this proficiency to the majority language will occur given adequate exposure and motivation to learn the language' (Cummins, 1986, p. 20). Research by Verhoeven (1994), for example, suggests that there is positive transfer between languages in literacy skills, sound systems (phonology) and communication skills (pragmatics). As may be expected, there is little transfer in lexicon (vocabulary) and syntax (e.g. grammar). Underlying the surface characteristics of both languages is one common core of developed ability or 'academic proficiency'. Beneath two protrusions on the water lies the one iceberg (see chapter 8).

The third statement concerns context. Community and school liaison, power and status relationships all need to be considered in schooling for language minority students. Cummins (2000b) suggests that **power relationships** are a key to understanding the position and interventions needed with language minority students. Power relationships range from collaborative to coercive. Where dominant–subordinate role expectations and relationships are found, culturally diverse students will typically be denied their identity and home language (Cummins, 1997). Collaborative approaches will enable and empower the student, amplifying their self-expression and identity, allocating power to the powerless (see Cummins, 2000b). This theme will be returned to later in this chapter.

Cummins' (1986, 2000b) suggests that minority language students are **'empowered'** or **'disabled'** by four major characteristics of schools.

(1)   **The extent to which minority language students' home language and culture are incorporated into the school curriculum**. If a minority language child's home language and culture are excluded, minimized or quickly reduced in school, there is the likelihood that the child may become academically 'disabled'. Where the school incorporates, encourages and gives status to the minority language, the chances of empowerment are increased. Apart from potential positive and negative cognitive effects, the inclusion of minority language and culture into the curriculum may have effects on personality (e.g. self-esteem), attitudes, and social and emotional well-being. This point is important because it raises a question about why bilingual education which emphasizes the minority language is successful. Is it due to such education

fostering cognitive and academic proficiency, as the interdependence hypothesis suggests? Or is it also due to students' cultural identity being secured and reinforced, thus enhancing self-confidence and self-esteem (or both)? Cummins (1986) sees minority students' language and culture existing on an **additive–subtractive** dimension. 'Educators who see their role as adding a second language and cultural affiliation to their students' repertoire are likely to empower students more than those who see their role as replacing or subtracting students' primary language and culture.' (p. 25)

(2) **The extent to which minority communities are encouraged to participate in their children's education**. Where parents are given power and status in the partial determination of their children's schooling, the empowerment of minority communities and children may result. When such communities and parents are kept relatively powerless, inferiority and lack of school progress may result. The growth of paired reading schemes is evidence of the power of a parent–teacher partnership. Parents listening to their children reading on a systematic basis tend to be effective agents of increased literacy.

As an illustration of the importance of community participation, Cummins (1996) cites the Pajaro Valley Family Literacy Project in a rural area surrounding Watsonville, California. Spanish speaking parents met once a month to discuss chosen books, write and discuss poems written by their children and themselves (Ada, 1988b). Books were related to prior experiences, critically analyzed and applied to everyday events. Parents read to their children – including television recordings of parents reading their children's stories. This gave children (and their parents) much pride in themselves, their growing literacy, their homes and heritage. Confidence in themselves and in the power of their own self-expression increased. The community's language, culture, and personal experiences were validated, celebrated and empowered.

Teachers are seen as being located along a dimension ranging from the **collaborative** to **the exclusionary**. Teachers at the collaborative end encourage parents of minority languages to participate in their children's academic progress through home activities or the involvement of parents in the classroom. Teachers at the exclusionary end maintain tight boundaries between themselves and parents (Cummins, 2000b). Collaboration with parents may be seen as irrelevant, unnecessary, unprofessional, even detrimental to children's progress.

(3) **The extent to which education promotes the inner desire for children to become active seekers of knowledge and not just passive receptacles**. Learning can be active, independent, internally motivated or passive, dependent and requiring external pulls and pushes. The **transmission** model of teaching views children as buckets into which knowledge is willingly or unwillingly poured and teacher-controlled 'legitimate facts' are placed in the 'bank' by students (Cummins, 2000b). The hidden curriculum of the 'banking' model may reinforce and symbolize the powerlessness of language minority students. There are those in control and those controlled. The alternative model is 'transformative' and requires **reciprocal interaction** involving:

a genuine dialogue between student and teacher in both oral and written modalities, guidance and facilitation rather than control of student learning by the teacher, and the encouragement of student/student talk in a collaborative learning context. This model emphasizes the development of higher level cognitive skills rather than just factual recall, and meaningful language use by students rather than the correction of surface forms. Language use and development are consciously integrated with all curricular content rather than taught as isolated subjects, and tasks are presented to students in ways that generate intrinsic rather than extrinsic motivation. (Cummins, 1986, p. 28)

If the 'banking' model is allied to the **disablement** of minority language students, then the 'transformative' model is related to the **empowerment** of students. This latter model aims to give students more control over their own learning, with consequent potential positive effects for self-esteem, cooperation and motivation.

(4) **The extent to which the assessment of minority language students avoids locating problems in the student and seeks to find the root of the problem in the social and educational system or curriculum wherever possible.** Psychological and educational tests tend by their very nature to locate problems in the individual student (e.g. low IQ, low motivation, backwardness in reading). At worst, educational psychologists and teachers may test and observe a child until a problem can be found in that child to explain poor academic attainment. Such a testing ideology and procedure may fail to locate the root of the problem in the social, economic or educational system. The subtractive nature of transitional bilingual education, the transmission model used in the curriculum, the exclusionary orientation of the teacher towards parents and the community and the relative economic deprivation of minority children could each or jointly be the real origin of a minority language child's problem. Therefore assessment and diagnostic activity need to be **Advocacy rather than Legitimization oriented** (Cummins, 2000b). Advocacy means the assessor or diagnostician advocating for the child, by critically inspecting the social and educational context in which the child operates. This may involve comments about the power and status relationships between the dominant and dominated groups, at national, community, school and classroom level (Forhan & Scheraga, 2000).

Empowerment thus becomes an important concept in transforming the situations of many language minorities. 'Empowerment means the process of acquiring power, or the process of transition from lack of control to the acquisition of control over one's life and immediate environment' (Delgado-Gaitan & Trueba, 1991, p. 138). Empowerment means movement for minority language students from coercive, superior–inferior (subordinate) relationships, to collaborative relationships, power sharing and power creating, where the identities of minorities are affirmed and voiced. Thus, for Cummins (1996), empowerment is 'the collaborative creation of power. Students whose schooling experiences reflect collaborative relations of power develop the ability, confidence and motivation to succeed academically. They participate competently in instruction as a result of having developed a secure sense of identity and the knowledge that their voices will be heard and respected in the classroom. (p. 15)

Empowerment can be furthered by education, but also needs to be realized in legal, social, cultural and particularly economic and political events. Delgado-Gaitan and Trueba (1991) argue for necessary sociocultural and political dimensions of empowerment to be added to the possibilities of empowerment through education. Empowerment also needs to include those language groups who generally receive minimal support and advocacy (e.g. Black English (Ebonics), Creole and Deaf People).

EMPOWERMENT AND PEDAGOGY

As a generalization, language minorities have less power and less chance of acquiring political power compared with language majorities. Such minorities are subservient to the majority who reproduce their dominance in particular classroom processes (see below). This powerlessness is enacted, transmitted and reproduced in the **classroom** by the authority relationship of, for example, a majority language teacher and a submissive language minority student (Delpit, 1988, 1995).

If classrooms transmit and reinforce power relations and powerlessness, is this reversible? Is language minority powerlessness reproduced inside 'weak' forms of bilingual education? Can this be reversed by 'strong' forms of bilingual education? It is important to ask 'how' and 'why' language minority children are at a disadvantage in the classroom. Can there be **attempted reversal and empowerment**? Delpit's (1988, 1995) analyses the 'Culture of Power' in classrooms.

(1) The 'Culture of Power' is enacted in the classroom by:
- teachers having power and dominance over students;
- the curriculum (e.g. via text books) determining a legitimate world view; the curriculum taught may be restricted to a majority language viewpoint (e.g. white, US, English language) and taught as supreme, incontestable and 'correct';
- majority language educators define narrowly what constitutes approved forms of intelligent behavior; what is regarded as 'intelligent behavior' is formulated by the language majority; this is imposed on students from a language minority whose own forms of intelligent behavior are ignored;
- school leading to employment (or unemployment) and hence to economic status (or a lack of status).

(2) The 'Culture of Power' is embedded in ways of talking and writing, ways of dressing, manners and ways of interacting (e.g. compare 'upper', 'middle' and 'lower' or 'working' class children).

(3) Success in school and employment often requires acquiring or mimicking the culture of those in power. This is essentially upper- and middle class culture. 'Children from other kinds of families operate within perfectly wonderful and viable cultures but not cultures that carry the codes or rules of power' (Delpit, 1988, p. 283). Language minority families have their own valid, well developed and valuable cultures already in place.

(4) Those outside of the 'Culture of Power' should be taught explicitly the rules and nature of that culture in order to become empowered. If styles of interaction, discourse patterns, manners and forms of dress, for example, are explained to a child, does this lead to the language minority child being empowered, or does this move such a child towards cultural separation?

Delpit (1995) has thus shown how in the US power imbalances are paralleled in the classroom. Schools sometimes tolerate but do not embrace linguistic diversity, and often refuse to acknowledge the politics that surrounds bilingual education. Therefore, it becomes important to educate bilingual students to understand the politics of bilingual education and the culture of power.

CONCLUSION

Underneath 'weak' and 'strong' forms of bilingual education lie different views about language communities, ethnic minorities and language itself. When language is viewed as a problem, there is often a call for assimilation and integration. Assimilationists will usually stress the majority language as the common leveler. When language is viewed as a right, the accent may vary between individual rights and language group rights. Such rights may be contested in law and expressed by political and grassroots movements.

Language may also be seen as a resource, a cultural and economic benefit, with a desire to maintain cultural and linguistic diversity. The political debate is often thus reduced to assimilation versus pluralism, integration versus multiculturalism. This debate relates directly to types of schooling: for example, submersion or heritage language, transitional bilingual education or dual-language education. 'Strong' forms of bilingual education may be seen as a form of reversing the powerlessness of those language minorities living within an assimilative and discriminatory political orientation. For language majorities, sensitization to language minorities may come through multicultural awareness. It is to multiculturalism we now turn.

KEY POINTS IN THE CHAPTER

- Four ideologies underpin discussions about languages in society and in schools: pluralist and assimilationist being the main 'opposites', but also with civic and ethnist ideologies being present.
- Assimilation is a belief that cultural groups should give up their heritage cultures and take on the host society's way of life. In contrast, pluralism

believes that these groups should maintain their heritage cultures in combination with the host culture.

- The identity or hybrid identities of immigrants is a key debate with modern views of identity suggesting social construction, constant change and negotiation and complexity.
- To maintain ethnic identity, boundaries are needed to remain a distinct group.
- A contrast between the equilibrium and conflict paradigms indicates basic political differences in language minority preferences and expectations.

SUGGESTED FURTHER READING

CRAWFORD, J., 2000, *At War With Diversity*. Clevedon: Multilingual Matters.
CRAWFORD, J., 2004, *Educating English Learners: Language Diversity in the Classroom*. Los Angeles: Bilingual Education Services.
CUMMINS, J., 2000, *Language, Power and Pedagogy: Bilingual Children in the Crossfire*. Clevedon: Multilingual Matters.
DICKER, S.J., 2003, *Languages in America: A Pluralist View* (2nd edition). Clevedon: Multilingual Matters.
McKAY, S.L. & WONG, S-L.C. (eds), 2000, *New Immigrants in the United States*. Cambridge: Cambridge University Press.
NORTON, B., 2000, *Identity and Language Learning: Gender, Ethnicity and Educational Change*. Harlow: Longman.
PAVLENKO, A. & BLACKLEDGE, A. (eds), 2004, *Negotiation of Identities in Multilingual Contexts*. Clevedon: Multilingual Matters.
SCHMIDT, R., 2000, *Language Policy and Identity Policy in the United States*. Philadelphia: Temple University Press.
SKUTNABB-KANGAS, T., 2000, *Linguistic Genocide in Education – or Worldwide Diversity and Human Rights*. Mahwah, NJ: Erlbaum.

STUDY ACTIVITIES

(1) Interview two local politicians with differing viewpoints on bilingual education. Attempt to locate on what dimensions there are differences and similarities between these two politicians. Try to explain why there are differences.

(2) Follow a political controversy in current or previous newspapers. This controversy may concern languages in school or bilingual education or language minorities. Portray in words the varying political dimensions of the controversy. Does the controversy fit neatly into a two-way split (e.g. left-wing compared with right-wing viewpoints)? Or does the controversy have a number of different sides to it? Do you feel there are aspects of the controversy that are implicit rather than explicit?

(3) Compose a short case study of a school with which you are familiar. Use Cummins's framework for describing and analyzing the school. Make a list of recommendations for how the school might raise its standards and quality through innovation and intervention with use of languages.

(4) Using a school you are familiar with, ask teachers and parents about school–home relationships. What forms of collaboration exist? What power relationships exist between teachers and parents? What part do parents play in literacy development?

CHAPTER 19

Bilingualism in the Modern World

Introduction

Occupational Bilingualism

Bilingualism and Tourism

Bilingualism and the Mass Media

Information Technology and Bilingualism

Bilingualism and the Internet

Bilingualism and the Economy
Bilingualism as an Economic Advantage
The Economic Usefullness of
Different Languages
Minority Languages and the Economy
Bilingualism and Economic Inequality

Conclusion

CHAPTER 19

Bilingualism in the Modern World

INTRODUCTION

This chapter takes a contemporary and **future look at bilingualism** and bilinguals. In the modern world, is a heritage (minority language) going to be an asset and/or a hindrance? Does tourism help sustain and/or dilute minority languages and their attendant cultures? Is bilingualism valuable for employment? Will bilinguals with two majority languages have a competitive advantage in developing global economies? Will the Internet and mass media ensure that English increasingly becomes the international language for global communication?

Forecasting the future is dangerous. The future of majority and minority languages in the world is **unpredictable**. Current economic, political, social and cultural change is swift (e.g. globalization), affecting all languages of the world (Block & Cameron, 2002; Harris & Bargiela-Chiappini, 2003). The flow of people (e.g. tourism, immigration, refugees), the flow of money and technology, the flow of information and images, and the flow of ideas and ideologies are all more rapid than hitherto. Therefore, five key modern themes are highlighted (employment, tourism, mass media, information technology and the economy) to show how languages within an individual and within society are likely to be subject to fast moving tides of local and global development.

OCCUPATIONAL BILINGUALISM

The ownership of two languages is increasingly seen as an asset as the 'communication world' gets smaller. As immediate communication by phone and computer across the world has become a reality, and as air travel has brought peoples and countries closer together, so the importance of bilingualism and multilingualism has been highlighted. As the amount of information available has dramatically increased, and the ease of delivering information round the world has quickened, so bilinguals, particularly those with 'English bilingualism', have become more important in the **employment market**.

In tourism, marketing, retailing, airlines, public relations, banking, performing arts, media, information and communications technology, accountancy, business consultancy, secretarial work, hotels, law and teaching, for example, bilingual and multilingual employees often have the competitive edge when applying for a post or for promotion. At the least, a bilingual has 'value added' by offering language competencies in employment. Where there is a **customer-interface**, then interacting in the language of the customer is good for business. In the growing prevalence of screen-based and information-based labor, bilinguals are often marketable and seen as more multi-skilled (Carreira & Armengol, 2001; McGroarty, 2002). Chorney (1998) surveyed the leading 250 export companies in Canada, and concluded that bilingualism was a major asset in finding employment in such large companies.

In the wake of 9/11, intelligence-gathering, diplomacy and national security have led to the need for those fluent in languages other than English. The US Defense Language Institute in Monterey, California has a 2500 student enrollment of around 2500, supplying the US army, navy, air force, Department of Defense, CAI and FBI with employees whose language skills are vital to their post (Tse, 2001).

However, there is a marked contrast between bilingual professions that carry a high prestige, and professions where bilinguals are in jobs that symbolize the lower status of many language minority bilinguals. In this latter case, language minority members may speak two languages, yet be in low paid jobs, and be marginalized in their employment prospects and chances of sharing wealth. We will first consider bilingual professions that are prestigious.

An example of bilingual professions that are prestigious surround the **tourism and travel business**. International flight attendants, instructors on ski slopes in mainland Europe, those who conduct safaris in Africa, those who cater for sun seekers in the Mediterranean all prosper when they are bilingual or multilingual. To communicate with clients, to inform those being instructed, to satisfy those seeking rest and excitement, the use of two or more languages enhances job performance.

For bilinguals and multilinguals who are skilled in two or more languages, being an **interpreter** or **translator** is often a prestigious post (V. Edwards, 2004). When politicians meet (e.g. European Commission, United Nations, on foreign visits) interpreters form the essential bridge and provide a smooth connection. Interpreting can also exist in a local language minority region.

In the highlands and islands of Scotland, translating facilities are available for those English-only speakers who need a translation when local government officials or elected community representatives are speaking Gaelic. Translating also can exist as a large-scale enterprise (e.g. in the United Nations and the European Union) where many documents have to be translated into official languages. Translation may also occur in language minority communities where, for example, a book or an article may be translated to or from the minority language.

Another example of a relatively prestigious bilingual profession is that of local **government officials**. When enquiries are made about health, social benefit or local taxes, it is often necessary to have people who can use the language(s) of the local people. In many language minority situations, bilinguals in local government may have to deal with superiors and paper work in the majority language, but deal orally or in writing in the minority language with some or many of the local population. Another example is when a local government official in Africa or India visits an indigenous ethnic group in a relatively remote part of the country. That local government official may need to talk in the dialect or local language of the people as well as talking to colleagues back in the town or city in a more widely used language.

In the **caring professions** (e.g. counselors, therapists, psychologists, doctors, nurses, religious leaders), one job performance factor is the bilingual abilities of such professionals. Take, for example, the midwife. The midwife is present at that very special moment of a mother's experience. Communication with the midwife is not only important, it is also very emotional and precious. Can the midwife assist in the moment of pain and joy in the preferred language of the mother? If not, the mother will need to switch to using her second language.

When people visit a psychiatrist or counselor, it may be important for them to discuss and reveal the innermost depths of their being in the language of their choice. To switch to a second or third language because the professional is monolingual may be unsatisfactory for client and professional. In a religious service, it can be important for a religious leader to conduct prayers or a funeral service in the language of the people. People may find praying in a second language unnatural, even awkward.

There are many times when the more prestigious professional (e.g. the consultant surgeon) only speaks the majority language, while the relatively less prestigious professional (e.g. the nurse on the hospital ward) is bilingual. This raises the occasional dilemma about whether it is more important to hire a monolingual who is more skilled at a profession, or a bilingual who is less skilled? (There will be many cases when bilinguals are as skilled or more skilled than the monolingual applicant for a post.)

This leads to the second part of this discussion about bilingual professions. In many **minority language situations**, those who are bilingual may be unemployed or in lower status jobs. Or the more prestigious jobs are sometimes filled by monolinguals and less prestigious posts by bilinguals. This may send a signal. Monolingualism symbolically connects with higher status employment, and bilingualism with lower status employment.

There is sometimes a vicious cycle of poverty, powerlessness, low expectations and lower motivation leading to under-achievement at school, with unemployment and lower status jobs becoming part of this cycle. For example, in cities in the United States where there are large proportions of Spanish speakers, many **teachers** are English language monolinguals. The cooks, cleaners, secretaries, teacher assistant and janitors in the school may often be bilinguals. For students in the school, such a differentiation between monolinguals and bilinguals in the roles they play may send out messages to the students and parents. There is a hidden curriculum in employment patterns within the school. The students may acquire the idea subconsciously that monolingual English speakers are prestigious, relatively well paid and in relatively secure jobs. Those who speak Spanish as their home language and can cope in English as a second language tend to be allocated the lower class, more menial jobs. The role models in the school convey the message that to be bilingual is to be associated with less status and more poverty and disadvantage, less power and more subservience (McGroarty, 1990).

This discussion of bilingual professions has revealed the dual nature in the link between bilingualism and employment. In the first case there are those who can use their bilingualism as an advantage: to sell, to satisfy clients' needs, to succeed in providing a service. Bilingualism has an economic potential; it is an asset used by an individual for advancement. Bilingualism can become a **marketable ability** to bridge languages and cultures, securing trade and delivery of services. In the second case, there are those people whose bilingual nature tends to mark them for lower status, more marginalized and precarious employment. Such bilinguals may be allocated the poorest paid jobs in schools and shops. Bilingualism is attached to **low status jobs** that symbolize the least powerful, the least affluent and least prestigious sections in a society.

BILINGUALISM AND TOURISM

In recent decades, tourism has been a growth industry. Increasing ease of travel and communications, the opening of national boundaries, more leisure time, earlier retirement, longer life and a greater disposable income have meant that vacations in other countries are part of the lifestyle of an increasing proportion of the affluent population of many developed countries. When people go on vacation, some are seemingly indifferent to the indigenous language and culture of the region they are visiting, especially if it is a minority language and culture. Others are curious, charmed, even captivated by different tongues and traditions, by varied communication and cultures.

Travel and tourism involves the **contact of cultures and languages**. This can be an enlightening and enriching experience. However, tourism is sometimes seen as the enemy of multiculturalism and multilingualism and especially of minority languages and cultures. Language minority activists can argue that tourism ruins unspoilt areas of great beauty with hotels, blocks of flats and marinas. Tourism can also pollute the cultural and linguistic environment. Tourists can be unaware of, and insensitive to cultural and linguistic diversity by expecting the language, food and other customs to be the same as at home.

If use is made of minority languages and cultures in tourist enterprises, this tends to follow an '**ethnic approach**', focusing on traditions, customs and cultural artifacts in a way that may portray them as 'quaint', 'archaic' or 'strange'. Whether we are talking about Breton embroidered costumes, Scottish tartan, Welsh harp music, Amish traditional dress, Native American rituals or Māori war dances, they may be presented as spectacles for gawking tourists rather than as part of real-life, contemporary living cultures. However, 'ethnic' tourism can bring money into the community.

Mass tourism has contributed to the spread of the **English language** and Anglo culture throughout the world, possibly at a cost to other languages and cultures. English is often the expected means of communication when tourists from different continents are abroad. Mass tourism can also weaken the cultural, linguistic and economic structure of a region by its tendency to provide casual, seasonal employment and also a mass influx of temporary workers from other regions. Because of all these negative implications, tourism is sometimes viewed with suspicion and concern by language minority groups.

Tourism that actively promotes the host language and culture has been called '**cultural tourism**'. With the growth of tourism throughout the world, more sophisticated and diverse strategies for boosting the tourist market have been devised. The importance of cultural tourism has been increasingly recognized and language minorities can raise their profile, create employment and find a niche economy in such cultural tourism.

BILINGUALISM AND THE MASS MEDIA

There has been an explosion in the number and distribution of newspapers and magazines, but, more importantly, radio and television have become important vehicles of mass communication, in the form of news, information and entertainment. The majority of households in Western countries possess at least one television set, and to own a television is the ambition of many families in less economically advanced world countries. Television (especially satellite television) has contributed to the creation of the **global village** – to the world-wide diffusion of important and immediate news, sport and culture. Television enables viewers to cross cultures. The development of satellite and cable technology has facilitated the transmission of programs world-wide. Television can contribute to multiculturalism, and to an empathy and insight into other cultures, languages and lifestyles.

However, there is another side to television. The largest television industry in the world is in North America. It provides a mass of programs, mainly light entertainment and news. These programs transmit **Anglo-American culture** to other parts of the world. Anglo-American music, cultural practices and lifestyles may be seen as prestigious and important, and, by implication, the indigenous cultures of other countries may seem outmoded and backward.

The **English language** is also diffused throughout the world by the mass media. The use of subtitling (cheaper than dubbing) means that the English language is experienced by audiences in many worldwide countries. Since the advent of satellite television, even more viewers have access to English language programs.

The widespread mass media diffusion of the **English** language has had some beneficial effects. It has contributed to the development of bilingualism. It has provided a means for speakers of other languages to develop competence in English as a useful language of international communication. In Scandinavian countries for instance, many English language films and other programs have traditionally been broadcast with subtitles. Only children's programs are dubbed. Motivation to learn English is usually high in Scandinavian countries, and television is one aid to competence. This is an additive bilingual situation, where the second language does not displace the first.

However, the English language has penetrated, via television, into many majority languages. This influx of **borrowings** from English via the mass media has provoked anxiety among language purists in both Japan and France. The French government has taken steps to reduce the quantity of non-French language broadcasting on radio and television.

One positive development caused by the proliferation of international satellite and cable channels is that there is an increasing international market for television programs. This, and the increasing use of subtitling, 'voice-overs' and dubbing, means that such programs and films can be made in many lesser used languages. The cost can then be recouped by selling them on the international market.

This is not to suggest that English language channels (and Internet use) are fully dominant in English-speaking countries (e.g. US and UK). In the UK,, there are Arabic and Asian language television channels on satellite watched by speakers of those languages. In the US, the Spanish channel Univision, for example, has grown from small beginnings in the early 1960s to a major provider with a large Spanish-speaking audience. Ramos (2002), a highly popular Spanish-language journalist in the US, indicates the growth and increasingly powerfulness of the Spanish TV contribution in the United States, not least in its political power and influence. Spanish language TV is now recognized for its influence on Latino voters, such that politicians (who support the dismantling of bilingual education) are enthusiastic to reach and persuade voters in their heritage language.

However, when majority language mass media (e.g. English) enter minority language homes, the effect may be a **subtractive bilingual situation**. For example, language minority children are exposed to the English language and Anglo-American culture on television from an early age. Minority language groups tend to be concerned about the potentially harmful effect on speakers of their language, especially teenagers and younger children, of the daily diet of majority language and culture. They are concerned that it further weakens the prestige and status of their own language and culture, further widening the gap between English (or another majority language) as the language of power, prestige, modern technology, fashion and entertainment and their own language, as an old-fashioned, outdated and backward language of yesterday. There is also concern that watching majority language television may affect children's acquisition of their native language, and hasten language shift to the majority language.

During recent decades, there has been a concerted effort by many minority language groups to gain access to radio and particularly television (V. Edwards, 2004). Minority language activists have seen **minority language radio and television** as vitally important to the maintenance of their language for the following reasons.

(1) Minority language media adds to the prestige and status of a language in the eyes of its speakers.
(2) Minority language media can add to a sense of unity and identity among its speakers.
(3) Minority language media helps to keep minority language speakers, especially children and young people, from being overwhelmed by the influence of majority language and culture. It acquaints them with their own heritage and culture and gives them pride in it.
(4) Minority language media can help disseminate a standard form of the language and also promotes new and technical vocabulary. Mass media can help the standardization of a minority language across a variety of registers.
(5) Minority language media can help the fluency of minority language speakers and can also help learners acquire the language.
(6) Minority language media creates well-paid, high prestige jobs for minority language speakers. The radio and television industry can help boost the economy of minority language regions.

The value of minority language media in the maintenance of minority languages and the reversal of language shift has been disputed by Fishman (1991). Fishman argues that radio and television should not be hailed as the rescuers of a minority language. He maintains that many minority language groups spend valuable resources in the lengthy and expensive task of establishing and maintaining minority language media, at the cost of more basic and fundamental issues such as the intergenerational transmission of the minority language. Fishman (1991) suggests that the impact of majority language television, particularly English language television in the UK and North America, is so immense, that it cannot be countered by the much lesser influence of a minority language.

But attempting to do something to counteract majority language mass media is much better than doing nothing. In the struggle there is vitality and vigor. There are benefits in having minority language media in the prestige, maintenance and promotion of minority languages, cultures and economies. Siguán (1993) claims that Galician television has contributed greatly to the increase in **social prestige** of the language. In Catalonia, the Catalan television channels are now watched by up to 40% of the population. In Wales, the establishment of a Welsh language television channel in 1982 led to the creation of many independent television companies in Wales, which have boosted the **economy** of the country. Such minority language television is regarded as important in **standardizing** the language in a wide range of registers across the north and south of Wales. Welsh television has also been viewed as a major force in the creation and a maintenance of a sense of identity and unity among Welsh speakers.

INFORMATION TECHNOLOGY AND BILINGUALISM

With the rapid spread of technology and networked information has gone the rapid **spread of English**. The inherent danger is that minority languages, cultural diversity and therefore bilingualism come under threat. The information that transfers across the Internet tends often to be in English. Over 150 million people in the world are estimated to access the Internet in English. The language of digitized encyclopedias and the multiplicity of software tends also to be in English, as does the language of games software.

Minority languages may seem in comparison to be part of heritage and history, and may fail to attain the status and prestige of modern, high-prestige and high-profile international languages used by information technology. The danger lies in the identification of advanced technological society with the English language, and subsequently minority languages being identified with home and history, ritual and religion. The danger is of a tiered information society: those who have the linguistic abilities to access information; those who cannot access new forms of communication and information as they do not own a language used in the information society.

Yet it is possible to harness technology to **aid minority language education.** For example, software can be displayed in or translated into the heritage language. Email and information exchange can be in that minority language. As more businesses begin to advertise using web pages, regional networks have developed using local languages on the Internet. As schools, colleges, universities, local government, libraries, record offices and local information agencies go online, their local pages are sometimes bilingual.

What is also important in preserving minority languages in a technological age is to ensure that there is appropriate **terminology** in the minority language. It is necessary to extend minority language vocabulary to embrace technological and computer terms in languages other than English. Such modernization aids the symbolic status of the language, particularly among the impressionable young. Such a modernization of corpus also ensures the minority language attempts to move into modern domains, and that information technology is a supporter and not a destroyer of bilingualism in children.

It is also possible to harness technology to aid minority language employment. The information superhighway makes residence in language minority rural areas more possible through improved speed and access in communications, and employment that allows people to **work at home**, using high speed computer links to receive and deliver services and products.

BILINGUALISM AND THE INTERNET

The Internet provides new possibilities for bilinguals: conversations across countries and continents, playing out multiple identities, a vicarious sense of belonging to other speakers of the heritage language, and a private space to be different, distinct and linguistically diverse.

When students use communication technology, bilingual proficiency can be enhanced. Through the Internet, for example, **authentic language practice** is possible via purposeful and genuine activities (e.g. the use of email). There may be

World-Wide Web Sites for Bilingualism

1. Center for Applied Linguistics (US)
    http://www.cal.org/
2. Language Policy Research Unit (US)
    http://www.asu.edu/educ/epsl/lpru.htm
3. James Crawford's Language Policy Web Site and Emporium (US)
    http://ourworld.compuserve.com/homepages/JWCRAWFORD/
4. Bilingualism database
    http://www.edu.bham.ac.uk/bilingualism/database/dbase.htm
5. The Office of English Language Acquisition, Language Enhancement, and Academic Achievement for Limited English Proficient Students (US)
    http://www.ed.gov/about/offices/list/oela/index.html
6. National Clearinghouse for English Language Acquisition & Language Instruction Educational Programs (US)
    http://www.ncela.gwu.edu/
7. National Association for Bilingual Education (US)
    http://www.nabe.org/
8. OISE, University of Toronto, Second Language Education on the Web (Canada)
    http://www.oise.utoronto.ca/~aweinrib/sle/
9. CILT (Centre for Information of Language Teaching and Research) (UK)
    http://www.cilt.org.uk/
10. Language Policy Research Center (Israel)
    http://www.biu.ac.il:80/HU/lprc/
11. Research Centre on Multilingualism (Belgium)
    http://www.kubrussel.ac.be/onderwijs/onderzoekscentra/ovm/ovm.htm
12. Research Unit for Multilingualism and Cross-Cultural Communication (Australia)
    http://www.rumaccc.unimelb.edu.au/
13. Welsh Language Board (Wales)
    http://www.bwrdd-yr-iaith.org.uk/
14. Centre for Language Immersion and Multilingualism (Finland)
    http://www.uwasa.fi/hut/svenska/ImmLing.html
15. Centre for Research on Bilingualism (Sweden)
    http://www.biling.su.se/
16. Center for Research on Education, Diversity & Excellence (CREDE) (US)
    http://www.crede.ucsc.edu/
17. USC Center for Multilingual, Multicultural Research (US)
    http://www-bcf.usc.edu/~cmmr/
18. Center for Language Minority Education (US)
    http://www.clmer.csulb.edu/
19. California Association for Bilingual Education
    http://www.bilingualeducation.org/
20. Multilingual Matters
    http://www.multilingual-matters.com/

increased motivation to acquire a language via contact with real students in other countries (e.g. Skourtou, 2002) and accessing authentic language sources to complete curriculum activity (e.g. a project on another country). Some examples are on the previous page.

Email, chat rooms, and message boards are already one of the Internet activities for language students, giving the feeling of the global village where barriers to communication (such as cost and the time of travel) are removed. There are increasing numbers of foreign language servers on the Internet accessible via 'sensitive maps' of sites in each country. They provide useful, relevant and topical information that is in a different language. **Linguistic competence** develops as a by-product of interest in the information.

By its nature, the Internet brings people speaking different languages into **closer contact**. By exchanging information with students in other countries, students can build increasing independence in language use, vary their language according to audience, and use language for real purposes. For example, Skourtou (2002) portrays a successful, Internet-based Greek–Canadian sister-class project between schools that provided 'an electronic environment for teaching and learning English as a foreign or second language (EFL/ESL) for Greek elementary school students in Greece as well as for teaching and learning Greek as a second language (GSL) for students of Greek origin in Canada' (p. 85).

Students can take part in conversations over the Internet with native speakers, using not only written text but increasingly video and audio conferencing as well. Exchange visits can be reinforced with preparatory and follow-up Internet links, and there are possibilities of **virtual exchanges** and 'telepresence'.

Technology also holds the promise of conversations between speakers of different tongues, minority and majority. The Tongues project at Carnegie Mellon seeks to integrate speech recognition (turning spoken words into text), a machine translator (converting text to other languages) and a speech synthesizer that turns translated text back into audible words in the language of the listener's choosing. This will enable **conversations** in two (or more) languages, and help protect minority language use and users.

The Internet provides teachers and learners with ready-to-use banks of **multimedia language resources**: a wealth of video and audio recordings from all over the world, pictorial and written information, and activities generated by different language centers in different countries. Providers of information and training for language teachers can use the Internet to publicize events, courses, materials, services and a subscription-based, remote training, advice and information service.

BILINGUALISM AND THE ECONOMY

Bilingualism as an Economic Advantage

Compared with the mainstream language majority, a language minority may experience high unemployment, low pay, poverty and powerlessness. Yet bilinguals have linguistic capital. Bilinguals typically have **marketable language skills** and intercultural knowledge. Bilinguals are often economically impoverished yet linguistically accomplished. Can such dual language competence be an economic asset?

In an increasingly bilingual and multilingual world, with trade barriers falling, with new markets growing, and with economic competition rapidly developing on a global scale, **competence in languages** is increasingly important (V. Edwards, 2004). An example is Southern Florida which has become a main center for South American business, and where Spanish language skills have become a bridge between the business cultures of the US and Latin America (Fradd & Boswell, 1996). The growth of multinational corporations in Southern Florida has increased with the emergence of markets in Latin America requiring Spanish, and not just English, as the language of trade. The growth of legal, financial and banking services in Miami is another example where bilinguals (Spanish and English) have distinct economic and employment advantages. It has been estimated that nearly half of the labor force in Florida requires some level of Spanish language skills in order to meet the needs of international business, tourism and Spanish language media enterprises (Fradd & Boswell, 1996). Yet demand for highly competent Spanish speakers can outstrip demand, including in Florida (Tse, 2001).

Monica Heller (1999a) suggests that, to gain advantage in the new global economy, bilinguals will need to adopt a different concept of their identity. The old politics of identity concern maintaining a heritage language and culture, conserving and protecting traditions, and perpetuating a well defined minority cultural identity. In contrast, Heller (1999a, 2002) talks about a new pragmatic identity for language minorities, which allows them to take advantage of their multiple linguistic and cultural resources to participate in a global economy. The nature of the New World economy is an **ability to cross boundaries**, and many bilinguals are relatively skilled in such behavior. She suggests that it is not multilingualism or a hybrid dual language system that is valued in the new economy, but parallel monolingualism (Heller, 2002).

In such a context, language minorities can act as **brokers** between different monolingual economic and political zones. However, this requires bilinguals to have linguistic resources that are sufficiently well developed to operate in either language group. From a Canadian context, Heller (1999a) argues that 'minorities are now in a good position to market their linguistic capital' (p. 29). To do so, they have to move away from the politics of ethnicity and tradition towards a politics based on capital, globalization and a new international political and economic order. However, language minorities are often politically and economically marginalized, with little chance of escape.

The Economic Usefulness of Different Languages

This immediately raises the question of **which languages** may be useful for economic advancement? In many countries of the world, it is English as a second or foreign language that has visible economic value. As Coulmas (1992) suggests,

> no Japanese businessman ever tries to operate on the American market without a sufficient command of English, whereas the reverse case, of American business people who expect to be able to do business in Japan without being proficient in Japanese, is not at all rare. On the one hand, this is a reflection of the arrogance of power, but on the other hand, it testifies to the fact that the opportunities for realizing the functional potential of English on the Japanese market are far better than those of realizing the functional potential of Japanese on the American market. (pp. 66–67)

As Willy Brandt, a former Chancellor of the old Federal Republic of Germany once said: 'If you wish to buy from us, you can talk any language you like, for we shall try to understand you. If you want to sell to us, then you must speak our language'.

Alongside the English language, the French, German, Japanese, Portuguese and Spanish languages have historically been regarded as important trading languages. However, in the future, this list of **modern languages for marketing and trading purposes** is likely to grow significantly. For example, Arabic and Bahasa Melayu, Mandarin and Cantonese, Swahili and Hausa, Bengali and Hindi/Urdu may each become increasingly valuable. Although the world is getting economically richer, the proportion of the wealth created and spent by Eastern countries may proportionally increase in relation to the West, and therefore positively affect the economic attractiveness of major eastern languages, and particularly the employability of bilinguals and multilinguals.

This scenario reflects the important half-truth discussed by Coulmas (1992, p. 152) who suggests that 'in spite of the non-economic values attached to language, what prevails in matters of language is often that which is profitable'. [The other half of the truth is that language is also related to less tangible, measurable and affective characteristics such as the social, cultural and particularly religious value of a particular language.]

In the context of Ireland, Ó Riagáin (2000) tends to agree. **Profit-margins** lead language life. With the growth of economic prosperity in Ireland since the 1960s came ever-widening international trade contacts, export markets, foreign investment, incorporation into international capitalism, and economic marriage with mainland Europe. English and major European languages gained. This 'created severe problems for policies designed to maintain Irish as a minority language' (p. 206). Such economic expansion was in the private sector, away from state control, whereas the state (since 1926) had conducted language planning mostly as a top-down public sector event. Thus, Ó Riagáin (2000) concludes that the 'complex sequence of maintenance, shift, revival etc. apparent in Ireland over this [last] century is intimately related to changes in the economic base of the community within the wider society' (p. 212). The lower economic value of the Irish language may make it difficult to preserve that language which reflects a cherished culture, home values and valued Irish traditions.

However, in the Nuffield Languages Inquiry (2000) in the UK, it was admitted that

> English is not enough. We are fortunate to speak a global language but, in a smart and competitive world, exclusive reliance on English leaves the UK vulnerable and dependent on the linguistic competence and the goodwill of others . . . Young people from the UK are at a growing disadvantage in the recruitment market. The UK workforce suffers from a chronic shortage of people at all levels with usable language skills . . . Mobility of employment is in danger of becoming the preserve of people from other countries. (p. 6)

Minority Languages and the Economy

In suggesting that bilingualism has economic advantages, the only languages to be highlighted so far have been majority languages. English, Spanish, German, French and Arabic, for example, are relatively prestigious majority languages. What is the place of local **minority languages** in the economy? Will bilinguals from language minorities have no economic advantage, no valuable trading language in their minority language, and no chance of getting out of the poverty trap that many bilingual's experience?

Heller (1999a) suggests that the economy of many countries is moving from the extraction and processing of material resources under the control of the nation state to an economy based on services and information under the control of multinational corporations and corporate capitalism. With a global economy, the new struggle for language minorities will be to exploit their linguistic resources, social networks and potential internationalism for economic and personal gain. The new economy requires the crossing of linguistic boundaries, and bilinguals are ahead of monolinguals in having this potential. Bilinguals can become the pivotal **bridge makers and go-betweens** in global economy operations. Crossing borders can be geographical and linguistic for bilinguals and multilinguals. However, this may be restricted to bilinguals whose languages cross frontiers and are not only used locally or regionally.

The harsh reality for many of the world's bilinguals is that their minority language has little or no economic value. The pressure is on them to move into a majority language, for example, English in the US. Where there is economic value associated with an **immigrant** language it is frequently in sweat shops, frugal factories, and fast food restaurants and is not connected with wealth, affluence or influence. A language is supported by businesses where factory workers, shop workers and managers work partly or mainly through their heritage language. On occasions, the immigrant language is a trade language with another trading country (e.g. Spanish, Urdu, Panjabi, Hindi), with profitability and local niche economies.

Where and when there is some small economic value associated with an **indigenous minority language**, it is often associated with non-sustainable developments in rural areas. Such bilinguals all too frequently work in barely profitable industries in remote language heartland areas. In Europe, for example, the move from regional and state economies to a single European market policy (with interlocking business structures in different European countries encouraging mobility in businesses across European countries), may leave a distinction between core and periphery, between those in important urban business areas and those in rural peripheries (e.g. rural areas and scattered communities in Ireland, Wales and Scotland). Since many indigenous minority languages in Europe are found in regions that are relatively sparsely populated, economically underdeveloped, with poorer rural road and transport systems, there is a danger that there will growing inequality between core and periphery.

In the economic restructuring that has occurred in the last 60 years, increased competition has led to the need for more efficiency to maintain profit. Industries and services have frequently had to 'automate, emigrate or evaporate'. **Emigration of industries** has been to countries such as India, Taiwan, Mexico, Brazil and Singapore, where wages, and therefore production costs, are relatively low. Such outside investment may sometimes offer work and wages to language minority members, but may also have negative consequences for language minorities.

One negative consequence is that economic investment may not reach a language minority. For example, where such minorities live in rural areas, economic growth may be in the urban 'core' rather than the rural periphery. Alternatively, the higher grade jobs may be in relatively affluent city areas, and the lower grade, poorly paid work in the more remote areas.

A different scenario is when a peripheral area attracts **inward investment** (e.g. factories are located in remoter areas). The tendency is for the local language minorities to provide relatively cheap workers, while the better paid (language majority) **managers** either operate from their far-away city headquarters or move into the periphery language community. In both cases (given below), the managers may have a negative effect on language maintenance:

(1) By working from city headquarters, there is a geographical separation of majority language manager and minority language proletariat that represents a status, and a social, cultural, economic and power division. Such a division has prestige consequences for the majority and minority language. Each language is identified with greater or lesser affluence, higher and lower status, more or less power.

(2) By living in the language minority community, a manager who does not learn the local language evokes a class distinction. The manager speaks the majority language; the workers the minority language. One is a higher socioeconomic class; the other a lower socioeconomic class. There is a **social class division**, and a separation or fracture within the social class structure of the community (Morris, 1992). Social tensions may result that lead to divisions along both social class and language dimensions. As Morris (1992) found in her research, one solution is language minority managers who are able to operate across social classes inside their language group.

The absence of community-based, ethnically-based businesses increases the risk of the emigration of more able, more skilled and more entrepreneurial people away from the area, hence leaving the language itself in peril. Also, a language community without economic activity is in danger of starving the language of one essential support mechanism. An **economically wealthy language** has a higher probability of being a healthy language. An economically impoverished language is placed at great risk.

There are also success stories. For example, the development of the Cuban **enclave economy** in Miami shows the possibility of a minority language economy developing in a region. Following the influx of Cubans into Miami in the 1960s, a Cuban enclave economy developed. Based on sufficient capital, a capable labor force, a ready market for products and a sufficient Cuban population to support Cuban-owned businesses, economic success of the enclave soon resulted.

This eastern area of the US also demonstrates a **salary advantage** for bilinguals in some language minority areas. Boswell's (1998) research showed that in Florida, bilinguals (Spanish/English) had an income advantage over monolingual English speakers of, on average, 2000 dollars. Also, such bilinguals had an average income advantage of 7000 to 8000 dollars over those who are monolingual in Spanish. This is partly because Florida is a major focus of trade with Latin America (about one-third of all US trade) and the Caribbean (approximately half of US trade).

Henley and Jones (2000) found that bilinguals in Wales were earning 8% to 10% more salary specifically for their bilingualism. This **earnings advantage** is statistically separate from educational and occupational achievement. The advantage is also not explained by 'discrimination' towards bilinguals. Rather the intrinsic 'dual communication' advantage of bilinguals is joined by their wider networks of contacts among both Welsh and English language communities. Also, Henley and Jones (2000) suggest that the cognitive advantages of bilinguals (see chapter 7) provide extra human capital that then affects their salaries.

Bilingualism and Economic Inequality

Historically, antagonism towards immigrants (particularly in times of economic recession) is typically directed at newcomers who are blamed for taking away jobs from long-standing citizens. **Immigrants** are then blamed for economic and social ills in society. However, immigrants can have a stimulating effect on the economy by (a) opening many new businesses, and (b) keeping businesses from relocating outside the country by providing inexpensive labor, which (c) keeps down the costs of goods and services. A 1997 United States National Academy of Sciences Panel found that immigrants add approximately 10 million dollars per year to the country's economic output such that 'the vast majority of Americans are enjoying a healthier economy as a result of the increased supply of labor and lower prices that result from immigration' (James P. Smith, economist and the Panel's Chairperson, quoted in Dicker, 2003, p. 183).

While there are ethnic group differences, the overall picture is of low wage employment among language minority members, relatively fewer opportunities for promotion and upward mobility, low vocational expectations and motivation, more economically disenfranchised communities and hence a possible economic poverty trap. However, it is not an inevitable condition of language minorities that they are economically deprived, impoverished or that they lack entrepreneurial enterprise. In the US, poverty and inequality are not equally shared by all Latinos with a difference between US Cubans and Puerto Rican, Mexican and Dominican language groups. With the Spanish-speaking population of the US growing, and with Spanish an important trading language in Latin America and elsewhere, there is a possibility that Spanish may be of increasing economic value in the years ahead.

CONCLUSION

It seems increasingly economically valuable to be bilingual. For some individuals, this is to gain employment and try to avoid poverty. For others, bilingualism may be of value to work locally for international and multinational corporations. For yet others, who wish to travel abroad to do their trade, languages also become increasingly important.

The concept that speaking English is all one needs, whether in Europe or the US, is naive. While English is often at the leading edge of economic modernization and technological development, selling and marketing, and tailoring products and services to suit local markets requires other languages. The importance of knowledge of languages other than English in economics and foreign trade was acknowledged by the US in a report accompanying the formulation of the Foreign Language Assistance for National Security Act of 1983. 'It is precisely this combination of foreign language ability and business expertise . . . that is now needed and will be required even more in the future by US companies if they are to compete successfully in these (Asian, the Middle East, Eastern Europe) markets.' (John McDougall, Executive Vice President of the Ford Motor Company).

Moving from a minority language to a majority language for perceived economic purposes may not reap the expected rewards. There is no guarantee that those who become linguistically assimilated (e.g. speak English-only) in countries like the US will gain employment. The evidence from García and Otheguy (1994) and Morales and Bonilla (1993) is that the ability to speak English does not give equal or automatic access to jobs and wealth. Linguistic assimilation does not mean incorporation into the economic structure of the country. If there is a growth of ethnic businesses (e.g. in urban areas), and a development of language minority businesses in peripheral, rural areas, then bilingualism rather than English monolingualism may become more economically valuable.

The economic importance of languages, and the path to self-perpetuating change, is neatly summed up by Strubell (2001) in terms of a positive 'Catherine wheel' cycle:

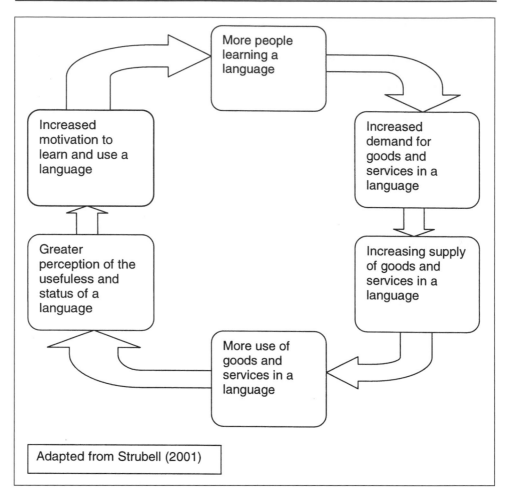

Adapted from Strubell (2001)

KEY POINTS IN THE CHAPTER

- In a world economy and ease of international communications, bilinguals and multilinguals are increasingly required in many occupations.
- The growth of tourism has potential economic benefits for many minority languages, but is allied to the rapid spread of English and preference for historical culture than contemporary living culture.
- Minority language mass media and use in information technology is required for the status of a language but is often in competition with the dominant anglophone mass media.
- Minority language groups are often identified with relatively high unemployment, low pay, poverty and powerlessness. However, local niche economies,

working from home, and community initiatives can support and sustain a language minority.

- Bilingualism can be more valuable than majority language monolingualism, giving a competitive edge for an increasing number of vocations.

SUGGESTED FURTHER READING

BLOCK, D. & CAMERON, D. (eds), 2002, *Globalization and Language Teaching*. London: Routledge.

EDWARDS, V., 2004, *Multilingualism in the English-speaking World*. Oxford: Blackwell.

FISHMAN, J.A. (ed.), 2000, *Can Threatened Languages be Saved?* Clevedon: Multilingual Matters.

HALL, J.K. & EGGINGTON, W.G., 2000, *The Sociopolitics of English Language Teaching*. Clevedon: Multilingual Matters.

LAVER, J. & ROUKENS, J., 1996, The global information society and Europe's linguistic and cultural heritage. In C. HOFFMANN (ed.), *Language, Culture and Communication in Contemporary Europe*. Clevedon: Multilingual Matters.

SKOURTOU, E., 2002, Connecting Greek and Canadian Schools through an internet-based sister-class network. *International Journal of Bilingual Education and Bilingualism* 5, 85–95.

STUDY ACTIVITIES

(1) Carry out a survey in your locality and find out how many different jobs use bilingual skills. Alternatively, analyze job advertisements in local papers for language skills required.

(2) Survey the employment and unemployment pattern of people from local language minorities.

(3) How much (a) provision and (b) use is made of different languages on terrestrial, cable and satellite television received by a sample of people in local language minorities. Also, what languages do they use with IT (e.g. use of the Internet).

(4) Make a poster or handout advertising the sites available for using a minority language on the Internet.

(5) In a small discussion or focus group, examine a selection of the dualisms or dimensions presented below. These attempt to sum up some of the debates and important dimensions of thinking in this book. Regard this as a 'summative' question that requires other chapters of the book to be considered and integrated.

   (i) Briefly state what are the different viewpoints alluded to in those dualisms/dimensions you have chosen.

   (ii) Indicate how these dualisms/dimensions relate to different views of bilingualism, bilingual education and multicultural education. What are the implications for the kind of language and cultural approach adopted in a school?

   (a) Linguistic compared with the Sociocultural/Sociolinguistic view of bilinguals.

   (b) Individual compared with societal analysis of bilingualism/diglossia.

   (c) Language skills compared with language competences

   (d) Fractional compared with a Holistic view of bilinguals.

(e) Subtractive compared with an Additive view of bilinguals.
(f) Preservationists compared with Modernizers.
(g) The Rights (individual and group) view compared with the Empowerment view.
(h) Assimilationist compared with the Pluralist view.
(i) The Functional view compared with the Conflict view.
(j) The deprivation, remedial, problem, disabled view of bilinguals compared with the resource, beneficial, talent diversity view of bilinguals.

Bibliography

Note: All WWW addresses were correct as at June 23 2005.

ABEDI, J., 2004, The No Child Left Behind Act and English language learners: Assessment and accountability issues. *Educational Researcher* 31 (1), 4-14.

ABEDI, J., HOFSTETTER, C.H. & LORD, C., 2004, Assessment accommodations for English language learners: Implications for policy-based empirical research. *Review of Educational Research* 74 (1), 1-28.

ACAC, 1993, *Developing a Curriculum Cymreig*. Cardiff: ACAC.

ADA, A.F., 1988a, Creative reading: A relevant methodology for language minority children. In L.M. MALAVE (ed.), *NABE '87. Theory, Research and Application: Selected Papers*. Buffalo: State University of New York.

ADA, A.F., 1988b, The Pajaro Valley experience: Working with Spanish-speaking parents. In T. SKUTNABB-KANGAS & J. CUMMINS (eds), *Minority Education: From Shame to Struggle*. Clevedon: Multilingual Matters.

ADA, A.F., 1995, Fostering the home–school connection. In J. FREDERICKSON (ed.), *Reclaiming Our Voices: Bilingual Education, Critical Pedagogy and Praxis*. Ontario, CA: California Association for Bilingual Education.

ADA, A.F., 1997, Mother-tongue literacy as a bridge between home and school cultures. In J.V. TINAJERO & ALMA FLOR ADA (eds), *The Power of Two Languages: Literacy and Biliteracy for Spanish Speaking Students*. New York: Macmillan/McGraw-Hill.

ADA, A.F. & SMITH, N.J., 1998, Fostering the home–school connection for Latinos. In M.L. GONZALEZ, A. HUERTA-MACIAS & J.V. TINAJERO (eds), *Educating Latino Students: A Guide to Successful Practice*. Lancaster, Pennsylvania: Technomatic.

ADAMS, J.W., 1997, *You and Your Deaf Child* (2nd edn). Washington, DC: Gallaudet University Press.

ADLER, J., 2001, *Teaching Mathematics in Multilingual Classrooms*. Dordrecht: Kluwer.

AFOLAYAN, A., 1995, Aspects of bilingual education in Nigeria. In B.M. JONES & P. GHUMAN (eds), *Bilingualism, Education and Identity*. Cardiff: University of Wales Press.

AITCHISON, J., 1991, *Language Change: Progress or Decay*. Cambridge: Cambridge University Press.

ALLARDT, E., 1979, Implications of the ethnic revival in modern, industrialized society. A comparative study of the linguistic minorities in Western Europe. *Commentationes Scientiarum Socialium* 12. Helsinki: Societas Scientiarum Fennica.

ALLARDT, E. & STARCK, C., 1981, *Sprakgranser och Samhallsstruktur*. Stockholm: Almquist and Wiksell.

ALLEN, P., CUMMINS, K., HARLEY, B., LAPKINS, S. & SWAIN, M., 1989, Restoring the balance: A response to Hammerly. *Canadian Modern Language Review* 45 (4), 770–776.

AMERICAN PSYCHOLOGICAL ASSOCIATION, 1982, Review of Department of Education report entitled: '*Effectiveness of Bilingual Education: A Review of Literature*', Letter to Congressional Hispanic Caucus, April 22nd.

ANDERSON, C., 2003, Criticism. Phillipson's Children. *Language and Intercultural Communication* 3 (1), 81-95.

ANDERSSON, T. & BOYER, M., 1970, *Bilingual Schooling in the United States* (2 volumes). Austin, TX: Southwest Educational Laboratory.

ARNAU, J., 1997, Immersion education in Catalonia. In J. CUMMINS & D. CORSON (eds), *Bilingual Education*. Volume 5 of the *Encyclopedia of Language and Education*. Dordrecht: Kluwer.

ARNBERG, L., 1987, *Raising Children Bilingually: The Pre-School Years*. Clevedon: Multilingual Matters.

ARTIGAL, J.M., 1991, *The Catalan Immersion Program: A European Point of View*. Norwood, NJ: Ablex.

ARTIGAL, J.M., 1993, Catalan and Basque immersion programmes. In H. BAETENS BEARDSMORE (ed.), *European Models of Bilingual Education*. Clevedon: Multilingual Matters.

ARTIGAL, J.M., 1997, Plurilingual education in Catalonia. In R. JOHNSON & M. SWAIN (eds), *Immersion Education: International Perspectives*. Cambridge: Cambridge University Press.

ARTILES, A.J., 2003, Special education's changing identity: Paradoxes and dilemmas in views of culture and space. *Harvard Educational Review* 73 (2), 164-202.

ARTILES, A.J. & ORTIZ, A.A., 2002, English language learners with special education needs. In A.J. ARTILES & A.A. ORTIZ (eds), *English Language Learners with Special Educational Needs*. Washington, DC & McHenry, IL: Center for Applied Linguistics & Delta Systems Co..

ARVISO, M. & HOLM, W., 2001, Tséhootsooídi Olta'gi Diné Bizaad Bíhoo'aah: A Navajo immersion program at Fort Defiance, Arizona. In L. HINTON & K. HALE (eds), *The Green Book of Language Revitalization in Practice*. San Diego: Academic Press.

ATTINASI, J.J., 1998, English Only for California children and the aftermath of Proposition 227. *Education* 119 (2), 263–283.

AUGUST, D., 2002, *Transitional Programs for English Language Learners: Contextual Factors and Effective Programming*. Baltimore MD: CRESPAR, John Hopkins University.

AUGUST, D. & HAKUTA, K., 1997, *Improving Schooling for Language-minority Children*. Washington, DC: National Academy Press.

AUGUST, D. & HAKUTA, K., 1998, *Educating Language-minority Children*. Washington, DC: National Academy Press.

BACA, L.M. & CERVANTES, H.T., 1998, *The Bilingual Special Education Interface* (3rd edn). Upper Saddle River, NJ: Prentice Hall.

BACHI, R., 1956, A statistical analysis of the revival of Hebrew in Israel. *Scripta Hierosolymitana* 3, 179–247.

BACHMAN, L.F., 1990, *Fundamental Considerations in Language Testing*. Oxford: Oxford University Press.

BACHMAN, L.F. & PALMER, A.S., 1996, *Language Testing in Practice: Designing and Developing Language Tests*. Oxford: Oxford University Press.

BAETENS BEARDSMORE, H., 1986, *Bilingualism: Basic Principles*. Clevedon: Multilingual Matters.

BAETENS BEARDSMORE, H., 1993a, The European school model. In H. BAETENS BEARDSMORE (ed.), *European Models of Bilingual Education*. Clevedon: Multilingual Matters.

BAETENS BEARDSMORE, H. (ed.), 1993b, *European Models of Bilingual Education*. Clevedon: Multilingual Matters.

BAETENS BEARDSMORE, H., 1997, *Manipulating the Variables in Bilingual Education. Report on the Conference on European Networks in Bilingual Education*. Alkmaar, Europees Platform voor het Nederlandse Onderwijs, 1997, 8–16.

BAETENS BEARDSMORE, H., 1999, Language policy and bilingual education in Brunei Darussalam. *Bulletin Des Seances* (Academie Royale Des Sciences D'Outre-Mer) 45 (4), 507–523.

BAETENS BEARDSMORE, H. & SWAIN, M., 1985, Designing bilingual education: Aspects of immersion and 'European School' models. *Journal of Multilingual and Multicultural Development* 6 (1), 1–15.

BAKER, C., 1985, *Aspects of Bilingualism in Wales*. Clevedon: Multilingual Matters.

BAKER, C., 1988, *Key Issues in Bilingualism and Bilingual Education*. Clevedon: Multilingual Matters.

BAKER, C., 1990, The effectiveness of bilingual education. *Journal of Multilingual and Multicultural Development* 11 (4), 269–277.

BAKER, C., 1992, *Attitudes and Language*. Clevedon: Multilingual Matters.

BAKER, C., 1993, Bilingual education in Wales. In H. BAETENS BEARDSMORE (ed.), *European Typologies of Bilingual Education*. Clevedon: Multilingual Matters.

BAKER, C., 1995, Bilingual education and assessment. In B.M. JONES & P. GHUMAN (eds), *Bilingualism, Education and Identity*. Cardiff: University of Wales Press.

BAKER, C., 1999, Sign language and the deaf community. In J.A. FISHMAN (ed.), *Handbook of Language and Ethnic Identity*. New York: Oxford University Press.

BAKER, C. 2000a, *A Parents' and Teachers' Guide to Bilingualism* (2nd edn). Clevedon: Multilingual Matters.

BAKER, C., 2000b, *The Care and Education of Young Bilinguals: An Introduction for Professionals*. Clevedon: Multilingual Matters.

BAKER, C., 2000c, Three perspectives on bilingual education policy in Wales: Bilingual education as language planning, bilingual education as pedagogy and bilingual education as politics. In R. DAUGHERTY, R. PHILLIPS & G. REES (eds), *Education Policy in Wales: Explorations in Devolved Governance*. Cardiff: University of Wales Press.

BAKER, C., 2002, Bilingual education. In R.B. KAPLAN (ed.) *The Oxford Handbook of Applied Linguistics*. Oxford: Oxford University Press.

BAKER, C., 2003a, Language planning: A grounded approach. In J-M. DEWAELE, A. HOUSEN & LI WEI (eds), *Bilingualism: Beyond Basic Principles*. Clevedon: Multilingual Matters.

BAKER, C., 2003b, Education as a site of language contact. *Annual Review of Applied Linguistics* 'Language Contact and Change' 23, 95–112.

BAKER, C., 2004, Biliteracy and transliteracy in Wales: Language planning and the Welsh national curriculum. In N.H. HORNBERGER (ed.) *Continua of Biliteracy: An Ecological Framework for Educational Policy, Research and Practice in Multilingual Settings*. Clevedon: Multilingual Matters.

BAKER, C., 2005, Bilingual education. In K. BROWN (ed.), *Encyclopedia of Language and Linguistics* (2nd edn). Oxford: Elsevier.

BAKER C. & HINDE J., 1984, Language background classification. *Journal of Multilingual and Multicultural Development* 5 (1), 43–56.

BAKER, C. & HORNBERGER, N.H., 2001, Jim Cummins: A biographical introduction. In C. BAKER & N.H. HORNBERGER (eds) *Introductory Reader to the Writings of Jim Cummins*. Clevedon: Multilingual Matters.

BAKER, C. & JONES, M.P., 2000, Welsh language education: A strategy for revitalisation. In C.H. Williams (ed.) *Language Revitalisation: Policy and Planning*. Cardiff: University of Wales Press.

BAKER C. & JONES, S.P., 1998, *Encyclopedia of Bilingualism and Bilingual Education*. Clevedon: Multilingual Matters.

BAKER, K.A., 1987, Comment on Willig's 'A meta analysis of selected studies of bilingual education'. *Review of Educational Research* 57 (3), 351–362.

BAKER, K.A., 1992, Ramirez *et al.*: Misled by bad theory. *Bilingual Research Journal* 16 (1&2), 63–89.

BAKER, K.A. & DE KANTER, A.A., 1981, *Effectiveness of Bilingual Education: A Review of Literature*. Washington, DC: Office of Planning, Budget and Evaluation, US Department of Education.

BAKER, K.A. & de KANTER, A.A., 1983, *Bilingual Education*. Lexington, MA: Lexington Books.

BAKER, P. & EVERSLEY, J., (eds), 2000, *Multilingual Capital: The Languages of London's Schoolchildren and their Relevance to Economic, Social and Educational Policies*. London: Battlebridge.

BALDAUF, R.B., 2005, Coordinating Government and Community Support for Community Language Teaching in Australia. *International Journal of Bilingual Education and Bilingualism* 8 (2&3), 132–144.

BALI, V., 2001, Sink or Swim: What happened to California's bilingual students after Proposition 227? *State Politics and Policy Quarterly*, Spring 2001, 295–317.

BARKER, V. & GILES, H., 2002, Who supports the English-only movement?: Evidence for misconceptions about Latino group vitality. *Journal of Multilingual and Multicultural Development* 23 (5), 353–370.

BARKER, V., GILES, H., NOELS, K., DUCK, J., HECHT, M. & CLEMENT, R., 2001, The English-only movement: A communication analysis of changing perceptions of language vitality. *Journal of Communication* 51 (1), 3–37.

BARONA, M.S. & BARONA, A., 1992, Assessment of bilingual preschool children. In R.V. PADILLA & A.H. BENAVIDES (eds), *Critical Perspectives on Bilingual Education Research*. Tempe, AZ: Bilingual Press.

BARRON-HAUWAERT, S., 2004, *Language Strategies for Bilingual Families: The One-Parent-One-Language Approach*. Clevedon: Multilingual Matters.

BARTH, F., 1966, *Models of Social Organization* (Occasional Paper No. 23). London: Royal Anthropological Institute.

BARWELL, R., 2002, Understanding EAL issues in mathematics. In LEUNG, C., *Language and Additional/Second Language Issues for School Education.* York, UK: NADLIC.

BARWELL, R., 2005a, Ambiguity in the mathematics classroom. *Language and Education* 19 (2), 118–126.

BARWELL, R., 2005b, Empowerment, EAL and the national numeracy strategy. *International Journal of Bilingual Education and Bilingualism* 8, (4), 313–327.

BATIBO, H.M., 2005, *Language Decline and Death in Africa: Causes, Consequences and Challenges.* Clevedon: Multilingual Matters.

BATT, L., KIM, J. & SUNDERMAN, G., 2005, *Limited English Proficient Students: Increased Accountability Under NCLB.* Harvard University: Policy Brief from the Civil Rights Project.

BAUGH, J., 1999, *Out of the mouths of slaves: African American language and educational malpractice.* Austin, TX: University of Texas Press.

BAYLEY R. & SCHECTER S. (eds), 2003, *Language Socialization in Bilingual and Multilingual Societies.* Clevedon: Multilingual Matters.

BEKERMAN, Z., 2003, Reshaping conflict through school ceremonial events in Israeli Palestinian-Jewish education. *Anthropology & Education Quarterly* 34 (2), 205–224.

BEKERMAN, Z., 2005, Complex contexts and ideologies: Bilingual education in conflict-ridden areas. *Journal of Language, Identity, and Education* 4 (1), 1–20.

BEKERMAN, Z. & SHHADI, N., 2003, Palestinian-Jewish bilingual education in Israel. Its influence on cultural identities and its impact on intergroup conflict. *Journal of Multilingual and Multicultural Development* 24 (6), 473–484.

BEL, A., 1993, Some results of the immersion programme in Catalonia. *Notícies del SEDEC/Newsletter of the Servei d'Enseynament del Catalonia.*

BENALLY, A. & VIRI, D., 2005, *Diné Bizaad* [Navajo Language] at a crossroads: Extinction or revival? *Bilingual Research Journal* 29 (1), 86–108.

BENSON, C., 2004, Do we expect too much of bilingual teachers? Bilingual teaching in developing countries. *International Journal of Bilingual Education and Bilingualism* 7 (2&3), 204–221.

BENYON, J. & TOOHEY, K., 1991, Heritage language education in British Columbia: Policy and programs. *Canadian Modern Language Review* 47 (4), 606–616.

BEN-ZEEV, S., 1977a, The influence of bilingualism on cognitive strategy and cognitive development. *Child Development* 48, 1009–1018.

BEN-ZEEV, S., 1977b, The effect of bilingualism in children from Spanish–English low economic neighborhoods on cognitive development and cognitive strategy. *Working Papers on Bilingualism* 14, 83–122.

BERNHARDT, E.B. (ed.), 1992, *Life in Language Immersion Classrooms.* Clevedon: Multilingual Matters.

BERNHARDT, E.B. & SCHRIER, L., 1992, The development of immersion teachers. In E.B. BERNHARDT (ed.), *Life in Language Immersion Classrooms.* Clevedon: Multilingual Matters.

BERTHOLD, M., 1992, An Australian experiment in French immersion. *Canadian Modern Language Review* 49 (1), 112–125.

BERTHOLD, M., 1995, *Rising to the Bilingual Challenge: Ten Years of Queensland Secondary School Immersion.* Canberra: National Languages and Literacy Unit of Australia.

BHATIA, T.K. & RITCHIE, W.C. (eds), 2004, *The Handbook of Bilingualism.* Malden, MA: Blackwell.

BIALYSTOK, E., 1987a, Influences of bilingualism on metalinguistic development. *Second Language Research* 3 (2), 154–166.

BIALYSTOK, E., 1987b, Words as things: Development of word concept by bilingual children. *Studies in Second Language Learning* 9, 133–140.

BIALYSTOK, E., 1988, Levels of bilingualism and levels of linguistic awareness. *Developmental Psychology* 24 (4), 560–567.

BIALYSTOK, E., 1997, Effects of bilingualism and biliteracy on children's emerging concepts of print. *Developmental Psychology,* 33 (3), 420–440.

BIALYSTOK, E., 2001a, *Bilingualism in Development: Language, Literacy and Cognition.* Cambridge: Cambridge University Press.

BIALYSTOK, E., 2001b, Metalinguistic aspects of bilingual processing. *Annual Review of Applied Linguistics* 21, 169–181.

BIALYSTOK, E., 2001c, Literacy: The extension of languages through other means. In R.L. COOPER, E. SHOHAMY & J. WALTERS (eds), *New Perspectives and Issues in Educational Language Policy: A Festschrift for Bernard Dov Spolsky.* Amsterdam: John Benjamins.

BIALYSTOK, E. & CODD, J., 1997, Cardinal limits: Evidence from language awareness and bilingualism for developing concepts of number. *Cognitive Development* 12 (1), 85–106.

BIALYSTOK, E., CRAIK, F.I., KLEIN, R. & VISWANATHAN, M., 2004, Bilingualism, aging, and cognitive control: Evidence from the Simon task. *Psychology and Aging* 19 (2), 290-303.

BIALYSTOK, E. & HERMAN, J., 1997a, Does bilingualism matter for early literacy? *Bilingualism: Language and Cognition* 2 (1), 35 44.

BIALYSTOK, E. & MAJUMDER, S., 1999, The relationship between bilingualism and the development of cognitive processes in problem solving. *Applied Psycholinguistics* 19 (1), 69–85.

BJÖRKLUND, S., 1997, Immersion in Finland in the 1990s: A state of development and expansion. In R.K. JOHNSON & M. SWAIN (eds), *Immersion Education: International Perspectives.* Cambridge: Cambridge University Press.

BJÖRKLUND, S. & SUNI, I., 2000, The role of English as L3 in a Swedish immersion program in Finland. In J. CENOZ & U. JESSNER (eds), *English in Europe: The Acquisition of a Third Language.* Clevedon: Multilingual Matters.

BLACHFORD, D.R., 1997, Bilingual education in China. In J. CUMMINS & D. CORSON (eds), *Bilingual Education.* Volume 5 of the *Encyclopedia of Language and Education.* Dordrecht: Kluwer.

BLACHFORD, D.R., 2004a, The sociopolitical and economic foundation behind minority language education policies in China Since 1949. In R.W. HEBER (ed.) *Issues in Aboriginal/ Minority Education: Canada, China, Taiwan.* Regina, Saskatchewan: Indigenous Studies Research Centre, First Nations University of Canada.

BLACHFORD, D.R., 2004b, Language spread versus language maintenance: Policy making and implementation process. In M. ZHOU (ed.) *Language Policy in the People's Republic of China: Theory and Practice Since 1949.* Boston: Kluwer.

BLACKLEDGE, A., 2000a, *Literacy, Power and Social Justice.* Stoke on Trent: Trentham.

BLACKLEDGE, A., 2000b, Power relations and the social construction of 'literacy' and 'illiteracy': The experience of Bangladeshi women in Birmingham. In M. MARTIN-JONES & K. JONES, *Multilingual Literacies: Reading and Writing Different Worlds.* Amsterdam/Philadelphia: John Benjamins.

BLACKLEDGE, A., 2001, The wrong sort of capital? Bangladeshi women and their children's schooling in Birmingham, UK. *International Journal of Bilingualism* 5 (3), 345–369.

BLACKLEDGE, A. & PAVLENKO, A., 2001, Negotiation of identities in multilingual contexts. *International Journal of Bilingualism* 5 (3), 243–257.

BLOCK, D. & CAMERON, D., 2002, Introduction. In D. BLOCK & D. CAMERON (eds) *Globalization and Language Teaching.* London: Routledge.

BLOOMFIELD L., 1933, *Language.* New York: Holt.

BORLAND, H., 2005, Heritage languages and community identity building: The case of a language of lesser status. *International Journal of Bilingual Education and Bilingualism* 8 (2&3), 109–123.

BOSWELL, T.D., 1998, Implications of demographic changes in Florida's public school population. In S.H. FRADD & O. LEE (eds), *Creating Florida's Multilingual Global Work Force: Educational Policies and Practices for Students Learning English as a New Language.* Tallahassee, FL: Florida Department of Education.

BOURDIEU, P., 1977, The economics of linguistic exchanges. *Social Science Information* 16, 645-668.

BOURDIEU, P., 1991, *Language and Symbolic Power.* Cambridge: Polity Press.

BOURHIS, R., 2001a, Reversing language shift in Quebec. In J.A. FISHMAN, (ed.), *Can Threatened Languages be Saved?* Clevedon: Multilingual Matters.

BOURHIS, R., 2001b, Acculturation, language maintenance, and language shift. In J. KLATTER-FOLMER & P. VAN AVERMAET (eds), *Theories on Maintenance and Loss of Minority Languages.* Münster: Waxmann.

BOURHIS, R., GILES, H. & ROSENTHAL, D., 1981, Notes on the construction of a subjective vitality questionnaire for ethnolinguistic groups. *Journal of Multilingual and Multicultural Development* 2 (2), 145–166.

BOURNE, J., 2001a, Discourses and identities in a multilingual primary classroom. *Oxford Review of Education* 27 (1), 103–114.

BOURNE, J., 2001b, The role of the bilingual support assistant. *Community Languages Bulletin*, Spring 2001, Issue 8, p. 8. London: CILT.

BOURNE, J., 2001c, Doing 'what comes naturally': How the discourses and routines of teachers' practice constrain opportunities for bilingual support in UK primary schools. *Language and Education* 15 (4), 250–268.

BOYD, S. & LATOMAA, S., 1999, Fishman's theory of diglossia and bilingualism in the light of language maintenance and shift in the Nordic Region. In G. EXTRA & L. VERHOEVEN (eds), *Bilingualism and Migration*. Berlin/New York: Mouton de Gruyter.

BOYSSON-BARDIES, B., 1999, *How Language Comes to Children: From Birth to Two Years*. Cambridge, MA: MIT Press.

BRAINE, M.D., 1987, Acquiring and processing first and second languages. In P. HOMEL, M. PALIJ & D. AARONSON (eds), *Childhood Bilingualism: Aspects of Linguistic, Cognitive and Social Development*. Hillsdale, NJ: Lawrence Erlbaum.

BRANAMAN, L. & RHODES, N., 1998, *A National Survey of Foreign Language Instruction in Elementary and Secondary Schools*. Washington: Center for Applied Linguistics.

BRECHT, R.D. & INGOLD, C.W., 2002, *Tapping a National Resource: Heritage Languages in the United States*. Washington, DC: ERIC/CLL.

BREEN, M.P., 2002, Principles for the teaching of EAL/ESL children in the mainstream: Lessons from experience and professional development. In LEUNG, C., *Language and Additional/Second Language Issues for School Education*. York, UK: NADLIC.

BRELJE, H.W. (ed.), 1999, *Global Perspectives on the Education of the Deaf in Selected Countries*. Hillsboro, OR: Butte Publications.

BRIGHT, W. (ed.), 1992, *The International Encyclopedia of Linguistics*. Oxford: Oxford University Press.

BRISK, M.E., 1998, *Bilingual Education: From Compensatory to Quality Schooling*. Mahwah, NY: Lawrence Erlbaum.

BROHY, C., 2000, Compulsory or free section: Implementation and outcomes of bilingual models in Switzerland. Paper presented at the 5th European Conference on Immersion, Vaasa, August 2000.

BROHY, C., 2001, Generic and/or specific advantages of bilingualism in a dynamic pluralingual situation: The case of French as official L3 in the school of Samedan (Switzerland). *International Journal of Bilingual Education and Bilingualism* 4 (1), 38–49.

BROHY, C., 2005, Trilingual education in Switzerland. *International Journal of the Sociology of Language* 171, 133–148.

BROWN, D. (ed.), 1997, *Education Policy and Language Learning for a Multilingual Society*. Durban: University of Natal.

BRUCK, M., 1978, The suitability of Early French immersion programmes for the language-disabled child. *Canadian Journal of Education* 3 (4), 51–72.

BRUCK, M., 1982, Language impaired children's performance in an additive bilingual programme. *Applied Psycholinguistics* 3 (1), 45–60.

BRUTT-GRIFFLER, J., 2002, *World English: A Study of Its Development*. Clevedon: Multilingual Matters.

BRUTT-GRIFFLER, J. & VARGHESE, M., 2004, Introduction. *International Journal of Bilingual Education and Bilingualism* 7 (2&3), 93–101.

BULL, B.L., FRUEHLING, R.T. & CHATTERGY, V., 1992, *The Ethics of Multicultural and Bilingual Education*. New York: Teachers College Press.

BULLOCK REPORT (DEPARTMENT OF EDUCATION AND SCIENCE), 1975, *A Language for Life*. London: HMSO.

BULWER, J., 1995, European Schools: Languages for all? *Journal of Multilingual and Multicultural Development* 16 (6), 459–475.

BURCH, S., 2000, In a different voice: Sign language preservation and America's deaf community. *Bilingual Research Journal* 24 (4), 1–19.

BUTTITTA, I., 1972, *Io Faccio il Poeta*. Milan: Fetrinelli.

BYRAM, M., 1998, Cultural identities in multilingual classrooms. In J. CENOZ & F. GENESEE (eds), *Beyond Bilingualism: Multilingualism and Multilingual Education*. Clevedon: Multilingual Matters.

CALDWELL, J. & BERTHOLD, M., 1995, Aspects of bilingual education in Australia. In B.M. JONES & P.S.S. GHUMAN (eds), *Bilingualism, Education and Identity*. Cardiff: University of Wales Press.

CALERO-BRECKHEIMER, A. & GOETZ, E.T., 1993, Reading strategies of biliterate children for English and Spanish texts. *Reading Psychology* 14, 177–204.

CALIFORNIA STATE DEPARTMENT OF EDUCATION, 1984, *Studies on Immersion Education. A Collection for United States Educators*. Sacramento, CA: California State Department of Education.

CANADIAN EDUCATION ASSOCIATION, 1991, *Heritage Language Programs in Canadian School Boards*. Toronto: Canadian Education Association.

CANADIAN EDUCATION ASSOCIATION, 1992, *French Immersion Today*. Toronto: Canadian Education Association.

CANADIAN HERITAGE OFFICIAL LANGUAGES, 2004, *Annual Report 2002-2003*.

CANTONI, G. (ed.), 1996, *Stabilizing Indigenous Languages*. Flagstaff, AZ: Northern Arizona University.

CAREY, S.T., 1991, The culture of literacy in majority and minority language schools. *Canadian Modern Language Review* 47 (5), 950–976.

CARLISLE, J.F., BEEMAN, M., DAVIS, L.H. & SPHRAIM, G., 1999, Relationship of metalinguistic capabilities and reading achievement for children who are becoming bilingual. *Applied Psycholinguistics* 20 (4), 459–478.

CARRASQUILLO, A.L., 1990, Bilingual special education: The important connection. In A.L. CARRASQUILLO & R.E. BAECHER (eds), *Teaching the Bilingual Special Education Student*. Norwood, NJ: Ablex.

CARRASQUILLO, A.L. & RODRÍGUEZ, V., 2002, *Language Minority Students in the Mainstream Classroom* (2nd edn). Clevedon: Multilingual Matters.

CARREIRA, M. & ARMENGOL, R., 2001, Professional opportunities for heritage language speakers. In J.K. PEYTON, D.A. RANARD & S. MCGINNIS (eds), *Heritage Languages in America: Preserving a National Resource*. McHenry, IL: Delta Systems.

CARROLL, J.B., 1968, The psychology of language testing. In A. DAVIES (ed.), *Language Testing Symposium. A Psycholinguistic Perspective*. Oxford: Oxford University Press.

CARROLL, L., 1872, *Through The Looking-Glass, And What Alice Found There*. London: MacMillan & Co.

CARTER, T.P. & CHATFIELD, M.L., 1986, Effective bilingual schools: Implications for policy and practice. *American Journal of Education* 95 (1), 200–232.

CASTELLANO, J.A. & DÍAZ, E.I. (eds), 2002, *Reaching New Horizons: Gifted and Talented Education for Culturally and Linguistically Diverse Students*. Boston: Allyn & Bacon.

CAZABON, M., LAMBERT, W. & HALL, G., 1993, *Two-Way Bilingual Education: A Progress Report on the Amigos Program*. Santa Cruz, CA: National Center for Research on Cultural Diversity and Second Language Learning.

CAZDEN, C.B., 1992, *Language Minority Education in the United States: Implications of the Ramirez Report*. Santa Cruz, CA: National Center for Research on Cultural Diversity and Second Language Learning.

CENOZ J., 1998, Multilingual education in the Basque Country. In J. CENOZ & F. GENESEE (eds), *Beyond Bilingualism: Multilingualism and Multilingual Education*. Clevedon: Multilingual Matters.

CENOZ, J., 2000, Research on multilingual acquisition. In J. CENOZ & U. JESSNER (eds), *English in Europe: The Acquisition of a Third Language*. Clevedon: Multilingual Matters.

CENOZ, J., 2003, The additive effect of bilingualism on third language acquisition: A review. *International Journal of Bilingualism* 7 (1), 71–87.

CENOZ, J., 2004, Teaching English as a third language: The effect of attitudes and motivation. In C. HOFFMANN & J. YTSMA, J. (eds), *Trilingualism in Family, School and Community*. Clevedon: Multilingual Matters.

CENOZ J. & GENESEE, F., 1998, Psycholinguistic perspectives on multilingualism and multilingual education. In J. CENOZ & F. GENESEE (eds), *Beyond Bilingualism: Multilingualism and Multilingual Education*. Clevedon: Multilingual Matters.

CENOZ, J. & HOFFMANN, C., 2003, Acquiring a third language: What role does bilingualism play? *International Journal of Bilingualism* 7 (1), 1–5.

CENOZ, J. & JESSNER. U. (eds), 2000, *English in Europe: The Acquisition of a Third Language*. Clevedon: Multilingual Matters.

CENOZ, J. & PERALES, J., 1997, Minority language learning in the administration: Data from the Basque Country. *Journal of Multilingual and Multicultural Development* 18 (4), 261–270.

CENOZ, J. & VALENCIA, J.F., 1994, Additive trilingualism: Evidence from the Basque Country. *Applied Linguistics* 15, 195–207.

CENTER FOR APPLIED LINGUISTICS, 2001, *Expanding Educational Opportunity in Linguistically Diverse Societies*. Washington: Center for Applied Linguistics.

CENTER FOR THE IMPROVEMENT OF EARLY READING ACHIEVEMENT, 2003, *Put Reading*

First: The Research Building Blocks for Teaching Children to Read (2nd edn). Washington, DC: Partnership for Reading.

CHAMBERS, G.N., 1999, *Motivating Language Learners*. Clevedon: Multilingual Matters.

CHESHIRE, J., 2002, Who we are and where we're going: Language and identities in the new Europe. In P. GUBBINS & M. HOLT (eds), *Beyond Boundaries: Language and Identity in Contemporary Europe*. Clevedon: Multilingual Matters.

CHICK, J.K., 2002, Constructing a multicultural national identity: South African classrooms as sites of struggle between competing discourses. *Journal of Multilingual and Multicultural Development* 23 (6), 462-478.

CHORNEY, H., 1998, Bilingualism in employee recruitment and the role of symbolic analysts in leading export-oriented forms. In A. BRETON (ed.) *New Canadian Perspectives: Economic Approaches to Language and Bilingualism*. Ottawa: Department of Canadian Heritage.

CHRISTIAN, D., 1994, *Two-Way Bilingual Education: Students Learning Through Two Languages*. Santa Cruz, CA: National Center for Research on Cultural Diversity and Second Language Learning.

CHRISTIAN, D., MONTONE, C., LINDHOLM, K. & CARRANZA, I., 1997, *Profiles in Two-Way Immersion Education: Students Learning Through Two Languages*. Washington, DC: Center for Applied Linguistics.

CLAPHAM, C. & CORSON, D. (eds), 1997, *Language Testing and Assessment*. Volume 7 of the *Encyclopedia of Language and Education*. Dordrecht: Kluwer.

CLARKSON, P.C., 1992, Language and mathematics: A comparison of bilingual and monolingual students of mathematics. *Educational Studies in Mathematics* 23, 417–429.

CLARKSON, P.C. & GALBRAITH, P., 1992, Bilingualism and mathematics learning: Another perspective. *Journal for Research in Mathematics Education* 23 (1), 34–44.

CLINE, T., 1993, Educational assessment of bilingual pupils: Getting the context right. *Educational and Child Psychology* 10 (4), 59–68.

CLINE, T., 1997, Educating for bilingualism in different contexts: Teaching the deaf and teaching children with English as an additional language. *Educational Review* 49 (2), 151–158.

CLINE, T. & FREDERICKSON, N. (eds), 1995, *Progress in Curriculum Related Assessment with Bilingual Pupils*. Clevedon: Multilingual Matters.

CLINE, T. & FREDERICKSON, N. (eds), 1996, *Curriculum Related Assessment. Cummins and Bilingual Children*. Clevedon: Multilingual Matters.

CLINE, T. & FREDERICKSON, N., 1999, Identification and assessment of dyslexia in bi/multilingual children. *International Journal of Bilingual Education and Bilingualism* 2 (2), 81–93.

CLOUD, N., 1994, Special education needs of second language children. In F. GENESEE (ed.), *Educating Second Language Children*. Cambridge: Cambridge University Press.

CLOUD, N., GENESEE, F. & HAMAYAN, E.V., 2000, *Dual Language Instruction: A Handbook for Enriched Education*. Boston: Heinle & Heinle.

CLYNE, M., HUNT, C.R. & ISAAKIDIS, T., 2004, Learning a community language as a third language. *International Journal of Multilingualism* 1 (1), 33–52.

COELHO, E., 1998, *Teaching and Learning in Multicultural Schools*. Clevedon: Multilingual Matters.

COLLIER, V.P., 1989, How long? A synthesis of research on academic achievement in a second language. *TESOL Quarterly* 23 (3), 509–531.

COLLIER, V.P., 1992, A synthesis of studies examining long-term language minority student data on academic achievement. *Bilingual Research Journal* 16 (1&2), 187–212.

COLLIER, V.P., 1995, Acquiring a second language for school. *Directions in Language and Education* 1 (4), 1–12. (National Clearinghouse for Bilingual Education).

COMEAU, L., GENESEE, F. & LAPAQUETTE, L., 2003, The Modeling Hypothesis and child bilingual codemixing. *International Journal of Bilingualism* 7 (2), 113–126.

CONKLIN, N. & LOURIE, M., 1983, *A Host of Tongues*. New York: The Free Press.

COOK, V.J., 1992, Evidence for multicompetence. *Language Learning* 42 (4), 557–591.

COOK, V.J., 2002a, Background to the L2 user. In V. COOK (ed.), *Portraits of the L2 User*. Clevedon: Multilingual Matters.

COOK, V.J., 2002b, Language teaching methodology and the L2 user perspective. In V. COOK (ed.), *Portraits of the L2 User*. Clevedon: Multilingual Matters.

COOPER, R.L., 1989, *Language Planning and Social Change*. Cambridge: Cambridge University Press.

COBO-LEWIS, A.B., EILERS, R.E., PEARSON, B.Z. & UMBEL, V.C., 2002, Interdependence of Spanish and English knowledge in language and literacy among bilingual children. In D.K.

OLLER & R.E. EILERS (eds), *Language and Literacy in Bilingual Children*. Clevedon: Multilingual Matters.

COULMAS, F., 1992, *Language and Economy*. Oxford: Blackwell.

COUNCIL OF EUROPE, 2001, *Common European Framework of Reference for Languages: Learning, Teaching, Assessment*. Cambridge: Cambridge University Press.

CRAWFORD, J., 1999, *Bilingual Education: History, Politics, Theory and Practice* (4th edn). Los Angeles: Bilingual Educational Services.

CRAWFORD, J., 2000, *At War with Diversity: US Language Policy in an Age of Anxiety*. Clevedon: Multilingual Matters.

CRAWFORD, J., 2003, *Hard Sell: Why is Bilingual Education so Unpopular with the American Public?* (EPSL-0302-102-LPRU). Tempe, AZ: Arizona State University, Language Policy Research Unit.

CRAWFORD, J., 2004, *Educating English Learners: Language Diversity in the Classroom*. Los Angeles, CA: Bilingual Education Services.

CREESE, A., 2004, Bilingual teachers in mainstream secondary school classrooms: Using Turkish for curriculum learning. *International Journal of Bilingual Education and Bilingualism* 7 (2&3), 189–203.

CRYSTAL, D., 1995, *The Cambridge Encyclopedia of the English Language*. Cambridge: Cambridge University Press.

CRYSTAL, D., 1997a, *English as a Global Language*. Cambridge: Cambridge University Press.

CRYSTAL, D., 1997b, *The Cambridge Encyclopedia of Language* (2nd edn). Cambridge: Cambridge University Press.

CRYSTAL, D., 2000, *Language Death*. Cambridge: Cambridge University Press.

CUMMINS, J., 1975, Cognitive factors associated with intermediate levels of bilingual skills. Unpublished manuscript, Educational Research Centre, St Patrick's College, Dublin.

CUMMINS, J., 1976, The influence of bilingualism on cognitive growth: A synthesis of research findings and explanatory hypotheses. *Working Papers on Bilingualism* 9, 1–43.

CUMMINS, J., 1977, Cognitive factors associated with the attainment of intermediate levels of bilingual skills. *Modern Language Journal* 61, 3–12.

CUMMINS, J., 1978, Metalinguistic development of children in bilingual education programs: Data from Irish and Canadian Ukrainian English programs. In M. PARADIS (ed.), *Aspects of Bilingualism*. Columbia: Hornbeam Press.

CUMMINS, J., 1979, Cognitive/academic language proficiency, linguistic interdependence, the optimum age question. *Working Papers on Bilingualism* 19, 121–129.

CUMMINS, J., 1980a, The construct of language proficiency in bilingual education. In J.E. ALATIS (ed.), *Georgetown University Round Table on Languages and Linguistics 1980*. Washington, DC: Georgetown University Press.

CUMMINS, J., 1980b, The entry and exit fallacy in bilingual education. *NABE Journal* 4 (3), 25–59.

CUMMINS, J., 1981a, *Bilingualism and Minority Language Children*. Ontario: Ontario Institute for Studies in Education.

CUMMINS, J., 1981b, The role of primary language development in promoting educational success for language minority students. In CALIFORNIA STATE DEPARTMENT OF EDUCATION (ed.), *Schooling and Language Minority Students. A Theoretical Framework*. Los Angeles, CA: California State Department of Education.

CUMMINS, J., 1983a, *Heritage Language Education: A Literature Review*. Ontario: Ministry of Education.

CUMMINS, J., 1983b, Language proficiency, biliteracy and French immersion. *Canadian Journal of Education* 8 (2), 117–138.

CUMMINS, J., 1984a, *Bilingualism and Special Education: Issues in Assessment and Pedagogy*. Clevedon: Multilingual Matters.

CUMMINS, J., 1984b, Wanted: A theoretical framework for relating language proficiency to academic achievement among bilingual students. In C. RIVERA (ed.), *Language Proficiency and Academic Achievement*. Clevedon: Multilingual Matters.

CUMMINS, J., 1986, Empowering minority students: A framework for intervention. *Harvard Educational Review* 56 (1), 18–36.

CUMMINS, J., 1992a, Heritage language teaching in Canadian schools. *Journal of Curriculum Studies* 24 (3), 281–286.

CUMMINS, J., 1992b, Bilingual education and English immersion: The Ramirez Report in theoretical perspective. *Bilingual Research Journal* 16 (1&2), 91–104.

CUMMINS, J., 1993, The research base for heritage language promotion. In M. DANESI, K.

McLEOD & S. MORRIS (eds), *Heritage Languages and Education: The Canadian Experience*. Oakville: Mosaic Press.

CUMMINS, J., 1996, *Negotiating Identities: Education for Empowerment in a Diverse Society*. Ontario, CA: California Association for Bilingual Education.

CUMMINS, J., 1997, Cultural and linguistic diversity in education: A mainstream issue? *Educational Review* 49 (2), 105–114.

CUMMINS, J., 1999a, Alternative paradigms in bilingual education research: Does theory have a place? *Educational Researcher* 28 (7), 26–32 (plus p. 41).

CUMMINS, J., 1999b, The ethics of Doublethink: Language rights and the bilingual education debate. *TESOL Journal* 8 (3), 13–17.

CUMMINS, J. 2000a, *Language, Power and Pedagogy: Bilingual Children in the Crossfire*. Clevedon: Multilingual Matters.

CUMMINS, J. 2000b, Putting language proficiency in its place: Responding to critiques of the conversational/academic language distinction. In J. CENOZ & U. JESSNER (eds), *English in Europe: The Acquisition of a Third Language*. Clevedon: Multilingual Matters.

CUMMINS, J. & CORSON, D. (eds), 1997, *Bilingual Education*. Volume 5 of the *Encyclopedia of Language and Education*. Dordrecht: Kluwer.

CUMMINS, J. & DANESI, M., 1990, *Heritage Languages. The Development and Denial of Canada's Linguistic Resources*. Toronto: Our Schools/Ourselves Education Foundation and Garamond Press.

CUMMINS, J. & MULCAHY, R., 1978, Orientation to language in Ukrainian–English bilingual children. *Child Development* 49, 1239–1242.

CUNNINGHAM-ANDERSSON, U. & ANDERSSON, S., 2004, *Growing Up in Two Languages: A Practical Guide* (2nd edn). London: Routledge.

CZIKO, G.A., 1992, The evaluation of bilingual education: From necessity and probability to possibility. *Educational Researcher* 21 (2), 10–15.

DAGENAIS, D., 2003, Accessing imagined communities through multilingualism and immersion education. *Journal of Language, Identity, and Education* 2 (4), 269–284.

DANESI, M., 1991, Revisiting the research findings on heritage language learning: Three interpretive frames. *Canadian Modern Language Review* 47 (4), 650–659.

DANESI, M., McLEOD, K. & MORRIS, S. (eds), 1993, *Heritage Languages and Education: The Canadian Experience*. Oakville: Mosaic Press.

DANIEL-WHITE, K., 2002, Reassessing parent involvement: Involving language parents in school work at home. *Working Papers in Educational Linguistics* 18 (1), 29–49.

DANOFF, M.N., COLES, G.J., McLAUGHLIN, D.H. & REYNOLDS, D.J., 1977, *Evaluation of the Impact of ESEA Title VII Spanish/English Bilingual Education Programs Volume 1*. Palo Alto, CA: American Institutes for Research.

DANOFF, M.N., COLES, G.J., McLAUGHLIN, D.H. & REYNOLDS, D.J., 1978, *Evaluation of the Impact of ESEA Title VII Spanish/English Bilingual Education Programs Volume 3*. Palo Alto, CA: American Institutes for Research.

DATTA, M., 2000, Bilingual readers. In M. DATTA (ed.) *Bilinguality and Literacy: Principles and Practice*. London: Continuum.

DAVIES, A., 1996, Review article: Ironising the myth of linguicism. *Journal of Multilingual and Multicultural Development* 17 (6), 485–496.

DAVIES, A., 2003, *The Native Speaker: Myth and Reality*. Clevedon: Multilingual Matters.

DAVISON, C. & WILLIAMS, A., 2001, Integrating language and content: Unresolved issues. In B. MOHAN, C. LEUNG & C. DAVISON, *English as a Second Language in the Mainstream: Teaching, Learning and Identity*. Harlow, England: Longman.

DAWE, L.C., 1982, The influence of a bilingual child's first language competence on reasoning in mathematics. Unpublished PhD dissertation, University of Cambridge.

DAWE L.C., 1983, Bilingualism and mathematical reasoning in English as a second language. *Educational Studies in Mathematics* 14 (1), 325–353.

DE BOT, K. & MAKONI, S., 2005, *Language and Aging in Multilingual Contexts: An Applied Linguistics Approach*. Clevedon: Multilingual Matters.

DE COURCY, M., 2002, *Learners' Experiences of Immersion Education: Case Studies of French and Chinese*. Clevedon: Multilingual Matters.

DE COURCY, M., WARREN, J. & BURSTON, M., 2002, Children from diverse backgrounds in an immersion programme. *Language and Education* 16 (2), 112–127.

DE HOUWER, A., 1990, *The Acquisition of Two Languages from Birth: A Case Study*. New York: Cambridge University Press.

DE HOUWER, A., 1995, Bilingual language acquisition. In P. FLETCHER & B. MACWHINNEY (eds), *The Handbook of Child Language*. Oxford: Blackwell.

DE HOUWER, A., 2003, Home languages spoken in officially monolingual Flanders: A survey. *Plurilingua* 24, 79-96.

DE HOUWER, A., 2004, Trilingual input and children's language use in trilingual families in Flanders. In C. HOFFMANN & J. YTSMA (eds), *Trilingualism in Family, School and Community*. Clevedon: Multilingual Matters.

DE HOUWER, A., 2005, Bilingual development in the early years. In K. BROWN (ed.), *Encyclopedia of Language and Linguistics* (2nd edn). Oxford: Elsevier.

DEAF EX-MAINSTREAMERS GROUP (ed.), 2003, *Between a Rock and a Hard Place*. Ossett, West Yorkshire, UK: DEAF Ex-Mainstreamers Group.

DEAF EX-MAINSTREAMERS GROUP, 2004, *Deaf Toolkit: Best Value Review of Deaf Children in Education, from Users' Perspective*. Ossett, West Yorkshire, UK: DEAF Ex-Mainstreamers Group.

DEL VALLE, S., 1998, Bilingual education for Puerto Ricans in New York City. *Harvard Educational Review* 68 (2), 193–217.

DEL VALLE, S., 2003, *Language Rights and the Law in the United States: Finding Our Voices*. Clevedon: Multilingual Matters.

DELGADO-GAITAN, C., 1990, *Literacy for Empowerment: The Role of Parents in Children's Education*. New York: Falmer.

DELGADO-GAITAN, C. & TRUEBA, H., 1991, *Crossing Cultural Borders: Education for Immigrant Families in America*. New York: Falmer.

DELPIT, L.D., 1988, The silenced dialogue: Power and pedagogy in educating other people's children. *Harvard Educational Review* 58 (3), 280–298.

DELPIT, L.D., 1995, *Other People's Children: Cultural Conflict in the Classroom*. New York: New York Press.

DEMMERT, W.G., 2001, *Improving Academic Performance among Native American Students: A Review of the Research Literature*. Charleston, WV: ERIC Clearinghouse on Rural Education and Small Schools.

DEUCHAR, M. & MUNTZ, R., 2003, Factors accounting for code-mixing in an early developing bilingual. In MULLER, N. (ed.) *(In)vulnerable Domains in Multilingualism*. Amsterdam: John Benjamins.

DEUCHAR, M., & QUAY, S., 1999, Language choice in the earliest utterances: A case study with methodological implications. *Journal of Child Language* 26 (2), 461–475.

DEUCHAR, M. & QUAY, S., 2000, *Bilingual Acquisition: Theoretical Implications of a Case Study*. Oxford: Oxford University Press.

DEUSEN-SCHOLL, N., 2003, Toward a definition of heritage language: Sociopolitical and pedagogical considerations. *Journal of Language, Identity, and Education* 2 (3), 211–230.

DEWAELE, J-M., 2000, Three years old and three first languages. *Bilingual Family Newsletter* 17 (2), 4–5.

DEWAELE, J-M., 2002, Book review of Masayo Yamamoto: 'Language Use in Interlingual Families'. *Applied Linguistics* 23 (4), 546-547.

DI PIETRO, R., 1977, Code-switching as a verbal strategy among bilinguals. In F. ECKMAN (ed.), *Current Themes in Linguistics*. Washington, DC: Hemisphere Publishing.

DÍAZ, E. & FLORES, B., 2001, Teacher as sociocultural, sociohistoric mediator: Teaching to the potential. In M. REYES & J. HALCÓN (eds), *The Best for Our Children: Critical Perspectives on Literacy for Latino Students*. New York: Teachers College Press.

DIAZ, R.M., 1985, Bilingual cognitive development: Addressing three gaps in current research. *Child Development* 56, 1376–1388.

DICKER, S.J., 2000, Official English and bilingual education: The controversy over language pluralism in US society. In J.K. HALL & W.G. EGGINGTON (eds), *The Sociopolitics of English Language Teaching*. Clevedon: Multilingual Matters.

DICKER, S.J., 2003, *Languages in America: A Pluralist View* (2nd edn). Clevedon: Multilingual Matters.

DICKS, J.E., 1992, Analytic and experiential features of three French immersion programs: Early, middle and late. *Canadian Modern Language Review* 49 (1), 37–60.

DIEBOLD, A.R., 1964, Incipient bilingualism. In D. HYMES (ed.), *Language in Culture and Society*. New York: Harper and Row.

DIXON, R.M., 1997, *The Rise and Fall of Languages*. Cambridge: Cambridge University Press.

DOGANCAY-AKTUNA, S., 1997, Language planning. In N. HORNBERGER & D. CORSON (eds), *Research Methods in Language and Education*. Volume 8 of the *Encyclopedia of Language and Education*. Dordrecht: Kluwer.

DOLSON, D.P. & MEYER, J., 1992, Longitudinal study of three program models for language-minority students: A critical examination of reported findings. *Bilingual Research Journal* 16 (1&2), 105–157.

DONOVAN, S. & CROSS, C., 2002, Executive summary. In S. DONOVAN & C. CROSS (eds), *Minority Students in Special and Gifted Education*. Washington, DC: National Academy Press.

DÖPKE, S., 1992, *One Parent–One Language: An Interactional Approach*. Amsterdam: John Benjamins.

DORIAN, N.C., 1981, *Language Death: The Life Cycle of a Scottish Gaelic Dialect*. Philadelphia: University of Pennsylvania Press.

DORIAN, N.C., 1989 (ed.), *Investigating Obsolescence: Studies in Language Contraction and Death*. Cambridge: Cambridge University Press.

DORIAN, N.C., 1998, Western language ideologies and small-language prospects. In L.A. GRENOBLE & L.J. WHALEY, *Endangered Languages: Current Issues and Future Prospects*. Cambridge: Cambridge University Press.

DÖRNYEI, Z., 1994, Motivation and motivating in the second language classroom. *The Modern Language Journal* 78 (3), 273–284.

DÖRNYEI, Z., 1998, Motivation in second and foreign language teaching. *Language Teaching* 31 (3), 117–135.

DÖRNYEI, Z., 2001a, New themes and approaches in second language motivation research. *Annual Review of Applied Linguistics* 21, 43-59.

DÖRNYEI, Z., 2001b, *Teaching and Researching Motivation*. Harlow: Longman.

DÖRNYEI, Z. & CSIZER, K., 1998, Ten Commandments for motivating language learners: Results of an empirical study. *Language Teaching Research* 2 (3), 203–229.

DÖRNYEI, Z. & SCOTT, M.L., 1997, Communication strategies in a second language: Definitions and taxonomies (Review Article). *Language Learning* 47 (1), 173–210.

DOSANJH, J.S. & GHUMAN, P.A., 1996, *Child-Rearing in Ethnic Minorities*. Clevedon: Multilingual Matters.

DOYLE, A., CHAMPAGNE, M. & SEGALOWITZ, N., 1978, Some issues on the assessment of linguistic consequences of early bilingualism. In M. PARADIS (ed.), *Aspects of Bilingualism*. Columbia: Hornbeam Press.

DULAY, H.C. & BURT, M.K., 1978, *Why Bilingual Education? A Summary of Research Findings* (2nd edn). San Francisco, CA: Bloomsbury West.

DULAY, H.C. & BURT, M.K., 1979, Bilingual education: A close look at its effects. *Focus*, No. 1.

DUNCAN, S.E. & DE AVILA, E.A., 1979, Bilingualism and cognition: Some recent findings. *NABE Journal* 4 (1), 15–50.

DUQUETTE, G., 1999, *Vivre et enseigner en milieu minoritaire*. Sudbury, Ontario: Presses de l'Université Laurentienne.

DUTCHER, N., 1996, *Overview of Foreign Language Education in the United States*. NCBE Resources Collection Series, No. 6, Spring 1996. Washington, DC: National Clearinghouse for Bilingual Education.

DUTCHER, N., 2004, *Expanding Educational Opportunity in Linguistically Diverse Societies* (2nd edn). Washington, DC: Center for Applied Linguistics.

EALAW (English as an Additional Language Association of Wales), 2003, *The Achievement of Ethnic Minority Pupils in Wales*. Cardiff: National Assembly for Wales.

EASTMAN, C.M., 1992, Codeswitching as an urban language, contact phenomenon. *Journal of Multilingual and Multicultural Development* 13 (1&2), 1–17.

ECHEVARRÍA, J. & GRAVES, A., 1998, *Sheltered Content Instruction*. Boston: Allyn & Bacon.

ECHEVARRÍA, J., VOGT, M, & SHORT, D., 2000, *Making Content Comprehensible for English Language Learners: The SIOP Model*. Boston, MA: Allyn and Bacon.

ECIS (See European Council of International Schools).

EDELSKY, C., 1991, *With Literacy and Justice for All: Rethinking the Social in Language and Education*. London: Falmer.

EDELSKY, C., HUDELSON, S., FLORES, B., BARKIN, F., ALTWERGER, B. & JILBERT, K., 1983, Semilingualism and language deficit. *Applied Linguistics* 4 (1), 1–22.

EDUCATION COMMISSION OF THE STATES, 2004, *ECS Report to the Nation*.

EDUCATION DEPARTMENT OF HONG KONG, 1997, Medium of Instruction Guidance for Secondary Schools.

EDWARDS, J., 1985, *Language, Society and Identity*. Oxford: Blackwell.

EDWARDS, J., 1994a, *Multilingualism*. London: Routledge.

EDWARDS, J., 1994c, Ethnolinguistic pluralism and its discontents. *International Journal of the Sociology of Language* 110, 5–85.

EDWARDS, J., 2002, Forlorn hope? In LI WEI, J-M. DEWAELE & A. HOUSEN (eds), *Opportunities and Challenges of Bilingualism*. Berlin: Mouton de Gruyter.

EDWARDS, V., 1995a, Community language teaching in the UK: Ten years on. *Child Language Teaching and Therapy* 11 (1), 50–60.

EDWARDS, V., 1995b, *Reading in Multilingual Classrooms*. Reading: University of Reading.

EDWARDS, V., 1996, *The Other Languages: A Guide to Multilingual Classrooms*. Reading: Reading and Language Information Centre.

EDWARDS, V., 1998, *The Power of Babel: Teaching and Learning in Multilingual Classrooms*. Stoke-on-Trent: Trentham.

EDWARDS, V., 2004, *Multilingualism in the English-speaking World*. Oxford: Blackwell.

EDWARDS, V. & NEWCOMBE, L.P., 2005, New initiatives in intergenerational language transmission. *International Journal of Bilingual Education and Bilingualism* 8 (4), 298–312.

EDWARDS, V. & NWENMELY, H., 2000, Language, literacy and world view. In M. MARTIN JONES & K. JONES, *Multilingual Literacies: Reading and Writing Different Worlds*. Amsterdam/Philadelphia: John Benjamins.

EDWARDS, V. & REDFERN, A., 1992, *The World in a Classroom: Language in Education in Britain and Canada*. Clevedon: Multilingual Matters.

ELLIS, N., 1992, Linguistic relativity revisited: The bilingual word-length effect in working memory during counting, remembering numbers and mental calculation. In R.J. HARRIS (ed.), *Cognitive Processing in Bilinguals*. Amsterdam: North-Holland.

EPSTEIN, J., 1992, *School and Family Partnerships*. Baltimore: Center on Families, Communities, Schools and Children's Learning (John Hopkins University).

ERRASTI, M. P., 2003, Acquiring writing skills in a third language: The positive effects of bilingualism. *International Journal of Bilingualism* 7 (1), 27–42.

ESCAMILLA, K., CHAVEZ, L. & VIGIL, P., 2005, Rethinking the 'Gap': High stakes testing and Spanish-speaking students in Colorado. *Journal of Teacher Education* 56 (2), 132–144.

ESTYN, 2001, *Y Cwricwlwm Cymreig. The Welsh Dimension of the Curriculum of Wales: Good Practice in Teaching and Learning*. Cardiff: ESTYN.

ETXEBERRÍA, F., 2004, Trilinguals at four? Early trilingual education in the Basque Country. In C. HOFFMANN & J. YTSMA, J. (eds), *Trilingualism in Family, School and Community*. Clevedon: Multilingual Matters.

EUROPEAN COMMISSION, 1996, *Euromosaic: The Production and Reproduction of the Minority Language Groups in the European Union*. Luxembourg: Office for Official Publications of the European Communities.

EUROPEAN COUNCIL OF INTERNATIONAL SCHOOLS, 1998, *The ECIS International Schools Directory*. Saxmundham, Suffolk: John Catt Educational Ltd.

EUROPEAN UNION, 2001, *Europeans and Languages: Eurobarometer Survey 54*.

EVAS, J., 2000, Declining density: A danger for the language? In C.H. Williams (ed.) *Language Revitalization: Policy and Planning in Wales*. Cardiff: University of Wales Press.

EXTRA, G. & YAGMUR, K. (eds), 2004, *Urban Multilingualism in Europe: Immigrant Minority Languages at Home and School*. Clevedon: Multilingual Matters.

FABBRO, F., 1999, *The Neurolinguistics of Bilingualism: An Introduction*. Hove: Psychology Press.

FABBRO, F., 2002, The Neurolinguistics of L2 Users. In V. Cook (ed.), *Portraits of the L2 User*. Clevedon: Multilingual Matters.

FALTIS, C.J., 1993a, *Joinfostering: Adapting Teaching Strategies for the Multilingual Classroom*. New York: Macmillan.

FALTIS, C.J., 1993b, Critical issues in the use of sheltered content teaching in high school bilingual programs. *Peabody Journal of Education* 69 (1), 136–151.

FALTIS, C.J., 1997, *Joinfostering: Adapting Teaching for the Multilingual Classroom* (2nd edn). Upper Saddle River, NJ: Prentice Hall.

FALTIS, C.J. & HUDELSON, S.J., 1998, *Bilingual Education in Elementary and Secondary School Communities*. Boston: Allyn & Bacon.

FANTINI, A., 1985, *Language Acquisition of a Bilingual Child: A Sociolinguistic Perspective.* San Diego, CA: College Hill Press.

FEINBERG, R.C., 2002, *Bilingual Education: A Reference Handbook.* Santa Barbara, CA: ABC-CLIO.

FERGUSON, C., 1959, Diglossia. *Word* 15, 325–340.

FERGUSON, C.A., HOUGHTON, C. & WELLS, M.H., 1977, Bilingual education: An international perspective. In B. SPOLSKY & R. COOPER (eds), *Frontiers of Bilingual Education.* Rowley, MA: Newbury House.

FERGUSON, G., 2003, Classroom code-switching in post-colonial contexts. In S. MAKONI & U.H. MEINHOF (eds), *Africa and Applied Linguistics.* AILA Review Volume 16. Amsterdam: John Benjamins.

FEUERVERGER, G., 1997, 'On the edges of the map': A study of heritage language teachers in Toronto. *Teacher and Teacher Education* 13 (1), 39–53.

FEUERVERGER, G., 2001, *Oasis of Dreams: Teaching and Learning Peace in a Jewish-Palestinian Village in Israel.* New York: RoutledgeFalmer.

FIGUEROA, R.A., 2002, Toward a new model of assessment. In A.J. ARTILES & A.A. ORTIZ (eds), *English Language Learners with Special Educational Needs.* Washington, DC & McHenry, IL: Center for Applied Linguistics & Delta Systems Co..

FISHMAN, J.A., 1965, Who speaks what language to whom and when? *La Linguistique* 2, 67–68.

FISHMAN, J.A., 1971, The sociology of language. In J. FISHMAN (ed.), *Advances in the Sociology of Language, Volume 1.* The Hague: Mouton.

FISHMAN, J.A., 1972, *The Sociology of Language.* Rowley, MA: Newbury House.

FISHMAN, J.A., 1980, Bilingualism and biculturalism as individual and as societal phenomena. *Journal of Multilingual and Multicultural Development* 1, 3–15.

FISHMAN, J.A., 1989, *Language and Ethnicity in Minority Sociolinguistic Perspective.* Clevedon: Multilingual Matters.

FISHMAN, J.A., 1990, What is reversing language shift (RLS) and how can it succeed? *Journal of Multilingual and Multicultural Development* 11 (1&2), 5–36.

FISHMAN, J.A., 1991, *Reversing Language Shift.* Clevedon: Multilingual Matters.

FISHMAN, J.A., 1993, Reversing language shift: Successes, failures, doubts and dilemmas. In E.H. JAHR (ed.), *Language Conflict and Language Planning.* New York: Mouton de Gruyter.

FISHMAN, J.A. (ed.), 1999, *Handbook of Language and Ethnic Identity.* New York: Oxford University Press.

FISHMAN, J.A. (ed.), 2000, *Can Threatened Languages be Saved?* Clevedon: Multilingual Matters.

FISHMAN, J.A., 2001a, 300-plus years of heritage language education in the United States. In J.K. PEYTON, D.A. RANARD & S. MCGINNIS (eds.), *Heritage Languages in America: Preserving a National Resource.* McHenry, IL: Delta Systems.

FISHMAN, J.A., 2001b, From theory to practice (and vice versa). In J.A. FISHMAN, (ed.), *Can Threatened Languages be Saved?* Clevedon: Multilingual Matters.

FISHMAN, J.A., 2001c, Reversing language shift. In R. MESTHRIE (ed.) *Concise Encyclopedia of Sociolinguistics.* Oxford: Elsevier Science.

FISHMAN, J.A., 2006, 300-plus years of heritage language education in the United States. In G. VALDÉS, J.A. FISHMAN, R. CHÁVEZ & W. PÉREZ (eds), *Towards the Development of Minority Language Resources.* Clevedon: Multilingual Matters.

FORHAN, L.E. & SCHERAGA, M., 2000, Becoming sociopolitically active. In J.K. HALL & W.G. EGGINGTON (eds), *The Sociopolitics of English Language Teaching.* Clevedon: Multilingual Matters.

FRADD, S.H. & BOSWELL, T.D., 1996, Spanish as an economic resource in metropolitan Miami. *Bilingual Research Journal* 20 (2), 283–337.

FRANCIS, N. & REYHNER, J., 2002, *Language and Literacy Teaching for Indigenous Education.* Clevedon: Multilingual Matters.

FREDERICKSON, N. & CLINE, T., 1990, *Curriculum Related Assessment with Bilingual Children.* London: University College London.

FREDERICKSON, N. & CLINE, T., 1996, The development of a model of curriculum related assessment. In CLINE, T. & FREDERICKSON, N. (eds), *Curriculum Related Assessment. Cummins and Bilingual Children.* Clevedon: Multilingual Matters.

FREDERICKSON, N. & CLINE, T., 2002, *Special Educational Needs, Inclusion and Diversity: a Textbook.* Buckingham (UK): Open University Press.

FREEMAN, R., 1995, Equal educational opportunity for language minority students: From policy to practice at Oyster Bilingual School. *Issues in Applied Linguistics* 6 (1), 39–63.

FREEMAN, R., 1998, *Bilingual Education and Social Change* Clevedon: Multilingual Matters.

FREEMAN, R., 2004, *Building on Community Bilingualism*. Philadelphia: Caslon Publishing.

FREEMAN, Y.S., FREEMAN, A. & FREEMAN, D., 2003, Home run books: Connecting students to culturally relevant texts. *NABE NEWS*, 26 (3), 5–12, 28.

FREEMAN, Y.S., FREEMAN, D.E. & MERCURI, S., 2002, *Closing the Achievement Gap: How to Reach Limited-Formal-Schooling and Long-Term English Learners*. Portsmouth, NH: Heinemann.

FRIERE, P., 1970, *Pedagogy of the Oppressed*. New York: Seabury Press/Continuum.

FRIERE, P., 1973, *Education for Critical Consciousness*. New York: Continuum.

FRIERE, P., 1985, *The Politics of Education*. South Hadley, MA: Bergin and Garvey.

FRIERE, P. & MACEDO, D., 1987, *Literacy: Reading the Word and the World*. South Hadley, MA: Bergin and Garvey.

FROUDE, J., 2003, *Making Sense in Sign: A Lifeline for a Deaf Child*. Clevedon: Multilingual Matters.

GAARDER, A.B., 1977, *Bilingual Schooling and the Survival of Spanish in the United States*. Rowley, MA: Newbury House.

GAL, S., 1979, *Language Shift: Social Determinants of Linguistic Change in Bilingual Austria*. New York: Academic Press.

GALAMBOS, S.J. & HAKUTA, K., 1988, Subject-specific and task-specific characteristics of metalinguistic awareness in bilingual children. *Applied Psycholinguistics* 9, 141–162.

GÁNDARA, P. *et al.*, 2000, *The Initial Impact of Proposition 227 on the Instruction of English Learners*. University of California, Davis: UC Linguistic Minority Research Institute.

GANDHI, M., 1927 (English edition, 1949), *The Story of My Experiments with Truth*. London: Cape.

GARCÍA, E., 1983, *Early Childhood Bilingualism*. Albuquerque, NM: University of New Mexico Press.

GARCIA, E., 2002, Bilingualism and schooling in the United States. *International Journal of the Sociology of Language* 155/156, 1–92.

GARCÍA, O., 1988, *The Education of Biliterate and Bicultural Children in Ethnic Schools in the United States. Essays by Spencer Fellows of the National Academy of Education*, Vol. 4, pp. 19–78.

GARCÍA, O., 1991, Latinos and bilingual education in the United States: Their role as objects and subjects. *New Language Planning Newsletter* 6 (2), 3–5.

GARCÍA, O., 1992, For it is in giving that we receive: A history of language policy in the United States. Paper presented to a conference 'American Pluralism: Toward a History of the Discussion', State University of New York at Stonybrook, June 7th 1992.

GARCÍA, O., 1993, Understanding the societal role of the teacher in transitional bilingual classrooms: Lessons from sociology of language. In K. ZONDAG (ed.), *Bilingual Education in Friesland: Facts and Prospects*. Leewarden: Gemeens Chappelijk Centrum voor Onderwijsbegeleiding in Friesland.

GARCÍA, O., 1997, Bilingual education. In F. COULMAS (ed.), *The Handbook of Sociolinguistics*. Oxford: Blackwell.

GARCÍA, O. & BAKER, C. (eds) 2006, *Bilingual Education: An Introductory Reader*. Clevedon: Multilingual Matters.

GARCÍA, O. & OTHEGUY, R., 1985, The masters of survival send their children to school: Bilingual education in the ethnic schools of Miami. *Bilingual Review* 12 (1&2), 3–19.

GARCÍA, O. & OTHEGUY, R., 1988, The language situation of Cuban Americans. In S.L. McKAY & S.C. WONG (eds), *Language Diversity: Problem or Resource?* New York: Newbury House.

GARCÍA, O. & OTHEGUY, R., 1994, The value of speaking a LOTE in US business. *Annals of the American Academy of Political and Social Science* 532, 99–122.

GARCÍA, O. & TRAUGH, C., 2002, Using descriptive inquiry to transform the education of linguistically diverse US teachers and students. In LI WEI, J-M. DEWAELE & A. HOUSEN (eds), *Opportunities and Challenges of Bilingualism*. Berlin: Mouton de Gruyter.

GARCIA, R. & DIAZ, C.F., 1992, The status and use of Spanish and English among Hispanic youth in Dade County (Miami) Florida: A sociolinguistic study. *Language and Education* 6 (1), 13–32.

GARCIA, S.B., 2002, Parent–professional collaboration in culturally sensitive assessment. In A.J. ARTILES & A.A. ORTIZ (eds), *English Language learners with Special Educational Needs*. Washington, DC & McHenry, IL: Center for Applied Linguistics & Delta Systems Co..

GARDNER, H., 2003, Multiple intelligences after 20 years. Paper presented at the American Research Association, Chicago, Illinois, April 21, 2003.

GARDNER, N., 2000, *Basque in Education in the Basque Autonomous Community*. Vitoria-Gasteiz: Euskal Autonomi Erkidegoko Administrazioa.

GARDNER, R.C., 1985, *Social Psychology and Second Language Learning*. London: Edward Arnold.

GARDNER, R.C. & LAMBERT, W.E., 1972, *Attitudes and Motivation in Second Language Learning*. Rowley, MA: Newbury House.

GARRETT, P., COUPLAND, N. & WILLIAMS, A., 2003, *Investigating Language Attitudes: Social Meanings of Dialect, Ethnicity and Performance*. Cardiff: University of Wales Press.

GAWNE, P., 2003, Gaelic-medium education in the Isle of Man. In M. SCOTT & R. NÍ BHAOILL (eds), *Gaelic-Medium Education Provision: Northern Island, the Republic of Ireland, Scotland and the Isle of Man*. Belfast: Cló Ollsciol na Banríona.

GEARY, D., CORMIER, P., GOGGIN, J., ESTRADA, P. & LUNN, M., 1993, Mental arithmetic: A componential analysis of speed-of-processing across monolingual, weak bilingual and strong bilingual adults. *International Journal of Psychology* 28 (2), 185–201.

GEARY, D. & PAN, Y., 2003, A bilingual education pilot project among the Kam people in Guizhou Province, China. *Journal of Multilingual and Multicultural Development* 24 (4), 274-289.

GENERAL ACCOUNTING OFFICE, 1987, *Bilingual Education. A New Look at the Research Evidence*. Washington, DC: General Accounting Office.

GENESEE, F., 1983, Bilingual education of majority-language children: The immersion experiments in review. *Applied Psycholinguistics* 4, 1–46.

GENESEE, F., 1984, Historical and theoretical foundations of immersion education. In CALIFORNIA STATE DEPARTMENT OF EDUCATION (eds), *Studies on Immersion Education: A Collection for United States Educators*. California: California State Department of Education.

GENESEE, F., 1987, *Learning Through Two Languages*. Cambridge, MA: Newbury House.

GENESEE, F., 1992, Second/foreign language immersion and at-risk English-speaking children. *Foreign Language Annals* 25, 199-213.

GENESEE, F., 1998, A case study of multilingual education in Canada. In J. CENOZ & F. GENESEE (eds), *Beyond Bilingualism: Multilingualism and Multilingual Education*. Clevedon: Multilingual Matters.

GENESEE, F. (ed.), 1999, *Program Alternatives for Linguistically Diverse Students*. Santa Cruz: Center for Research on Education, Diversity & Excellence, University of California.

GENESEE, F., 2001, Bilingual first language acquisition: Exploring the limits of the language faculty. *Annual Review of Applied Linguistics* 21, 153–168.

GENESEE, F., 2002, Portrait of the bilingual child. In V. Cook (ed.), *Portraits of the L2 User*. Clevedon: Multilingual Matters.

GENESEE, F., 2003, Rethinking bilingual acquisition. In J-M. DEWAELE, A. HOUSEN & LI WEI (eds), *Bilingualism: Beyond Basic Principles*. Clevedon: Multilingual Matters.

GENESEE, F., BOIVIN, I. & NICOLADIS, E., 1996, Talking with strangers: A study of bilingual children's communicative competence. *Applied Psycholinguistics* 17 (4), 427–442.

GENESEE, F. & GÁNDARA, P., 1999, Bilingual education programs: A cross national perspective. *Journal of Social Issues* 55 (4), 665–685.

GENESEE, F. & HAMAYAN, E., 1994, Classroom-based assessment. In F. GENESEE (ed.), *Educating Second Language Children*. Cambridge: Cambridge University Press.

GENESEE, F., LINDHOLM-LEARY, K.J., SAUNDERS, W. & CHRISTIAN, D., 2005, *Educating English Language Learners: A Synthesis of Empirical Evidence*. New York: Cambridge University Press.

GENESEE, F., PARADIS, J. & CRAGO, M.B., 2004, *Dual Language Development & Disorders: A Handbook on Bilingualism and Second Language Learning*. Baltimore: Paul H. Brookes.

GENESEE, F., TUCKER, G.R. & LAMBERT, W.E., 1975, Communication skills in bilingual children. *Child Development* 46, 1010–1014.

GERSTEN, R. & WOODWARD, J., 1994, The language minority student and special education: Issues, trends and paradoxes. *Exceptional Children* 60 (4), 310–322.

GIBBONS, P., 2002, *Scaffolding Language, Scaffolding Learning: Teaching Second Language Learners in the Mainstream Classroom*. Portsmouth, NH: Heinemann.

GILES, H., 2001, Ethnolinguistic vitality. In R. MESTHRIE (ed.) *Concise Encyclopedia of Sociolinguistics*. Oxford: Elsevier Science.

GILES, H., BOURHIS, R. & TAYLOR, D., 1977, Towards a theory of language in ethnic group relations. In H. GILES (ed.), *Language, Ethnicity and Intergroup Relations*. London: Academic Press.

GILES, H. & COUPLAND, N., 1991, *Language: Contexts and Consequences*. Milton Keynes: Open University Press.

GOLDSTEIN, B.S., 2002, Walking the talk: The joys and challenges of critical pedagogy. In A.J. ARTILES & A.A. ORTIZ (eds), *English Language Learners with Special Educational Needs*. Washington, DC & McHenry, IL: Center for Applied Linguistics & Delta Systems Co..

GOLEMAN, D., 1995, *Emotional Intelligence*. New York: Bantam Books.

GOLLAN, T.H. & ACENAS, L-A.R., 2004, What is TOT? Cognate and translation effects on tip-of-the-tongue states in Spanish–English and Tagalog–English bilinguals. *Journal of Experimental Psychology: Learning, Memory, and Cognition* 30 (1), 246–269.

GOLLAN, T.H., MONTOYA, R.I. & WERNER, G., 2002, Semantic and letter fluency in Spanish–English bilinguals. *Neuropsychology* 16 (4), 562–576.

GÓMEZ, L., FREEMAN, D. & FREEMAN Y., 2005, Dual language education: A promising 50-50 model. *Bilingual Research Journal* 29 (1), 145–164.

GONZALEZ, J.M., 1979, Coming of age in bilingual/bicultural education: A historical perspective. In H.T. TRUEBA & C. BARNETT-MIZRAHI (eds), *Bilingual Multicultural Education and the Professional: From Theory to Practice*. Rowley, MA: Newbury House.

GORAL, M., LEVY, E.S., OBLER, L.K., 2002, Neurolinguistic aspects of bilingualism. *International Journal of Bilingualism* 6 (4), 411–440.

GORDON, M.M., 1964, *Assimilation in American Life: The Role of Race, Religion and National Origins*. New York: Oxford University Press.

GRADDOL, D., 1997, *The Future of English?* London: British Council.

GRADDOL, D. & MEINHOF, U.H. (eds), 1999, *English in a Changing World*. AILA Review 13. Oxford: Catchline (The English Trading Company).

GREEN, D.W., 1998, Bilingualism and thought. *Psychologica Belgica* 38 (3/4), 251–276.

GREENE, J., 1998, *A Meta-Analysis of the Effectiveness of Bilingual Education*. Claremont, CA: Tomas Rivera Policy Institute.

GREGORY, E., 1993, Sweet and sour: Learning to read in a British and Chinese school. *English in Education* 27 (3), 53–59.

GREGORY, E., 1994, Cultural assumptions and early years' pedagogy: The effect of the home culture on minority children's interpretation of reading in school. *Language, Culture and Curriculum* 7 (2), 111–124.

GREGORY, E., 1996, *Making Sense of a New World: Learning to Read in a Second Language*. Paul Chapman, London.

GREGORY, E., LONG, S. & VOLK, D., 2004, Introduction: Syncretic Literacy Studies: Starting Points. In E. GREGORY, S. LONG, & D. VOLK, (eds) *Many Pathways to Literacy: Young Children Learning with Siblings, Grandparents and Communities*. London: RoutledgeFalmer.

GREGORY, E. & WILLIAMS, A., 2000, Work or play? 'Unofficial' literacies in the lives of two East London communities. In M. MARTIN-JONES & K. JONES, *Multilingual Literacies: Reading and Writing Different Worlds*. Amsterdam/Philadelphia: John Benjamins.

GRENOBLE, L.A. & WHALEY, L.J., 1998, Toward a typology of language endangerment. In L.A. GRENOBLE & L.J. WHALEY, *Endangered Languages: Current Issues and Future Prospects*. Cambridge: Cambridge University Press.

GRIMES, B.F., 2000, *Ethnologue (14th edn) Volumes 1 & 2*. Dallas, TX: SIL International.

GRIN, F., HEXEL, D. & SCHWOB, I., 2003, Language diversity and language education: An introduction to the Swiss model. In P. CUVELIER, L.T. DU PLESSIS & L. TECK (eds), *Multilingualism, Education and Social Integration*. Pretoria, South Africa: Van Schaik.

GROSJEAN, F., 1982, *Life with Two Languages*. Cambridge, MA: Harvard University Press.

GROSJEAN, F., 1985, The bilingual as a competent but specific speaker-hearer. *Journal of Multilingual and Multicultural Development* 6 (6), 467–477.

GROSJEAN, F., 1992, Another view of bilingualism. *Cognitive Processing in Bilinguals* 83, 51–62.

GROSJEAN, F., 1994, Individual bilingualism. In R.E. ASHER & J.M. SIMPSON (eds), *The Encyclopedia of Language and Linguistics* (Volume 3). Oxford: Pergamon.

GROSJEAN, F., 2001, Bilingualism, individual. In R. MESTHRIE (ed.) *Concise Encyclopedia of Sociolinguistics*. Oxford: Elsevier Science.

GUBBINS, P & HOLT, M., 2002, *Beyond Boundaries: Language and Identity in Contemporary Europe*. Clevedon: Multilingual Matters.

GUPTA, A.F., 1997, When mother-tongue education is not preferred. *Journal of Multilingual and Multicultural Development* 18 (6), 496–506.

GUZMAN, J., 2002, English: New evidence on the effectiveness of bilingual education. *Education Next* 2 (3), 58–65.

HAGEMEYER, A., 1992, *The Red Notebook*. Silver Spring, MD: National Association of the Deaf.

HAKUTA, K., 1986, *Mirror of Language. The Debate on Bilingualism*. New York: Basic Books.

HAKUTA, K., 2001, A critical period for second language acquisition? In D. BAILEY, J. BRUER, F.

SYMONS & J. LICHTMAN (eds), *Critical Thinking about Critical Periods.* Baltimore: Paul Brookes Publishing Co.

HAKUTA, K., 2002, Comment. *International Journal of the Sociology of Language* 155/156, 131–136.

HAKUTA, K., BUTLER, Y.G. & WITT, D., 2000, *How Long Does it Take English Learners to Attain Proficiency?* University of California Linguistic Minority Research Institute Policy Report 2000–1.

HAKUTA, K. & D'ANDREA, D., 1992, Some properties of bilingual maintenance and loss in Mexican background high-school students. *Applied Linguistics* 13 (1), 72–99.

HALL, D., GRIFFITHS, D., HASLAM, L. & WILKIN, Y., 2001, *Assessing the Needs of Bilingual Pupils* (2nd ed.). London: David Fulton Publishers.

HALL, J.K. & EGGINGTON, W.G. (eds), 2000, *The Sociopolitics of English Language Teaching.* Clevedon: Multilingual Matters.

HALL, K., 1993, Process writing in French immersion. *Canadian Modern Language Review* 49 (2), 255–274.

HALL, K., 2002, Asserting 'needs' and claiming 'rights': The cultural politics of community language education in England. *Journal of Language, Identity, and Education* 1 (2), 97–119.

HALLIDAY, M.A.K., 1973, *Explorations in the Functions of Language.* London: Edward Arnold.

HAMMERLY, H., 1988, French immersion (does it work?) and the development of the bilingual proficiency report. *Canadian Modern Language Review* 45 (3), 567–578.

HANSEGÅRD, N.E., 1975, Tvåspråkighet eller halvspråkighet? Aldus, Series 253, Stockholm, 3rd edn.

HARDING-ESCH, E. & RILEY, P., 2003, *The Bilingual Family: A Handbook for Parents* (2nd edn). New York: Cambridge University Press.

HARLEY, B., 1991, Directions in immersion research. *Journal of Multilingual and Multicultural Development* 12 (1&2), 9–19.

HARLEY, B., 1994, After immersion: Maintaining the momentum. *Journal of Multilingual and Multicultural Development* 15 (2&3), 229–244.

HARNISCH, H. & SWANTON, P. (eds), 2004, *Adults Learning Languages: A CILT Guide to Good Practice.* London: CILT.

HARRIS, J., 1984, *Spoken Irish in Primary Schools. An Analysis of Achievement.* Dublin: Instituid Teangeolaiochta Eireann.

HARRIS, J. & MURTAGH, L., 1999, *Teaching and Learning Irish in Primary School: A Review of Research and Development.* Dublin: Instituid Teangeolaiochta Eireann.

HARRIS, S. & BARGIELA-CHIAPPINI, F., 2003, Business as a site of language contact. *Annual Review of Applied Linguistics' Language Contact and Change'* 23, 155-169.

HARRY, B., 1992, *Cultural Diversity, Families and the Special Education System: Communication and Empowerment.* New York: Teachers College Press.

HARTMAN, D. & HENDERSON, J. (eds), 1994, *Aboriginal Languages in Education.* Alice Springs, Australia: IAD Press.

HARWOOD, J., GILES, H., PIERSON, H., CLÉMENT, R. & FOX, S., 1994, Vitality perceptions of age categories in California and Hong Kong. *Journal of Multilingual and Multicultural Development* 15 (4), 311-318.

HELLER, M., 1982, Negotiations of language choice in Montreal. In J. GUMPERZ (ed.), *Language and Social Identity.* Cambridge: Cambridge University Press.

HELLER, M., 1994, *Crosswords: Language Education and Ethnicity in French Ontario.* Berlin and New York: Mouton de Gruyter.

HELLER, M., 1999a, *Linguistic Minorities and Modernity: A Sociolinguistic Ethnography.* New York: Longman.

HELLER, M., 1999b, Heated language in a cold climate. In J. BLOMMAERT (ed.) *Language Ideological Debates.* Berlin: Walter de Gruyter.

HELLER, M., 2002, Globalization and the commodification of bilingualism in Canada. In D. BLOCK & D. CAMERON (eds) *Globalization and Language Teaching.* London: Routledge.

HELLER, M. & MARTIN-JONES, M., 2001, Introduction: Symbolic domination, education, and linguistic difference. In M. HELLER & M. MARTIN-JONES (eds), *Voices of Authority: Education and Linguistic Difference.* Westport, CT: Ablex Publishing.

HENLEY, A. & JONES, R.E., 2000, *Earnings and Linguistic Ability in a Bilingual Economy.* Research Paper 2001-18. Aberystwyth: School of Management and Business.

HERNÁNDEZ-CHÁVEZ, E., BURT, M. & DULAY, H., 1978, Language dominance and proficiency testing: Some general considerations. *NABE Journal* 3 (1), 41–54.

HICKEY, T., 1997, *Early Immersion Education in Ireland: Na Naíonraí*. Dublin: Institiuid Teangeolaiochta Eireann.

HICKEY, T., 1999, Parents and early immersion: Reciprocity between home and immersion pre-school. *International Journal of Bilingual Education and Bilingualism* 2 (2), 94–113.

HICKEY, T., 2001a, Mixing beginners and native speakers in minority language immersion: Who is immersing whom? *Canadian Modern Language Review* 57 (3), 443–474.

HICKEY, T., 2001b, Second language writing systems: Reluctant readers of a minority language. In V. COOK & B. BASSETTI (eds), *Second Language Writing Systems*. Clevedon: Multilingual Matters.

HICKEY, T. & Ó CAINÍN, P., 2001, First language maintenance and second language acquisition of a minority language in kindergarten. In M. ALMGREN, A. BARRENA, M-J. EZEIZ ABARRENA, I. IDIAZABAL & B. MACWHINNEY (eds) *Research on Child Language Acquisition: Proceedings of 8th Conference for the Study of Child Language*. Somerville, MA: Cascadilla Press.

HINTON, L., 1998, Language loss and revitalization in California: Overview. *International Journal of the Sociology of Language* 132, 83–93.

HINTON, L. & HALE, K. (eds), 2001, *The Green Book of Language Revitalization in Practice*. San Diego, CA: Academic Press.

HOFFMAN, E., 1989, *Lost in Translation: A Life in a New Language*. New York: Dutton.

HOFFMANN, C., 1985, Language acquisition in two trilingual children. *Journal of Multilingual and Multicultural Development* 6 (6), 479–495.

HOFFMANN, C., 1998, Luxembourg and the European Schools. In J. CENOZ & F. GENESEE (eds), *Beyond Bilingualism: Multilingualism and Multilingual Education*. Clevedon: Multilingual Matters.

HOFFMANN, C., 2000, Balancing language planning and language rights: Catalonia's uneasy juggling act. *Journal of Multilingual and Multicultural Development* 21 (5), 425–441.

HOFFMANN, C., 2001, Towards a description of trilingual competence. *International Journal of Bilingualism* 5 (1), 1–18.

HOFFMANN, C. & YTSMA, J. (eds), 2004, *Trilingualism in Family, School and Community*. Clevedon: Multilingual Matters.

HOLBOROW, M., 1999, *The Politics of English*. London: Sage.

HOLM, A. & HOLM, W., 1990, Rock Point, A Navajo way to go to school. In C.B. CAZDEN & C.E. SNOW (eds), *The Annals of the American Academy of Political and Social Science*, Vol. 508, 170–184.

HOLM, A. & HOLM, W., 1995, Navajo language education: Retrospect and prospects. *Bilingual Research Journal* 19 (1), 141–167.

HOLOBOW, N.E., GENESEE, F. & LAMBERT, W.E., 1991, The effectiveness of a foreign language immersion program for children from different ethnic and social class backgrounds. *Applied Psycholinguistics* 12 (2), 179–198.

HOLT, D.D., 1993, *Cooperative Learning: A Response to Linguistic and Cultural Diversity*. McHenry, IL: Center for Applied Linguistics and Delta Systems.

HORNBERGER, N.H., 1988, *Bilingual Education and Language Maintenance: A Southern Peruvian Quechua Case*. Dordrecht, Holland: Foris.

HORNBERGER, N.H., 1989, Continua of biliteracy. *Review of Educational Research* 59 (3), 271–296.

HORNBERGER, N.H., 1991, Extending enrichment bilingual education: Revisiting typologies and redirecting policy. In O. GARCÍA (ed.), *Bilingual Education: Focusschrift in Honor of Joshua A. Fishman (Vol. 1)*. Amsterdam/Philadelphia: John Benjamins.

HORNBERGER, N.H., 1994, Literacy and language planning. *Language and Education* 8 (1&2), 75–86.

HORNBERGER, N.H. (ed.), 1997, *Indigenous Literacies in the Americas: Language Planning from the Bottom-Up*. Berlin: Mouton de Gruyter.

HORNBERGER, N.H., 2002, Language shift and language revitalization. In R.B. KAPLAN (ed.) *The Oxford Handbook of Applied Linguistics*. Oxford: Oxford University Press.

HORNBERGER, N.H., 2003a, Continua of biliteracy. In N.H. HORNBERGER (ed.) *Continua of Biliteracy: An Ecological Framework for Educational Policy, Research, and Practice in Multilingual Settings*. Clevedon: Multilingual Matters.

HORNBERGER, N.H.(ed.), 2003b, *Continua of Biliteracy: An Ecological Framework for Educational Policy, Research, and Practice in Multilingual Settings*. Clevedon: Multilingual Matters.

HORNBERGER, N.H., 2004, The continua of biliteracy and the bilingual educator: Educational linguistics in practice. *International Journal of Bilingual Education and Bilingualism* 7 (2&3), 155–171.

HORNBERGER, N.H. (ed.), 2005, Heritage/community language education: US and Australian perspectives. Special Issue of *International Journal of Bilingual Education and Bilingualism* 8, 2&3.

HORNBERGER, N.H. & CHICK, J.K., 2001, Co-constructing school safetime: Safetalk practices in Peruvian and South African classrooms. In M. HELLER & M. MARTIN-JONES (eds) *Voices of Authority: Education and Linguistic Difference*. Westport, CT: Ablex Publishing.

HORNBERGER, N.H. & CORSON, D. (eds), 1997, *Research Methods in Language and Education*. Volume 8 of the *Encyclopedia of Language and Education*. Dordrecht: Kluwer.

HORNBERGER, N.H., HARSCH, L. & EVANS, B., 1999, Language education of language minority students in the United States (The Six Nations Education Research Project: The United States). *Working Papers in Educational Linguistics* 15 (1), 1–92.

HORNBERGER, N.H. & KING, K.A., 2001, Reversing Quechua language shift in South America. In J.A. FISHMAN (ed.) *Can Threatened Languages Be Saved?* Clevedon: Multilingual Matters.

HORNBERGER, N.H. & SKILTON-SYLVESTER, E., 2003, Revisiting the continua of biliteracy: International and critical perspectives. In N.H. HORNBERGER (ed.) *Continua of Biliteracy: An Ecological Framework for Educational Policy, Research, and Practice in Multilingual Settings*. Clevedon: Multilingual Matters.

HOUSE, D., 2002, *Language Shift among the Navajos*. Tuscon, AZ: University of Arizona Press.

HOUSEN, A., 2002, Process and outcomes in the European Schools model of multilingual education. *Bilingual Research Journal* 26 (1), 1–9.

HOUSEN, A. & BAETENS BEARDSMORE, H., 1987, Curricular & extra-curricular factors in multilingual education. *SSLA* 9, 83–102.

HOWARD, E.R. & CHRISTIAN, D., 2002, *Two-Way Immersion 101: Designing and Implementing a Two-Way Immersion Education Program at the Elementary Level*. University of California at Santa Cruz: CREDA.

HOWARD, E.R., CHRISTIAN, D. & GENESEE, F., 2004, *The Development of Bilingualism and Biliteracy from Grade 3 to 5: A Summary of Findings from the CAL/CREDE Study of Two-Way Immersion Education*. University of California at Santa Cruz: CREDA.

HOWARD, E.R., SUGARMAN, J., CHRISTIAN, D., LINDHOLM-LEARY, K., ROGERS, D., 2005, *Guiding Principles for Dual Language Education*. Washington, DC: Center for Applied Linguistics.

HOWE, M.A.J., 1997, *IQ in Question: The Truth about Intelligence*. London: Sage.

HUDSON, A., 2001, Diglossia. In R. MESTHRIE (ed.) *Concise Encyclopedia of Sociolinguistics*. Oxford: Elsevier Science.

HUDSON, A., 2002, Outline of a theory of diglossia. *International Journal of the Sociology of Language*, 157, 1-48.

HUDSON, L., 1966, *Contrary Imaginations. A Psychological Study of the English Schoolboy*. Harmondsworth, Middlesex: Penguin.

HUDSON, L., 1968, *Frames of Mind*. Harmondsworth, Middlesex: Penguin.

HUFFINES, M.L., 1991, Pennsylvania German: 'Do they love it in their hearts?' In J.R. DOW (ed.), *Language and Ethnicity. Focusschrift in Honor of Joshua Fishman*. Amsterdam/Philadelphia: John Benjamins.

HUGUET, A., VILA, I. & LLURDA, E., 2000, Minority language education in unbalanced bilingual situations: a case for the linguistic interdependence hypothesis. *Journal of Psycholinguistic Research* 29 (3), 313–333.

HUSBAND, C. & KHAN, V.S., 1982, The viability of ethnolinguistic vitality: Some creative doubts. *Journal of Multilingual and Multicultural Development* 3 (3), 193–205.

HUSS-KEELER, R.L., 1997, Teacher perception of ethnic and linguistic minority parental involvement and its relationship to children's language and literacy learning: A case study. *Teacher and Teacher Education* 13 (2), 171–182.

HYLTENSTAM, K. & STROUD, C., 1996, Language maintenance. In H. GOEBL, P.H. NELDE, Z. STARY & W.WÖLK (eds) *Contact Linguistics: An International Handbook of Contemporary Research*. Berlin: Walter de Gruyter.

IANCO-WORRALL, A.D., 1972, Bilingualism and cognitive development. *Child Development* 43, 1390–1400.

IATCU, T., 2000, Teaching English as a third language to Hungarian–Romanian bilinguals. In J. CENOZ & U. JESSNER (eds), *English in Europe: The Acquisition of a Third Language*. Clevedon: Multilingual Matters.

IMOFF, G., 1990, The position of US English on bilingual education. In C.B. CAZDEN & C.E.

SNOW (eds), *The Annals of the American Academy of Political and Social Science, Vol. 508*, 48–61. London: Sage.

ISAACS, E., 1976, *Greek Children in Sydney*. Canberra: Australian National University Press.

JACOBSON, R., 1990, Allocating two languages as a key feature of a bilingual methodology. In R. JACOBSON & C. FALTIS (eds), *Language Distribution Issues in Bilingual Schooling*. Clevedon: Multilingual Matters.

JACQUES, K. & HAMLIN, J., 1992, PAT scores of children in bilingual and monolingual New Zealand primary classrooms, *Delta (NZ) 46*, 21–30.

JAMES, M. & WOLL, B., 2004, Black Deaf or Deaf Black? Being Black and Deaf in Britain. In A. PAVLENKO & A. BLACKLEDGE (eds) *Negotiation of Identities in Multilingual Contexts*. Clevedon: Multilingual Matters.

JANKOWSKI, K.A., 1997, *Deaf Empowerment: Emergence, Struggle and Rhetoric*. Washington, DC: Gallaudet University Press.

JEYNES, W.H., 2003, A meta-analysis: The effects of parental involvement on minority children's academic achievement. *Education and Urban Society 35* (2), 202–218.

JIMÉNEZ, R.T., GARCÍA, G.E. & PEARSON, P.D., 1995, Three children, two languages and strategic reading: Case studies in bilingual/monolingual reading. *American Educational Research Journal 32* (1), 67–97.

JOHNSON, R.K. & SWAIN, M., 1994, From core to content: Bridging the L2 proficiency gap in late immersion. *Language and Education 8*, 211–229.

JOHNSON, R.K. & SWAIN, M., 1997, *Immersion Education: International Perspectives*. Cambridge: Cambridge University Press.

JOHNSTONE, R., 2002, *Immersion in a Second or Additional Language at School: A Review of the International Research*. Stirling (Scotland): Scottish Centre for Information on Language Teaching.

JOHNSTONE, R., HARLEN, W., MACNEIL, M., STRADLING, B. & THORPE, G., 1999, *The Attainments of Pupils Receiving Gaelic-Medium Primary Education in Scotland*. Stirling (Scotland): Scottish Centre for Information on Language Teaching.

JONES, D.V, 2000, Talk and texts in bilingual mathematics lessons in Wales. *Welsh Journal of Education 9* (2), 102–119.

JONES, D.V. & MARTIN-JONES, M., 2004, Bilingual education and language revitalization in Wales: Past achievements and current issues. In J.W. TOLLEFSON & A.B.M. TSUI (eds) *Medium of Instruction Policies: Which Agenda? Whose Agenda?* Mahwah, NJ: Erlbaum.

JONES, G.M., 1997, Immersion programs in Brunei. In J. CUMMINS & D. CORSON (eds), *Bilingual Education*. Volume 5 of the *Encyclopedia of Language and Education*. Dordrecht: Kluwer.

JONES, G.M., MARTIN, P.W. & OZÓG, A.C.K., 1993, Multilingualism and bilingual education in Brunei Darussalem. In G.M. JONES & A.C.K. OZÓG (eds), *Bilingualism and National Development*. Clevedon: Multilingual Matters.

JONES, W.R., 1959, *Bilingualism and Intelligence*. Cardiff: University of Wales Press.

JONES, W.R., 1966, *Bilingualism in Welsh Education*. Cardiff: University of Wales Press.

JONG, E.J DE, 2002, Effective bilingual education: From theory to academic achievement in a two-way bilingual program. *Bilingual Research Journal 26* (1), 1–9.

KANNO, Y., 2003, Imagined communities, school visions, and the education of bilingual students in Japan. *Journal of Language, Identity, and Education 2* (4), 285–300.

KAPLAN, R.B. & BALDAUF, R.B., 1997, *Language Planning from Practice to Theory*. Clevedon: Multilingual Matters.

KARMANI, S., 2005, Petro-linguistics: The emerging nexus between oil, English, and Islam. *Journal of Language, Identity, and Education 4* (2), 87–102.

KARMANI, S. & PENNYCOOK, A., 2005, Islam, English, and 9/11. *Journal of Language, Identity, and Education 4* (2), 157–172.

KAUR, S. & MILLS, R., 1993, Children as interpreters. In R.W. MILLS & J. MILLS (eds), *Bilingualism in the Primary School*. London: Routledge.

KENNER, C., 2000, Children writing in a multilingual nursery. In M. MARTIN-JONES & K. JONES, *Multilingual Literacies: Reading and Writing Different Worlds*. Amsterdam/Philadelphia: John Benjamins.

KENNER, C., 2004a, *Becoming Literate: Young Children Learning Different Writing Systems*. Stoke on Trent: Trentham.

KENNER, C., 2004b, Living in simultaneous worlds: Difference and integration in bilingual script-learning. *International Journal of Bilingual Education and Bilingualism 7* (1), 43–61.

KESSLER, C. & QUINN, M., 1980, Positive effects of bilingualism on science problem-solving abilities. In J.E. ALATIS (ed.), *Georgetown University Round Table on Languages and Linguistics 1980*. Washington, DC: Georgetown University Press.

KESSLER, C. & QUINN, M.E., 1982, Cognitive development in bilingual environments. In B. HARTFORD, A. VALDMAN & C.R. FOSTER (eds), *Issues in International Bilingual Education. The Role of the Vernacular*. New York: Plenum Press.

KESTER, E.S. & PEÑA, E.D., 2002, Language ability assessment of Spanish-English bilinguals: Future Directions. *Practical Assessment, Research and Evaluation* 8 (4), 1–8. http://pareonline.net/getvn.asp?v=8&n=4

KIBBEE, D.A., 1998, Presentation: Realism and idealism in language conflicts and their resolution. In D.A. KIBBEE (ed.), *Language Legislation and Linguistic Rights*. Amsterdam & Philadelphia: John Benjamins.

KIM, K., RELKIN, N., LEE, K-M. & HIRSCH, J., 1997, Distinct cortical areas associated with native and second languages. *Nature*, Volume 388, 10th July, 171–174.

KINDLER, A.L., 2002, *Survey of the States' Limited English Proficient Students and Available Educational Programs and Services: 2000–2001 Summary Report*. Washington, DC: National Clearinghouse for English Language Acquisition and Language Instruction Educational Programs.

KING, K.A., 2001, *Language Revitalization Processes and Prospects*. Clevedon: Multilingual Matters.

KIRKNESS, V.J., 2002, The preservation and use of our languages: Respecting the natural order of the creator. In B. BURNABY & J. REYHNER (eds), *Indigenous Languages Across the Community*. Flagstaff, AZ: Northern Arizona University Center for Excellence in Education.

KLOSS, H., 1977, *The American Bilingual Tradition*. Rowley, MA: Newbury House.

KLOSS, H., 1998, *The American Bilingual Tradition*. McHenry, IL: Center for Applied Linguistics and Delta Systems.

KNIGHT P. & SWANWICK, R., 1999, *The Care and Education of a Deaf Child*. Clevedon: Multilingual Matters.

KOLERS, P., 1963, Interlingual word association. *Journal of Verbal Learning and Verbal Behavior* 2, 291–300.

KOWAL, M. & SWAIN, M., 1997, From semantic to syntactic processing: How can we promote it in the immersion classroom? In R.K. JOHNSON & M. SWAIN, *Immersion Education: International Perspectives*. Cambridge: Cambridge University Press.

KRASHEN, S., 1985, *The Input Hypothesis: Issues and Implications*. London: Longman.

KRASHEN, S., 1996, *Under Attack: The Case Against Bilingual Education*. Culver City, CA: Language Education Associates.

KRASHEN, S., 1999, *Condemned Without a Trial: Bogus Arguments Against Bilingual Education*. Portsmouth, NH: Heinemann.

KRASHEN, S., 2002, Developing academic language: Early L1 reading and later L2 reading. *International Journal of the Sociology of Language* 155/156, 143–151.

KRASHEN, S., 2004, The acquisition of academic English by children in two-way programs: What does the research say? Paper presented at the National Association of Bilingual Education Conference, February 2004, Albuquerque, NM.

KRASHEN, S., TSE, L. and McQUILLAN, J., 1998, *Heritage Language Development*. Culver City, CA.: Language Education Associates.

KRAUSS, M., 1992, The world's languages in crisis. *Language* 68, 6–10.

KRAUSS, M., 1995, Language loss in Alaska, the United States and the World. *Frame of Reference* (Alaska Humanities Forum) 6 (1), 2–5.

KRAUSS, M., 1998, The scope of the language endangerment crisis and recent response to it. In K. MATSUMARA (ed.) *Studies in Endangered Languages*. Papers from the International Symposium on Endangered Languages. Tokyo, November 18-20, 1995. Tokyo: Hituzi Syobo.

KRAUSS, M., 2000, Statement by Michael E. Krauss, Director Emeritus, Alaska Native Language Center, University of Alaska Fairbanks, July 20, 2000, at Hearing on S.2688, the Native American Languages Act Amendments Act of 2000.

KROLL, J.F. & DE GROOT, A.M.B., 1997, Lexical and conceptual memory in the bilingual: Mapping form to meaning in two languages. In DE GROOT, A.M.B. & KROLL, J.F. (eds), *Tutorials in Bilingualism: Psycholinguistic Perspectives*. Mahwah, NJ: Erlbaum.

LADD, P., 2003, *Understanding Deaf Culture: In Search of Deafhood*. Clevedon: Multilingual Matters.

LADO, R., 1961, *Language Testing*. New York: McGraw Hill.

LAITIN, D.D., 1997, The cultural identities of a European State. *Politics and Society* 25 (3), 277–302.

LAMBERT, W.E., 1974, Culture and language as factors in learning and education. In F.E. ABOUD

& R.D. MEADE (eds), *Cultural Factors in Learning and Education*. 5th Western Washington Symposium on Learning, Bellingham, Washington.

LAMBERT, W.E., 1980, The social psychology of language. In H. GILES, W.P. ROBINSON & P.M. SMITH (eds), *Language. Social Psychological Perspectives*. Oxford: Pergamon.

LAMBERT, W.E. & CAZABON, M., 1994, *Students' Views of the Amigos Program*. Santa Cruz, CA: National Center for Research on Cultural Diversity and Second Language Learning.

LAMBERT, W.E. & TUCKER, R., 1972, *Bilingual Education of Children. The St Lambert Experiment*. Rowley, MA: Newbury House.

LANDRY, R., ALLARD, R. & THÉBERGE, R., 1991, School and family French ambiance and the bilingual development of Francophone Western Canadians. *Canadian Modern Language Review* 47 (3), 878–915.

LANDRY, R. & BOURHIS, R.Y., 1997, Linguistic landscape and ethnolinguistic vitality: An empirical study. *Journal of Language and Social Psychology* 16 (1), 23–49.

LANZA, E., 1997, *Language Mixing in Infant Bilingualism: A Sociolinguistic Perspective*. Oxford: Oxford University Press.

LAOSA, L.M., 2000, *Non-language characteristics of instructional services for language minority students*. Washington, DC: National Clearinghouse for Bilingual Education.

LAPKIN, S., SWAIN, M. & SHAPSON, S., 1990, French immersion research agenda for the 90s. *Canadian Modern Language Review* 46 (4), 638–674.

LASAGABASTER, D., 2000, Three languages and three linguistic models in the Basque Country. In J. CENOZ & U. JESSNER. *English in Europe: The Acquisition of a Third Language*. Clevedon: Multilingual Matters.

LASAGABASTER, D., 2001, Bilingualism, immersion programmes and language learning in the Basque Country. *Journal of Multilingual and Multicultural Development* 22 (5), 401–425.

LAURÉN, C., 1994, Cultural and anthropological aspects of immersion. In *Language Immersion: Teaching and Second Language Acquisition: From Canada to Europe. Second European Conference 1994, Vaasa Finland*, Issue 192, pp. 21–26.

LAURÉN, C., 1997, Swedish immersion programs in Finland. In J. CUMMINS & D. CORSON (eds), *Bilingual Education. Volume 5 of the Encyclopedia of Language and Education*. Dordrecht: Kluwer.

LAURÉN, U., 1991, A creativity index for studying the free written production for bilinguals. *International Journal of Applied Linguistics* 1 (2), 198–208.

LAURIE, S.S., 1890, *Lectures on Language and Linguistic Method in School*. Cambridge: Cambridge University Press.

LEBLANC, R., 1992, Second language retention. *Language and Society* 37, 35–36.

LEBRUN, N. & BAETENS BEARDSMORE, H., 1993, Trilingual education in the Grand Duchy of Luxembourg. In H. BAETENS BEARDSMORE (ed.), *European Models of Bilingual Education*. Clevedon: Multilingual Matters.

LEE, J-W. & SCHALLERT, D.L., 1997, The relative contribution of L2 language proficiency and L1 reading ability to L2 reading performance: A test of the threshold hypothesis in an EFL context. *TESOL Quarterly* 31 (4), 713–739.

LEOPOLD, W.F., 1939–1949, *Speech Development of a Bilingual Child. A Linguists' Record* (4 volumes). Evanston, IL: Northwestern University Press.

LEUNG, C., 2005, Mathematical vocabulary: Fixers of knowledge or points of exploration? *Language and Education* 19 (2), 127-135.

LEWIS, E.G., 1977, Bilingualism and bilingual education: The ancient world of the Renaissance. In B. SPOLSKY & R.L. COOPER (eds), *Frontiers of Bilingual Education*. Rowley, MA: Newbury House.

LEWIS, E.G., 1981, *Bilingualism and Bilingual Education*. Oxford: Pergamon.

LEWIS, W.G., 2004, Addysg Gynradd Gymraeg: Trochi a Chyfoethogi Disgyblion, *Welsh Journal of Education* 12 (2), 49–64.

LI WEI, DEWAELE, J-M. & A. HOUSEN, A., 2002, Introduction: Opportunities and challenges of bilingualism. In LI WEI, J-M. DEWAELE & A. HOUSEN (eds), *Opportunities and Challenges of Bilingualism*. Berlin: Mouton de Gruyter.

LI WEI, MILLER, N. & DODD, B., 1997, Distinguishing communicative difference from language disorder in bilingual children. *Bilingual Family Newsletter* 14 (1), 3–4.

LI WEI, MILROY, L. & PON SIN CHING, 1992, A two-step sociolinguistic analysis of codeswitching and language choice: The example of a bilingual Chinese community in Britain. *International Journal of Applied Linguistics* 2 (1), 63–86.

LIN, A.M., 1996, Bilingualism or linguistic segregation? Symbolic domination, resistance and code switching in Hong Kong schools. *Linguistics & Education* 8 (1), 49–84.

LIN, J., 1997, Policies and practices of bilingual education for the minorities in China. *Journal of Multilingual and Multicultural Development* 18 (3), 193–205.

LINDHOLM, K.J., 1987, *Directory of Bilingual Education Programs* (Monograph No. 8). Los Angeles: University of Southern California, Center for Language Education and Research.

LINDHOLM, K.J., 1991, Theoretical assumptions and empirical evidence for academic achievement in two languages. *Hispanic Journal of Behavioral Sciences* 13 (1), 3–17. Also in A.M. PADILLA (ed.), 1995, *Hispanic Psychology: Critical Issues in Theory and Research*. Thousand Oaks, CA: Sage.

LINDHOLM, K.J., 1994, Promoting positive cross-cultural attitudes and perceived competence in culturally and linguistically diverse classrooms. In R.A. DEVILLAR, C. FALTIS & J. CUMMINS (eds), *Cultural Diversity in Schools: From Rhetoric to Practice*. Albany, NY: State University of New York Press.

LINDHOLM-LEARY, K.J., 2000, *Biliteracy for Global Society: An Idea Book on Dual Language Education*. Washington, DC: NCBE (see: http://www.ncbe.gwu.edu/).

LINDHOLM-LEARY, K.J., 2001, *Dual Language Education*. Clevedon: Multilingual Matters.

LINDHOLM-LEARY, K., 2005, *Review of Research and Best Practices on Effective Features of Dual Language Education Programs* (see http://www.lindholm-leavy.com/resources/review_research.pdf).

LINDHOLM, K.J. & ACLAN, Z., 1991, Bilingual proficiency as a bridge to academic achievement: Results from bilingual/immersion programs. *Journal of Education* 173 (2), 99–113.

LINDHOLM-LEARY, K. & BORSATO, G, 2006, Academic achievement. In F. GENESEE, K.J. LINDHOLM-LEARY, W. SAUNDERS & D. CHRISTIAN (eds), *Educating English Learners: A Synthesis of Empirical Evidence*. New York: Cambridge University Press.

LINQUANTI, R., 2001, *The Redesignation Dilemma: Challenges and Choices in Fostering Meaningful Accountability for English Learners*. Santa Barbara, CA: Linguistic Minority Research Institute, University of California.

LITTLEBEAR, R.E., 1996, Preface. In G. CANTONI (ed.) *Stabilizing Indigenous Languages*. Flagstaff: Northern Arizona University Press.

LITTLEBEAR, R.E., 1999, Some rare and radical ideas for keeping indigenous languages alive. In J. REYHNER, G. CANTONI, R. ST CLAIRE & E. PEARSONS YAZZIE (eds), *Revitalizing Indigenous Languages*. Flagstaff, AZ: Northern Arizona University Press.

LO BIANCO, J.L., 2001, *Language and Literacy Policy in Scotland*. Stirling: Scottish CILT.

LOTHERINGTON, H., 1998, Trends and tensions in post-colonial language education in the South Pacific. *International Journal of Bilingual Education and Bilingualism* 1 (1), 65–75.

LUCAS, T., HENZE, R. & DONATO, R., 1990, Promoting the success of Latino language-minority students: An exploratory study of six High Schools. *Harvard Educational Review* 60 (3), 315–340.

LUKMANI, Y.M., 1972, Motivation to learn and learning proficiency. *Language Learning* 22, 261–273.

LUYKX, A., 2003, Weaving languages together: Family language policy and gender socialization in bilingual Aymara households. In R. BAYLEY & S. SCHECTER (eds), *Language Socialization in Bilingual and Multilingual Societies*. Clevedon: Multilingual Matters.

LYON, J., 1996, *Becoming Bilingual: Language Acquisition in a Bilingual Community*. Clevedon: Multilingual Matters.

LYONS, J.J., 1990, The past and future directions of Federal bilingual-education policy. In C.B. CAZDEN & C.E. SNOW (eds), *Annals of the American Academy of Political and Social Science*, Vol. 508, 119–134. London: Sage.

MACÍAS R.F., 2000, The flowering of America: Linguistic diversity in the United States. In S.L. McKAY & S-L.C. WONG (eds), *New Immigrants in the United States*. Cambridge: Cambridge University Press.

MACINTYRE, P.D., BAKER, S.C., CLÉMENT, R. & NCONROD, S., 2001, Willingness to communicate, social support, and language-learning orientations of immersion students. *Studies in Second Language Acquisition* 23, 369-388.

MACKEY, W.F., 1970, A typology of bilingual education. *Foreign Language Annals* 3, 596–608.

MACKEY, W.F., 1976, *Bilinguisme et contact des langues*. Paris: Klincksieck.

MACKEY, W.F., 1978, The importation of bilingual education models. In J. ALATIS (ed.), *Georgetown University Roundtable: International Dimensions of Education*. Washington, DC: Georgetown University Press.

MACKEY, W.F., 1991, Language diversity, language policy and the sovereign state. *History of European Ideas* 13, 51–61.

MACNAB, G.L., 1979, Cognition and bilingualism: A reanalysis of studies. *Linguistics* 17, 231–255.

MACNEIL, M.M., 1994, Immersion programmes employed in Gaelic-medium units in Scotland. *Journal of Multilingual and Multicultural Development* 15 (2&3), 245–252.

MACSWAN, J., 2000, The threshold hypothesis, semilingualism, and other contributions to a deficit view of linguistic minorities. *Hispanic Journal of Behavioral Sciences* 22 (1), 3–45.

MACSWAN, J. & ROLSTAD, K., 2003, Linguistic diversity, schooling and social class: Rethinking our conception of language proficiency in language minority education. In C.B. PAULSTON & G.R. TUCKER (eds.) *Sociolinguistics: The Essential Readings.* Oxford: Blackwell

MAHER, J., 1997, Linguistic minorities and education in Japan. *Educational Review* 49 (2), 115–127.

MALAKOFF, M., 1992, Translation ability: A natural bilingual and metalinguistic skill. In R.J. HARRIS (ed.), *Cognitive Processing in Bilinguals.* Amsterdam: North-Holland.

MALDONADO, J.A., 1994, Bilingual special education: Specific learning disabilities in language and reading. *Journal of Educational Issues of Language Minority Students* 14, 127–147.

MALHERBE, E.C., 1946, *The Bilingual School.* London: Longman.

MAN, L.W. & LU, D., 2006, Persistent use of mixed code: An exploration of its functions in Hong Kong. *International Journal of Bilingual Education and Bilingualism* 9, in press.

MANEVA, B. & GENESEE, F., 2002, Bilingual babbling: Evidence for language differentiation in dual language acquisition. In B. SKARABELA, S. FISH & A. DO (eds), *BUCLD 26: Proceedings of the 26th Annual Boston University Conference on Language Development,* Volume 1, 383–392. Somerville, MA: Cascadilla Press.

MANGUBHAI, F., 2002, Language-in-education policies in the South Pacific: Some possibilities for consideration. *Journal of Multilingual and Multicultural Development* 23 (6), 490–511.

MANZER, K., 1993, Canadian immersion: Alive and working well in Finland. *Language and Society* 44, 16–17.

MARINOVA-TODD, S.H., MARSHALL, D.B. & SNOW, C.E., 2000, Three misconceptions about age and L2 learning. *TESOL Quarterly* 34 (1), 9–34.

MARTÍ, F. *et al.,* 2005 *Words and Worlds. World Languages Review.* Clevedon. Multilingual Matters.

MARTIN, D., 1997, Towards a new multilingual language policy in South Africa. *Educational Review* 49 (2), 129–139.

MARTIN-JONES, M., 2000, Bilingual classroom interaction: A review of recent research. *Language Teaching* 33 (1), 1–9.

MARTIN-JONES, M. & JONES, K., 2000, Introduction: Multilingual literacies. In M. MARTIN-JONES & K. JONES, *Multilingual Literacies: Reading and Writing Different Worlds.* Amsterdam/Philadelphia: John Benjamins.

MARTIN-JONES, M. & ROMAINE, S., 1986, Semilingualism: A half baked theory of communicative competence. *Applied Linguistics* 7 (1), 26–38.

MARTIN-JONES, M. & SAXENA, M., 2003, Bilingual resources and 'funds of knowledge' for teaching and learning in multi-ethnic classrooms in Britain. *International Journal of Bilingual Education and Bilingualism* 6 (3&4), 267–282.

MÄSCH, N., 1994, The German model of bilingual education. In R. KHOO, U. KREHER & R. WONG (eds), *Towards Global Multilingualism: European Models and Asian Realities.* Clevedon: Multilingual Matters.

MASHIE, S.N., 1995, *Educating Deaf Children Bilingually.* Washington, DC: Gallaudet University.

MATTHEWS, T., 1979, *An Investigation Into the Effects of Background Characteristics and Special Language Services on the Reading Achievement and English Fluency of Bilingual Students.* Seattle, WA: Seattle Public Schools, Department of Planning.

MAY, S., 1996, Indigenous language rights and education. In C. MODGIL, S. MODGIL & J. LYNCH (eds), *Education and Development: Tradition and Innovation* (Volume 1). London: Cassell.

MAY, S., 2000, Uncommon languages: The challenges and possibilities of minority language rights. *Journal of Multilingual and Multicultural Development* 21 (5), 366–385.

MAY, S., 2001, *Language and Minority Rights: Ethnicity, Nationalism and the Politics of Language.* London: Longman.

MAY, S., 2004, Maori-medium education in Aotearoa/New Zealand. In J.W. TOLLEFSON & A.B.M. TSUI (eds), *Medium of Instruction Policies: Which Agenda? Whose Agenda?* Mahwah, NJ: Erlbaum.

MAY, S. & HILL, R., 2004, Bilingual education in Aotearoa/New Zealand: At the crossroad. In K.

MCALISTER, K. ROLSTAD & J. MACSWAN (eds), *ISB4: Proceedings of the 4th International Symposium on Bilingualism.* Somerville, MA: Cascadilla Press.

MAY, S., HILL, R. & TIAKIWAI, S., 2004, *Bilingual/Immersion Education: Indicators of Good Practice.* New Zealand: Ministry of Education.

McCARTY, T.L., 1997, American Indian, Alaska Native, and Native Hawaiian bilingual education. In J. CUMMINS & D. CORSON (eds), *Bilingual Education.* Volume 5 of the *Encyclopedia of Language and Education.* Dordrecht: Kluwer.

McCARTY, T.L., 1998, Schooling, resistance, and American Indian languages. *International Journal of the Sociology of Language* 132, 27–41.

McCARTY, T.L., 2002a, Bilingual/bicultural schooling and indigenous students: A response to Eugene Garcia. *International Journal of the Sociology of Language* 155/156, 161–174.

McCARTY, T.L., 2002b, Between possibility and constraint: Indigenous language education, planning, and policy in the United States. In J.W. TOLLEFSON (ed.) *Language Policies in Education: Critical Issues.* Mahwah, NJ: Erlbaum.

McCARTY, T.L., 2003, Revitalising indigenous languages in homogenizing times. *Comparative Education* 39 (2), 147–163.

McCARTY, T.L., 2004, Dangerous difference: A critical-historical analysis of language education policies in the United States. In J.W. TOLLEFSON & A.B.M. TSUI (eds), *Medium of Instruction Policies: Which Agenda? Whose Agenda?* Mahwah, NJ: Erlbaum.

McCARTY, T.L. & BIA, F., 2002, *A Place To Be Navajo: Rough Rock and the Struggle for Self-Determination in Indigenous Schooling.* Mahwah, NJ: Lawrence Erlbaum.

McCARTY, T.L. & WATAHOMIGIE, L.J., 1999, Indigenous community-based language education in the USA. In S. MAY (ed.), *Indigenous Community-Based Education.* Clevedon: Multilingual Matters.

McCONNELL, B., 1980, Effectiveness of individualized bilingual instruction for migrant students. Unpublished PhD dissertation, Washington State University.

McGROARTY, M., 1990, Bilingualism in the workplace. *Annals of the American Academy of Political and Social Science* 511, 159–179.

McGROARTY, M., 1997, Language policy in the USA: National values, local loyalties, pragmatic pressures. In W. EGGINGTON & H. WREN (eds), *Language Policy: Dominant English, Pluralist Challenges.* Philadelphia: John Benjamins.

McGROARTY, M., 2002, Language Uses in Professional Contexts. In R.B. KAPLAN (ed.) *The Oxford Handbook of Applied Linguistics.* Oxford: Oxford University Press.

McKAY, P. *et al.*, 1997, *The Bilingual Interface Project Report.* Department of Employment, Education, Training and Youth Affairs, Canberra.

McKAY, S.L., 1988, Weighing educational alternatives. In S.L. McKAY & S.C. WONG (eds), *Language Diversity: Problem or Resource?* New York: Newbury House.

McKAY, S.L. & WONG, S-L.C. (eds), 2000, *New Immigrants in the United States.* Cambridge: Cambridge University Press.

McKINNIE, M.P. & PRIESTLY, T., 2004, Telling tales out of school: Assessing linguistic competence in minority language fieldwork. *Journal of Multilingual and Multicultural Development* 25 (1), 24–40.

McLAUGHLIN, T & McLAUGHLIN, D., 2000, Reversing Navajo language shift, revisited. In J.A. FISHMAN, (ed.), *Can Threatened Languages be Saved?* Clevedon: Multilingual Matters.

McLEAY, H., 2003, The relationship between bilingualism and the performance of spatial tasks. *International Journal of Bilingual Education and Bilingualism* 6 (6), 423–438.

McMAHON, A.M., 1994, *Understanding Language Change.* Cambridge: Cambridge University Press.

McNAMARA, T. F., 1996, *Measuring Second Language Performance.* London: Longman.

McNAMARA, T. F., 2003, Looking back, looking forward: Rethinking Bachman. *Language Testing* 20 (4), 466–473.

McQUILLAN, J. & TSE, L., 1995, Child language brokering in linguistic minority communities: Effects on cultural interaction, cognition and literacy. *Language and Education* 9 (3), 195–215.

McQUILLAN, J. & TSE, L., 1996, Does research matter? An analysis of media opinion on bilingual education, 1984–1994. *Bilingual Research Journal* 20 (1), 1–27.

MECHELLI, A., CRINION, J.T., NOPPENEY, U., O'DOHERTY, J., ASHBURNER, J., FRACKOWIAK, R.S. & PRICE, C.J., 2004, Neurolinguistics: Structural plasticity in the bilingual brain. *Nature*, 431, 757 (14 October 2004).

MEHLER, J., JUSCZYK, P., LAMBERTZ, G., HALSTED, N. BERTONCINI, J., AMIEL-TISON, C., 1988, A precursor of language acquisition in young infants. *Cognition* 29, 143–178.

MEISEL, J.M., 2004, The bilingual child. In T.K. BHATIA & W.C. RITCHIE (eds), *The Handbook of Bilingualism*. Malden, MA: Blackwell.

MEJÍA, A-M. DE, 2002, *Power, Prestige and Bilingualism: International Perspectives on Elite Bilingual Education*. Clevedon: Multilingual Matters.

MENKEN, K. & BARRON, V., 2002, What are the characteristics of the bilingual education and ESL shortage? *AskNCELA No. 14*. Washington: National Clearinghouse for English Language Acquisition and Language Instruction Educational Programs.

MERCER, J.R., 1973, *Labeling the Mentally Retarded*. Berkeley, CA: University of California Press.

MET, M., 1998, Curriculum decision-making in content-based language teaching. In J. CENOZ & F. GENESEE (eds), *Beyond Bilingualism: Multilingualism and Multilingual Education*. Clevedon: Multilingual Matters.

MET, M. & LORENZ, E.B., 1997, Lessons from US immersion programs: Two decades of experience. In R.K. JOHNSON & M. SWAIN, 1997, *Immersion Education: International Perspectives*. Cambridge: Cambridge University Press.

MEYER, M.M. & FIENBERG, S.E., 1992, *Assessing Evaluation Studies: The Case of Bilingual Education Strategies*. Washington, DC: National Academy Press.

MIGUEL, G.S., 2004, *Contested Policy. The Rise and Fall of Federal Bilingual Education in the United States 1960-2001*. Denton, TX: University of North Texas Press.

MILLS, J., 2004, Mothers and mother tongue: Perspectives on self-construction by mothers of Pakistani heritage. In A. PAVLENKO & A. BLACKLEDGE (eds), *Negotiation of Identities in Multilingual Contexts*. Clevedon: Multilingual Matters.

MITCHELL, D.E., DESTINO, T., KARAM, R.T. & COLÓN-MUÑIZ, A., 1999, Changes in educational policy: The politics of bilingual education. *Educational Policy* 13 (1), 86–103.

MITCHELL, R. & MYLES, F., 1998, *Second-Language Learning Theories*. London: Arnold.

MOHAN, B., 2001, The second language as a medium of learning. In B. MOHAN, C. LEUNG & C. DAVISON, *English as a Second Language in the Mainstream: Teaching, Learning and Identity*. Harlow, England: Longman.

MOHANTY, A.K., 1994, *Bilingualism in a Multilingual Society: Psycho-Social and Pedagogical Implications*. Mysore, India: Central Institute of Indian Languages.

MOHD-ASRAF, R., 2005, English and Islam: A clash of civilizations? *Journal of Language, Identity, and Education* 4 (2), 103–118.

MOLL, L.C., 1992, Bilingual classroom studies and community analysis. *Educational Researcher* 21 (2), 20–24.

MOLL, L.C., 2001, The diversity of schooling: A cultural-historical approach. In M. REYES & J. HALCÓN (eds), *The Best for Our Children: Critical Perspectives on Literacy for Latino Students*. New York: Teachers College Press.

MONTECEL, M.R. & CORTEZ, J.D., 2002, Successful bilingual education programs: Development and the dissemination of criteria to identify promising and exemplary practices in bilingual education at the national level. *Bilingual Research Journal* 26 (1), 1–10.

MORALES, R. & BONILLA, F., 1993, *Latinos in a Changing US Economy*. London: Sage.

MORGAN, B., 2004, Teacher identity as pedagogy: Towards a field-internal conceptualisation in bilingual and second language education. *International Journal of Bilingual Education and Bilingualism* 7 (2&3), 172–188.

MORISON, S.H., 1990, A Spanish–English dual-language program in New York City. In C.B. CAZDEN & C.E. SNOW (eds), *The Annals of the American Academy of Political and Social Science*, Vol. 508, 160–169. London: Sage.

MORRIS, D., 1992, The effects of economic changes on Gwynedd society. In L. DAFIS (ed.), *Lesser Used Languages: Assimilating Newcomers*. Carmarthen, Wales: Joint Working Party on Bilingualism in Dyfed.

MORRISON, S., 2001, *9/11 Brings U.S. Defense Language Needs Into Focus*. ERIC/CLL.

MOSELEY, C. & ASHER, R.E., 1994, *Atlas of the World's Languages*. London: Routledge.

MOSES, M.S., 2000, Why bilingual education policy is needed: A philosophical response to critics. *Bilingual Research Journal* 24 (4), 333-354.

MÜHLHÄUSLER, P., 2002, Ecology of languages. In R.B. KAPLAN (ed.) *The Oxford Handbook of Applied Linguistics*. Oxford: Oxford University Press.

MULLER, A. & BAETENS BEARDSMORE, H., 2004, Multilingual interaction in plurilingual classes – European School practice. *International Journal of Bilingual Education and Bilingualism* 7 (1), 24–42.

MUÑOZ, C., 2000, Bilingualism and trilingualism in school students in Catalonia. In J. CENOZ & U. JESSNER. *English in Europe: The Acquisition of a Third Language*. Clevedon: Multilingual Matters.

MUYSKEN, P., 2000, *Bilingual Speech: A typology of Code-mixing*. Cambridge: Cambridge University Press.

MYERS-SCOTTON, C., 1972, *Choosing a Lingua Franca in an African Capital*. Edmonton, Champaign (IL): Linguistic Research.

MYERS-SCOTTON, C., 1992, Comparing codeswitching and borrowing. *Journal of Multilingual and Multicultural Development* 13 (1&2), 19–39.

MYERS-SCOTTON, C., 1993, *Duelling Languages: Grammatical Structure in Codeswitching*. Oxford, New York: Oxford University Press.

MYERS-SCOTTON, C., 1997, Code-switching. In F. COULMAS (ed.), *The Handbook of Sociolinguistics*. Oxford: Blackwell.

MYERS-SCOTTON, C., 2002, *Contact Linguistics*. Cambridge: Cambridge University Press.

MYERS SCOTTON, C. & URY, W., 1977, Bilingual strategies: The social functions of code-switching. *Linguistics* 193, 5–20.

NATIONAL CLEARINGHOUSE FOR ENGLISH LANGUAGE ACQUISITION, 2005, *The Growing Numbers of Limited English Proficient Students: 1992/93-2002/03*. Washington: NCELA.

NATIONAL READING PANEL, 2000, *Teaching children to read: An evidence-based assessment of the scientific research literature on reading and its implications for reading instruction*. Washington, DC: National Institute of Child Health and Human Development.

NELDE, P.H., 1997, Language conflict. In F. COULMAS (ed.), *The Handbook of Sociolinguistics*. Oxford: Blackwell.

NELDE, P.H., LABRIE, N. & WILLIAMS, C.H., 1992, The principles of territority and personality in the solution of linguistic conflicts. *Journal of Multilingual and Multicultural Development* 13 (5), 387–406.

NETTEN, J. & GERMAIN, C., 2004, Theoretical and research foundations of intensive French. *The Canadian Modern Language Review* 60 (3), 275–294.

NETTLE, D. & ROMAINE, S., 2000, *Vanishing Voices: The Extinction of the World's Languages*. Oxford: Oxford University Press.

NICHOLLS, C., 2005, Death by a thousand cuts: Indigenous language bilingual education programmes in the Northern Territory of Australia, 1972-1998. *International Journal of Bilingual Education and Bilingualism* 8 (2&3), 160–177.

NICOLADIS, E., 1998, First clues to the existence of two input languages: Pragmatic and lexical differentiation in a bilingual child. *Bilingualism: Language and Cognition* 1, 105–116.

NICOLADIS, E. & GENESEE, F., 1996, Word awareness in second language learners and bilingual children. *Language Awareness* 5 (2), 80–90.

NICOLADIS, E. & GENESEE, F., 1997, Language development in preschool bilingual children. *Journal of Speech-Language Pathology and Audiology* 21 (4), 258–270.

NORTON, B., 2000, *Identity and Language Learning: Gender, Ethnicity and Educational Change*. Harlow: Longman.

NORTON, B. & TOOHEY, K., 2002, Identity and language learning. In R. B. KAPLAN (ed.) *The Oxford Handbook of Applied Linguistics*. Oxford: Oxford University Press.

NUFFIELD FOUNDATION, 2000, *Languages: The Next Generation: The Final Report and Recommendations of The Nuffield Languages Inquiry*. London: The Nuffield Foundation.

Ó GLIASÁIN, M., 1996, *The Language Question in the Census of the Population*. Dublin: Linguistics Institute of Ireland.

Ó MURCHÚ, H., 2003, Gaelic-medium education in the Republic of Ireland. In M. SCOTT & R. NÍ BHAOILL (eds), Gaelic-medium education in the Republic of Ireland. *Gaelic-medium Education Provision: Northern Ireland, the Republic of Ireland, Scotland and the Isle of Man*. Belfast: Cló Ollsciol na Banríona.

Ó RIAGÁIN, P., 1997, *Language Policy and Social Reproduction: Ireland 1893-1993*. Oxford: Oxford University Press.

Ó RIAGÁIN, P., 2000, Irish language production and reproduction 1981–1996. In J.A. FISHMAN, (ed.), *Can Threatened Languages be Saved?* Clevedon: Multilingual Matters.

OCHSE, E., 2001, EFL with adult deaf students: Two cultures, two approaches. In G. CORTESE &

D. HYMES. 'Languaging' in and Across Human Groups Perspectives on Difference and Asymmetry. Genova, Italy: Tilgher. (Textus (English Studies in Italy), 14, 447–472).

OKA, H., 1994, Studies on bilingualism and their implication in Japan. In R. MICHAEL BOSTWICK (ed.), Immersion Education International Symposium Report on Second Language Acquisition through Content-based Study: An Introduction to Immersion Education. Numazu, Japan: Katoh Gakuen.

OLLER, D.K. & EILERS, R.E. (eds), 2002, Language and Literacy in Bilingual Children. Clevedon: Multilingual Matters.

OLLER, J.W., 1979, Language Tests at School. London: Longman.

OLLER, J.W., 1982, Evaluation and testing. In B. HARTFORD, A. VALDMAN & C. FOSTER (eds), Issues in International Bilingual Education. New York: Plenum Press.

OLLER, J.W. & PERKINS, K., 1980, Research in Language Testing. Rowley, MA: Newbury House.

ORELLANA, M.F., EK, L., & HERNÁNDEZ, A., 1999, Bilingual education in an immigrant community: Proposition 227 in California. International Journal of Bilingual Education and Bilingualism 2 (2), 114–130.

ORTIZ, A.A., 2002, Prevention of school failure and early intervention for English language learners. In A.J. ARTILES & A.A. ORTIZ (eds), English Language Learners with Special Educational Needs. Washington, DC & McHenry, IL: Center for Applied Linguistics & Delta Systems Co.

ORTIZ, A.A. & YATES, J.R., 2002, Considerations in the assessment of English language learners referred to special education. In A.J. ARTILES & A.A. ORTIZ (eds), English Language Learners with Special Educational Needs. Washington, DC & McHenry, IL: Center for Applied Linguistics & Delta Systems Co.

OTHEGUY, R., 1982, Thinking about bilingual education: A critical appraisal. Harvard Educational Review 52 (3), 301–314.

OTHEGUY, R. & OTTO, R., 1980, The myth of static maintenance in bilingual education. Modern Language Journal 64 (3), 350–356.

OVANDO, C.J., 1990, Essay review: Politics and pedagogy: The case of bilingual education. Harvard Educational Review 60 (3), 341–356.

OVANDO, C.J., 2003, Bilingual education in the United States: Historical development and current issues. Bilingual Research Journal 27 (1), 1–24.

OVANDO, C.J., COLLIER, V.P. & COMBS, M.C., 2003, Bilingual and ESL Classrooms: Teaching in Multicultural Contexts (3rd edn). New York: McGraw Hill.

PAKIR, A., 1994, Making bilingualism work: Developments in bilingual education in ASEAN. In R. KHOO, U. KREHER & R. WONG (eds), Towards Global Multilingualism: European Models and Asian Realities. Clevedon: Multilingual Matters.

PARADIS, M., 2000, The neurolinguistics of bilingualism in the next decades. Brain and Language 71, 178–180.

PARADIS, M., 2004, A Neurolinguistic Theory of Bilingualism. Amsterdam/Philadelphia: John Benjamins.

PARRILLO, V.N., 1996, Diversity in America. Thousand Oaks, CA: Pine Forge Press.

PARRISH, T.B., LINQUANTI, R., MERICKEL, A., QUICK, H.E., LAIRD, J. & ESRA, P. 2002, Effects of the Implementation of Proposition 227 on the Education of English learners, K-12: Year 2 report. Palo Alto, CA: American Institutes for Research, and San Francisco: WestEd.

PAULSTON, C.B., 1980, Bilingual Education: Theories and Issues. Rowley, MA: Newbury House.

PAULSTON, C.B., 1992, Sociolinguistic Perspectives on Bilingual Education. Clevedon: Multilingual Matters.

PAULSTON, C.B., 1994, Linguistic Minorities in Multilingual Settings. Amsterdam/Philadelphia: John Benjamins.

PAULSTON, C.B., 1997, Language policies and language rights. Annual Review of Anthropology 26, 73–85.

PAVLENKO, A., 1999, New approaches to concepts in bilingual memory. Bilingualism: Language and Cognition 2 (3), 209–230.

PAVLENKO, A., 2000, What's in a concept? Bilingualism: Language and Cognition 3 (1), 31–36.

PAVLENKO, A., 2001a, Bilingualism, gender, and ideology. International Journal of Bilingualism 5 (2), 117–151.

PAVLENKO, A., 2001b, 'In the world of the tradition, I was unimagined': Negotiation of identities in cross cultural autobiographies. International Journal of Bilingualism 5 (3), 317–344.

PAVLENKO, A., 2002a, Poststructuralist approaches to the study of social factors in second language learning and use. In V. COOK (ed.), *Portraits of the L2 User*. Clevedon: Multilingual Matters.

PAVLENKO, A., 2002b, Emotions and the body in Russian and English. *Pragmatics and Cognition*, 10, 201-236.

PAVLENKO, A., 2003a, 'I never knew I was a bilingual': Reimagining teacher identities in TESOL. *Journal of Language, Identity, and Education* 2 (4), 251–268.

PAVLENKO, A., 2003b, The making of an American: Negotiation of identities at the turn of the twentieth century In A. PAVLENKO & A. BLACKLEDGE (eds) *Negotiation of Identities in Multilingual Contexts*. Clevedon: Multilingual Matters.

PAVLENKO, A., 2004b, 'Stop doing that, *Ia Komu Skazala'*: Language choice and emotions in parent-child communication. *Journal of Multilingual and Multicultural Development* 25 (2&3), 179–203.

PAVLENKO, A., 2005a, Bilingualism and thought. In J. KROLL & A. DE GROOT (eds), *Handbook of bilingualism: Psycholinguistic Approaches*. Oxford: Oxford University Press.

PAVLENKO, A., 2005b, *Emotions and Multilingualism*. New York: Cambridge University Press.

PAVLENKO, A. & LANTOLF, J.P., 2000, Second language learning as participation and the (re)construction of selves. In J.P. LANTOLF (ed.) *Sociocultural Theory and Second Language Learning*. Oxford: Oxford University Press.

PAVLENKO, A. & PILLER, I., 2001, New directions in the study of multilingualism, second language learning, and gender. In A. PAVLENKO, A. BLACKLEDGE, I. PILLER & M. TEUTSCH-DWYER (eds) *Multilingualism, Second Language Learning, and Gender*. Berlin: Mouton De Gruyter.

PEAL, E. & LAMBERT, W.E., 1962, The relationship of bilingualism to intelligence. *Psychological Monographs* 76 (27), 1–23.

PEER, L, & REID, G. (eds), 2000, *Multilingualism, Literacy and Dyslexia: A Challenge for Educators*. London: David Fulton.

PELLERANO, C. & FRADD, S.H., 1998, *Coral Way Elementary School: A Success Story in Bilingualism and Biliteracy*. Washington, DC: National Clearinghouse for Bilingual Education.

PENNYCOOK, A., 1994, *The Cultural Politics of English as an International Language*. New York: Longman.

PENNYCOOK, A. & MAKONI, S., 2005, The modern mission: The language effects of Christianity. *Journal of Language, Identity, and Education* 4 (2), 137–156.

PÉREZ, B. & TORRES-GUZMÁN, M., 1996, *Learning in Two Worlds: An Integrated Spanish/English Biliteracy Approach* (2nd edn). New York: Longman.

PERLMANN, J., 1990, Historical legacies: 1840–1920. In C.B. CAZDEN & C.E. SNOW (eds), *English Plus: Issues in Bilingual Education*. London: Sage.

PETRIDES, K.V., FURNHAM, A. & FREDERICKSON, N., 2004, Emotional intelligence. *The Psychologist* 17 (10), 574–577.

PEYTON, J.K., RANARD, D.A., & MCGINNIS, S., 2001, Charting a new course: Heritage language education in the United States. In J.K. PEYTON, D.A. RANARD & S. MCGINNIS (eds), *Heritage Languages in America: Preserving a National Resource*. McHenry, IL: Delta Systems.

PHILLIPSON, R., 1992, *Linguistic Imperialism*. Oxford: Oxford University Press.

PHILLIPSON, R., 2003, *English-Only Europe? Challenging Language Policy*. London: Routledge.

PILLER, I., 2001, Private language planning: The best of both worlds? *Estudios de Sociolingüística* 2 (1), 61–80.

PILLER, I., 2002, *Bilingual Couples Talk: The Discursive Construction of Hybridity*. Amsterdam: John Benjamins.

PINTNER, R. & ARSENIAN, S., 1937, The relation of bilingualism to verbal intelligence and school adjustment. *Journal of Educational Research* 31, 255–263.

POPLACK, S. & MEECHAN, M., 1998, Introduction: How languages fit together in codeswitching. *International Journal of Bilingualism* 2 (2), 127–138.

PORTES, A. & HAO, L., 1998, E pluribus unum: Bilingualism and loss of language in the second generation. *Sociology of Education* 71 (October), 269–294.

PORTES, A. & HAO, L., 2002, *The Price of Uniformity: Language, Family, and Personality Adjustment in the Immigrant Second Generation*. Princeton University: The Center for Migration and Development.

POWERS, S. & GREGORY, S., 1998, *The Educational Achievements of Deaf Children*. London: Department for Education and Employment.

POWERS, S., GREGORY, S., LYNAS, W., MCCRACKEN, W., WATSON, L., BOULTON, A. &

HARRIS, D., 1999, *A Review of Good Practice in Deaf Education*. London: Royal National Institute for Deaf People.

PROCTOR, P., 2003, Degree of bilingualism and English reading achievement. Paper presented at the Fourth Symposium on Bilingualism, Arizona State University, April 2003.

QUAY, S., 1994, Language choice in early bilingual development. Unpublished PhD, University of Cambridge.

QUAY, S., 2001, Managing linguistic boundaries in early trilingual development. In J. CENOZ & F. GENESEE (eds), *Trends in Bilingual Acquisition*. Amsterdam/Philadelphia: John Benjamins.

QUEZADA, M., WILEY, T.G. & RAMIREZ, J.D., 1999, How the reform agenda shortchanges English learners. *Educational Leadership* 57 (4), 57–61.

RAHMAN, T., 2005, The Muslim response to English in South Asia: With special reference to inequality, intolerance and militancy. *Journal of Language, Identity, and Education* 4 (2), 119–136.

RAMANATHAN, V., 2005, *The English-Vernacular Divide: Postcolonial Language Politics and Practice*. Clevedon: Multilingual Matters.

RAMÍREZ, J.D., 1992, Executive summary. *Bilingual Research Journal* 16 (1&2), 1–62.

RAMÍREZ, J.D. & MERINO, B.J., 1990, Classroom talk in English immersion, early-exit and late-exit transitional bilingual education programs. In R. JACOBSON & C. FALTIS (eds), *Language Distribution Issues in Bilingual Schooling*. Clevedon: Multilingual Matters.

RAMÍREZ, J.D., WILEY, T.G., KLERK, G. de, LEE, E. & WRIGHT, W.E. (eds), 2005, *Ebonics: The Urban Education Debate* (2nd edn). Clevedon: Multilingual Matters.

RAMÍREZ, J.D., YUEN, S.D. & RAMEY, D.R., 1991, *Final Report: Longitudinal Study of Structured English Immersion Strategy, Early-exit and Late-exit Programs for Language-minority Children. Report Submitted to the US Department of Education*. San Mateo, CA: Aguirre International.

RAMOS, J., 2002, *No Borders: A Journalist's Search for Home*. New York: HarperCollins.

RAMPTON, B., 1995, Language crossing and the problematisation of ethnicity and socialization. *Pragmatics* 5 (4), 485–513.

REBUFFOT, J., 1993, *Le Point sur L'Immersion au Canada*. Anjou, Quebec: Centre éducatif et Culturel.

REID, S., 1993, *Lament for a Nation: The Life and Death of Canada's Bilingual Dream*. Vancouver: Arsenal Pulp Press.

RESNICK, L.B. & RESNICK, D.P., 1992, Assessing the thinking curriculum: New tools for educational reform. In B.R. GIFFORD & M.C. O'CONNOR (eds), *Changing Assessments: Alternative Views of Aptitude, Achievement and Instruction*. Boston: Kluwer.

RESNICK, M.C., 1993, ESL and language planning in Puerto Rican education. *TESOL Quarterly* 27 (2), 259–275.

REYHNER, J. & EDER, J., 2004, *American Indian Education: A History*. Norman: University of Oklahoma Press.

REYHNER, J. & TENNANT, E., 1995, Maintaining and renewing native languages. *Bilingual Research Journal* 19 (2), 279–304.

REYNOLDS, A.G., 1991, The cognitive consequences of bilingualism. In A.G. REYNOLDS (ed.), *Bilingualism, Multiculturalism and Second Language Learning*. Hillsdale, NJ: Lawrence Erlbaum.

REYNOLDS, D., BELLIN, W., AB IEUAN, R., 1998, *A Competitive Edge: Why Welsh Medium Schools Perform Better*. Cardiff: Institute of Welsh Affairs.

RHEE, J., 1999, Theories of citizenship and their role in the bilingual education debate. *Columbia Journal of Law and Social Problems* 33 (1), 33–83.

RICCIARDELLI, L.A., 1992, Creativity and bilingualism. *Journal of Creative Behavior* 26 (4), 242–254.

RICHARDS, J. & ROGERS, T., 2001, *Approaches and Methods in Language Teaching* (2nd edn). Cambridge: Cambridge University Press.

RILEY, R.W., 1998, *Helping All Children Learn English*. Washington, DC: US Department of Education.

RIVERA, C. (ed.), 1984, *Language Proficiency and Academic Achievement*. Clevedon: Multilingual Matters.

ROBERTS, C., 1985, Teaching and learning commitment in bilingual schools. Unpublished PhD thesis, University of Wales.

ROBERTS, G., 1994, Nurse/patient communication within a bilingual health care setting. *British Journal of Nursing* 3 (2), 60–67.

ROBINSON, C.D.W., 1996, *Language Use in Rural Development: An African Perspective*. New York: Mouton de Gruyter.

ROBSON, A., 1995, The assessment of bilingual children. In M.K. VERMA, K.P. CORRIGAN & S. FIRTH. (eds), *Working with Bilingual Children*. Clevedon: Multilingual Matters.

ROLSTAD, K. MAHONEY, K.S. & GLASS, G.V., 2005, Weighing the evidence: A meta analysis of bilingual education in Arizona. *Bilingual Research Journal* 29 (1), 43–67.

ROMAINE, S., 1995, *Bilingualism* (2nd edn). Oxford: Basil Blackwell.

ROMAINE, S., 2000a, *Language in Society: An Introduction to Sociolinguistics* (2nd edn). Oxford: Oxford University Press.

ROMAINE, S., 2000a, Multilingualism, conflict, and the politics of indigenous language movements. *Estudios de Sociolingüística* 1 (1), 13–26.

ROMAINE, S., 2002, Can stable diglossia help to preserve endangered languages? *International Journal of the Sociology of Language* 157, 135–140.

RONJAT, J., 1913, *Le developpement du langage observe chez un enfant bilingue*. Paris: Champion.

ROSENTHAL, R., 1966, *Experimenter Effects in Behavioral Research*. New York: Appleton-Century-Crofts.

ROSSELL, C.H., 1992, Nothing matters?: A critique of the Ramirez *et al.* longitudinal study of instructional programs for language-minority children. *Bilingual Research Journal* 16 (1&2), 159–186.

ROSSELL, C.H. & BAKER, K., 1996, The educational effectiveness of bilingual education. *Research in the Teaching of English* 30 (1), 7–74.

RUEDA, R., 1983, Metalinguistic awareness in monolingual and bilingual mildly retarded children. *NABE Journal* 8, 55–68.

RUIZ, R., 1984, Orientations in language planning. *NABE Journal* 8 (2), 15–34.

RUMBERGER, R.W., CALLAHAN, R.M. & GÁNDARA, P., 2003, Has Proposition 227 reduced the English learner achievement gap? *UCLMRI Newsletter* 13 (1), 1–2.

SAER, D.J., 1922, An inquiry into the effect of bilingualism upon the intelligence of young children. *Journal of Experimental Pedagogy* 6, 232–240 and 266–274.

SAER, D.J., 1923, The effects of bilingualism on intelligence. *British Journal of Psychology* 14, 25–38.

SAER, D.J., SMITH, F. & HUGHES, J., 1924, *The Bilingual Problem*. Wrexham: Hughes and Son.

SALE, L., SLIZ, L. & PACINI-KETCHABAW, V., 2003, Creating an inclusive climate for newly arrived students. In S.R. SCHECTER & J. CUMMINS (eds), *Multilingual Education in Practice: Using Diversity as a Resource*. Portsmouth, NH: Heinemann.

SANTAMARÍA, L.J., FLETCHER, T.V. & BOS, C.S., 2002, Effective pedagogy for English language learners in inclusive classrooms. In A.J. ARTILES & A.A. ORTIZ (eds), *English Language learners with Special Educational Needs*. Washington, DC & McHenry, IL: Center for Applied Linguistics & Delta Systems Co..

SCHERMERHORN, R.A., 1970, *Comparative Ethnic Relations*. New York: Random House.

SCHINKE-LLANO, L., 1989, Early childhood bilingualism: In search of explanation. *Studies in Second Language Acquisition (SSLA)* 11 (3), 223–240.

SCHLOSSMAN, S., 1983, Is there an American tradition of bilingual education? *American Journal of Education* 91, 139–186.

SCHMIDT, R., 2000, *Language Policy and Identity Policy in the United States*. Philadelphia: Temple University Press.

SCHWARTZ, A.M., 2001, Preparing teachers to work with heritage language learners. In J.K. PEYTON, D.A. RANARD & S. MCGINNIS (eds), *Heritage Languages in America: Preserving a National Resource*. McHenry, IL: Delta Systems.

SEARS, C., 1998, *Second Language Students in Mainstream Classrooms*. Clevedon: Multilingual Matters.

SECADA, W.G., 1991, Degree of bilingualism and arithmetic problem solving in Hispanic First Graders. *Elementary School Journal* 92 (2), 213–231.

SECRETARY'S COMMISSION ON ACHIEVING NECESSARY SKILLS (SCANS), 1991, *What Work Requires of Schools. A SCANS Report for America 2000*. Washington, DC: US Department of Labor.

SENESAC, B.V.K., 2002, Two-way bilingual immersion: A portrait of quality schooling. *Bilingual Research Journal* 26 (1), 1–15.

SHARWOOD SMITH, M.A., 1989, Crosslinguistic influence in language loss. In K. HYLTENSTAM & L.K. OBLER (eds), *Bilingualism Across the Lifespan: Aspects of Acquisition, Maturity and Loss*. Cambridge: Cambridge University Press.

SHAW, P., 2003, Leadership in the diverse school. In S.R. SCHECTER & J. CUMMINS (eds) *Multilingual Education in Practice: Using Diversity as a Resource*. Portsmouth, NH: Heinemann.

SHOHAMY, E., 1997, Critical language testing and beyond. Plenary Paper presented at the American Association of Applied Linguistics (AAAL), Orlando, March 1997.

SHOHAMY, E., 1999, Unity and diversity in language policy. Paper presented at the AILA Conference, Tokyo, August 1999.

SHOHAMY, E., 2001, *The Power of Tests: A Critical Perspective on the Uses and Consequences of Language Tests*. London: Longman.

SIEGEL, J., 1996, *Vernacular Education in the South Pacific: A Report of AusAID*. New England, Australia: University of New England.

SIEGEL, J., 1997, Formal vs. non-formal vernacular education: The education reform in Papua New Guinea. *Journal of Multilingual and Multicultural Development* 18 (3), 206–222.

SIERRA, J. & OLAZIREGI, I., 1989, *EIFE 2. Influence of Factors on the Learning of Basque*. Gasteiz, Spain: Central Publications Service of the Basque Government.

SIGUÁN, M., 1993, *Multilingual Spain*. Amsterdam: Swets and Zeitlinger.

SIMON, D-L., 2001, Towards a new understanding of codeswitching in the foreign language classroom. In R. JACOBSON (ed.) *Codeswitching Worldwide II*. Berlin: Mouton de Gruyter.

SINGLETON, D., 2003, Critical period or general age factor(s)? In M. MAYO & M. LECUMBERRI (eds), *Age and the Acquisition of English as a Foreign Language*. Clevedon: Multilingual Matters.

SINGLETON, D. & RYAN, L., 2004, *Language Acquisition: The Age Factor*. (2nd edn). Clevedon: Multilingual Matters.

SJÖHOLM, K., 2004, English as a third language in bilingual Finland: Basic communication or academic language. In C. HOFFMANN & J. YTSMA, J. (eds), *Trilingualism in Family, School and Community*. Clevedon: Multilingual Matters.

SKEHAN, P., 1988, Language testing. *Language Teaching*, 21 (January) 1–13 and (October) 211–22.

SKEHAN, P., 1998, *A Cognitive Approach to Language Learning*. Oxford: Oxford University Press

SKOURTOU, E., 2002, Connecting Greek and Canadian schools through an internet-based sister-class network. *International Journal of Bilingual Education and Bilingualism* 5 (2), 85–95.

SKUTNABB-KANGAS, T., 1977, Language in the process of cultural assimilation and structural incorporation of linguistic minorities. In C.C. ELERT, S. ELIASSON, S. FRIES & S. URELAND (eds), *Dialectology and Sociolinguistics*. UMEA: UMEA Studies in the Humanities.

SKUTNABB-KANGAS, T., 1981, *Bilingualism or Not: The Education of Minorities*. Clevedon: Multilingual Matters.

SKUTNABB-KANGAS, T., 1991, Swedish strategies to prevent integration and national ethnic minorities. In O. GARCÍA (ed.), *Bilingual Education: Focusschrift in Honor of Joshua A. Fishman*. Amsterdam/Philadelphia: John Benjamins.

SKUTNABB-KANGAS, T., 1999a, Education of minorities. In J.A. FISHMAN (ed.), *Handbook of Language and Ethnic Identity*. New York: Oxford University Press.

SKUTNABB-KANGAS, T., 1999b, Linguistic human rights – Are you naive, or what? *TESOL Journal* 8 (3), 6–12.

SKUTNABB-KANGAS, T., 2000, *Linguistic Genocide in Education – or Worldwide Diversity and Human Rights*. Mahwah, NJ: Erlbaum.

SKUTNABB-KANGAS, T. & PHILLIPSON, R. (eds), 1994, *Linguistic Human Rights: Overcoming Linguistic Discrimination*. Berlin: Mouton de Gruyter.

SKUTNABB-KANGAS, T. & TOUKOMAA, P., 1976, *Teaching Migrant Children Mother Tongue and Learning the Language of the Host Country in the Context of the Socio-Cultural Situation of the Migrant Family*. Tampere, Finland: Tukimuksia Research Reports.

SMYTH, G., 2003, *Helping Bilingual Pupils to Access the Curriculum*. London: David Fulton.

SNEDDON, R., 2000a, Language and literacy: Children's experiences in multilingual environments. *International Journal of Bilingual Education and Bilingualism* 3 (4), 265–282.

SNEDDON, R., 2000b, Language and literacy practices in Gujarati Muslim families. In M. MARTIN-JONES & K. JONES, *Multilingual Literacies: Reading and Writing Different Worlds*. Amsterdam/Philadelphia: John Benjamins.

SNEDDON, R. & PATEL, K., 2003, The Raja's Big Ears: The journey of a story across cultures. *Language and Education* 17 (5), 371–384.

SNOW, C.E., BURNS, M.S. & GRIFFIN, P., 1998, *Preventing Reading Difficulties in Young Children*. Washington, DC: National Academy Press.

SNOW, C.E. & HOEFNAGEL-HÖHLE, M., 1978, The critical period for language acquisition: Evidence from second language learning. *Child Development* 49, 1114–1128.

SNOW, M.A., 1990, Instructional methodology in immersion foreign language education. In A.M.

PADILLA, H.H. FAIRCHILD & C.M. VALADEZ (eds), *Foreign Language Education: Issues and Strategies*. London: Sage.

SOLTERO, S.W., 2004, *Dual Language: Teaching and Learning in Two Languages*. Boston: Pearson Education.

SPACK, R, 2002, *America's Second Tongue: American Indian Education and the Ownership of English, 1860-1900*. Lincoln, NB: University of Nebraska Press.

SPADA, N. & LIGHTBOWN, P.M., 2002, L1 and L2 in the education of Inuit children in northern Quebec: Abilities and perceptions. *Language and Education* 16 (3), 212–240.

SPOLSKY, B., 1989b, Review of 'Key Issues in Bilingualism and Bilingual Education.'. *Applied Linguistics* 10 (4), 449–451.

SPOLSKY, B., 1998, *Sociolinguistics*. Oxford: Oxford University Press.

SPOLSKY, B., 2004, *Language Policy*. Cambridge: Cambridge University Press.

SPOLSKY, B. & SHOHAMY, E., 1999, *The Languages of Israel: Policy, Ideology and Practice*. Clevedon: Multilingual Matters.

SRIDHAR, K.K., 1996, Societal multilingualism. In S.L. McKAY, & N.H. HORNBERGER, *Sociolinguistics and Language Teaching*. Cambridge: Cambridge University Press.

STOTZ, D. & ANDRES, F., 1990, Problems in developing bilingual education programs in Switzerland. *Multilingua* 9 (1), 113–136.

STREET, B.V., 1994, What is meant by local literacies. *Language and Education* 8 (1&2), 9–17.

STREET, B.V., 1995, *Social Literacies: Critical Approaches to Literacy in Development, Ethnography and Education*. Longman, New York & London.

STREET, B.V., 2000, Literacy events and literacy practices: Theory and practice in the new literacy studies. In M. MARTIN-JONES & K. JONES, *Multilingual Literacies: Reading and Writing Different Worlds*. Amsterdam/Philadelphia: John Benjamins.

STREET, B.V., 2002, Understanding literacy issues in contemporary multiethnic schooling contexts, with particular reference to EAL pupils. In C. LEUNG, *Language and Additional/Second Language Issues for School Education*. York, UK: NADLIC.

STREET, B.V., 2003, What's 'new' in New Literacy Studies? Critical approaches to literacy in theory and practice. *Current Issues in Comparative Education* 5, 1–14.

STRITIKUS, T.T., 2001, From personal to political: Proposition 227, literacy instruction, and the individual qualities of teachers. *International Journal of Bilingual Education and Bilingualism* 4 (5), 291–309.

STRITIKUS, T.T., 2003, The interrelationship of beliefs, context, and learning: The case of a teacher reacting to language policy. *Journal of Language, Identity, and Education* 2 (1), 29–52.

STRITIKUS, T.T. & GARCIA, E., 2003, The role of theory and policy in the educational treatment of language minority students: Competitive structures in California. *Education Policy Analysis Archives* 11 (26), 1–25.

STRONG, M., 1995, A review of bilingual/bicultural programs for deaf children in North America. *American Annals of the Deaf* 140 (2), 84–94.

STROUD, C., 2001, African mother-tongue programmes and the politics of language: Linguistic citizenship versus linguistic human rights. *Journal of Multilingual and Multicultural Development* 22, 339–355.

STROUD, C., 2004, The performativity of codeswitching. *International Journal of Bilingualism* 8 (2), 145–166.

STRUBELL, M., 2001, Catalan a decade later. In J.A. FISHMAN (ed.), *Can Threatened Languages be Saved?* Clevedon: Multilingual Matters.

STUBBS, M., 1991, Educational language planning in England and Wales: Multicultural rhetoric and assimilationist assumptions. In F. COULMAS (ed.), *A Language Policy for the European Community*. New York: Mouton de Gruyter.

SWAIN, M., 1993, The output hypothesis: Just speaking and writing aren't enough. *Canadian Modern Language Review* 50, 158–164.

SWAIN, M., 1997, French immersion programs in Canada. In J. CUMMINS & D. CORSON (eds), *Bilingual Education*. Volume 5 of the *Encyclopedia of Language and Education*. Dordrecht: Kluwer.

SWAIN, M. & JOHNSON, R.K., 1997, Immersion education: A category within bilingual education. In R.K. JOHNSON & M. SWAIN, *Immersion Education: International Perspectives*. Cambridge: Cambridge University Press.

SWAIN, M. & LAPKIN, S., 1982, *Evaluating Bilingual Education: A Canadian Case Study*. Clevedon: Multilingual Matters.

SWAIN, M. & LAPKIN, S., 1991, Additive bilingualism and French immersion education: The roles of language proficiency and literacy. In A.G. REYNOLDS (ed.), *Bilingualism, Multicultur-alism and Second Language Learning*. Hillsdale, NJ: Lawrence Erlbaum.

SWAN, D., 1996, *A Singular Pluralism: The European Schools 1984–1994*. Dublin: Institute of Public Administration.

TAKAKI, R., 1993, Multiculturalism: Battleground or meeting ground? *Annals of the American Academy of Political and Social Science* 530, 109–121.

TANG, G., 2001, Knowledge framework and classroom action. In B. MOHAN, C. LEUNG & C. DAVISON, *English as a Second Language in the Mainstream: Teaching, Learning and Identity*. Harlow, England: Longman.

TANKERSLEY, D., 2001, Bombs or bilingual programmes?: Dual language immersion, transformative education and community building in Macedonia. *International Journal of Bilingual Education and Bilingualism* 4 (2), 107–124.

TANNENBAUM, M. & HOWIE, P., 2002, The association between language maintenance and family relations: Chinese immigrant children in Australia. *Journal of Multilingual and Multicultural Development* 23 (5), 408–424.

TAYLOR, D.M., CRAGO, M.B. & McALPINE, L., 1993, Education in Aboriginal communities: Dilemmas around empowerment. *Canadian Journal of Native Education* 20 (1), 176–183.

THOMAS, W.P., 1992, An analysis of the research methodology of the Ramirez Report. *Bilingual Research Journal* 16 (1&2), 213–245.

THOMAS, W.P. & COLLIER, V.P., 1995, *Language Minority Student Achievement and Program Effectiveness. Research Summary*. Fairfax, VA: George Mason University.

THOMAS, W.P. & COLLIER, V.P., 1997, *School Effectiveness for Language Minority Students*. Washington, DC: National Clearinghouse for Bilingual Education.

THOMAS, W.P., & COLLIER, V.P., 2002a, *A National Study of School Effectiveness for Language Minority Students' Long-Term Academic Achievement. Final report*. Washington, DC: Center for Research on Education, Diversity & Excellence.

THOMAS, W.P., & COLLIER, V.P., 2002b, Accelerated schooling for all students: Research findings on education in multilingual communities. In S. SHAW (ed.), *Intercultural Education in European Classrooms: Intercultural Education Partnership*. Stoke-on-Trent: Trentham.

THOMAS, W.P., COLLIER, V.P. & ABBOTT, M., 1993, Academic achievement through Japanese, Spanish or French: The first two years of partial immersion. *Modern Language Journal* 77 (2), 170–179.

THOMPSON, L., 2000, *Young Bilingual Learners in Nursery School*. Clevedon: Multilingual Matters.

THOMPSON, M.S., DICERBO, K.E., MAHONEY, K. & MACSWAN, J., 2002, Exito en California? A validity critique of language program evaluations and analysis of English learner test scores. *Education Policy Analysis Archives* 10, 7 (January 25).

TOLLEFSON, J.W., 1986, Language planning and the radical left in the Philippines. *Language Problems and Language Planning* 10 (2), 177–189.

TOLLEFSON, J.W., 1991, *Planning Language, Planning Inequality*. London: Longman.

TOLLEFSON, J.W., 2002, Limitations of language policy and planning. In R.B. KAPLAN (ed.) *The Oxford Handbook of Applied Linguistics*. Oxford: Oxford University Press.

TOOHEY, K., 2000, *Learning English at School: Identity, Social Relations and Classroom Practice*. Clevedon: Multilingual Matters.

TORIBIO, A.M., 2004, Spanish/English speech practices: Bringing chaos to order. *International Journal of Bilingual Education and Bilingualism* 7 (2&3), 133-154.

TORRANCE, E.P., 1974a, *Torrance Tests of Creative Thinking: Directions Manual and Scoring Guide*. Lexington, MA: Ginn.

TORRANCE, E.P., 1974b, *Torrance Tests of Creative Thinking: Norms-Technical Manual*. Lexington, MA: Ginn.

TORRES-GUZMÁN, M.E., ABBATE, J., BRISK, M.E. & MINAYA-ROWE, L., 2002, Defining and documenting success for bilingual learners: A collective case study. *Bilingual Research Journal* 26 (1), 1–10.

TOSI, A., 1988, The jewel in the crown of the modern prince: The new approach to bilingualism in multicultural education in England. In T. SKUTNABB-KANGAS & J. CUMMINS (eds), *Minority Education: From Shame to Struggle*. Clevedon: Multilingual Matters.

TOSI, A., 1991, High-status and low-status bilingualism in Europe. *Journal of Education* 173 (2), 21–37.

TOUKOMAA, P. & SKUTNABB-KANGAS, T., 1977, *The Intensive Teaching of the Mother Tongue to*

Migrant Children at Pre-school Age (Research Report No. 26). Department of Sociology and Social Psychology, University of Tampere.

TREFFERS-DALLER, J., 1992, French–Dutch codeswitching in Brussels: Social factors explaining its disappearance. *Journal of Multilingual and Multicultural Development* 13 (1&2), 143–156.

TREFFERS-DALLER, J., 1994, *Mixing Two Languages: French–Dutch Contact in a Comparative Perspective*. Berlin/New York: Mouton de Gruyter.

TROIKE, R.C., 1978, Research evidence for the effectiveness of bilingual education. *NABE Journal* 3 (1), 13–24.

TRUEBA, H.T., 1991, The role of culture in bilingual instruction. In O. GARCÍA (ed.), *Bilingual Education: Focusschrift in Honor of Joshua A. Fishman (Volume 1)*. Amsterdam/Philadelphia: John Benjamins.

TSE, L., 1995, Language brokering among Latino adolescents: Prevalence, attitudes, and school performance. *Hispanic Journal of Behavioral Sciences* 17 (2), 180–193.

TSE, L., 1996a, Language brokering in linguistic minority communities: The case of Chinese- and Vietnamese-American students. *Bilingual Research Journal* 20 (3&4), 485–498.

TSE, L., 1996b, Who decides?: The effects of language brokering on home–school communication. *Journal of Educational Issues of Language Minority Students* 16, 225–234.

TSE, L., 2001, *'Why don't they learn English?' Separating Fact from Fallacy in the US Language Debate*. New York: Teachers College Press.

TUCKER, G.R., 1998, A global perspective on multilingualism and multilingual education. In J. CENOZ & F. GENESEE (eds), *Beyond Bilingualism: Multilingualism and Multilingual Education*. Clevedon: Multilingual Matters.

TUCKER, G.R. and D'ANGLEJAN, A., 1972, An approach to bilingual education: The St Lambert Experiment. In M. SWAIN (ed.), *Bilingual Schooling: Some Experiences in Canada and the United States*. Ontario: Ontario Institute for Studies in Education Symposium Series No. 1.

TUNMER, W.E. & HERRIMAN, M.L., 1984, The development of metalinguistic awareness: A conceptual overview. In W.E. TUNMER, C. PRATT & M.L. HERRIMAN (eds), *Metalinguistic Awareness in Children*. Berlin: Springer-Verlag.

TUNMER, W.E. & MYHILL, M.E., 1984, Metalinguistic awareness and bilingualism. In W.E. TUNMER, C. PRATT & M.L. HERRIMAN (eds), *Metalinguistic Awareness in Children*. Berlin: Springer-Verlag.

TUOMINEN, A., 1999, Who decides the home language? A look at multilingual families. *International Journal of the Sociology of Language* 140, 59–76.

UNITED NATIONS EDUCATIONAL, SCIENTIFIC AND CULTURAL ORGANIZATION (UNESCO) 1953, *The Use of Vernacular Languages in Education*. Paris: UNESCO.

UNITED NATIONS EDUCATIONAL, SCIENTIFIC AND CULTURAL ORGANIZATION (UNESCO), 1994, *The Salamanca Statement and Framework for Action on Special Needs Education*. Paris: UNESCO.

UNITED STATES DEPARTMENT OF EDUCATION, 1992, *The Condition of Bilingual Education in the Nation: A Report to the Congress and the President*. Washington, DC: Department of Education.

UNITED STATES DEPARTMENT OF EDUCATION, Office of Special Education and Rehabilitative Services, Office of the Assistant Secretary, 2004, *National Symposium on Learning Disabilities in English Language Learners, October 14-15, 2003*. Washington, DC: US Department of Education.

USMANI, K., 1999, The influence of racism and cultural bias in the assessment of bilingual children. *Educational and Child Psychology* 16 (3), 44–54.

VAID, J., 2002, Bilingualism. In V.S. RAMACHANDRAN (ed.), *Encyclopedia of the Human Brain*. San Diego, CA: Academic Press.

VAID, J. & HULL, R., 2001, A tale of two hemispheres: A meta-analytic review of the bilingual brain. Poster presented at the Third Symposium on Bilingualism, University of the West of England, April 2001.

VALDÉS, G., 1997, Dual language immersion programs: A cautionary note concerning the education of language-minority students. *Harvard Educational Review* 67 (3), 391–428.

VALDÉS, G., 1998, The world outside and inside school: Language and immigrant children. *Educational Researcher* 27 (6), 4–18.

VALDÉS, G., 2001, *Learning and Not Learning English: Latino Students in American Schools*. New York: Teachers College Press.

VALDÉS, G., 2003, *Expanding Definitions of Giftedness: The Case of Young Interpreters from Immigrant Communities*. Mahwah, NJ: Lawrence Erlbaum.

VALDÉS, G., 2004, Between support and marginalisation. The development of academic language in linguistic minority children. *International Journal of Bilingual Education and Bilingualism 7* (2&3), 102–132.

VALDÉS, G., 2006, The foreign-language teaching profession and the challenges of developing language resources. In G. VALDÉS, J.A. FISHMAN, R. CHÁVEZ & W. PÉREZ (eds), *Towards the Development of Minority Language Resources.* Clevedon: Multilingual Matters.

VALDÉS, G., BROOKS, H. & CHÁVEZ, C., 2003, Bilinguals and bilingualism. In G. VALDÉS, *Expanding Definitions of Giftedness: The Case of Young Interpreters from Immigrant Communities.* Mahwah, NJ: Lawrence Erlbaum.

VALDÉS, G. & FIGUEROA, R.A., 1994, *Bilingualism and Testing: A Special Case of Bias.* Norwood, NJ: Ablex.

VALDÉS, G., FISHMAN, J.A., CHÁVEZ, R. & PÉREZ, W., 2006, *Towards the Development of Minority Language Resources.* Clevedon: Multilingual Matters.

VARGHESE, M., 2004, Professional development for bilingual teachers in the United States: A site for articulating and contesting professional roles. *International Journal of Bilingual Education and Bilingualism 7* (2&3), 222–237.

VARGHESE, M., MORGAN, B., JOHNSTON, B. & JOHNSON, K.A., 2005, Theorizing language teacher identity: Three perspectives and beyond. *Journal of Language, Identity, and Education 4* (1), 21–44

VELTMAN, C., 2000, The American linguistic mosaic: Understanding language shift in the United States. In S.L. McKAY & S-L.C. WONG (eds), *New Immigrants in the United States.* Cambridge. Cambridge University Press.

VERHOEVEN, L.T., 1994, Transfer in bilingual development: The linguistic interdependence hypothesis revisited. *Language Learning 44* (3), 381–415.

VILLARREAL, A., 1999, Rethinking the Education of English Language Learners: Transitional Bilingual Education Programs. *Bilingual Research Journal, 23* (1), 11–45.

VOLTERRA, V. & TAESCHNER, T., 1978, The acquisition and development of language by bilingual children. *Journal of Language 5,* 311–326.

VON GLEICH, U. & WÖLCK, W., 1994, Changes in language use and attitudes of Quechua Spanish Bilingual in Peru. In P. COLE, G. HERMON & M.D. MARTIN (eds), *Language in the Andes.* Newark, DE: University of Delaware.

VYGOTSKY, L.S., 1962, *Thought and Language.* Cambridge, MA: MIT Press.

WA THIONG'O, Ngugi, 1985, The language of African literature. *New Left Review,* April-June, 109-127.

WAGNER, S.T., 1980, The historical background of bilingualism and biculturalism in the United States. In M. RIDGE (ed.), *The New Bilingualism.* Los Angeles, CA: University of Southern California Press.

WARNER, S.L.N., 1999, *Kuleana*: The right, responsibility, and authority of Indigenous peoples to speak and make decisions for themselves in language and cultural revitalization. *Anthropology & Education Quarterly 30* (1), 68–93.

WARNER, S.L.N., 2001, The movement to revitalize Hawaiian language and culture. In L. HINTON & K. HALE (eds), *The Green Book of Language Revitalization in Practice.* San Diego: Academic Press.

WELLS, G., 1986, *The Meaning Makers: Children Learning Language and Using Language to Learn.* London: Heinemann.

WELLS, G. & CHANG-WELLS, G.L., 1992, *Constructing Knowledge Together: Classrooms as Centers of Inquiry and Literacy.* Portsmouth, NH: Heinemann.

WELSH LANGUAGE BOARD, 1999, *A Strategy for the Welsh Language: Targets for 2000–2005.* Cardiff: Welsh Language Board.

WESCHE, M.B., 1993, French immersion graduates at university and beyond: What difference has it made? In J.M. ALATIS (ed.), *The Georgetown Roundtable on Languages and Linguistics 1992.* Washington, DC: Georgetown University Press.

WESCHE, M. & SKEHAN, P, 2002, Communicative, task-based, and content-based language instruction. In R.B. KAPLAN (ed.) *The Oxford Handbook of Applied Linguistics.* Oxford: Oxford University Press.

WHORF, B.L., 1956, *Language, Thought and Reality.* New York: Wiley.

WIESE, A-M., 2004, Bilingualism and biliteracy for all? Unpacking two-way immersion at second grade. *Language and Education 18* (1), 69–92

WIESE, A-M. & GARCIA, E.E., 2001, The Bilingual Education Act: Language minority students and US Federal educational policy. *International Journal of Bilingual Education and Bilingualism* 4 (4), 229–248.

WILEY, T.G., 1996a, *Literacy and Language Diversity in the United States*. McHenry, IL: Center for Applied Linguistics and Delts Systems.

WILEY, T.G., 1996b, Language planning and policy. In S.L. McKAY, & N.H. HORNBERGER (eds), *Sociolinguistics and Language Teaching*. Cambridge: Cambridge University Press.

WILEY, T.G., 2001, On defining heritage language education and their speakers. In J.K. PEYTON, D.A. RANARD & S. MCGINNIS (eds), *Heritage Languages in America: Preserving a National Resource*. McHenry, IL: Delta Systems.

WILEY, T.G., 2002, Accessing language rights in education: A brief history of the US context. In J.W. TOLLEFSON (ed.) *Language Policies in Education: Critical Issues*. Mahwah, NJ: Erlbaum.

WILEY, T.G., 2005a, Discontinuities in heritage and community language education: Challenges for educational language policies. *International Journal of Bilingual Education and Bilingualism* 8 (2&3), 222-229.

WILEY, T.G., 2005b, Ebonics: Background to the current policy debate. In J.D. RAMIREZ, T.G. WILEY, G. DE KLERK, E. LEE & W. WRIGHT, *Ebonics: The Urban Education Debate* (2nd edn). Clevedon: Multilingual Matters.

WILEY, T.G., 2005c, *Literacy and Language Diversity in the United States* (2nd edn). McHenry, IL: Center for Applied Linguistics and Delts Systems.

WILEY, T.G., DE KLERK, G. & WRIGHT, W., 2005, Introduction. In J.D. RAMIREZ, T.G. WILEY, G. DE KLERK, E. LEE & W. WRIGHT, *Ebonics: The Urban Education Debate* (2nd edn). Clevedon: Multilingual Matters.

WILEY, T.G. & LUKES, M., 1996, English-Only and Standard English ideologies in the US. *TESOL Quarterly* 30 (3), 511–535.

WILEY, T.G. & WRIGHT, W., 2004, Against the undertow: Language-minority education policy and politics in the 'age of accountability'. *Educational Policy* 18 (1), 142–168.

WILLIAMS, Cen, 1994, Arfarniad o Ddulliau Dysgu ac Addysgu yng Nghyd-destun Addysg Uwchradd Ddwyieithog. Unpublished PhD thesis. Bangor: University of Wales.

WILLIAMS, Cen, 1996, Secondary education: Teaching in the bilingual situation. In C. WILLIAMS, G. LEWIS & C. BAKER (eds), *The Language Policy: Taking Stock*. Llangefni (Wales): CAI.

WILLIAMS, Cen, 2000, Welsh-medium and bilingual teaching in the further education sector. *International Journal of Bilingual Education and Bilingualism* 3 (2), 129–148.

WILLIAMS, C.H., 1991a, Language planning and social change: Ecological speculations. In D.F. MARSHALL (ed.), *Language Planning, Volume III*. Philadelphia: John Benjamins BV.

WILLIAMS, C.H., 1991b, *The Cultural Rights of Minorities: Recognition and Implementation* (Discussion Papers in Geolinguistics No. 18). Staffordshire: Staffordshire Polytechnic.

WILLIAMS, C.H., 1996, Geography and contact linguistics. In H. GOEBL, P.H. NELDE & Z.S.W. WÖLCK, W. (eds), *Contact Linguistics: An International Handbook of Contemporary Research*, Vol. 1. Berlin, New York: Walter de Gruyter.

WILLIAMS, C.H., 1998, Introduction: Respecting the citizens – Reflections on language policy in Canada and the United States. In T. RICENTO & B. BURNABY (eds), *Language and Politics in the United States and Canada: Myths and Realities*. Mahwah, NJ: Erlbaum.

WILLIAMS, C.H., 1999, The communal defence of threatened environments and identities. *Geografski vestnik* 71, 105–120.

WILLIAMS, C.H., 2000, Restoring the language. In G.H. JENKINS & M.A. WILLIAMS (eds), *'Let's Do Our Best for the Ancient Tongue': The Welsh Language in the Twentieth Century*. Cardiff: University of Wales Press.

WILLIAMS, C.H., 2004, The geography of language. In U. AMMON, N. DITTAR, K.J. MATTHEIER & P. TRUDGILL (eds), *Sociolinguistics: An International Handbook of the Science of Language and Society, Volume 1* (2nd edn). Berlin: Walter de Gruyter.

WILLIAMS, G., 1992, *Sociolinguistics: A Sociological Critique*. London: Routledge.

WILLIAMS, I.W., 2003, *Our Children's Language: The Welsh-Medium Schools of Wales 1939-2000*. Talybont (Wales): Y Lolfa.

WILLIG, A.C., 1981/82, The effectiveness of bilingual education: Review of a report. *NABE Journal* 6 (2&3), 1–19.

WILLIG, A.C., 1985, A meta-analysis of selected studies on the effectiveness of bilingual education. *Review of Educational Research* 55 (3), 269–317.

WILLIG, A.C. & RAMIREZ, J.D., 1993, The evaluation of bilingual education. In B. ARIAS & U.

CASANOVA (eds), *Bilingual Education: Politics, Research and Practice*. Berkeley, CA: McCutchan.

WILSON, W.H., 1998, The sociopolitical context of establishing Hawaiian-medium education. *Language, Culture and Curriculum* 11 (3), 325-338.

WILSON, W.H., & KAMANA, K., 2001, 'Mai loko mai o ka 'I'ni: Proceeding from a Dream': The 'Aha Punana Leo connection in Hawaiian language revitalization. In L. HINTON & K. HALE (eds.), *The Green Book of Language Revitalization in Practice*. San Diego: Academic Press.

WINSLER, A. DIAZ, R.H. ESPINOSA, L. & RODRIGUEZ, J.L., 1999, When learning a second language does not mean losing the first: Bilingual language development in low-income, Spanish-speaking children attending bilingual preschool. *Child Development* 70 (2), 349–362.

WONG FILLMORE, L., 1979, Individual differences in second language acquisition. In C. FILLMORE, D. KEMPLER & W. WANG (eds), *Individual Differences in Language Ability and Language Behavior*. New York: Academic Press.

WONG FILLMORE, L., 1982, Instructional language as linguistic input: Second language learning in classrooms. In L. WILKINSON (ed.), *Communicating in the Classroom*. New York: Academic Press.

WONG FILLMORE, L., 1991a, When losing a second language means losing the first. *Early Childhood Research Quarterly* 6, 323–346.

WONG FILLMORE, L. & SNOW, C., 2000, *What Elementary Teachers Need to Know About Language*. Washington: Center for Applied Linguistics.

WORLD BANK, 1997, *Project Appraisal Document, Guatemala, Basic Education Reform Project*. Washington, DC: World Bank.

WRAY, A., EVANS, B., COUPLAND, N. & BISHOP, H., 2003, Singing in Welsh, becoming Welsh: Turfing a 'grass roots' identity. *Language Awareness* 12 (1), 49–71.

WRIGHT, W.E., 2004, What English-Only really means: A study of the implementation of California language policy with Cambodian-American students. *International Journal of Bilingual Education and Bilingualism* 7 (1), 1–24.

WRIGLEY, O., 1996, *The Politics of Deafness*. Washington, DC: Gallaudet University Press.

WURM, S.A., 2001 (2nd edn), *Atlas of the World's Languages in Danger of Disappearing*. Paris: UNESCO.

YAMAMOTO, M., 2001, *Language Use in Interlingual Families: A Japanese-English Sociolinguistic Study*. Clevedon: Multilingual Matters.

YAMAMOTO, M., 2002, Language use in families with parents of different native languages. *Journal of Multilingual and Multicultural Development* 23 (6), 531–554.

YATIM, A.M., 1988, Some factors affecting bilingualism amongst trainee teachers in Malaysia. Unpublished PhD thesis, University of Wales.

YEH, C.J., CHEN, J., KWONG, A., CHIANG, L., WANG, Y-W. & PU-FOLKES, F., 2002, Educators of Asian bilingual students: Pedagogical techniques, strategies and challenges. *Journal of Multilingual and Multicultural Development* 23 (4), 296–315.

YTSMA, J., 2000, Trilingual primary education in Friesland. In J. CENOZ & U. JESSNER. *English in Europe: The Acquisition of a Third Language*. Clevedon: Multilingual Matters.

YUKAWA, E., 1997, *L1 Japanese Attrition and Regaining: Three Case Studies of Two Early Bilingual Children*. Stockholm: Centre for Research on Bilingualism, Stockholm University.

ZAPPERT, L.T. & CRUZ, B.R., 1977, *Bilingual Education: An Appraisal of Empirical Research*. Berkeley, CA: Bay Area Bilingual Education League.

ZHOU, M., 2001, The politics of bilingual education and educational levels in ethnic minority communities in China. *International Journal of Bilingual Education and Bilingualism* 4 (2), 125–149.

Index

Author Index

Abbate, J., 285
Abbott, M., 268
Abedi, J., 361, 362
Ab Ieuan, R., 249
ACAC, 298
Acenas, L-A.R., 147
Aclan, Z., 268
Ada, A.F., 326, 334, 416
Adams, J.W., 373
Adler, J., 174
Afolayan, A., 251
Aitchison, J., 75
Allard, R., 74
Allardt, E., 73, 410, 411
Allen, P., 275
Altwerger, B., 183
American Psychological Association, 263
Amiel-Tison, C., 98
Anderson, C., 87
Andersson, S., 117
Andersson, T., 189
Armengol, R., 423
Arnau, J., 272
Arnberg, L., 117
Arsenian, S., 147
Artigal, J.M., 249
Artiles, A.J., 348, 349, 352, 355, 367
Arviso, M., 244
Ashburner, J., 151
Asher, R.E., 44
Attinasi, J.J., 196
August, D., 197, 217, 222, 260, 262, 264, 267, 280, 283, 287, 289, 303, 335

Baca, L.M., 209, 348, 353, 354, 367
Bachi, R., 130,
Bachman, L.F., 15, 16

Baetens Beardsmore, H., 16, 251, 252, 253, 254, 256, 277, 284, 289, 313
Baker, C., ix, 7, 18, 25, 32, 34, 50, 52, 53, 106, 117, 126, 127, 131, 161, 164, 176, 186, 192, 214, 225, 229, 235, 238, 240, 242, 249, 252, 256, 260, 265, 284, 297, 305, 313, 340, 358, 364, 371, 373, 379, 404
Baker, K.A., 263, 264, 265
Baker, P., 22
Baker, S.C., 310
Baldauf, R.B., 50, 239
Bali, V., 196
Bargiela-Chiappini, F., 422
Barker, V., 394
Barkin, F., 183
Barona, A., 353
Barona, M.S., 353
Barron, V., 300
Barron-Hauwaert, S., 97, 101, 117,
Barth, F., 410, 411
Barwell, R., 174
Batibo, H.M., 44, 46, 64, 69, 78, 255
Batt, L., 199, 200
Baugh, J., 240
Bayley, R., S., 96
Beeman, M., 199
Bekerman, Z., 238
Bel, A., 249
Bellin, W., 249
Benally, A., 73, 238, 240, 243, 244
Benson, C., 314
Benyon, J., 240
Ben-Zeev, S., 155, 156, 161
Bernhardt, E.B., 307, 310
Berthold, M., 239, 249
Bertoncini, J., 98
Bhatia, T.K., 18

480

Subject Index